P9-DWK-673

George Sand

Also by Curtis Cate

Antoine de Saint-Exupéry: His Life and Times

George Sand

A Biography

by Curtis Cate

Illustrated with Photographs

Houghton Mifflin Company Boston

Library of Congress Cataloging in Publication Data
Cate, Curtis, 1924–
George Sand : a biography.
Bibliography: p. Includes index.
1. Sand, George, pseud. of Mme. Dudevant, 1804–1876—Biography.
PQ2413.C3 843'.7 [B] 75-8680
ISBN 0-395-19954-9
Printed in the United States of America

V 10 9 8 7 6

To Elena

"Qui pourrait s'en étonner? C'est un Caméléon, c'est un prisme aux mille couleurs que cette personne dont le caractère, aussi remarquable que le talent, offre un composé de tous les contrastes. Raison et folie, enfantillage et philosophie, ordre et désordre, impassibilité et violence, tout se trouve dans cette tête qui sait raisonner comme un homme, et déraisonner comme une femme."

— Sosthènes de La Rochefoucauld

Preface

Some twenty years ago, when André Maurois presented his biography of France's most celebrated and controversial woman author to his fellow countrymen, he wrote an almost apologetic preface in which, among other things, he explained that he had been led to an appreciation of George Sand's writings by Marcel Proust, who had been brought up by his mother to admire the effortless fluidity of style exhibited in novels like *La Petite Fadette* and *François le Champi*. If such an apologia was needed for the French, how much more necessary it must have been for American and British readers who, as likely as not, had never read a George Sand novel and for whom she was (and probably still is) little more than a name variously associated with Musset, Chopin, the smoking of cigars, and mannish forms of dress. Today Proust ranks alongside of Kafka, Joyce, and Thomas Mann as one of the great authors of our century, but few would think of placing George Sand among the literary masters who preceded them. But such was not the opinion of her contemporaries. One of them, the poetess Elizabeth Barrett, felt that she was the glorious exception to the general, "chauvinistic" rule about the relative paucity of female talents in the creative arts. "One woman indeed now alive," she wrote to her future husband, Robert Browning, in July 1845, "seems to me to justify an opposite opinion — that wonderful woman George Sand; who has something monstrous in combination with her genius, there is no denying at moments . . . but whom, in her good and evil together, I regard with infinitely more admiration than all other women of genius who are or have been."

Separated as we are from the early nineteenth century by the Himalayan mountain range of authors who made the modern novel what it is (from Tolstoi to Hemingway, from Thackeray to Vladimir Nabokov), we have some trouble understanding how a major literary critic like Sainte-Beuve could, as late as 1840, consider George Sand to be the finest and most original of French prose writers. Nor was this a purely French or limited opinion. Heinrich Heine considered her the greatest writer France had produced since the July Revolution of 1830, a great "prose poet" whom he did not hesitate to place above Victor Hugo.

"The Queen of the new literary generation," as the poet Béranger had dubbed her in 1833, was a few years later known all over Europe. When the great mezzo-soprano Pauline García, who had inspired *Consuelo* and its sequel, *La Comtesse de Rudolstadt,* visited Saint Petersburg and Moscow, she and her husband Louis Viardot were astounded by the veneration in which George Sand was held. "Here you are the foremost writer, the foremost poet of our country," Louis Viardot wrote to her in November of 1843. "Your books are in everybody's hands, your portraits are everywhere to be seen, you are ceaselessly talked about, and we are congratulated on the luck we have in being among your friends." Alexandre Dumas, who visited Russia fifteen years later, was equally surprised to find how familiar educated Russians were with George Sand's works, as well as with those of Hugo, Balzac, and himself. "Even Dickens, who began appearing in our country at about the same time, came after her in the admiration of the public," Dostoevski was to write. Indeed, "during the 1840s George Sand's glory was so high and the faith in her genius so great that we, her contemporaries, all expected of her in the near future something immense and unheard of, not to say definitive solutions."

These definitive solutions were not in the end forthcoming. It was indeed expecting too much to suppose that "definitive solutions" to the political, social, and religious problems of the European continent could be provided in works of fiction. Dostoevski in this case had clearly succumbed to his century's infatuation with the novel. Today writers, like critics, tend to be more modest. No one would now dare to claim that *Hamlet* or *Don Quixote* had actually altered the course of human history, any more than did *The Brothers Karamazov* or Thomas Mann's *The Magic Mountain,* both of which are a good bit more profound than George Sand's most intellectual novel, *La Comtesse de Rudolstadt.* But just as Dickens' novels helped to spur on a change in his country's poor laws and social attitudes, so George Sand's novels, in a Europe dominated by Metternich's Holy Alliance (Austria, Prussia, and Russia), helped to propagate the "sublime" ideals and revolutionary beliefs of her ultra-Romantic generation.

That there was a measure of luck, as well as of female genius, in her extraordinary success, there can be no doubt. George Sand had the good fortune to be born in 1804, the year of Napoleon's imperial coronation. She was twenty-six years old and in the full springtime of creativity when the reactionary Bourbons were finally overthrown in 1830 and a new, relatively liberal regime inaugurated with the stoutly middle-class Louis-Philippe. The first great Romantic generation — if we can regard Goethe, Robert Burns, and Rousseau as essentially pre-Romantics — had by that time spent its force. Keats had died in 1821, Shelley in 1822, the same year as E. T. A. Hoffmann, the creator of a new literary genre — the "fantastic tale" — which was to exercise an almost hypnotic influence on his successors (among them George Sand). Walter Scott, who had done the same for the novel, was already in his dotage and destined to die in 1832, one year after Aurore Dudevant's — the future George Sand's — arrival in Paris. In France the first Romantic generation was still represented by Lamartine, but the aging Chateaubriand, who was close to sixty, had by this time virtually abandoned fiction for politics and memoir writing. George Sand's contemporaries — led by Victor Hugo and Alexandre Dumas (both born in 1802), Balzac (born in 1799), Alfred de Vigny (born in 1797), Prosper Mérimée (born in 1803), and last but not least, Alfred de Musset (born in 1810), the *enfant terrible* of this second Romantic generation — thus shared the exhilarating feeling of having a clean field before them, one calling for the "renovation" of the arts and a radical break with the pompous academicism of the Napoleonic era and its conservative aftermath.

Chronological good luck was abetted, in the case of George Sand and her contemporaries, by geographic concentration. Prior to

1830 no European city could claim to be the capital of the continent's Arts. The poets were scattered all the way from England to Italy, and the most illustrious and influential of them all, Byron, finally died in Greece. The sculptor Canova, who had lived in Rome, was as influential as the painter David, who had lived and worked in Paris and Brussels. The Italians, who had dominated the world of music and opera for most of the eighteenth century, had been completely overshadowed by the Austrians and Germans — Mozart, Haydn, Beethoven, and Schubert, who had made Vienna the musical capital of Europe. But with Schubert's death in 1828 Vienna suddenly lost that position. Rossini, who had succeeded Mozart as the most influential opera writer of the day, had already chosen to settle down in Paris, and his example was soon to be followed by Meyerbeer, Liszt, and Chopin, all of whom became George Sand's friends. The dramatic young Géricault, followed by the no less flamboyant Delacroix, had broken the classic spell woven by David and Canova, making Paris the center of the plastic arts. Victor Hugo, with *Hernani* (1830), and Dumas, with *Antony* (1831), had done the same for the Romantic stage. Paris had even become the center of Romantic poetry, having managed (though for nonpoetic reasons) to attract Germany's Heinrich Heine and Poland's great epic poet Adam Mickiewicz.

The blessings conferred on her by favorable chronology may also be regarded as the curse of George Sand's writing. Had she been a poetess, like Marceline Desbordes-Valmore or Elizabeth Barrett Browning, it might well have been different. But the Romantic cult of heroic posturing, overflowing emotion, and mawkish sentimentalism — "One must write with the heart as well as with the mind," as Théophile Gautier, a typical Romantic, put it — was not made to produce great novels. One of the first to realize it was Stendhal, a curiously anti-Romantic Romantic who detested Chateaubriand's exalted rhetoric and who finally developed a brisk storytelling style which Dwight Macdonald, if I rightly recall, once likened to that of a public accountant. Another was Balzac, who gradually veered away from the absurd implausibilities and grotesque plots that had marked many of his early literary efforts. George Sand, on the other hand, let her heart as well as her conscience run away with her so much that her later works failed to maintain the promise of the first.

This is why so much of George Sand's fiction is now difficult to read. *Indiana* and *Valentine,* her first two novels, were written in a simple unpretentious style which makes them as enjoyable as anything written by Jane Austen. *Leone Leoni* can stand comparison with the Abbé Prévost's *Manon Lescaut,* which inspired it. *Mauprat* is as exciting as the best of George Eliot, though it does not reach the sublime intensity of *Wuthering Heights,* a literary miracle that is unique in its genre. On the other hand, *Lélia,* the strange prose oratorio (it is a "novel" in name only) which created a sensation for the embarrassing candor of its erotic revelations, is now as difficult to digest as Etienne de Sénancour's mist- and dream-drenched *Obermann* or the crypto-Gaelic verses of Ossian.

The same can be said of *Jacques,* a novel written in the exchange-of-letters style made fashionable by Rousseau's *Nouvelle Héloïse* and Choderlos de Laclos' *Les Liaisons dangereuses.* This strange story of a husband who agrees to "disappear" so that his wife may live in tranquil peace with her lover — a plot suggested to George Sand by the circumstances of her private life — enjoyed a vogue that it is virtually impossible for us to understand today. Not being Romantics, we can no longer experience the same thrill when we stumble across a phrase like this one, then considered the height of unconventional audacity: "I have not changed my mind, I am not reconciled to society, and marriage, to my way of thinking, is one of the most barbarous institutions it has engendered. I have no doubt that it will be abolished if the human species makes some progress toward justice and reason; a more human and no less sacred link will replace it, assuring the existence of children who will be born of a man and a woman without forever shackling the freedom of one and the other." For thousands, indeed for tens of thousands of fluttering Romantic hearts this pious wish had the force of a cabalistic truth, as enunciated by this new sibyl in man's clothing who had chosen to call herself George Sand. Just what this new form of hallowed wedlock would be, neither she nor her successors could say with any degree of precision. But the mere prospect was enough to arouse the wildest hopes.

Matthew Arnold, in an appreciative essay written a few months after George Sand's death, claimed that the three characteristic features of her work were "the cry of agony and revolt, the trust in beauty and nature, the aspiration towards a purged and renewed human society." In many of her novels the three are inextricably intertwined — as, for example, in *Jeanne,* which Balzac considered a masterpiece and Dostoevski a novel of genius. But where the element of anguish dominated to the detriment of everything else — as in *Lucrezia Floriani* and *Elle et Lui* — the results were less successful. Today these novels are of interest chiefly for the light they throw on George Sand's relations with Chopin and Alfred de Musset. The acuity of analysis places them in that category of psychological novel in which the French, and not least of all French women — from Madame de Lafayette to Françoise Sagan — have long excelled. But their limited and almost petty scope place them well below the level of Benjamin Constant's *Adolphe* or Alphonse Daudet's *Sapho.*

George Sand's *The Story of My Life* and her *Lettres d'un voyageur* are something else again, and Ivan Turgenev was certainly not mistaken in considering them the best things she ever wrote. The latter are particularly remarkable, being much more than the "letters of a traveler," as their title suggests. Neither Dumas nor Mérimée, who also wrote travel essays, ever attained the lyrical intensity achieved by George Sand in these highly personal meditations on music, art, politics, friendship, love, Alpine scenery, and Venetian habits — the last described with a verve and insight that no other woman writer, not even Mary McCarthy, has ever managed to rival.

Remarkable too are George Sand's pastoral novels, which won her the appellation "the Walter Scott of Berry." No French writer of the nineteenth century wrote as much about country life, and here she was clearly a pioneer, helping to establish a literary genre that was virtually nonexistent before her. But fascinating though they are as chronicles of provincial and peasant life, novels like *La Mare au diable, François le Champi,* and *Les Maîtres Sonneurs* are of necessarily limited appeal, written for readers who can derive enjoyment from a work like Turgenev's *A Huntsman's Notes.* It takes something of a connoisseur, like the French musicologist Thérèse Marix-Spire, to appreciate the delicacy with which George Sand could depict not only the sights but in particular the *sounds* of nature; just as it takes a connoisseur of French, like Henry James, to be able to note that her language "had to the end an odor of the hawthorn and the wild honeysuckle — the mark of the *climat souple et chaud,* as she somewhere calls it, from which she had received *l'initiation première.*" For much of the beauty of these pastoral descriptions is unfortunately washed away in translation.

The least successful of George Sand's novels, because the most implausible, are those in which she gave free rein to her social idealism, inventing plots as far-fetched and complex as those of some of Shakespeare's lighter comedies in order to arrange for unconventional love affairs and passions between high-souled plebeians and noble-hearted ladies. One can argue that the earthy cynicism of Balzac was often just as arbitrary, but he made no attempt to preach. In novels like *Le Compagnon du Tour de France* or *Le Meunier d'Angibault,* on the other hand, George Sand could be insufferably didactic: didactic enough to inspire one of Igor Stravinsky's more cruel quips: "On the one hand there is Luther, Protestantism, Kant, and that *vieille vache de Sand,* on the other, Catholicism and *le bon vin.*" Nothing could so enrage that voluptuary of sinfulness, Charles Baudelaire, than this tendency to righteous predication, which once caused him to explode: "She has always been a moralist. Only, previously she indulged in antimorality. She has thus never been an artist. She has the famous flowing style dear to the bourgeois. She is stupid, she is ponderous, she is long-winded; she has in moral ideas the same depth of judgment and the same delicacy of feeling as concierges and kept women."

George Sand, oddly enough, was aware of this literary failing but made little effort to correct it. "The pleading must be carried on without anybody's noticing it," she once wrote to her fellow novelist Eugène Sue. "This is the secret of the novel. I have never found it in practice." Careless in the composition of her dialogues, which often sounded more like monologues or dissertations, she felt that it was a novelist's *duty* to present his readers with an unambiguous and clear-cut point of view. Let others write novels for the simple sake of enjoyment; she had to write novels that were instructive and thus beneficial to society. This made her a utilitarian, opposed to the aristocratic doctrine of Art for Art's sake. Yet this same priestess in pantaloons, who felt that the message was more important than the form, was able to become a close friend of the fastidious Gustave Flaubert's, for whom the form was everything. Another believer in Art for Art's sake, Oscar Wilde, was even moved to pay her this extraordinary homage: "For the aristocracy of the intellect she had always the deepest veneration, but the democracy of suffering touched her more. Of all the artists of this century she was the most altruistic. She felt everyone's misfortunes but her own."

This last statement was certainly an exaggeration. It was from the coarse-grained stuff of her personal misfortunes that much of her fiction was woven — from *Indiana,* which reflected the ennui of an unhappy marriage, to *Mademoiselle Merquem,* inspired by her daughter's marriage to a man who, though talented, was both a drunkard and a rake. There was also a great deal of anguished breast-beating in her letters, in which words like *chagrin* (grief) and *mal* (woe) recur with almost obsessive frequency. Wilde, of course, was writing about her more than eighty years ago, when only a small portion of her letters had been published. But today we are in a more privileged position, thanks to the definitive edition of her letters which Garnier Frères began publishing ten years ago.

When finally completed years from now, this monumental task of epistolary concentration may well make George Sand the most meticulously documented woman in nineteenth-century France, if not in French history. A quarter of a century ago, when the great Sand scholar Georges Lubin began this labor of love, some three thousand of her letters had been inventoried and published. Since then, working with a care and diligence which should be a model for other editions of this kind, he has managed to unearth 16,000 more. More than 5000 of them have already been published in ten fat volumes, the total of which may run to twenty-five when he is finally through.

These figures, though impressive, are not quite as monumental as they sound. At a time when the telephone did not exist, it was not uncommon for people to write two, three, or more letters a day. An average of three per day would make more than 1000 in a year, or 40,000 in forty years — which was roughly speaking the span of

George Sand's creative life. No, what makes these published letters awe-inspiring is not their number, nor even the fact that so many of them have survived — thereby disproving Anthony West's fanciful assertion, in *Mortal Wounds,* that George Sand was a tenacious letter-mutilator and destroyer. The extraordinary thing about these letters is the length to which many of them run and the detailed information about George Sand's life which they reveal. The occasional snatches of dialogue to be found in this biography are not invented; they were simply culled from certain of these letters. Thus the dramatic confrontation with her husband that took place in the Nohant drawing room on October 19, 1835, and which the reader will find in Chapter 23, has been presented much as George Sand herself described it in a lengthy memorandum she wrote for her lawyer, Michel de Bourges. Similarly, the blow-by-blow description, contained in Chapter 32, of the terrible row with Solange and Clésinger which precipitated the final break with Chopin in July of 1847, has been taken from the seventy-one-page letter (only recently published by Lubin) which George Sand wrote, immediately after the uproar, to another lawyer, friend, and confidant, Emmanuel Arago.

That she was, as a French librarian once remarked to me, a formidable *pisseuse d'encre* (ink pisser) the ten published volumes of her *Correspondance* make amply clear. Charity may not have been George Sand's nemesis, but it certainly kept her busy. The pains she went to in writing letters of criticism and encouragement to proletarian poets, unhappy wives and husbands, workingmen down on their luck, and perplexed socialists of every hue were quite simply extraordinary. Less interesting, to be sure, than the prophetic letters she wrote to Mazzini in the immediate wake of the 1848 Revolution, or to Flaubert during and after the Commune of 1871, these offer us a revealing insight into the kind of hair-shirt complex that was so pronounced a feature of her do-good, mysticoreligious personality.

For it should not be forgotten, in judging this voluminous correspondence, that the same woman who found time to write so many long and detailed letters also managed to write close to sixty novels, twenty-five plays, a long autobiography, and enough miscellaneous essays to fill a dozen volumes. As Alexandre Dumas *fils* wrote to her in April of 1871: "There are three of you in this century — you, Balzac, and he." By which he meant his father, who had died a few months earlier. He was thinking of course in quantitative terms. Though her own output fell somewhat short of the eighty-five novels Balzac managed to churn out in the prodigiously short space of twenty years, it was enough to make her too a *monstre sacré* and the most prolific authoress the world has yet seen.

The wonder of it was that writing as rapidly as she did, she could maintain an elegance and richness of style which forced the admiration even of those who were dubious about the content. Henry James, who can be classed in this latter category, put it beautifully when he remarked that "people may like George Sand or not, but they can hardly deny that she is the great *improvisatrice* of literature — the writer who best answers to Shelley's description of the sky-lark singing 'in profuse strains of unpremeditated art.' No writer has produced such great effects with an equal absence of premeditation." Her regularity in filling twenty pages of "copy" during the four to six hours a night she usually devoted to the task was already legendary in her lifetime. But this bountiful discipline, which she owed to the teaching of her grandmother, was anything but mechanical and as much a product of will power and determination as of boundless and unpremeditating energy. Her letters frequently portray her as absolutely worn out by the harrowing effort to meet some critical deadline. "I shall die without having worked a single day for myself," she complained to the composer Gounod early in 1852, and similar laments against the "forced drudgery" of her existence echo through scores of other letters.

If, as the saying has it, necessity is the mother of invention, never was it more so than in the case of George Sand. Like Scott, Balzac, Dumas, Dickens, Dostoevski, and so many other "galley slaves" of nineteenth-century literature, she was forced to turn out novel after novel above all else to keep from sinking further into debt. The country house she inherited from her grandmother at Nohant was very far from being the kind of rich estate that enabled gentlemen like Tolstoi and Turgenev, and even Flaubert, to live lives of relative ease. Its annual income barely sufficed to maintain a household staff which included a coachman, a cook and an assistant, several maids and gardeners. Alimony being then as unknown as divorce, she had to provide the rest from her writing after being separated from her husband.

That she was something of a spendthrift and had no head for efficient estate management, George Sand was the first to admit. In a letter written to the banker-philanthropist Edouard Rodrigues when she was close to sixty, she reckoned that over the preceding thirty years she had given away at least 500,000 francs, without counting the two dowries she had offered to her real and to her adopted daughter — the equivalent of roughly one million dollars in charitable donations, given for the most part to peasants in distress or to the families of politically persecuted republicans. All told, this amounted to about sixty years of income from her estate. George Sand was thus forced to write less from an inveterate taste for hard work (about which she frequently complained to her close friends) than from a need to sustain the generosity which made her known as "the Good Lady of Nohant."

A cynic might well conclude from this that so much industry, expended on behalf of so much generosity, was the result of an almost psychotic need for virtuous self-sacrifice. Even the most exalted motives, as Jean-Paul Sartre has demonstrated, can be "proved" to be self-seeking or enhancing — at least for those who are of this belittling temper. Recalling Oscar Wilde's remark — "Like Goethe, George Sand had to live her romances before she could write them" — one could likewise claim that the first were more or less planned to provide novelistic material for the second. Yet was this really so? Jules Sandeau could not have foreseen that his love affair with Aurore Dudevant would one day inspire his novel *Marianna* any more than she could have realized that his exasperating indolence would later be pilloried in the person of the flighty Paris student Horace Dumontet. But the suspicion is one it is easy to entertain in the case of an established woman author known to have had more than one adventure.

It is tempting, to be sure, but also facile to regard as willed what was in fact fortuitous. Like her fellow-Romantics, George Sand wanted to live "the life of the heart" at its fullest and most intense. But this does not mean that she could plot out her adventures and their dramatic conclusions in advance. It is as arbitrary to claim that George Sand planned her ill-starred journey to Venice in the winter of 1833–1834 to keep her romance with Alfred de Musset from dying of boredom in Paris as it is to claim — as Anthony West has done — that it was undertaken to "ditch" Musset in a conveniently distant place, while the disencumbered authoress moved on happily to exotic Istanbul. This belated honeymoon was originally to have taken the two lovers south to Rome and Naples, where the end result, admittedly, might have been equally calamitous and far less picturesque. But whether it was to keep or to "dump" Musset, this was an expensive modus operandi far exceeding George Sand's humble means. Which is why I have suggested the more plausible, even if less exciting, explanation that the primary motives for both authoress and poet were of a literary nature.

The truly surprising thing about George Sand's romance with Musset is not that it received its first coup de grâce in Venice; it is that given his high-strung nature and sadomasochistic inclinations, it should later have undergone a spectacular, Phoenixlike rebirth in Paris. "How can she go on taking it?" her editor François Buloz was moved to exclaim, unable to understand how a strong-willed woman who reminded him of Catherine the Great could be made to tremble like a leaf by a young man who was more than six years her junior. The answer bears a curious resemblance to George Sand's failings as a writer — those failings which once moved a conditional admirer to exclaim: "The only fault I find with her is that she is so insufferably virtuous." Here too virtue was her undoing, and she was ill served by her relentless desire to do good. Not content to be Musset's mistress — enough to tax the patience of the most long-suffering of women — she wanted to be his savior, somewhat like the Edmée of *Mauprat,* and to cure the schizophrenic poet of his chronic relapses into debauchery and drunkenness.

George Sand would clearly not have been George Sand but for this latent martyr complex and driving compulsion to act as a kind of *Mater dolorosa* to the living. Her willingness to put up with Chopin's jealous scenes for a good half-dozen years, if not longer, cannot be explained in any other way, particularly since it was reinforced by a self-imposed chastity which was a distinct hardship for a woman who suffered fits of feverish desire with the advent of each spring.

A less virtuous woman would have unburdened herself of the delicate composer years before, or at least made less effort to be faithful. For no matter what certain Chopin biographers have suggested, her passing flirtation with Louis Blanc, recently revealed by the painstaking Georges Lubin, seems to have been her only "parallel" affair prior to the final break in July of 1847.

An objective, detailed, and step-by-step account of George Sand's relations with Chopin — a book that has yet to be written — might well be entitled "From Passion to Pity." The compassion, in any case, was considerably stronger than the passion, and the urge to be a nursemaid and mother far more powerful than the desire to be a mistress. No less typically, this protective urge was expressed with a Romantic intensity which an older (and consequently wiser) George Sand came close to deploring. "Kindness, which should be a clear-sighted and judicious virtue, was in my case a torrential and tumultuous élan," she explained to her young friend Juliette Adam when she was already in her sixties. "As soon as someone had inspired a great feeling of pity in me, I was possessed. I flung myself on the opportunity to be beneficent with a blindness which, as often as not, caused me to do harm."

There are times, in reading the story of this momentous life, when one is tempted to say: "How can a woman of such exceptional intelligence have committed so many blunders?" Not all of these can be ascribed to the bright-eyed idealism which caused her to embrace Pierre Leroux's Christian Communism and to lend her tireless pen to a demagogic windbag like Ledru-Rollin. It was perhaps the pity George Sand felt for Liszt's lot as Marie d'Agoult's lover which prompted her to "brief" Balzac on her pretentious vanity and to encourage him to write a novel about the "galley slaves of love." But if so, it was a pity heavily smudged by spite. If a sullen thirst for revenge, after being maltreated by her husband, helps to explain her affair with Stéphane Ajasson de Grandsagne, this extraordinary "fling" is no easier to condone than George Sand's sudden "passion" for Pietro Pagello in Venice. This "good woman of genius," as Pauline Viardot-García liked to call her, who could be the soul of kindness to so many was the same woman who could crucify her lovers in her novels.

It is clear that "the Good Lady of Nohant" was anything but a monolithic personality and singularly complex. There is a measure of truth in the acid comment her daughter, Solange, once scribbled, after her death, on one of George Sand's letters: *"Bien malin celui qui débrouillera ma mère."* (A shrewd one it will be who will unravel my mother.) No wonder her contemporaries were so often baffled by this strange sibyl with the huge, devouring black eyes who could be as mute and mysterious as the Sphinx. This seeming extrovert who wore trousers and smoked cigarettes at a time when no "lady" did so could be positively timid with people she did not know. "She wished to seem cold, distrustful, and even annoyed," a German visitor, Karl Gutzkov, noted in April of 1842, adding perspicaciously: "She betrayed her fear of being betrayed."

There is a little-known episode that graphically illustrates this diffident taciturnity. One day in July of 1833, when she was still a youngish twenty-nine, she went to call on Etienne de Sénancour, whose neo-Gothic novel *Obermann* had greatly influenced her own prose poem *Lélia.* The sexagenarian "philosopher" received her courteously, nodding to her to be seated while waiting for her to open the conversation. "Now it seems that Madame Sand never begins an encounter with persons she is seeing for the first time," a contemporary later recalled. "As for Virginie de Sénancour" — the philosopher's daughter — "she did not dare break the silence. They spent several minutes looking at each other. There was a ceremonious exchange of bows, and then the visitor left without having uttered a single word."

This, of course, was an extreme case. But this tendency to silence, the strange product of timidity and pride, was enough to make her seem a "ruminant," as Marie d'Agoult liked to say. More charitable was Franz Liszt, who had known her before she began to be plagued by a certain difficulty in hearing, and who had rightly sensed how much modest generosity was concealed behind those pensive silences. When the already famous Miss Evans (the English writer George Eliot) called on him at Weimar in the early 1850s, he was reminded of the other George's spongelike way of absorbing everything she saw and heard. George Eliot's "long, ungainly face then took on an expression of such intense attention that it became interesting," Liszt later told his secretary Janka Wohl. "But Madame

Sand was at her ease in listening, she thus made you more eloquent. Miss Evans, on the other hand, seemed to covet your utterances and thus put you on your guard."

I doubt that one could find a more succinct description of one of George Sand's major gifts: as a listener and thus as an inspirer of geniuses as varied as Alfred de Musset, Liszt, Chopin, Alexandre Dumas *fils,* and not least of all Flaubert, who may well — I personally suspect it — have been encouraged by her to give *L'Education sentimentale* its subtle platonic ending. That this admirable capacity for listening could be extraordinarily intense we know from the painting Delacroix began of George Sand listening to Chopin play the piano — a canvas later cut in two by some art-loving vandal, with the result that the Chopin half is today in the Louvre, and the rest in Copenhagen (see photo insert page 12 in this book).

It is also thanks to Delacroix that we have a portrait of another and no less representative George Sand, caught in an expression of almost mystic contemplation (see photo insert page 1). Those of her contemporaries who were fortunate enough to see this magnificent painting were later understandably perplexed in trying to "square" it with the somewhat heavy-featured, almost bovine creature the older Madame Sand had turned into. Such transformations, of course, are anything but rare. In George Sand's case this metamorphosis seems to have singularly marked, if not as rapid as is often the case with Latin women. The anything but flattering portrait made of her by the well-meaning Luigi Calamatta makes her look like a heavy-lidded fowl framed in ungainly chiffon flaps. Though George Sand herself liked to claim that ugliness, from adolescence on, had been her natural state, we know that this was anything but the case. Heine, in a typically tongue-in-cheek tribute, written sometime in the 1840s, described her as a "distinguished beauty" — with features of an almost "Greek regularity," softened, however, by "the sentimentality which is suffused over them like a veil of sorrow," soft, tranquil eyes whose "fire has perhaps been extinguished by frequent tears" and which "recall neither Sodom nor Gomorrah," magnificent shoulders (comparable to those of the Venus de Milo, no less!), small hands and feet, and a bosom the hidden charms of which he admitted he was incompetent to describe and must leave to the effrontery of bolder contemporaries to describe. When her friend and fellow writer Hortense Allart came upon the sentence in *The Story of My Life* in which George Sand had written: "I had but one instant of freshness and never one of beauty," she exclaimed: "One cannot be more modest in not wishing to show off . . . But who will give her back to us as beautiful as she was in the beginning, at the time of [her affair with] Mérimée?"

The "finely chiseled lightness in her features" which, as the Goncourt brothers noted in 1862, had not come through in portraits that had "thickened and fattened her face," obviously posed a challenge which few of the artists of her time could cope with. But the striking diversity in the pictures that have survived has been curiously enhanced by a few spurious additions. One, painted by Delacroix, was used on the jacket cover of the American edition of André Maurois's *Lélia* when it first appeared some twenty years ago. The portrait, that of a most alluring lady in a broad-brimmed hat, was indeed by Delacroix, but it was the portrait of his mistress, Madame Dalton. Another illustration in this same edition, one which had already been used in Frances Winwar's *The Life of the Heart* (and which recently reappeared in Eleanor Perényi's life of Liszt), shows a distinctly masculine George Sand, her head oddly tilted under a tall top hat. The accompanying caption specified: "George Sand, by Delacroix. 1830." But not until 1834 did she actually meet Delacroix, who would never have dreamed of painting a portrait of George Sand in a top hat, even if she had wanted it, which is doubtful. All we know about this portrait is that it was actually painted by Couture and that it was later identified by George Sand's granddaughter as being of her father, Maurice Sand, but even this attribution is open to question.

This is, obviously, a classic case of stereotypic image-making. Since George Sand was known to have been a woman who smoked, wore masculine attire, and had adopted a man's name, a picture had to be produced that showed her in a top hat. No such portrait existed — with the possible exception of a full-length painting showing two gentlemen in toppers who have been "identified" as being George Sand and Chopin, though the resemblance in each case is more than vague.

The idea that George Sand always wore trousers and ran around in a top hat is, in fact, closer to legend than reality. Though her name will always be associated with these vestimentary innovations, she was far from being the first woman to wear trousers. As she herself took pains to point out in her autobiography, her mother and other women of modest means had taken to wearing trousers during the sans-culotte days of the French Revolution in order to gain access to the cheap standing-room area (reserved for men) in a theater's "pit." In the province of Berry a local squire later began dressing his daughters in male attire for hunting, and it was this which first prompted the young Aurore Dupin to climb into trousers, simply because they were so much more practical for cross-saddle riding. George Sand's sole merit, if such it can be called, was to have made a domestic habit out of what was originally a utilitarian disguise. But it was a habit which, like riding, she gave up relatively early on, when she was in her middle forties.

George Sand's mannish ways and affectations were thus only the more visible and superficial aspect of a far more complex personality. Had it been otherwise, the same Frédéric Chopin who is reported to have exclaimed: "What an antipathetic woman, this Sand! Is it really a woman?" after their first encounter could not later have fallen so completely under her spell. Nor, if her masculinity had been so blatant and overpowering, could a dedicated skirt-chaser like Alfred de Musset conceivably have described her to a friend as being "*la femme la plus femme*" — the most womanly woman — he had ever met. Nor would Flaubert, for whom she had become a kind of second mother, have been able to write after her death: "Poor dear great woman! . . . One had to know her as I knew her to understand how much of the feminine there was in this great man, the immensity of tenderness to be found in this genius."

For professional debunkers, of course, George Sand has always been a sitting duck. She was, inevitably, the femme fatale who destroyed Musset, the black-widow spider who sapped Chopin's lifeblood and inspiration. A good example of this character assassination is Henri Guillemin's recent onslaught, *La Liaison Musset-Sand* (devoted to the fateful Venice trip), which the *Times Literary Supplement* aptly dismissed as "242 pages of methodically indexed venom."

Another example is provided by the third volume of Chopin's *Correspondance,* translated into French and edited by Bronislas Sydow, who was doubtless well intentioned, and by two French ladies who, in compiling supposedly objective footnotes, seized on every chance to blacken the record where they could.

In dealing with a life as rich and eventful as George Sand's this is easy sport. As an object of public notoriety and scandal she attracted hostile comment and criticism much as a lightning rod attracts lightning. The gossipmonger is confronted with a positive embarrassment of riches. Why, then, waste time with a humdrum compliment when a cruel quip is so much more piquant? Why waste one's time quoting the younger Liszt's admiring comment — "She is beyond doubt or comparison the 'strongest' woman (in the Biblical sense) and the most astonishingly gifted" — when one can fall with relish on this later description of her literary methods, as recorded by Janka Wohl: "Madame Sand took pleasure in capturing the butterfly with a sticky brush and in gaining its trust while she locked it into a box with aromatic herbs and flowers — this was the love period. Then she stuck a needle into it and let it writhe in a death agony — this was the dismissal, which always came from her. After which she dissected her 'object' and stuffed it for her collection of heroes for novels."

Another provider of rich fare was Heinrich Heine, one of the most ingenious coiners of bons mots there has ever been. (On Musset: "A young man with a promising past.") In the last years of his life, when he was preparing an edition of his Complete Works, the ailing poet (slowly dying of syphilis) devoted a particularly vicious paragraph to the melancholy Czech composer Josef Dessauer, a friend of Chopin's who had inspired George Sand's play *Maître Favilla.* Dessauer, whom Heine termed a "crawling insect" and a "boastful flea," had, he suggested, enjoyed George Sand's "intimacy" along with Chopin and Franz Liszt, who was referred to more cryptically as a "spider." These "sad insults," emanating from a "suffering soul, deserving nonetheless of a better end," as George Sand wrote to Dessauer, are typical of the spiteful rumors her career never ceased to engender. Heine had developed a pathological hatred for Dessauer ever since the day he had vainly sought to borrow money from him for a trip to Spain. He also seems to have resented the fact that George Sand could succumb to the influence of the "philosophical Capucin" Pierre Leroux while rejecting the advances which he, who had studied philosophy under Hegel, had made to her in 1838, at a time when he was anxious to disengage himself from the vampire grip of his sensuous Parisian mistress, Eugénie Mirat.

Heine's insinuation that Dessauer and Liszt had both enjoyed the favor of George Sand's bed was as fanciful as the claim put forward by a recent Heine biographer, Friedrich Hirth, who would have us believe that the German poet was one of her many "victims." Such allegations appeal to a sensation-hungry age which would like to believe that the "real" George Sand was a voracious nymphomaniac, moving insatiably from the exhausted body of one genius to the next in vain search of an inexhaustible virility.

Juliette Adam was much closer to the truth in her comment on George Sand's relations with Musset and Mérimée: *"Elle était amante et ne savait pas être maîtresse"* — which may be translated into tougher Anglo-Saxon as: "She knew more about loving than about making love." The total number of her "victims," even by the most generous count, does not reach twenty, and previous biographies notwithstanding, I personally doubt that the Swiss poet Charles Didier ever managed to bed her. Her behavior in 1836 and 1837, when she was at her most flirtatious and "unhinged," was, all things considered, less that of an insatiable Messalina than that of a frustrated Penelope, doing her best to play off one "hopeful" against another. Similarly, the malady she suffered from, as I have suggested in the chapter entitled *Lélia,* was not nymphomania but nympholepsy: a yearning for the unattainable and "sublime" induced by an arch-Romantic and mystical imagination.

No less insidious has been the legend woven around George Sand's "lesbian" propensities. This, of course, is not a recent discovery. But in an age increasingly inclined to regard the abnormal as the norm, it was as inevitable that this quality should be added to George Sand's virtues as that Chopin should be revealed to have been a homosexual (which is what the French musicologist Bernard Gavoty has suggested in a recent biography). Anthony West, in

Mortal Wounds, takes it more or less for granted that the young Aurore Dupin's tomboy antics and transvestite attire were a public manifestation of heterosexual inclinations — which was apparently enough to make her a "practicing lesbian" from adolescence on. With whom? Well, with Marie Dorval, the actress, as everybody knows . . .

But how much do we actually know, and from whom was it derived? The question deserves to be looked into, for it is a classic example of how myths are born. The first thing to be noted is that Marie Dorval was the only woman whose name was linked at the time in this kind of relationship with George Sand. Now a lesbian who limits herself to one affair of this kind, no matter how "practiced" she may be, is clearly a special type of lesbian. What makes the story stranger is that we find virtually the same pattern in the case of her "partner," Marie Dorval. Here was an actress who was notoriously fond of men and who for years cuckolded her husband almost every day of the week. She had a rival in the person of Juliette Drouet (Victor Hugo's love-crazed mistress), who graciously let it be known to anyone willing to listen that Madame Dorval had harbored a passion for her "of the same nature as that of Sappho for the young lesbians," as the critic Gustave Planche reported it to George Sand. Marie Dorval also had a lover, Alfred de Vigny, who had developed the curious habit of visiting his mistress in the morning simply because he felt that aristocratic decorum called for his staying home at night with his mother and his frigid English wife. The mere idea that that "monstrous woman" George Sand should visit Marie Dorval at night, when the actress's domestic and theater chores were over, was enough to make the jealous poet suspect the worst. The Paris literary world then being what it still is today — a beehive of malicious gossip — it was not long before these suspicions had hardened into "facts" which were bandied back and forth from one salon to the next. The final touches were later added by Arsène Houssaye, a glib gossipmonger who was barely eighteen years old when these "events" occurred. Stripped of its rococo embellishments, the original "evidence" is thin indeed: the insinuations of a jealous actress, the suspicions of a jealous lover. Not much. But of such gossamer material are legends often made.

"Where would I be, Good Lord, with my best friends if I had listened to what they have so often told me about each other!" George Sand once wrote to the actor Pierre Bocage. But from those who were not her friends the author of *Lélia* could expect no such indulgence. Her reputation as a lethal femme fatale once established, nothing could weaken or destroy the image. What in the behavior of other *femmes de lettres* was regarded as acceptable was in her case considered monstrous. Rare were those who, like the unusually sympathetic Madame Fauvety, were prepared to take up the cudgels for George Sand when *Elle et Lui* was published, shortly after Alfred de Musset's death, in 1859: "All of us Parisians know what Musset was like, the scorn with which he treated women, the great [actress] Rachel included! Madame Sand literally tried to drag him from the taverns of low resort. She has more than the right, she has the feminine duty to prove that she didn't 'torture' Musset. There's good reason to be dumfounded when one thinks of the cruelty with which George Sand is now judged, as opposed to the indulgence that was shown to Madame de Staël, who deceived Benjamin Constant with Camille Jordan, and was then unfaithful to the latter with her son's tutor . . ."

One may well wonder, with Madame Fauvety, why George Sand should have been judged with one yardstick and Madame de Staël with another. The answer is not, I think, to be found in any upsurge of moral righteousness in the French, no longer willing to forgive Madame Sand for the peccadilloes that had readily been forgiven Madame de Staël. The Second Empire, for all its external decorum, was as tolerant of liaisons as had been the First, and the France of Louis-Philippe and Napoleon III was in this respect considerably less hidebound than Queen Victoria's Britain. What George Sand's contemporaries could not forgive her was the iconoclasm of her dress, the audacity with which she smoked cigarettes and pipes and laid claim to domestic prerogatives that up until then had been regarded as exclusively masculine. Madame de Staël had made no such claims, contenting herself with the traditional role of hostess-mistress that had been established and confirmed over the centuries at the court of the Kings of France. In transgressing the limits of this traditional role, George Sand made herself two sets of enemies. She antagonized the men, stubbornly attached to their masculine prerogatives, and she shocked the women, most of whom were still traditionalists brought up to believe that to smoke was unladylike and sinful and not to wear a skirt positively barbarous behavior.

Yet the surprising thing about this "rebel" who shocked so many of her contemporaries was how conservative she remained in many important matters. André Maurois was right to say that spencers, sentry-box greatcoats, and trousers notwithstanding, George Sand was never really an Amazon. Generally speaking, she preferred the company of men to that of women, and she had altogether too low an opinion of the political intelligence of most members of her sex to be a suffragette. She favored divorce and deplored the conditions of female servitude characterizing existing marriage laws, but she did not think that marriage was a contemptible bourgeois institution. Though her own proved disastrous, she continued to the end to uphold marriage as a kind of social ideal, God-ordained and granted. She did not consider needlework, jam-making, and cooking — in all of which she was surprisingly proficient — as inherently degrading. Adamantly opposed to the promiscuous doctrine of "free love" which the followers of Saint-Simon and Fourier were trying to propagate, she felt little sympathy for the kind of "free wife" which Senkovski and other European liberals were trying to promote. She was the very opposite of a "female chauvinist" and refused to view woman's plight as so endemically desperate as to warrant an antimasculine crusade. As Dostoevski rightly pointed out here too: "George Sand associated herself with every forward movement and not with a campaign solely destined to assure the triumph of women's rights."

All this makes George Sand a distinctly baffling personality for those who now champion the "liberation" of women. Simone de Beauvoir, to name but one, accords her several passing mentions in *The Second Sex* and that is all. If George Sand was in any sense a prototype of the modern emancipated female, she was also a singularly monitory prophet, more conscious of the pitfalls that were to be skirted than of the boons and blessings this new revolution was likely to confer.

Hightly critical of those nineteenth-century priestesses who, she felt, had ill-served the cause of their downtrodden sex by their often misguided clamors, George Sand would have been even more critical of those who today have been promoting lust and license as a necessary forward step on the road to the final "emancipation" of man- and womankind. Nothing, certainly, would have appalled her more than the pornographic glut which has recently swamped the newsstands of the Western world. Not because she was a puritan but because she was a poet. On this subject she and Isak Dinesen, so different in other respects, would have seen eye to eye. Both would have recoiled before the shameless curiosity of the roving camera eye, now mounted tanklike on a pornocratic juggernaut which is busy grinding the last taboos to dust. This is not the "progress" George Sand dreamed about, still less the "freedom" she championed. If only because from the tyranny of the taboo we have moved, with dizzying speed, to the servitude of sex.

The gospel she herself undertook to preach was not that of unlimited sex but of boundless love. She called this gift — for such she conceived it to be — "the fire of Heaven" — causing Henry James to remark: "In her view love is always love, is always divine in its essence and ennobling in its operation." It may sound quaint, it may sound old-fashioned, it was certainly romantic, it may even have been mystical in its idealism, but it was this which makes George Sand timeless — like Teresa of Avila. In one of her earliest short stories, "La Marquise," she noted that the noblewoman's unfulfilled passion for a lowly actor, far more than the irksome embraces of her official paramour, was what "to a certain extent had made a woman of her." The capacity to love was, for George Sand, woman's distinctive virtue, just as the capacity to reason is what distinguishes man from the beast. Sex without love may be enjoyed by the mindless and totally uninhibited, but for many others it is closer to hell than to heaven. And this is why, were she alive today, George Sand would at the very least have smiled, and more likely have shuddered at the crude idea that erotic felicity is within every woman's easy reach — the no longer forbidden fruit of polymorphous curiosity, promiscuous indulgence, and professional technique.

Contents

Illustrations *following page 396*

PART I

Youth

1. Major Dupin's Daughter

FRAGMENTARY AND MYSTERIOUS, as though veiled by a lifting fog, are our first childish memories, and who is there among us who has not been struck by the random nature of his or her first recollection? Why it should have been a particular fold in the bedroom curtain, a certain flower in the pattern of the wallpaper, the sudden stops and starts in the erratic movement of flies buzzing overhead that should have remained so vividly present when so much else had washed away, George Sand in later life could not explain. She could only attribute it to the interminable succession of waking hours she had spent on her infant back, staring at the ceiling from the soft captivity of her crib — a feeling of confinement made all the more baffling as the light began to fade by the curiously unfocused, double halo of the candles that were brought in to dispel the evening gloom.

But among these first disconnected perceptions was one that stood out sharply. Half a century later she could still vividly recall the russet hue of the marble mantelpiece she had struck with her forehead as she fell. Gone was all memory of pain, as though erased by the shock that had jolted her infant mind into coherent recollection, but not of the red blood that had welled forth from the cut which had marked her brow from then on. And there, looming up before her as though it had only happened yesterday, was the tear-streaked face of the tipsy maid who had dropped her, the anguished figure of her uniformed father, so different, she felt, from the apparent indifference of her mother, who had gripped her tiny wrists and sought to quiet her screams as a terrifying doctor bent over and hooked a pair of wriggling leeches to the lobes of her ears.

It had happened in the country, before her parents had moved back into Paris to the modest third-floor flat on the Rue de la Grange-Batelière, near which Aurore Dupin had been born two years earlier. Of this latter event, which took place on the twelfth day of Messidor in the Year XII of the Republic — which is to say, on July 1, 1804 — she had, of course, not the slightest recollection, any more than she had of Napoleon's coronation, celebrated some months later. But her mother always enjoyed recalling how Aurore came into the world one festive evening, when her father (who was musically as well as martially inclined) was playing the violin and she was stretched out on a chaise longue in a pink dress, watching her sister Lucie go through the motions of a minuet.

To have married an army officer whom she had met in Milan during Napoleon's first Italian campaign in 1800, an officer, furthermore, who was the grandson of the illustrious Maréchal de Saxe, might have seemed the final consummation of a dream for the lowly born Sophie-Victoire Delaborde; her own father had been a humble tavern keeper who had sold birds on the banks of the Seine and the Canal Saint-Martin. But their life was anything but luxurious. In the small Rue de la Grange-Batelière flat it was Sophie Dupin who did the sewing and mending, made the beds, swept the floors, and attended to the cooking. Though she was seldom in bed before one and always rose at six, she never complained of overwork or fatigue. Meals were served in a kind of antechamber, next to the small kitchen, and the bedroom beyond became a living room in daytime. Each morning Aurore's cot was pushed back into the alcove and hidden behind a door; when not away at boarding school, her elder sister, Caroline (five years her senior and only a half sister, as she was later to discover) slept on the couch, whose green velvet cover was rolled back to make a bed.

To keep the restless Aurore from playing with the bedroom stove while she was busy in the kitchen with the pot-au-feu, her mother would fence her in behind four straw-seated chairs, which were all they possessed. There being no cushion available, the child had to content herself with an empty foot warmer, on whose hard metal surface she would sit when tired of standing. Using it as a stool, she would prop her elbows on the seat of a chair and tear doggedly at the rushes with her fingernails, as though trying to reveal some hidden treasure. While her little fingers were thus engaged in dismantling what furniture there was, her tongue was no less idle, inventing long, rambling stories which her mother called her "novels."

At ten months she could walk, and she could read quite well by the time she was four, well enough, indeed, to be able to amaze a salon full of aged ladies by reading off the brand name of a sweet her paternal grandmother had just handed her. It did not occur to Madame Dupin de Francueil to find such a feat precocious, for in this respect the child was no more advanced than her cousin Clothilde, the daughter of her mother's sister, with whom she was brought up. Indeed, the two mothers — named Lucie and Sophie-Victoire Delaborde before their respective marriages to Amand Maréchal and Maurice Dupin — took turns drilling their two daughters, teaching them the Lord's Prayer, the Ave Maria, as well as the verses of La Fontaine, which the young ones were soon rattling off like parrots while barely understanding a word of what they were reciting.

Given the poverty of their wardrobe, Aurore's mother did not take her to skip rope or play with hoops in the fashionable Tuileries Gardens, where their modest attire might have inspired smug remarks. Not until she was considerably older did Aurore realize that the principal cause of their tight straits was the extravagant expenses her father had to incur as aide-de-camp to Joachim Murat, the dashing cavalryman who had married Napoleon's sister Caroline and who had been appointed governor of Paris. The officer's salary he received was quite insufficient to pay for the silver-buttoned dolmans and scarlet brandenburgs, the fur-lined shakos and golden epaulets he needed for state occasions, to say nothing of harnesses and saddles, and the ostler he needed to take care of his horses.

Months would pass without his seeing his wife or his daughter, as his duties took him (with the resumption of hostilities) across the Rhine to Berlin and East Prussia, and then from Tilsit, on the Niemen, as far south as Venice. At last, in January of 1808, Maurice Dupin was back in Paris, a bit plumper about the waist than he had been when he had begun courting Sophie-Victoire Delaborde eight years earlier in Italy but still an unusually handsome man, with his faintly aquiline nose, a pair of dark lustrous eyes, and whiskers and eyebrows that were so jet black that they looked as though they had been dyed in India ink. He doted on his only daughter, who had grown even more precious since the death, some eighteen months earlier, of a short-lived son, and to amuse Aurore at suppertime, he would tie his napkin into knots and give himself rabbit ears, a jester's bell cap, or a monkish cowl.

In the spring of 1808 he was off again, this time to Madrid, whither Murat had been dispatched posthaste by Napoleon, following on a revolt against the Spanish Queen's Francophile favorite, Manuel de Godoy, the unpopular prime minister who had involved Spain in hostilities with England and thus contributed to the destruction of the Spanish fleet at Trafalgar. As the weeks passed it became increasingly clear from Colonel Dupin's letters that his sojourn in the Spanish capital might be a long one. The thought was enough to unleash all of his wife's jealous suspicions. A winter spent in the frozen wastes of Poland and East Prussia was one thing, but a summer spent in the hot, passionate climate of Spain was a different matter. What might not be the temptations, particularly for a handsome man, made even more alluring by the martial glamour of his attire!

Though she was by this time seven months pregnant, Aurore's mother could wait no longer. A Madame Fontanier, she learned, was leaving shortly for Spain to join her quartermaster husband. Her sole companion for the trip being a twelve-year-old groom, there were two empty seats in her calèche which she was glad to offer to Sophie Dupin and her four-year-old daughter.

Spain, which it took them two weeks to reach, offered an unforgettable contrast to the gently rolling country through which they had been passing. Aurore felt overpowered by the watchful stillness of the steep Basque valleys through which they had to wind. The puffing of the horses as they pulled wearily uphill, the painful creak of the axles, the swaying and rocking of the carriage as they lurched round the precipitous bends combined with the ever wilder aspect of the landscape to fill her with anguished forebodings. Too young to appreciate the "sublime" beauty of the Pyrenees, which were later to inflame her romantic imagination, she expected at any moment to see the rough dirt road come to an abrupt end or dwindle into a goat track, too steep to enable them to continue, too narrow to allow them to turn back.

Not far from Burgos they stopped at an inn for dinner. Shortly after their arrival a large coach was driven into the stable yard, followed by several others and generous clouds of dust. Coachmen, grooms, and ostlers went to work changing the horses with extraordinary precipitation. Outside, a throng of villagers ran up, shouting: *"La reina! La reina!"* One of the inn's serving girls picked Aurore up and brought her close to the largest coach. "There, look at the Queen!" she said. The person inside looked anything but regal: her high-bodiced dress was yellow with dust and, like her young daughter next to her, she seemed unnaturally dark and ugly. The pathetic "Queen" she was looking at was the Infanta María Luísa, daughter of that spineless Bourbon Carlos IV. She was now fleeing to Bayonne to place herself under the custody of Napoleon, who had promised but failed to secure for her the throne of the new kingdom of Lusitania (northern Portugal).

The farther south they progressed, the grimmer the spectacle of wartime havoc became. At one village where they stopped for the night every house had been looted and gutted by the French invaders, and there were just one chair, one bench, and one table left in the pillaged inn. The only thing the innkeeper could offer them for supper was raw onions. Aurore ate several, but neither her mother nor Madame Fontanier would touch them. Both sat through the night, while Aurore was stretched out on the single remaining table, on a "mattress" composed of carriage cushions.

At last they reached Madrid, the hot, dusty, seething Madrid of Goya's wartime sketches. On every side a sullen populace was preparing to rise against the French "protectors," but of this the little Aurore was blissfully unconscious as she climbed out of the calèche and into her father's arms. Promptly forgotten were the perils and discomforts of the journey, as she and her mother were led into the palace that was now to be their home. It had been the residence of Manuel Godoy, overthrown by the popular uprising just two months earlier. Its ground-floor apartments were now occupied by Murat.

As his aide-de-camp, Aurore's father had been given lodgings on the third floor, where the scale may have been smaller but where the crimson damask hangings were no less princely. This was the dream world of Aurore's fairy tales come true, but the reality was overpowering. The gilded armchairs, the gilt divans, the gilded beds, even the ornate cornices seemed to be made of solid gold, and everywhere she felt pursued by watchful faces, silently staring down from huge portrait frames. Having never before had a chance to see herself in full reflection, she was at once awed and fascinated by the dark-haired, dark-eyed stranger she could see walking hesitantly across the carpets toward the Psyche mirror, whose persistently cold touch came as much of a surprise to her as did the size of the questioning reflection.

Most of the Spanish servants having been evicted along with their former master, the palace's apartments were as dirty and untidy as they were grand. Cats, dogs, and even rabbits wandered in and out more or less at will, and one of them, a white rabbit with ruby red eyes, became so attached to Aurore that it would go to sleep on her knees or crouch for long minutes on the hem of her dress while she filled its tall ears with stories. Never had she had so many toys to keep her amused — dolls in cloth-of-gold dresses waiting to be laid to rest in tiny tasseled beds, richly caparisoned horses, dwarflike figures in painted wood — playthings that had already been severely manhandled by the infantas of Spain and whose work of demolition she joyously completed.

Though in the end they only spent eight weeks in Madrid, to Aurore at the time they seemed interminably long. Often she would have to spend a good part of the day alone, while her mother accompanied her father to some official reception. The Spanish maid Teresa, who was supposed to keep watch over her, preferred to scurry off on mysterious "errands," locking the door as she went, or leaving Aurore to the care of her father's manservant, Weber, an unwashed Alsatian who stank so dreadfully that she felt faint each time he picked her up in his arms.

Aurore was delighted by her mother's eventual confinement, for it put an end to the solitude she had found so depressing. Sophie Dupin no longer left the palace, spending much of the day stretched out on a chaise longue. When the time came for her to be delivered of the "little brother or sister" Aurore had long been promised, the child was sent out to play on the hot, sun-warmed balcony. The mirrored doors were closed and not an anguished birth-giving cry reached her young ears. Her father called her back a little later, but as she stepped into the bedroom, she hardly noticed the fuzzy-haired newcomer so upset was she by the pale, drawn features of her mother, whom she rushed to embrace with tears in her eyes. It took her some time to realize that the small wrinkled face she was repeatedly shown was that of a baby brother, whom her mother would gently rock against her bosom with a look of infinite distress. The unusual pallor of the infant's blue eyes made it clear that something was amiss.

Two weeks later their belongings were packed and they made ready to leave, like the rest of Murat's entourage. The fate of Spain had been decided, or so Bonaparte rashly thought, and her Bourbon monarch, Carlos IV, had been obliged to abdicate, along with his son Fernando, in favor of Napoleon's older brother, Joseph. To Murat, his principal lieutenant in the peninsula, had been given the throne of Naples, where Maurice Dupin was due to follow him after a few weeks of home leave in France.

All were overjoyed by the news, and none more so than Murat's aide-de-camp, who could not wait to shake the hot dust of Madrid from his boots and spurs. At Nohant, some 600 miles to the north and east in the central French province of Berry, his widowed mother, he knew, would welcome her only son: she would be only too happy to have him and his young family spend a few weeks in the eighteenth-century country house she had bought some fifteen years before. Aurore, who had never seen Nohant, having been born and brought up in Paris and its immediate vicinity, wanted to be off immediately. Her father managed to get hold of a calèche for his wife and children, but he himself rode a fiery Andalusian charger, known as "Leopardo the Untamable," which Fernando VII had given him as a present during a visit to the royal palace of Aranjuez.

If the journey down from France had been rough and uncomfortable, the return was a nightmare. All over the peninsula, during these summer weeks of 1808, the Spaniards were rising up against the unwanted intruders who had highhandedly decided to abduct the royal family and put a French ruler in his place. Murat and his escorting regiments had to fight more than one engagement as they headed north. Aurore's father rode on ahead with Murat and his suite, trotting back as often as he could on his spirited mount to see how his wife and children were doing among the carriages and carts of the baggage train. Once, when they halted near a French camp, whose white tents dotted the plain in neat military rows, Aurore crept up behind an officer friend of her father's, wanting to surprise him with a pinch, but all her little fingers encountered was an empty sleeve. A cannonball had carried away his left arm.

It was by now mid-July and the midday heat was merciless. Like the soldiers accompanying them, Sophie Dupin and her children were wracked by an awful thirst. Aurore grew feverish, like her baby brother, and increasingly numb to the incomprehensible swirl of events in which they were caught up. At a roadside inn, not far from Medina del Río Seco, her mother brought her over to the window, saying: "Look, that's a battle, and your father's perhaps in it." Aurore went on munching her green apple, contentedly admiring the gory beauty of the sunset, the gay puffs of smoke, the arching stabs of fire, the distant boom of the cannon, as though she were watching a fireworks display especially arranged for her enjoyment. Even the spectacle of the carnage, the following morning, seemed to her no more real than had the dolls she and her cousin Clothilde had so often and eagerly dismembered during their "war games" in Paris. The air, however, was infected, the stench sickening. "What are all tose rags out there?" asked Aurore innocently, gazing out over a plain littered with formless debris. Her mother, instead of answering, buried her face in her hands. There was a sinister crunch as one of their wheels hit an obstacle on the roadway. Aurore wanted to lean out to see what it was but was pulled back by her mother, who knew that what they had just run over was a corpse.

Their calèche was soon requisitioned for the transportation of the wounded, and they found themselves on a farm cart, wedged in among baggage, sick soldiers, and sutlers. Aurore too was sick —

with scabies, which she quickly transmitted to her baby brother and mother. On they lumbered — past gutted farmsteads, over corpse-strewn roads, along ditches where the meager pools of water secreted dark gobs of blood. Already plagued by thirst, they were now tortured by hunger. Raw onions, green lemons, and sunflower seeds were all they could find to eat — to the silent dismay of Aurore's mother, who had to wean her tiny boy on this unpalatable diet. One evening she had Aurore sit down next to a group of soldiers who were eating a hot soup with relish. The soldiers gladly fed her out of their mess kits, but when Aurore's mother came closer, she saw black wicks floating on the broth's greasy surface next to lumps of soaked bread. The bouillon Aurore was being fed — to her evident satisfaction — had been made from melted candle ends!

At last they reached the Basque foothills and their ordeal became less painful, as the fields grew greener and the heat less burning. They regained possession of their calèche. At the roadside inns they now found beds with sheets as well as tasty cakes and cheeses. At Fuenterrabia, near the French border, Aurore was given the first bath she had had in weeks. But the pleasant feel of cleansing water gave way to disgust as her sick body was powdered with sulphur and she was forced to swallow lumps of it mixed into sugared butterballs.

Worn out by days of ceaseless jolting over rough dirt roads, Aurore's mother now insisted that they continue to Bordeaux by sea rather than by land. A sloop was hired and their calèche lowered and stowed beneath the craft's small deck. Aurore was given a bouquet of roses to offset the nauseating stench of sulphur, and off they sailed in an atmosphere of near holiday rejoicing. The wind-whipped Bay of Biscay for once was calm, and the voyage up the coast was agreeably smooth and uneventful, until they headed into the estuary of the Gironde. Here the sloop hit a hidden reef and began to ship water. While the skipper and his two assistants strained desperately toward the shore, Aurore's father tore off his jacket and readied a shawl with which he proposed to strap his two children on his back if he had to swim to land with his wife. The ever-rising water had already reached the wheel hubs of their carriage when they finally grazed up against a stone embankment and were hauled up a rescue ladder lowered by several men on shore.

Fearful as ever, Aurore's mother beseeched her father to let their belongings founder with the leaking sloop rather than risk his life further, but Maurice Dupin would not rest until he had cut the calèche loose with his saber and dragged it up to dry land. Then he helped the harassed skipper beach his stricken craft.

Aurore spent the rest of the journey in a feverish daze, from which she only emerged when their carriage rolled into a little elm-shaded square next to a squat, moss-covered church and on through two stone gateposts into the circular courtyard beyond. They had reached Nohant.

2. Nohant

THE FIRST PERSON Aurore saw, as she was lifted out of the carriage, was her grandmother, a pale, rosy-cheeked lady who looked, to her young eyes, very tall and imposing, though she in fact stood barely five feet tall. She wore an old-fashioned brown silk dress with a low waistline — markedly different from the high-bodiced Empire gowns worn by her mother — and even more startling for Aurore was the sight of her ancien régime wig, whose tubular blond curls half hid her forehead beneath a little round bonnet adorned by a distinctive lace cockade.

After hugging Aurore's father with the intense maternal tenderness she felt for her only son, the old lady turned and opened her arms to Aurore's mother, who stopped her, saying: "Dear Mama, do not touch me or these children. You don't know the hardships we've been through, we're all ill."

"A few pimples!" exclaimed Maurice Dupin with a laugh, "which have made such an impression on Sophie's lively imagination that she fancies they've got scabies." With that he swung Aurore up from the ground and placed the child in his mother's arms.

"Scabies or not," said the grandmother, pressing Aurore to her bosom, "I shall take care of this one."

The bed on which Aurore was laid, in her grandmother's ground-floor room, was a handsome four-poster with tasseled valances and a double set of curtains which could be drawn closed to keep out the light. The little girl felt ashamed and disgusted at the idea that she was defiling the luxurious silk cushions she was lying on, no less than the elegant cretonne wallpaper with its leafy East Indian motifs. But her grandmother displayed no sign of repulsion as she fussed and fretted over her.

They were soon joined by a chubby boy of nine, who walked in with a huge bouquet of flowers, which he playfully thrust into Aurore's face, with that gruff impetuousness children often display when unsure as to just how they should behave. "This is Hippolyte," her grandmother introduced him. "Now, my children, kiss one another." The two young ones embraced, without Aurore's realizing that she was kissing her half brother.*

The "doctor" who later came to look her over was a solemn-faced gentleman dressed in a hazel gray frockcoat and white silk stockings (beneath the eighteenth-century breeches), on the top of whose head was perched a buttoned-down hunting cap. A former abbé who had prudently chosen, after the outbreak of the 1789 Revolution, to become *le citoyen* François Deschartres, he had served Aurore's grandmother for almost twenty years, first as Maurice Dupin's tutor and later as the manager of her estate. A self-taught agronomist who liked to experiment with new seeds and planting methods calculated to double normal crop yields, he had also managed to accumulate a considerable knowledge of chemistry and "physics" through the assiduous perusal of learned tomes; though he had never obtained a formal degree in medicine, he was reasonably adept in wielding a surgeon's knife and scalpel. The verdict he now handed down, as Nohant's unofficial doctor, was reasonably encouraging: Aurore had been suffering from scabies — of that there was no doubt — but the illness had largely run its course and her lingering fever was due more to prolonged fatigue than to anything else.

The fresh country air soon restored Aurore to good health, though her mother kept forcing little butterballs of sulphur down her reluctant throat. Her baby brother, Louis, was less fortunate. The pimples covering his body disappeared, but his face remained flushed with fever. His pale blue eyes had a vacant look, and one day Aurore overheard Deschartres saying, at a moment when nei-

* In fact, an illegitimate half brother, the unexpected product of a casual affair which the twenty-year-old Maurice Dupin had had with a Nohant serving girl before going off to the wars. For more details see the notes to this chapter, and the accompanying genealogical chart, at the end of this book.

ther of her parents was present: "But this child is blind." Had his normal growth been stunted in his mother's womb by the rigors of their carriage journey across Spain, or had the infant deliberately been blinded at the time of his birth by the Madrid doctor, vengefully determined that this French child at least would "never see the Spanish sun"? In her mounting anguish Aurore's mother was ready to believe anything. They spent long hours out of doors, well wrapped and blanketed with shawls and cushions, but the feverish infant was beyond saving. On the eighth of September 1808 the little body grew cold and it was a lifeless child whom Deschartres finally removed from the mother's desperate arms.

Eight days after his son's death, Maurice Dupin decided to ride over to the town of La Châtre, some three miles to the south, to dine with friends. Sophie was much upset to find herself thus left alone for an evening with a mother-in-law she had never liked and who had done everything possible to thwart her marriage to her son. She even broke down and wept in the presence of Madame Dupin de Francueil, who had difficulty restraining her from venturing out into the rainy night to look for her husband.

Exhausted by her recent tribulations, Sophie finally agreed to retire upstairs to bed. But at six o'clock the next morning, when she rose, her husband was still not back. Aurore was already up and her mother had just slipped into a white skirt and sleeved jacket when an ashen-faced Deschartres burst in without knocking.

"Maurice! Where's Maurice?" cried Aurore's mother desperately.

Deschartres stood there, his jaw muscles working convulsively, his speech reduced to short staccato sentences. "He had a fall! . . . No, don't go, don't go, stay here! . . . Think of your daughter! . . . Yes, it's serious . . . very serious . . ." Then, with what seemed like a superhuman effort, he blurted out: "He's dead!" His knees suddenly buckling, the anguished tutor sat down, uttered a brief convulsive laugh, and burst into tears.

Sophie staggered back and collapsed into a chair behind the bed. Aurore rushed to her side and began breathlessly kissing her bare arms, between contagious sobs which her mother, in her cries of distress, was too grief-stricken to feel or hear.

Gradually the grim truth was unfolded. A tragic mishap had

befallen Maurice Dupin as he came riding home from La Châtre the previous evening. Having crossed the arched bridge spanning the Indre River at the foot of the sloping town's main street, he had spurred his horse into a gallop. In the dark, pelting rain neither he nor his spirited charger — the same "untamable" Leopardo he had brought back from Spain — could see the heap of stones and rubble that had been piled up by the thirteenth poplar, at a point where there was a bend in the road. As the horse's hoofs struck the stones, it had half-sunk to the ground, as though about to roll over, then reared up with such sudden force that it had sent its rider flying over its rump. He had landed on his back, snapping the vertebra in his neck, and had expired a moment later in the arms of his faithful Alsatian manservant, Weber, who had been riding behind him.

Maurice Dupin was subsequently laid to rest in the same cypress-shaded graveyard where his baby son, Louis, had been buried one week earlier. But for weeks after the funeral his spirit continued to haunt the stricken household and the superstitious servants, who claimed that they had seen him in full-dress uniform slowly descending the curving stairs or meditating in the empty downstairs chamber he had wanted to turn into a billiard room.

Though much affected by this tragedy, Aurore was much too young to grasp its implications. She would lapse into long melancholy reveries, sitting for hours on a stool by her mother's feet, her arms limp, her mouth open, and with a vacant gaze which made her look almost idiotic. From these states of torpor she would pass without transition to outbursts of capricious energy, chasing the birds in the garden and rolling on the ground in a childish tantrum when the gardeners laughed at her vain efforts. She would pound Weber's calves with her little fists, imploring him to lift her up onto his saddle, but the faithful Alsatian ostler, whose first action, after his master's death, had been to sell the wild Leopardo, had strict orders not to let her get close to a horse.

A five-year-old girl named Ursule, the niece of her grandmother's personal maid, Mademoiselle Julie, was brought over from La Châtre to keep her company. Aurore, though almost eighteen months her junior, took an immediate fancy to this vivacious country girl, who was made to dress in black during the first months of mourning and who, though of much humbler birth, ate her meals at the same table and even slept at night in the same big bed with Aurore's mother.

Like all children, they fought epic battles, as soon forgotten and forgiven as begun, and in the grove which filled the southwestern corner of the property they amused themselves building magic edifices, to which they gave pompous names — like "The Fairy's Castle" or "The Palace of the Sleeping Beauty." One of their greatest joys was to ride the Nohant donkey, an ageless beast which was allowed to roam unhaltered through garden, field, and village, and which occasionally extended its explorations to dining room and kitchen in search of Aurore's grandmother from whom it could always count on receiving some succulent reward. Comfortably ensconsed in hampers, one on each bulging flank, the two girls would watch the trees and hedgerows sway slowly past, as their venerable ass plodded patiently across the fields toward the church of Saint-Chartier, almost two miles to the north, where they always went for Sunday mass. After the service they would be taken next door into the half-abandoned castle, a massive pile of weather-beaten stone, flanked by four tall turrets, where, seated in drafty flagstoned halls, they would restore themselves on the bread and victuals they had brought along.

At Nohant, as earlier in Paris, Aurore's mother personally busied herself with her daughter's education — teaching her to read the fairy tales of Madame d'Aulnoy and Charles Perrault. In introducing Aurore to the rudiments of orthography, she even managed to improve her own faulty spelling and writing. Though she could not read a note of music, Sophie could sing beautifully and was marvelously adroit with her hands. She could repair the harpsichord whenever a key went soft or sour by replacing a broken string or quill. She personally made all of Aurore's clothes as well as her own hats and dresses — not for nothing had she once been a *modiste* in Paris — and she once surprised her mother-in-law, who had no aptitude for sewing, by presenting her with a percale dress that her nimble seamstress' fingers had embroidered from top to bottom in a couple of days.

Though momentarily united by a common sorrow — the disappearance of the man both treasured above all others — no two women could have differed more in looks, temperament, and upbringing than Aurore's mother and grandmother. The first, with her dark eyes and ringlets, had a Spanish temper, if not a Spanish face, and was a bundle of contradictions. She was both proud and humble, timid and outspoken. She could be sweet and irascible by turns, tongue-tied at one moment and furiously voluble the next. She was "as crafty as a fox and suddenly as naïve as a child," as George Sand was later to describe her mother. Of a passionate disposition, she was serenely confident in her good looks and yet given to smoldering fits of jealousy. She could flare up at the slightest provocation, then burst into tears, overcome by a sense of remorse at the enormities she had been uttering.

In private she could be devastatingly caustic in her judgments of the sots and parvenus of the "aristocratic world," peppering her speech with pithy morsels of Parisian slang, and then be as paralyzed as a schoolgirl when in "superior" company. Like many of the lowly-born, she was nagged by a sense of social inferiority, being at once defiantly proud of her humble origins and secretly intimidated by the aristocratic milieu into which the hazards of love had thrust her. Never could she forget that her father, Antoine Delaborde, had been a simple tavern keeper and a *maître oiselier* who had hawked bullfinches and canaries on the banks of the Seine, and never was she more conscious of being a *fille du peuple* than when she found herself in the presence of her mother-in-law's ancien régime companions, most of them widows of noble husbands who had been guillotined or otherwise swallowed up in the convulsions of the French Revolution.

Aurore's grandmother had lost her own husband, Louis-Claude Dupin de Francueil, several years before the epic storming of the Bastille. Born in 1748, one year before Goethe and three years after that memorable battle of Fontenoy at which French and British officers had doffed their cocked hats with such exquisite gallantry before opening murderous fire upon each other, she was a characteristic product of the beautifully mannered age that saw powdered wigs replace flowing locks and buckled slippers drive loutish boots from the vulnerable polish of well-waxed parquets. All her life she had been surrounded by household domestics, who hastened to right a fallen log or to hold a door open for her to pass, and this privileged exemption from all muscular exertion had left its mark. She still took eighteenth-century snuff, quickening the tempo of her sniffs whenever put out or upset, but so stiff had her body grown through lack of exercise and years of elegant inertia that if she let drop her snuffbox or a glove, she would have to wait till Aurore or someone else bent down to retrieve it.

It was, of course, only gradually, as she grew older, that Aurore came to realize what a gulf separated the two women. Charmed as she often was by Sophie's natural wit and ebullience, Madame Dupin de Francueil could never really forgive her daughter-in-law for having "stolen" the affections of her son, Maurice. The latter had been born in 1778, one year after her marriage to a man (Louis-Claude Dupin de Francueil) who was more than thirty years her senior and who died before the next decade was up. Left fatherless when he was barely nine, Maurice had become the dominating passion of her life. It was a passion she had later found herself having to share, in her fifty-fourth year, with a twenty-nine-year-old "hussy" who, in the camp-following wake of Napoleon's armies, had pursued Maurice from Milan to Paris and La Châtre, and who, she felt, was as socially unfit to wed her son as certain of her friends had once felt it was "beneath her" to marry a "commoner" who earned his livelihood as a royal tax collector. But whereas Aurore de Saxe's marriage to Louis-Claude Dupin de Francueil could ultimately be justified because of his considerable wealth, no such justification could be invoked to condone Maurice Dupin's clandestine marriage with the plebeian as well as penniless Sophie Delaborde.

Had the Saxon blood triumphed over the other strains in her ancestry, and had Aurore (the future George Sand) been born blond and blue-eyed like her grandmother, it is possible that the sentimental tug of war that a doting mother and a jealous wife had waged over the person of Maurice Dupin would not, after his sudden death, have been extended to his daughter. But from her Swedish great-grandmother, the beautiful and spirited Aurora of Koenigsmark, the young Aurore Dupin had inherited a most un-Swedish head of jet black hair and the same large, dark eyes as her father.

Indeed, not only her looks but certain of her mannerisms, her moody switches from dreamlike lethargy to wild exuberance, and even her voice were so reminiscent of her father that her grandmother would often call her "Maurice" or speak of her to others as "my son," thereby betraying an unconscious emotional transference.

Just when Aurore Dupin discovered that she had royal blood in her veins, George Sand was unable to specify when she set out to write her autobiography almost half a century later. Most probably, it was one of those insidious and oft-repeated truths that parents or governesses use in an effort to correct the younger generation's barbarous behavior: "My little girl, when one happens to be the great-great-granddaughter of a King, one lifts the spoon to one's mouth, one doesn't put one's chin in the soup." And while her mother, in scolding or spanking her daughter (which she did often), had more forceful ways of bringing her headstrong daughter to heel, Deschartres, who had never reconciled himself to his one-time master's misalliance, could be counted on to remind her that she was descended, on her father's side, from a Polish King of Saxon origin named Friedrich Augustus.

Augustus the *physically* strong — as Thomas Carlyle liked to call him, as much for his prowess in crumpling silver plates (a sport at which he was a match for Peter the Great) as for his numerous bedroom conquests — is reported, among other things, to have sired three hundred illegitimate children. The most illustrious of these royal bastards, one born to him by the tempting Aurora of Koenigsmark, was Maurice de Saxe, the future victor of Fontenoy. As enterprising a Lothario as he was a soldier, Saxe had many gallant adventures, including one with a lady of highly exploitable virtue and even more exploitable good looks, who began life as Marie-Geneviève Rainteau and who finished it, after giving birth to an uncommonly attractive daughter and an even handsomer son, as Mademoiselle de Verrières de Furcy, having added two aristocratic *de*'s to the names of two localities, one of them so obscure that it seems to have vanished from the contemporary map of France. The uncommonly attractive daughter, named Aurore de Saxe in honor of her Saxon grandfather, Friedrich Augustus, and his Swedish king charmer of a mistress, Aurora of Koenigsmark, was Aurore Dupin's grandmother. The even handsomer son, born just two years later (1750) and baptized Charles Godefroi Marie de Beaumont, was the future George Sand's great-uncle.

He merits a place in any account of her life because no one did more to try to smooth the often tense relations between his aristocratic half sister and her plebeian daughter-in-law. "He was the handsomest old man I have ever seen in my life," George Sand could later write, and for once she was probably not exaggerating. His father, Godefroy Charles Henry de la Tour d'Auvergne, the grandson of Louis XIV's great general, Henri de Turenne, had with his legitimate wife begotten two unhappily crippled sons, one of whom ended up a hunchback. But with the winsome Marie de Verrières he produced a blond Adonis of such surpassing good looks that even his legitimate wife was ready to forget the boy's adulterous origins and to treat him as her own son. Had he not been a bastard, the young Charles Godefroi would one day have succeeded to his father's title as Duc de Bouillon, and had he been reasonably ugly, he might well have ended up a general, in the militant Turenne tradition. But his good looks proved his undoing. Hardly had the young chevalier been appointed colonel in his father's regiment than he attracted the roving eye of a noblewoman who happened to be having an affair with his father. When the irate paterfamilias was informed by his spies that he was being cuckolded by his mistress, with the gallant concourse of his bastard son, he hounded the interloper out of his regiment and threatened to have him locked up in the Bastille for life if he refused to take religious orders.

A jolly, quick-witted salon charmer, the chevalier turned Abbé de Beaumont was about as fit for the ministry as his cynical contemporary Talleyrand, the one-time bishop of Autun. He was also no mean diplomat and a shrewd enough judge of human frailties not to have sought too strenuously to discourage his nephew Maurice Dupin's "regrettable" passion for the attractive though humbly born Sophie-Victoire Delaborde. More tolerant and easygoing than his half sister, he harbored no prejudices about birth and pedigree; all he asked of a woman was that she be amiable and pretty. Aurore's mother being pretty, he treated her with avuncular affection, ready to chide her when her quick tongue and temper got the better of her patience in judging others but no less ready to defend her against Deschartres' barbed quips and innuendoes.

At Nohant, where he came to spend some weeks with his half sister to help console her for the untimely death of her son, Maurice, his was a soothing and salutary presence. He still fancied the carefully powdered pigeon-wing peruke and the Prussian pigtail of the eighteenth century, and in his buckled shoes, his black satin breeches, and his purple quilted robe, he looked as though he had just stepped out of a full-length family portrait. But the old-fashioned solemnity of his attire was more than offset by a bubbling and inventive spirit which gradually dispelled the post-mortem gloom that had settled on the household. At the dinner table the silence was less brittle, and the talk in the salon was more lively. For his half sister's birthday the good-humored abbé even put on a playlet for which he wrote the lines and personally built the stage set in the unoccupied upstairs chamber next to the bedroom where Aurore slept with her mother. Deschartres, acting as a one-man orchestra, tootled away industriously on his flageolet, while the four-and-a-half-year-old Aurore brought down the house with a bolero, full of exuberant entrechats and pirouettes that made her grandmother laugh for the first time in months.

It was also the good abbé who finally prevailed on his "niece" Sophie Dupin to return to Paris to be near her daughter Caroline, whom she had left there in a boarding school, and to entrust her younger daughter's education to her grandmother. Disregarding little Aurore's pleas that she not be "given away for money," Sophie agreed to sign a paper naming Madame Dupin de Francueil as her granddaughter's lawful teacher and guardian. In return, the impecunious Sophie was granted a pension of 1500 francs, to be paid to her from the annual income of the Nohant estate. This was added to the 1000 francs a year she continued to receive from a property in Westphalia, which had been "bequeathed" to Maurice Dupin by right of imperial conquest.

The parting, when it came, was passionate and tearful. Aurore's grandmother, for all her soft-spoken airs, overawed her, and she even missed her mother's brusque reprimands and spankings. So long as her mother had been at Nohant, Aurore had been allowed to run around, to roll on the ground, to use the local *berrichon* dialect with the servants, and generally to kick up her childish heels. Now she was told to keep out of the kitchen, to avoid excessive familiarity with the servants, to curtsy to visiting grown-ups, and not to raise her voice when playing indoors. Where she had once felt free and uninhibited, she now felt an omnipresent constraint. She was reminded at every turn that she was a lady-to-be, a lady who displayed the respect due to her elders and betters by addressing them in the third person.

When, at last, it was time to leave for Paris, the family berlin was dragged from the coach house and its voluminous recesses and pockets were stuffed with an extraordinary profusion of edibles, books, perfume bottles, decks of cards, maps, and moneybags, without which Aurore's grandmother could not face the rigors of the three-day journey. Well enveloped in foot rugs and pillows, Madame Dupin de Francueil and her personal maid, Mademoiselle Julie, stretched out comfortably in the back of the coach, while Aurore sat on a little bench with her back to the coachman, trying not to kick the servant seated opposite.

Because this was the first of a hundred such trips she was to make between Nohant and Paris, it later came to occupy a special niche in George Sand's recollections of her youth. After traversing the dreary flatlands of the Sologne (to the north of Bourges) — with their stunted trees, tangled thickets, and monotonous fens — they penetrated the leafy forest south of Orléans. The sky disappeared above their heads and suddenly it was night. Though her son, Maurice, had never ventured into this brigand-infested wood without first arming himself and his servants, Madame Dupin de Francueil resolutely urged on the nervous coachman. To her maid she explained that holdups had been more frequent before the Revolution, when there were no roadside ditches and the underbrush was not cut back; the highwaymen, when caught, were then strung up on the spot.

"One winter," the old lady went on, not realizing that her granddaughter was all ears, "I remember seeing a tall woman, with long black hair floating in the wind, remain intact for a long time, while the crows circled around and fought for pieces of her flesh. It was a dreadful sight and the stench pursued us to the gates of the city." Aurore, at these words, broke into a cold sweat, and never, for years to come, could she pass through this robbers' haven without being haunted by the vision of all those wild-haired corpses, swinging from the bare-branched oaks in the wintry moan of the wind.

3. Between Two Worlds

In Paris Aurore was lodged with her grandmother in an apartment overlooking the spacious gardens behind the Rue Neuve-des-Mathurins, not far from where the Opéra now stands. The rich carpets spread over the floors, the sky blue damask hangings, the logs blazing in all the fireplaces made for a luxury she had never known in her parents' cramped quarters on the Rue de la Grange-Batelière and which even surpassed the rustic comforts of Nohant. Yet Aurore was only truly happy here when her mother stopped by in the afternoon and took her out for long walks. No matter how tired her little legs might get, there was a never-ending delight in feeling her mother's hand curled around her own and in simply being able to touch her dress. The toy-shop windows before which they would linger, the trained dogs they would see prancing on the pavements, the engravings and caged canaries that loquacious hawkers would try to press on them as they ambled up the boulevards, even the exotic Bains Chinois, with their upswooping pagoda roofs, bulbous rock gardens, and squinting figurines, where they often stopped for refreshment — everything was a source of babbling wonder and enchantment and as much shared in by the smiling mother as by the excited child.

She was, however, much less fond of the Chinese hairdo into which she was forced by her mother, shocked to see her daughter still dressed — "like a little old woman" — in the low-waisted frocks, so hideously outmoded by the armpit-high belt line of Empire fashion. Aurore's dark locks, instead of being able to cascade freely down over her shoulders, were now pulled sharply back from the forehead and wound into a thick black bun, which an uncomfortably tight ribbon kept in artificial place on top of her head.

Equally painful were the artificial barriers that were raised, on her grandmother's instructions, between herself and her twelve-year-old sister, Caroline. Her father, at the time when they had lived on the Rue de la Grange-Batelière, had treated Caroline as if she were his own daughter, even though she had been brought into the world by an unmarried Sophie Delaborde a full year before her mother had met Maurice Dupin. That Caroline was thus only a half sister, and an illegitimate one at that, Aurore had hitherto never suspected, nor was she yet old enough to understand exactly what this meant. But one afternoon, when her gentle beanstalk of a sister unexpectedly rang the doorbell of the Rue Neuve-des-Mathurins apartment, Madame Dupin de Francueil ordered Rose, the sturdy red-haired maid, to show her out immediately. "My granddaughter no longer knows her, and I don't know her at all," she declared in an unusually harsh, dry voice, adding that she would dismiss her maid if Caroline was ever seen there again.

That evening Aurore was led off to bed, sobbing and crying for her sister. She refused to be mollified by the black-faced doll with gleaming eyes and dazzling white teeth which her grandmother offered her in a pathetic endeavor to regain her affection, and was later seized with convulsions and vomiting — due to a sudden onset of measles.

As soon as she was recovered and well enough to go out, her grandmother wrapped her up warmly and took her in a carriage to her mother's apartment, a tiny, dark, low-ceilinged flat whose shabby furniture contrasted sharply with that of the Rue Neuve-des-Mathurins. The door was opened by Caroline, an angelic-looking Caroline with a charming turned-up nose, who hugged her little sister with a joyous cry. Politely though coldly, she drew up an armchair for Madame Dupin de Francueil to sit on and then went to fetch her mother, who was visiting a neighbor. There was a moment of tension when the two women found themselves face to face, but the elder managed to avert the threatening storm by declaring in a calm, dignified voice: "When you sent Caroline over to me, you doubtless misunderstood my intentions as to the relations which should exist between her and Aurore. Never did it occur to me to cross my granddaughter in her affections. I shall never object to her coming to see you or to her seeing Caroline *in your home* . . ."

By making this gracious concession, Aurore's grandmother restored a measure of peace to the two households. Once a week, on Sundays, when Caroline was let out of boarding school, Aurore was brought back by her mother to what she liked to call *chez nous* (our home) — a home where she could play games with her older sister and see her familiar earthenware plate filled with a generous helping of the pot-au-feu, which simmered quietly away in the stewpot above the hearth.

At five o'clock Caroline would go off alone to have dinner with her aunt Lucie Maréchal, while Aurore and her mother went to eat with the Abbé de Beaumont, a bon vivant who knew how to appreciate as well as employ a cordon bleu cook. Here, in a tall-windowed Louis XIV apartment, they would find the convivial abbé ensconced in a huge armchair on one side of the warm fireplace, with Aurore's grandmother seated opposite in another. Between them, with her long skirt slightly drawn up over two emaciated shanks ending in a pair of pointed shoes, would be the comfortably stretched out and gaily chattering form of Madame de la Marlière, the widow of a count who had perished beneath the guillotine. Though she was herself descended (even if illegitimately) from the King of Sardinia, she was without the aristocratic prejudices that distinguished most of Madame Dupin de Francueil's friends and she treated Aurore's mother with affable bonhomie, reason enough for Aurore to find her the least objectionable of her grandmother's "old countesses," and this notwithstanding the robust vigor of her language, a strange Provençal accent, and a chin so pointed that it invariably left its bruising mark on each of the tender cheeks Aurore had to expose, when arriving and departing, to her abrasive kiss.

After several months, the decision was taken to return to Nohant. Aurore had begun to languish in Paris, and it was felt that she could do with a change of air. So visibly anxious was the child not to be separated from her mother that Madame Dupin de Francueil finally relented and invited her daughter-in-law to accompany Aurore to the country.

The months that followed were among the happiest the young Aurore was ever to experience at Nohant. A peaceful understanding seemed to reign between her mother and grandmother, and though both were occasionally to be seen quietly sobbing or mopping their eyes in some secluded corner, there was now more gaiety in the house, and Sophie suffered less from the blinding headaches that had oppressed her after her husband's sudden death. The new Empress Marie-Louise had just borne Napoleon a son, and the rejoicing inspired by this happy event offered a momentary distraction from the shortages caused by Britain's continental blockade and the six francs — an appallingly high price — one now had to pay for a pound of sugar.

Aurore's mother continued to give her lessons in reading and writing, while her grandmother initiated her to the mysteries of music. Half paralyzed though her fingers already were, the old lady could still accompany herself on the small, shrill harpsichord which stood in her bedroom and under which Aurore liked to crawl, curling up on the rug next to the dog Brillant in order to be totally enveloped by the music. Her grandmother's voice, though it was unsteady and had begun to crack, imparted an ancient charm to the seraphic melodies she would sometimes decipher from the score, sometimes sing by heart. Gluck and Piccinni, whom she had personally met in Paris in the 1770s, were her gods, but so vast was her familiarity with eighteenth-century music that George Sand, who was to become something of a connoisseur herself, could later recall her singing fragments from Leo, Hasse, and Durante that she never again heard sung by anybody else.

Gradually, as she became more practiced in writing, Aurore was turned over to the tutelage of Deschartres to be taught the rudiments of French and later of Latin grammar. The lessons, attended by Ursule as well as by her half brother, Hippolyte (who being older was already learning, or supposed to be learning, mathematics), were given upstairs in Deschartres' room on the first floor, which always smelled overpoweringly of lavender soap. With the two girls he was a fairly satisfactory pedagogue, able to elucidate whatever needed explanation in a clear, calm, concise manner. But with Hippolyte, who was a singularly restless boy, he would regularly lose his temper, begin to storm and rant, tripping over words and launching into stammering tirades that grew increasingly incoherent the more wrathful he became.

That Hippolyte fully merited many of the blows and beatings that were meted out to him by the pompous tutor, there can be no doubt. He was a born hell-raiser whose taste for mischief-making at times verged on the destructive. He once came near to setting the house on fire by hurling flaming brands up the chimney flue, afterward explaining that he had only been "sacrificing to the gods of the underworld." On another occasion he undertook to "study the theory of volcanoes" by rigging up a cauldron over a thick log stuffed with gunpowder, the resultant explosion being strong enough to project the contents of the stewpot all over the kitchen. He tied saucepans to the tails of howling dogs and forced the paws of meowing cats into walnut-shell "clogs," which made them slip and fall pathetically with every step.

A poor student Hippolyte may have been — for want of application far more than for want of brains — but one thing was certain: as a mimic he was remarkably gifted. Years later George Sand could write that "no one has ever made me laugh as he did," which may well have been the case. Once, when *le grand homme* — as Deschartres was called behind his back — had left to go sell some animals at a country fair, Hippolyte, who was supposed to be studying in the room of the "great man," decided to put his absence to profitable use. He climbed into the tutor's hunting jacket, which reached down to his knees, put on his button-down cap, and began pacing to and fro, with his feet pointed outward and his hands clasped magisterially behind his back. Taking a piece of chalk, he marked up the blackboard, growing steadily more worked up over the "crass ignorance" of his "loutish" pupil. Not content with that, he went to the window and began shouting at one of the gardeners, who was soundly berated for the inept way in which he was pruning his trees. Upset by this unwarranted tongue-lashing, the simple-minded fellow was even more startled to see the real Deschartres appear under the trees and stop to listen to his well-imitated voice. He had returned from the fair earlier than expected, early enough to be able to creep upstairs unobserved and to surprise the mimic in the act of venting his tutorial fury on his indolent charge: "You don't do a lick of work, you write like a polecat, you spell like a picklock! Here!" — paf! paf! — "take this on your ears, you beast!" And get it on the ears he did. For, as George Sand was later to recall the scene, "while the false Deschartres was cuffing an imaginary Hippolyte, the real Deschartres was cuffing the real Hippolyte."

In late October of this same year (1811), just as the first frosts were whitening the hardened earth, Aurore and her grandmother returned to Paris with Deschartres and Hippolyte. Aurore's education as a seven-year-old *demoiselle*-to-be was now begun in earnest. She was paired off with a slender blond girl of her own age, Pauline de Pontcarré, the granddaughter of one of Madame Dupin de Francueil's aristocratic friends, and three times a week they received joint instruction in handwriting, dancing, and music. Hippolyte, on those days when he could be let out of boarding school, would join them, executing entrechats and *battements* with a bearlike clumsiness that shook the house to its foundations. Deschartres, when present, would work himself into another rage, while the teacher, a professional ballet dancer with the rollicking name of Gogault, would lay aside his pocket fiddle, mop his harassed brow, and declare with a weary sigh that never in all his years of dancing at the Opéra had he ever encountered a plow horse like this one!

The writing sessions were even more excruciating. For Monsieur Loubens, their *professeur de belles lettres* — as an abbé friend of Aurore's grandmother sarcastically called him — was a calligraphic martinet who believed that to write correctly one must hold one's head high, keep one's elbow off the tabletop, and hold the pen with three fingers while resting the weight of the hand on the fourth. These precise prerequisites requiring unnatural muscular exertion, he began by placing his pupils in a kind of pedagogic harness. A whalebone crown was placed upon the victim's head and fastened to a waist belt by a taut shoulder strap; the elbow was raised by means of a wooden bar screwed to the table edge; pen and index finger were slipped through a double brass-ring mount over a knuckled handrest equipped with boxwood rollers. Digital paralysis and headaches were the first fruits of this elaborate paraphernalia, and far from enabling the two young ladies and the future squire to develop a fine aristocratic hand, it produced three painful scrawls which became increasingly illegible.

Only in music did Aurore and her friend make appreciable headway, receiving instruction from Pauline's mother, who also taught them a bit of geography and history in the Pontcarré home. The piano on which Aurore practiced in her grandmother's apartment was placed between two dining room windows overlooking a busy street, so that she was constantly distracted by the rattle of passing wheels, the oaths of whip-cracking coachmen, and the plaintive crank and wheeze of itinerant barrel organs. There was an incessant coming and going in their house, for their second-floor neighbor was a certain General Maison, whose orderlies and grooms kept running up and down the stairs and filling the inner courtyard with cries as they scrubbed and polished his carriages, loaded and unloaded the mule trains, and galloped off on mysterious military missions.

Throughout this winter of 1811–1812 Napoleon's officers and soldiers were kept busy preparing the immense campaign against Russia. Unlike the choleric Deschartres, who never stopped denouncing the "tyrant" as a Corsican upstart and parvenu, both Aurore and her mother were fervent Bonapartists, as had been Maurice Dupin up until the imperial coronation of December 1804, when he realized that the one-time Jacobin from Ajaccio had ceased to be the first soldier of the French Revolution and made himself into another European autocrat. Aurore's grandmother understandably shared her son's distaste for the Empire's nouveau riche panache, for she had always been a monarchist, albeit a fervent admirer of Rousseau and Voltaire. Her cozy bedroom, where she received her aristocratic friends — the unheated salon being only used for "formal" receptions that never took place — was in fact a buzzing hive of anti-Napoleonic gossip. But never did the young Aurore hear one of these ancien régime critics suggest that the "conqueror" — *l'ambitieux,* as they called him — might this time be headed for disaster. Like the most delirious of his supporters, they considered him invincible. "And when we have taken Russia, what shall we do with it?" somebody one day asked one of her grandmother's friends.

Such was the universal sentiment in April of 1812, when the

springtime softness of the air and the first fragrant blossoms made the rigors of a Russian winter seem absurdly distant and unreal. It was time to be leaving Paris and to return to Nohant again — not only for Aurore and her grandmother but also for Hippolyte who, far from being disciplined at boarding school, had fallen in with a band of kindred devils who had taught him how to do even less work and raise even greater hell.

This time Aurore's mother did not come with them. Though she had a standing invitation to spend her summers at Nohant, she apparently found the atmosphere of this country house too cramped and rustic for her lively Parisian taste. The summer months drifted by in the weekly expectation that at any moment Aurore's mother might appear — as, on parting and to console the fretful child, she had told her daughter she might do "a little later." But neither in July, when Aurore celebrated her eighth birthday, nor in October, when the white-wigged Abbé de Beaumont turned up for his half sister's annual fete, did her mother deign to appear.

The disastrous news from Russia, which finally filtered out after weeks of eerie silence, had the effect of prolonging their stay at Nohant. "Up until then," as George Sand was later to recall these dark, heroic days, "I had regarded my nation as invincible, and the imperial throne as that of God himself." At Christmastime they learned that Napoleon was back in Paris. But it was weeks before the grim truth, which a censored press and fallacious imperial bulletins carefully concealed, began to reach them in letters written by Paris friends who had talked to this or that survivor.

Aurore had gradually accustomed herself to the idea of periodic separations from her mother, who showed little inclination to join them at Nohant. Following on the French victories at Lützen, Bautzen, and Dresden, the Berry countryside was inundated with foreign prisoners, many of whom were now to be seen trudging up the tree-lined highway leading from La Châtre to Châteauroux. One day an exhausted German sat down on the cool stone step of the little pavilion which formed the northwest corner of the Nohant property. The stagnant green waters of the moat that separated the grove from the highway being unsafe for drinking, Aurore and Hippolyte brought him a bottle of wine to drink and a hunk of peasant bread. "*Enfants très pons!*" cried the grateful foreigner, squeezing their small hands in his friendly paw. When Madame Dupin de Francueil heard about it, the tears came into her eyes. Captured by the Austrians in northern Italy, her own son, Maurice, had once had to beg his way back to the French lines in a semistarving condition. A barrel of wine was installed in the pavilion, and for some days Hippolyte and his half sister ran a kind of roadside canteen, doling out hunks of country bread and glasses of wine to footsore prisoners. The latter would thank their young hosts by gathering round and singing German and Tyrolean folk songs with an instinctive sense of choral harmony that left Aurore spellbound.

That winter she was brought back to Paris to resume her lessons in drawing and dancing. Her grandmother's warm bedroom was once again thronged by "old countesses" — superannuated relics of the past, like Madame de Troussebois, with her Egyptian mummy's face, or the haughty Madame de Bérenger, with her absurdly short-haired wig (closely cropped in the latest Emperor Titus style) — who clucked and gloated over Napoleon's reverses.

New Year's found the Cossacks crossing the Rhine. The impossible, the inconceivable, was happening at last. For a moment the exultant chatter of the Royalists was stilled, giving way to a vague malaise. Feeling no vocation for heroism, Aurore's grandmother decided to return to Nohant, which being not far from Bourges, France's geographic center, was less exposed to foreign incursion than Bonaparte's threatened capital. Sophie Dupin, however, refused to be alarmed: let Aurore return to Nohant with her grandmother, she would stay on with Caroline and both would be quite safe, for Aurore could rest assured that the Emperor would hurl back the Cossacks, not one of whom would ever enter Paris.

They set off in late January in an overloaded calèche. The weather was appalling, the slushy roads dark with marching soldiers, artillery caissons, and carts filled with cannonballs and powder. Fresh horses were difficult to obtain at the relay posts, and they had to spend more nights than usual in uncomfortable inns. At one point they found themselves sharing the bread they had stored in the coach trunks with a company of famished soldiers who had not eaten in two days.

Hardly had they reached Nohant than Aurore's grandmother fell seriously ill. For two days she remained in a sleep so profound that it resembled a coma. Now for the first time, just as she seemed about to lose her, Aurore realized how fond of her grandmother she had grown, in spite of everything. After the old lady regained consciousness, it was found that the salt poultices administered by Deschartres had left a large festering scar, which took two months to heal.

By the end of March, at about the time the Allies were marching into Paris, a letter from one of her "old countesses" informed Madame Dupin de Francueil that the Emperor Alexander of Russia was going to place Louis XVI's brother on the throne of France. But the news, far from gladdening her Royalist heart, only caused her to remark to Aurore: "So here are our cousins on the throne again, but believe me, my little girl, it is nothing to boast about." *

Shortly thereafter Aurore's mother turned up at Nohant, full of extraordinary stories about the "barbarians" who had invaded the French capital. For a moment she had thought her last hour had come when a cannonball, fired from the heights of Montmartre at the Napoleonic victory column on the Place Vendôme, had ended up embedded in her apartment ceiling, after tearing a two-foot hole in the mansard roof and dropping through two floors. Persuaded that this was the opening round in a murderous cannonade intended to level the heart of Paris, she had fled from the house with Caroline, only to see elegantly dressed ladies hastening across the boulevards in their sycophantic zeal to smother the caracoling conquerors beneath their flowered wreaths and kisses.

In the end Sophie only stayed one month, and a not particularly happy one at that. She felt stifled in this country house, ruled over by a mother-in-law whose latent hostility was unconsciously rekindled by her upsetting presence. Her elder daughter Caroline, whom she was not allowed to bring with her, was full of vehement reproaches each time she was left alone in Paris, while Aurore unwittingly aroused her grandmother's possessive jealousy by showing

* Maurice de Saxe's half sister, Maria Josepha, had married Louis XV's son Louis and borne him three sons. The first became Louis XVI; the second, the Comte de Provence, became Louis XVIII; the third, the Comte d'Artois, became Charles X. As the illegitimate daughter of Maurice de Saxe, Aurore de Saxe (George Sand's grandmother) was thus the bastard first cousin of all three.

her mother more spontaneous affection than she could to the older lady.

The four of them were thus caught up in a web of feminine sympathies and animosities which Mademoiselle Julie, Madame Dupin de Francueil's personal maid, did her best to exacerbate. Unlike Rose, who remained devoted to "Madame Maurice" (as Sophie Dupin was known to the servants), perhaps because it was her dead husband who had originally hired her, Mademoiselle Julie lost no opportunity to poison her mistress' mind against her daughter-in-law, whom she kept under close surveillance. Aurore had by this time acquired a room of her own. But often, on hearing her mother's footsteps on the stone stairwell around eleven o'clock at night, she would tiptoe barefoot across the corridor to Sophie's room and cuddle up to her under the blankets of the broad double bed. Tipped off by her "police lieutenant," Mademoiselle Julie, Aurore's grandmother came up one night and intercepted her. Rose was called out of her room and scolded for letting such things happen. For, as the *châtelaine* of Nohant informed her — as well as Aurore's mother, when she joined them in the corridor — it was neither healthy nor "chaste" for a nine-year-old daughter to sleep with her mother!

This was too much for the sharp-tongued Sophie. "If there's anyone here who lacks chastity, it's you for having such ideas!" she snapped. "It's by speaking too early of such things to children that one robs their minds of innocence, and if that's the way you intend to raise my daughter, you would have done better to have left her to me."

The incident spurred her decision to return forthwith to Paris. Aurore, when she saw her mother packing, was desperate. She threw herself into her arms, she hugged her thighs, asking to be taken too. Her mother sat her on her knees and sought to reason with her. Her grandmother, she explained, could at any time reduce her annual income to 1500 francs a year by withholding further payment of the additional 1000 francs she gave her to make up for her lost widow's pension — the income she had once derived from a property in Westphalia which had vanished with the collapse of the Napoleonic Empire. Without those extra thousand francs there would simply not be enough to pay for Caroline's boarding school and her own expenses, to say nothing of the costs of feeding and dressing Aurore. "We would end up so poor that you could no longer stand it . . ."

"Never, never!" cried Aurore, too young to understand such considerations. "We'll be poor, but we'll be together . . . We'll work, we'll eat beans in a little attic, as Mademoiselle Julie says, and what's so wrong with that?"

The often repeated threat, used to intimidate the querulous Aurore, thus became the kernel of a new idea. To calm her agitated daughter, Sophie promised to borrow the needed money from her sister and to open a hat shop in Orléans, where life was less expensive than in Paris. It wouldn't be a princely life, but by living thriftily, as they had once done on the Rue de la Grange-Batelière, they could save enough to get Caroline and Aurore married off to honest workers "who will make you happier than marquesses and counts." When everything was ready, she would return to Nohant and inform Madame Dupin de Francueil that she was removing Aurore forever.

Aurore, on hearing this, could not contain herself. She skipped about the room, laughing and shrieking with delight. Eagerly she helped her mother pack her bundles, trunk, and bonnet boxes, knowing that the sooner she left Nohant the sooner she would be back to fetch her.

At the dinner table that afternoon her grandmother was surprised by her sprightliness, all the stranger in a little girl whose eyelids were red and swollen from much weeping. But as dusk fell, Aurore was besieged by childish doubts. Her mother now seemed downcast, preoccupied rather than elated by the little plot they had hatched between them. At nine o'clock, when Aurore went up to bed, she decided she would stay awake to say a last goodbye to her mother, who was to leave early the next morning. After Rose had tucked her into bed and snuffed out her candle, Aurore heard her descending the stone stairs to help Mademoiselle Julie put her grandmother to bed. This was an elaborate ceremony, which began with a frugal supper, after which the old lady's head and shoulders were enveloped in an extraordinary accouterment of night bonnets, woolen shawls, silk coverlets, and padded quilts. Thus wrapped and cushioned, she listened to Mademoiselle Julie's confidential account of all the intimate goings-on she had witnessed or heard about during the day. This was followed by a second report Rose had to make to her concerning the latest housekeeping problems. Sometimes it was two o'clock in the morning before Madame's ritual *coucher* was over, and only then could Rose retire upstairs to the little antechamber next to Aurore's bedroom.

Knowing that her mother would be coming upstairs long before then, she got up and by blowing repeatedly on the glowing embers in the fireplace — for she had no matches — she managed to relight her snuffed-out candle. She then tore several pages from an exercise book and poured out her heart on to the paper, laboriously rewriting each tear-smudged word. She wanted her mother to promise *in writing* that she would soon return to Nohant and take her away to live with herself and Caroline. Tiptoeing across the corridor, she entered her mother's bedroom and hid the letter behind a framed pencil drawing of her grandfather, Louis-Claude Dupin de Francueil, shown in a frock coat and pigeon-wing peruke, stoop-shoulderedly bent over his writing table. "Place your reply behind this same portrait of old Dupin. I'll find it tomorrow after you have left," Aurore had written at the top of the letter. Now she added a second message — "Shake the portrait" — on another sheet of paper, which she tucked into her mother's nightcap.

Back in her little room Aurore remained seated on her bed, listening with a beating heart. At last the twelve chimes of midnight were resonantly struck by the clock in Deschartres' room, separated from her own by a thin wall. She heard the tutor's slow deliberate steps coming up the circular stairwell and down the tiled corridor, followed by a majestic opening and closing of doors. Her mother came up a quarter of an hour later, accompanied by Rose, who was to help her finish packing.

One hour later, after Rose had gone to bed, Aurore stealthily opened her bedroom door and crept across the corridor. She found her mother in tears, reading her pathetically unhappy letter. Opening her arms, her mother clasped her to her bosom, stroked her dark hair, and did her best to console her. She was now overcome with remorse at the idea that she had aroused such wild hopes in her daughter. She was no longer sure their little plan would work. It would be better if Aurore forgot everything they had said. She was certain she would get used to her grandmother, even if it took time.

Tearfully Aurore reproached her with going back on her word. So pathetic were her pleas that her mother finally relented. Yes, she promised, she would come back in three months' time to fetch her. She even agreed to give her pledge in writing. Aurore would find it after she had left. Only thus could she persuade the distraught child to return to bed.

The next morning, as the gray light of dawn began to filter in through the window, Aurore heard doors being opened and bundles moved downstairs. Opening the door, she rushed out barefoot and flung herself into her mother's arms, beseeching her to take her with her. Her mother begged her to go back to bed; couldn't Aurore see that she was only adding to the pain of their parting?

Meekly Aurore returned to her room. When at last the carriage wheels that were bearing her mother away could be heard rolling out through the front gate, she sobbed so unrestrainedly that even the tough-minded Rose was moved to tears and came in to console her.

Finally Aurore dozed off, emotionally exhausted. After waking, she crossed the corridor and threw herself onto the rumpled bed-covers, hugging and kissing the pillow that still bore the imprint of her mother's head. Before she could look for the written message, Rose walked in to strip the sheets. The mattresses were turned and shaken, the shutters finally closed, and Aurore invited to leave the dark, abandoned room.

Only later in the day was she able to re-enter her mother's bed-room unobserved. With a trembling heart she hurried over to the portrait and unhooked it from the door. No letter fell out from behind it. Aurore turned the drawing over with dismay and stared at its blank back. Her mother had left nothing.

Not once during the weeks that followed did her mother's letters contain the slightest, veiled allusion to the little "plot" they had hatched between them. Orléans, the hat shop, their joint life with

Caroline — all were discreetly forgotten. There was no hiding the bitter truth, which became more evident with each passing day: her mother did not love Aurore as much as she was loved by her daughter. It was her first great amorous disappointment, the first of a long series of passionate frustrations that were later to make George Sand feel like an old, emotionally spent woman before she was forty. This kind of unbalance between a child's impetuous attachment and the casual response of the parent is of course anything but rare. To some extent it is inevitable, as George Sand was lucid enough to recognize in looking back with the wise eyes of middle age on this early sentimental shock: "My mother had for me, as for all the beings she had loved, more passion than tenderness. In her soul there were formed, as it were, great gaps of which she was quite unaware. Alongside of treasures of love there were abysses of forgetfulness and lassitude. She had suffered too much, often she needed not to suffer anymore; whereas I was avid for suffering, so much young energy in this regard did I still have to expend."

Her mother, now absent, was constantly in Aurore's thoughts, and though she could still laugh at her half brother Hippolyte's uproarious imitations of the ladies and gentlemen who came to dine at Nohant, she would often grow moody and even burst into tears. Her grandmother, like her mother, offered her scant solace, for there was no more talk of their returning to Paris for the winter.

Shortly before Sophie's departure, a desperate Aurore had told her that if need be she would *walk* to Paris to rejoin her. But before Aurore could even make the attempt, her grandmother suffered a paralytic seizure. One day, in the middle of dinner, she suddenly felt faint and closed her eyes, remaining deathly pale and motionless for a full hour. It was the first of a series of cataleptic seizures that were to recur at two-month intervals. Overcome with guilt at the idea that she had been planning to abandon her ailing grandmother at a moment when she most needed her, Aurore gave up all idea of trying to run away.

Her grandmother's growing infirmity made it even more difficult for Aurore to lead a normal life in her presence. All manifestations of childish exuberance now fatigued the old lady, who though increasingly given to somnolence, could be irritably awakened by the slightest sound. Seated in a tall-backed armchair in her downstairs bedroom, the doors and window of which were kept carefully closed, she would subside at noon into a three-hour siesta, which the hushed household was ordered to respect, before Mademoiselle Julie came in to revive her sluggish circulation with footbaths and frictions. Save for the morning harpsichord lesson, now reduced to half an hour, Aurore only saw her at mealtimes and in the evening, when she would play cards with her or watch her play solitaire and patience.

Though Sophie, in her distressingly rare letters, exhorted her daughter to "run, play, walk, grow bigger, get back your good red cheeks," and think only of "gay things," Aurore was subject to frequent spells of listlessness, for which Hippolyte would tease her mercilessly. She still clung to the conviction that she would one day be joining her mother and would help her to make and sell hats. Such being the vocation she imagined for herself, she could work up little enthusiasm for "abstract" and totally unpractical studies — like arithmetic, Latin, Greek, French versification, and a carefully sexpurged botany — which were taught to her by Deschartres.

Her mother's absence also made itself felt in other ways. For lacking her support and encouragement, Aurore now found herself virtually isolated in her Napoleonic hero worship. Not only her grandmother, a firm supporter of the Bourbon restoration, and Deschartres, as vehement as ever in his denunciations of the "tyrant" (now happily banished to Elba), but even the simple-minded peasants of Nohant seemed to have turned their backs on the Empire and embraced the monarchy. The new hero, lavishly praised in the letters Madame Dupin de Francueil received from her Royalist friends in Paris, was the Russian Emperor Alexander I, whose flabby, blond, side-whiskered face Aurore was asked to admire (in a miniature portrait shown to her) as though it were that of a universal genius, another Frederick the Great.

Her irritation gave way to private rejoicing in March of 1815, when Nohant, like the rest of France, was electrified by the news that the Corsican "adventurer," whose genius Deschartres was so determined to belittle, had unexpectedly landed in Provence and was marching triumphantly on the capital. Everywhere he was being greeted with delirious enthusiasm, those who only yesterday had dragged the tricolor in the mud to cries of *"A bas le tyran!"* now being the first to cry *"Vive l'Empereur!"* How seemingly honest people could shift their allegiances so swiftly was more than Aurore could understand. It filled her with a vague disgust and sense of shame.

But not all of Aurore's exalted daydreaming could save her hero from defeat at Waterloo. Paris once again was occupied by foreign soldiery, and the feeble, gout-ridden, cane-supported figure of Louis XVIII heaved back onto the shaky throne he had been forced so ignominiously to vacate a couple of months earlier. For Aurore these were distant, dimly comprehensible mishaps. But for her patriotic as well as Bonapartist mother they were unendurably real. The military swagger of foreign conquerors was humiliation enough without the vindictive hue and cry of French "legitimists" clamoring for the heads of "traitors" like Marshal Ney. Sickened by the spectacle of this "black reaction" (as Stendhal was to call it), Aurore's mother entrusted her elder daughter, Caroline, to the care of her sister, Lucie Maréchal, and fled to the provincial backwaters of Nohant where, as one can imagine, she was greeted by her younger daughter with delirious transports of delight.

The entire province of Berry was soon inundated with veteran soldiers from the short-lived Army of the Loire, which a monarchy more than ever fearful of a post-Napoleonic insurrection had disbanded. A regiment of lancers that had been decimated at Waterloo was stationed in their neighborhood, and for several weeks its commander, General Colbert, established his headquarters at Nohant.

Never, in the twenty years since Madame Dupin de Francueil had acquired the estate, had the Louis XVI mansion and its adjacent carriage houses, barns, and stables been the scene of so much hustle and bustle. Twice daily Colbert would be joined by a fellow general with the chest-swelling name of Subervie, who would ride over from his billet at the nearby Château d'Ars to be entertained at lunch and dinner with a dashing retinue of lancers.

As the widow of one of Murat's aides-de-camp, Aurore's attractive mother was much courted by the lancers, who paid her gallant compliments and made discreet advances. Aurore too came in for her share of attention, not only from the young aides-de-camp who would play amusing games with her and Hippolyte but also from the winsome and spirited General Subervie, who one day playfully pulled her ears. Aurore avenged herself by taking a sheet of paper and carefully snipping out a white rosette — the hated white cockade of France's ancien régime "legitimists" — which she pinned over the tricolor cockade on the general's black bicornuate hat.

That Madame Dupin de Francueil was a Royalist these Napoleonic veterans could tell at a glance from her old-fashioned, pre-Empire mode of dress. But they were full of respect for a lady who was the daughter of the illustrious Maréchal de Saxe, had been the mother of a brave hussar, and was to boot a gracious hostess. She in turn refrained from saying anything that might vex their Bonapartist sympathies. Deschartres, however, was less tactful, and one day he clumsily provoked Colbert with some slighting reference to Napoleon's defeats. The general, a plump, red-faced man who had endeared himself to his hostess by his fine salon manners and his skilled keyboard tinkling when singing old romances, now brusquely flared up.

"No, we weren't defeated!" he cried, his dark eyes flashing. "We were betrayed and still are. If we hadn't been, and if we could rely on all our officers, I promise you that our brave soldiers could still show those Prussian and Cossack fellows that France is not a prey they can devour with impunity!"

Deschartres, thoroughly cowed, said nothing. Aurore's grandmother took the general gently by the arm, removed the table knife he had begun brandishing in his excitement, and had him sit down, but with such maternal solicitude that he was quite overcome. He kissed her two hands, begged her to forgive his bellicose words, and then burst into tears.

The old lady was right, and the general knew it. So grudgingly did his colleagues. There was no more talk of a resumption of hostilities, of partisan warfare, of a desperate last-ditch stand. Among themselves they might protest, but in their warrior hearts they knew that sooner or later they would have to resign themselves to the inevitable. They would have to accept a lackluster regime, calling not for individual heroism but for collective submission. Those who could manage it could look forward to eventual promotions and to a decent, if not exciting, military career; those who couldn't would have to leave the army and find other employment.

When the time came for General Colbert to move on with his men, Aurore's grandmother openly wept his departure, so attached had she, the monarchist, become to this stoutly Bonapartist soldier. He was followed by other officers, who were billeted at Nohant throughout this dry, hot summer, as columns of brilliantly uniformed *chasseurs,* carbineers, dragoons, cuirassiers, and artillery-men tramped, trotted, or rattled past. There were particularly heart-rending scenes when the order was finally issued to substitute the white fleur-de-lis banner of the Kings of France for the tricolor of the Republic and to burn the imperial eagles. In the ample stable yard and in the tree-shaded village square of Nohant Aurore and her mother actually saw battle-hardened troopers break down and cry like children over the flames that were consuming the proud Napoleonic emblems, while others spat on the Royalist white cockade they were required to pin to their peaked shakos.

It was, nevertheless, with a distinct feeling of relief that Madame Dupin de Francueil and most of her household saw the last of these veteran campaigners disappear down the dusty roads. The old lady was emotionally exhausted by the reawakening of so many bitter-sweet memories and Aurore's mother saddened by the realization that her happiest years lay behind her and that never again would she love someone as she had loved Maurice Dupin. The over-worked staff were in bad need of rest, and Deschartres, as mayor of the tiny commune of Nohant, was quite worn out from the daily apportionment of hundreds of billets. Two months of catering to forty officers, aides-de camp, and orderlies, matched by an equal number of horses, had consumed an entire year of Madame Dupin de Francueil's income and ravaged her cellar.

Probably no one was sorrier to see the troopers leave than Aurore and Hippolyte, whose studies had been agreeably interrupted by the glorious bedlam. The sixteen-year-old Hippolyte was in no mood to return to his textbooks and more than ever consumed by one desire: to be rid of Deschartres' pedagogic tyranny and to launch out on his own, no matter how. He had absorbed a certain amount of mathematics on the understanding that this would help get him admitted to the navy, but he was quite ready to sacrifice this humble smattering of knowledge for a dashing career in the cavalry. This latter prospect was openly encouraged by his and Aurore's first cousin, René de Villeneuve, who visited Nohant that autumn. Though a well-known Bonapartist — he had been Louis Bonaparte's court chamberlain and his wife had served as lady-in-waiting to Queen Hortense — René de Villeneuve had just married off a daughter to an officer in Louis XVIII's Royal Guard. Skillfully exploiting this noble connection — for his son-in-law was among other things a count — he was able not only to promise but to obtain a post for Hippolyte in a regiment of hussars.

The news that he was to leave for the garrison town of Saint-Omer, in northern France, depressed Aurore as much as it delighted her half brother. Her mother had already returned to Paris in the late autumn of 1815, and in March of the next year Hippolyte set out over the same northbound route. Now, for the first time, Aurore was left alone with her grandmother and Deschartres. The two years that followed were, in George Sand's later words, "the longest, the most dreamlike, the most melancholy years there had yet been in my life." She had no one to play with, nor was her grandmother any longer disposed to spend the winter months in Paris.

With fewer distractions the lonely girl had more time and energy to devote to her lessons. Grudgingly she labored at arithmetic, so abhorrent to her nature that it induced headaches and dizziness; dutifully she studied Latin, her early enthusiasm waning the further she progressed in that "dead language"; submissively she learned thousands of French verses, the full beauty of which she was often too young to savor. Geography she found intriguing and history fascinating, whether it was the "sacred" history of the Bible or the "profane" history of classical antiquity and post-Roman Europe. Here she could give free rein to her fancy, embellishing in her compositions the traits of heroic kings and queens, darkening the character of villains, magnifying minor figures she felt the chronicler had unduly slighted, and occasionally indulging in superlative exaggerations — with fiery suns and mysterious moons, sweet-scented flowers and monumental ruins, sacred flutes and Ionian lyres, clashing shields and wild whinnying horses all playing their epic parts — which would make her grandmother laugh when these naively purple passages were read to her out loud.

She also tried her hand at purely literary descriptions of things or places she had seen. One of them, a description of the *"Vallée noire"* (black valley) lying a few miles to the north, so impressed her grandmother that the old lady extolled it to her friends as a "masterpiece." But another was sufficiently high-flown to elicit this written comment: "Your fine phrases certainly made me laugh, I only hope you're not going to talk like that."

Just as George Sand was to feel about her later writings, so the young Aurore Dupin was dissatisfied with these early literary ventures. They looked singularly feeble next to the grandeur of Homer's *Iliad* or the heroic élan of Tasso Torquato's *Jerusalem Delivered,* both of which so enthralled her that she felt cheated by their "shortness." That these two epic poems should have been the first works (after the Bible and the early fairy tales) to have impressed her deeply is certainly revealing. Her favorite figures already were virile rather than passive — as were to be the heroines of George Sand's more progressive novels (such as the dashing Edmée de Mauprat); they were closer to Pallas Athene and Joan of Arc than to Aphrodite or Lancelot's Guinevere. "I made them act and speak, I wilfully altered the course of their adventures," she later explained her mental tampering with Tasso's great epic, "not because I thought I could do better than the poet, but because the amorous preoccupations of these characters bothered me, and I wanted them to feel as I felt, that is, enthusiastic only for religion, war, and friendship."

Today it might seem highly abnormal to the champions of unlimited permissiveness and precocious "sex education," but at the age of eleven Aurore Dupin was still blissfully ignorant of the facts of life. The universe of her imagination had not been affected by cynical parental gossip, mandatory lectures with their clinical explicitness, or the cataracts of pornographic imagery that today engulf the growing child. Left to her own devices by the prolonged absences of her mother and the casual supervision of her grandmother, Aurore could cultivate that sense of penumbral awe and mystery which is every whit as vital to a young being's healthy development as its corrosive opposite — the harsh, midday light of "scientific" knowledge and technical maîtrise. Nor in later life did she come to regret this "anomaly" — George Sand being able to write that "I have seen mothers, of an indelicate and jealous surveillance, always suspect some impurity in the chaste day-dreams of their daughters, and cast stones or filth into this pure, peaceful lake which still only reflected the sky."

Aurore, as a good child of the Napoleonic Empire which had (superficially at least) reconciled revolutionary France and the Catholic faith, had been brought up on the New Testament. Her mother, who had taught her to pray and been responsible for her early Biblical instruction, was instinctively, ardently, almost thoughtlessly religious. She went to church every Sunday, doubling her weekday prayers if she was forced to miss a Mass, even though she avoided confessions and detested sanctimonious bigots. Hers was a naive, unquestioning "coalman's faith" — *une foi de charbonnier,* as the French say — in which Christ's miracles were as straightforwardly accepted as his teachings. Not so Madame Dupin de Francueil, who had little use for devotion and even less sympathy for "miracles" and superstitions. An eighteenth-century rationalist, she was a deist, like Voltaire, convinced that God was a necessary invention for the orderly functioning of human society. She admired the Gospel as an "excellent philosophy," once purged of all fabulous hyperbole and treated as a salutary moral tonic. She likewise held Jesus Christ "in great esteem" as a human being of exemplary candor and goodness. But so allergic was she to the merest whiff of dogma or the most casual mention of "faith" that Aurore had to hide the tears she shed for Christ's sufferings and crucifixion for fear of being mocked. Taught to doubt the veracity of Christ's miracles and to question his divinity, Aurore could not eradicate a youthful longing for the divine which caused her to invent a god of her own, able to mediate between herself and the all too remote and threatening Almighty, whether personified by the Judaic Jehovah or the pagan Jupiter.

The god she thus invented was called Corambé, a strange composite of the qualities she had most admired in the heroes and heroines of Homer's *Iliad* and Tasso's *Jerusalem Delivered.* He was as charitable as Jesus, as radiant and beautiful as the archangel Gabriel, possessed of the grace of the nymphs and the poetic feeling of Orpheus. He — but it was often a She, whom Aurore could not help imagining clothed in female garb, like her mother, the human being she adored above all others — was as wise as Pallas Athene and as chaste as Diana, as artistically gifted as the Muses, as melodiously inspired as Apollo.

Her veneration for this extraordinary He/She figure — "whom I wanted to love like a friend, like a sister, at the same time revering him like a god" — first took the form of verses, or what George Sand later called "chants," which celebrated her hero-goddess' or her god-heroine's beneficent incarnations and remedial interventions in this or that human plight or vicissitude. But as her poetic daydreaming increasingly took possession of her mind, to such an extent that later she could speak of a "kind of sweet hallucination," she could not content herself with imagining her playmates (the daughters of tenant farmers) to be nymphs disguised as shepherdesses. During the two hours of "recreation" that were allowed between midday and two o'clock for romping in the fields, picking autumn fruit, gathering winter fodder, or sliding down the hay chutes, she would steal into the grove and take refuge in a "sanctuary" she had discovered hidden away behind a protective screen of hawthorn and privet. Here on a mossy couch, shaded by three lovely maples arching up from a common base, she built an altar made of shapely stones and pebbles which she festooned with floral wreaths and hanging chaplets of ivy leaves from which abandoned bird's nests and pink and white shells (pulled from the placid waters of the nearby moat) were strung like sacred oil lamps. To this "sanctuary" she would bring her "offerings" — birds and butterflies, lizards, beetles, and green frogs — which she or her playmates had managed to trap in the woods or fields and which, far from sacrificing to her god — the very idea made her shudder — she would "liberate" from the box or the trap in which the poor creature was imprisoned.

One day, however, the sanctuary was discovered by one of her playmates and the magic charm was broken forever. Her beloved Corambé ceased to frequent the sacred spot; it was abandoned by the dryads and cherubs of her dreams. Her elaborate ceremonies and sacrifices now suddenly struck her as so puerile that she buried the hanging garlands and the festoons at the foot of the tree, beneath the ruins of an altar she meticulously destroyed. Her dream world had been defiled and in the process had been revealed to be a myth unworthy of the adult she now aspired to become.

Like any intelligent adolescent, Aurore was torn between the conflicting pulls of brain and body. At times she would succumb to a kind of cerebral "possession," and momentarily forgetting her outdoor friends and amusements, she would for days on end lead a life of vicarious adventure in her bedroom, or remain closeted in her grandmother's boudoir, unable to tear herself from some enthralling new book. "I was of a strong constitution," George Sand could later recall, "and throughout my childhood I was expected to become a beauty, a promise which I failed to keep. I may have been partly to blame, for at the age where beauty flourishes, I already spent my nights reading and writing."

In twelve months, between her twelfth and thirteenth years, Aurore Dupin grew three inches, finally reaching her mother's height — at which point she stopped. Though only five-foot-three, which by our standards would be short, she was already a remarkably robust young girl who was seldom sick. Her grandmother let her roam the countryside at will. With her friends, the sons and daughters of Nohant's tenant farmers, Aurore helped milk the cows and goats, danced wild country dances in the stubble, devoured wild apples, pears, and berries. Often she would accompany Deschartres on his agricultural rounds. But while the "great man" would long-windedly complain because that ox over there had been bought at the market for such and such a price, only to develop skin disease or a rotting foot, Aurore would be thinking what a bore it was to be a proprietor and master, eternally having to call one's tenants to account, when it was so much pleasanter to lose oneself in bucolic contemplation of the landscape.

Her grandmother's fingers now being too stiff and arthritic for piano-playing exercises, Aurore was entrusted to the musical supervision of the La Châtre organist, whose deplorable taste and lack of sensitivity almost killed her love for music. A heavy-handed key pounder named Gayard, he would turn up at Nohant on Sundays in his old-fashioned pigtail, pigeon-wing hairdo, and square-cut eighteenth-century livery, devour a hearty lunch, tune harpsichord and piano, and give Aurore a two-hour lesson before retiring to the kitchen to disport himself with the maids. The sight of his fat dirty fingers and the smell of powder covering his unwashed body made these musical sessions particularly nauseous for Aurore, who would breathe a sigh of relief when, after a second copious repast, he would ride out of the village, his pockets bulging with the tasty tidbits and dainties he had wheedled from the kitchen staff.

The other six days of the week could fortunately be devoted to repairing the ravages of the seventh. For Madame Dupin de Francueil, though no longer able to sing, or rather bleat, in her thin, cracked voice the old eighteenth-century airs of Porpora and Pergolesi that had so enchanted Aurore in the past, could still "keep time" and criticize her granddaughter's playing.

Nothing — neither her lessons, nor her rustic recreations, nor the occasional charade-improvising evenings to which she was invited by friends in La Châtre — could make Aurore forget her mother's absence and the little "plot" they had hatched between them. She still dreamed of being a milliner; she was still stoically determined to sacrifice the reprehensible comforts of Nohant for the life of hardworking poverty she wanted to share with her mother. In this imaginary scheme of things there was no more place for bookish education than there was for the titles and wealth she rejected out of hand — with that ungrateful petulance teen-agers are apt to display when frustrated in their dreams of meritorious martyrdom.

Her grandmother would take her to task for neglecting her studies, but the scoldings would only stiffen Aurore's resolve *not* to become well educated. One day, after being thus rebuked, she walked out of her grandmother's room and, in a fit of pique, threw her textbooks and notebooks on the floor, exclaiming out loud: "Yes, It's true, I don't study because I don't want to! But I have my reasons." Julie, who had followed her out, scolded her for her stubbornness, saying that she deserved to be sent back to her mother.

"My mother!" cried Aurore. "But that's all I want, that's all I ask for — to be sent back to my mother!"

When Julie reported these words to her mistress, the old lady was mortally offended. The same woman who had disputed her son's heart and finally wrested him from her was now alienating her granddaughter's affections. Too proud to show how hurt she was by Aurore's stubborn "ingratitude," she had Julie order her to go upstairs to her room. Since she detested her grandmother, Julie informed her, she would not see her anymore, and in three days' time they would bundle her off to Paris.

For the next three days Aurore was pointedly ostracized. The normally smiling servants were ordered not to speak to her. Deschartres was as tight-lipped as a mummy. Wherever she went there was an embarrassed silence. Only after her grandmother had finished her meal was Aurore allowed to come down to the dining room, and only when the old lady was once more installed in her ground-floor room was she told to go run around in the garden. Each time Aurore passed her grandmother's bedroom door, the bolt would be rammed shut, as though in anticipation of an enemy assault.

Upstairs in her room Aurore communed privately with Corambé, spilling out her woes and asking for His commiseration, which He readily granted. Now at last her martyrdom was real, she was being made to suffer for excessive love of her mother. She was filled and sustained by a feeling of wronged righteousness.

The third day, seeing that nothing was being done to prepare for her trip to Paris, she came downstairs to have a frank talk with her grandmother. But when she turned the handle after knocking on Madame Dupin de Francueil's door, she found it as sternly bolted as ever.

Early the next morning Aurore was told to go downstairs and beg her grandmother's forgiveness for the sorrow she had caused her. The old lady was still in bed, bundled up in her usual array of night bonnets, coverlets, and shawls. Aurore dropped on to her knees by her bedside and took her old veined hands in her own. But before she could kiss them, her grandmother stopped her. "Now stay on your knees and listen carefully to what I have to say to you," she said in a sharp, embittered tone that sounded strangely different from her usually placid and deliberate mode of speech. "What I am going to say to you now you have never heard before and will never hear again from me. These are things that are only said once in a lifetime, because they are things one does not forget."

With that she launched into the story of her life. She told how she, Aurore de Saxe, had been born the natural daughter of the great Maurice de Saxe, himself the illegitimate son of King Frederick Augustus of Poland. Her father having died when she was only two, she had been adopted by her aunt, Maurice de Saxe's half sister, Maria Josepha, who had married Louis XV's eldest son and who was known at the Court of Versailles as *la dauphine*. Her royal aunt had supervised her education, sent her to the Ecole de Saint-Cyr — the finest school for young ladies in the realm — and had not permitted her to see her mother, Mademoiselle de Verrières, who had had the misfortune to be born Marie Rainteau, a commoner.

At the age of fifteen, she continued, she had been married to the Comte de Horn. But the marriage had never been consummated, thanks to some "unspeakable" malady against which she and her half brother, the future Abbé de Beaumont, were warned on the wedding day by one of the count's valets and his personal physician. After her husband's death, which occurred not long afterward, she had entered a Paris convent, but this had not kept her from receiving visits from a sexagenarian admirer, Louis-Claude Dupin de Francueil, an entertaining salon conversationalist who had personally known Jean-Jacques Rousseau, Voltaire, and many of the eighteenth-century *philosophes*. Handsome, gracious, elegantly dressed and perfumed, gay, kindly, and affectionate, Monsieur Dupin de Francueil was a person of universal if somewhat dilettantish genius who could design houses and decorate interiors, mend clocks, cook, embroider clothes, paint portraits, repair locks, write poems, compose music, and even mend the fiddles his nimble fingers liked to play. He was a walking encyclopedia and so brimful of wit and knowledge that she could not recall ever having spent a dull hour in his company. Still, she had long hesitated to accept his generous offer to marry her because of the thirty-year difference in their ages, which to his dying day had led him to call her "*ma fille*" (which in French can mean "my girl" or "my daughter"), just as playfully she called him "my Papa," or later "my old husband." She had also had to overcome the well-entrenched prejudice, according to which it was a misalliance for one who was the granddaughter of a King and the widow of a count to marry a person who was not of noble birth. But Louis-Claude Dupin de Francueil was fortunately rich; indeed, his father, also a royal tax collector, had at one time been so wealthy that he had been able to buy the Château de Chenonceaux, one of the jewels of the Loire valley, as well as a magnificent town house in Paris he had later sold to Voltaire's friend and patroness, Madame Du Châtelet.

These financial considerations having easily stifled all aristocratic objections, they had gone to London to be married, in 1777. One year later she had borne him a son, named Maurice after his illustrious grandfather, Maurice de Saxe. Nine years later, in 1788, Monsieur Dupin de Francueil had died, and now twice widowed, she had had to face the turmoil of the French Revolution alone. The subsequent upheavals had dealt a severe blow to her fortune and even caused her to be imprisoned for some months in the Couvent des Anglaises, a convent run by English nuns which had momentarily been transformed into a revolutionary jail. Notwithstanding her noble connections, she had managed to save her head from the guillotine, thanks to the exemplary sang-froid of Deschartres, who at considerable personal risk had burned some highly incriminating documents linking her to Louis XVI's brother, the Comte d'Artois. Though half ruined, she had managed to save enough of her husband's fortune to be able to buy Nohant in 1793 and later to help Aurore's father purchase the uniforms he needed as a dashing young hussar.

But what — and at this point we must imagine the old lady raising her eyebrows in a look of emphatic scorn — what, in comparison, could be said of Aurore's mother? Far from having any royal blood in her veins, she was of such humble birth that she did not even know who her paternal grandfather was. This, of course, was no fault of hers, but what was one to think of the daughter — Aurore's half sister, Caroline — who had been born to her when she was still in her teens of an unknown father who had chosen to abandon her, for reasons Sophie-Victoire Delaborde had never been willing to explain. (That her own son, Maurice, had similarly seduced a pretty local lassie named Anne-Marie Chatiron, the daughter of a humble La Châtre carpenter, and that the fruit of their clandestine amours was Aurore's half brother, Hippolyte, the old lady conveniently neglected to mention, it being understood, at any rate by her, that the peccadilloes of a man are quite different from those of a woman.) And what was one to think of this same young mother, who had calmly left her young daughter Caroline in Paris after starting an affair with a quartermaster general, with whom she had traveled to Milan in 1800? No wonder she had begun making eyes at the handsome Maurice Dupin the moment their paths had crossed in the French headquarters at Milan and Asola! Humble her origins might be, but Sophie-Victoire Delaborde knew a good match when she saw one! Her quartermaster had been forgotten and abandoned overnight, while she set her cap at this dashing young hussar, pursuing him from one camp or headquarters to the next, from Paris to Boulogne, from Boulogne to Sedan and back to Paris, even following him down to La Châtre, from which Deschartres had vainly sought to dislodge her during one period of leave — until finally she had prevailed on Maurice to marry her just one month before Aurore was born!

Who could seriously believe, she went on, that Sophie had maintained an absolutely virtuous existence during the eight years that had elapsed since her husband's untimely death? Instead, Madame Dupin de Francueil gave Aurore to understand that there was some appalling new secret in her mother's present existence over which a veil had to be thrown, something so unmentionable that she would forever be prejudicing her future if she seriously tried to rejoin her. The mere thought of it should make her tremble! For the truth, the old lady finally blurted out in a hollow, emotionally exhausted voice, the truth was that her mother was *une femme perdue* — a lost woman — and Aurore an utterly blind child intent on plunging to her doom.

Too paralyzed to move, though time and again she wanted to protest, Aurore knelt there by the bedside, her hands drawn back in self-protection, listening to her grandmother's rasping voice blow and crack over her bowed head like the whiplashes of a cruel wind. When at last the storm was over, she rose to her feet, turned, and walked out without a word. She ran upstairs, locked herself into her room, then broke into convulsive sobs.

Perhaps it was Romantic exaggeration which later caused George

Sand, in recalling this scene, to say that her own fits of weeping, unlike most, had never managed to assuage her but that, on the contrary, "as soon as tears come to my eyes, sobs seize my throat, I suffocate, my breathing erupts in cries and groans; and as I have a horror of noise and suffering, and keep myself from howling, I have often collapsed, as though lifeless, to the floor . . ." This time, however, her hysterical cries were loud enough to bring Rose running to comfort her. Finally mastering her sobs, Aurore went downstairs and sat through a silent lunch, forcing herself to eat. She opened her notebooks and pretended to study, when all she was conscious of was the smarting irritation she could feel behind her tear-swollen eyelids. She no longer knew if she loved or hated anyone or anything; all she felt was a supreme, overwhelming indifference. "It was as though I had an enormous internal burn and a kind of searing void in the place of my heart. I felt a kind of scorn for the entire universe, a bitter disdain for life, whatever it might hold in store for me; I no longer loved myself. If my mother was contemptible and detestable, then I, the fruit of her loins, was also detestable. A hideous, an almost irreparable wrong had been done to me; an attempt had been made to stop up in me the well-springs of moral life, faith, love and hope."

Time, however, is a great healer. As the days passed Aurore discovered to her surprise that she loved her mother more than ever, without hating her grandmother for having been so brutally frank. But inside her something was broken. There was no more delightful daydreaming. There were no plans or "plots" for the future. Corambé gradually faded from her consciousness, unable to offer reassuring answers to questions she was now too dispirited to ask. "I lived like a machine."

To mask her inner disarray she returned to her childish games and amusements in the garden and in the surrounding fields, romping through pastures, wheat sheaves, and hedges in heavy peasant clogs, and turning the house upside-down with her rowdy companions. At table she talked out of turn, saying anything that came into her head, and broke into pointless laughter at the slightest pretext. Willfully she was turning into a hellion, an "enfant terrible," as Rose called her. For her sophisticated, old-fashioned grandmother it was a painful spectacle. "You were once a charming young girl," she finally said to her, "you mustn't now turn into an absurd young lady. You have lost your composure, your grace, your sense of the appropriate. You have a good heart but a pitiful head. It is time to change all that. You need proper masters, and I cannot find them here. So I have decided to place you in a convent, and we are going to Paris for that reason."

And so she would see her mother? Aurore could not restrain her joy.

Yes, the old lady answered coldly. She would see her mother.

4. From Deviltry to "Sacred Sickness"

Like Teresa of Avila, who entered her first convent unwillingly only to fall in love with monastic life forever, Aurore Dupin cared little at first for the cloistral existence to which her grandmother was condemning her but ended up spending three surprisingly happy years in an austere but strangely vibrant religious community.

Her lingering hope, as they rattled into Paris over the old coach road, was that her mother would ridicule the idea of a religious education. But once again she was in for a shock. While her mother found it ironic that Madame Dupin de Francueil, with her abhorrence of clerical devotion, should wish to entrust Aurore to the tutorship of pious nuns, she herself warmly supported the idea, saying that a year or two of convent education would do her daughter a world of good and prepare her for a brighter future than the drudgery of a milliners' career.

The Couvent des Anglaises, to which Madame Dupin de Francueil finally decided to send her thirteen-year-old granddaughter in November of 1817, was one of the three truly distinguished boarding schools for young ladies then existing in Paris. Composed of a rambling group of vine- and jasmin-draped buildings situated on the eastern flank of the Sainte-Geneviève hill (which is now, but was not then, dominated by the ponderous, neoclassic dome of the Panthéon), it included a chapel, a vaulted cloister, a cemetery, a broad garden shaded in spring and summer by magnificent horse chestnuts, and an even larger kitchen garden, behind whose tall grillwork gates and fence were grown the vegetables, fruits, and melons needed to nourish the convent's one hundred and twenty inmates. First established in seventeenth-century Paris, the convent had become a sanctuary for British Catholic ladies seeking refuge from Roundhead persecutions. The noblest of these exiles were buried beneath the elegantly scrolled and epitaphed flagstones over which one trod when walking round the quadrangle to the chapel. Others were honored by memorial wall tablets, likewise composed in an English it took Aurore some time to understand. A select few were even preserved for posterity in an imposing array of portraits (princes and prelates as well as ladies of the realm) that hung in the chambers of the mother superior, the portly, worldly-wise, shrewd yet subtle Madame Canning.

In 1793, at the height of the Robespierre terror, when all titles had been scrapped and there was hardly a monastery in France that had not been transformed into a revolutionary prison, Aurore's grandmother had been jailed in the Couvent des Anglaises as a *ci-devant* aristocrat. Aurore's untitled mother had also spent a few days here, after being arrested for allegedly singing a seditious, "counter-revolutionary" song. Both were thus familiar with the interior of the religious "prison" where Aurore was now confined, behind forbidding walls and windows which were not only barred but covered with a kind of canvas sacking — to keep the "angelic" inmates from tempting glimpses of the sinful outer world. Their parents could come to talk to them in the parlor and even slip them presents of sweets and dainties through the grillwork bars; twice a month they could be taken home for dinner, and on New Year's Day they were allowed to spend the night at home. Aurore, however, was less privileged. Shortly before returning to Nohant — in early February of 1818 — her grandmother prevailed on her mother not to take Aurore out for the fortnightly half holiday. When her aristocratic cousin René de Villeneuve (the same who had got Hippolyte admitted to the Hussars) offered to take her out, Aurore proudly refused, preferring monastic seclusion to a betrayal of her slighted mother. For one long year Aurore thus deliberately forfeited her rare holidays, but such was her relief at having ceased to be a bone of contention between her mother and grandmother that George Sand could later write that "I think I was the only one of the children I knew there who was truly satisfied. The others had relatively happy families and homesteads to regret; I didn't."

Yet Aurore's life at the Couvent des Anglaises was anything but milk and roses. Because she knew no English — the language used for classroom work and at mealtimes, and regularly spoken by the nuns, who were all English, Scottish, or Irish (unlike their charges, most of whom were French) — she was made to join the junior class, composed of girls younger than herself, and had to sleep in a third-floor dormitory situated directly below the eaves. The room was so glacial, particularly in those first wintry weeks of 1818, that Aurore would lie in her cold bed, vainly trying to drop off to sleep, while the chapel bell marked the slow passage of the hours. Being by nature a night owl and a late riser, she had been allowed at Nohant to go to bed late and to get up when she chose. But here she and her thirty dormitory companions were rudely awakened at six, then forced to "wash" their hands and faces in pitchersful of freezing and sometimes frozen water. Her hands developed chilblains, her swollen feet bled in the excessively tight shoes. Poorly clad in a purple serge dress, she shivered on her bench and trembled drowsily on her knees through the candlelit mass, only faintly revived by the cup of tea and the piece of bread she was given for the seven o'clock breakfast. A lukewarm stove, placed near the teacher's chair, was the only source of heat in the stone-cold classroom, and not until midday did she really begin to thaw out. At the Couvent des Anglaises she froze, developing streaming colds and suffering sharp rheumatic pains which were to plague her for the next fifteen years.

The cramped, low-ceilinged classroom where Aurore and her junior class companions were forced to spend the larger part of each day was in some ways even grimmer than the dormitory. Wretchedly ventilated, it smelled like a chicken coop permeated by coal dust and smoke. Its walls were covered with a bilious egg yellow wallpaper and adorned by an ugly plaster crucifix. The smoke-smudged ceiling was unwashed, the floorboards were warped, the tables, stools, and benches ink stained and unvarnished. As though this were not tribulation enough, the classroom was ruled over by an irascible martinet of an instructress, who avenged herself for the antipathy she aroused in the young girls by publicly insulting them and forcing them to kneel down and kiss the floor each time they uttered an "evil word."

Less than this would have been needed to turn Aurore into a rebel. The junior class, she discovered, was divided into three camps or categories: there were the naturally submissive and devout, who were called *les sages* (the wise ones), there were the resolutely unsubmissive who were known as *les diables* (the devils), and there were the lukewarm in-betweeners, known as *les bêtes* (the dolts), who were ready to laugh at the antics of the "devils" when the teacher was out of the room and just as quick to dissociate themselves when she returned.

Aurore, as one of the oldest girls in the junior class, immediately chose to become a "devil." She learned to slip out of the classroom during the brief intermissions when their teachers were changed; she joined in nighttime prowls through the convent's sprawling buildings in search of a secret door leading to the cavernous catacombs and cellars. With the other "devils" she partook of clandestine picnics — cakes, pâtés, pies, basketsful of grapes and cherries, all smuggled into the convent with the connivance of a sympathetic porter; she also became adept in strewing melon rinds on the stairs, filling the pianos with chicken bones, and throwing jam pies so that they would remain, for a brief while, menacingly stuck to the ceiling. For her persistent deviltry she was known to the nuns as "madcap" and "mischievous," while her favorite nickname with her contemporaries was *calepin,* given to her because she was always scribbling messages or secret letters — furtively passed from hand to hand and ingeniously added to during classroom sessions — on little pocket-size notebooks.

Aurore's literary verve also found expression in the almost daily letters she wrote to her grandmother. They soon became a kind of satirical journal in which she made fun of the detested mistress of the junior class. Madame Dupin de Francueil was much amused by these tokens of rebellious disrespect. Not so the Reverend Mother Canning, whose suspicions were aroused by the extraordinary number of letters Aurore Dupin left on the heavy oak chest in her antechamber, where all outgoing mail had to be deposited. Though the inmates of the Couvent des Anglaises were allowed to seal the letters they wrote to parents and nearest kin — all other letters being left open for inspection — the mother superior could not resist un-sealing several of Aurore's epistles. What she read both shocked and shook her. Summoned to her office and ordered to cease these "calumnies," Aurore insisted that her black descriptions of the hated mistress of the junior class were the simple truth, adding, with singular temerity, that she would go on writing what she liked and that should the privacy of her letters be further violated, she would ask to be removed to another convent. Her grandmother supported Aurore in this dispute, letting Madame Canning know that she would not tolerate any tampering with her granddaughter's mail. Aurore's letters from then on went uncensored, but to remove her from the "baleful" influence of the "devils," the mother superior had her "kicked upstairs" to the senior class.

This unexpected "promotion" turned out to be a blessing in disguise. Aurore was now admitted to a spacious, well-heated hall, where there was a large fireplace as well as a good, warm stove. Its six luminous windows looked out on to the garden's horse chestnut trees, already heavy with bright April leaves and pink candelabra blossoms. Ever sensitive to air and light, she felt as though she were "entering paradise."

Neither the discomforts of the upstairs dormitory — to which she was long condemned as a punishment for deviltry — nor the chaste rigor of the rules they were subjected to (no kissing between girls, no walking about in pairs, it had to be in threes — *numquam duo, semper tres* — and so on) could mar the deep, unexpected happiness Aurore derived from this cloistral existence. With each passing day she became more practiced in English, and she even managed, between escapades, to acquire some knowledge of Italian. Though much later, in *The Story of My Life,* George Sand belittled the "smattering of music and drawing" she picked up at the convent, her grandmother's letters of this period speak of her making great progress, not only with the pencil but also with the harp.

She was also taught how to dance, under the octogenarian tutelage of a Monsieur Abraham, who had once initiated Marie Antoinette into the subtleties of Versailles etiquette. Faithful to the silk-stockinged livery of the ancien régime, he would turn up in his muslin jabot, his buckled slippers, his carefully curled and powdered wig, and airily dangling a tiny violin between his ringed fingers, he would show the fifteen or twenty young ladies entrusted to his care in the mother superior's parlor — for as a man he was forbidden access to the convent — how to offer one's glove or retrieve one's fan, how to bow, curtsy, and withdraw with degrees of diminishing deference, in the presence of princes, dukes, marquesses, counts, viscounts, barons, knights, presidents, vidames, and mere abbots. These too were occasions ready-made for merriment, so pompous and mannered did the "graces" taught by the aged gentleman seem to his giggling charges, who would first try his patience with loutish "blunders" and then redeem themselves by affecting exaggerated poses — enough to bring wrinkled smiles of approval to his curiously discolored, red- and blue-veined face.

When, at long last, Aurore was allowed to leave the dormitory and occupy a cell of her own, she felt more than ever at home. Situated beneath the eaves, like the dormitory, it was an oven in the summer months, an ice box in winter, and so tiny that to close the door, after entering, she had to back into the embrasure of the small dormer window. The sloping roof was so low that, if not careful, she cracked her head against a rafter on getting up in the morning. Between the plain wooden bed, a diminutive chest of drawers, and a rush chair, there was just room for the small Louis XV harp her grandmother had once played and which she had specially brought up from Nohant to give her. Yet because this tiny cubicle was hers, because she could retire here for one hour each day, she came to love this tiny mansard cell. The faded wallpaper was covered with verses, dates, names, and proverbs left there by previous occupants, but there was still space enough to add chiseled drawings and "epic poems" of her own.

Aurore Dupin may not have been the very worst "devil" at the Couvent des Anglaises — as George Sand later claimed in her autobiography — but one thing seems certain: already in her fourteenth and fifteenth years she was displaying that couldn't-care-less audacity, that brash straightforwardness which were later to make her one of the most "aggressive" and scandalous women of her day. What none of the other girls dared do, she did, with a tranquil assurance the nuns seem to have found irresistible. Whereas the other girls were summarily expelled from the gloomy basement where Sister

Teresa, a Scottish converse nun, used to distil the mint grown in the garden, Aurore alone was allowed to move about the bubbling alembics and retorts, inhaling the delicious aroma of the leaves she helped gather up for boiling and watching with fascination as the precious emerald liquid oozed out drop by drop. Similarly, the dream-wish of every girl in the convent was to be "adopted" by Sister Mary-Alicia Spiring, the kindest, most intelligent, and (at thirty years) still the most beautiful of all the nuns. Only one girl had ever been adopted as Sister Alicia's "daughter," but in comparison with Aurore Dupin she had been a saint. But this did not keep Aurore from asking that she be adopted — for what merit was there, after all, in guiding someone who was by nature good and obedient? So ingeniously, so convincingly did she plead her cause that the good Sister Alicia finally gave in — to the astonishment of Aurore's friends, who knew how busy she was running the mother superior's office. Every evening, shortly before nine o'clock, Aurore could thus spend a few privileged minutes in the cell of her "mother," telling her in all frankness of her latest dissipations. Taking her "torment" (as she playfully called her) by the shoulders, the kind sister would give Aurore a good shaking, as though to expel the demon inhabiting her, and then send her off to bed with a soft caressing laugh which would make Aurore feel spiritually cleansed and at peace with the world.

The circumstances of this curious "adoption" are less interesting than the motives. At fifteen Aurore was still in desperate search of parental affection. Her father was dead, her grandmother too old, while her mother, on whom her filial passion had so long been focused, was growing increasingly remote, not to say estranged. Now definitely eliminated from any decisive say in Aurore's education, Sophie seemed resigned to letting things take their course. Dependent as she was on Madame Dupin de Francueil's financial support, she made no attempt to defy the old lady's strict injunctions.

"The only violent love I had experienced, filial love, had left me as though worn out and broken," George Sand later wrote. "I had a kind of cult for Madame Alicia, but it was a tranquil love; I needed an ardent passion. I was fifteen years old. All my needs were in my heart, and my heart was bored, if I may so express it."

There comes a time when even pranks can pall, and such a time had come for Aurore. Like Augustine, the convent's patron saint, she found herself wondering if the pleasure she derived from the illicit did not stem more from the fact that it was illicit. Every afternoon at four o'clock the girls had to file into the chapel for a ritual half-hour of "devotion," which was supposed to be spent in prayer, meditation, or the perusal of some sacred text. As a "devil" Aurore had usually spent this half-hour napping or whispering with her neighbors when the mistress' roving eye was not trained on her. But now out of sheer boredom she began reading an abridged copy of *The Lives of the Saints.* The first "life" she read was that of Simeon Stylites, the Syrian anchorite who, so legend claimed, had spent thirty-six years living on top of a pillar. Far from finding this exploit absurd, she was struck by its poetic force: a person who could steel himself to such a level of solitude was no common mortal.

The more she read about the early Christian hermits and martyrs, the more impressed she was by their stoic fortitude. Their exemplary sufferings imparted a new meaning to the magnificent painting hanging behind the choir — a painting which showed a tormented, white-skinned Christ fainting into the arms of a red-robed angel in the garden of the Mount of Olives. She found herself being deeply moved by the mystery of Christ's passion. And as her moist eyes moved on to another painting in which Saint Augustine was depicted seated beneath a fig tree, his heaven-raised brow smitten by a ray of celestial light and the soul-shaking words, *"Tolle, lege"* (Take, read), which had moved him to read the Gospels, she too was moved by an imperious desire to read about the Berber saint's epic sinfulness and conversion. She found herself rereading the Gospels — those same Gospels her grandmother at Nohant had taught her to treat with Voltairean skepticism.

Aurore's own conversion, however, was not the direct product of these readings. Still less was it willed. For as George Sand later wrote, "With love it is as with faith. One does not find it when one seeks it, one finds it at the moment when one least expects it."

One evening, she was wandering listlessly through the darkened cloister when she saw several heavily veiled nuns making for the chapel. For Aurore the standard tricks had lost the charm of novelty. She and her "devil" friends had poured ink into the font, they had tied Sister Alippe's cat Whisky to the little cloister bell — all this was "old hat." But the one thing she had never done was to venture into the chapel at a time when normal access to it was forbidden.

She now entered the chapel alone. In the fading light, it was filled with a mysterious calm and beauty that went straight to her heart. The nave, like the choir, was dark, save for a faint rivulet of light running down the marble flagstones from a little silver lamp suspended near the altar. A single star was framed in a panel of deep, sea blue glass. Warm summer scents of jasmine and honeysuckle flooded in through an open transept door, and she could hear the faint flutelike trill of warbling birds.

She watched in silence as a black-veiled nun came forward to light her candle from the suspended choir lamp. There was a quiet upraising of arms, a trembling flicker of a flame, a profound prostration before the altar, and then the dark incognito figure returned like a phantom from where it had come.

The minutes passed, silently, uncounted. The solitary nun closed her missal, extinguished her candle, and retired. Already the bell was sounding for evening prayer, but still Aurore stayed on, rooted to the spot by a sense of deep, ineffable bliss. "I had forgotten everything. I do not know what was going on inside me. I was breathing an atmosphere of an unspeakable sweetness, and I was breathing it via the soul even more than through the senses," as George Sand later sought to describe this first mystic experience. Aurore felt giddy and as though enveloped in an aureole of light. "*Tolle, lege,*" someone whispered in her ear. She turned, expecting to see Sister Mary-Alicia, but she was quite alone.

When this "characteristic sort of consciousness once has set in," William James wrote in *The Varieties of Religious Experience,* "the mystic feels as if his own will were in abeyance, and indeed sometimes as if he were grasped and held by a superior power." This was the feeling Aurore Dupin now experienced. Suddenly, without warning, she felt her heart being seized and possessed by faith. "So thankful, so delighted was I by it that a torrent of tears streamed down my face. I also felt that I loved God, that my thinking embraced and fully accepted this ideal of justice, tenderness and holiness I had never really called into doubt, but with which I had never found myself in direct communication. Now at last I felt this communication suddenly established, as though some invincible obstacle had been removed between the source of infinite ardor and the subdued fire in my soul."

Hearing someone whimpering in the nave, the nun who had come to lock up the chapel came forward to investigate. Aurore rose to her feet and hurried out without a word. The next day, when asked where she had been during the evening prayer, she answered quite simply: "In the chapel." The reply, coming from a notorious "devil," was so startling that it silenced the teacher, who even forgot to punish the truant for her absence.

"From that day on all struggle ceased, and my devotion assumed the character of a passion. The heart once seized, reason was resolutely shown the door, with a kind of fanatical joy. I accepted everything, I believed in everything, without battles, without suffering, without regret, without false shame."

Each evening, during the brief recreation period, she could hardly wait to enter the chapel and relive a few moments of rapt, mystic fervor. Her "devil" friends found her oddly changed. Some made cruel sport of her. Others were more sympathetic, but none sought to follow her example. This would have been difficult in any case, for Aurore now threw herself into devotion with the same passion she had shown for deviltry. She went to see her father confessor, the sympathetic and sensible Abbé de Prémord, who had hitherto refused her absolution, realizing the hypocrisy of the ritual *examen de conscience* (examination of conscience) she was in the habit of mechanically reciting. This time, however, the abbé had her sit down and tell him her life story. It took her three hours. He then made her kneel and receive the absolution, telling her to give thanks unto God for unlocking the portals of her heart.

The rest of the summer and the first autumn weeks were spent in a state of deep beatitude. She communed every Sunday and sometimes two days in succession. Like Saint Teresa of Avila, she could no longer sleep, she hardly ate, she walked about in a kind of trance, oblivious of the movements of her body. She mortified her flesh by wearing a filigrain-wire chaplet about her neck, and instead of pain she felt only an agreeable sensation when her abrasions began to bleed. "In a word, I was living in ecstasy, my body was unfeeling, I no longer existed."

Years later George Sand could look back on this *maladie sacrée* — this "sacred sickness" — with a sense of adult relief at having been able to survive its furious fevers. For at the time it looked as though she were destined to succumb. Dubbed "Saint Aurore" by her friends, she derived a saintly satisfaction from helping a humble converse nun wash the chapel floor and polish the oak stalls. When she informed Sister Mary-Alicia of her determination to become a nun, her kindly mentor smiled, told her that neither her mother nor her grandmother would hear of such a thing, and that a religious vocation was not something that could be chosen overnight. But Aurore was only half convinced. And if it was the "merit of suffering" she sought — like the sacred humility with which the converse Sister Helen scrubbed the chapel floors — then she did not need to look for it in a convent.

Her health, however, soon began to suffer from an excess of spiritual exaltation. She was seized by stomach cramps, had no appetite, could not sleep. Dragging herself to the chapel, she felt listless and distracted: the prayers had lost their savor, the mass had lost its fervor. God, for reasons she could not comprehend, had decided to withdraw His grace from her.

Persuaded that she was being punished for her continued sinfulness, she took to exaggerating minor misdemeanors and to inventing all sorts of sins each time she confessed. His patience finally exhausted by the litanies of self-reproach he was forced to listen to, the Abbé de Prémord consulted the mother superior and Sister Mary-Alicia, who assured him that Aurore had been behaving with exemplary docility. He then took her gently to task for her pious "exaggerations," which were worrying her kinsfolk, alienating her friends, and which threatened to turn the piety she professed into an object of general revulsion. Let her go out and play games with her friends instead of prostrating herself in the chapel during recreation hours! Let her skip rope, let her play ball, and she would see — her appetite would return, she would be able to sleep soundly, her brain would be better able to appreciate the "faults" she claimed to have committed.

Startled by these injunctions, which the abbé imposed on her by way of "penance," Aurore meekly submitted. Soon the color returned to her cheeks, she ate with renewed appetite, she slept soundly and laughed gaily, like the fifteen-year-old adolescent she still was. Her friends, overjoyed by this sudden metamorphosis, came flocking back to her.

At this crucial juncture in her life, as George Sand was reluctantly forced to admit years later, she had been saved by a Jesuit. "Without him, I believe I would now either be mad or a cloistered nun. He cured me of a delirious passion for the Christian ideal. But in this was he a Catholic Christian or a worldly Jesuit?"

Too submissive to return to her former deviltry, Aurore was still too spirited and inventive to remain totally subdued. With several friends from the senior class she took to improvising charades and then to preparing scenarios for which she provided the script. Now nicknamed *l'auteur* (the author) and *boute-en-train* (live wire), she was the animator of a theater group that became the marvel of the convent.

Late in the autumn of 1819 Madame Dupin de Francueil returned to Paris and was surprised to find Aurore gay and in good health and spirits, quite different from the sad, sickly girl about whom she had received such disturbing reports. Aurore, though now serene and happy, had not abandoned her decision to take the veil, and though she said nothing, her grandmother got wind of it from the mother of Aurore's friend, Pauline de Pontcarré. Resolutely anticlerical, Madame Dupin de Francueil decided to end this adolescent "dream" by taking her granddaughter back with her to Nohant.

Thus ended three of the happiest years Aurore Dupin had known. Years later, in reviewing the mystic élan that had overtaken her during her stay at the Couvent des Anglaises, George Sand could condemn its excesses almost as harshly as had her grandmother. The habit nuns have of considering themselves the brides of Christ, she felt, could only nourish "hysterical mysticism, the most repugnant of the forms mysticism can take. This ideal love of Christ is only without danger at an age when human passions are mute. Later it lends itself to aberrations of feeling and to the chimerae of a troubled imagination. Our English nuns were not mystical in the least, fortunately for them." And, she could have added, fortunately for herself. Had it been otherwise, Aurore Dupin might have become Sister Marie-Augustine (her convent name). Christendom might not have gained a saint, but the world would never have known George Sand.

5. Hellion on Horseback

Far from experiencing a feeling of joyous liberation from the rigors of convent discipline, Aurore felt disoriented by her sudden return to "normal" life. Her grandmother was now, in the early spring of 1820, almost seventy-two years old and well aware that she had not much longer to live. "My little girl," she kept repeating, "I must marry you fast, for I am on my way out." The idea was repellent to Aurore, who was not yet sixteen. But fortunately the various matches proposed by her great-uncle, the jovial Abbé de Beaumont, led to nothing, and even her grandmother had to admit that Aurore was a "foolish little girl" who needed at least six more months to mature.

Aurore was thus relieved when the time came to pack their belongings for the return trip to Nohant. But her joy was brutally shattered by her mother's adamant refusal to accompany them. She hated the country, and above all Nohant, where she had endured agonies of suffering. Also, Caroline was now a grown-up young lady and she couldn't leave her alone in Paris. "I shall return to Nohant only when your grandmother is dead," she added truculently.

Aurore's persistent hope, throughout these years, had been that somehow her mother and her grandmother could be reconciled. But the passage of time seemed only to have increased her mother's hostility. Sadly Aurore paid a last call on her convent friends before she set out with her grandmother in the large blue calèche that had replaced the lumbering old berlin. At Nohant the workmen were redoing her little bedroom, substituting a soft lilac for the gaudy orange wallpaper with the flamboyant foliage, but fortunately her hearselike four-poster had been spared. She spent the first night in her mother's large Louis XVI bed, with the gilt pomegranate trimmings, and woke at the astonishingly late hour of nine — she who had spent three years listening to the early chapel bell — to find the garden trees in glorious blossom and the nightingales piping and trilling in the nearby branches above the distant chant of farmhands laboring in the fields.

A maid brought her a pink gingham frock to replace the purple serge dress she had worn at the convent, and for the first time in three years she was free to comb her hair as she pleased, without risking a reprimand for "sinfully" uncovering her temples. The dogs who had growled at her the evening before now leaped and frolicked around her in belated recognition. The servants and the Nohant peasants who trudged in to pay their respects found her *"plus grossière"* — plumper (though it sounded like "grosser" in the quaint patois of Berry) — and even Deschartres had trouble recognizing "Mademoiselle," as Aurore was henceforth respectfully called.

In September Hippolyte Chatiron returned to Nohant on leave, a proud hussar corporal who rolled his r's and strutted about with fine military swagger, saying that the horse hadn't yet been born he couldn't tame. To prove it, he took Aurore out into a grassy meadow and had her mount an as yet unbroken mare named Colette. Hippolyte proved such an able instructor and Aurore such a fearless pupil that within a week she and Colette were jumping hedgerows and ditches, scrambling up steep inclines, and wading through deep water. He taught her to ride cross-saddle, and not to be outdone by his dashing hussar's shako, she took to wearing a man's cap to keep her flying hair in place.

But all too soon the fun-loving Hippolyte had to return to his regiment, leaving Aurore alone once again with her grandmother and Deschartres. Both declared themselves appalled by her "crass ignorance," which three years of mind-numbing religious education had done little to alleviate. Aurore was so stung by their criticism that she stayed up late, working at her English and reading history books until two or three in the morning. Already displaying that astounding energy which was to make her one of the female prodigies of the nineteenth century, she would limit herself to four or five hours of sleep and be off galloping down the country roads and across the fields long before her grandmother rose at nine. After lunch she would sing and play the piano for Madame Dupin de Francueil, then read to her from the gazette or sketch in her boudoir, while Deschartres read the latest news. The day would end with another long session, Aurore reading out loud to her grandmother, after which Mademoiselle Julie would help the old lady into her satin nightgown, lace bonnets, and cockades, moisten her wrists and forehead with expensive perfumes, slip special rings over her gnarled fingers, and carefully pillow and cushion her — for she always slept in a semirecumbent position.

But one January night — they had now entered the year 1821 — Aurore was reading out loud from a book when her grandmother stopped her: "I must have dozed off," she explained. "I have grown much weaker. I can no longer read and I can no longer listen." To humor her, Aurore took up a deck of cards and they played several hands together. But the old lady's thoughts were clearly elsewhere. Finally she declared that she had rejected the suggestion of her great-nephew, René de Villeneuve, that Aurore be married to an "immensely rich man" — a fifty-year-old general whose credentials might have been impeccable but for the saber slash scarring his face. No, Aurore could rest assured: never would she be forced to marry against her will or be asked to break with her mother by celebrating a "fine marriage."

Touched by her grandmother's unusually penitent tone, Aurore went up to bed in a happy frame of mind, feeling that the conflict that had divided the two women and herself might be coming to an end. But at seven o'clock the next morning she was woken by Deschartres, who told her that her grandmother had tried to get up during the night, had suffered a paralytic stroke, and collapsed onto the cold floor, where she had lain for hours. Wrapped up in blankets, the old lady was nursed back to consciousness, but it was soon clear that her mind was affected. At times it seemed as though she had regained her old wit and lucidity, but such moments were brief.

For the next ten months Aurore acted as nursemaid to her grandmother, sitting up for half the night to humor the old lady who, no longer able to tell night from day, would complain that Deschartres, Mademoiselle Julie, and Aurore were trying to "isolate" her from the normally active world. Often they would have to light a score of candles, concealed behind her bed, to persuade Madame Dupin de Francueil that it really was the day and that she wasn't going blind. To keep from falling asleep during these long nocturnal vigils, spent in her grandmother's airless room, Aurore drank black coffee and helped herself to generous pinches of snuff. But she soon discovered that nothing restored her flagging energies as much as an early morning gallop on Colette.

Her "anchoritic" existence, however, was not quite as solitary as she made it seem in a letter full of melancholy and nostalgia which she wrote about this time to her old convent friend Emilie de Wismes. For she had already found a substitute for Hippolyte — in the person of Stéphane Ajasson de Grandsagne, a young gentleman from La Châtre who was just two years her senior. They apparently met by accident one day when Aurore was out roaming the countryside on horseback; and while this may be local legend rather than strict fact, it is certain that during the winter and spring of 1820–1821 they did a great deal of trotting and galloping together — enough to cause comment in the neighborhood.

Stéphane Ajasson de Grandsagne was a handsome, well-built young man, with curly hair and long Byronic sideburns, a pair of delicately arched eyebrows, and two ironic dimples at the pursed corners of his mouth. "He lacked neither knowledge, nor intelligence, nor wit," George Sand later described her first "beau." His father, Comte François Ajasson de Grandsagne, who had been mayor of La Châtre under the Napoleonic Empire, had had the misfortune to sire ten children, whose expensive upbringing had ruined what was left of the family fortune. Stéphane, the youngest of four sons, had thus been forced to give up his scholarly interest in the classics (he read Greek and Latin fluently) and devote his student energies to medicine and science. Had he been richer, Madame Dupin de Francueil might well have considered him a good match for Aurore. But having been forced by a miserly mother to strain his health in excessive study, he was not only impecunious but said to be consumptive.

Such was the young gentleman who first taught Aurore to fire a pistol and encouraged her to wear masculine clothes when riding. He had picked up this idea from another La Châtre nobleman, Comte Omer de Villaines, whom he had one day met accompanied by a "young boy" dressed in a male blouse and cap. The old count explained that he dressed his daughter like a boy so that she could go hunting with him, "climbing and jumping without being bothered by the clothes which render women powerless at an age when they have the greatest need of developing their strength."

The moment Aurore heard this she abandoned all inhibitions and from then on wore men's clothes when riding, finding them an immense relief from the awkward, tight-fitting sheath dresses then in vogue. Deschartres encouraged this inclination, doubtless because he was a hardened bachelor who had spent most of his adult life tutoring boys. With that taste for devilish exaggeration she had already demonstrated at the convent, and which was to make her the talk of Paris before she was thirty, Aurore derived a singular relish from sallying forth on horseback disguised as a man. One day, in a village where she was unknown, she sat down to sketch a Gothic castle; several ladies came out to admire the drawing and asked how much *Monsieur* would be willing to sell it for!

Determined to "improve" her lamentable education, Deschartres gave Aurore lessons in geology, mineralogy, and medicine. He made Aurore look on stoically while he set broken bones or amputated infected arms and fingers, allowing her to undertake some elementary first-aid chores on her own. But his knowledge of medicine being largely self-taught and rudimentary, he suggested that she take lessons in anatomy and osteology from someone better trained than himself — like Stéphane Ajasson de Grandsagne. The young physician-to-be was only too delighted to oblige. His visits to Nohant became increasingly frequent, and while Madame Dupin de Francueil dozed downstairs, "teacher" and "pupil" spent increasingly long hours studying the complexities of muscles, bones, and sockets. He brought Aurore arms, legs, and skulls to copy, while a La Châtre doctor even lent her a human skeleton, which remained for several weeks stretched out on top of her chest of drawers.

Though two centuries had passed since physicians had been burned for practicing anatomical dissections, the idea that a young lady should indulge in such unorthodox activities soon had tongues wagging. Everything Aurore did went counter to local practice and tradition. She rode forth brazenly, dressed like an amazon in a round Spanish-style hat rather than demurely seated on the crupper of her valet's horse. She shot and hunted like a man and derived a morbid pleasure from the study of dead bones. Nor, so local rumor had it, did her iniquities stop there. She spent hours in her bedroom closeted with a supposedly studious young man, while at night she dabbled in the occult sciences. Her page, André, also reputed to be her lover as well as her accomplice in exercises of black magic, had even seen her and Deschartres stealthily exhume the skeletons in the Nohant graveyard! In a word, she was the incarnation of evil and in league with the powers of darkness.

Even her most innocent diversions — such as the long rides and the target practice she indulged in with her cousin René de Villeneuve, when he came to Nohant in May to act as a witness for the drawing up of Madame Dupin de Francueil's will — were maliciously interpreted by the chatterboxes of La Châtre. The fact that her cousin only looked thirty, though he was in fact forty-five, and that the two of them would often stay up *alone* till two or three in the morning, only added to the gossip. These "sinful" tête-à-têtes were largely devoted to discussing the novelists, essayists, and philosophers Aurore had been reading — for René de Villeneuve was as widely read as he was beautifully mannered. Not for a moment did it occur to him that Aurore's robust outdoor life might be regarded as eccentric, and far from berating her for the late hours she kept, he encouraged her to go on burning the midnight oil and to continue the diary she had begun keeping — in preparation for the day when she would start writing novels of her own.

That summer, when Aurore's uncle, the Archbishop of Arles, came to Nohant to "offer absolution" to the free-thinking Madame Dupin de Francueil, he ordered Aurore to get down on her knees before him and to beg forgiveness, saying: "You ride, you sing Italian songs, and I am told you shoot with a pistol." * Aurore, how-

* Jean-Claude Leblanc de Beaulieu, to give him his full name, was the bastard son of Claude Dupin de Francueil and Madame d'Épinay, the author of some celebrated eighteenth-century memoirs. For further information on this kinship, see notes to this chapter.

ever, flatly refused to confess any "sins," and when he demanded to know if by any chance she had been reading Voltaire and other "infamous" authors, she roundly answered: "At the present time I am reading the Fathers of the Church and I find many contradictory points of view." Unwilling to take her word for it, the vexed divine marched into his aunt's library and would have burned and mutilated a large number of "seditious" volumes had he not been stopped in the nick of time by an outraged Deschartres.

Though she would not have had to do much hunting to find one church father contradicting another, it was not one of them who created havoc with the naive Christianity Aurore had picked up at the convent. Still less was it Voltaire, whom she only read much later — in obedience to her grandmother's curiously "pious" request that she sample none of his works before reaching the age of thirty. The book that smote her like a thunderbolt was Chateaubriand's *Le Génie du christianisme,* which the curé of La Châtre kindly lent her, in the simple-minded belief that it would fortify her Catholic convictions. But Chateaubriand's romantic apologia for the virtues of Christianity had precisely the opposite effect. Suddenly Aurore realized how much self-indulgent masochism lay concealed in the doctrine of Christian self-abasement that Thomas à Kempis had taught in his *Imitation of Christ.* "This sublime and stupid book," George Sand wrote years later, "can make saints but will never make a man." *The Imitation of Christ* was a book made for the cloister and tonsured monks. "It is mortal to the soul of anyone who has not broken with human society and the duties of human life." The Christianity extolled by Chateaubriand, on the other hand, was positive, outgoing, optimistic, not limited to morality and doctrine. For Christianity's real mission, even if its priests and practitioners had not always understood it, was to encourage genius, purify taste, "give vigor to thought," develop the "virtuous passions" and appreciation for the fine arts. In this scheme of things there was no harm in paying homage to Newton as well as to Bossuet, to Racine as well as to Pascal. In short, it was a religion "made to appeal to all the enchantments of the imagination and to all the interests of the heart . . ."

Fed up with the fashionable but trivial novels she had been reading for distraction, Aurore now delved into Locke and Condillac,

Montesquieu and Bacon, Bossuet, Aristotle, Pascal, and Montaigne, obediently perusing the passages her grandmother had marked out for her to read. She even tackled Leibnitz, and though much of what she read was way above her head, she was moved by his sturdy belief in the virtues of knowledge and in his optimistic refusal to believe that the God-created universe could be anything but good.

She also read the great poets — Dante, Pope, Milton, Virgil, Shakespeare (Dante in Italian, most of the others in translation). But the decisive mace stroke against her naive Christianity was dealt by Jean-Jacques Rousseau, "the man of passion and sentiment *par excellence,*" as George Sand was to describe him.

Her gradual disenchantment with the established Church would probably have occurred in any case, but her readings of Rousseau accelerated this spiritual drift. Instinctively she sided with the "liberals," as they were beginning to be called, and though not yet prepared to associate the Church with the color black — as Stendhal did in *Le Rouge et le Noir* — she was, like Byron, for all emancipation movements, beginning with that of the Greeks against the Ottoman Turks and of the Italians against Austrians and Spaniards — movements which the Catholic Church was doing nothing to encourage.

For Aurore Christianity had to be liberal, generous, and enthusiastic, or it ceased to be Christianity: it simply became a religious sham, a pious fraud. At the convent she had been spiritually uplifted by the beauty of the services. But in the provincial backwaters of Nohant she had to put up with set prayers recited in faulty Latin, hear the choristers sing off key, and try to ignore the snoring of sleeping women while the priest droned on in an interminably stupid sermon, occasionally interrupted by a robust oath uttered against some misbehaving hound that one of the parishioners had insisted on dragging into church.

Thus, curiously enough, it was her sense of religious absolutism that drove her to become a nonconformist. What Rousseau had declared — that man is essentially good but society iniquitous — applied to religion as well. It too was established, and thus conservative, conformist, and only too often petty. In such a stuffy climate the individual could not flourish. He was doomed, like

Hamlet, to feel at odds with a world that was out of joint. He was destined, like Alceste in Molière's *Le Misanthrope,* to be hamstrung at every turn by hypocritical conventions. He was fated, like Chateaubriand's René, to be a lonely sufferer. Like René, Aurore too was a romantic "outsider."

Increasingly she felt like an orphan — with no father to guide her, a grandmother in her dotage, a tutor who had virtually turned over to her the administration of the Nohant estate, and an absent mother whose rare letters were full of reproach. Her solitude was aggravated in November of 1821 when Stéphane de Grandsagne left La Châtre for Paris, where he was due to enter the Faculty of Medicine. Aurore gave him a list of books to buy, suggesting that he leave them with her mother, who would have them sent on. We know little of what happened when the high-strung Sophie Dupin met the studious and scientifically minded Stéphane, save that at one point he made a passing reference to Aurore's "warlike character." Sophie, who had been receiving strange reports about her daughter's behavior, took her seriously to task in her next letter. Aurore's reply, while respectful in tone, was a veritable declaration of filial independence. If she spent so much time out of doors, it was because a closed, indoor existence would have made her as sickly as her grandmother. It was an insult to Monsieur de Grandsagne's sense of honor to suggest that he might have taken advantage of their studious encounters in her room and an affront to her sense of virtue and propriety to suggest that she might have succumbed to his amorous advances. And why, she defiantly asked, "must a woman be ignorant? . . . Supposing that I should one day have sons and that I should have derived enough benefit from my studies to teach them, don't you think the lessons of a mother are worth as much as those of a tutor? But to reach this point one must be married, and, for that say you, I shall only find a giant or a coward. In that case I might never get married, for I no longer believe in giants and care not for cowards . . . I won't look for a man capable of becoming the slave of his wife, because he would be an imbecile; but I don't believe that a man of intelligence and wit would want his wife to seem timid and fearful when she was neither one nor the other."

The hand that penned these emphatic lines was that of the seventeen-year-old Aurore Dupin, but the voice was already that of George Sand. One of the first to feel the full force of this "warlike" disposition was the curé of La Châtre, who was rash enough to ask her, during a confession, if she were not beginning to feel the first stirrings of love for a certain person — unnamed, but it was clearly Stéphane Ajasson de Grandsagne who was meant. Aurore answered heatedly that she did not know what love was, but that it was none of his business. Infuriated by this priestly prying into her intimate life, she ceased confessing and going to Mass.

Worn out by the many sleepless nights she had to spend by her ailing grandmother's bedside, sickened by the ugly gossip her uninhibited behavior aroused, her imagination kindled by the morbidly romantic books she was reading, she now sank into a state of profound depression. She took to walking by the river Indre, tempted by the idea of flinging herself into the water like Shakespeare's Ophelia. Once, while crossing a ford with Deschartres, she was overcome by a suicidal urge and deliberately prodded her horse into the deep, swirling waters. But her stout mare began battling the current, and Aurore, brought to her senses by Deschartres' anguished shouts as he plunged out to save her, let her faithful Colette swim her to the bank.

Her grandmother, meanwhile, had slowly been subsiding into a silent state of apathy. Three days before Christmas she had Aurore awakened in the middle of the night to give her a mother-of-pearl knife — why she was unable to explain. Later that same night, she woke from a fitful sleep and murmured: "You are losing your best friend."

They were her last words. Shortly afterward she fell into a deep, comatose sleep. She died at four o'clock in the morning the day after Christmas. Aurore was by now so exhausted that she could not even cry. Mademoiselle Julie dressed the old lady in her lace bonnet and her ribbons, slipping the rings over her cold fingers, as though in preparation for one more night. A grave was dug in the little cemetery between the Nohant church and the garden so that she might lie beside her beloved son, Maurice.

At one o'clock in the morning, on the day of burial, Deschartres knocked on Aurore's door and insisted that she accompany him out into the freezing night, across the icy, snow-covered paths. He had watched the farm hands preparing the grave and had noticed that the nails in Maurice Dupin's coffin had rusted clean away. Later, when he was alone, he had lifted the lid and kissed the skull, now detached from the skeleton, of the man he had once tutored and adored. Now he asked Aurore to do the same. A less hardy soul might have recoiled in horror, but Aurore, who had watched the blood flow under Deschartres' scalpel, lowered herself into the grave and kissed her father's frozen skull with a sense of filial exaltation.

This too, she realized, was the act of a rebel. For had any neighbor or servant seen them, they would have thought them mad or worse — indulging in midnight witchcraft. But the privacy of this distinctly macabre homage to a father she had all too briefly known made the act seem more natural to Aurore than the public lamentations she had to witness the following morning when her grandmother was finally laid to rest.

That night everyone went to bed early, worn out by the emotional strain of these climactic days — all, that is, save Aurore, who slipped into her grandmother's room for one last nostalgic glimpse. The bed, which had not been made, still bore the imprint of her aged body. The room smelled of the benzoin and incense that had been burned during the long wake. Aurore half pulled the curtain, lit the night lamp, which still contained some oil, and stoked the dying embers in the hearth; then stretching out in an armchair, she listened to the faint moan of the December wind blowing down the chimney. She felt too tired to comprehend all that had happened. But one thing she knew: her youth was now over.

PART II

Marriage & Motherhood

6. Casimir Dudevant

The new year — 1822 — was already upon them when Aurore's cousin René de Villeneuve reached Nohant, soon followed by her mother, her Aunt Lucie, and her Uncle Amand Maréchal. The first embraces were joyous, as Aurore hugged her mother and was entertained by her aunt's lively Parisian chatter, and for a brief moment it looked as though all the conflicts and frictions were a thing of the past. But this illusion lasted barely a quarter of an hour. The mere sight of Deschartres, with his cold and disapproving air, and of René de Villeneuve, whom Madame Dupin de Francueil had named Aurore's guardian, was enough to bring all of Sophie's past injuries and humiliations boiling to the surface. Aurore was appalled by the torrent of invective now poured out against her grandmother, listening in an icy silence which only exacerbated her mother's pent-up fury.

Madame Dupin de Francueil's will was officially read on January 2 and immediately contested by Sophie, who heatedly declared that the law was on her side since she was Aurore's mother and thus her legitimate guardian. The subsequent legal wrangling consumed the better part of two weeks and was finally terminated by the justice of the peace in La Châtre, who named René de Villeneuve a *surrogate* guardian for the seventeen-year-old heiress of Nohant. He could offer advice, but the headstrong Sophie was under no obligation to heed it.

She followed up this triumph by putting a brusque end to the generous proposal René de Villeneuve had made to Aurore — that she come to live with his family at the Château de Chenonceaux, that jewel of the river Cher, which he and his brother, Auguste, had inherited from their (and Aurore's) great-grandfather Claude Dupin and his wealthy second wife, Louise-Marie Madeleine de Fontaine. Destroyed too at one stroke was the dream Aurore's grandmother had so long and fondly cherished: that Aurore one day be wedded to one of René de Villeneuve's sons. Sophie was determined to take her daughter back to Paris with her, away from the baleful influence of Mademoiselle Julie and Deschartres.

Relations between mother and daughter were by now so tense that when Sophie airily suggested at the dinner table that she was doing Aurore a favor by "being willing" to keep her in Paris with her, Aurore brusquely flared up: "You are *willing* to keep me with you! And when did I ever request it? Didn't you *force* me into it?" All the predictions her grandmother had one day made to her in a moment of remarkable lucidity were now dramatically confirmed. "Your mother," the old lady had said, "is odder than you think . . . . She is so uncultured that she likes her young ones the way birds do, with great care and much ardor in early childhood. But once they have found their wings, instead of reasoning or relying on instinctive tenderness, she flies to another tree and chases them off with pecks. At present you could not live three days with her without feeling wretchedly unhappy."

This was exactly what had happened to Aurore's half sister, Caroline, who had finally managed to escape by marrying a young firearms inspector named Pierre-Nicolas Cazamajou. Their mother was now left with only one child to tyrannize. And tyrannize her she did. She relented to the point of allowing Aurore to bring along her maid, Sophie Cramer, and her favorite dog, Pluchon, but she refused to let her travel with more than a small handful of books.

In Paris they spent several relatively calm weeks in the apartment of Aunt Lucie Maréchal, who knew how to handle her sister's tantrums. But as soon as Aurore and her mother had occupied Grandmother Dupin's apartment, on the Rue Neuve-des-Mathurins, the sparks began to fly. Not only had the old lady's prolonged infirmity eaten heavily into the income of the Nohant estate, but under Deschartres' fumbling stewardship it had been losing rather than earning money. To pay the numerous staff of servants Madame Dupin de Francueil had insisted on maintaining, many sacrifices had been made, including Aurore's wardrobe, which had been reduced to just one dress. What had saved them financially was the income derived from several state pensions and from tenants occupying a house they owned on the Rue de la Harpe in Paris. Aurore also knew that Deschartres had borrowed 18,000 francs from her grandmother to buy a piece of land not far from Nohant — a loan he could never possibly repay. Sophie summoned the "great man" to Paris to explain these anomalies and reduced him to such embarrassed stammerings that Aurore, feeling pity for his plight, boldly declared that the missing 18,000 francs had not been a loan but a gift she had personally turned over to Deschartres at her grandmother's request. Her mother then flew into a violent rage and accused her of lying; to punish her, she sent the maid Sophie packing and got rid of Pluchon.

But this was only the beginning of her misfortunes. When her cousin René de Villeneuve called on them one day and courteously inquired if he could take Aurore home with him for dinner, her mother haughtily replied that Madame de Villeneuve would have to come and make the request in person! This was too much for the normally urbane René de Villeneuve. Never, he retorted, would his wife set foot in Sophie's apartment! He didn't need to add that his wife, born the daughter of the Comte de Guibert who had been a minister of war under Louis XVI, was a social snob who would rather have died than consort with people of Sophie's species. With a frigid bow René de Villeneuve walked out, and it was twenty years before Aurore saw her favorite cousin again.

Her other cousin, the more roughhewn Auguste de Villeneuve, was even blunter when he too came to call. He chided Aurore for going out for walks in public with her half sister, Caroline — who was dismissed as "socially impossible." Let Aurore marry a commoner if she wished, but one thing he was sure of — no "gentleman of fortune and birth" would condescend to call on her here, even after she had attained her majority.

Though she had royal blood in her veins, Aurore Dupin was thus declared a social outcast because of her mother's plebeian origins. She had to choose between one world or the other — the aristocratic or the lower middle class. The choice had in fact been made — by her mother — but it made Aurore feel a misfit. The romantic fiction she had devoured at Nohant was no longer just literature; it had become a harsh, everyday reality. Like Chateaubriand's René, like Byron's Lara, she was the tormented sufferer, one who bore the stigma of a secret, ineradicable sin.

Aurore accepted her lot with resignation. But her submissiveness only added fuel to her mother's exasperation. Years of sterile widowhood, during which she had never found a man to replace her beloved Maurice, had left Sophie Dupin frustrated and embittered. She had entered the age of menopause, and lacking a man to assuage her passionate feelings, she sought an emotional outlet in tempestuous "scenes." If Aurore was reading a book, she would snatch it away, saying it made no sense to her and must therefore be bad. And not only bad, perverse — like Aurore's behavior at Nohant! "The filth of the little town had overwhelmed my mother's lively and yet feeble imagination," George Sand was later to recall. "It had penetrated so deeply as to destroy the simplest powers of reasoning." At times, indeed, Aurore wondered if her mother were not now mentally deranged as she watched her in the evening, angrily tearing the ribbons and flowers from a hat she had found "charming" in the morning and disguising her lovely dark hair beneath hideous blond, auburn, and silver white wigs, which were changed from day to day.

To escape from this crippling confinement Aurore would appeal to her mother's stoutly Catholic convictions and ask to be allowed to pay one more visit to her convent friends. The permission was at first granted readily enough, but not for long. Ever ready to believe the worst of her daughter, Sophie was soon complaining to the old Abbé de Beaumont that Aurore's frequent visits to the Couvent des Anglaises were being used to mask an amorous "intrigue" she was carrying on with some young man she had met. The jocular old abbé first discounted these reports: such behavior on her part was inconceivable. But he finally agreed to put in a word of friendly warning: "Behave yourself, my Aurore, as an honorable girl should behave!"

"So, my uncle, you believe me guilty?" she asked.

"I would much like to doubt it," replied the abbé, giving his great-niece every chance to absolve herself. Instead, she bowed her head, while a tear trickled down her cheek. Then suddenly springing to her feet, she threw her arms about the old abbé's neck, hugged him briefly, and said: "Uncle, farewell!" Picking up her bonnet, she called to her mother and walked out, proudly refusing to return — to her great-uncle's considerable chagrin.

This time it was not her mother but Aurore herself who slammed the door on an old friendship. But why this desperately proud behavior, why this sudden pique? Was there, after all, some substance to her mother's suspicions? This is one of the riddles in Aurore Dupin's early life to which we still do not know the answer. But at least one George Sand scholar has pointed out that at this time, the late winter and early spring of 1822, Stéphane Ajasson de Grandsagne was studying medicine and science in the Latin Quarter — which is to say, right around the corner from the Couvent des Anglaises!

Spring only added to the mounting tension between mother and daughter. The constant strain, the repeated rows began to affect Aurore's health and looks. Even her mother was forced to admit that her child needed a change of air, and one day, while dining with one of the Abbé de Beaumont's friends, she was pleasantly surprised to be invited to make a visit to the country with her "ailing" daughter.

The almost total strangers who thus extended their hospitality to Aurore and her mother were a retired cavalryman named James Roëttiers du Plessis and his young wife, Angèle. At Le Plessis-Picard, some fifteen miles southeast of Paris, near the highway leading to Melun and Fontainebleau, they owned a Louis XVI country house, in a delightful rustic setting of flower beds and vegetable gardens, spacious lawns and meadows. Their property even included a lovely wood full of bounding deer and long leafy alleys down which one could gallop at full speed.

A cavalry officer who had fought under Napoleon, James Roëttiers, at forty-two, was beginning to lose his hair, but his bright blue eyes had lost nothing of their captivating twinkle. He had been a gay blade in his youth, but once married to his wealthy young niece, who had inherited the Le Plessis property, he had become a model husband and the father of five daughters. The four eldest were dressed in boys' clothing (to compensate for the son he would have liked to have had); and in their red trousers and silver-buttoned jackets they looked like little drummer boys of varying shapes and sizes. Their mother, Angèle, was already gray-haired, though only twenty-seven. But she was of such a generous and good-natured disposition that Aurore was immediately won over to her, as she was to her husband.

Soon abandoned by her own mother, who could not wait to return to Paris, Aurore was adopted as a member of the du Plessis family, fitted out with new clothes (which she badly needed), and henceforth called "our daughter" by her hosts. She just as naturally took to calling Madame Angèle "Mother" and James Roëttiers "Father."

Originally, Aurore had only been invited to spend a week at Le Plessis. In early April she accordingly returned to Paris with the Roëttierses, who wanted to indulge in a bit of theatergoing. Each day they picked up Aurore at her mother's apartment and took her to the theater and the elegant cafés. Her mother, far from exhibiting any jealousy, was happy to be relieved of having to keep her daughter amused and entertained, and in late April, when the Roëttierses left Paris, she agreed to let Aurore return with them to the country.

James Roëttiers, who had briefly known Aurore's father in Italy during the Napoleonic campaigns of 1800, was full of paternal solicitude for his newly adopted "daughter." Aurore's mother, he knew, wanted to see her married, and though the prospect had little charm for Aurore herself, it did at least offer her the possibility of freeing herself from her mother's crippling tutelage. Naturally hospitable, the Roëttierses maintained an almost permanently full house, entertaining friends and neighbors as well as officers stationed at Melun and Fontainebleau, more than one of whom were soon courting the small, brilliantly dark-eyed heiress of Nohant.

The first of these epauleted suitors was a fairly handsome second lieutenant of humble peasant origin named Jean-Baptiste Garinet. Unfortunately, like many Napoleonic soldiers, he had not had time to acquire a good education, and worse still from the marital point of view, he was relatively poor. His advances, culminating in a formal proposal, were accordingly rejected by Aurore, whose heart meanwhile had been captured by another.

Of this second suitor, Prosper Tessier, we know little, beyond the fact that he was a thirty-year-old infantry lieutenant. As a doctor's son he had presumably received a better education than Garinet—enough at any rate to charm the seventeen-year-old Aurore. He was a good horseman and good company, and she enjoyed galloping with him down the branch-vaulted paths and across the leafy clearings. At the end of one such stimulating race, when they found themselves alone in the faintly rustling forest, he proposed to her. Why, he asked, did Aurore hold out so stubbornly against him? Why did she not yield to the dictates of her throbbing heart and make both of them happy? Would it really be a crime, punishable by God, if she let herself fall with a sigh into his welcoming arms? Given a little encouragement, he declared, he could easily arrange to have himself appointed aide-de-camp to a general stationed at Fontainebleau so that they could remain together.

Aurore's response was one of tearful stupefaction. Too late she realized that she had fallen in love with a man who wanted her to be his mistress, with someone who could threaten to leave her because he found her too fatally enthralling. "I love you too much," he declared in what he must have thought was a heroic confession. "So I must leave you, flee from you." Well, if that was all she meant to him, if he found it that easy to be parted from her, then let him leave! For if, as Aurore later wrote to a friend, "he had loved me for myself, he would have known how to master himself and preferred to see me happy and pure beside him rather than embarrassed and humiliated in his arms."

One week later the frustrated seducer left, just as he had promised, and Aurore never saw him again. His brusque departure, like his bold advances, left her emotionally shattered. Her first amorous infatuation had ended in humiliation, leaving a wound which was not completely healed for years.

In early June she was proposed to once again. This time she accepted with alacrity. The man who thus caught her "on the rebound" was also an officer, though he had gone into semiretirement from the army in order to obtain a law degree. Aurore had first met him in Paris one April evening when she was seated with the Roëttierses, enjoying an aftertheater ice cream at the fashionable Café Tortoni, on what was then called the Boulevard de Gand (now the Boulevard des Italiens). "Look, here's Casimir!" Angèle Roëttiers had exclaimed as they were accosted by a slender, elegantly dressed young man, whose slightly stiff military bearing was offset by a gay, smiling face. His father, Colonel François Dudevant, had once commanded James Roëttiers' cavalry regiment, while the son was on such friendly terms with the du Plessis family that he had jokingly been promised the hand of their eight-year-old daughter, Winefride.

Taking a seat next to Angèle Roëttiers, the young stranger had asked her in a whisper about the dark-haired young lady. "This is my daughter!" Madame Roëttiers replied in her forthright way. "Ah, then she's my wife?" Casimir Dudevant responded. "I thought it was to be Winefride, but since this one seems of an age better suited to mine, I'll accept her if you want to give her to me."

When, a week or two later, Casimir Dudevant came out to visit them at Le Plessis, he made no attempt to woo Aurore, like certain of the other officers, but took part quite naturally in the lively games she played with the Roëttiers children and their friends. Continuing the old family joke he had begun at Tortoni's, he started calling Aurore "my wife," while she laughingly called him "my husband." Thus a feeling of playful camaraderie was gradually established between them. He was twenty-six and had seen something of the world, she was a tender seventeen and though intellectually precocious, she had led a relatively solitary and sheltered existence. Suddenly exposed to ardent young suitors, she felt the need for a confidant, for a kind of older brother who could give her frank and disinterested advice. As she wrote in a letter to her half brother, Hippolyte: "I have here a companion I like a lot, with whom I jump and laugh as I do with you."

From fraternal companionship it was but a short step to the idea of marriage — a "solution" Aurore welcomed, to escape her mother's carping surveillance. Several of the young gentlemen to whom she had been introduced at Le Plessis were richer, probably too rich to be interested in her small fortune. Casimir Dudevant, on the other hand, as James Roëttiers explained to her, came from a Gascon family of relatively modest means. His father, Colonel Dudevant, had been made a Baron of the Empire under Napoleon and had married an aristocratic lady who had brought him a number of properties. But because Casimir was an illegitimate son, born of a housemaid before the colonel had married his present wife, he might only inherit half of these holdings, even though he was the sole heir, in which case his fortune would be less than what Aurore inherited at Nohant.

What had begun as a joke now became a serious matter. On his second visit to Le Plessis, in early June, Casimir Dudevant formally proposed to her, explaining that though this was contrary to usual practice, he would not press the matter further without her consent. He added that though he hadn't found her beautiful or even pretty the first time they had met, he'd been struck by her "good and reasonable" air. Touched by this direct and frank approach and by the "eternal friendship" he promised her in lieu of a sudden, May-time passion, Aurore agreed to an opening of negotiations between their respective parents. Old Colonel Dudevant journeyed up from his country house in Gascony to meet Aurore's mother, who was charmed by his distinguished bearing, his silver gray hair, his affable disposition. She was much less impressed by Casimir, saying, "I would have liked a handsome son to give me his arm," but she gave her tentative agreement nonetheless.

Two weeks later Sophie returned to Le Plessis "like a bomb," as George Sand later described it. Casimir, she had learned, had once served as a café waiter and such a person was not fit for her daughter! This incredible "discovery" was greeted with general laughter, to the fury of the irascible Sophie. Neither the patient explanations of James Roëttiers du Plessis nor the detailed account Casimir Dudevant gave of his army career and the life he had led as a law student lodged in his father's Paris apartment could calm her. Dragging Aurore out of the house, she raved and ranted hysterically against the "intrigues" of the Roëttiers household, claiming that they were making a "business" of marrying off heiresses to adventurers in return for handsome bribes! Aurore offered to return to Paris that very evening, but calming down as suddenly as she had exploded, her mother said that, all things considered, she would return to Paris alone, since Aurore obviously felt so much at home here.

A few days later Aurore followed her back to Paris, where they were soon joined by Hippolyte Chatiron, who had just resigned from the army. Fed up with the slowness of his promotions — five years to become a sergeant — he had decided to give up his career as a hussar. His presence turned out to be a godsend, for unlike Aurore, all too easily hurt and provoked by her mother's sharp tongue, he alternately flattered and made fun of Sophie Dupin, laughing off her fits of rage with a disarming insouciance.

Several times the marriage was decided, then postponed, as Aurore's temperamental mother went into new tantrums, expressing a violent distaste for the shape of Casimir's nose and deliberately taunting him each time they met. She insisted that the bridegroom provide a marriage settlement (60,000 francs was the amount finally agreed to), and though Aurore considered this a humiliating condition, old Baron Dudevant swallowed his pride and accepted it. Finally on September 17, 1822, Aurore Dupin and Casimir Dudevant were married, first civilly, and then religiously, at the church of Saint Louis d'Antin. Leaving Paris, the newlyweds spent a few weeks at Le Plessis with their friends the Roëttierses, and in mid-October, the French Ministry of War having accepted his resignation from the army, Casimir Dudevant set out for Nohant with his young wife.

At Nohant, where she spent the cold snowy winter of 1822–1823, Aurore soon found herself pregnant. While her husband, Casimir, went out hunting — his favorite pastime — she was confined indoors. Normally she would have spent her time reading, but now, in her expectant condition, she took up sewing and knitting, which her grandmother had never bothered to teach her, embroidering bonnets and tiny clothes for the baby she could feel stirring within her.

Aurore Dudevant found this new kind of domestic work singularly comforting. "I have often heard women of talent say that household work, and needlework particularly, were mind-numbing and insipid and part of the slavery to which our sex has been condemned," George Sand was to write some thirty years later. "I have no taste for the theory of slavery, but I deny that these chores are its consequence. They have always seemed to me to have a natural, invincible attraction for us, for I have felt it in all periods of my life and they have sometimes calmed great agitations of the mind. Their influence is mind-numbing only for those who spurn them and who don't know how to look for what can be found in everything — skillful work, well done. Doesn't the man who spades have an even rougher and more monotonous task than the woman who sews? Yet the good laborer who spades fast and well is not bored by his spading, and he will tell you with a smile that he *likes the toil and the sweat of it.*"

Was she completely satisfied, was she truly happy with her married life? Not entirely, to judge from a letter she wrote to Emilie de Wismes in January of 1823 in which she agreed with her old convent friend that "the dissensions which are born from the diversity of tastes and characters are only too real in most households . . . Each time one or the other of the two spouses wishes to stick to his ideas and never yield, he will be unhappy. It is essential, I believe, that one of the two, in marrying, should practice self-abnegation, should renounce not only his will but even his opinion, should firmly strive to see through the other's eyes, to like what he likes, etc. What torture, what a life of bitterness, when one is united to someone one detests! What a sad uncertainty, what a charmless future when one is married to a stranger! But also, what an inexhaustible source of happiness when one obeys what one loves! Each privation is a new pleasure . . . The only question remaining is if it's up to the man or the woman to *remake* himself thus on the model of the other, and since *all power is on the side of the beard,* and since, besides, men are incapable of such a degree of attachment, it is necessarily up to us to bend in obedience."

This was not to be her feeling for long. But in this cold month of January 1823 Aurore was too wrapped up in the joyful sufferings and tribulations caused by her pregnancy to think otherwise. In late May she and her husband left Nohant, and after tarrying for several days with the Roëttierses, they rented a small furnished suite at the Hôtel de Florence in Paris (on the Rue Neuve-des-Mathurins) run by Napoleon's former chef Gallyot. And it was here, in a small, rear-court pavilion whose windows looked out on to a tiny garden, that at six o'clock on the morning of June 30, 1823, Aurore Dudevant gave birth to a son — named Maurice, like her father and great-grandfather, the unforgettable and unforgotten Maréchal de Saxe. "It was the most beautiful moment of my life," George Sand was later to recall, "this moment when, after an hour of deep sleep which had followed on the terrible pains of delivery, I saw on waking this tiny tot asleep on my pillow. I had dreamed so much of him beforehand and I was so weak that I wasn't sure I wasn't still dreaming. I was afraid to stir, lest the vision fade . . ."

Deschartres arrived shortly afterward, looking more provincial and superannuated than ever in his cornflower blue frock coat and gold buttons. Now that there was a new master at Nohant, he had decided to give notice. He unswaddled the tiny Maurice and turned him over and over, examining every inch of his wrinkled pink flesh with medical thoroughness. Not once did he caress him — Aurore could not recall ever having seen Deschartres caress anyone — but he did hold the sleeping infant on his knees for a while before rising to his feet to announce that the time had come for him to "live for myself."

It was virtually the last glimpse she was to have of her "great man." In August, to escape the heat, Aurore and Casimir, accompanied by the little Maurice, whom she insisted on suckling herself, traveled back out to Le Plessis, where they spent a few merry weeks with the Roëttierses, taking long walks and acting in vaudeville plays. They returned to Nohant early in October. Compared to the dizzying gaiety of Le Plessis — where at one point forty houseguests had been lodged for a full week — Nohant seemed to Aurore a "desert." As she wrote to Emilie de Wismes, now married in her turn to a viscount: "My little country house is really pretty, only it's in a region where there is nobody to see. I don't regret society, but I would like to see two or three friends who would often come to draw or to sing with me. My dear Casimir is the most active of men, he never stops coming in, going out, singing and playing with his child; only with the greatest difficulty in the evening can I get an hour or two to read. But I have read somewhere that to love perfectly one must have similar principles and souls, with contrary habits and tastes."

She might indeed have read it, but living it was another matter.

As the months passed, it became increasingly clear that her tastes and Casimir's were radically different. He put order into the household, he straightened out the garden paths, he got rid of the aging dogs and horses, he cleared out the dead trees. Nohant, from the point of view of economic husbandry, was unquestionably "improved," but in the process some of the ramshackle old charm was gone.

Casimir, as she wrote to a neighbor, was "good, simple, and frank"; he undoubtedly meant well, he tried to be a tender husband, but for her romantic yearnings this was not enough. Though it was a luxury they could ill afford, he bought her a new piano. But once installed, he made no attempt to conceal his callous indifference to music. Each time she sat down at the keyboard, he would make a face and leave the room. To humor him, she gave up playing and singing. She tried to interest him in reading, but in vain. Dutifully he would read a few lines, sometimes a few pages, then bored or drugged by the quantities of wine he had drunk at table, he would doze off and let the book drop to the floor. Every effort Aurore made to discuss literature, poetry, or ethics proved equally barren. Intellectually, Casimir was on a level with her half brother, Hippolyte, who had been invited to stay with them at Nohant with his recently wedded wife. Ponderous barracks-room jokes, local political gossip, the practical problems involved in running their estate — these were the limits of Casimir's conversational powers. Aurore sought desperately to hide from the bitter truth, but it was too patent to be ignored.

She had rushed headlong into marriage to escape her mother's temperamental tyranny, only to discover that she had moved from one prison to another. For a mistress she had substituted a master, but no better than the petulant Sophie did the more tolerant and easygoing Casimir understand what Aurore's romantic nature craved. At eighteen, she had reached that age where, as she later told him, "one feels a need to love exclusively. Everything one does must concern one's beloved. One wants one's talents and graces to be for him alone. You did not notice mine. My knowledge was wasted, since you did not share it. I didn't say so to myself, but this is what I felt. I pressed you in my arms, I was loved by you, but something I could not explain was missing from my happiness."

Her one consolation was her plump, bouncing son, Maurice, who by March of 1824 was drinking wine and sinking his six baby teeth into eggs, bread, and pancakes. But such maternal satisfactions could not dispel the feeling of overpowering ennui that now oppressed her. Robbed of its cultural sparkle, Nohant now seemed like a tomb. Increasingly gloomy, she broke down frequently and cried, and one morning at breakfast she burst into tears.

Unable to explain what was troubling her, Aurore agreed with her husband that her "feeble" brain must have been affected by sad memories of her dead grandmother. Casimir offered to take his wife to Paris. There she spent every evening she could at the theater and her afternoons walking "Bibi" — as Maurice was now called — in the Tuileries Gardens. But the thought of returning to Nohant and of finding herself locked up again in a dismal tête-à-tête with her husband was more than she could face. Gratefully they accepted one more invitation from their friends the Roëttierses du Plessis on the understanding that they would pay their share of household expenses. Casimir, meanwhile, would explore the outskirts of Paris, in the hope of finding some more permanent place of residence.

In the joyous atmosphere of Le Plessis Aurore regained her old joie de vivre, acting in plays, riding and hunting in the woods, and playing noisy games with the children. If anything, they were too noisy, too turbulent — for many of the adults at any rate. Little could they guess that all this frenetic activity on Aurore's part was essentially a mask for the despair that was eating away at her heart. Her husband found her enthusiasm for childish games exasperating and even "mad." One day, while playing with a young friend on the house's sand-covered terrace, Aurore inadvertently spilled a few grains of sand into Casimir's coffee cup. Angrily he got up and told her to stop, or he would slap her. "I don't believe it!" she answered mischievously, picking up another handful of sand with which to chase her young tormentor. A moment later she received a stinging slap on the face. Stunned by this rebuke, Aurore left the "grown-ups" on the crowded terrace and went off to sulk with her young friends in another part of the garden. That her own husband could thus lift his hand against her, brutally and in public, left her dazed and humiliated. That night she informed Casimir that she was sharing his bed under duress, since they were guests in another person's home.

This unpleasant incident did nothing to narrow the rift that was inexorably widening between them. Often Aurore would slip away on her own, and seated beneath a tree in the wood, she would dream of a different life and burst into tears. Twice Casimir had to go back to Nohant to supervise the harvest, and each time she felt oddly "lost," writing tender letters in which she called him "my angel, my dearest love, my good friend," complained of the rheumatism that had caused her legs to swell, bewailed the emptiness of the big double bed without him, and added: "How I shall kiss you on your return!"

Doubtless she meant it, for she was still bent on being a dutiful wife. But there was already something hollow in these passionate phrases. At twenty Aurore was still erotically undeveloped. Try as she might to respond to her husband's ardent caresses, there was something forced and artificial in her amorous frenzy, which was never fully consummated — particularly with a man for whom she had first felt a kind of fraternal affection but whom she had never truly loved. Marriage, to satisfy her, would have had to bring her a sense of passionate ecstasy, but this the straightforward and prosaic Casimir could not provide. It must have hurt his masculine pride to realize that he could not overcome his wife's basic frigidity. With other less complicated women he had presumably been more successful, and they may have included the wife of Jean-Louis Lambert, the notary who handled their affairs in Paris.

Just when Aurore got wind of this extramarital "flirtation" we do not know for sure, but it is pointedly referred to in a later letter. At Le Plessis, at any rate, she avenged herself by flirting briefly with one of the houseguests. Arousing her husband's jealousy was one of the surest ways of forcing him to pay more attention to her. Still, it was humiliating enough for her to have to write, at the end of one of her letters to him: ". . . rest well, sleep . . . and *sleep alone*."

In September Aurore, Casimir, and the little Maurice said goodbye to Le Plessis and moved with a manservant and a maid to a cottage Casimir had discovered near the village of Ormesson, in the

Montmorency valley, northwest of Paris. The cottage, though distinctly humble, was set in a rambling, English-style garden, with lawns, groves of venerable elms and oaks, a handsome stone fountain, and even a romantic tomb shaded by dark cypress trees placed there for ornamental effect (and which later inspired certain pages of *Lélia*). Often left to herself by Casimir, who had business to attend to in Paris, Aurore read Montaigne's *Essays*, went for long walks around the nearby lake of Enghien, and amused herself in the evenings playing charades with two neighboring families. She found the solitude of her surroundings relatively soothing after the frantic gregariousness of Le Plessis.

Aurore would not have minded spending the entire winter here, but for the gardener, who developed a pronounced dislike for the child; he claimed that Maurice was "ruining" *his* lawns. Shortly before Christmas Casimir had a heated falling-out with him. Paris, which they had long avoided as too prohibitively expensive, now seemed the only haven. They accordingly moved into the city, first put up by Aurore's Aunt Lucie Maréchal, later lodged in a furnished apartment, with a charming view on an inside garden, in an old town house on the Rue du Faubourg-Saint-Honoré.

In all, the four months spent at Le Plessis, the ten weeks at Ormesson, and the three months in Paris cost Casimir Dudevant 30,000 francs, or one half of his marriage settlement. It was a high price to pay for marital felicity, and particularly for a happiness that was more fleeting than ever. For in Paris, evenings at the theater and the company of friends and relatives notwithstanding, Aurore sank anew into a state of deep depression. She went to call on the Abbé de Prémord, who had so sagaciously counseled her in the past, and found him so aged and feeble and his voice so cracked and wheezy that she had trouble understanding him. He lectured her paternally on the dangers of melancholy and finally suggested that she spend a few days in her old convent. Casimir, at his wits' end as to how to combat her moroseness, readily consented, and the new mother superior, Madame Eugénie, agreed to this "retreat."

The nuns welcomed her back with friendly solicitude, and for a moment Aurore found herself wondering if she hadn't made a hideous mistake in not taking the veil. She found such ease and liberty in this state of captivity, in a strict discipline assuring one hours of reflection, in the monotony of duties sparing one the anxieties of the unforeseen. But her "good mother" Mary-Alicia was as firm as ever in discouraging her monastic inclinations, reminding her that she now had a charming baby boy, and that life being short, this was all one needed for "happiness in this world."

As a special favor, Aurore was allowed to have her son brought to her each morning, since he was not yet a man and was small enough to be placed in the revolving cylinder, in the convent's outer wall, through which the nuns received their provisions. "Rabbits!" cried the little boy on first seeing the strange dark veils, wimples, and white robes worn by the nuns, who were soon spoiling him with sweets and dainties. But when Aurore presented him to Sister Helen, whose penitential floor scrubbing had once struck her as so saintly, the converse nun took her to task for seeking an "earthly happiness" which was naught but vanity, a snare and a delusion, as it is written in the Scripture. "Bah!" she concluded, as the child began to cough. "He's too pink and rosy. He's probably consumptive."

Horrified, Aurore picked up her darling Maurice and hurried out of the convent. She spent a sleepless night at home, listening anxiously to her child's every breath. The next morning she was reassured by the doctor, who told her that the boy was not sick at all. But the shock administered to Aurore by the religious fanatic she had once admired cured her of all further desire to re-enter her old convent. The time was passed when she could aspire to sainthood.

7. Romance in the Pyrenees

In mid-June of 1825 the humdrum life of Nohant was enlivened by the visit of Aimée and Jane Bazouin, two school friends whom Aurore had known at the Couvent des Anglaises. They were accompanied by their wealthy father, who spared no pains to lavish on his two surviving daughters all the luxuries that fine carriages and horses, spacious country houses, rare birds and flowers, and the delights of indolent travel could confer. Saddened by the death of their oldest sister, Chérie, Aimée Bazouin had lost all zest for life and was visibly wasting away, victim of that debilitating "spleen" which Byron and other romantic poets had made so fashionable. It was in the hope that the health-giving waters of the Pyrenees would work wonders on this morbid affliction that her generous father had decided, for the second successive summer, to undertake the pilgrimage to Cauterets.

Situated some twenty miles south of Lourdes, in the very heart of the Pyrenees, the little village of Cauterets had in the space of five or six years begun to enjoy an extraordinary prestige, a prestige which at this time far exceeded that of its grotto-studded neighbor later made so famous by Bernadette Soubirous. No miracle had been needed to open Cauterets' hot sulphurous springs, which — if the *Guide Bleu* is to be trusted — still pour out one and a half million liters of curative waters a day (more than any other thermal spa in the world). But those who, from 1820 on, headed for this mountain Mecca did so as much to find spiritual "uplift" as to be cured of catarrh, chronic coughing, and other bronchial derangements. Like Rousseau and later Byron, who had made a cult of Alpine vistas, they set out to steep their soaring souls in the exhilarating ozone of the "sublime," amid a cyclopean landscape of vertiginous peaks where "horrendous" waterfalls, "hideous" gorges, "terrifying" torrents, and "satanic" abysses plunged them into ecstasies of somber stupefaction and romantic melancholia. They were in search of a nature that was as wild and uncontrolled as their own beating hearts, as storm-tossed and tormented as a Géricault painting.

Aurore herself was not in overly good health. She was subject to fits of furious heartbeating and wracked by a chronic cough, severe enough at times to bring up blood as well as phlegm. Though she later attributed these symptoms to the nervousness induced by her unhappy psychological state, at the time she was sure she was consumptive. Little urging was needed to persuade her that a visit to the Pyrenees would do her a world of good; and when, after several days of joyful riding around and sketching the Nohant countryside, the Bazouin sisters said goodbye to her, it was on the understanding that Aurore and her husband, Casimir, would soon be joining them at Cauterets, before they moved on to the Dudevant country house, situated in the Gascon lowlands.

On the fifth of July Aurore celebrated her twenty-first birthday — as much in sadness as in joy. Only her brother, Hippolyte, seemed in a mood for merriment as his hosts prepared to leave for the south. "Farewell, Nohant," she wrote in her private journal, as the carriage was being readied downstairs, "I may never see you again." She may honestly have thought that she was doomed to a premature demise, like her friend Chérie Bazouin, and on seeing her servants lined up to say goodbye to her with tears in their eyes, she too could not help crying.

She read a few pages of Ossian as the carriage rolled south, but the nordic mists and clouded moons of the fashionable crypto-Gaelic bard only accentuated her feeling of despondency. She was oppressed once again by the feeling of incompatibility that had weighed on her for months. What kind of escape was this? "I've passed through charming regions; I've seen lovely horses," she noted in her diary during their stopover at Périgueux, long enough to include a sightseeing tour of the old ramparts. "This town strikes me as agreeable, but I am deathly sad. I cried a great deal while out walking. But what good does it do to cry? One must get used to feeling death in one's heart while keeping a smiling face."

At Tarbes a bright blue sky, the sight of torrential waters gushing past walls made of huge river boulders, above all the sea of gay, multicolored peasant costumes through which they wandered at a local fair offered her a few moments of distraction from her husband's corrosive impatience to reach their destination. But not until the following morning, when their stagecoach began the rugged climb toward the dazzling chain of snow-draped mountains, did this tedious 400-mile journey at last seem like a holiday. Disregarding the burning heat and the blinding dust, Aurore sat up on the swaying box next to Casimir so as to miss nothing of the soaring scenery, with its towering, slate gray mountain slopes, its thundering gorges, its overhanging precipices, and its stretches of placid, sky-reflecting waters framed by soft-scented lindens in full aromatic bloom.

Some distance from the tiny mountain village of Cauterets, Aimée and Jane Bazouin were posted at a road crossing to greet them. Joyfully they fell into each other's arms. Aurore was taken aback by the cleanliness of the hamlet's dirt streets, which seemed to match the crystalline purity of its rivulets, the bracing tang of its air. No less surprising were its houses, all built out of roughhewn slabs of marble. Equally roughhewn were the plain bedrooms that had been reserved for them at the large, red-shuttered hotel — at a cost as exorbitant as the furnishings were crude.

The next day, on waking up, Aurore went to the window for an early morning glimpse of the peaks that had so thrilled her. But there was not a peak to be seen. All around her she could hear the gushing roar of cataracts, but there was not a cataract in sight. The vertiginous landscape had been flattened by a blanket of mountain fog. Only gradually, as in a Chinese painting, did a chalet, then a tree, and finally a patch of green upland with its diminutive herd emerge through the wisps of cotton, suspended as though vertically, far above her head.

As soon as they had settled in, Casimir went off on shooting excursions into the mountains, leaving a fretful Aurore behind to "take the waters," like the other "invalids" who had invaded this mountain resort to cure their real or imaginary ailments. "Monsieur *** "

— by which was meant her husband — "is mad about hunting," she noted in her diary. "He kills chamois and eagles. He gets up at two in the morning and comes back at nightfall. His wife complains of it. He doesn't seem to foresee that a time will come when she will be glad that it is so."

The time came — sooner than expected. But during the first days at Cauterets she thought she would go out of her mind. The regime she was made to undergo to cure the pain in her chest and the recurrent fits of coughing began with a heavy dousing in hot spring water that drenched her from head to foot, after which she was wrapped in blankets like a mummy and carried back to her hotel room on a portable chair. The rest of the day was supposed to be spent in a recumbent position, from which she was only released in the evening, spent in the company of this or that fashionable lady and her circle of admirers. "Did I come to Cauterets to indulge in evening entertainments and to find another Paris in this land of eagles and chamois?" she complained in her diary. Aurore had never felt at home in "society," and she was still too much the prim schoolgirl not to be dismayed when she heard one lady declare, with a rapacious gleam in her eye, that her prime purpose in "taking the waters" of Cauterets was to be got with child!

In thinking that she would meekly submit to the health cure normally prescribed to persons of her sex and condition, Casimir Dudevant had once again misjudged his wife. Aurore soon found a kindred soul in the person of Zoé Leroy, the twenty-eight-year-old daughter of a well-to-do Bordeaux wine merchant, who was lodged with her family in the house across the street — a street so narrow that they could talk to each other from their windows without having to go downstairs. As romantically rebellious as Aimée Bazouin was down-to-earth and socially submissive, as expansive as Jane Bazouin was dreamy and demure, Zoé Leroy was the ideal companion a frustrated Aurore was seeking to accompany her on excursions into the surrounding Pyrenees.

These excursions normally began on horseback but were continued on foot when the ground grew too steep and rocky. Those unaccustomed to the hazards of mountaineering would be seated in a chair, firmly attached to a litter, and thus transported across yawning chasms and abysses by hardy Basque guides, who would leap agilely from rock to rock and from ledge to ledge. For the adventurous Aurore this was tame sport. Since the guides, as she wrote to her mother, "stink to high heaven and one dies of cold after one or two in the afternoon, particularly on the mountaintops, I preferred to walk and I jumped like them from one rock to the next, often stumbling and bruising my shins, but always laughing at my mishaps and clumsiness."

While her friends Aimée and Jane Bazouin were left to undertake "little health cures which perfectly maintain an illness," as she noted in her diary, Aurore and Zoé ventured forth on ever larger and bolder excursions. They were soon joined by one of Zoé's friends, a young gentleman from Bordeaux who had come to Cauterets to be near the young lady to whom he was engaged to be married. Almost as dark-haired and dark-eyed as the young Baronne Dudevant, Aurélien de Sèze was both younger and better looking than her husband, Casimir. His father, Victor de Sèze, had been the rector of the Bordeaux Academy; one of his uncles had defended Louis XVI at the trial which preceded his and Marie Antoinette's execution; his mother, Suzanne Caroline de Raymond de Sallegourde, had inherited the Château d'Eyran, near Bordeaux, where he had been born in 1799; he himself was a magistrate in good standing and already launched on a successful career in the Bordeaux judiciary. But it was neither his good looks nor his aristocratic connections which made an impression on Aurore. It was the elegance of his speech, the elegance of his wit, the elegance of his thought; it was his peculiar turn of conversation, as open to the discussion of literary and philosophical themes as her husband's was closed to them. It was, as she later wrote, his "frank, tender, ardent air" — again so different from her husband's unemotional, benevolent indifference.

Discretion may not always be the better part of valor, but it can be a powerful stimulus to love. Often, as they rode out of Cauterets together, Aurore found herself flanked by Aurélien de Sèze and his fiancée, the lovely Laure Le Hoult. There would be some casual banter, after which Aurore would give him a knowing smile and spur on her horse, galloping ahead to join Zoé Leroy and other members of the party. But the ardent young magistrate lost little time complaining to her about this excess of discretion. One day, while Casimir was off on another of his shooting expeditions in the mountains, Aurore rode off with Aurélien on a little expedition of her own to the village of Saint Sauveur, situated almost midway between Cauterets and Lourdes. Her companion seemed dejected. How could Aurore believe he was seriously contemplating marriage with someone as uninteresting as Laure Le Hoult, whom he had discovered to be a beautiful statue, no more. Her beauty had misled him, and only now, in the presence of someone who was as vibrant and intriguing as the other was cold and uninspired, did he realize the full extent of his mistake. There was now only one person who mattered, only one person in the world he wanted.

Aurore felt her heart leap with joy. For days a new feeling of rapture and excitement had been quickening within her, but instinctively she had been on her guard against it. She had been hurt too deeply three years earlier to be ready to yield to an impulse that might once again betray her. But on hearing Aurélien put her own thoughts and feelings into words, she knew she could no longer hide the truth from herself. She too was in love.

When, on the way back to Cauterets, he slipped his arm about her waist, she gave him a reproving frown, but the tremor it caused her was not one of anger. Vainly, to cool his ardor, she kept repeating what she had already told him: she was not the gay, mischievous, madcap person she might seem to be in public. All that was a disguise she wore to hide the anguish that was eating at her heart. Her real, her inner, life was one of melancholy and despair, a joyless life offering no hope for the future. Whatever marriage might be, it was not romance. As for love, she had experienced it once and it had left a bitter taste. Then, Aurélien protested, he would be her consoler. Overcome by the exaltation of sentiments so perfectly shared, Aurélien bent down and kissed her neck. She rebuked him for the liberty he had taken, but that kiss, she felt instinctively, had sealed a bond between them.

The next day they went off on another excursion, this time to the Lac de Gaube, a glacier-fed lake situated at an altitude of more than 7000 feet. Aurélien rowed her out, and letting the boat drift in the placid waters, he opened his penknife and carved the letter A into the gunwale. He had just noticed that the first three letters of their two names were the same. While her beating heart belied her casual words, Aurore strove to appear indifferent. Whenever he glanced up at her, she would look dreamily away, her gaze concentrated on the shimmering reflections in the lake's icy blue waters. But how tempted she was, as he bent over his labors, to stretch out her hand and to run her fingers through his dark locks!

Later, while waiting for the porters to appear with her litterchair, he took advantage of the privacy offered by a mass of overhanging rock to take her into his arms. What could have been more natural? "Aurélien is honest and delicate," she later wrote, "but he is a man. Our tête-à-tête moved him deeply." But where, she wondered, did one draw the line between delicate emotion and seductive intent? For him this might be one more adventure, no more. But if there was to be anything between them, it had to be different, it had to be unique! Instinctively she drew back, treating his apologies, like his advances, as the wiles of a seducer.

It was their first lovers' quarrel and he took it badly. Deeply hurt at the idea that she could have doubted his sincerity, his tact, his honorable intentions, he let three days go by without saying a word, without looking at her once. She was too proud to make any advances of her own but too vulnerable to be happy without his. For Aurore these were three days of all-consuming anguish. Desperately she rode off into the mountains alone, dismounting to fall on her knees and to implore God to cure her of this baleful, unrequited passion. But a moment later she would be on her feet again, her tortured brain anxiously turning over ways in which she could approach her tormentor.

Never had the "society" of Cauterets seemed to her more frivolous, the table talk more vapid! The third evening, at a dinner party given by a Bordeaux lady who had come to "take the waters," Aurore heard Aurélien, *her* Aurélien, the one who had carved *their* initial into the rowboat's wood, announce his intention of accompanying his fiancée's family on an excursion to Gavarnie. What exquisite indifference, what casual disdain! Feeling suddenly faint, she rose and had to be helped home by a friend. That night, stretched out next to her husband's snoring form, she did not sleep a wink.

The next day, at a luncheon given by the same neighbor, Aurélien offered Aurore his hand as they went into the dining room. And how did she feel today? he inquired with icy politeness.

"What concern is it of yours?" she answered irritably. "Why this sudden interest in my health?"

He answered with a sigh: "My one desire is that you should show more fairness towards me."

This soft-spoken plea sufficed to galvanize her amorous energies. To the astonishment of her husband, who had not realized what a passion his wife had developed for vertiginous vistas and soaring peaks, she insisted that they too must make the excursion to Gavarnie. The local gossips raised their eyebrows, Aimée and Jane Bazouin remonstrated, saying that Aurore was overdoing it, but she stuck to her decision. What if the excursion was full of risks and took three days? If need be, she would do the trip in two. The poor health of her son, Maurice? His mild attack of dysentery was now virtually over, and besides, there was his nursemaid, Fanchon, to take care of him.

On the appointed day they set out for Gavarnie, first riding downhill toward Lourdes, then up a parallel valley through scenery more tortured and dramatic than any Aurore had so far seen. Aurélien, guessing her real motives, maneuvered his horse so that for a while they could ride side by side. He compared the cliffs and cataracts past which they rode to the stormy passions and sufferings of lovers. How much grander they were than the flat, monotonous, level lives of those who neither love nor hate, of those who live a stolid, bovine life devoid of emotional upheavals and upsets! Aurore, after weakly trying to defend the merits of a contented life, finally agreed that he was right. But she stressed the importance of virtue.

"What is virtue, in the sense you give to it? A convention, a prejudice?" he countered. But instead of pressing the argument, Aurélien tactfully let it die, and when, a little later, he said, "Rest assured, Madame, that I think as you do and that I was only joking a moment ago," she could have leaped with joy.

"I hope so for your sake," she replied, with deceptive calm, while her pounding heart added, "and *also for mine.*"

"God! How happy we were together! How we understood each other!" she later recalled this blessed moment. "What charm there was in even the most general conversation about entirely alien matters! With what delight I listened to you talking about the most insignificant things! They seemed to become interesting merely for falling from your lips. No one talks like you, no one has your accent, your laugh, your turn of wit, your way of looking at things and presenting ideas. No one," she concluded, "no one, Aurélien, but me."

In the village of Saint-Sauveur, which they reached at sundown, a country ball was in progress. Through the open, ground-floor windows of the diminutive town hall came the melodious screech of an off-key fiddle, the shrill piping of a flageolet, the tambourine jingle of tiny bells adorning the guitarlike tympanon. They paused for a moment to admire the red-faced villagers prancing back and forth over the reverberating floor, then wandered down to the little public garden. It was by now quite dark, dark enough for them to tarry for a moment beneath a tree without being recognized by other members of their party. Earnestly Aurélien sought to dispel the misunderstanding that had cropped up between them. He would rather give up Aurore completely, he declared, than pass in her eyes as a crass seducer.

Again, it was what she wanted to hear. But, she asked, wouldn't it be possible for him to stop making advances to her without assuming a cold and distant air?

"What!" he cried. "Me, put on a distant air with you! Oh, you don't know what it costs me! You don't know how dear you are to me!"

Overhead the first evening stars were beginning to twinkle in the mauve sky, above the dark, barely visible undulations of the hills. This was the hour of mystic rapture that had so moved her at the Couvent des Anglaises. Aurore thanked him. Her eyes brimmed with tears and there was a sob in her throat. Protectingly, soothingly, Aurélien opened his arms and pressed her to him.

Overjoyed to know that Aurélien belonged to her and to no one else, Aurore rose the next day at dawn feeling thoroughly refreshed. She no longer needed to seek him out for private tête-à-têtes. She could even play the part of a dutiful wife, pressing her horse forward and following her husband wherever he went. For fifteen hair-raising miles they rode along a narrow bridle path, skirting precipices and gorges and seemingly bottomless abysses. Casimir kept turning round to scold her, saying she should stick with the guides and the main party, who were following more slowly and sure-footedly behind. It was mad of her to take such risks, not expected of a person of her sex; she was showing off, she was attracting unnecessary attention, she was "singularizing" herself. Turning in her saddle, Aurore would point at Zoé Leroy, following right behind. "We are singularizing ourselves!" she would shout, to make herself heard above the sound of falling water, and the two friends would burst into joyous laughter at the idea that well-bred ladies ought not to be more "singular" than men.

They were allowed a few minutes of repose to admire the nature-made "Bridge of Snow" — strong enough to support shepherds and their migratory flocks. They gaped briefly at the great, gnarled curtains of glacier ice. They were overwhelmed by the thunder and drenched by the spray of the 1300-foot waterfall foaming down the cliff faces of the massive amphitheater of Gavarnie. But already it was time to leave. The sun was sinking and Aurore's teeth had begun to chatter from the cold.

So back they headed, at an even faster, more reckless pace. Galloping round dizzying bends, leaping over boulders with a wild zest which was fully shared by their sure-footed mountain horses, Aurore and Zoé reached the "chaos" of Goumélie a good half-hour ahead of the slower moving caravan. They were thus able to enjoy the Luciferian spectacle of tumbled rocks and tortured stone in peace, untroubled by the shattering commentaries of gentlemen suffering from colic or the complaints of chairborne ladies whose delicate insides had been upset by the swaying of their litters and the purgative waters they had too copiously imbibed.

While the other members of the party prepared to settle down for the night at the halfway stop of Luz, Aurore rode impetuously on, determined to reach Cauterets that night so as to be by her son's side. At Saint-Sauveur, while their horses were being saddled, she and Aurélien managed to give Casimir the slip. They walked down to the public garden, but finding it full of people, they climbed a slope commanding a fine view of the torrential river. Since this was goodbye, Aurélien pleaded, let him at least give her a kiss. Aurore finally relented, letting him kiss her on the cheek. Then pushing him away, she ran back into the village, where an impatient Casimir was angrily looking for her. He gave her a sharp tongue-lashing, which she accepted meekly, unwilling to betray the secret he had come close to discovering. When, late that night, they finally rode into Cauterets, exhausted, they could both congratulate themselves on having covered 100 miles in just two days.

No sooner was he rested from these exertions than Casimir was off again, hunting chamois and eagles, leaving Aurore to spend her last days at Cauterets as she pleased. It pleased her to spend those she could in less exhausting rides and walks with Aurélien. Each encounter turned her head a little further, made her feel more giddily, ecstatically in love. With jealous possessiveness she insisted that he stop flirting with Laure Le Hoult, that he choose once and for all between them. To reassure her of the sincerity of his feelings, he wrote several letters which further enflamed her passion. What elegance they had, what style and delicacy of feeling. How different they were from the plodding, uninspired missives her husband dutifully wrote to her! Now reconciled to the idea that theirs should be a platonic idyll, Aurélien begged her forgiveness each time he pressed his amorous advances too ardently, saying: "Continue to resist me. Fear not that I should take offense. I would hold myself in horror were I to sully the purity of an angel . . . You are worthier than I, *dear sister,* inspire me with your purity, it enchants me, it redoubles my tenderness for you."

But all too soon it was time to leave. The late August nights were frosty. Already the heavy autumn mists were blanketing the rocky valleys, and purple-cheeked shepherds were moving their shuffling flocks down from the chilling uplands. Fearful lest the brusque change of temperature play havoc with little Maurice's health, as they descended into the Gascon lowlands, Aurore and Casimir chose to stop for several days at the fashionable spa of Bagnères-de-Bigorre. The heat here was as oppressive as the air of the high mountains had been cool and refreshing. Though Maurice basked happily in the hot sunshine and gurgled with pleasure at the sight of so many brightly colored equipages, Aurore already regretted the more primitive charm of Cauterets. But she was consoled by the surprise appearance of Aurélien, who had let his fiancée and her family return to Bordeaux without him.

Aurore and Aurélien once again contrived to see each other alone, each semiclandestine meeting adding to their sense of intimate attachment. Innocently Casimir agreed to Aurore's suggestion that they all ride over to Lourdes on a grotto-visiting excursion before saying goodbye to Aurélien. The eighteen-mile ride, through verdant valleys, seemed like a picnic after the exploits of Gavarnie. But on reaching the famed Grotte du Loup (the Grotto of the Wolf), there was a moment of uncomfortable suspense when, one after the other, they were made to crawl on their bellies into the low mouth of the cave. Further on the rock ceiling rose and they were able to stand up and follow the guides with torches in their hands. On reaching the rim of the vast echoing well, they could see nothing but inky blackness both above and beneath. The guides, to prove that there was water below, pried away stones and sent them tumbling into the abyss. Bouncing off the rocky sides as they went down, they echoed like cannon bursts before plunging with a dull splash into the invisible water.

Taking advantage of the flickering, torchlit obscurity and the reverberating thunder of the vault, Aurélien put his arm round Aurore and drew her to him, solemnly promising to love her and respect her all his life "like my mother, like my sister."

Bruised, muscle-sore, and dirtied by hours of energetic crag-climbing and cave-crawling, famished, exhausted, and drenched to the bone by the pouring rain through which they had to gallop home, Aurore and Casimir were not back in Bagnères-de-Bigorre until well after 10:00 P.M. Aurélien had said goodbye to them at Lourdes before setting out on the direct road for Bordeaux, but Aurore was sustained by the thought that she would be receiving letters from her loved one, as well as news of him through their mutual friend Zoé Leroy.

"Oh, I shall never forget the Pyrenees!" she wrote to Zoé a few days later. "It is the loveliest country in the world. On leaving it, I seemed to be leaving an enchanted spot, only to rediscover, along with the bare, uniform plains of other regions, the sad realities of life."

8. A Curiously Platonic Triangle

OF THE JOURNEY to Nérac, through the lowlands of Gascony, Aurore later could remember nothing so indifferent was she to the passing scenery, so full of thoughts of Aurélien. Equally uninspiring for her soaring spirit was the first sight of the Dudevant "château" at Guillery, a modest country house, five windows broad, which was just as modestly furnished. But the absence of luxury bothered Aurore less than the monotony of the surrounding flatlands — miles and miles of sandy forests full of dwarfish scrub oaks and cork trees. "In these sad regions," as she wrote to Zoé Leroy, "one only encounters desolating thoughts . . . I thus spend my days . . . drawing or writing in my bedroom. I am looked upon as the gloomiest soul on earth, and people are astounded to hear that I was the *life of the party* in the Pyrenees."

Though Aurore got on well with Casimir's father — *Mousu le varon,* as he was known to his peasant neighbors — she found the baronial fare too Pantagruelian for her taste. The grease sauces sickened her so much that often she abstained from eating, hungry though she was, particularly when returning from her kindly host's hunting expeditions (undertaken against the wolves and other wildlife infesting the surrounding forests). Physically she was not well, and psychologically she felt no better. Though she had not become Aurélien's mistress, her conscience was wracked by the awareness that she was now leading a double life. She had to hide the several letters Aurélien managed to get through to her — concealing them in her bodice, as was then the romantic fashion — and suffer agonies each time Casimir caressed her. He accused her of being frigid, not understanding the cause.

She yielded to moods of dark despair. No matter what she did, one of the two men in her life was bound to suffer. At times she was so despondent that she yearned for a quick and easeful death that would deliver her from the inextricable contradictions of her plight. Each time she reread Aurélien's letters, she felt uplifted, delighted — "no sacrifice seemed too great to merit the happiness of being loved by you," she later wrote to him. "But in the silence of the nights, I would look with envy at my sleeping husband and my sleeping son. They are calm and tranquil, I said to myself, but nothing can calm *me*."

As there was no easy way out of this impasse, the only thing to do was to plunge more deeply into it. Consciously she may not have realized it, but this in effect was what she did in accepting Zoé's invitation to visit her at the Leroy family's country house at La Brède. Zoé being a good friend of Aurélien de Sèze's and La Brède a charming lakeside village on the outskirts of Bordeaux, Aurore had a second "imperious" reason for insisting that she and Casimir undertake a visit to the city, where he had a number of Dudevant relatives.

We know little about the precise circumstances of the lovers' first reunion in Bordeaux beyond the fact that it was intense and dramatic. Five weeks had gone by since their last encounter at Lourdes, five weeks during which Aurore had had ample time to ponder the hopelessness of her passion. The conclusion she had come to was that there was not a man on earth, not one, who would in the long run content himself with merely possessing a woman's *heart*. Sooner or later she would have to yield the rest as well. But this she could not bring herself to do (or so at least she tried to persuade herself). The impasse was total, and as she later summed it up: "If I must grant him his victory, I shall die, and if I refuse it to him, I shall lose my heart."

The joy she felt at seeing Aurélien again was thus tempered by a feeling of despair which got the better of her the moment they found themselves alone, in the hotel where she and Casimir were lodged. Too depressed to be able to explain just what was troubling her, Aurore leant her head on Aurélien's shoulder and burst into tears. Taking her into his arms, he kissed her; and it was in this compromising embrace that the two of them were surprised a moment later by Casimir.

Aurélien was asked to leave Aurore's room, while the irate husband demanded an explanation of his wife. Suspecting the worst, he accused her of infidelity and swore that she would never see Monsieur de Sèze again. On hearing the terrible words, Aurore sank to her knees, sobbing uncontrollably. Each time she tried to get up, her legs gave way beneath her. Her husband, who had never seen her in such a hysterical state, now felt overcome with pity and remorse. Perhaps he had been too harsh.

In a kind of waking dream Aurore saw Aurélien reappear at the door and speak to Casimir, but she was too weak and faint to comprehend what it was they said. The only thing she understood, slowly, gradually, was that something miraculous was happening. Husband and lover were conversing in placid, measured tones.

After Aurélien had left, Casimir told his wife that he was ready to forget and to forgive. She would even be left as free as she had been before to deceive him, if such was her inclination; it was a matter he left to her sense of honor and discretion. Tearfully Aurore thanked him for this expression of continued trust, and in her miserable and distracted state of mind, she impulsively declared herself ready to sacrifice everything, even her feelings for Aurélien de Seze, in order to save their marriage.

Not until the following morning was she able to read the two letters Aurélien had given her and which she had luckily not tucked away in her bodice, where Casimir, in loosening her stays, would certainly have found them. All the doubts she had entertained were now wondrously dispelled. How wrong she had been to accuse Aurélien, in one of her letters, of merely wanting to seduce her! Here he solemnly pledged himself to an absolutely chaste love, an eternal and abiding respect, encouraging her once again to resist any improper advances his ardent nature might impel him to make. She had done Aurélien a grave injustice. He was not like other men, after all. He was indeed her guardian angel, her soul mate, her brother!

Within twenty-four hours of this crisis the three of them set out together for La Brède. Aurore could hardly believe it. Abandoning herself to the soft sway of the carriage, the gentle clop-clop of horses' hoofs, and the amiable chatter of her two men, both so eager to soothe and console her, she now felt less ill and upset, though still weak from emotional exhaustion. And when her husband, in a movement of generous forgiveness, pressed her little hand in front of Aurélien, it gave her a rare thrill of pleasure.

In the Leroys' country house Aurore poured out her heart to her friend Zoé, telling her everything that had happened. She was given a new letter from Aurélien, but not until evening, when she had a moment to herself, could she find time to read it. Ah, but what a letter, the kind of letter a woman pines for, but which her husband had never once thought of writing! It moved Aurore to tears. Aurélien told her how he had spent the previous night making repeated trips underneath her window, anxiously gazing up to see if the lamp in her room was still burning. Carefully he had noted each passing hour of the night, as though dating the start of a new letter, a letter written in a spirit of total self-sacrifice. He was ready to take the blame for everything that had happened. He was prepared to be denounced as a scheming seducer if it could mitigate her husband's fury against her. He was even prepared never to see her again if this was the price needed to restore her husband's confidence and trust.

Aurélien sacrifice himself for her? The offer, intended to be generous, caused her another night of sleepless misery.

At sunrise Casimir rode off to hunt as though this were a day like any other. Aurore, however, greeted it with dread. It had been agreed the previous evening that while her husband was away, she and Aurélien would have an early morning tryst. Thoughtful as ever, her friend Zoé came in to help her dress. But Aurore was alone when, at seven o'clock, with a nervously beating heart, she entered the bower at the bottom of the garden and found Aurélien waiting for her. Only now could he put the question he hadn't dared ask during yesterday's carriage ride: what had happened in Bordeaux after he had left?

Aurore sighed. Her husband, incredibly enough, had forgiven her. He had left her free to act as she pleased. He had made it a question of *her* sense of honor and fidelity. This was the elegant revenge he had found for his wounded self-esteem; this was his way of torturing her. Oh, Aurélien, she pleaded, what, but what, should she do now?

White-faced, he steadied himself against a tree trunk. "Yes, I understand . . ." he murmured. "I have nothing to answer . . . You are right, you are right . . . Oh, just let me die!"

Appalled by his anguished words, alarmed by his deathly pallor, Aurore sought desperately to comfort him.

"Enough, enough!" he said. He didn't need to have her prove the need for sacrifice. He felt its necessity as much as she did. "But neither you nor I can answer for my life thereafter. Farewell! I am returning to my mother. She will speak to me, her voice will give me courage." And on that ringing romantic note he left her.

Aurore dragged herself back to her room and flung herself, with a moan, into Zoé's arms. She had lost her Aurélien, lost him forever! But the good Zoé would not hear of their parting on a note of mutual reproach. She went to reason with Aurélien and found him in an equally despondent frame of mind.

A little later she brought him to Aurore's room. He apologized for his recent outburst, said he had regained his composure and that he had conceived a plan to govern their future relations. They were henceforth to renounce all expressions and demonstrations of passionate love. They were to abandon all attempts to see each other clandestinely and alone. They would write no more letters to each other. Having nothing reprehensible to hide from Aurore's husband, they could be sincere and open in all their dealings. They need not become strangers or indifferent to each other; they could continue to love each other, like brother and sister.

Aurore clutched at this new hope as a drowning man clutches at a log. She wept, Zoé wept with her. But theirs were tears of gratitude, tears of delirious relief. Yielding in his turn to the emotional euphoria of the moment, Aurélien declared that Casimir was a generous, forgiving husband, a noble, great-hearted soul! Yes, echoed Zoé enthusiastically, what marvelous reunions they would all have together — with Aurore and her husband, Aurélien, their close Bordeaux friends, her sisters and herself!

Cheered by these radiant visions of the future, the three of them went for a long walk beneath the splendid oaks Montesquieu had planted more than eighty years before to grace the chateau where he wrote *The Spirit of Laws.* Aurore could not tear her eyes from Aurélien's unnaturally pale face. "A mother does not look at her sick child with more solicitude and tenderness," she later recalled, "than I did, that day when we were walking in the woods of Montesquieu. I was so weak that I could barely drag myself along. But I was leaning on Zoé's arm, and the help of a real friend is such a boon!"

Zoé proved it again by volunteering to accompany Aurore back to Bordeaux. The three of them even managed to make the trip in the same carriage, relieved of Casimir's embarrassing presence. Aurore wept for much of the way, deeply moved by a letter Aurélien read aloud to her.

In Bordeaux there was another crisis on the eve of her and Casimir's departure, when Aurore arranged to have herself escorted home from the theater by Aurélien de Sèze. Casimir, irritated by her sudden "disappearance," was doubly annoyed to be sent out to buy some cough drops — an excuse which gave his wife time to read the tender missive Aurélien had just given to her. (Only a couple of months earlier, he declared, he would have laughed at anyone who loved the way he now loved!) Returning with the unnecessarily *expensive* drops — he deliberately stressed the word — Casimir gave vent once again to his not unreasonable suspicions. Aurore got him to agree that she did not look like a liar or a seductress — was not sincerity written all over her face? She admitted that she might at times have gone a bit too far and given Aurélien too much encouragement, innocent though it all was. She went on to explain that she and Aurélien had discussed their relations with great frankness and had decided to found them henceforth on *respect* and nothing more.

"We went on talking for a long time," Aurore later wrote to Aurélien. Casimir "seemed divided between the need to believe me and a sense of shame which made him fearful of being deceived, by *you* at least. At times he was ready to esteem you, more often he was afraid that it might be a plan thought up to deceive me and to make me play into your hands behind a specious veil."

Shaken by her husband's accusations, which brought the blood rushing repeatedly to her face, Aurore spent another agitated night, finally dropping off to sleep a mere hour before Zoé came in to wake her. Her faithful friend accompanied her to the wharf, where a paddle-boat steamer was waiting to take Baron Dudevant and his wife up the Gironde estuary as far as Langon. Aurélien, who had joined them on the dockside, was permitted in the presence of a frozen-faced Casimir to give Aurore a fraternal peck on the cheek.

Smoke poured from the grimy funnel, the wooden pales began to churn the placid water into a boiling green froth, and slowly the pier drifted backward and away. No word, no gesture was exchanged between them, but as the figure of Aurélien gradually shrank and receded, until she could no longer distinguish his dark top hat from Zoé's shawl and bonnet, Aurore knew that he had eyes only for her and that spiritually he was still by her side.

Casimir soon withdrew to the saloon, leaving his wife alone with the little album in which she recorded her thoughts or sketched whatever happened to catch her fancy. "Will you explain to me what it is I feel?" she now wrote, addressing herself to Aurélien. "Will you tell me whence comes this delightful calm I breathe? My thoughts are so refreshing! and this fresh river air revives me so . . . Tell me, my brother, how can we still be so happy when we have just parted for more than two months? Ah, you tell me. I hear you. We know each other at last. We are pure. Our feelings have risen to perfection. They have acquired a celestial gleam. We are proud of each other, we are united for life, nothing can divide us, we are one."

Fortunately for her amorous meditations, Casimir was by now dozing off in the saloon, leaving her free to pursue her silent dialogue with her beloved. At Langon, which they finally reached at one o'clock, they disembarked to take the stagecoach to Bazas, where their own horses, brought by a groom, were waiting to take them the rest of the way to Guillery. But they were held up by repeated delays and had to halt for the night at Casteljaloux, after riding through a dark, wolf-infested pine forest.

Aurore wrote Aurélien a second letter before they left early the next morning. But after reaching Guillery, where she was happily reunited with her darling son, Maurice, she abandoned the album, which she found too cramping, and began filling a notebook with letters written but not sent. The twenty-two letters she wrote to Aurélien de Sèze, between October 11 and November 14, were Aurore's first serious literary effort. In them she poured out her heart, dwelt at delectable length on the sublime, passionate, often troubling moments they had spent together in the Pyrenees, examined her past, exposed her obsessions (the family problems due to her mixed ancestry and semiplebeian birth), and offered occasional glimpses of her present life at Guillery. These letters, full of novelistic dialogue (from which we have briefly quoted), reveal many of the facets of the complex personality George Sand was to become: not only a passionate romantic in search of a heroic love but an introspective analyst of feeling, a social and literary critic, a moralist and memoir writer, a literary landscape artist endowed with a keen love of nature.

Aurore had arranged to keep Aurélien informed of her welfare through their mutual friend Zoé Leroy, with whom she corresponded directly. Probably she hit on the idea of composing an "Intimate Journal" as a subterfuge to get around their agreement not to write love letters to each other. The "Journal" may also have been intended as a gift, to be entrusted to Aurélien the next time they met. Whatever her intentions, they were brusquely upset in early November when Casimir discovered Aurore's secret notebook and read the first sixteen letters.

A week of bitter recriminations followed, which left Aurore once again anguished and emotionally exhausted. She could no longer find solace in writing to Aurélien. To add to her misery, her son, Maurice, suffered a serious mouth infection. Nowhere in her letters to Aurélien, she proudly pointed out to her husband, was there the slightest suggestion that she had become or ever considered the possibility of becoming his mistress. Theirs had been a pure, platonic idyll — one could almost call it "fraternal." If Casimir was going to accuse her of infidelity, she declared, then she would leave him!

Surprised by the vigor of her reaction, Casimir backed down; the breakup of their marriage was a disaster he wished at all costs to avoid. He was ready to take her to Bordeaux, he was even ready to let her see Aurélien de Sèze *alone* — provided she could assure him that she could see him *without love*.

Aurore found it difficult to tell her husband the blunt truth: that it was his callous indifference to her tastes and talents which had led her to share her intellectual enthusiasms with someone who was more receptive. But since he was going back to Nohant — to look into their anything but brilliant financial affairs — he might do well to go into the library and do a bit of educational reading instead of spending all of his time hunting. If their marriage was in serious trouble, it was because all real communication had ceased between them. More than physical coexistence was needed to keep a household happy and a wife contented. And if he wanted to know how it felt to be a virtually abandoned wife, well, he should read the diary she had begun keeping at Cauterets.

Casimir did not have a chance to read her scathing comments on marriage until, drenched to the skin from having to travel on the stagecoach roof, he was drying out his soaked limbs at Périgueux. It was a shock to have his wife hold the mirror to his face and to see his imperfections so sharply reflected through her eyes. How stupid, how insensitive he had been not to realize that there had been a reason — other than feminine caprice — for her bursting into tears during the walk they had taken along the ramparts of this very town four months earlier. Casimir began a long, fumbling, self-pitying letter of apology, in which he begged Aurore to forgive his "grumbling character" and promised to change his callous ways: "Never had I understood until now how much you were necessary to my happiness, I enjoyed it not ungratefully but almost indifferently . . . I wanted to take my pleasure egotistically, whereas today all my thoughts are turned toward you, I only want to do what will give you pleasure . . . In communicating my ideas, I fancy I am talking to you, this relieves me, does me good . . ." And so forth.

A week passed before Aurore received this letter, a week in which, relieved of her husband's inquisitorial presence, she was free again to write to Aurélien. A letter dispatched to him directly, in which she told how her letters to him had been discovered, elicited a prompt reply which made a partial shambles of the theoretical accord they had reached at La Brède. But Aurélien de Sèze was not a lawyer for nothing, and after the first amorous professions of a love that would never die, of memories sweet enough to last a lifetime, he added a few paragraphs containing some lavish compliments for a husband who had shown himself so magnanimous and forgiving: "Never was there created a more delicate heart, a nobler soul! . . . So let Casimir no longer think of me in anger, Aurore. Have him read this letter! Either I know him badly or he will appreciate my wishes, he will believe in their sincerity.

"My feelings have been purified in the crucible of adversity," he concluded with marvelous sophistry. "The word *love* expresses nothing of what I feel for you, since I neither wish to seduce nor to deceive you . . . I love you, Aurore, but with a calm, a sweetness which love does not permit. I love you like the most cherished sister."

Casimir, meanwhile, had started to so some laborious scribbling of his own. Anxious to redeem himself in his wife's critical eyes, he made a painstaking effort to establish the kind of intellectual rapport she had said was lacking between them. In a second, marathon epistle, which he began writing during brief stagecoach halts and finally completed at Nohant, he attempted to "communicate his ideas." On reaching Châteauroux, he had bumped into Aurore's half brother, Hippolyte, and his new wife. Startled to see him looking so downcast and dejected, Hippolyte had invited him in to lunch, and there poor Casimir had made a clean breast of his marital woes. "A tear trickled from my eyes, he noticed it, he consoled me. I like your brother a lot. He's a good friend. He told me he's going to write to you. My wound has opened once again, I can feel the tears flowing. Tomorrow I shall visit your father's tomb, and your grandmother's also. I shall go there to find some consolation . . ." The letter contained a dozen folio pages of this kind of sentimental drivel, and one can just imagine Aurore's reaction when she had to wade through it some ten days later.

The first and (as it turned out) only significant upshot of this brief trip to Nohant was a budding friendship between the two men. As Casimir readily admitted, he had hitherto felt only indifference toward Hippolyte — only to discover now, in his hour of distress, that he was a splendid fellow. The splendid fellow got so worked up over Casimir's account of Aurore's misdoings with Aurélien de Sèze that he too seized pen and paper and dashed off an angry letter — a letter Aurore answered with a stinging rebuttal which completely cowed the none-too-intelligent Hippolyte. Though successful in winning his brother-in-law's sympathy, Casimir failed conspicuously when it came to improving his mind. From the Nohant library he pulled out the *Pensées* of Pascal, which his wife had suggested he read. Dutifully he placed the little volume next to his pillow for nighttime reading, but what followed, as his pathetic letter makes all too clear, was a one-sided battle between Pascal and Bacchus, with the God of Wine flooring the philosopher in every encounter.

Realizing that her passionate correspondence with Aurélien would have to cease once Casimir returned from Nohant, Aurore poured out her soul in six more letters written between November 8 and November 14. Sealing her final letter with a kiss — "Aurélien, I am going to sign *our name* [AURélien, AURore], I place my lips upon it. May yours find their trace" — she said goodbye to her precious notebook (twenty-two letters covering thirty-seven densely filled pages) and dispatched the precious gift to her beloved. Then, after a day spent in solemn rumination, she sat down and wrote an astonishing twenty-page letter to her husband.

Though George Sand — one of the most prolific letter writers of all time — was later to write letters that were twice as long, this was far and away the longest Aurore had yet attempted. It was also the most explicit. She wasn't begging her husband's forgiveness, she made clear at the outset, since basically she was innocent. Casimir had only himself to blame for the troubles that had overtaken him (". . . you were the *innocent cause* of my going astray . . ."). As a husband Casimir had been good to her — "this was your only true merit in my eyes" — but nothing more. He had shown no consideration for her tastes, so strikingly different from his: "I carefully hid my bitter reflections. I became disgusted with everything, the mere idea of living appalled me, I decided to adopt your tastes but was unable to do so; for in living like you without doing anything, I was bored to tears and you didn't notice it . . ."

Then had come the fateful journey to the Pyrenees. "The sight of those mountains inspired me with a thousand new ideas, my mind was exalted, my heart opened to vivid impressions. I felt the need to like and to admire with someone who could feel as much enthusiasm as I." Aurore then delivered herself of a step-by-step account of her growing attachment to Aurélien de Sèze. "Oh my friend, you who are so good, so noble, so generous, so capable of appreciating virtue," she concluded, "don't ever tell me that I have been taken in by false illusions, and that seeing Aurélien and loving him simply as a brother would have been impossible, and that he himself would soon have tired of it. Never say this to me, I beg of you on my knees. You don't know how much it hurts me. You are depriving me of the sweetest, most gracious idea of my life. If you strip our conduct of the lovely colors under which it appeared to us, if you reduce us to the level of vulgar souls, if in a word you succeeded in persuading me that he [Aurélien] is a scoundrel and I a feeble, faithless woman, I shall never get over it."

She peppered this impassioned plea with two pinches of romantic blackmail — "I shall hide all my sufferings and I shall die, for I don't know how to be unhappy and live" and ". . . my esteem for him will only be torn from me with my life" — and then produced a seven-point plan, intended to define her future relations with her husband and Aurélien de Sèze:

1. They would not go to Bordeaux that winter, the recently opened wounds being still too fresh.
2. She promised never again to write secretly to Aurélien, but she would be allowed to write to him occasionally, on the understanding that Casimir would see all the letters she sent and received.
3. She would be allowed to write frequently to Zoé, with the same stipulations.
4. If they spent the winter in Paris, Casimir would undertake to improve his education.
5. If they spent the winter in Nohant, he would read the library books with which he was unfamiliar and they would discuss them together.
6. Casimir would put an end to his fits of rage, just as she would give up her spells of moodiness, and together they would learn to view the past with equanimity.
7. With the passage of time she would be allowed occasionally to speak to him about Aurélien and Zoé without his losing his temper at the mere mention of these two names.

And, she added, as a "final article" (unnumbered), "another year, our affairs permitting, we shall go spend the winter in Bordeaux." If, however, Casimir felt that this was not feasible, the trip would be postponed, "but you will allow me to count on it one day or the other."

This "Confession," as it has often been called, was delivered to Casimir on his return from Nohant during the latter part of November. The less than perfect spouse must have winced more than once at this candid exposé of his shortcomings. But finally recovering from the shock, he decided the best thing to do was to yield to the caprices of his headstrong wife.

They were to have made a second visit to Bordeaux at Christmastime, but Aurore's health, undermined by weeks of emotional crisis, would not permit her to leave Guillery, and Casimir had to make the trip alone. "For some time I have found it impossible to apply myself to anything," Aurore wrote to Zoé Leroy four days before Christmas. "I have a continual headache and feeling of oppression. An hour of study kills me. Drawing fatigues my eyesight, singing tires my lungs. I have to interrupt myself twenty times in writing a letter." The doctors advised against any precipitate return to the colder and foggier north — before diagnosing an acute attack of quinsy, which kept her bedridden for three weeks. She was repeatedly bled by leeches, a treatment which filled her with disgust and which may well have prolonged, rather than relieved, her illness.

From Bordeaux Casimir wrote to reassure her that "here you enjoy a brilliant reputation, everyone talks of your extraordinary wit, of your talents, of the anything but ordinary woman that you are . . . You can imagine how proud I am that it is to me that people should be coming to say all this. I have a swollen head, as you can imagine." But these flattering words offered Aurore scant solace for her own absence from the city of her beloved. The taboos imposed on their correspondence were crippling. There was little they could do in their "open letters" but limit themselves to innocuous descriptions of social events, speak of encounters with mutual friends and relatives, and keep the old fires smothered beneath a hatch of feigned indifference.

After Casimir's return in early January, Guillery and its surrounding pine and cork forests were blanketed by exceptionally heavy snowfalls, followed by a thaw which caused the Garonne to flood its banks. Famished wolves ate most of the Dudevants' hunting dogs.

One of them even came up one night and began gnawing at the shutters protecting the French window behind which Aurore lay in bed reading. Thinking it was one of their dogs, she rose and was about to open the shutter when her husband, who had been sleeping in the next room, woke up and cried: "No, no, it's the wolf!" — before rolling over to his other side and falling back to sleep.

Not until February, when the carnival season was drawing to a close, could Aurore and Casimir make the long-postponed trip to Bordeaux. They put up at the Hôtel de France, to which Aurélien de Sèze paid daily visits, along with a number of Casimir's uncles, aunts, and cousins, who apparently found Aurore "charming." Later she described them as "very honorable" people, but at the time she most probably found them a nuisance, for their presence — like that of her watchful husband — made private chats with the man she loved all but impossible. Casimir had to busy himself with the sale of a house that had been part of his marriage settlement and which was officially valued at 30,000 francs — for they were by now so short of funds that they had to borrow from local moneylenders who charged exorbitant rates of interest.

Aurore also saw a great deal of Zoé Leroy. While visiting her one day in late February Casimir burst in, his face as white as a sheet, crying: "He's dead!" Thinking he meant Maurice, whom she had left with the governess at the hotel, Aurore sank to her knees and would have fainted dead away had Zoé not cried: "No, no, your father-in-law!" Aurore's sinking heart jumped with joyful relief, but a moment later she was stricken with remorse and burst into tears. For she was genuinely fond of the old, silver-haired Baron Dudevant, who had been such a sympathetic host at Guillery.

To his widow, a pathetically dried up, introverted, unloved, and mean old lady, Aurore was less attached. When, after the funeral, the old baron's will was read at Guillery, Casimir discovered that he had been virtually disinherited by his stepmother, who had persuaded her husband to limit his son's share of the Dudevant properties to 50,000 francs, payable to Casimir in five annual installments. This was the noble-born but childless baroness's revenge against an illegitimate heir who did not happen to be her son.

In March Aurore and Casimir returned to Bordeaux. But though the smiles were necessarily subdued and the talk deceptively casual, Aurore must have been secretly thrilled to be able to see Aurélien de Sèze every day. Ten years later the memory of these all too brief encounters was still so vividly present that George Sand (as she had by then become) could write to her old friend Zoé Leroy: "There is in the simple name of the city you inhabit an electric effect, an entire past which is aroused, an entire life which rebegins, and such emotions are not good. So many things have happened since then, and yet the old wound is still often reopened. I think one must live with it, just as the *grognards* did with the scars they brought back from their campaigns. Bordeaux was my crossing of the Berezina."

9. A Distinctly Maculate Conception

WITH THE ADVENT of spring the Dudevants returned to Nohant. It was a relief to be back after an absence of eight months, but during the first weeks Aurore was hard-pressed, "slaving like a convict from morning till nightfall, to put some order into the affairs of my house and village," as she wrote to a friend in early April of 1826. In anticipation of ever greater harvests from the new wheat fields he had sown, Casimir recruited a small army of carpenters, masons, and farm hands to build new barns around the stable yard adjacent to the house. Though the cost of these additions was ruinous, she had to admit that her husband could not have made better use of their money. "This countryside brings back all of my past, each tree, each stone retraces a chapter of my history," she wrote to Zoé Leroy. "So you will understand, my friend, that I'm breathing the air that's good for me, without doubting my steadfast friendship and the regret I feel at being so far from you."

This was as close as she could come, in her first letter to Zoé, to suggesting that while physically she was at Nohant, she had left her heart in Bordeaux. Anxious to humor her, Casimir gave her a new mare and later presented her with a gold necklace on Maurice's saint's day. Aurore promptly christened her new horse "Fairy." The simple-minded Casimir probably attributed this choice of name to his wife's Anglomania; for in addition to Pascal's *Pensées* she had been urging him to study English. But Aurélien de Sèze, to whom she promptly communicated the news, was not for a moment deceived. In his answering letter he declared that he was emphatically opposed to the name "Fairy," though Aurore was not to think that this was due to jealousy on his part, since one of his dogs already bore this name. He ended by suggesting that if she absolutely had to choose an English name, then why not "Rosabella" — the name given to the "stout hackney" on which Mary Stuart made good her escape "from the Scottish castle where she was kept a prisoner."

This too was about as close as he could come to suggesting that Aurore's married life was a form of captivity. For Aurélien could never be sure that his letters would not be read by an understandably jealous husband. The captive, in any case, showed no wish to escape, remarking in her second letter to Zoé that she had lost all "taste for great things," the journey to the Pyrenees having been the "last flash of a brilliant flame. At present I trot about in a round straw hat, and I'm usually taken for a humble miller's wife rather than for the *frisky* dame of yore."

Bored by the sedentary life of Nohant, the frisky dame of Cauterets continued to be wracked by burning pains in the chest, a chronic cough, and what she called an "inseparable" sore throat. The hot weather brought only partial relief, even though, as she wrote to Zoé in late June, "like all who suffer from the effects of winter, heat, or what the doctors call *insolation,* makes me live again. So I bask in the sun, the way dogs do."

In midsummer Casimir left on a brief trip to Bordeaux to collect the money still due to him from the house he had sold earlier in the year. Aurore now felt doubly frustrated, not to say cheated. While her husband was free to look up Zoé and Aurélien, she had to stay behind to oversee the early harvest preparations, tramping through the fields in mannish trousers and a belted blouse.

Active as ever, she resumed her "apothecary" studies under the guidance of the handsome Charles Delavau, who taught her how to prepare different drugs, apply leeches (for bleeding), cauterize and stitch up wounds. There were the occasional wild outings when she felt full of the devil and just *had* to shock the neighbors — as happened one night when Casimir had gone to bed early and she and Hippolyte rode laughingly into La Châtre and startled its staid burghers by singing serenades under the windows of their friend Alexis Pouradier Duteil, a fun- and pun-loving lawyer and a right merry tippler to boot.

In September Aurore's first "beau," Stéphane Ajasson de Grandsagne, made a sudden reappearance in her life. Already suffering from tuberculosis, a condition aggravated by chronic malnutrition and overwork, he had to interrupt his Paris studies and come down to the country for a rest. In a long letter to Zoé, Aurore described him as a friend "who is everything a friend can be without inspiring love," someone with whom she could say she had "journeyed through life," since they were of the same age and county. "Half consumptive, half mad, he came to spend part of his convalescence here," she went on in the high-flown romantic style to which both she and Zoé were much addicted. "His hollow cheeks, his wild eyes, his stooped shoulders . . . have cast a black shadow over my thoughts and steeped me in melancholy . . . I'm afraid of death . . . I think of Maurice and I weep . . . yet I'm healthy enough . . . am I too going mad?"

If the news that Zoé's sister-in-law had just lost a newborn child was enough to inspire these morbid apprehensions, it was because Aurore herself secretly yearned for another child. More specifically, she wanted a sister to keep her Maurice company, as once she had been the playmate and companion for the older Hippolyte. But the idea that this daughter might be fathered by Casimir was profoundly repugnant to her. The ideal father, the lover she ardently caressed and who possessed her in her dreams, was the inaccessible Aurélien, who now seemed as despairingly remote as Sirius. But this sentimental surrogate failed to satisfy the cravings of her body — a body wracked once again, as a golden-leafed autumn turned into a bare-branched winter, by familiar rheumatic pains and a burning irritation in the chest. "To avoid being as stricken as I was last year, I wrap myself in flannel, knitted cardigans, panties, and woolen stockings," she wrote to her mother in October. All to no avail, to judge by another letter written just before Christmas in which she complained of exhausting chest pains, insomnia, and absence of appetite. "Everything revolts me and the only thing I can stomach is clear water, which doesn't fatten me, as you can imagine."

In mid-January of 1827 she hied herself to Paris for reasons which are anything but clear. During her two-week stay Aurore suffered one more "deep grief" (the French word *chagrin* recurs with obsessive frequency in her letters of this period), and as she wrote to Zoé, "I wept bitter tears from a source I had thought dried up forever. I would pour out my heart to you, my friend, and I would be greatly consoled if I were but near you. But there are things I dare not commit to paper."

Had she secretly hoped to meet Aurélien de Sèze and then discovered that he was too hard-pressed by his judicial commitments as an up-and-coming assistant attorney general to be able to leave Bordeaux? Had she made unsuccessful advances to someone else? Had she suffered or deliberately provoked a new miscarriage? Had she discovered some new peccadillo on the part of her husband, which, her growing indifference notwithstanding, had secretly wounded her pride? Aurore's letters to Aurélien, which might have shed some light on these mysteries, were later destroyed, while her letters to Stéphane Ajasson de Grandsagne, which might have been even more instructive, have simply vanished.

The one thing we know for sure is that Aurore was back home by early February in time to take part in the pre-Lent festivities. She attended several carnival balls in La Châtre. At Nohant the Dudevants put on a rustic ball of their own to celebrate the simultaneous weddings of André Cailleau (Aurore's former page) and his sister Fanchon (who had become Maurice's nurse). "The marriage festivities were held in our coach houses," Aurore wrote to her mother, "with dancing in one and eating in the other. It was of a luxury difficult to imagine — three candle stubs for lighting, plenty of cheap wine for refreshments, an orchestra composed of a hurdy-gurdy and the shrillest (and thus best-loved) bagpipe in the neighborhood. We invited a number of people from La Châtre and indulged in all sorts of larks, such as disguising ourselves as peasants and doing it so well that we could no longer recognize each other . . . Stéphane Grandsagne, whom I think you know, was a swaggering peasant, and pretending to be drunk, he sidled up and began berating our *Sous-Préfet,* an agreeable fellow who was about to walk out in a huff when he recognized us at last."

Stéphane's presence in the region seems to have been brief, for he soon returned to Paris to resume his studies in natural history under the great fossilist Cuvier. Hippolyte, who frequently invited him for dinner to his house on the Rue de Seine, was overawed by the encyclopedic sweep of his knowledge and the brilliance of his intellect, but he was equally disturbed, as he wrote to Aurore, by their friend's wild extravagance in entertaining friends (when he had the money to burn) and his bohemian indifference to regular hours.

"What you tell me about Stény saddens me no end," Aurore wrote back to her half brother in April. "He takes neither care of his health, nor of his affairs, and spares neither his body nor his purse. Worse still, he does not take kindly to good advice . . . I foresee that *St.*, with all the means he has for making good in the world, will never achieve anything . . . The fondness I feel for him will always be held against me, and though people don't dare show it openly, I often read signs of disapproval on the faces of people who force me to defend him . . . *Sten.* will always be dear to me, no matter how unfortunate he may be. He is already unfortunate, and the more so he becomes, the less interest will he inspire. Such is the rule of society. I at least will do my best to repair his misfortunes. He will find me when others have turned their backs on him, and even should he sink as low as his eldest brother" — a ne'er-do-well mariner who had ended up hawking musical instruments and his services as a public scribe — "I shall still love him with compassion after having ceased to love him through esteem."

Still plagued by intermittent coughing and by pains in the chest — "it's a bad habit I've contracted these past three winters," she wrote to her mother — Aurore did her best to deny that her ailments might have a "moral cause." Her excessively lively disposition, she claimed, was a "gift" she had inherited from Sophie. "I also practice medicine, surgery, pharmacy," she went on. "I mend broken noses, patch up fingers, I make potions and juleps for colds, I prepare poultices and even administer enemas. All this consumes my time and uses up my garden flowers, and I spend the day making syrups, jams, and liqueurs." But she still had energy enough to go on riding excursions with her friends — when not galloping from one farmstead to the next on her medical "rounds" — and on one such equestrian outing, in late June of 1827, she suffered a bad fall while recklessly trying to climb a ruined wall.

The hope that had sustained her for months was that Casimir,

Maurice, and she could make another summer trip to the Pyrenees, stopping off at La Brède and Bordeaux on the way down or coming back. But having had to borrow money the previous year to make ends meet, they could not afford another expensive trip to Cauterets or Bagnères-de-Bigorre — a trip which in any case held little charm for a spiritually, if not physically, cuckolded husband. As a compromise, Casimir offered to take Aurore on a two-week trip to the no-less-famous spa of Mont-Dore in the heart of mountainous Auvergne.

The sight of pine-covered mountains proved painful as well as pleasant. Everywhere she was reminded of the loftier and more dramatic Pyrenees, so rich in sentimental associations. Once again she decided to keep a journal, noting her impressions in a red-leather notebook — impressions which, even more than her surviving letters, offer us penetrating glimpses into her thoughts and obsessions.

"*Mont d'Or. Monday* (13 August)

"What a strange life this is! It's even agreeable. I'm getting reconciled to it. Still, I don't yet feel assured enough to stay in the drawing room. Everyone keeps staring at me as the latest arrival. How stupid it is to pay attention to me! I return to my room. It's a charming room! Four feet by four, but a delightful warmth, an alcove for Maurice and myself, with two twin beds. Another room for Casimir, white curtains, many windows, and a delightful cleanliness.

"But what to do? It's raining . . . And supposing I wrote to someone? Yes, to my mother, for example! To my mother, oh God! 'Oh, mother, what have I done to you? Why don't you love me? And yet I'm good . . . Oh, how I would have loved you, mother, if only you had wanted it! But you betrayed me, you lied to me, mother . . . You broke my heart. You opened a wound which will bleed all my life. You embittered my character and warped my judgment. You introduced into my soul a dryness, a bitterness I find in everything. Do you think I've forgotten all that when now you caress me? . . . When I see another girl, happy, adored, protected in her mother's arms, I twist my hands and I think of you who abandoned me . . .' "

A little further on: "But then, good Lord, to whom shall I write?

. . . To Stéphane? He's a madman, a real pedant. I hate science. To Gustave? * He's a beast, and beasts bore me . . . I shall write to Zoé. She's so good, an angel! Yes, but she would show my letter and I don't want to be remembered . . ."

Show her letter to whom? The name was significantly omitted, as too secret, too sacred, to be uttered. Try as she might to forget and be forgotten, it was to Aurélien de Sèze that her thoughts kept inexorably returning.

"My head feels sick," she noted later. "Vainly have I sought these last few days to dull my senses with fatigue. This grief, this grief can't sleep and won't keep quiet. Oh anguish!"

In search of distraction she visited the thermal baths and was impressed by the monumental grandeur of the vaulted arcades, the heavy pillars, and the massive gray walls built of volcanic lava rock. Back in her hotel room she was suddenly gripped with a desire to record the happenings of her youth and adolescence. "Yesterday's thoughts will offer a diversion from today's. But above all, not one word about the present, I would write about it with a fiery pen dipped in gall." With that she proceeded to draw up a synopsis for what, a quarter of a century later, was to become *The Story of My Life*. Here are a few samples:

Chapter 7. "I was of a gay yet dreamy disposition. For there are contrasts in all human characters and above all in mine. The most natural expression for my features was one of meditation. There was in this absent look, it seems, a fixity resembling that of the snake when it fascinates its prey. At least, this was the high-flown comparison employed by my provincial adorers. One of them, in particular, succumbed, while I preferred Colette [her horse] to him."

Chapter 16. "When I married I had a son, and there are a couple of chapters here which have disappeared clean from my memory . . . And when I look at my sickly complexion, my anticipated old age, when I feel extinguished and frozen in my heart, when I feel dreadful pains in my body, the bitter fruits of despair, stifled sobs and sleepless nights, I realize I've lived. I don't need to recall which days began my ruin and which days finished it."

* Gustave Papet, a nineteen-year-old Nohant neighbor who lived in the nearby Château d'Ars, with its handsome Renaissance façade.

The projected twentieth chapter boldly stated a theme that was to run like a leitmotif through all of George Sand's works and correspondence: "The heart remained as pure as a mirror — *ch'ogni respiro appanna.* It was ardent, it was sincere, but it was blind. It could not be tarnished, it was shattered." Years before, she had inscribed that lovely verse of Metastasio's in one of her little notebooks, and the image of the mirror "which no breath can cloud" had remained engraved on her mind, not to say her heart. Yes, the flesh might be tempted, it might succumb, it might sin, but the soul, because it was all fire and passion, remained as pure, undefiled, and immaculate as the most miraculous of all conceptions.

Chapter 21. "I left for the Pyrenees . . . But what's that I hear? The dinner bell already? I must have been daydreaming instead of writing." Perhaps it was just as well that she should have been interrupted; at this point the past was uncomfortably close to the present.

As she had done in the Pyrenees, she sallied forth on horseback, accompanied by admirers. One was a gentleman from Champagne named Joseph-Sulpice Blavoyer who (as will be seen later on) came to George Sand's rescue when her fortunes were at a particularly low ebb. Together they galloped over the wooded hills and scrambled to the top of Auvergne's highest peak, the 6000-foot-high Puy de Sancy. But instead of being exhilarated, she was strangely saddened by the bluish thread of water — the headwaters of the Dordogne — she could see, tumbling westward toward "those sub-blessed lands . . . homeland of those fiery souls" — she was thinking of Aurélien de Sèze — "region of those burning summers I shall never see again."

Blavoyer was not the only man who found himself attracted by her dark, hypnotic eyes. The morning of her second Sunday at Mont-Dore, she noted in her journal: "I shall certainly get a declaration today unless I'm careful. I must try to avoid it. This kind of thing spoils everything . . . How a woman who has the misfortune not to be coquettish is often bored with being a woman!"

By ten o'clock that same evening, her fears had been confirmed: "This man understands nothing, he guesses nothing. He's mad. He takes hot showers, but what he needs is ice! Heavens, one more of them in love! . . .

" 'Monsieur, I don't mind being loved, but I do not wish to be adored.'

" 'Then you should not be so agreeable.'

" 'The compliment is banal. But never mind . . . If we're going to start behaving like characters in a novel, we shall become insufferable.'

" 'You won't make me believe that you are this insouciant in character. Not with eyes like yours.'

" 'My eyes are perhaps impertinent, but my character is what I tell you it is.' "

And so it went. His pressing overtures rebuffed, Monsieur F *** — as she designated him in her journal — hied himself off to the town of Clermont for several days, only to return more vainly enamored than ever. At the gala ball given on the eve of Casimir's and her departure, Aurore's pink dress created a sensation and she was the belle of the evening. "Since in this world people are tasteless enough to find me charming," she noted in her journal, "I am leaving in order not to have to live any longer with people who have no common sense and who would like me to lose the little I possess."

The trip to Auvergne may not have relieved Aurore emotionally, but it momentarily restored her to good health. "I have a frightening appetite and I've acquired the habit of sleeping, which I find most agreeable," she wrote to her mother in early September. From the mountains she also brought back a new passion for botany, into the study of which she now threw herself with characteristic intensity.

In this she was encouraged by one of her neighbors, Jules Néraud, who, on a lovely strip of hillside not far from Nohant, had planted a garden full of exotic shrubs and flowers he had brought back from his travels in the South Seas. Intrigued by the flaming beauty of the first dahlias she had ever seen — Néraud's were indeed the first to be grown in the province of Berry — Aurore had one day plucked the head off a stem as she was riding past his garden hedge and had been overjoyed a few days later to receive (as generous punishment for her "theft") a basketful of dahlia bulbs, which were promptly planted in the Nohant garden. A small, weatherbeaten little man who had lost half his teeth and whose skin had been tanned by five years spent under the burning Madagascan sun, Néraud proved a singularly inspiring and enthusiastic teacher — unlike Deschartres, whose pedantic emphasis on Greek and Latin nomenclature had come close to killing Aurore Dupin's early love of nature.

That the teacher would soon conceive an overpowering passion for his pupil was not yet evident in September of 1827, when Casimir invited Jules Néraud and his wife, along with three La Châtre friends — the frail, fair-haired Charles Duvernet, the bearded giant Alphonse Fleury, and the witty, pock-marked lawyer Alexis Pouradier-Duteil — to accompany them on an overnight riding expedition to the ruined castle of Châteaubrun, overlooking the picturesque valley of the Creuse. Just why Casimir should have been in such a filthy mood the next morning is not clear, but as the horses were being dragged out to be saddled, he struck his own over the nose with a riding crop. The frightened beast backed up and almost crushed Aurore against the stable wall, whereupon she told her husband that this was no way to treat a horse.

"No way to treat a horse!" he shouted, losing all control. "Why, you little so-and-so!" (The language was so coarse that George Sand later refused to repeat the exact words as they were "too unprintable.") "If I want to beat my horse, I'll damn well do it! And if you get off any more remarks like that, I'll give you the same treatment!"

Aurore was too startled by the sudden savagery of this outburst to be able to reply. But going off to one side to hide her grief, she burst into tears.

The incident left its mark — even more deeply than had the rough slap Casimir had administered to her three years earlier on the sandy terrace of the Roëttiers du Plessis' house. Back at Nohant she relapsed into her chronic despair. Though she tried to put up a brave front, if only for the sake of her son, Maurice, it was increasingly clear to Aurore that her marriage was on the rocks. Casimir's pathetic efforts to improve his education — through the reading of Pascal and tortured sessions with an English grammar — had barely lasted a season and done nothing to improve his short temper. The more conscious he became of his intellectual inferiority, the more irascible, intemperate, and coarse-mouthed he became. A lover of the fermented grape, like the simple Gascon he was, he now began drinking in earnest. Hippolyte, who came to stay with them several weeks, did nothing to discourage this penchant, being himself a heavy drinker, and when he had to return to Paris in mid-October, Casimir insisted on accompanying him.

Aurore's friends — including Stéphane Ajasson and his slightly older brother, Jules de Grandsagne — immediately came flocking in to see her. Forced to keep to her bed by a sudden fever and palpitations of the heart, she received her friends in the downstairs bedroom, next to the dining room, which her grandmother had once occupied. Charles Delavau, her doctor, advised a new application of leeches, which Aurore refused. The root cause of her accelerated heartbeats was almost certainly psychological and probably due to more than simple marital misery. Was Aurore in an agony of indecision because she wanted to indulge in an extramarital adventure, or had she already started an illicit affair which she was afraid would be discovered? Again, we are reduced to conjectures.

There are too many references in other letters to a state of recurrent ill health to conclude, like André Maurois, that Aurore's ailments were "only of the conscience," if not an elaborate bluff. But this does not mean that medical motives alone prompted her to make a hasty trip to Paris in early December, for she probably welcomed the chance of once more seeing that stimulating (even if somewhat pedantic) "madman," Stéphane Ajasson de Grandsagne.

Accompanied by Jules de Grandsagne and by her manservant, André, Aurore reached Paris on December 5. She rented three rooms at the same Hôtel de Florence where she had given birth to Maurice in June of 1823. Jules Ajasson took up his quarters in a tiny garret just above her suite, and his brother, Stéphane, came to call on them every day.

Everything about this trip was odd, beginning with this curious presence of an elder brother who was supposed to act as Aurore's escort and chaperon on behalf of the absent husband. The goings-on had a distinctly Mardi Gras flavor. Not long before, the prankish Hippolyte had solemnly arranged a meeting between Aurore's mother and Dr. Lavarac, a brilliant La Châtre physician whom her daughter would do well to consult. The unsuspecting Sophie had been so taken in by the bogus gab and garb that she had failed to recognize Stéphane Ajasson de Grandsagne. At a second luncheon, attended this time by Aurore, the "brilliant" doctor was introduced to her mother by his real name and officially forgiven for having pulled her petticoated leg. Back at the Hôtel de Florence this innocent piece of mischief was the subject of much mirth and merriment. Stéphane and Hippolyte "are as stupid as donkeys," Aurore reported back to Casimir. "They spend the day calling each other 'My son' or 'Old dog,' and either exchanging fisticuffs or falling into each other's arms. Jules in the midst of it all maintains a serious mien, caresses the bottle and eats with the phlegmatic calm of a Scotsman."

As a former medical student, Stéphane Ajasson was able to have Aurore examined by the foremost doctors of the day. Landré-Beauvais, dean of the Paris Faculty of Medicine, had her strip, tapped her chest, listened with a stethoscope, and finally declared that there seemed to be some slight impediment to the intake of air in her left lung but that it was nothing serious. Dr. Husson, of the Hôtel-Dieu, could find absolutely nothing wrong with her. Dr. Broussais claimed to have discerned "an irritation of the heart and stomach" for which he prescribed an "appropriate" remedy. The consensus seems to have been that while there was nothing wrong with her heart, Baroness Dudevant would do well to have her tonsils removed, or she would risk a new attack of quinsy.

In a letter written to Casimir on December 15, Aurore said that she would have been willing to part with her tonsils had the doctors not insisted that she would need an eight-day rest thereafter — a lapse of time she considered an unbearable hardship on the increasingly fretful Maurice, whom she had left in her husband's care at Nohant. Three days later she took the stagecoach back to Châteauroux, accompanied by both Jules and Stéphane. Her stay in Paris had lasted just thirteen days, but during that time a lot more had happened than had been indicated in the six letters (an unusually high number) she had felt impelled to write to Casimir.

In early January of 1828 she wrote to her mother to say that she was once again feverish and suffering from a sore throat. The same news was conveyed in another letter to Aurélien de Sèze, who expressed surprise, in answering, that Aurore should have given him so few details about her Paris trip and limited herself to a laconic announcement of some impending "amputation of the tonsils." And he added, plaintively enough: "I didn't even know they were swollen."

What she wrote to him in her next letter, early in February, we do not know. But to judge by one sentence in his reply — "Don't write too much" — she had probably informed him that she was pregnant. With their friend Zoé Leroy, Aurore was at once more guarded and more candid. Yes, she had to admit with a sense of shame that she had let two months go by without writing even though she owed Zoé a letter of condolence for her father's recent death. But if Aurore had remained silent, it was because she was a wretchedly unhappy person. "My thoughts were so somber, my heart so stricken that my letter would have augmented rather than lessened your sorrow . . . Have pity on me but do not accuse me. Those who are unhappy do not know how to console, but they love no less strongly than the others . . . I no longer ask you to love me as before. I no longer deserve the friendship of anyone. Like the wounded animal which goes off to die in a corner, I won't go to seek support and succor among my own kind . . ."

An astonishing admission! And one that throws a revealing light on what had really happened in Paris in December. For the anguished cry which rings through this letter is that of a guilty conscience. Aurore was conscious of having been unfaithful — not to her husband, that was something which could no longer occasion her remorse, but to Aurélien, her spiritual, platonic love. But since this was something she couldn't admit to her friend Zoé, still less to Aurélien, all she could do was to beat her aching chest and groan.

In early May, Zoé wrote again from Bordeaux to say that she had heard from a sister, living in Paris, that Aurore was "pregnant and suffering. I didn't know it. Aurélien, who cannot usually be accused of taciturnity, hadn't said anything to me about it, even though he claims the contrary" — an interesting statement, since it proves that Aurélien had already been informed, months before Aurore's child was born (contrary to what most of George Sand's biographers have claimed). "I took him severely to task," added the innocent Zoé, "and promised that I would inform you of his negligence, now that I am no longer ignorant of the truth. I would like to be exactly informed of your state of health. Is it a sister for Maurice you are asking of Heaven? . . ."

Zoé's intuition had not misled her. Alternately plagued by guilt and buoyed by hope, Aurore was continuously ill throughout this long, expectant spring. She was unable to sleep, "suffering a great deal from the stomach and with such precipitated beatings of the heart," as she wrote to her mother, "that I feel as though there were water boiling away under my clothes." Casimir, for his part, took the news in his by now well established stride. "You know how lazy-minded and furious-footed he is," Aurore wrote to a friend in Paris. "Neither the cold nor the mud keeps him from being out of doors, and he only comes inside to eat and to snore."

Upset by stomach pains every time she ate, she finally decided to stay at Nohant and to rely on the local doctor rather than make the painful trip to Paris, as she had done for the birth of Maurice. While Casimir, more industrious than ever, was out in the fields from dawn to dusk in his farmer's blouse (his latest agricultural enterprise being a scheme to grow tobacco, with seeds sent to him by Aurélien de Sèze!), Aurore stayed indoors playing Italian airs on the harp and the piano. Hippolyte's annual arrival was celebrated with the uncorking of numerous bottles of champagne and almost daily fishing expeditions to the nearby Indre. Finally, in early September, they were joined by Aurélien, who was at Nohant on the thirteenth when Aurore gave birth to a baby daughter who was given the name of Solange.

Years later, in writing the story of her life, George Sand sought to gild over the embarrassing fact that her daughter was born nine months after the trip she had made to Paris to see Stéphane Ajasson de Grandsagne. The birth, she claimed, was premature. The previous evening Hippolyte's daughter had issued such piercing cries from the stairwell that for one dreadful moment Aurore had thought she had tumbled down the stone steps and broken every bone in her body. "I immediately began to feel the labor pains, and on waking up the next morning I barely had time to prepare the little bonnets and woolies I had fortunately finished."

In the same passage, Aurélien de Sèze (identified only as "one of our Bordeaux friends") was depicted as being astonished to come upon Aurore in the drawing room taking out the baby clothes she had kept in her workbox. "What are you doing?" he was supposed to have asked. "Well, as you can see, I'm hurrying for someone who's arriving sooner than I thought." Having not been in Paris the previous December, he may well have believed her.

The news, in any case, was received with wild rejoicing — above all by Hippolyte, who galloped madly into La Châtre to fetch the doctor, then got uproariously drunk with Aurélien. The country house at Nohant had already seen some strange doings, and was to see some even stranger. But the sight of the normally prim and proper attorney general of Bordeaux prancing around in a drunken bear-like dance with Hippolyte Chatiron must have provided rare entertainment.

From Hippolyte, of course, this wild carouse came as no surprise, any more than did the delightful answer he gave to his half sister when he staggered into her ground-floor bedroom, slipped, and fell heavily on his bottom. All of Aurore's nervous, pent-up tensions were suddenly released as she burst into hysterical laughter, a laughter she could even less control on seeing Hippolyte drag himself to his knees and solemnly declare, through his hiccups: "It'sh not the wine I shwear . . . which . . . no, it'sh the friendship I feel for you which preventsh me from shtandin' on my feet!"

The only one to miss the fun was that poor, pedantic "madman" — Stéphane Ajasson de Grandsagne.

10. The End of an Idyll

THE EUPHORIA over Solange's birth proved both short-lived and deceptive. Far from delighting Casimir, it only succeeded in aggravating his growing irritability and short temper. Local gossip soon had it that he was not the father, and according to Louise Vincent, Stéphane Ajasson de Grandsagne would answer, when twitted by his friends about his occasional visits to Nohant: "I am going to see my daughter." *

No one, curiously enough, did more to substantiate such rumors by his actions than Casimir himself. Four years earlier he had often spent hours at a time romping over the floor with his infant son, Maurice, but for the plump Solange there was no time for such exhibitions of tenderness and parental solicitude. There are cuckolded husbands who manage to put up a brave front and successfully conceal the source of their secret shame, but Casimir was too simple-minded, blunt, and straightforward to be capable of such dissimulation. Besides, what with many husbands is no more than a suspicion may with him have been a certainty. Years later, in explaining her reasons for wanting a divorce, George Sand wrote that "by an almost indiscernible progression . . . a secret antipathy grew up between us . . . an antipathy which led us to a complete separation of bodies from the day I conceived the hope of having a second child." The wording is admittedly ambiguous, but literally inter-

* No date or source is offered for this "information" in Louise Vincent's two-volume study, *George Sand et le Berry.* She also claimed that Aurore herself sometimes called her daughter "Mademoiselle Stéphanie." Presumably she picked up these reports from the local inhabitants during her laborious research in the Nohant countryside.

preted, this could mean that Aurore had stopped sleeping with her husband even before Solange was conceived.

One thing is certain: once delivered of Solange, Aurore insisted on their sleeping in separate bedrooms. Casimir occupied the "master's bedroom," whose ground-floor windows looked out on the front courtyard and driveway with their flowered mound and lilac bushes, while she occupied her grandmother's old room looking out on the garden. The two rooms were separated by a corridor, which was a simple matter to cross, as Casimir soon proved — by paying stealthy visits to Pepita, the Spanish maid whom Aurore had installed in a tiny chamber next to her bedroom, and who looked after Solange. One night, when Aurore was supposed to be sleeping, she distinctly heard Casimir enter Pepita's room. The telltale creaking of Pepita's bed, the muffled whispers and the groans and grunts of erotic rapture which followed made it all too obvious what was going on.

Aurore, significantly, did nothing. Her later explanation was that she had merely entertained "suspicions" and had not wanted to destroy what was left of marital "harmony" between herself and her husband. The explanation is not entirely convincing. More probably, Aurore shrank from provoking another scene because her own conscience was anything but clear, and because she knew that Casimir could smother her with humiliating reproaches.

There was thus established a fragile modus vivendi which made life under the same roof possible, if not always congenial. Considering herself released from previous pledges, Aurore now wrote several letters to Aurélien de Sèze which were so full of confidential revelations that he refused to show them to Zoé Leroy — who had to write to Aurore to protest this "ferocious" ostracism.

Though still plagued by secret torments, Aurore seems to have been relieved, psychologically no less than physically, by her second childbirth. The letters she wrote during the winter of 1828–1829 show her in rare good health and spirits. Unable to undertake the annual winter trip to Paris — the four-month-old Solange being still too young to stand the rigors of the two-day trip — Aurore decided to liven up the traditional carnival season. This she did by persuading the aristocratic *sous-préfet* of La Châtre to make fun of the town's strait-laced burghers by staging a candlelit "ball" at which "top-drawer" snobs were invited to rub gown hems and shoulders with a *canaille* (or riffraff) of second- and even third-drawer caliber. This social outrage was compounded by the gleeful wretchedness of the "orchestra" — consisting of Aurore, who tinkled the keyboard and the jovial Alexis Duteil, who sawed away on a screechy fiddle. So intensive, indeed, was the merriment and mischief-making that not until early March of 1829 could *Madame Horreur* (as Aurore had dubbed herself in a piece of satirical doggerel) find time to write to her mother to say that "never in Paris have we lived such an active and dissipated life as the one we have just spent during the Carnival" — what with horseback rides, visits, receptions, and dinners which had caused them to spend more time in La Châtre than at home. With Hippolyte to entertain them with his songs and his jokes, even the dreary Lenten evenings were unseasonably merry, and as Aurore wrote in the same letter to her mother: "We laugh, sing and dance like mad, and it's been years since I've been in such good health."

But shortly after these lines were written Aurore once more fell into a state of deep depression. Exactly what brought it on we do not know, any more than we know exactly what happened. Casimir later claimed to have intercepted a letter written by Aurore to Stéphane Ajasson de Grandsagne, in which she asked her scientific friend to send her some poison because she wanted to put an end to her life. Did she mean it seriously? Or was this a letter deliberately written to be seen by Casimir, perhaps to make it clear to what lengths she was prepared to go if he continued to bait her with embarrassing questions regarding Solange's parentage? Again we are reduced to conjectures.

In early May, at any rate, Casimir allowed Aurore and the two children to accompany him on a trip to Bordeaux. Originally they were to have spent three weeks there before moving on to stay a month with Casimir's mother-in-law at Guillery. But May melted into June and June was overtaken by July before Aurore could bring herself to leave. She complained of dizzying headaches which could only be alleviated, she claimed, by morning visits to the local baths. But the recurrent frequency of the ailment and the uniformity of the "cure" soon convinced her husband that Aurore's "ill health" was really a pretext for paying daily visits to Aurélien de Sèze. His supicions were almost certainly justified. The "ailing" wife insisted on staying a total of nine weeks, thus forcing her husband to borrow 3000 francs; and if Casimir's later testimony is to be trusted, it took the combined efforts of himself and Aurélien — acting for once in extraordinary unison — to make Aurore understand that her continuing presence in Bordeaux could only culminate in a public scandal.

As a price for being "reasonable," Aurore insisted that Aurélien be invited to revisit Nohant in September. This happy prospect seems to have stimulated her literary energies. Two weeks after returning to Nohant she finished writing a brief account of her youthful trip to Spain and a far more detailed account of the trip she and Casimir had made to Mont-Dore two summers previously. She also experimented with a puppet theater for the amusement of her houseguests at Nohant. One of them was the young Baron Gonzalvo de Nervo, whose sister had married the aristocratic *sous-préfet.* In mid-September he may well have caused Aurore something of a shock when he submitted her handwriting to a graphological analysis: "Sense of order, strength, chaste, tight reasoning, much logic, much wit. There is in the heart a mystery I cannot fathom. The imagination is cold and will grow colder than the passage of the years would incline." How much the young Baron read into her writing, how much he was influenced by what his sister and brother-in-law had told him about Aurore we do not know, and the mystery in this case is compounded by the penciled note which the Belgian collector, Spoelberch de Lovenjoul, added much later to the surviving scrap of paper on which the analysis was written: "Allusion is here made to Aurélien de Sèze."

That Aurélien was as present as ever in her thoughts cannot be doubted. In a letter written three days after this handwriting session, Aurore suggested that her friend Charles Meure (who was also a royal prosecutor) look up Aurélien in Paris and even plan to journey down with him in the same stagecoach to Châteauroux. She added: "I feel in a very lively manner (*without this being apparent*). My nerves are excessively irritable (without anyone suspecting it). My imagination is forever galloping ahead without going anywhere, because it is linked to a character which is too soft and to a health which is too frail for the mind ever to be able to produce a good or bad result."

This pessimistic self-appraisal was a direct reflection of the increasingly separate and secluded life she now chose to lead at Nohant in an effort to forget the omnipresent reality: what George Sand later described as "a gaiety without expansion, an interior without intimacy, a solitude which noise and drunkenness rendered even more absolute about me." For there was no hiding the unpleasant truth — which was that not only Casimir, but Hippolyte and only too often Alexis Duteil as well, were hitting the bottle with distressing frequency. "There is nothing worse than drunkards who are witty and good-natured, one cannot get angry with them," was George Sand's wry comment years later. "But when my nerves were on edge, when the company grew obscene and vulgar, when even my poor brother, so long submissive and repentant as a result of my remonstrances, became brutal and nasty, I turned a deaf ear and as soon as I could, I discreetly withdrew to my little room."

This little sanctuary was her grandmother's former boudoir, linked by a single communicating door to the large bedroom in which the children slept. Crammed with books, plant specimens, pressed butterflies, a canary cage, curious shells and stones — for Aurore had not lost her taste for the natural sciences — this scholarly cubicle was furnished with a wardrobe whose single door or panel opened down, instead of out, to form a horizontal desk top on which she could write. Here, along with her feathered quills, her bottles of black ink, her sheets of paper and wax seals, there also lived a cricket for whom she conceived a strong attachment, even letting it feed off her writing paper before helping it back into the drawer in which it had made its home. For weeks its strident *cri-cri* accompanied her nocturnal lucubrations, until one evening the unusual silence caused her to hunt for her vanished friend. She finally found the remnants of two hind legs, which the careless maid, in closing the window, had crushed in the jamb. Dropping them inside a trumpet lily, Aurore preserved the remains for some weeks, seeing in her companion's untimely end a symbolic presage of the slow death of the passion for Aurélien that had sustained her all these years.

The story of the cricket's death was included among a series of disconnected episodes which she now turned into a novelette called *La Marraine* (*The Godmother*). For as she wrote to Jane Bazouin in early October: "Since you put it into my head to write something, dear Jane, I have neither appetite nor sleep." In acknowledging receipt of the manuscript, Jane Bazouin congratulated Aurore on her character delineations but took her gently to task for the "scorn of the human species" and the despondent note that were sounded throughout.

Maurice was now six years old and it was high time, his mother felt, that someone better qualified than Hippolyte be found to give him instruction in reading and writing. The Liberal deputy, François Duris-Dufresne, with whom Hippolyte one day struck up a conversation in the Paris-Châteauroux stagecoach, suggested that Madame Dudevant write to his brother-in-law, the ardently Napoleonic general Bertrand, whose younger son had been taught to read "in a few lessons" by a remarkable young tutor named Jules Boucoiran. Though distrustful of short-cut methods of instruction ("some of which are not exempt of charlatanism"), Aurore wrote to the young man, who agreed to give Maurice a three-month cram course in reading.

Jules Boucoiran's arrival at Nohant proved a blessing for Aurore. This bashful, introverted youth of twenty-one may have been gauche and inhibited in the company of others — particularly Casimir's rowdy drinking chums — but he shared Aurore's enthusiasm for literature. At Nohant he became what Hippolyte's wife, Emilie, was too somnolent and placid to be: a confidant, a kind of private secretary, and not least of all — though Aurore disapproved of his frequenting "less well educated" people — a highly valuable informant, able to report to her the latest kitchen gossip.

In November Casimir had to journey up to Paris to see a Bordeaux "shipping merchant" (for such he claimed to be) about a business venture that was expected to net a handsome profit. Aurore seized on this opportunity to make a little trip of her own — in the opposite direction. Its ostensible purpose was to visit Alexis Duteil's sister-in-law, Félicie Molliet, who was now living at Périgueux. By the direct route, via Châteauroux and Limoges, the distance (150 miles) could normally be covered in eighteen hours by stagecoach. Instead, Aurore chose (or at least pretended to have chosen) a more circuitous route via the mountainous province of La Marche. Though she left Nohant on the evening of November 25, she did not reach Périgueux until the early morning of the twenty-ninth — more than three days later. She dashed off a letter to her husband to explain that at each stop she had found the stagecoach full and had had to wait for the next, or even spend the night. The next day she wrote a second letter to say that she was feeling better than she had felt for months, that her friend Félicie — "fresh, fat, and lovely" — was taking marvelous care of her, treating her to four meals a day and forcing her to sleep twelve hours a night, that Madame Molliet's "singularities" and perpetual quarrels with her husband kept them in constant stitches. And so on.

If she didn't make a lightning trip to Bordeaux before this letter was written, she certainly made one after it. For six days passed before she wrote to Casimir again. A quarter of a century later, when the memory of these events had grown a trifle blurred, George Sand inadvertently let the cat out of the bag by writing that "In the autumn" — of 1829 — "I went to spend several days at Périgueux . . . I pushed on as far as Bordeaux, to embrace Zoé." It was not only the good Zoé whom Aurore wanted to embrace, but above all Aurélien. Casimir, who was not taken in by the elaborate camouflage, later identified the site of their clandestine tryst as the Hôtel Richelieu in Bordeaux.

Just how ardent their embraces were there is no way of saying, but given their respective temperaments, they were probably more passionate then platonic. On December 8, after her return to Périgueux, Aurore wrote a sprightly letter to "my dear little Jules" — as, with motherly solicitude, she was already calling Maurice's tutor, Boucoiran — to report that: "My health is still fine, and besides, I'm in a mood to sing the *Nunc Dimittis.* You don't know, you heretic, what that means? I will tell you." The cryptic promise notwithstanding, the good tutor was probably not told just what "salvation of the Lord" it had been given Aurore's eyes to behold and in exactly what tranquillity of spirit it had been given to "His servant" to depart.

Upon her return to Nohant in mid-December, Aurore discovered that her eighteen-day absence had been fruitfully exploited by Hippolyte, who had replaced Casimir as Pepita's lover. In this lusty enterprise he had fared so well that the Spanish maid had been moved to sigh: "Ah, Monsieur, it's so much better than Monsieur Dudevant!" Boucoiran must have been startled to hear Hippolyte boast of his amorous savoir-faire at a time when his wife and daughter were living under the same roof, but then, what wasn't the garrulous Hippolyte capable of saying when he was in his cups!

Aurore decided to put an end to this hanky-panky by having Maurice's cot moved into her crowded boudoir-study, next to her narrow bed, while her former page, André, slept in the large bedroom "to keep an eye on Pepita with whom I'm not pleased," as she wrote to her husband the day after her return.

Casimir by this time had been away for three full weeks but seemed in no hurry to return. Aurore had rightly sensed that the "shipping merchant" who had talked him into investing 10,000 francs in a cargo vessel called the *Jeune Caroline* was a swindler. She wrote to her husband several times imploring him to stay away from his partner's wines and champagnes, which had such a deleterious effect on his business acumen. "One shouldn't conclude business matters after a meal when one has the misfortune not to be sober," she berated him in a long, stern letter written shortly before Christmas. After suggesting that he might do better investing his money in the improvement of the Nohant estate, she reminded him tartly that he was a poor bargainer who had established an unfortunate reputation for buying at higher prices than anyone else in the neighborhood. "I have no regret," she concluded her lecture, "seeing you spend your money for your pleasure, and my only reproach is that you don't spend enough. But it infuriates me to see you spend it in yawning. I enjoy seeing you in a society where there are ladies, there you behave well and are reasonable. But with men, and particularly at gatherings where you are among yourselves, you want to be the noisiest and you are the most absurd. It's when they are among themselves, the saying has it, that women lose themselves. I think it applies with equal force to men."

When the crestfallen Casimir finally returned to Nohant in early January of 1830, he had to admit that his seven-week absence had produced absolutely nothing — his Bordeaux "shipping merchant" remaining as vague as ever about the "fabulous" cargo that the *Jeune Caroline* was due to bring back from the Indies. Backed by Hippolyte and Duteil, Aurore now insisted that she be given a monthly allowance of 1000 francs for the strict and (she claimed) "economical" management of the Nohant estate. Casimir, having made a fool of himself in Paris, had no choice but to acquiesce.

Aurore's first action, under the new "regime," was to get rid of Pepita, whose culminating sin was to take Maurice into the village and to stuff the poor boy, just recovering from a bout of indigestion, with hot bread and wine. She was replaced by André's wife, Françoise. Determined to prove that she could personally add to the annual revenue of the Nohant estate, Aurore now tried her hand at decorating snuffboxes and wooden cigar cases with painted birds and flowers — an idea first given her by the *sous-préfet*'s wife. But the hours of microscopic concentration she had to devote to the making of these miniatures did little more than strain her eyesight.

This new handicraft and the express desire to look into the strange affair of the *Jeune Caroline* gave Aurore an excuse for making a seven-week trip to Paris in late spring. Leaving Solange at Nohant, she took along Maurice, wishing to have his picture painted by the noted portraitist Blaize. She was also anxious to reestablish contact with Jules Boucoiran, who had left her service shortly before Christmas, more or less dismissed by the irascible Casimir, who seemed to feel that his presence at Nohant was one more "whim" on the part of his erudite wife.

What followed, if not altogether premeditated, did at least pay tribute to Aurore's talent for improvisation. In Paris she and Maurice were put up by Madame Julie-Justine Gondoüin Saint-Agnan. Her "aunt" — so named because she was the sister of Aurore's foster father, James Röettiers du Plessis — was something of a bon vivant and not above having a lover, though she was clever enough to hide it. Aurore could thus count on her discretion, notwithstanding a number of "chance" encounters that were altogether too providential to have been totally unplanned. Almost the first person she saw was Emile Paris, a Bordeaux friend with whom she, Casimir, and Aurélien had explored the grottoes of Lourdes. Another "old friend" who came to call, not once but repeatedly, was Stéphane Ajasson de Grandsagne. "I don't know how he learned I was here," Aurore wrote to her husband.

Two weeks after her arrival Aurore wrote again to Casimir — this time to say that she had just received an "urgent" letter from Zoé reminding her of an earlier promise to visit her in Bordeaux. The summons was just too urgent to be politely refused; besides, Aurore had just discovered that there were fast new stagecoaches that could cover the distance to Bordeaux in thirty-six hours. "I am very undecided and even quite annoyed at having to make this trip," she went on with an exquisite hypocrisy which can have fooled no one but herself, "for I shall see very little of Aurélien, who is in the country, nor of Emile [Paris], who is staying on here a little longer. I'll tell you what has decided me, it's a moment of *high dudgeon* and chagrin which gives me a yearning and a need for *moving around!*" This was followed by a strange story about a row Aurore had just had with her "crazy" mother, simply because she had neglected to sit through an entire play in the same theater box. All of which had so upset her that she absolutely had to be off!

By the time Casimir received this letter, Aurore was already on her way. On reaching Bordeaux she dashed off a second missive to say that Zoé did not want her family to know that she had come down specially for her, and that for this reason, "I avoid seeing them and return here to the hotel for dinner the moment the brothers arrive." Casimir must have thought it odd that Zoé, who had been so "pressing" in her invitation a few days earlier, should now seem positively embarrassed by Aurore's presence in Bordeaux. He may even have begun to wonder if Zoé had ever written to Aurore at all.

If Zoé was surprised by this sudden visit, Aurore must have been even more dismayed by an unforeseen event which played havoc with her dreams. For though it was now mid-May — that season of the year which habitually aroused all of her animal energies and appetites, after the cold, cough- and rheumatism-inducing winter — the moment was poorly chosen for passionate embraces. She spent three days in Bordeaux (one more than she had promised Casimir), but found Aurélien de Sèze "much changed, much aged and sad." He had just lost his father, the brilliant rector of Bordeaux University, he and his family were in mourning, and even if he had been in the mood, which seems doubtful, he could not now indulge in reckless romance.

Though Aurore put a brave face on it, later writing to Casimir that the "dash" down to Bordeaux and back had done her "nothing but good," it must have pained her to realize that there were social limits which Aurélien could simply not transgress in responding to her passion. In private he could, as she had once written to a friend, be very much the "sublieutenant"—that is, drink, dance, flirt, and make gallant advances. But in Bordeaux he was a public figure and a respected member of the bench who could not afford to go on a wild bohemian fling with a married lady in one of the city's better-known hostelries. His name might not be Romeo, any more than hers was Juliet; he was no monk and she no Héloise, but theirs, like all sublime romances, was hedged with insuperable impediments.

Years later George Sand could write that "The absent being, I could almost say the *invisible* being, whom I had made the third term of my existence (*God, he, and I*), was tired of this superhuman aspiration to a sublime love. Generous and tender, he did not say so, but his letters became rarer, his expressions warmer or cooler according to the meaning I wished to attach to them. His passions needed something more nourishing than enthusiastic friendship and epistolatory exchanges. He had made me a vow which he had religiously observed and without which I would have broken with him. But he had not made a vow excluding the joys and pleasures he could find elsewhere. I felt that I was becoming a terrible drag-chain for him, or else that I had ceased to be more than a mental amusement. I leant too modestly toward the latter opinion, and only later did I discover that I was mistaken . . . I continued to love him for a long time thereafter, in silence and despair. Then I came to think of him with calm, with gratitude, and I never think of him without a deep-felt friendliness and a well-founded esteem . . . I don't know if I am right in regarding pride as one of the first duties of a woman, but I don't have it in me not to look down on a passion that is too insistent."

Thus was ended, neither suddenly nor bitterly, Aurore's first great romantic passion. Unlike those that were to follow, it left no trace of bitterness or mutual recrimination.

PART III

From Jules Sandeau to George Sand

11. Jules Sandeau

IF AURORE'S FLYING TRIP to Bordeaux marked the twilight of one romance, her seven-week stay in Paris ushered in the dawn of another. She found the city so changed that, as she wrote to Casimir, "I no longer recognize anything . . . The new galleries [of the Louvre] are admirable. There was in the glasswork of the vault a moonlight effect which was mingled with the glimmer of the lighted globes. One could have thought oneself in a fairy palace."

Her professional interest in art — now that she was trying to sell as well as decorate her painted snuffboxes and cigar cases — led her to make repeated visits to the Louvre and Luxembourg picture galleries, where she was overawed by the robust richness of the Titians, the Tintorettos, and the Rubens there exposed. A glutton for music, she managed to take in four operettas during her first week; and when her funds ran low, she rationed herself to a brioche or two in order to see Weber's *Der Freischütz* and Rossini's *William Tell,* as well as a ballet-pantomime by Halévy and Scribe.

She also took in a number of plays, including Alexandre Dumas' new melodrama *Stockholm, Fontainebleau et Rome,* which impressed her because, as she wrote home, "they assassinated Monaldeschi" — the lead actor — "before our eyes. *It's the latest genre.* Every evening I see an execution, a hanging, a suicide, or at least a poisoning, with an accompaniment of cries, convulsions, and death agonies. It's charming. I'm growing a bit blasé and my sensitivity has been so dulled that I laughed my head off . . . when Monaldeschi smeared his chest with red currant jam in lieu of blood. The bad, the false, the stilted have in my opinion invaded the stage and literature."

Such theatrics seemed scandalous innovations in a country which had been taught for generations to believe, along with Sophocles, Aeschylus, and Aristotle, that violent actions may be described in verse but should on no account be presented on the stage. These were the classical conventions to which Racine, Corneille, and even Molière had adhered but which Shakespeare had blithely disregarded, and it was in the name of Shakespeare, the anticlassicist par excellence, that Victor Hugo, Dumas, and their followers were determined to bury the "Ancients" (or *perruques,* as they were contemptuously called, after the wigs worn by the pre-Napoleonic generation) and to emancipate an excessively regimented art. Little could Aurore Dudevant have guessed, in ridiculing the melodramatic extravagances of the new cult — not for nothing was she Madame Dupin de Francueil's granddaughter — that the time would soon come when she would be regarded as one more Romantic rebel and impious iconoclast.

Nohant, after this stimulating exposure to the gale winds of artistic controversy, seemed to her more than ever a cultural backwater, and La Châtre, with its irregular cobbled streets and sullen gabled houses, "which seem to want to turn their backs on each other," more than ever a fortress of provincial mediocrity. "I remember often going to spend insipid evenings with people who were even more insipid," George Sand was later to recall. "I had several leagues to cover on my way home and not a week would pass without my finding myself alone on the highway, between midnight and two o'clock in the morning. These were well nigh the only hours of reverie and solitude for which there was room in a life as subject to domestic chores as mine. I then pondered my situation, I examined my destiny . . . I was convinced that beyond the limits of my life of labor and renunciation, there was a choice life, an affable, elegant, enlightened society where gifted persons could be welcomed and have a chance to share their feelings and ideas. I didn't know that genius, whether locked up in a cell or roaming at large, is always solitary, oppressed, suffering, ignored . . . It was with awe that I considered the immense superiority which the lowliest literary hack enjoyed over myself. All those who composed verses I took to be poets, and I would have ridden ten leagues for a passing glimpse of Monsieur de Balzac."

There was in this, as in virtually everything she wrote, a strong whiff of Romantic exaggeration. For though she may already have heard of Balzac and perhaps even read his first noteworthy novel, *Le Dernier Chouan,* her gods of the moment were Walter Scott, E. T. A. Hoffmann, and Victor Hugo — the same Hugo who had created such a storm the previous February with his dramatic staging of his swash-buckling *Hernani.* Nor, to judge by the letters she wrote during this eventful year of 1830, was Aurore Dudevant quite as politically naive as the later George Sand may have thought. To be sure, the political upheavals of this spring and summer — the imposition of a drastic press censorship, the dissolution of a rebellious Chamber of Deputies, Charles X's foolhardy decision to rule by royal decree with the aid of his archreactionary minister, the Prince de Polignac, left a skeptical Aurore singularly unmoved. "I don't want to talk politics," she wrote to Charles Meure, the King's attorney of Clamecy, in late June. "It's all above my head and much too boring besides."

While patriotism is not always the last refuge of a scoundrel, as Samuel Johnson claimed, politics can often offer a convenient haven for mediocre minds. This was the one area of conversation in which Casimir Dudevant could assert his masculine authority. At table he would cut his wife short, peremptorily declaring: "Don't be silly, you've no idea what you're talking about!" and a suddenly cowed Aurore would lapse into a brittle silence, while her husband nodded significantly at Hippolyte or joked with Alexis Duteil about the inveterate inability of women to understand the first thing about politics. It was now Aurore's turn to find refuge for her wounded self-esteem, and she found it, not unnaturally, in her wood-painting craft. "I spend six hours a day, copying real flowers," she wrote to Julie Gondoüin Saint-Agnan, who would have laughed if she could have seen Aurore's narrow den, now so crowded with paint bottles, strips of boxwood, pots of glue, and varnish that she had to move Maurice's little bed back into the big yellow bedroom and herself sleep in a hammock!

From these monastic labors Aurore was finally torn by the "three glorious days" of late July, which saw an outraged Paris populace rip up paving stones, overturn carriages, barricade the streets, and snipe away at the Royalist troops mustered to "restore order," while the fatuous Charles X, comfortably installed in the Château de Saint-Cloud (separated from Paris by one of the loops of the Seine), kept stolidly repeating: "It was the concessions he made which cost my brother [Louis XVI] his throne. I'm not going to repeat the same mistake!"

News of the insurrection was slow in filtering down to La Châtre, as mail coaches were held up and searched by Royalist constabulary in a belated effort to keep the provinces from being "inflamed" by incendiary reports from the capital. Anxious to know what had happened to her mother and to Aunt Lucie — whose husband, Amand Maréchal, was an arms inspector in the Royal Household and lodged next door to the Tuileries palace — Aurore galloped into La Châtre every day to pick up what news she could from acquaintances gathered on the main square. On the last day of July travelers on the stagecoach from Châteauroux brought the glad tidings that "victory was with the citizens," but a letter from Jules Boucoiran which was "read by the entire town" spoke of much bloodshed and shooting.

For a good ten days no one really knew who was in control of the country, as the wildest rumors raced from mouth to mouth. The *sous-préfet* dutifully tendered his resignation, while a tricolor flag was hoisted over his doorway. When a Royalist regiment from Bourges was reported to be marching on the "rebel town," the Liberals of La Châtre, led by Casimir, Hippolyte, and the ardently republican Jules Néraud, improvised a National Guard company of 120 men and made ready to do battle. The whole business had a faintly comic air, the first concern of these militant "constitutionalists" being to fit themselves out with the appropriate military gear before sallying forth with their flintlocks, bayonets, and sabers. In his splendid grenadier's uniform and under the bushy bonnet, even the ugly Alexis Duteil almost cut a handsome figure, and Aurore was much amused to see him sprout a lopsided mustache, thrown off balance by the pockmarked depression under one nostril.

"You are lucky to be a man," she wrote to Jules Boucoiran. "With you anger can provide a diversion from sorrow." In the end, however, she did not have to mourn the death of a single friend or relative in Paris. Nor did any family property suffer from the wild fusillades or energetic erection of barricades. True to his prankish form, Hippolyte put it out that his house on the Rue de Seine had been "leveled" by a cannonade fired across the Seine from the Louvre at the "rebellious" Left Bank, and his vivid description of this totally imaginary disaster earned him many solemn expressions of condolence from the hoodwinked gentry of La Châtre.

On July 30, while the confusion was at its height, Aurore rode over to Le Coudray, overlooking the Vallée Noire, to call on her friend Charles Duvernet. With him were some familiar faces — that of Gustave Papet, now an eighteen-year-old student of medicine, and that of the towering Alphonse Fleury, whose newly cultivated beard — in the style made fashionable by the Romantics — was soon to earn him the nickname of "The Gaul." But there was also among them a newcomer, a fair-haired youth with pale blue eyes who, on seeing Aurore arrive, moved shyly off and sat down on a grassy mound beneath a pear tree to read a book. Intrigued by his diffidence, Aurore gradually led her friends toward the grassy mound, which happened to be her favorite spot in the Duvernets' garden, so as to be introduced to the young man who seemed so anxious to avoid her. His name, she was informed, was Jules Sandeau.

Though he was not, like the others, a "local boy" — he had been born at Aubusson, the famous tapestry center — his father had spent the past fourteen years at La Châtre as a collector of royal taxes, and it was to the quaint town, with its rambling streets winding uphill toward the steepled church and the square-walled citadel, that the young man always joyfully returned for his holidays. At the Royal College of Bourges he had won an impressive number of prizes in rhetoric, literature, and drawing. He had dabbled in poetry, composing a Byronic ode in honor of Greece's newly won freedom from the hated Turk, as well as a 200-verse encomium on the pun. Even his biographer, Mabel Silver, later had to admit that this adolescent verse-making was for the most part dreadfully pompous and wooden, but then this was a pompous age. Even if it no longer believed, with the eighteenth century, that Voltaire was a great poet, it went in heavily for exalted declamation and facile rhyming, in the style André Chénier had vulgarized and Chateaubriand sought to raise to the level of great art. At nineteen Jules Sandeau could be forgiven for wallowing in Victor Hugo and poetic daydreaming, while his less-inhibited and more down-to-earth friends rode off to hunt.

This first encounter, though brief, was decisive for both Aurore Dudevant and Jules Sandeau. Her friends were eager to ride into La Châtre to pick up the latest news, and there was no time to indulge in a literary or philosophical discussion. But mounted on her horse, Aurore cut as provocative a figure as she did on foot. Reaching the point where their respective roads parted, she turned to Duvernet and said: "Charles, tomorrow you must bring all your friends over for dinner." The young Sandeau must have guessed that the *all* was meant to include himself. Aurore nodded, gave her horse an imperious crack over the rump with her riding crop, and galloped impetuously away, looking more than ever like the wild, romantic heroine he had dreamed about for years.

This first chance encounter was followed by many others, greatly facilitated by Casimir's providential departure for Paris early in August. "From the very first day his [Sandeau's] expressive gaze, his brusque, frank manners, his gauche timidity with me made me want to see and examine him," Aurore later wrote to a mutual friend. Each examination became a little more searching, more intimate, more secretive. The need to obtain the "latest news" about developments in Paris gave Aurore a ready-made pretext for galloping into La Châtre, where she would meet up with her friends and go for delightful strolls through the Couperies, a rock-studded ravine overlooking the quietly flowing Indre a mile or two to the south. Informed by a maid that "Madame's friends have arrived," Aurore would thrill at the sight of the red cord tied around his gray top hat, which distinguished it at a glance from the gray toppers with blue cords worn by his friends. Her "little Jules," she then knew, was in the drawing room with the others.

Their friends, sensing the attraction between them, would leave Aurore and Jules to themselves when they went for a "stroll" through Nohant's little grove. It was here, on a little bench, that their hands first touched and that they simultaneously declared their love for one another. "I don't know just how it happened," Aurore later recalled. "A quarter of an hour earlier I was alone, seated on the stone steps and holding a book which my eyes alone were reading. My thoughts were entirely absorbed by a single, gracious, sweet, delightful thought, a thought that was vague, uncertain, mysterious. I saw Jules in my mind's eye, I heard his voice, I went over everything I had heard him say about himself, everything I had guessed, and my heart burned with love without it occurring to me to yield or to preserve myself from it. Forgotten was the future, the morrow. He had come to call the previous evening, and that was all that mattered. Then suddenly I heard a voice that made me thrill from head to foot. I turned around. It was he. I had expected him so little."

The enthusiasm with which she had greeted the July Revolution was now channeled in a more private direction. The more disgusted she became with political developments, the readier she was to concentrate all of her passionate energies on her new love. For with each passing day it became clearer that *their* revolution had been corrupted and betrayed. Where the stupid Charles X had tried to govern with his retinue of diehard nobles, burning to undo everything that had been accomplished under the first revolution, the Directoire, and Napoleon, the "Citizen-King," Louis-Philippe, was getting ready to install a regime of money-grubbing bankers. Aurore was disgusted by the spectacle of "hordes of ambitious and servile scoundrels who yesterday claimed to be adversaries of the Powers that Be and who today are showering them with incense," as she wrote to Charles Meure — who felt that all things considered, the new regime was an improvement on the old, a sentiment she could not share. "I may be wrong, but servility is ingrained in the character of so many people that an attitude of opposition can be permitted in that of others" — among whom she classed herself, adding: "I am naturally disposed to side with the weak against the strong."

Of the genuineness of her republican sympathies there can be no doubt. As she emphatically declared in another letter sent to Charles Meure in mid-September: "Sir, I am a republican and you are a fine one to doubt it! I have no use for rose water, and even less for the lukewarm. I need a full-fledged republic, or else I'll have none of it . . . If I were a man," she went on in the same resolute vein, "I would take the trouble to provide a seasoned justification for my republicanism. I would indulge in serious study, something I haven't done and don't need to do . . . I am so well known for being a person of no consequence, feeble-minded and somewhat lunatic" — a dig at Casimir and other "male chauvinists" of his ilk — "that I'm not afraid of influencing the people around me and of leading them dangerously astray. A woman is always a woman, and don't think this is something I complain of. On the contrary, it's so convenient! It's so comforting . . . to have no common sense, to go around speaking one's mind at will without having to go to prison for it, not to have to pit men of one party against those of another, and not to have one's conscience troubled by those heavy reproaches which must weigh on the minds of prominent leaders in the midst of their humdrum errors."

With the onset of autumn and the consolidation of the Citizen-King's Bourgeois Monarchy, her interest in politics waned. Her heart and mind were now absorbed by another kind of passion. One day at Nohant, while Aurore and her friends were seated on the grass for an open-air reading of Hoffmann's *Don Juan,* Duteil began furtively stroking the hand of an attractive servant girl named Claire. He was promptly put in his place with a swift kick administered by Hippolyte's wife, Emilie, who had been rash enough to hire the all too prepossessing maid. Duteil was not the only male in the neighborhood to be aroused by Claire's tempting contours, for Casimir was soon creeping up the stone stairs at night for visits to her bedroom.

Aurore was not in much of a position to complain now that her own erotic energies had found a new and conveniently close stimulus. "Since July 30th I haven't touched a paintbrush," she had to admit in mid-October in a letter sarcastically addressed to *Madame la citoyenne Duchesse de Saint-Agnan,* who had been waiting for more than three months for the glove box Aurore had promised to paint for her. "I spend my life out of doors and only come in to eat and sleep." What she carefully avoided adding — something that would not overly have surprised the friend who had jokingly accused her in May of being a "female Don Juan," with lovers in Paris, Bordeaux, and even Le Havre! — was that all this galloping and running around was anything but politically motivated.

The first meeting of hands, which had so thrilled her and Jules on the little bench in the Nohant grove, was inevitably followed, though probably not immediately, by their first hesitant embrace. Years later, in his partly autobiographical novel *Marianna,* Sandeau sought to transcribe the breathless excitement of this moment: "He was there, so fine, so poetic, so full of adolescent grace! His brow was so pure and so dreamy! His hair, faintly stirred by the breeze, gave off such an intoxicating scent! There was an instant of hallucination during which, in a movement of instinctive tenderness, . . . she lent toward Henry" — which is to say, Jules — "and taking his head between her hands, she pressed him to her heart. Chaste embrace! No one can say how it came about that their lips touched! It was but a rapid kiss, as quick as lightning! But the spark that falls on saltpeter does not touch off a prompter or swifter explosion. Madame de Belnave" — Aurore — "tore herself, pale and trembling, from the arms that had embraced her; and in a quavering voice, which she sought to calm, she complained of the freshness of the evening . . ."

We have Aurore's word for it (in a letter written one year later) that she did not give way immediately. She let her little Jules put his arms about her, she let him kiss her, she let him caress her, doubtless she caressed and kissed him too, but for three long months she refused to let herself go completely. It wasn't that she didn't want him. But she was afraid of being hurt once more — this time by a lover who was seven years her junior. The tension grew unbearable. Jules pleaded, sighed, groaned, wept, reproached her with not loving him, spoke desperately of putting an end to his days, and experienced such agonies of expectant torment that it looked to her at times as though he were about to faint or even to "die of suffering in my arms" (as she later described it). Finally she gave in, abandoning herself to his feverish embraces as passionately as she had resisted them.

Their relations were now far too intimate for them to arrange "accidental" meetings in the Nohant grove. The woods, which dotted the countryside, were much safer. "The rumors in La Châtre are rifer than ever," she wrote to Boucoiran in late October. "Those who have little love for me say that I *love* Sandot [sic] (you understand the full import of the word), those who don't like me one bit say that I *love* both Sandot and Fleury; those who detest me say that Duvernet and you to boot don't frighten me. Thus I have four lovers at once. It's not too many for someone with lively passions like myself. Nasty-minded imbeciles! I feel sorry they were ever born!"

In mid-October Hippolyte journeyed up to Paris, leaving his wife, Emilie, to keep Aurore company in the evenings. The morose sister-in-law regularly went to bed at 9:00 P.M., while Aurore retired to her den to write letters, draw, and paint into the small hours of the morning. In early November Charles Duvernet left for Paris in his turn, soon to be followed by the twenty-one-year-old Fleury, who had to return to his law studies, and the nineteen-year-old Sandeau, who had to return to — exactly what he didn't know. For though he had begun to study law, he was increasingly tempted to try his hand at writing.

Aurore, after fourteen intoxicating weeks, felt herself more than ever alone and abandoned. The onset of winter brought on a serious attack of rheumatism that forced her to keep to her bed for fifteen days, wracked by "terrible pains in all my entrails" (as she described them in a letter to Jules Boucoiran). But the misery was psychological as well as physical. She was tired of living under the same roof with an increasingly short-tempered and critical husband. Casimir's brief lieutenancy in the National Guard had bolstered his wounded self-esteem, while her management of the Nohant estate had proved so extravagant that she had already outrun the annual budget of 12,000 francs before the month of December was even started. Her box-painting "industry" had not netted her a penny and had been all but forgotten in the recent political and emotional upheavals. At the beginning of the year it had looked as though she was at least going to become mistress in her own house, but eleven months later she was back where she had started, reduced to begging for further "advances" from her "lord and master."

One day, while Casimir was out hunting, she opened his desk and went through his papers. She may have been looking for traces of the promissory notes Casimir had so recklessly signed in favor of his "Bordeaux shipping merchant," or she may have wanted to see exactly how well he had been doing financially with his purchase of new lands, the cultivation of beetroot, and other agricultural projects. Whatever the reason, she came upon an envelope addressed to her but marked: "Do not open until after my death!"

"The packet being addressed to me, I had the right to open it without indiscretion," she explained the next day in a letter to Jules Boucoiran, "and my husband being in fine health, I could read his will in peace and quiet. Heavens! What a will! Nothing but curses! He had poured into it all of his anger and ill humor against me, all his reflections on my *perversity,* all his feelings of scorn for my character, and left it there as a token of his tenderness! I thought I was dreaming, I who have hitherto closed my eyes, not wishing to see how much I was despised. This finally aroused me from my slumbers . . .

"I have made up my mind, and I can say *irrevocably* . . . Without waiting one day more, weak and sick though I still am, I announced my wish [to Casimir] and explained my motives with a skill and calm which petrified him. He didn't expect to see someone like me suddenly rise up and talk back to him. He stormed, argued, begged, but I remained inflexible. *I want an allowance and I shall go to Paris forever, my children will stay at Nohant.* That was the result of our first discussion. I refused to give way on anything. It was a feint, as you can imagine. I have no desire to abandon my children entirely, but I let myself be accused of indifference, I said I was prepared for anything. When he was finally convinced of it, he became as tender as a lamb. Today he is in tears. He came to tell me that he would rent Nohant, that he would clean out the house, that he couldn't live alone, that he would take Maurice to Paris and put him in a boarding school. That's something I don't yet want. The child is too young and delicate. Besides, I don't want my house emptied of servants who saw me born and whom I almost love as friends . . . In fact, I intend to spend part of the year, *six months at least,* at Nohant with my children, and even with my husband, who will learn from this lesson to be more circumspect and from whom in any case I shall become independent. He has treated me up till now as though I were odious to him . . . I am proving to him that I do not wish to be treated like a burden, but wanted and sought after like a free companion who will only live by his side if he is worthy of it."

The reason this forthright letter was addressed to Boucoiran was simple: Aurore was desperately anxious to get him back as Maurice's tutor. "If you are at Nohant, I can breathe and sleep in peace. My child will be in good hands, his education will progress, his health will be looked after, his character will neither be spoiled by neglect nor ferocious discipline . . . If I leave my son to my husband's devices, he will be spoiled today, beaten tomorrow, forever neglected, and all I shall find in him is a nasty rapscallion." What was she to do if Boucoiran refused? "If you abandon me, I shall have to bow and submit once again. Ah, and what advantage he'll take of it!"

By the terms of an agreement concluded between them at the time of their marriage, Aurore had been assured an annual allowance of 1500 francs. Having no head for finance and almost priding herself on her "absence of order," she had never claimed it, preferring to let Casimir settle the bills as they came along through their Paris businessman, Louis-Nicolas Caron, and his successor, Achille Salmon. She now laid claim to this allowance, which Casimir could hardly refuse her since almost all of their income was derived from the Nohant estate and the town house on the Rue de la Harpe in Paris, both of which Aurore had inherited from her grandmother. Casimir accordingly agreed to give her an allowance of 250 francs a month for each month she spent away from Nohant.

Julie Gondoüin Saint-Agnan having made it clear to Aurore that she was no longer welcome to stay with her as a houseguest — she had not forgotten her "Don Juanish" exploits of the previous May — Aurore had to find somewhere to live. Though Hippolyte laughed at the idea that she could possibly survive in an expensive city like Paris on a mere 250 francs a month, he generously offered his sister the use of his apartment in the house he owned on the Rue de Seine. Solange, it was agreed, would stay at Nohant until Aurore had found a suitable place of her own in Paris, while Maurice would be left in the care of Boucoiran (who, fortunately for Aurore, agreed to return to Nohant in January, for a two-year term of service as tutor).

Holed up in her little den, with a single oil lamp to light her curious wardrobe-desk, Aurore scratched furiously away, far into each night, keeping herself awake on a strange diet of chocolate (which she ate in lumps), milk, or occasionally lemonade. Her latest brain child was a novelette called *Aimée,* for which she hoped to find a publisher in Paris. In Mid-December she wrote to Félix Pyat, a school friend of Jules Sandeau's who had turned from law to writing journalistic articles and plays, to say that she would be coming up to Paris soon with a "work which only needs a beginning and an end. I realize that beginnings have been done away with by the latest trend of fashion, but catastrophes are indispensable, and five or six people have absolutely got to be killed off at the end. I shall ask you to take care of this for me, you who are *so well versed* in drama, so I hear, and who must be skilled in daggerwork. To each one his trade. I have so far only killed flies and butterflies and I have some trouble spilling human blood."

Three days after New Year's she left Nohant for Paris. The parting was more than a little painful, for Hippolyte, who could be cruel as well as crude in his jesting, had persuaded the seven-year-old Maurice that his mother was leaving him forever! It took all of Aurore's powers of persuasion, as well as a great deal of maternal self-control, to convince the hysterical child that she would be back in just three months. Having lived through such scenes with her own mother, Aurore knew just how her son felt. But unlike Sophie Dupin, she managed to keep her word.

12. *"Vive la vie d'artiste!"*

AURORE REACHED PARIS on the sixth of January 1831 and immediately had herself driven in a fiacre to her brother's house at 31 Rue de Seine Saint-Germain. At Nohant she had been careful to say nothing about Jules Sandeau, though he was one of her main reasons for leaving Nohant. Had she been free to act as she pleased, she would have had Jules move into Hippolyte's apartment with her, but the presence of a sullen concierge and his equally slovenly and suspicious wife made this impossible. Thirty-one Rue de Seine Saint-Germain thus became her official address and place of work. But her real home was the small, sparsely furnished room that Jules Sandeau had rented in a boarding house–hotel situated on the corner of the Quai des Grands Augustins and the Rue Gît-le-Coeur (and what could have been more poetic than this name of "Heart-Rest Street"?).

Over the uneven paving stones and cobbles, on which she slipped and swayed "like a boat on ice" in her awkward shoes, it was a five-minute walk, no more, from her official lodging place to the love nest on the quai. Hippolyte's apartment, though much larger, had no view, whereas from Jules Sandeau's corner room she could admire the towers of Notre-Dame to the right, the old seventeenth-century houses and stone embankments of the Ile de la Cité just opposite, and to the left the picturesque Pont Neuf, over which the carriages rattled to and fro past sidewalk "barbers" who, for a modest fee, combed and clipped the capital's shaggy dogs.

Theirs was a *vie de bohème* — even if there were no real painters or composers among them. With the exception of Gustave Papet, known as "Milord" because the generous allowance he received from his well-to-do father permitted him to pay the occasional restaurant bills, all of Sandeau's friends were or had been impecunious students of medicine or law. Often too poor to afford wine, Aurore and Jules lived soberly off tea, cheese, beefsteaks, and an occasional cutlet when not reduced to a meatless diet of fried potatoes and apple fritters bought from a street vendor. But with what youthful ardor they would debate the events of the day — Jules in his dirty artist's frock coat and unbuttoned shirt, sprawled over three chairs, nervously tapping the ground with his foot or breaking the fire tongs in the heat of the discussion; the "bearded Gaul" — which is to say the ardently republican Fleury — "plotting some great conspiracy" in one corner, while Emile Regnault, a medical student from Bourges, clambered onto the table to make himself heard. So tumultuous were their debates that more than once they were greeted by angry thumping on the thin wall dividing their room from their neighbor's, a fiddler who tried to silence them with sudden blasts on a French horn.

The first weeks in Paris were exceptionally busy, as Aurore divided her time between museum-going, drawing lessons, occasional evenings at the theater (when she could spare the time from her writing), and visits to persons who might help launch her on "the stormy seas of literature" (as she wrote to Boucoiran). She had no clear idea how she was going to survive as a "woman of independent means," and whether it was to be with the writer's pen or artist's brush she did not know. François Duris-Dufresne offered to introduce her to his fellow deputy Lafayette, the white-haired "patriarch of Liberalism" who knew many influential people in the "world of the arts," but she felt that to importune so famous a man for a talent as obscure as her own was an impertinence she could not afford.

She did, however, follow her kindly mentor's suggestion in going to call on Count Auguste de Kératry, a Breton deputy who had dabbled in literature and even acquired a certain notoriety with a novel entitled *Les Derniers des Beaumanoir*. Though Stendhal had called Kératry "the greatest charlatan among all our liberal writers" and though Aurore cared little for his poorly constructed novel and even less for its climactic scene — in which a priest rapes a "dead" woman he is supposed to bury and who turns out to be still living — she buttered him up unscrupulously, even going so far as to "recall" how it had made her weep! Delighted by this outlandish flattery — such a tribute, Kératry said, meant more to him than any amount of drawing room applause — the sixty-two-year-old deputy-author readily consented to read Aurore's novelette.

Their second encounter went less smoothly. In the interim the politician-author had read Aurore's manuscript and found it insufferably naive in its moralizing. "Believe me," he told the would-be authoress, as he escorted her to the door, "don't make novels, make children." To which Aurore, who had just been introduced to the twenty-five-year-old wife he had recently married, retorted: "Keep the precept for yourself."

Equally discouraging was the reaction of the second literary sponsor to whom Aurore showed her manuscript. This was Hyacinthe de Latouche, who had taken over the editorship of the moderate *Figaro* and turned it overnight into a critical journal of opinion. Cranky and capricious — he once closed his gate to a noted actor when he saw him driving up to his country cottage with a melon in his hand (he had, for some reason, a deep distaste for melons) — Latouche was not universally popular, and still less admired, in Paris literary circles.

Unlike the opportunistic Kératry, Latouche was a stout republican who had rushed back to Paris the previous July and had helped the historian Louis-Adolphe Thiers draft a protest against Charles X's high-handed Ordinances before manning a gun on the barricades. A rugged individualist who had no use for fads and still less for cults, Latouche had aroused the fury of Victor Hugo and his literary coterie — the *Cénacle* as they called themselves — by scoffing at the monarchist sympathies and self-congratulating pretentiousness of these "little princes of poetry." In 1824, when his friend Charles Nodier had agreed to become curator of the Arsenal Library, Latouche had challenged him to a duel for accepting a post offered by Charles X. He later quarreled with Alexandre Dumas (who had also manned a gun on the July 1830 barricades) when the latter decided to ingratiate himself with Louis-Philippe's regime in the hope that it would allow the Comédie Française to stage his plays.

Cruel though his bons mots often were, Latouche was not vindictive. But a series of painful setbacks had turned this inordinately sensitive man into a misanthropic hypochondriac. At school a ball had blinded him in one eye, which, though sightless, would still light up with a strange, bloodshot glow every time he grew animated or angry. He had failed in his law studies — being far too bohemian for regular office hours — and had just missed winning the French Academy's annual award for a verse play. An ardent Bonapartist, he had served as secretary to Marshal Brune, only to see him assassinated and his body flung into the Rhone. Latouche's marriage to a woman almost as temperamental and high-strung as himself had ended in a separation shortly after the birth of a son. A tempestuous love affair with the actress (and later poetess) Marceline Desbordes had lasted somewhat longer and had also produced a son. But his two boys, whom he adored, had died within a couple of months of each other in 1816. He had achieved a modest triumph coauthoring a verse play with Emile Deschamps, but his later hopes were dashed when an elegant translation of Schiller's *Mary Stuart,* on which he had labored for months, was overshadowed at the last moment by a rival's wretched adaptation — which nevertheless had Paris audiences weeping copious tears.

So it came about that this gifted wit, who spoke Italian like a native, had some knowledge of Spanish, Portuguese, and even Polish, knew English well enough to translate Shakespeare and Robert Burns, German fluently enough to translate Schiller, Ludwig Tieck, and Goethe, who had done as much as anyone to ensure the success of the Romantic movement in France and who could number Alfred de Vigny, Lamartine, Stendhal, Chateaubriand, Madame Récamier, and Balzac (whom he personally launched) among his friends, gradually yielded to facility. His journalistic flair led him to ghostwrite the "Memoirs" of a woman implicated in a sensational murder, thus producing a spectacular best seller which went through four editions in five days. An alleged translation of letters exchanged between two desperate lovers, condemned by a dread Barcelona plague, turned out to have been invented from start to finish. He similarly "unearthed" a scintillating correspondence between Pope Clement XIV (who was poisoned for having dared to ban the Jesuit order in

1773) and the famous harlequin actor Carlo Bertinazzi, and when challenged to produce the original texts, he came up with several letters written in such flawless Italian that he found himself being accused of "infidelities" in his French "translation."

Though Hyacinthe de Latouche was also a native of Berry, the honest Duris-Dufresne felt it was his duty to warn Aurore against their Berrichon countryman. She herself hardly needed special introduction, for her father, Maurice Dupin, had once played the violin in an orchestra organized by Latouche's father at La Châtre. But she had made doubly sure of being received by the redoubtable plagiarist and critic by asking Charles Duvernet's mother (a cousin of Latouche's) for a letter of recommendation. To it Aurore now added a note explaining her naive desire to contribute to her modest income by writing.

The reply she received was couched in a typically ironic vein: "Madame, I make it a practice to pity those who ask of the arts more than the happiness they confer on those who cultivate them . . . But you are the friend of my friends, and I am at your service . . . the few lines of yours which I have read lead me to suspect that it is not your fault if you write; you have succumbed, I believe, to the fatality of talent. One must, you say, like you to find you amiable; for me you already seem amiable. I shall go to see you tomorrow at 7:30 in the evening, if you do not forbid it. And when you entrust your writings to me, I shall continue to be severe. Goodwill is only too often the laziness of friendship, is it not? H. de Latouche."

Aurore's first impression of this waspish man of letters was not favorable. His exquisite diction, what the critic Sainte-Beuve was later to call his "sirenlike" voice, struck her as stilted. Only later, when she got to know him better, did she realize that this was no aristocratic affectation but the graceful mode of discourse of a man who improvised scathing epigrams and paradoxes as effortlessly as a conjurer juggling with six balls.

Having let her fear the worst, Latouche could afford to be generous in inviting Aurore to accompany him the next Sunday to a poetry-reading session which his neighbor Madame Récamier, now a faded beauty of fifty-three, was holding in her country house, south of Paris. Fearing that as an "aspiring author" she might be asked to "shine" for the delectation of Chateaubriand and other distinguished guests, Aurore prudently declined the invitation.

A few days later she could write to Charles Duvernet to say that his cousin, Hyacinthe de Latouche, had read her little opus. "I was charming in his presence, I curtsied, I took small pinches of snuff, scattering as little as possible over his fine white carpet, I didn't put my elbows on my knees, I didn't sprawl over his chairs. In a word, I was on my best behavior, such as you have never seen me." Latouche had listened, had found it all charming but had had to confess that "it made no sense. To which I replied: 'That's right.' It had to be redone completely. To which I answered: 'That's possible.' I would do well to begin all over. To which I added: 'Enough.' "

The senseless novel was accordingly forgotten. But, Latouche suggested suavely, since she had chosen to live as poorly as himself, why did she not consider writing for his newspaper, the *Figaro,* which paid seven francs for every column published? Still full of illusions about the merits of her brain child, Aurore first declined the offer. She and Jules Sandeau had just concocted an "incredible" article that had apparently appealed to Louis Véron, editor of the fortnightly *Revue de Paris.* Véron being one of several million Frenchmen who believed that women are wonderful so long as they don't write or prattle about politics, science, and other matters that are way over their heads, Jules had signed *their* article with the masculine name of Sandeau. "And (*quite entre nous*) he wrote three quarters of it, for I am suffering from fever. Besides, I don't possess his talent for the *sublime* which the *Revue de Paris* goes in for . . .

"I'm delighted for Sandeau's sake," Aurore went on in the same letter to Charles Duvernet. "This proves that he can make a go of it, and I've decided to associate him with my work or to associate myself with his (as you wish). All so that he may lend me his name, for I don't wish to appear with mine, and that I should lend him my help when he needs it. Please keep this *literary association* secret and to yourself . . . I'm so cruelly maligned at La Châtre (as you must know) that this would be all that was needed to finish me off."

Two weeks later the two literary associates were unpleasantly surprised when their "incredible" article was returned to them by the *Revue de Paris* on the grounds that the author was too obscure to be of interest to its readers. Aurore now had to swallow her pride and pay another call on the editor of the *Figaro.* Latouche's vanity must have been secretly flattered by this sudden capitulation, for he finally agreed to publish their joint brain child after personally reworking it. He even suggested ways in which Aurore's novelette might be salvaged — recommendations she eventually disregarded, preferring instead to consign the misbegotten opus to the flames. On the strength of her recommendation Sandeau and Félix Pyat were both hired at a menial fee of forty to fifty francs a month — they were after all natives of Berry, like Latouche, even if their journalistic credentials were dubious — and before this month of February was over, Aurore too found herself working for the *Figaro.*

For young provincials dying to win their journalistic spurs this was an exciting time to be in Paris. The "Three Glorious Days" of the preceding July had unleashed an extraordinary ferment, after years of stifling regimentation, and the young rebels now boldly paraded their political colors. To distinguish themselves from the ultra-Bourbon Carlists, who dressed in green, republicans and Bonapartists sported flaming red waistcoats, while the Saint-Simonians (who were out to promote a new industrial society) fancied horizon blue. Paris, as Jules Sandeau was later to write, "still smelled of powder, as though in the immediate aftermath of battle. The air was alive with a feeling of revolt and a spirit of insurrection haunted streets, books, and theaters . . . Everything was called into question: social as well as religious institutions, husbands as well as gods and kings. All one heard was blasphemies against the laws, the savage ridiculing of marriage, and wild aspirations for a better future. Public places teemed with twenty-year-old legislators who found Christ somewhat aged and who wanted to supplant him in the task of guiding mankind."

In mid-February several thousand artisans and workers went on a rampage, sacking the archbishopric, then occupied by the arrogant and widely detested Comte de Quélen. The sight of cobblers, carpenters, blacksmiths, and blackguards parading around in chasubles and miters, mumbling bogus prayers and solemnly sprinkling the onlookers with unholy water flicked from chamber pots was greeted by Aurore with devilish glee. "Yes," she wrote to her friend Charles Meure, the sedate King's attorney of Clamecy, who confessed himself a trifle dismayed by such events, "I've seen a nice little revolution indeed! I saw the episcopal library float away on the yellow waters of the Seine . . . I don't need to tell you that I was everywhere and saw everything with my own eyes. I like noise, storms, even danger, and if I were selfishly inclined, I would like to see a revolution every morning, so amusing do I find it. In addition to which, being penniless and with nothing to lose but my life (about which I care little), and with all my parents and friends being so cowardly that they wet their breeches and hide in their cellars as soon as the bugles sound, I really have nothing to lose."

From the kindly Duris-Dufresne she obtained seats in the visitors' gallery of the Chamber of Deputies, the stormy sessions of which were one of her "gayest pastimes." Not content with being a passive spectator, she asked the deputy from the Indre to provide Jules Sandeau and herself with information about the principal turncoats in the Chamber — those who, having changed their professed principles and opinions and trimmed their sails to the prevailing winds so often, had come to resemble what the French call *girouettes,* or weathercocks. The result, to which she contributed, was Jules Sandeau's first article in the *Figaro* — a piece of E. T. A. Hoffmann fantasy making fun of a Chamber of Deputies debate.

The *Figaro,* which Latouche then edited in an Italian-style villa located in suburban Montmartre, bore no resemblance to the respectable Paris newspaper which now slavishly caters to the conventional tastes of France's *haute bourgeoisie.* It was a four-page daily, of small tabloid format, which went in heavily for satire and blistering critiques of Louis-Philippe's "toadyish" ministers and the "bloodthirsty" Tsar Nicolas I of Russia. Almost any piece of gossip was grist to Latouche's journalistic mill, for he was the kind of cook who cares more about the succulence of the sauce than the original quality of the meat. He had no office to speak of, preferring to preside over his team of hatchet men in a spacious drawing room. Visitors, whom he received in large numbers, were ushered in and offered a seat by the fireplace with an astonishing lack of formality. No attempt was made at privacy and whatever was said could be heard by clerks and subeditors — his *eaglets,* he liked to call them — who were scattered about the salon at individual desks.

As a special mark of favor Aurore was given a desk and a little carpet not far from the fireplace. Latouche would toss her a subject to "embroider" and a sheet of paper, specially cut to space, into which the resulting article would have to fit. Brevity had never been her strong point, and before she knew it, she would have thrown ten pages into the fire without having come to real grips with the subject. "The others had wit, verve, and facility," she later recalled. "Everyone talked and laughed. Latouche was brilliantly caustic. I listened, I enjoyed myself hugely, but what I produced was worthless, and at the end of the month I would have earned twelve francs and fifty centimes or fifteen francs all told for my collaboration, far too well paid at that."

George Sand, in recalling these exhilarating times a quarter of a century later, was being too modest. At least one of the three articles devoted to the great violin virtuoso Paganini, which the *Figaro* published during March of 1831, was almost certainly written by her, and we know there were others besides. One of them, published in the *Bigarrures* (or "Medley") column, a standard third-page feature dealing heavily in epigrams and puns, purported to be the text of a decree "about to be published" by the Paris prefect of police. All citizens capable of bearing arms, this bogus decree announced, would have to convene from seven in the morning until eleven at night to guard the approaches to the Palais Royal . . . To cow villains and evildoers, seven-foot ditches were to be dug around every house, all windows were to be fitted out with bars, each Paris household was to be armed with twenty flintlocks for the use of tenants and domestics, and so on.

Vexed by this rough-handed lampooning of the government's panicky efforts to "maintain the peace," the public prosecutor appealed to Louis-Philippe to take action. "You really think I must get angry?" the Citizen King was reported to have asked him. "Yes, Majesty, you must get angry." "And so the King got angry," wrote the author of this report to her friend Charles Duvernet, "and now they've seized the copies of the *Figaro* and are starting a *lawsuit against it.* If particular articles are incriminated, mine will *certainly* be included. I shall declare myself its author and shall get myself jailed. Great Heavens! What a scandal at La Châtre! What horror and despair in my family! But my reputation will also be made and I shall find a publisher to buy my platitudes and fools to read them. I'd give 9 francs 50 centimes," she recklessly added (perhaps because this was all she had on her at the time), "for the happiness of being condemned."

Unfortunately (or perhaps fortunately) for Aurore, this happiness was not vouchsafed her. The prefect of police, who was more thick-skinned and sensible than his colleague of the royal bench, decided it would be wiser to let the whole ridiculous business die a quiet death. The *Figaro* was not arraigned, nor Aurore imprisoned, and instead of a quick immortality, she was condemned to a continuing anonymity and the drudgery of having to spend eight hours a day — from 9:00 A.M. till 5:00 P.M. — trying to think up new journalistic gags in Latouche's "office."

"Phew!" she wrote to Boucoiran on the subject of journalism. "If you only knew what it's like! But de Latouche pays 7 francs a column, and with that one can eat, drink, and even go to the theater, *following the advice you gave me* . . . When one wants to write, one must see everything, know everything, laugh at everything. Ah, believe me, *vive la vie d'artiste!* Our motto is *liberty!*"

The little tip Boucoiran had given her was that the simplest way to see a play or an opera was to avoid the hideously expensive boxes and to choose the parterre (or pit) — the downstairs portion of the theater where the spectators either stood or sat on benches. For the relatively cheap price of two and a half francs, fifty, any *man* who wanted to could thus obtain standing room admission. Ladies, on the other hand, could only sit in the less plebeian boxes — one of many reasons that had prompted Balzac to declare that no one could be a Parisian lady on less than 25,000 francs a year. Since Aurore lacked the means to be a lady, the obvious solution was to go to the theater disguised as a man.

Aurore had a tailor make her a *redingote-guérite* (a sentry-box riding coat) in heavy gray cloth, with waistcoat and trousers to match. She took a particular delight in her metal-heeled boots, so much stronger than her flimsy woman's shoes, in which she could "fly around from one end of Paris to the other." A gray top hat perched saucily over her dark hair and a woolen cravat wound round her neck, made her look like a first-year university student. Her almost childish appearance — so evident in the sketches and paintings made of her at this time — doubtless contributed as much to the success of her disguise as the strange huskiness of her voice, which had earlier caused her grandmother to mistake her for her son, Maurice.

Having discovered a cheap way of going to the theater, Aurore made up for lost time with vengeance. "I've seen Dumas' *Napoléon* at the Odéon. The play is pitiful," she wrote to her husband toward the end of January. "Yesterday I went to the [theatre of the] Italians. I saw Madame Malibran in *Otello.* She made me weep, shudder, and suffer as though I had been watching a scene from real life. This woman is the foremost genius of Europe, as lovely as a Raphael madonna, simple, energetic, naive, she's the foremost singer and the foremost tragedian. I'm mad about her."

Well she might be. And mad not only about María Malibran, the great Spanish contralto who was now the highest-paid diva in Europe, but mad also about the Théâtre des Italiens, which under the dynamic guidance of a music lover named Edouard Robert, the friend and successor of Rossini, was now threatening the supremacy of the Paris Opera. For it was not only in the realms of poetry and drama that Paris (with Lamartine, Vigny, Dumas, Hugo, and the young Alfred de Musset) had become the center and focus of the Romantic movement. Vienna, which (with Mozart, Haydn, Beethoven, and Schubert) had been the musical capital of Europe for more than fifty years, was now totally eclipsed. As Chopin, drawn to Paris like Rossini, Meyerbeer, and Liszt, was to exclaim later in this same year of 1831 after hearing María Malibran's "miraculous" voice: "Marvel of marvels! . . . Only here can one know what singing really is!"

Aurore's enthusiasm for María Malibran gave her new zest for writing. *La Prima Donna,* which she dashed off in a single week, was a rather stupid tale about a diva who, having been misguided enough to marry a duke, begins to waste away; to restore her flagging energy and health, her husband allows her a triumphal return to the operatic stage, where she surpasses herself as Juliet, only to sink back lifeless into the arms of her Romeo partner. How much of this piece of marzipan was Aurore's, how much of it Jules Sandeau's, there is no way of telling. But it was considered sufficiently *sublime* to suit the taste of Louis Véron, the opera-loving editor of *La Revue de Paris,* who might have died of apoplexy had he but known that it was partly, if not mostly, written by a woman.

In early March Véron was named director of the Paris Opera and replaced at the *Revue de Paris* by a gentleman named Charles Rabou, who was apparently less ill disposed toward women authors. This stroke of good fortune only confirmed Aurore in her resolution to pursue a literary career. Having an aim in life at last had cured her of her spleen and even given her a ferocious appetite. But still, her conscience was troubled by the extravagant demands of her new craft. In their craving for ever newer and more scandalous subjects, the "mad dogs" of the Romantic movement had left not only Chateaubriand but even Victor Hugo far behind. A pack of sub-Hugos were now in full chase, led by a certain Lassailly, who had had the hero of one of his novels kill off a small army of rivals before killing his mistress by tickling her feet. Another sub-Hugo named Xavier Forneret had had his hero commit suicide by swallowing his mistress' eyeball! Even Balzac was momentarily swept off his feet by the new craze. As Aurore wrote to Boucoiran: "Literature is in the same chaos as politics. There's one preoccupation, one uncertainty which overshadows everything. Everyone wants to dabble in the new and ends up dabbling in the ridiculous. Balzac is on the crest of the wave, for having depicted a soldier's love for a tigress, and an artist's love for a castrato. What is all this, Good Heavens! Monsters are in fashion. Let us produce monsters. I'm giving birth to a most agreeable one right now."

If Aurore was saved from these Romantic aberrations, it was largely due to the restraining influence of Latouche, who had too much critical acumen and good taste to enjoy wallowing in the grotesque. Her association with Latouche was also providential in another respect, for he was a remarkable musicologist, a great admirer of Rossini, and one of the first Frenchmen to hail the genius of Beethoven, Berlioz, and (later) Chopin. The avuncular, not to say paternal, interest the forty-five-year-old editor showed for the journalistic labors of his twenty-six-year-old protégée was certainly stimulated by their common passion for music: a passion he was glad to encourage by offering her free tickets for operas and chamber music concerts. Aurore could now sit, dressed like a lady, in a box at the Opéra or attend concerts at the Conservatoire, whose limited number of seats were normally sold out three months in advance. Narrow, uncomfortable, damp, and feebly lit by gaslights though it was, the Conservatoire "resounded like a Stradivarius" (as Thérèse Marix-Spire has aptly written), and under the inspired leadership of its first violinist, François-Antoine Habeneck — podium-raised conductors had yet to make their appearance — its orchestra was acknowledged by musical connoisseurs to be the finest in Europe. Here Aurore heard her first Beethoven symphonies — perhaps including the Ninth, which had its Paris première in this same month of March 1831. Though she didn't go into a convulsive fit and have to be carried out, as had happened to María Malibran on hearing Beethoven's Fifth Symphony for the first time, the impact of what she heard was great enough to convince her (as she later wrote) that music was the most universal, the most expressive, "the most beautiful of all the arts."

In mid-March their Berrichon circle was increased by the unexpected arrival of Charles Duvernet. With the connivance of his mother, an excellent harpist, he made a clandestine trip to Paris to take in a bit of opera with Aurore — using the tickets obligingly supplied them by his cousin Latouche — and to hear Paganini, who staged his Paris première at the Opéra on March 9. News of the famous violinist's first visit to the French capital had drained the provinces of music lovers and touched off such a fever of anticipation that the poet Alfred de Vigny was ready to wager that his performances would be a let down. But the maestro not only equaled, he even managed to surpass his hyperbolic legend. Aurore, to judge by the article she probably composed for the *Figaro* (it was unsigned, like the others), succumbed to the general frenzy, resorting to superlatives to describe this strange, foot-dragging, black-clad figure who looked like a "creation of God in the image of the devil"; whose magic bow could "weep like a voice broken by sorrow," mock one as cruelly as Hamlet, laugh as wildly "as that poor mad Ophelia." And so on.

Paganini's sensational performances served to promote the Hoffmannesque idea that art is sacred, requiring of its practitioners an absolute devotion. This idea, which was to reappear like a leitmotif in George Sand's novels and novelettes, now inspired a second short story entitled *La Fille d'Albano,* which Aurore and Jules Sandeau successfully sold to a new magazine called *La Mode.* In this rather insipid tale — inspired by a painting Aurore had once admired at the Luxembourg gallery — the daughter of a famous Italian painter is talked out of marrying a French country gentleman (named Aurélien!) by her brother, who cannot bear the idea that someone who is "as beautiful as Correggio's Virgin . . . with so much poetry in her gaze, so much fire in her soul, so much genius in her hands," should end up vegetating "among lawmakers and money-grubbers, amass a fortune, produce children, and become the first servant of a family and a man."

It sounded wonderful on paper, even if it was difficult to reconcile real life with such an exalted ideal. Judged by this strict criterion, Aurore herself was already disqualified; having married and had children, she had put domestic welfare ahead of Art. She was probably not troubled by the contradiction, for she did not yet consider herself an "artist."

*

Early in April, Aurore bade a tearful goodbye to Jules Sandeau and returned for three months to Nohant. There she found her son, Maurice, singularly "corrected and improved" by his tutor's lessons, Solange bigger, chubbier, more unruly, though of an almost angelic beauty, Casimir "eating and roaring his head off," and Boucoiran disguised behind an incongruous pair of whiskers which suited him about as well as "lace on a hedgehog," as she wrote to her mother. Still doubtful about her literary talent, Aurore returned to her drawing. She sketched a self-portrait for Jules Sandeau, did a pencil study of Duris-Dufresne, and painted snuffboxes for her young friends in Paris.

"The countryside here is lovely," she wrote to Emile Regnault in early May. "In the evening the scent of lilac and lily of the valley wafts into my room in waves, along with yellow and black-striped butterflies, nightingales which sing under my window, and May bugs which stub their noses against my lamp." But she couldn't help regretting Paris, where "one laughs at everything," and disliking La Châtre, where "people take everything so seriously." Each night she locked herself into her den and penned a letter to her little Jules, counting the days and even the hours when they would be reunited in early July. "Still, I hold out against the need to flee, those palpitations which make my heart leap when I see a stagecoach pass by my windows, galloping toward Paris and leaving clouds of dust behind it." For to leave Nohant meant leaving her children, and this was "an immense sacrifice" she begged her younger, unmarried friends in Paris to understand.

In Paris, meanwhile, Sandeau had received an encouraging note from Balzac, after sending him a copy of *La Prima Donna.* Jules forwarded the letter to Aurore, who was pleased to learn that the industrious author of *Physiologie du Mariage* was of the opinion that their story held out "more than mere hopes" for the future.

She was even more pleased to learn that her young friends had found a three-room apartment on the corner of the Quai Saint-Michel, an apartment she was to share with Jules Sandeau when she returned to Paris in July. The view from its fifth-floor balcony, directly opposite Notre-Dame, was apparently spectacular. But what pleased Aurore most was the apartment's third room, the existence of which she was determined to conceal from her husband. This would be "the black chamber, the mysterious room, the phantom's hideout, the monster's lair . . . the vampire's cavern," as she imaginatively described it in a letter to Emile Regnault — the clandestine cabinet in which Jules would be hidden away, should her husband ever take it into his head to visit the premises.

The return to Paris in early July required a certain finesse. Not wishing to be met at the stagecoach terminus by her brother, Hippolyte, who had returned to his own apartment on the Rue de Seine, and who might be overly curious to know where his sister was living, she arranged to "tarry" in Orléans (supposedly to visit the cathedral) and then in Etampes (supposedly to spend a few days at Hyacinthe de Latouche's country place). In fact, she stayed with Jules Sandeau and his friends — which did not keep her from writing to her brother: "Don't worry. I'm in good health and staying near Etampes with a woman friend of mine. There are some people who in their sublime austerity might find a contact with talent and wit unworthy of them. I have not yet reached this degree of moral superiority."

Hippolyte, on receiving this sarcastic note, promptly wrote to Casimir to say that "your wife wants her freedom, she wants movement, dissipation. You haven't been a bad husband for her, as people are generally willing to grant you, both here and in the country. Let her do as she pleases. If she fares badly, she won't have you or her parents to blame, since she will have been following her wishes completely and entirely."

Casimir chose to heed the advice, evincing no desire to hasten up to Paris and to surprise his wife in the arms of a lover. Once installed in her fifth-floor mansard apartment, Aurore forgot all her earlier precautions about the "two-room flat" she was supposed to be occupying alone. "I have three lovely little rooms which look out over the river with a magnificent view and a balcony," she wrote to her son, Maurice, in a letter that his father was certain to read at Nohant.

The first weeks in Paris were unpleasantly hot and hectic, as Aurore rushed around buying furniture and hangings and borrowing the money to pay for them. Casimir having refused to increase her allowance for the month of July, she borrowed 200 francs from her mother and 500 francs from Duris-Dufresne, who thus showed that he was not a "liberal" for nothing. Latouche also advanced her 200 francs, promising her and Jules Sandeau 1000 more (to be paid in two installments) if they could dash off a "posthumous novel" — in four small volumes of about 240 pages each — supposedly written by a recently deceased author named Alphonse Signol. "And to facilitate the purchase of quill pens, we shall pay you, if you like, 125 francs with the delivery of each of the small volumes. All this is little, but I trust that the story you will tell will keep you entertained."

While their bosom friends Emile Regnault and Alphonse Fleury moved into their old lodging house — a mere hundred yards distant — Aurore and Jules Sandeau were reduced for several weeks to sleeping on two mattresses in their fifth-floor mansard flat. "You can imagine what it has taken in memory, legwork, time, and patience to buy everything from a dustpan to candle snuffers," she wrote to Charles Duvernet on July 19. "It's never-ending. The worst of it is the money it all costs . . . The *other one,* as you aptly call him," — by which was meant Casimir — "has just written me to say he hasn't the means to send me a penny. I don't care, that's something for the duffers who've given us credit to worry about. The Gaul [Fleury] and I are relying on a good patriotic *killing* or a good *cholera morbus*" — medical slang for dysentery — "to deliver us of this infamous retinue of creditors. Besides, aren't we due to have a republic? The first article of the new Charter will, I hope, decree the cancellation of all debts and the deportation of all creditors. We will let them off with their lives, because we are great-hearted and generous, but let them beware of ever recalling the past."

To Casimir she wrote the next day in a less jovial tone to say that she hadn't expected her husband and her brother to leave her to rely on the charity of strangers to pay for urgent debts: "For the past three days I've been living off a single 5-franc piece, and I've had to put off payment of a lock and a mantelpiece. One word from you and you could have spared me all this, . . . no matter how economically one lives, there's no easy mean between begging and paying. I only know of one — the Morgue opposite my windows and to which I see dead people being carted every day because they were short of 20 francs . . . I won't go beg my brother for bread; another thing I know is that I have a stomach like anyone else. I wish you a good appetite."

This fatuous suicide threat must have sounded to Casimir more like momentary petulance than serious blackmail. She had also used it on Hippolyte, and with some effect, to judge by a letter he sent to Casimir: "She does everything in her power to keep her family at arm's length, after which she accuses me of selfishness and indifference toward her. She told me she went hungry for three days, when my wife and I have invited her twenty times to the house without her once accepting . . . A spoiled child of fortune . . . she recently wrote me a letter in which she said that if I connive with you to make her unhappy, to deprive her of her children and to keep her in perpetually tight straits, she will throw herself into the Seine. She told me to warn you, so that you shouldn't have her death on your conscience.

"I went to reason with her, to show her the absurdity of all these fancies . . . She seemed unconvinced by what I said, and I even had the impression she considered me a kind of spy. She was busy soaping a dress, and her little place, very neat and tidy, speaks well of her sense of order and economy . . . I took it upon myself to advance her 500 francs until the month of October, in return for a receipt which I'm sure you will reimburse. For notwithstanding her extravagances which are more apparent than real, we mustn't leave her in a destitute state, given over to sad thoughts which could lead her to an extremity for which we would never be able to console ourselves."

August proved as hectic as July, though for other reasons. Having promised to return to Nohant in early September, when Boucoiran was due to leave for Nîmes to spend his holidays with his mother, Aurore had just four weeks in which to finish the "posthumous novel" she and Jules Sandeau had undertaken to deliver on short notice. The result, entitled *Le Commissionnaire* (*The Commissioner*), was an incredible grab-bag job put together from unpublished fragments of Alphonse Signol's manuscripts, to which Aurore, Jules Sandeau, Félix Pyat (the aspiring dramatist), and Emile Regnault (the medical student) added chapters of their own.

The publisher whom Latouche had found for this piece of literary contraband was a certain B. Renault. While they were at it, Aurore impetuously suggested, why not persuade Monsieur Renault to publish a more authentic Jules-Aurore or Sandeau-Dudevant work? It would be a story about two convent girls, one of whom chooses to become a nun (as the adolescent Aurore Dupin had dreamed of being), the other of whom ventures forth into the world and becomes an operatic diva. Renault liked the idea enough to sign a new contract along the same lines: 500 francs for a four-volume novel, each volume to be paid 125 francs on delivery, with an additional 500 francs to be paid to the two authors three months after publication.* The forthcoming novel, entitled *Les Pauvres Filles* (*The Poor Girls*), by a certain Sandeau, was accordingly announced on the back cover of Alphonse Signol's *Le Commissionnaire,* when that exceedingly bogus work made its appearance in September.

Aurore by this time had returned to Nohant, while her little Jules

* Though precise comparisons are impossible, given the enormous differences in purchasing power, domestic wages, cheapness of certain goods, and expensiveness of others, 500 francs in the early 1830s was roughly equal to $1000 today. Latouche claimed to be able to live off 1500 francs (about $3000) a year, but by his own admission he lived poorly.

had left for Niort, in the Vendée region of western France, to spend a few weeks with his parents. The two authors had agreed to split the work between them, each writing a volume and then comparing the results. Galvanized by this new literary challenge, Aurore showed what she could do under pressure. "It's 6 o'clock in the morning, and I've been working since 7 in the evening," she wrote to Emile Regnault (who had stayed behind in Paris, to maintain contact with the publisher) on September 9. "I've done one volume in 5 nights . . . I've not seen Charles [Duvernet], nor Alphonse [Fleury], nor Gustave [Papet]. I believe they don't know I've arrived. This is what I've been reduced to."

Nine days later she dispatched the first volume to Regnault, with a letter saying he could soon expect a second volume from Jules — described as "furiously blackening the paper." Meanwhile he was to take the manuscript to his "namesake" (Renault) and to extract another 125 francs, and if possible more, from the canny publisher. "Depict our impecuniousness in touching colors, describe the state of Jules's black frock coat, the rarity of his waistcoats, the decadence of my slippers and the decrepitude of my scarfs. Portray us as being in rags and tatters, tell him that Niort has opened a subscription to get Jules shaved and that La Châtre is putting on a charity drive to have me fed on public funds."

Letter and packaged manuscript went off on the morning of September 18. Later that same day Gustave Papet galloped over to Nohant with a secret message from Jules: he had quietly left Niort for a flying visit to Berry and was presently staying with Gustave a mile or two up the road at the Papet family's chateau. A clandestine meeting was arranged for that same evening. But due to some misunderstanding as regards the time, Aurore waited in vain for her lover to appear.

The next morning she rode over to the Château d'Ars to find out what was wrong. Persuaded that her little Jules had fallen ill — from the combined strain of overwork and the fatigue of his lightning trip — she berated him for having come all this way just to die of pleasure in her arms. And with that she rode away!

Charles Duvernet and Alphonse Fleury took over where Aurore had left off, saying that it was an act of folly to have made this flying visit, and seeing the state the poor fellow was in, they did their best at lunch to get him drunk.

Back at Nohant Aurore was overcome with remorse and sent word to Jules that she would expect him that afternoon at their secret meeting place. Once again he failed to appear. Climbing onto her horse, she galloped over to the Château d'Ars, where she found Jules preparing to leave without saying goodbye to her. There was another heated scene between them. He petulantly claimed that she wanted to be rid of him; she accused him of getting cold feet and not daring to come to see her. Stung to the quick, he told her to go to the devil and walked off in a huff.

That night, long after the two children in the next room had dropped off to sleep, Aurore was seated disconsolately in her little den, too nervously upset to be able to work or sleep, when there was a faint tap on her window. It was Jules. At the risk of waking the sleeping children, of arousing the fierce Pyrenean dog *Brave* (no respecter of trousers, as more than one visitor to Nohant had learned to his cost), and of being peppered with buckshot by an angry Casimir, Jules had come over with Gustave Papet (now quietly hiding in the roadside ditch) and had scaled the garden wall.

So here was her young Romeo, dying to clasp Juliet in his arms! Softly whispering between furious kisses, they tore and scratched, bit and hugged, moaned, gasped, and laughed into each other's ears. "It was a frenzy of joy such as I believe we have never experienced," Aurore wrote to Emile Regnault the following evening. "How can one scold people who are so reasonable and happy! In a few days you will have him to yourself and in two weeks the three of us will be back on the black bearskin couch, fighting and tearing each other's eyes out. I want him to come again tonight. Twice is not too much. After that it would be far too imprudent, for my husband is certain to learn that he's just three gunshots from Nohant. So far he doesn't know it. He's been harvesting the grapes. At night he sleeps like a hog.

"I'm a fool," she went on ecstatically, "I'm covered with tooth marks and bruises. I can hardly stand up. I'm in a frenzied state of joy. If you were here right now I would bite you till the blood came, just to have you share a bit of our frenzied happiness."

A week later Jules Sandeau returned to Paris, his black frockcoat in one piece and still unpeppered with grapeshot. Since their meetings had taken place at night, Aurore was shocked to see how thin, pale, and haggard he looked when at last she saw him in broad daylight just before he left for Châteauroux. Jules's mother, thinking to allay a fever and to improve his appetite, had given him an emetic before he left Niort, but this alone could not explain his peaked appearance.

"He's doing everything he can to kill himself," Aurore wrote anxiously to Emile Regnault, the future doctor. "He doesn't sleep. During the day he is as lazy and carefree as a dog, at night he goes without sleep in order to make up for lost time. . . . But I have other bones to pick with him. It's hard to explain. We'll talk about it, you and I, being both of us medics and not afraid to call a spade a spade . . .

"I was so happy to see him, I suffered such transports of delight in taking him into my arms!" she went on, hesitating to make a clean breast of what was troubling her. "But to know that this all-consuming love is slowly killing him, that this delirious happiness heats his blood and is wearing out his life, is just too dreadful for words! . . . Privations and absence irritate him and make him ill, my return makes him go wild and kills him. What is to be done? Treat him, give him drugs to calm him, make him sleep."

Regnault soon assured her that Jules was well and that there was nothing to worry about. But it was evident from his reply that he had not understood what was really troubling her. This she now undertook to make clear in a letter written on October 8, part of which was later clipped away, doubtless because the details it contained about their lovemaking were too intimate. The word "possession," followed by "How shall I force him to sleep? Shall I send him to sleep with you?" did survive the scissors, however. "These details are wretched," she went on. "I beg you to forgive me, but you don't know what a horrible anxiety, what a frightful remorse it is to see the being one would give one's life for dying in one's arms. To feel him growing thinner, wearing himself out, killing himself from day to day, and to realize . . . that your caresses are a poison, your love a fire which consumes and does not revive, leaving nothing but ashes, is just too dreadful. Jules refuses to understand it. He laughs it off. He scorns it like some childish terror, and when in the midst of his transports of delight, the idea grips and chills me, he answers that it's the death he envies and of which he'd like to die . . . For three months I let him die of suffering in my arms, I saw him a hundred times about to faint away as I resisted him. Finally I yielded for fear of killing him . . . Well, today I shudder at the idea that I've done him more harm by my devotion than by my resistance. I'm killing him, and the pleasure I give him is being purchased at the cost of his days."

It is easy to smile at these exaggerated apprehensions, which, as we shall see, were to cast the same mysterious shadow over George Sand's two most famous love affairs. Was Aurore really as erotically exhausting as she was here suggesting, or was she unconsciously casting herself in the role of the Romantic heroine, of La Belle Dame sans Merci, generously prepared to make an exception in this special case and to sacrifice her all too lethal desires to save her haggard, pale, and lovesick knight?

In mid-October Aurore rejoined Jules in Paris. Their joint industry — though it was more hers than his — had brought in close to 700 francs, allowing her to repay the sum she owed to Duris-Dufresne. This first debt paid, she and Jules found themselves penniless once more. Still wondering if she hadn't chosen the wrong vocation, she painted a portrait of her concierge, an affable woman who did her housekeeping and laundry. The portrait was hung up on a wall of the ground-floor café below. Unfortunately it was a poor likeness; the picture found no buyers and was soon prudently withdrawn from public view.

Aurore was bothered once again by a kind of latent fever which kept her in bed for some days with a burning pain in throat and chest. "I shall tell you nothing of Paris and its theaters," she wrote to her La Châtre friend Laure Decerfz, whose promised portrait (of herself) Aurore had been unable to frame for lack of funds. "My fever has not permitted me to run around except on Jules's legs . . . I'm waiting impatiently for my publisher to pay me, which will happen on the first of the month" — November — "and then I shall have to be very ill indeed not to go to listen to Madame Pasta before she leaves."

Not to be outdone by the new glitter and panache that Louis Véron had brought to the Paris Opera, the approaches to which were daily mobbed by music lovers battling to obtain seats to Meyerbeer's *Robert le Diable,* the manager of the Théâtre des Italiens had lured the celebrated Italian diva Giuditta Pasta back to Paris to succeed María Malibran in Rossini's *Tancredi.* As handsome and statuesque in features as María Malibran was small and almost ugly, "La Pasta," as she was known, was a classically pure and unruffled mezzo-soprano. The joint presence of these two great singers at the Théâtre des Italiens made this autumn of 1831 one of the most memorable in the musical history of Paris.

Inevitably it affected Aurore's and Jules Sandeau's new brain child. Their novel, already stuffed with autobiographical references (with echoes of Aurore's convent life, Bordeaux, the Pyrenees), was now embellished with elements of an almost journalistic topicality. Thus Rose, the convent girl who decides to become a diva, was given certain of María Malibran's features. She was also portrayed as being aroused to the sublime beauties of operatic music on hearing La Pasta sing in *Tancredi.*

"Blanche [the nun] and Rose are two stupid creatures, the most disgusting and boring composition I know of," Aurore wrote to Charles Duvernet in mid-November. "Thank God I shall soon be rid of them." The four volumes had by now spilled over into five, but toward the end Aurore and Jules had delayed bringing new chapters to the printers, insisting on first being paid by their niggardly publisher.

Casimir was also in Paris when the novel was finally published in mid-December. But fortunately for Aurore, who had been planning, if necessary, to hie herself to Nohant to avoid an embarrassing relapse into "conjugal intimacy," he chose to stay with Hippolyte and to leave her in peace. Casimir may not even have known that Aurore had helped give birth to a novel, for she was in no mood to boast of her achievement and had long since reassured her husband, as she had her worried mother-in-law, that the name of Dudevant would never cause a public scandal by appearing on the "cover of a printed book." The novel, renamed *Rose et Blanche* — or *The Actress and the Nun,* as it was subtitled — appeared over the signature of J. Sand — the abbreviated form of Sandeau which Latouche had suggested they adopt as their joint nom de plume.

"Far from having indulged in politics, I've written a wretched novel of no consequence which I haven't signed," Aurore wrote almost shamefacedly to her friend Charles Meure. The book, she explained to her mother, contained "many farces which I disapprove of and which I only tolerated to satisfy my publisher, who wanted it to be spicy." As Latouche had forthrightly commented, in an unsigned *Figaro* article: "The style has been marred by a singular demand on the part of the publisher . . . The mercantile publisher came ten times to the poor novelist's quarters to repeat: 'Monsieur, do not go in for the lofty genre. Try to rise to the level of low comedy, endeavor to write as poorly as possible.' "

Advice like this was enough to kill one's taste for writing. But for Latouche, who insisted that writing, not painting, was her predestined vocation, Aurore might have given up in disgust. Instead, she decided to redeem herself by writing another novel. But this time she would write it on her own and find some less "mercantile" scoundrel to publish it.

13. *Indiana*

DURING THESE crucial winter months, which saw her hesitantly launched on her literary career, Aurore's health was once again a source of serious concern to herself and her friends. In mid-November she came down with a severe attack of ptomaine poisoning, and two days later she suffered an apoplectic fit. "For two hours I was as cold as death, my teeth locked, and unconscious," as she wrote to Boucoiran. Emile Regnault, who though still only a medical student had become her personal physician, had to bleed her. For some days thereafter she suffered terrible headaches, breaking into clammy sweats followed by chills that made her teeth chatter. She had trouble breathing, and each time she began gasping for breath in a kind of asthmatic fit, Regnault, who now spent his nights on the couch so as to be near her in case of need, would whip out his lancet and bleed her again — with seemingly beneficial effect.

At Christmas she succumbed to a severe attack of lumbago, which confirmed her romantic conviction that she had not much longer for this world. She had hoped to spend New Year's with her children, but it was not until mid-January of 1832 that she was well enough to make the trip back to Nohant, where she found her eight-year-old Maurice grown suddenly less childish and more serious (under Boucoiran's tutorship), while the three-and-a-half-year-old Solange was as plump, bouncing, and rosy-cheeked as ever.

The onset of her monthly period made Aurore feel sick and feverish once more, and in the belief that it would help, she had herself bled in both arms. But the remedy this time seems to have done more harm than good, for a couple of days later she wrote a pathetic letter to Emile Regnault, asking him to preserve her, if possible, for several more years: "Here I can try all manner of remedies without Jules knowing about it and taking fright. Should I have myself bled every week? Should I try some more violent and active remedy? I've been taking etherized tincture of digitalis as you told me to. I put a small spoonful in a glass of water and I drink some night and day. Is this what I should do? I'm quite ready to try anything. When I let myself be ravaged by weariness and grief, I didn't care for life, but now that I'm happy, now that I'm loved, I would like not to be done for so soon . . ."

Though both Casimir and Hippolyte were persuaded that Aurore was a *malade imaginaire,* there is no reason to doubt the sincerity of this letter written to her favorite "doctor." Her troubles, once again, were probably of psychosomatic origin, though almost certainly aggravated by medicines which, in trying to cure her erratic heartbeat, had violently upset the stomach. Her mother was not the only one who had been dismayed by the occasional bawdy touches in *Rose et Blanche;* even Emile Regnault had found the novel's crude humor too contrived. Save for the characterization of Sister Olympe, the nun with a heart of gold who swears like a trooper, the ribald ornaments were the product of Jules Sandeau's adolescent wit.

Aurore's constant headaches, stomach pains, and nausea grew so unbearable that she finally called in the local doctor. Finding her pulse too weak, he wisely refused to bleed her and told her to stop the watery doses of digitalis that were burning up her insides and irritating her larynx. She resumed her milk diet, drank red currant water and sparkling Eau de Seltz. Her colic disappeared, her appetite came back, and within a week she was eating three hearty meals and sleeping eight hours a day.

Her fears of a premature demise thus dispelled, she sat down to the writing of her second novel. This one, to which she eventually gave the title of *Indiana,* was even more autobiographical than *Rose et Blanche.* The heroine, first named Noémi and then Indiana (the name of Aurélien de Sèze's sister), was depicted as unhappily married to a man far older than herself — a retired army officer named Colonel Delmare, whose sparse gray hair and mustache may faintly have recalled old Colonel Dudevant but whose gruff and querulous disposition was even more reminiscent of his son, Casimir.

Indiana, like Aurore in the second year of her marriage, is a tender nineteen, has dark hair, a soft, faintly husky voice, and eyes reddened from weeping. She and Colonel Delmare live in a "little manor house in the Brie" (shades of the Roëttiers house at Le Plessis-Picard!) with a cousin of Indiana's named Ralph (the name of Jules Sandeau's dog), a well-meaning but rather dull Englishman who, like Hippolyte, is on good terms with the hunt-loving husband. Indeed, the opening pages, describing the boredom of a rainy autumn evening, with nothing but the faint tick of the mantelpiece clock, the hiss and shudder of burning logs, the faint moan of the wind beneath the door, and the patter of raindrops against the windowpanes to break the silence, could almost have been a word-for-word description of one of those gloomy evenings Aurore had to spend alone with her husband at Nohant.

In the novel, the wordless monotony of this particular evening is disturbed by the news that robbers have been stealing coal on the property. The master of the house catches one of these poachers in the act of climbing over the garden wall and peppers him with grapeshot — exactly what Aurore had feared Casimir might do to Jules during the mad escapade of the previous September. His right hand wounded, the "brigand" loses his grip and is knocked unconscious by a twenty-foot fall. He is brought in under the front porch, where his neatly tailored hunting jacket and "noble features," carefully examined under the lamplight, make it clear that this is no common coal robber but a gentleman who has been indulging in some curious nocturnal trespassing. He is carried into the billiard room, his wounded hand is bandaged by Indiana, who, like Aurore Dudevant, knows something of first aid, and bled by Sir Ralph who, like Deschartres, is skilled in surgery.

The handsome interloper turns out to be a young nobleman named Raymon de Ramière. The real purpose of his wall-climbing incursions is likewise revealed to be Indiana's beautiful, black-eyed Creole maid, Noun, whom the bold young trespasser has been meeting for clandestine trysts in the property's greenhouse.

This too was not a particularly original situation. Half a century before, Beaumarchais had scandalized the Court of Versailles by depicting a nobleman's illicit amours with a lowly soubrette, and Mozart had shocked the staid Habsburgs in Vienna by putting Count Almaviva's exploits to delightfully gay music in *The Marriage of Figaro*. But what in the frivolous eighteenth century had been a subject for gay comedy now became a subject for nineteenth-century tragedy.

Stendhal, in *Le Rouge et le Noir* (published a year before she began working on *Indiana*), had portrayed the fatal love of a nobly born lady for a humble tutor. Reversing the roles, Aurore now portrayed a nobly born gentleman's cynical love affair with a lowly maid. In each case the passion felt by the feminine partner is largely unrequited. But whereas having Mathilde de la Mole for a mistress is for Julien Sorel a source of manly pride, the conquest and possession of the lowly Noun soon becomes, for Raymon de Ramière, a source of shame — as the author of *Indiana* took pains to point out in a bluntly worded passage which created a sensation when the book was published:

"Noun used to recall this day" — when Raymon had first met and seduced her — "with tenderness. She did not realize, poor child, that Raymon's love was not that old, and that what had been a day of pride for her was for him no more than a day of vanity. And then this courage which should have made her more loved displeased Mr. de Ramière. The wife of a French peer who would immolate herself in this way would have been a precious conquest, but a serving maid! What is heroism in the one becomes effrontery in the other. With one, a host of jealous rivals envies you; with the other, a host of scandalized lackeys condemns you. The lady of quality sacrifices twenty lovers she once possessed; the housemaid only sacrifices a husband she might have had."

The social impossibility of this love affair thus explicitly stated, it only remained to develop the imbroglio to its tragic conclusion. Here too Aurore needed little effort of imagination to have fiction improve on fact. Her own father had seduced a local damsel named Anne-Marie Chatiron, and the result had been her half brother, Hippolyte. Aurélien de Sèze, while sowing his wild oats, had likewise fathered an illegitimate child. Aurore's own husband, Casimir, had just repeated the exploit with Claire, a maid originally hired by Hippolyte's wife to take care of their daughter, Léontine. In this case though, the question of fatherhood was less clear-cut; for the pregnant maid was not prepared to say just who had placed her in this "state of paternity," as Aurore called it. The possible fathers included not only Casimir and Hippolyte, but Alexis Duteil, Jules Ajasson de Grandsagne, Charles Duvernet (all of whom seem to have had a go at her), and even — so rumor had it, but the idea made Aurore laugh till the tears came into her eyes — the simple Jules Boucoiran, who provided a convenient scapegoat for others more enterprising than himself.

In *Indiana* Noun, the Creole maid, made pregnant by her noble lover, is shattered by the realization that her seducer no longer loves her. The final blow is the discovery that Raymon has fallen in love with her mistress, Indiana. In despair, Noun drowns herself in the nearby river. It is now Indiana's turn to succumb to a fateful passion for this young Lovelace, whose interest in Indiana wanes once he realizes that he has a firm hold on her heart.

It would be an exaggeration to say that what follows in the novel was a literal transposition of what had happened between Aurore and Aurélien de Sèze. But the passionate sentiments attributed to Indiana are unquestionably those the author had felt for Aurélien, just as Indiana's growing antipathy for her husband was what Aurore felt for Casimir. At one point Indiana is described by four adjectives — "passionate and chaste, amorous and reserved" — which Aurore had long applied in imagination to herself. "Resist me, now, sweet and confident Indiana!" Raymon de Ramière is portrayed as thinking, in language astonishingly reminiscent of Aurélien's. "She had never seemed anxious to avoid him, and though he was in no haste to triumph in a love whose naive chastity had for him the attraction of singularity, he began to feel that it was a question of honor for him to lead it to such a result. He uprightly repulsed all malicious insinuations about his relations with Madame Delmare, modestly asserting that all that existed between them was a sweet and calm friendship. But for nothing in the world would he have wished to admit, even to his closest friend, that he had been passionately loved for six months without yet obtaining anything from this love."

No less autobiographical in origin was the author's scathing description of Indiana's husband, Colonel Delmare, portrayed not simply as an individual but as a social type: "Do you know what in the provinces is known as an *honest man?* It is he who does not trespass on his neighbor's fields, who does not exact a penny more than what his debtors owe him, who takes his hat off to all who salute him; it is he who does not rape girls in public places, who does not set fire to other people's barns, who does not waylay passers-by in a corner of his woods. Provided he scrupulously respects the life and purse of his fellow citizens, he is not called to account for anything else. He can beat his wife, mistreat his servants, ruin his children, they are nobody else's business. Society only condemns acts that are harmful to it; private life lies beyond its purview."

Colonel Delmare being, like Casimir, a former Napoleonic officer, Aurore went on to depict the failings of this kind of individual in the same unflattering terms: "He treated all delicacies of the heart as feminine puerilities and sentimental subtleties. A man devoid of wit, tact, and education, he enjoyed a greater measure of consideration than one obtains through talents or kindness . . . As he was not given to joking, he was ceaselessly preoccupied by the idea that people were making fun of him. Incapable of responding in a proper manner, he had only one way of defending himself: by imposing silence through threats . . . His was thus the most antipathetic nature, the heart least made to comprehend, the mind the least capable of understanding his wife."

The story of Indiana thus became Aurore's own: the story of an unhappy wife seeking to flee from the crippling bonds of marriage, specifically described as a form of slavery, as "the chain beneath which my life has been shattered and my youth spoiled." For like most husbands, Colonel Delmare is persuaded that "women are made to obey and not to advise." Called upon to tell him where she has spent the early morning, if not the entire night (after a visit to Raymon de Ramière's Paris house), Indiana proudly refuses to answer — just as Aurore had doubtless refused to answer embarrassing questions concerning Aurélien de Sèze or Stéphane Ajasson de Grandsagne.

"If I refuse to reply, it's absolutely for the form," the heroine declares. "I want to convince you that you have no right to address such a question to me."

"I don't have the right to, counfound it!" cries the flabbergasted colonel. "Who then is the master here, you or I? Who is it who wears a skirt and must wield the distaff? Do you propose to take the beard from my chin? That would be just like you, little woman!"

"I know I am the slave and you the lord" is Indiana's ringing answer. "The law of this country has made you my master. You can shackle my body, tie my hands, govern my actions. You have the right of the stronger, and society confirms it; but over my will, sir, you can do nothing. God alone can bend and break it."

And when the infuriated husband bellows: "Shut up, you foolish and impertinent creature! Your literary phrases bore us!" his wife defiantly answers: "You can impose silence upon me, but you cannot keep me from thinking . . . ," adding a moment later, after her cousin Ralph has intervened to keep her from being brutalized by her husband: "I have spent several hours outside your domination. I went to breathe the air of freedom, to show you that you are not morally my master and that upon nobody on earth do I depend but myself."

This was no longer just literature, it was virtually a manifesto. It was the passionate protest of an unemancipated woman, of a suffering wife who wanted to live and love as she pleased, regardless of society's hypocritical conventions. The force of the protest was magnified by being aimed with equal vigor at Indiana's disappointing lover, here made the prototype of masculine hard-heartedness and callous self-interest. His god, she writes to him in an impassioned letter, "is the god of men, he is the king, the founder and support of your race. Mine is the God of the universe, the creator, the mainstay and hope of all creatures. Yours has done everything for yourselves alone; mine has made all species for each other. You think yourselves the masters of the world; I think you are only its tyrants."

Not surprisingly, the protest goes unheeded, just as Indiana's efforts to overcome society's crippling constraints are ultimately unsuccessful. Indiana never becomes Raymon de Ramière's mistress, and in the first (and more dramatic) version of the novel she and her cousin Ralph end up throwing themselves over a cliff on a distant Pacific island. But the melancholy conclusion did not in any way detract from the universal and forceful scope of the message. Nor was Aurore unduly blowing her own horn in explaining to Emile Regnault, when she was halfway through the novel, that her unfortunate heroine was a "typical woman, weak as well as strong, at once weary of the air she breathes and capable of shouldering the heavens, timid in everyday life yet bold in days of battle . . . Such, I believe, is woman in general, an incredible mixture of weakness and energy, greatness and pettiness, a being forever composed of two opposed natures, now sublime, now wretched, skilled in deceiving, yet easily deceived."

Her novel finished, Aurore returned to Paris in early April, accompanied this time by Solange, who was eager to meet the "fiancé" (Emile Regnault) to whom she had been jokingly betrothed. The moment could not have been worse chosen. A few days later the cholera morbus Aurore and her Berrichon friends had so often joked about ceased to be a euphemism for diarrhea and became a grim reality. "All the drunks in Paris have been carried off like flies," Aurore wrote in a letter to her husband, in which she begged Casimir to avoid "all excess of drink." The epidemic claimed many sober victims as well, several of them in the very house in which she, Solange, and Jules Sandeau were living. For two frightening days, during which Sandeau almost went out of his mind and Emile Regnault slept on a mattress on the floor, it looked as though Aurore herself was stricken. But by drinking quantities of hot tea and keeping herself bundled up in blankets, she managed to shake off her fever. None of her Berrichon friends contracted cholera, but so nervous were they all that for several weeks they arranged to meet daily in the Luxembourg Gardens to make sure that no one was missing.

The proximity of the morgue, a neo-Greek edifice situated almost directly opposite on the Ile de la Cité, added a poignant note. Even worse than the sight of corpses stacked like cordwood on furniture-moving carts, which kept rolling back and forth across the Saint-Michel bridge, was, as George Sand later recalled, "the absence of parents and friends behind these funeral chariots." Swearing and impatiently cracking their whips, the coachmen would urge on their horses, while the pedestrians shrank back in horror and simple-minded workmen shook their fists at the sky, naively persuaded that this cholera plague was a form of mass poisoning, which their diabolical employers had deliberately plotted to thin their restive ranks.

From the fifth-floor balcony, which Aurore had turned into a tiny garden — with pots of geraniums, roses, jasmine, lilac, stock, and even a small orange tree — the plump, chubby-cheeked Solange looked down on the ceaseless bustle of the *quais,* commenting with guileless equanimity on the students and ragpickers, the petticoated ladies and *grisettes,* the organ grinders, hackney cabs, omnibuses, and hearses she could see passing beneath.

Aurore, meanwhile, had been asked to write a preface to her novel. Her first publisher, Renault, having gone bankrupt without paying the two authors of *Rose et Blanche* their due, Aurore had found another in the person of Henri Dupuy, a well-meaning fellow who seems to have feared that *Indiana* might be taken by some readers for a subversive and "dangerous" book. Heaven forbid that the reader should be left with this impression, she declared in the "philosophical and moral preface" which (as she wrote to Laure Decerfz at La Châtre) it had cost her "blood and sweat" to compose and which suited the novel about as well as "lace cuffs on a cow."

Formally announced by the printer on May 2, *Indiana* went on sale around the fifteenth of the month. A few days later Aurore wrote to Charles Duvernet to say that she hadn't had time to add a note to the copy she had sent him. "I was too busy with the binder, the glazer, the printer, the publisher, the compositor, the proof corrector, and the journalists to enjoy an instant of leisure and well-being. I am at last finished with all these chores and I have been paid my modest salary, without worrying about my glory or my shame, my success or downfall. All I desire is to go unnoticed amid this flood of bad or mediocre new books which have been spewing forth in battalion strength and spreading devastation, boredom, and disgust in the souls of honest readers. For me, as you know, the writer's trade means an annual income of three thousand francs, enough to cover basic expenses and to buy sugared almonds for Solange and *good tobacco* for my confounded nose."

Duvernet's cousin Latouche had meanwhile resigned his editorship of the *Figaro,* and deeply chagrined by the failure of his new play, *La Reine d'Espagne* (which Victor Hugo and his followers had mercilessly booed off the stage), he had retired to his tiny cottage at Aulnay, south of Paris. Aurore, who loved this little rustic retreat amid its flowering apple trees, woods, and meadows, had taken Solange out on the stagecoach several times to visit the misanthropic recluse to whom she owed so much. But when he heard that she was actually going ahead and publishing *Indiana* without prior consultation, he came storming into Paris and climbed the five flights to her and Jules Sandeau's flat to call her every name in the book — a dolt, a dunderhead, an old fogy, a goose, a booby, a dimwit, etc. For given time and his expert advice, she could have written an admirable book that would have done her credit.

"And meanwhile (*says I*) on what shall I live?" Aurore reported the subsequent exchange to Charles Duvernet. "Live off grass (*says he*). That's all right with me (*says I*), but it's a bit dry and Solange's teeth are not as long as mine when it comes to grazing . . . The upshot being that I still don't know what he thinks of *Indiana,* since he still hasn't read it. Janin" — another well-known critic who had also worked for the *Figaro* — "says it's admirable and doesn't bother to read it. Balzac claims it's sublime and will never read it. So do the same, my friend, and let's hear no more about it."

Aurore was doing all of them an injustice. Latouche's first reaction, to be sure, was negative. He had surprised her on the balcony about to autograph the first printed copy of *Indiana* to him. Intrigued, he had taken it out of her hands and begun reading it, exclaiming as he flicked the pages: "But this is a pastiche — school of Balzac! . . . A pastiche, I tell you! Balzac, do you hear, Balzac!"

But that same night (while Aurore was penning her plaintive letter to Duvernet) her cranky mentor returned to his Paris apartment and actually read the novel. The next morning she received the following note from him: "I didn't want to leave for the country without coming back to make honorable amends at your feet, Aurore.

"Forget the foolish things I said to you yesterday about the beginning of your book. Your book is a masterpiece. I spent the night reading it and I feel all the pride of friendship . . . The simplicity, the brilliance and the firmness of the style place you, at one leap, at the head of contemporary writers. No woman alive can subject you to the insolence of a comparison . . . Balzac and Mérimée are crushed and buried beneath *Indiana*. Ah, my child, how happy I am! H. de Latouche."

Balzac's reaction was somewhat different, but in its own way no less flattering. The novelist had become a good friend of both Aurore's and Jules Sandeau's, and they had been amused to see him use the money earned by his *La Peau de Chagrin* to transform his low-ceilinged apartment on the Rue Cassini into an "assemblage of marquises' boudoirs" — as George Sand later described it — with walls dripping in a feminine exuberance of silk and lace. Once, after entertaining them to a dinner of boiled beef, melons, and champagne (his standard fare), he had insisted on accompanying them home as far as the Luxembourg Gardens, arrayed in a lovely new dressing gown and with a handsome brass candlestick to light the way, explaining as they went that no robber would dream of attacking him — taking him either for a dangerous madman or a prince whom it would be wiser to respect. He had made a number of visits to their Quai Saint-Michel flat, pushing his robust paunch up the five flights of stairs and arriving all puffing and blowing — which did not for a moment keep him from laughing and talking nonstop. He would pick up any sheets of paper Aurore or Jules had left lying on the table, glance at them for a moment, and then would start describing the new book or stories he was planning or actually engaged in writing.

Not long before the publication of *Indiana,* he had brought up a copy of his Rabelaisian short stories — *Les Contes Drolatiques* — and insisted on reading extracts to Aurore. Shocked by their salacious gusto, she had exclaimed that they were the work of an "indecent" mind. Balzac had called her a prude, adding from the landing as he left: "You're a ninny!" But this momentary blowup had not affected their friendship.

"I was delighted by your preface," Balzac now wrote to acknowledge his receipt of *Indiana.* "It is very well written and full of sense, but as I had to work, I wanted to hold out against my pleasure, and to judge by the samples I have read, I considered it very dangerous for my imagination. It has given me great joy to see my friend G. Sand launched, and I shall give him my opinion about the book *once read,* something I can only do now with very few books."

Aurore thus found herself saddled with a nom de plume that was not entirely of her own choosing. "You may be surprised to find a G. instead of a J. placed next to Sand on the cover of my book," she wrote to Charles Duvernet. "If you want to know the cause, here it is. *George Sand* is me, *Jules Sand* is my brother. We are beginning, in spite of ourselves, to know quite a few people in the world of the arts. Jules, who finds my productions charming, doesn't wish to flaunt them as his own. I, who find my productions stupid, don't wish to dishonor him with them."

She was being a bit coy. In sober fact, her new publisher had wanted her to retain the old name of Sand, which *Rose et Blanche* and several short stories had at least made known, rather than risk launching her under an entirely new pseudonym. Latouche, whose Solomonian judgment had led to the initial amputation of the name Sandeau, then suggested that Aurore find herself a different Christian name for *Indiana*. She chose Georges (at first spelled with an *s*), apparently feeling that this name — derived from the Greek *georgos* (or husbandman) — was suitably close to the land for a provincial writer from Berry.

To her embarrassed surprise, Aurore found herself famous overnight. The sedate *Journal des Débats* described the novel as a "warm-hearted story and full of interest, which is marked by all the defects and virtues of the modern age." "This is the story of modern passion, the true story of a woman's heart, which alone has kept its primitive passions, while man has lost his," proclaimed the *Figaro* a couple of days later. "You have never seen a more painstaking analysis, a more exquisite dissection, a deeper anatomy of the human heart," the author's friend Félix Pyat exulted in *L'Artiste*, adding that her characters could stand comparison with Stendhal's. Not to be outdone, the noted critic Henri Boussuge compared Raymon de Ramière to Stendhal's Julien Sorel, adding that *Indiana* displayed an "immense superiority of style" over *Le Rouge et le Noir*.

The chorus of praise seems to have dismayed the startled author almost as much as the murderous gunfire which broke out near the Porte Saint-Martin and rapidly spread to the Ile de la Cité a couple of weeks after the book's appearance. Once again the barricades went up as huge crowds flooded down the streets singing the *Mar-*

seillaise and shouting *"Vive la République!"* Aurore, who was walking Solange in the Luxembourg Gardens when the turmoil started, had some trouble hurrying the terrified little girl home through streets thronged with panic-stricken pedestrians running in all directions. They made it safely back to their flat, where Solange would run to clasp her mother's knees each time the cannon rumbled and shots rang out below. Jules helped Aurore lift a mattress from the bed and block off the window of Solange's little room to protect her from stray bullets, and the child actually managed to sleep through the shouts and shooting. But Aurore spent a good part of the night on the balcony, listening with anguished horror to the piercing cries and dying groans of republican insurgents, as they were hacked to pieces by saber-swinging soldiers of the National Guard and their bodies tossed into the Seine.

The next morning the firing squads went to work, and the morgue was once again choked with corpses, whose "superposed heads were piled up behind the windows like mountains of hideous masonry," as George Sand later wrote. But the spectacle this time was even grimmer than it had been during the cholera epidemic, for a stream of blood now oozed from the building and down the embankment, mingling its redness with the muddy waters of the Seine. The stench of rotting bodies was so frightful that it was two weeks before Aurore could again touch red meat.

"To see the blood flow is a horrible thing," Aurore wrote to her La Châtre friend Laure Decerfz one week later, ". . . to see the straw lightly sprinkled on a lumbering cart pushed back to reveal twenty or thirty corpses, some in black suits, others in velvet waistcoats, but all torn, mutilated, blackened by powder, mud-splattered and bloodied; to hear the cry of wives who recognize their husbands or their children, is horrible. Yet even that is perhaps less awful than to see a poor fugitive being done to death beneath one's window, notwithstanding his pleas for mercy, and to hear the death rattle of the wounded man whom no one is allowed to succor and who is condemned by thirty bayonets.

"As you can imagine," she went on, "in the midst of these tragedies the arts are forgotten, lost, annihilated. If I were selfish, I would ardently wish for the maintenance of absolute powers, for there is much sad, rough truth in the paradox that the more *arbitrary is the law,* the more *individuals are free.* . . . If we had ten years of political calm, literature would doubtless enter a flourishing age, for after the reaction of the false against the true" — by which she meant the Romantic extravagances of the previous decade — "there would follow that of the true against the false, that which every reader craves for, which every writer dreams about and craves, but which cannot flourish in a century of furious clamor and on an earth full of hospitals. If I had written to you prior to June 6th, I would have spoken to you joyfully about the *success* of *Indiana* . . . this honest, completely literary success I did not solicit . . . But *June 6th has killed Indiana* for a month and has thrown me so brutally into real life that I presently seem incapable of *ever dreaming about novels.*"

Her pessimism, as it happened, was unjustified. The bloody riots of early June, which had come so close to upsetting Louis-Philippe's regime, were quickly forgotten, at any rate in the world of letters. For the nonce she found herself being mobbed, as novelists, journalists, salon wits, and "dispensers of glory" clambered up and down the five flights of stairs to her flat, eager to offer a new contract or, as often as not, to beg one more copy off the author.

The visits grew so intensive that her staircase became a "kind of Jacob's ladder of literature." One of her visitors requested six copies of *Indiana* — to be sent to Saint Petersburg, of all places — and seemed incensed when she asked him for sixty francs to pay for them. Another wanted a free copy for a library he was starting in a lunatic asylum. "Monsieur," answered the author, who had lost none of her aplomb, "I may need you one day. I have nothing to refuse you. Here is *Indiana.*"

The noted critic Jules Janin, who had described her in an article as being "young and beautiful," also climbed the five flights of stairs to pay his respectful homage. But on meeting her he asked Aurore who she was, being so shortsighted that he was incapable of telling a Negress from a Laplander. On seeing him appear, Solange, who had begun to tire of all these solicitous interlopers, greeted him with more than customary insolence: "Ah, it's you, you old rogue? You're a big fat pig."

"That child has a holy horror of literature," her mother explained in a letter to Laure Decerfz, which it took her three days to complete so frequent were the interruptions. The same Jules Janin, she claimed, had been rash enough to term *Indiana* "the most beautiful social novel of the age." The next day, so it was said, Victor Hugo had turned up at Janin's apartment, his face flushed with rage. "What, you scoundrel!" he cried, "You claim that *Indiana* is the best of all books! And mine? Do you take *Notre-Dame de Paris* for a whore?"

The wildest rumors were circulating, and this was doubtless one of them. According to another, the Saint-Simonians, advocates of a managerial revolution that was to remold society in a new industrial image and to usher in a regime of "free love" between absolutely equal sexes, were preparing to make the author of *Indiana* their "Popess." Aurore could smile at these reports and carry on as usual. But now, whether she liked it or not, she was a recognized celebrity. One week later, when the Opéra's 1750 seats were sold out for the resumption of Meyerbeer's *Robert le Diable,* she found herself included with the most famous names in the world of the arts — next to actresses like Mademoiselle Mars, Madame Dorval, Mademoiselle George, singers like María Malibran, composers like Hector Berlioz, critics, writers, and poets like Sainte-Beuve, Théophile Gautier, Gérard de Nerval, and Alfred de Musset. It was now too late to turn back and try to hide behind another name. Willy-nilly, she was stuck with her nom de plume. *"In Paris Madame Dudevant is dead,"* she wrote to a friend in La Châtre. *"But Georges Sand is known as a sprightly young fellow."*

14. Disenchantment and Despair

THE FIRST LETTER she signed with her new nom de plume of Georges Sand was addressed in early July of 1832 to her publisher, Henri Dupuy, and it was with the same publisher that several weeks later Aurore negotiated a contract for a new novel, to be called *Valentine*. The terms were not exactly generous: there was no advance, a down payment of 500 francs being due to her once the first volume was printed (tentatively fixed for late October), and the remaining 1900 francs to be paid her when the two volumes went on sale in December. But Aurore, who had spent several harassing weeks hunting for a new apartment, did not wish to antagonize her publisher at this moment. Jules Sandeau had stopped working for the *Figaro,* now edited by a Marseillais named Nestor Roqueplan, and what was more serious, he was soon due to be called up for military service. The only way he could avoid this was to hire a replacement from an agency specializing in this kind of operation. The cost was a little over 300 francs a quarter — a sum too big for Jules's meager finances. Dupuy accordingly agreed to pay the four quarterly installments in exchange for a guarantee (written into the contract) that the author of *Valentine* would reimburse him.

Two days later Aurore left Paris with Solange, while Jules Sandeau went to join his parents at Parthenay, some 120 miles to the west of La Châtre. At Nohant, which was stewing in a heat wave, she found the wells dry, the livestock dying of thirst, the flowers parched and wilted, but Maurice grown noticeably taller and handsomer, with a new row of pearly white teeth. Casimir was away at Châteauroux, acting as temporary judge at the court of assize, but

Hippolyte more than made up for his absence — "singing, laughing, smoking and drinking all day," as Aurore wrote to her mother.

Her own "holidays" were spent in a fever of industry. Having promised to deliver the first part of her new novel to the publisher by early October, she had not a minute to lose. She spent the better part of each day locked up in her den before going to bed at an early hour. "I've grown so used to it," she wrote to Emile Regnault toward the middle of August, "that I write with as much ease as if I were stitching a hem." She was working "like a horse," she wrote one week later to François Rollinat, the son of a prominent Châteauroux lawyer whose acquaintance she had recently made, adding: "My soul has gone to press and my faculties are in the hands of the typesetter. Infamous trade! Each day I devote to it, I'm left with nothing in the evening, that many more days which I cannot live for myself. But perhaps there's some good in that after all, for left to myself I would live too much!"

She did, however, find time to write daily letters to Jules, letters that were meant to stimulate his literary energies. But the pampered draft dodger found the home atmosphere of Parthenay anything but a spur to his imagination. Being more in love with her than she was with him, Sandeau spent an inordinate amount of time in his parents' garden, smoking cigars, stroking his dog, Ralph, dreaming of the happy days he had spent with his "poor Aurore" and the "poor child" (Solange) he had so much enjoyed bouncing on his knee in Paris. Yielding to the sensuous charm of so many breathless reminiscences, whose tooth marks still made him thrill from head to toe, he let the voluptuous past blot out the irksome present, conveniently forgetting that his loved one was working with grim intensity to honor debts she had generously underwritten for him.

At Nohant his "poor Aurore" was not even granted a mid-August respite after another heated row with Casimir, who refused to allow her to drive off on a four-day pleasure trip to the Château de Valençay (which Talleyrand had made his princely residence) with two young escorts, Gustave Papet and François Rollinat, whom the tireless gossips of La Châtre were bound to proclaim her lovers. Working against the clock, she finished a long short story, *La Mar-*

quise, in two weeks of drudgery, sold it to *La Revue de Paris,* and used the proceeds to reimburse Dupuy for the first quarterly installment due for Sandeau's military replacement. Though a distinguished piece of writing — from the purely stylistic point of view it was probably superior to *Indiana* — there was something romantically far-fetched in this curious tale about an eighteenth-century marquise's socially "impossible" passion for a lowly actor named Lélio.

The same theme — a socially impossible passion — was dealt with more ambitiously and plausibly in *Valentine.* Due to inherit a considerable fortune (like the young Aurore Dupin), Valentine de Raimbault has been betrothed to a diplomat she does not really like. Of an artistic temperament, she dreams of becoming a painter, for though musically gifted, she is instinctively too modest to wish to shine at salon concerts or on the opera stage, and too proud to become a humble music teacher. At a country fete, Valentine is invited to dance the bourrée by a young man named Bénédict, the nephew of a tenant farmer who, though of lowly origin, is exceptionally learned (like Stéphane Ajasson de Grandsagne), has the soul of a poet and a heavenly voice.

Music plays a major role in this novel, just as it did in *Rose et Blanche* and *La Prima Donna.* It brings the nobly born Valentine and the plebeian Bénédict together in a piano duet, and later, after Bénédict (like Goethe's Werther) has tried to shoot himself in despair at Valentine's marriage to another, its soothing charm is used to nurse the wounded man back to life. Being for "passionate souls the source of all poetry, the language of every strong passion," as Georges Sand specifically asserted, it is likewise music that inflames a fateful passion and embellishes the lovers' evening meetings in a garden pavilion (again curiously reminiscent of the one at Nohant). But theirs is destined to be a tragic, Romeo-and-Juliet kind of passion, not because they belong to two hostile families, but because they belong to two different aristocracies: hers being the aristocracy of birth, his the aristocracy of the spirit.

While in her imagination Aurore was thus transforming herself, the heiress of Nohant, into the nobly born Valentine, and the humbly-born Jules Sandeau into the musically gifted Bénédict, the remorseless current of real life was already carrying them in different directions. At the beginning of their association, it had probably not occurred to either Aurore or Jules to compare their literary talents. He was sensitive and shy, full of suppressed fire and enthusiasm, he was not lacking in imagination, and he could write in a lively style, even if his wit at times was a trifle heavy-handed. Besides, he was more than six years her junior, which meant that his talent had plenty of time to mature. If *Rose et Blanche* in the end owed more to her than to him, it really wasn't that important, for in any case it wasn't much to boast about. But *Indiana* was another matter. It was Aurore's work from start to finish. The novel, though not written in this intent, constituted a stimulus, if not a challenge. Now that the feminine member of their partnership had shown what she was capable of, it was up to the "other half" to prove himself, if only by his industry. But though he had assured Aurore, on parting, that he was going to "work like a dog" in his summer retreat at Parthenay, it was obvious by mid-September that little had come of this resolve.

In early August Aurore wrote to Latouche to ask if she might not rent his Quai Malaquais apartment now that he had retired to his ivy-covered cottage in the country. She had long since decided to give up the Quai Saint-Michel flat — the five flights of stairs were too exhausting and the northern exposure too sunless for the chill winter months. His reply reached her almost one month later, on the sixth of September: "You will have my apartment, and I love you with all my soul. It has taken me 3 weeks to overcome my abhorrence of paper . . . to the point of writing you this long letter. I have discovered a new illness, and I have it: it's *cartophobia.* H. de L."

In the hypochondriac editor and plagiarist, such a malady could be forgiven more readily than in a young and supposedly aspiring author of twenty-one. "I complain of Latouche to Jules and I scold Jules for wanting to resemble Latouche," Aurore wrote to their mutual friend Emile Regnault in mid-September. "But I have an excuse for this malady" — epistolary silence — "which neither of them have, which is to work like an ox and to find myself worn out with boredom in the evening."

Of the acrimonious correspondence that followed — between herself and Jules — only a six-line fragment has survived. "I kiss you most tenderly, I wish you more pleasure and as much satisfaction as for me. I ask you to love me a bit and for good reason. You can be sure of always finding me sincere and constant in my feelings for you. Your friend Aurore."

From the start of their increasingly intimate attachment, Aurore had been troubled by the nagging feeling that she was too old for Sandeau. But it was not only age: whereas she was Jules's first passion, Jules was not her first great love. Aurélien de Sèze, before him, had left her sentimentally disillusioned and — or so at least she fancied — emotionally exhausted. To Aurélien she had abandoned herself completely — to the extent of forgetting their extraordinary platonic pledge and making two mad trips alone to Bordeaux to see him. The second, undertaken at the worst possible moment, had left her with the feeling that she had been short-changed: Aurélien had not loved her the way she had loved him. In her letters to him she had poured out her heart and her obsessions, while his had remained essentially noncommittal. Peppered with prudent counsels which he offered with almost paternal solicitude, full of ironic digs at her naive Rousseauphilia and democratic enthusiasm, they were the letters of a friend far more than the letters of a lover. Then, almost miraculously, young Jules had come into her life — full of youthful fervor and enthusiasm, an ardent young wooer who was in many ways the antithesis of his predecessor: excitable and temperamental where Aurélien had been a model of composure, blissfully optimistic where the other had been worldly-wise and ironic, passionately republican where Sèze had been a condescending monarchist, a writer with a head full of dreams rather than a level-headed jurist. With Jules she had refound a sense of youth she had feared was gone forever.

The first months of their affair had been blissful, spiced by the heady realization that she was throwing bourgeois caution to the winds and reveling in a life of bohemian sin. Yet her original misgivings remained, and all it had needed to make her painfully aware of their presence was a letter she had received in early June of 1831, while she was at Nohant.

Unlike so many monarchists, who had transferred their allegiance from Charles X to Louis-Philippe overnight in order to improve their chances of administrative advancement, Aurélien de Sèze had refused to take the easy way out. He had resigned his post as advocate general in Bordeaux, thereby reaffirming his "legitimist" loyalty to the Bourbons (as opposed to the "upstart" house of Orléans, to which Louis-Philippe belonged) — at the cost of a promising career in the judiciate. But this man who had so nobly chosen not to compromise with his political principles was preparing to make the necessary compromise with something she considered far more sacrosanct — his "love" for Aurore — by contemplating marriage to someone from his own aristocratic milieu. She had done almost everything she could to flout convention and to escape the crippling bonds of marriage, but here was Aurélien preparing to bow to the exquisite hypocrisies of "genteel" society. Inevitably, it made her wonder if he had ever truly loved her.

The deep agitation into which this letter threw her was such that, without naming the sender, she made a frank confession about it the next day in a long letter written to Emile Regnault: "A former friend who is profoundly unhappy has written me a letter which has recalled the most burning sorrows of my life. These are no more than memories for me, but they are so gloomy and heart-rending that even from the depths of my present happiness I cannot look back on them without emotion . . . This is the mood in which I was yesterday, after reading this fatal letter. I succumbed to an unbearably nervous oppression, I vainly sought a sense of freshness and well-being in my little grove and my cherished bench. But my physical suffering, as dumb as brute matter, remained and I couldn't *sleep a wink* all night. I was in a state of irritation against the past. To relieve myself I insulted it, asking why my destiny had been so harsh and wretched during the loveliest years of my life, why, when I was twenty and enjoyed the beauty I have lost, possessed the serenity of a simple and trustful heart and that love of mankind which cannot subsist with experience, yes, why when I was made to be loved did I not meet Jules as he is today? I was then worthier of his ardent soul and I would have made him happier; instead, I wasted my affections on persons who were either cold or false" — poor Stéphane de Grandsagne, poor Aurélien de Sèze! — "I lost my youth going from one disappointment to the next."

So long as Jules Sandeau could merit her respect and admiration, she could stifle her past obsessions and forget that Ajasson de Grandsagne, through his sardonic atheism, and Aurélien de Sèze, with his antidemocratic irony, had poisoned the wellsprings of her youthful enthusiasms. But the more it dawned on her that Jules's literary talent and output could not match hers, that he was inclined to be indolent and even irresponsible, the more critical she found herself becoming. What she secretly craved was a kind of ideal lover — possessed of the capacity for work of a Stéphane Ajasson, the sense of responsibility and paternal solicitude of an Aurélien de Sèze, as well as the youthful fire and enthusiasm of Jules Sandeau. But unfortunately her little "hummingbird," as she liked to call her slight, fuzzy-haired lover, seemed, in this autumn of 1832, blissfully unconcerned by the financial problems of the morrow.

By early October *Valentine* was virtually finished. Sandeau, meanwhile, had produced nothing. Aurore's mounting exasperation, to which she gave free rein in her letters, was further aggravated by the general situation of her country. The bloody riots of the previous June, put down with a ferocity which had "rekindled the hatred of the Powers that Be, and the thirst for anarchy in drifting minds," as she had written to Laure Decerfz, the unseemly haste with which so many Frenchmen had ingratiated themselves with the new regime, the bourgeois smugness of a nation turning in upon itself had chilled the libertarian fervor with which she had greeted the July revolution of 1830. What two years earlier had seemed natural now struck her as naive, and far from placing her faith in the gospel of progress and in the doctrine of the limitless perfectibility of the human species, which Condorcet had made so fashionable, she was more tempted to share the romantic pessimism of the fashionable moralist Charles Nodier, for whom life was a vale of tears and the contemporary, post-Napoleonic, world one sinking inexorably to its doom.

This was not the first time her optimism had come to grief on the rocky shoals of reality. Brought up on Jean-Jacques Rousseau, she had learned by experience that the "system" propounded in *Emile* for the successful raising of a child was more likely to produce a spoiled brat than a responsible young man or a well-behaved daughter. This was something Hyacinthe de Latouche could understand, a staunch republican though he had remained. He at least had lived, he had been married, he had had mistresses, he had fathered and lost two children, he had suffered all manner of misfortunes. But how could little Jules and his young friends, none of whom were married and all of whom were half-a-dozen years younger than herself and a quarter of a century younger than Latouche, be expected to understand that "man is incorrigible" and that "the species does not improve"?

Though they were only a few years apart in age, it was now almost as though Aurore were separated from Jules Sandeau and his contemporaries by a "generation gap." Most of their Berrichon friends sided with Jules, apparently feeling that her gloom was exaggerated and the demands she was placing on her lover unreasonable. The delicate Charles Duvernet, who had recently married, was far too occupied with his incredibly plump wife to be able to offer consolation, and the only neighbor into whose sympathetic ear she could pour out her woes was Gustave Papet.

Sandeau meanwhile had returned to Paris. On the twenty-third of October Aurore left for the capital in her turn, ostensibly to move her furniture and belongings from the Quai Saint-Michel flat to Latouche's apartment on the Quai Malaquais but in effect to have it out with Jules. "I am leaving with fever in my blood and despair in my heart," she wrote in a despondent goodbye note to Papet, "but don't concern yourself about this. The others have already hurt me enough, with their halfway comprehension. I'm going to see Jules. If we cannot reach a meeting of minds, then no one can cure us . . . I've been constantly ill, and I'm still so ill that I don't know if I shall ever return from Paris," she concluded with a tragic flourish. "Farewell, Gustave. If I fail to return, think of me, feel pity for me, and alone among all of you, don't accuse me. Who has peered deeply enough into the depths of my heart to have the right to do so?"

Aurore's unannounced arrival took Jules Sandeau and his friends completely by surprise. Her determination to berate her lover for his regrettable indolence melted away in the passionate delight of their reunion.

"Jules is well and we love each other more than ever," Aurore could soon report to her "good Gustave." "We are mutually curing each other of our sufferings. Don't be anxious, my friend . . ."

Aurore was obviously trying hard to persuade herself that the row was over and the reconciliation complete. But though reluctant to admit it to herself, the charm was now broken. Jules Sandeau was too sensitive and high-strung not to feel it. A few quotations from *Marianna,* the novel he later embroidered around their love affair, give us a graphic idea of what followed:

"She took pleasure in discussing the interests of his future with Henry" — that is, Jules Sandeau. "But serious matters could not hold out long against the fever which consumed them . . . When Marianna" — which is to say, Aurore — "would turn to Henry and ask: 'Now what do you want to do?', he would answer: 'I want to love you!' and fling his arms about her neck." But the intensity of each embrace could no more cloud out the memory of the past than it could make her forget all concern for the future. "In vain she protested the youth of her heart. The time was passed when she could plunge avidly into happiness without imagining that the source was exhaustible. George had killed her self-confidence, that flower of the soul which blooms but once."

In the novel, George Bussy, the fictitious character Sandeau created around the figure of Aurélien de Sèze, is held uniquely responsible for destroying the heroine's capacity for love. The reality was more complex, for Stéphane Ajasson de Grandsagne had done as much to chill Aurore's idealistic enthusiasms as Aurélien de Sèze. But the withering consequences were essentially as Sandeau described them in *Marianna:* "She was marvelously skilled . . . at mocking and destroying the ideas, facts, and theories that gave Henry such moments of glorious exaltation . . . New religions and political convictions, social utopias, all crumbled beneath the weight of her sarcasm." And yet, hurt though it had been in the past, her passionate heart could not help but struggle against the blighting irony of her mind. "Not only did she conceal from Henry the discouragement of her soul, but she succeeded in long concealing it from herself . . . She had sacrificed too much to love, she had proclaimed it too loftily to be the highest good, to be able to withdraw from it at the first sign of faint-heartedness . . . She made a dogged effort to be happy; she turned her happiness into a question of self-esteem, stubbornly refusing to give in. But from then on it became a laborious, unremitting effort."

In early November Aurore returned to Nohant. She continued to receive letters from Jules, as though nothing had happened, but she missed the frequent letters Emile Regnault had written prior to her row with his friend Sandeau. "I know I have lost much . . . of that enthusiastic veneration your youthful head used to grant me," she wrote to her young critic on November 18. "This is the trouble with friendships where there is a disproportion of age and experience. One of the two is blind, the other must step down from the pedestal on which he has been placed despite himself. This is what has happened to me: the prism you were holding before your eyes has been shattered through one of those jolts by which life is tormented, and now seeing me better, you have suffered the dizziness which follows on a disappointment. You have done what we all do, dear Emile, in similar circumstances; you have gone from one extreme to the other, and moved from adoration to injustice . . . When you know more about life," she concluded, "you will understand that I deserved not reproaches but pity. Now I can get along without the pity of human beings. I believe in God. Come back, my friend, you too would suffer from losing one who is both a mother and a friend to you."

Though she was by now well into two new stories (*Cora* and *Le Toast*), Aurore's feverish brain was already toying with something more ambitious: the idea of contrasting the chilling negativism of age and experience with the positive but naive ardor of youth. This too was originally conceived as a short story (and given the title of *Trenmor*). But unlike the others, it soon outgrew its modest blueprint, turning into a monstrous confession that was one long *cri du coeur*.

15. *Lélia*

By the time Aurore returned to Paris in early December, *Valentine,* published several weeks earlier, was already the talk of the town. On December 9 the *Revue de Paris* followed up with her short story, *La Marquise.* It was now clear that *Indiana* was no flash in the pan, and that G. Sand — as the two novels were signed — was an author with a future.

Once again she was besieged by editors and publishers anxious to sign her up. This time they had only three flights of stairs to climb to reach the apartment that Hyacinthe de Latouche had occupied at 19 Quai Malaquais. Aurore's new abode looked out over an inner garden full of trees; the noonday sun flooded in through the windows, facing south and she was no longer troubled by the ceaseless rattle of carriage wheels on the rough cobbles of the *quais.* The blue-papered living room was large enough to accommodate a piano (for which Aurore persuaded Casimir to make her an advance), and there was a kitchen complete with stove and hooded flue as well as two bedrooms, in one of which Solange's little iron-posted bed was installed. "All I hear in the way of noise is the sound of a harp coming from somewhere and the tinkle of a fountain playing beneath my windows in the garden," she wrote to Jules Boucoiran.

A bare week after her arrival, a tall young man dressed in an extraordinarily shabby green frock coat came to call on her. With his strong chin, finely chiseled profile, prominent forehead, and chestnut hair, he would have been handsome but for his faintly myopic blue eyes and an absurdly puckered, cherry-red lower lip, which seemed to have been twisted into an expression of permanent disdain. The newcomer was Gustave Planche, a twenty-five-year-old critic whose trenchant articles in the *Revue des Deux Mondes* had already earned him a reputation as one of the most controversial, and disliked, literary figures in Paris. ("Mr. Hugo must make a violent break with his habits if he is to continue writing for the theater"; Balzac "makes a story the way one makes a suit or a house," etc.).

Planche had just written a particularly flattering review of *Indiana* and *Valentine* in which he roundly declared that it was "impossible to have more eloquence with less style." Along with the proofs of his article, which he gave Aurore as a token of his homage, he brought her a contract proposal drafted by the editor of the *Revue des Deux Mondes,* who was anxious to wean her away from the rival *Revue de Paris* (to which Hugo and Balzac were in the process of transferring their allegiance, partly out of annoyance with Planche's criticism of their work).

Founded in 1829, just four months after the *Revue de Paris,* the *Revue des Deux Mondes* had originally been launched as a political fortnightly. But under the liberating impact of the July Revolution, and the soaring prestige of a new generation of young Romantic writers eager to go Byron and Scott one better, it had gradually veered from diplomacy and politics to poetry and fiction. Its new editor, François Buloz, had in fact won his literary spurs working under the scrofulous, opera-loving Louis Véron for the *Revue de Paris* before moving over to its rival. A canny Savoyard and very much a self-made man, Buloz was an editorial workhorse with an innate flair for public tastes and a shrewd business sense. When he had taken over the *Revue des Deux Mondes* at the age of twenty-eight, the fortnightly was virtually on the rocks, with only 350 subscribers. In little over a year he had almost doubled this number, had obtained contributions from Alfred de Vigny, Victor Hugo, Balzac, Alexandre Dumas, and had conscripted the talents of the two leading critics of the up-and-coming generation — Gustave Planche and the twenty-seven-year-old Charles-Augustin Sainte-Beuve.

The contract Buloz offered to Madame Dudevant (as she was referred to in the text) gave her the right to have her short stories, articles, or novels published or serialized at least once a month. Depending on the regularity of the rhythm she could maintain, this contract offered her the possibility of earning as much as 4000 francs a year — considerably more than the 250-franc-a-month allowance she had obtained from her husband. In return, she had to grant the *Revue des Deux Mondes* an exclusive right to the publication of her short stories and the serializing of her novels. Though this meant breaking off relations with the *Revue de Paris,* the terms offered by Buloz were too flattering to be lightly dismissed. Besides, she had been vexed to discover that the 300 francs paid to her for *La Marquise* was a lower fee than what the new editor of the *Revue de Paris* was paying to the young novelist Eugène Sue (who was exactly her own age) and to the learned book collector P. L. Jacob, whose literary credentials were more than modest. The author of *Indiana* and *Valentine,* now far better known than either, was not going to put up with further discrimination simply because Georges Sand was in reality a woman.

As a token of her appreciation for his unexpected visit, she gave Planche the still unfinished text of a new story she was working on. Called *Trenmor* — a name she had borrowed from the crypto-Gaelic bard Ossian — this rambling, disconnected tale purported to be the story of a rehabilitated gambler who has returned to "normal" life after being condemned to five years of forced labor for petty thievery. But into this all too nebulous plot had been woven a second story — more exactly, a kind of ethereal dialogue carried on between an older, lovesick woman named Lélia and a young poet called Sténio, whom the world-weary ex-convict is somehow supposed to reconcile.

Buloz was frankly dismayed by what Planche showed him. When he brought back a revised contract proposal on December 18, Planche was so tongue-tied that he could not find the words to convey the blunt truth about Buloz's disappointment. But later that same day Aurore received a handwritten note in which the young critic admitted his embarrassment, adding that he felt that "Lélia and Sténio were lit by too rare and shadowy a light. Was I wrong?"

Georges Sand's reaction to this well-meant criticism was one of intense pique. She read Planche's articles on Alfred de Vigny and Prosper Mérimée, as well as his stinging rebuttal to Latouche's attack on the Romantics, which he had written for the *Revue des Deux Mondes.* The next time they met she made cruel fun of his "impossible reasoning," told him frankly that she felt almost as much hurt by his onslaught on Latouche as had been the poor recluse himself, and made it clear that she found him unbearably pedantic. In an answering letter the young critic humbly promised to see her as rarely as possible, "in order to escape the severity of your gaze."

By early January at least three Paris publishers were making serious overtures to Georges Sand. Notwithstanding her rebuke, Gustave Planche had even persuaded Buloz to offer her 5000 francs for her new book — it was no longer a short story — with a bonus of 1000 francs thrown in if the 1500 printed copies of the first edition were sold out within a period of nine months after publication. But to punish Buloz for his initially negative reaction, she preferred to sign a far less advantageous contract with Dupuy (who had published *Indiana* and *Valentine*), for which she obtained only 2000 francs for an edition of 1300 copies. Buloz's criticism had, however, borne fruit, for the new novel was no longer called *Trenmor* but boldly entitled *Lélia.* The spotlight had shifted from the former gambler and was now centrally focused on the spiritual anguish of a woman tormented by the depressing feeling that she will never be able to love again.

The giddy charm of the *vie de bohème* had long since worn off, and what Aurore Dudevant, the mother, and Georges Sand, the author, were now faced with was the problem of housing and feeding not only herself and her daughter but her indolent lover as well. It was she who had undertaken to pay the quarterly installments for Jules's military replacement. It was she who had paid the rent on their old apartment and who would now have to pay it on their new one. But since her physical presence seemed to have a crushing impact on him, paralyzing his capacity for work, it was essential that Sandeau have a place of his own to write in. She accordingly rented and partly furnished a tiny flat for him on the nearby Rue de l'Université. If her love for her little Jules was gradually drying up, she was determined to disguise it as long as possible behind a mask of maternal solicitude and generosity.

Her growing celebrity now brought on a dramatic widening of her friendships, no longer limited to Latouche and her Berrichon friends. After Gustave Planche, the critic Sainte-Beuve asked to be allowed to call on the author of *Indiana,* about which he had recently written a laudatory review in the weekly *National.* A few months earlier, Aurore and her La Châtre friend Laure Decerfz had almost split their sides with laughter over the more fatuous verses of Sainte-Beuve's *Poésies et Pensées de Joseph Delorme* — in which female breasts had been described as "swimming in delight," kisses as being "wet," unhappy Sundays "yellow," and the unloved bard had compared himself to "a stag moaning and troating on the brink of the abyss": romantic lapses Latouche had mercilessly panned and which were to justify Oscar Wilde's later dictum that "bad poetry springs from genuine feelings." But all this was now conveniently forgotten and the permission to call readily granted.

Aurore refused to be put off by the unsuccessful bard's unprepossessing looks. Behind the wobbly cheeks and the shifty weazel eyes, she soon realized, was a sharp mind which had already freed itself from its earlier infatuation with the poetic sentimentality of the Victor Hugo clique. In this plump tabby cat of a man, who betrayed his timidity by the almost canonical unction with which he kept rubbing his flabby hands, she also encountered a sympathetic echo of her own obsessions with human frailty, the temptations of the flesh, and her religious doubts about original sin and the infinite *miséricorde* of God.

Quite different from the epicene Sainte-Beuve was another friend who now burst into Aurore's life with the force of a whirlwind. This was Marie Dorval, an actress of humble origin who had dumfounded the critics by playing the part of a noble lady in Alexandre Dumas' *Antony* — a tragic melodrama which had created a scandal in May of 1831 by its blatant approval of adultery. Later, through the sheer fire and genius of her acting, she had saved Victor Hugo's *Marion de Lorme* from the panning it deserved. Like María Malibran, Marie Dorval was anything but handsome, being too small and frail to have a commanding stage presence. She had thin veined hands and a husky, almost commonplace voice in which the r's were too often burred. But what she lacked in natural attributes was more than matched by a passionate intensity and a lack of theatrical artificiality which had made her the darling of the Romantics. In breaking away from the stilted pomposity of classic French drama and Napoleonic academicism to achieve a style of acting that was more vibrant, heart-rending, and "sublime," she had in fact done for the French stage what Delacroix had done for painting.

One day, acting on a sudden impulse, Georges Sand (as she purposefully signed herself) dashed off an admiring letter. Marie Dorval's response was swift and dramatic, in keeping with her temperament. Aurore was telling Jules Sandeau about the letter she had sent off in the morning when suddenly the door to her Quai Malaquais apartment flew open and a small, strange woman wearing a feathered hat burst in. Her blue eyes lit up joyously as with a breathless cry she flung her arms around Aurore: *"Me voilà, moi!"* (Here I am, it's me!).

There was something so friendly and sincere in the letter Georges Sand had sent her, she explained, that she had decided it could only have been written by someone with the soul of an artist, like herself. It had reminded her of the enthusiastic letter she had written years before to Mademoiselle Mars, a letter to which the famous Comédie Française actress had responded with cold hauteur. Now that the same sincere, spontaneous homage was being paid to her, Marie Dorval was responding in an entirely different manner.

Georges Sand was as bewitched by Marie Dorval's intensity as was Jules Sandeau, who compared her slight form to the airy, half-broken feather she had stuck in her hat. Both were invited to dine the following Sunday *en famille,* this being the only evening of the week that Marie Dorval could spend away from the stage with her husband, the playwright and drama critic Jean-Toussaint Merle, and the three daughters she had had by a previous husband and a lover.

Present among the guests at this Sunday dinner was the actress' latest paramour, the pale-faced poet Alfred de Vigny, whose brooding presence Marie Dorval's husband accepted with unruffled equanimity. Vigny, who had met the author of *Indiana* some months earlier, had found her too frank and forthright for his genteel taste. "She's a woman who looks about twenty-five," he had noted in his diary. ". . . Her hair black and curled and tumbling down over her collar in the manner of Raphael's angels. Her eyes are large and black, formed like the exemplary eyes of mystics and the most magnificent Italian heads. Her face severe and immobile, the lower part unlovely, the mouth badly formed. No grace in her bearing, rough in speech. A man in turn of phrase, language, sound of voice, and boldness of expression."

The "elective affinities" that had so fascinated Goethe obviously did not exist between the somewhat bashful blue-eyed poet and the black-eyed author of *Valentine*. But they clearly did between Marie Dorval and Georges Sand. The actress was everything the unhappy authoress dreamed of being: vivacious, passionate, wholly dedicated to her art, absolutely uninhibited. She was a splendidly emancipated woman who had defied convention, shocked the traditionalists, and had triumphantly got away with it. In vain did the acerbic Gustave Planche try to warn Georges Sand against this sudden, ardent passion: he had been confidentially informed by a rival actress that Madame Dorval had "harbored a passion for her of the same nature as that of Sappho for the young Lesbians." The mere mention of this "calumny" made Georges Sand flare up and silence him with "virile threats" (as he rather curiously termed them in a plaintive letter).

Years later, in recalling this sudden infatuation for a person of her own sex, George Sand robustly declared that "With very few exceptions, I do not long endure the company of women. Not that I feel them inferior to me in intelligence; I consume so few of them in the habitual commerce of my life" — the gynaecophagic expression is hers — "that everyone has more of them around than I. But women, generally speaking, are nervous, anxious beings who, my reluctance notwithstanding, communicate their eternal disquiet to me apropos of everything. I begin by listening to them with regret, then I let myself be caught up in a natural interest for what they are saying, only to perceive that there was really nothing to get worked up about in their puerile agitations. . . .

"I thus like men better than women, and I say so without malice, seriously convinced that nature's goals are logical and complete, that the satisfaction of the passions is only a restricted and accidental part of that attraction which one sex feels for the other, and that aside from physical relations, different souls seek each other out in a kind of intellectual and moral alliance, to which each sex brings what is complementary for the other. Were it otherwise, men would flee women, and vice versa, whereas on the contrary, when the age of physical passion is over, the principal element of human civilization is in their calm and delicate relationships."

Georges Sand's friendship for Marie Dorval was thus in every way exceptional. She who normally sought the company of "serene souls" capable of lending a sympathetic ear to her problems and offering her the comfort of calm advice now found herself dealing with a high-strung woman who, as she later put it, was "the résumé of feminine anxiety carried to its highest power." Listening to Marie Dorval talk was like being exposed to a storm full of electrical discharges; it was, for Georges Sand at any rate, an exciting but at the same time exhausting experience. For Marie Dorval's flow of speech, intensified but not artificially affected by thirty years of stage experience (she had made her "debut" at the age of four!), was as elemental as it was earthy. She could move from one mood to another with stupefying ease and rapidity, rebounding from the deepest gloom to the maddest gaiety, shedding bitter tears at one moment, breaking into contagious laughter the next, while her expressive face and thin, nervous hands kept up a dazzling pantomime.

Of the two, it was Marie Dorval who had suffered more, and not simply because she was five years older than Georges Sand. The illegitimate daughter of two itinerant players, she had seen her fickle father abandon her embittered mother and run off with another actress when she was only five. Her mother had later died of tuberculosis, partly caused by malnutrition, and to keep from starving, the fifteen-year-old Marie had agreed to marry Allan Dorval, a fellow actor and ballet master who was twenty-one years older than herself. Before dying at an unexpectedly early age, he had given her two daughters, who had later turned into hellions.

Enthusiastically acclaimed in Strasbourg, Marie Dorval's dramatic talents had long been scorned in Paris because her figure was too small, her gesturing too little mannered, her husky voice insufficiently clear and ringing for the pompous theatrical conventions of post-Napoleonic France. Reduced to accepting bit parts and even to singing in operatic choruses, she had finally, out of sheer despair, become the mistress of the Italian orchestra conductor at the

Théâtre Saint-Martin, only to discover that he was carrying on an affair with another actress. So she had gone, from flirtation to flirtation, from one liaison to the next. The handsome actor Frédérick Lemaître, with whom she had had a brief romance, had proved as unfaithful as her orchestra conductor, being not only married but having another mistress besides. To avenge her wounded pride, Marie Dorval had "given herself" to Jean-Toussaint Merle, who had finally been badgered by his royal patroness, the Duchesse d'Angoulême, into "regularizing" his liaison and marrying his mistress. Sixteen years older than she, he was fortunately a tolerant husband, generously letting Marie entertain her lovers in her satin-lined boudoir but also generously allowing her to foot most of the household bills.

How, under the circumstances, could a woman have any confidence in men? Were they not all equally untrustworthy—hypocritically tender when not unscrupulously forgetful? The hot-blooded Alexandre Dumas, while pressing his amorous advances, had promised her the lead in his play *Antony,* then offered it to her famous Comédie Française rival, Mademoiselle Mars, whose impossible pretensions had proved too much to swallow. The same had happened with *Marion de Lorme:* Victor Hugo had only offered her the lead after quarreling with Mademoiselle Mars, who had insisted he rewrite the play according to her imperious dictates. But the cruelest blow of all had been dealt her by her poet-lover, Alfred de Vigny. After writing a verse play—*La Maréchale d'Ancre*—especially for her, he had gone behind her back and offered the lead role to Mademoiselle George, a faded star of the Napoleonic stage, to curry favor with her influential lover, Charles-Jean Harel, the director of the Odéon theater. Well might Marie Dorval say of men, after so many betrayals, what Byron had once said of the fair sex: "Woman cannot live with Man, nor can She live without him."

For someone recently emerged from the provincial backwaters of Berry, this new and sudden friendship with the most talked of actress in France was decidedly intimidating. "Do you think you can bear me?" Georges Sand wrote to her pathetically, shortly after their first meeting. "You don't know yet, nor do I. I'm such a boor, so stupid, so slow in thinking out loud, so gauche and tongue-tied, precisely when I have so many things I would like to get off my chest! Don't judge me by outward appearance, wait a bit to know what you can grant me in pity and affection. I feel that I love you with a rejuvenated heart, a heart you have remade anew. If it is a dream, like everything I have desired in life, don't rob me of it too quickly. It does me so much good!"

In early February Georges Sand wrote again, to ask if her friend could get her a seat for a special commemorative performance at the Comédie Française in which Marie Dorval was to play the part of the Countess and Mademoiselle Mars the part of Suzanne in Beaumarchais' *Le Mariage de Figaro*. "Farewell, my dear loved one," she concluded. "I wish someone loved me the way I love you." Back came two tickets and this note: "My friend, I have two box stalls for you. Be there, I beg you. I shall need to feel there is someone out there who loves me."

Eager to acclaim the actress whose dramatic style had so often been criticized as insufficiently classic and noble, Georges Sand spent the night after the Comédie Française performance composing an article in which she claimed that Mademoiselle Mars's mode of acting had always been stiff and unnatural, lacking the suppleness, mobility, and passion of Marie Dorval's. Published in the next issue of the weekly *L'Artiste,* it was furiously attacked in the *Courrier des Spectacles,* which bluntly declared that it was an injustice to the fair sex to believe that "this most impertinent of articles" could have been written by a woman. "We for our part believe that it is a nasty man in petticoats."

The article published in *L'Artiste* was enough to seal a lifelong friendship. "Dear soul," the author wrote to her friend Marie three days before it appeared, "do you think of me a little? I am ill, I was bled this evening. As soon as I have the strength to do so, I shall go to see you. *Ricourt*" — the editor of *L'Artiste* — "kisses your feet for this article, you for being so beautiful, me for understanding you so well. But I know that I am not worth one lock of your hair, and this is why I love you."

"Marie, why have we not seen each other for so long?" she complained in another letter sent off the next day. Then, after a brief visit made to Aulnay with Solange, to see Latouche in his ivy-covered cottage, she returned to find that her friend Marie had dropped by the Quai Malaquais apartment during her absence. "How unhappy I am to lose a day of my life when you could have been there!" she immediately wrote. "But tell me which day you can give me, to come after midnight for a chat . . . You, little woman, have many things in your life. I, nothing! . . . Only you, whom I kiss a thousand times."

The letter was signed "George" — without the s — to make the first name accord with the English-sounding Sand. Though it took her some weeks to get used to the new spelling, from May 1833 on this was the way she invariably wrote her name.

Almost half a century later, in describing the growing intimacy of the two *inséparables,* the novelist Arsène Houssaye could write that on returning from the theater after midnight, the famous actress, i.e., Marie Dorval, would find "the strange woman [George Sand] waiting for her prey while smoking cigarettes" in the little blue-curtained room where a teapot steamed in front of a lively fire. "A singularly amorous duo followed. The brunette loosened the blonde one's hair. The blonde one loosened the dark hair of the other. And these locks of hair were mingled amid the kisses and the bites. Never did Sappho speak so well to the beautiful Phaon. Never did Erinna reply to Sappho in a more caressing voice. And thus the nighttime hours passed, more radiant than those of sunlit day. For both . . . were frantic for the unforeseen and insatiable for love. It was not only wantonness of the heart, but a display of Oriental, Indian, and Japanese voluptuousness. The two bacchantes would take leave of each other at the crack of dawn, still drunk on the pallor of accomplished dreams. And that day the eloquent woman had more eloquence. And that day the woman of the theater had a softer caress in her voice, more fire in her gaze, greater energy in her passion."

Houssaye, in his indiscreet (and often inaccurate) *Confessions,* was simply embroidering the gossip he had picked up in different Paris salons. For in this respect, as Aurore Dudevant had by now discovered, the salons of the French capital could more than hold their own against the drawing rooms of La Châtre. Insanely jealous, Alfred de Vigny was ready to think the worst of these nocturnal rendezvous, even though he was one of their prime causes: stubbornly insisting on spending his nights at home with his frigid English wife and his mother, Vigny made a habit of visiting his mistress in the morning. Marie Dorval's afternoons being taken up with domestic chores and her evenings devoted to the theater, it was only after midnight that George Sand could hope to pour out her heart to her friend in an intimate tête-à-tête.

That the tête-à-tête occasionally become a *corps-à-corps* is possible, though I personally doubt it. The unpracticed Aurore, who had never been to Lesbos, still less to India or Japan, must in any case have been a gauche and timid lover. Nor, to judge by *Lélia,* the novel with which she was desperately wrestling during these troubled months, could this particular "solution" have brought much solace to her tormented soul. At least one passage in the book suggests that she, who had always dreamed of being a passionate romantic heroine, was obsessed by the idea that she was too masculine, fancying that this might explain her increasing coldheartedness and frigidity toward Jules Sandeau.

In his novel *Marianna,* written four years later, Sandeau was to give a graphic account of the last stormy weeks leading up to the fateful climax. Sensing that something had turned sour, his hero Henry (which is to say, Jules himself) "began finding fault with everything. Endowed with an inordinate sensibility, he could not be satisfied with an unhappy love . . . He set about tormenting his mistress' heart, he took pleasure in bringing tears to those eyes which had already wept so much."

Relatively mild at first, these lovers' quarrels were quickly washed away in tearful embraces. But soon these scenes ended with thundering storms "in which words sliced through the air and struck like bolts of lightning." Sandeau's indolence — for he "brooded over his sorrow as he had brooded over his joy" (as was candidly admitted in the novel) — irritated Aurore beyond all measure. No longer able to respond to her lover's "virile flame, his increasingly avid lip" (as she was to describe it in *Lélia*), she sought to deflect his amorous advances by urging him to work. "There were then furious outbursts, terrible rages, cutting reproaches, frightful recriminations." Life, as this sentence from *Marianna* makes clear, became a living hell for both of them.

The final break came in early March. Just what caused it we do not know. The facile explanation — first offered by one of George

Sand's friends (Henri Amic) some twenty years after her death — is that Aurore one day surprised Jules Sandeau in the arms of a washerwoman in his small Rue de l'Université flat. It is more than fanciful. Young Jules, still a passionate Romantic clinging to a "deathless" love, could not have wished to defile it through an act of random lechery. To have done so would have been to admit — something against which he was desperately struggling — that his romance with Aurore was already on the rocks.

The decision in any case was hers. On March 3, or thereabouts, George Sand wrote to Marie Dorval, who had become a kind of go-between for the two unhappy lovers, to ask if she would add the name of Gustave Planche to the guest list for a ball (probably a fancy-dress ball during this particularly wild carnival season). "Jules, evidently, will be with us," she added. "But at present he is doubtless with you, and he is happier than I am." Two days later she wrote again in haste, asking Marie to strike their three names from the list. "Gustave Planche was only going because of me and I wouldn't go for all the millions in the world. A hideous grief has descended upon me and my thoughts are closer to death than to pleasure. If you are good and full of pity, you will come to see me soon."

When Marie Dorval hurried over the next day, George Sand was out, having hied herself to the Rue de l'Université flat to console her brokenhearted Jules. "My friend, go to Jules, and take care of his body," she had already written to Émile Regnault. "The soul is shattered, you couldn't mend it. Don't try . . . Do your best to have Jules live, it will be horrible for him for a long time to come, but still, he's so young . . . We have no reproaches to make to each other, we have been struggling for some time against this dire necessity . . . The only thing left for us to do was to kill ourselves. But for my children, we would have done it . . . He will never have the right to keep me from being his mother. Go, my friend, go."

Her maternal solicitude was anything but fanciful. Jules Sandeau later told Balzac that in the immediate wake of their rupture, he had tried to kill himself by taking a dose of acetate of morphine, but his nervous stomach vomited it all up before any of it could be lethally absorbed.

His friends eventually decided that the best way of healing Sandeau's broken heart would be to send him on a long, leisurely trip to Italy. The necessary funds were collected and a passport obtained toward the end of March. George Sand's first important biographer, Vladimir Karénine, later claimed that Aurore also made a financial contribution, though the evidence is missing. But we know that she wrote to Charles Didier, a Swiss poet to whom she had been introduced in Hortense Allart's fashionable literary salon, to ask if he couldn't provide Jules with some letters of introduction to people in Italy.

Didier, who had spent three years in the peninsula, was only too happy to oblige. Ever since he had read *Indiana,* which had kept him awake for all of one "agitated" night, he had been eager to meet the author who signed herself G. Sand. His curiosity had been further whetted by the voluble Hortense Allart, herself a lady of letters and something of a novelist, who had gone into rhapsodies over Madame Dudevant (for it was an open secret by now who G. Sand really was), saying that once she began talking she was irresistible ("If I were a man I would be mad about her!"). Didier, though a man, had been frankly disappointed by Madame Dudevant's austere, dry, and incommunicative air. But he had been sufficiently intrigued by his first glimpse to call on her two days later at her Quai Malaquais apartment. He had found her domestically engaged in winding yarn and had noted in his diary: "Is she capable of passion? I believe she has crossed the Rubicon."

On March 21 he called on George Sand once again and found her ill. "She is beautiful and soft," he noted in his diary. "Her lovely pale face, framed by black hair, made a most graceful effect. A number of dirty provincials" — by which he meant Alphonse Fleury, Emile Regnault, Hippolyte Chatiron, and others — "kept dropping in and leaving. Then came Planche, with whom I chatted. She, suffering and silent, but following the conversation in her mind, as one could see from her eyes. Planche is not lacking in finesse or wit; but he's superficial, speaking of things he knows nothing about."

Nine days later Didier was back, with the letters of introduction Aurore had requested for Jules Sandeau. To the Swiss poet's delight, he was asked to stay for dinner along with Hortense Allart and Planche. "Found her sad," he noted that night, speaking of his hostess. "I think that Planche, with whom she is closely linked, exercises a bad influence on her, putting his literary theories between herself and her spontaneity. We stayed a moment together, the lady and myself. We read a page of *Oberman* * which went to the heart. Madame Dud[event] was soft and abandoned; she breathed love. I fear her liaison with P[lanche], a man who's not made for her."

In this at least the Swiss poet — who was a year younger than Aurore — was not mistaken. Just how intimate they already were, or were later to become, there is really no way of saying, for the evidence is scant and contradictory. But that Gustave Planche, during these difficult weeks, came to exercise a notable ascendancy over George Sand is unquestionable. Intellectually, if not physically, he filled the void left by Jules Sandeau.

There was something disarming about this young critic's almost groveling desire to promote her literary interests. Whereas the tough-minded François Buloz had been ready to reject her latest brain child out of hand, Planche had carefully emphasized its merits and offered to "decompose" its tangled elements so that what was blurred and inchoate to begin with might assume a definite, coherent form. Thanks in no small part to this encouragement, what had originated as a short story about a "rehabilitated" gambler had by early January of 1833 turned into a metaphysical novel about a woman's sentimental, religious, intellectual, and physical sufferings and travails.

No less powerful, though more distantly exerted, was Balzac's influence on the genesis of this soul-searching and, for many at the time, "scandalous" confession — so great indeed that the French scholar Pierre Reboul could claim without exaggeration that but for the prior appearance of *La Peau de Chagrin*, *Lélia* would never have been written. But though the similarity of theme is striking, no two books could have differed more in tone and treatment.

In the central episode of Balzac's novel a penniless but gifted young writer, Raphaël de Valentin — variously described as poet and piano player — flings himself into a life of wild dissipation

* *Obermann,* as it should be spelled, was a novel that had been published in 1804 by the "pre-Romantic" Etienne de Senancour, himself greatly influenced by the melancholy soul-suffering of Goethe's Werther.

(providentially financed by a windfall at the gambling table) after being repeatedly rebuffed by a beautiful but frozen-hearted countess. *Lélia* deals with the same general theme. Driven to despair by a beautiful woman (Lélia) who can no longer love him and who even pushes him into the arms of her profligate sister (Pulchérie) in the hope that this carnal tonic will cure him of his hopeless infatuation for her, a young poet named Sténio gives himself up to a life of strenuous debauch. But far from proving a remedy for his sentimental woes, it leaves him so broken in body and spirit that he finally hurls himself to death down a ravine. Balzac's story, like so much of what he wrote, was a rollicking, earthy tale, full of cynical psychological insights and wild implausibilities. *Lélia,* on the other hand, became an essentially metaphysical novel, assuming that it can be called a novel, for it was in reality the thinly disguised expression of Aurore Dudevant's intimate despair, a highly personal confession deeply influenced by Charles Nodier's pessimism and Pascal's idea that human beings are born, above all, to suffer on this earth.

"If I should ever reach the point of no longer loving anything," Aurore had written to Emile Regnault the previous November, "it would be a malady of the heart, a petrifaction of which I shall complain to God and my destiny, but for which I shall never seek the cause in those I have loved." The theme of *Lélia* was summed up in that one sentence. Where Balzac had written an essentially external account of a society woman's cruel treatment of an importunate young wooer, George Sand sought to expose the inner anguish of a woman who involuntarily and most unhappily has grown cruel and stony-hearted. And what she finally produced, after six months of agonizing labor, was not so much a novel as a lengthy lamentation, a romantic Book of Job, written from a woman's point of view.

That the well-meaning Gustave Planche unintentionally contributed to the somber, misanthropic tone of *Lélia* is certain. The son of a well-to-do pharmacist, he had preferred literature to medicine, much as Sandeau had abandoned his law studies for writing, but he was the very antithesis of the fervent, enthusiastic Jules. Something of his dreary family background, if not of his brief medical training, had seeped into his soul: he had the mind of a dissector and his approach to the arts was positively clinical. Unloved as a child, he had grown up nourishing a secret grudge against the world. He had long dreamed of writing a great novel, but a mere dream it had remained. The nonchalant, almost insolent way he had of slouching around with his hands in his pockets, like the unbelievably shabby green frock coat he refused to part with, even when given the money with which to buy a new one by the normally penny-pinching Buloz, was simply the external flaunting of his self-dissatisfaction. If he looked like a bohemian, it was not because he had the soul of a bohemian, it was rather a badge of gloomy defiance he sported to protest his inability to live the giddy life he had once dreamed of living— on an equal footing with the elegant men of letters whose company he had sought out in the literary salons of Charles Nodier, Victor Hugo, and Alfred de Vigny. What had begun as a mood had eventually become a habit he had neither the desire nor the energy to shake off, a prolonged exercise in anti- or counter-dandyism on the part of a profoundly frustrated young man who for one blissfully mad year (during which he ran through his mother's inheritance) had had money to burn, carriages to ride in, shiny top hats to hide his receding hairline, and yellow kid gloves with which to twirl a cane.

"His melancholy mood, his theories of universal disgust, his aversion for concessions made to anything remotely facile or agreeable in the arts," as George Sand was later to recall, ". . . filled me in my turn with a kind of spleen to which I was only too prone at the time I knew him. I perceived in him an eminent mind which generously sought to have me share the riches that had been amassed at the price of his happiness, but I was still at an age when one has greater need of happiness than knowledge . . ."

In search of solace she made several evening visits to various Paris churches, shedding "mystic tears" in her rapt contemplation of the crucifix and in the hope that these moments of hushed darkness, far from the furious bustle of a cruel world, would bring her spiritual relief. These she kept carefully secret from the corrosive Gustave Planche, though not from Marie Dorval, a devout believer like herself. But she now discovered, with a sense of anguished alarm, that she could no longer lose herself in the naive, celestial dreams of her adolescence. Like those atheists whom Dostoevski was to combat, she found herself anguished by the thought that a supposedly perfect God could have created a hideously imperfect world teeming with evil, unhappiness, and vice. She tried desperately to recall the arguments which that most optimistic of philosophers, Leibnitz — the Dr. Pangloss of Voltaire's *Candide* — had propounded in his *Theodicy* to explain this monstrous and baffling paradox. Leibnitz, George Sand later wrote, was her "last anchor of salvation! I had always said to myself that the day I understood him well, I would be safe from all disspiritments of the mind. I also remember that one day, when Planche asked me if I was familiar with Leibnitz, I hastily replied *No,* less from modesty than from the fear that I would have to listen to him discuss and *demolish* him."

It was Planche, however, in a commentary called "Autopsy of Lélia," which he penned on to a page of her private notebook, who helped her to unravel the tangled skein of her new novel — by identifying the five main characters with five distinct ideas or, to be more precise, human conditions. In this analytical schema, as he presented it:

1. Lélia	(personifies)	doubt.
2. Trenmor	—	expiation, Stoicism.
3. Sténio	—	poetry.
4. Magnus	—	superstition, compressed desire.
5. Pulchérie	—	the senses, opposed to *Psyche.*

The analysis, though substantially correct, was inevitably a simplification. For in this strange prose poem Lélia personifies maternal solicitude and compassion as well as a paralyzing doubt about her further capacity to love. She is portrayed, furthermore, as an austere, frigid, intellectually musclebound creature who is all desire and no enjoyment, as opposed to her wonderfully relaxed and wanton sister, Pulchérie, who takes her pleasures as they come, with the uninhibited lust for life of a Marie Dorval. Trenmor, the luckless gambler, is not simply a Stoic who has had to expiate his sins, he is a kind of elder statesman, a sympathetic sage and mediator who, having been exposed to the cruelest vicissitudes of life, can look back on it all with a certain philosophical detachment — much as Hyacinthe de Latouche could do (or at least claim to be doing) in his little "hermitage" at Aulnay. Nor is Sténio simply a poet. Whereas, in the first part of the book, he is the embodiment of youthful hope and enthusiasm, and clearly modeled on Jules Sandeau, toward the end he is a poet robbed of all his innocent illusions, a fierce blaspheming cynic, modeled on Stéphane Ajasson de Grandsagne (whence the name Sténio — an Italianate version of the nickname "Stény" by which Grandsagne was known at Nohant).

Lélia is more like an oratorio than a novel, with the various characters addressing and answering each other in polyphonic counterpoint against a symbolic landscape of Venetian palaces, moonlit ruins, and vertiginous ravines. "Some will say I am Lélia," George Sand admitted in a private letter, "but others could recall that I was formerly Sténio. I also had days of fearful devotion, of passionate desire, of violent struggles and timorous austerity when I was Magnus. I can also be Trenmor. Magnus is my infancy, Sténio my youth, Lélia is my maturity; Trenmor may perhaps be my old age. All of these types have lived within me . . ."

In *Rose et Blanche* Aurore had rather naively contrasted the lives of two sisters, one of whom seeks happiness by going out into the world, while the other prefers the sheltered serenity of convent life. In *Lélia* the roles are curiously and harshly reversed. The person who has reached a state of philosophical serenity, in which he is no longer tormented by unsatisfied desires, is Trenmor, the headlong gambler who has sinned, stolen, and been punished. The one who remains hideously frustrated, sexually repressed, and tormented by feverish erotic dreams, is, on the other hand, Magnus, the wild Irish monk who has vainly sought to throttle his animal instincts and desires.

In this sense *Lélia* can be considered a pre-Freudian novel. Not only is priestly celibacy specifically attacked as "a slow physical suicide" and the monastic spirit as one that "narrows the mind and dries up sensitivity," but there are even some sharp barbs at the misogynistic tendencies of the Church, as in the scene where the sex-crazed Irish priest raises his voice in public prayer, calling on God's "guardian angel . . . when he appears in our dreams, not to assume the delicate features, the tender gaze, the floating dress and the long hair of a woman."

Indeed, George Sand may well have associated the physical abnormality of monastic life with the abnormality of monogamy and the artificiality of marriage — here more pointedly and violently condemned than in any of her previous books. Thus Pulchérie, the carnal enjoyer and "believer," says to Lélia, the austere and tormented ascetic: "How many affronts is she [i.e., Woman] made to pay for the weaknesses she has surprised and the brutalities she has endured? Under what a mountain of ignominy and injustice must she accustom herself to sleeping and walking, to being lover, courtesan and mother, three conditions of woman's destiny which no woman can escape, whether she sells herself through a bargain of prostitution or a marriage contract." One of the many pessimistic notions Aurore had picked up from Charles Nodier and which echoes through *Lélia* is that individuals of the different sexes are not physically made to live eternally together; that erotically they were originally designed by nature for casual and temporary encounters; and that this being the case, love, in the sense of an enduring and constant emotion, is really a mental aberration calling for an impossible fidelity, an intellectual complication unknown to primitives, and thus the price that Man, and even more Woman, must pay for "civilized" society.

Though she had never read Havelock Ellis, still less Simone de Beauvoir, George Sand was inclined by her own experience to the same melancholy conclusion: that more rapes take place inside of marriage than outside of it. No matter which she chooses, Woman must pay the price. The dutiful wife must submit to the husband's bestial brutalities after she has fallen out of love with him. The woman who pursues pleasure by going from man to man is inevitably branded a slut. Even the woman who would like to give it all up finds no easy way out, only a troubled withdrawal into a kind of onanistic limbo, where the satisfactions are as synthetic as the torments of the flesh are real.

For this was the real nature of George Sand's pathetic confession in *Lélia,* and one of the many reasons why this novel seemed so shocking to most of her contemporaries. If Macbeth, and even more his wife, is the victim of "vaulting ambition," Lélia is the victim of a vaulting imagination which tragically and ceaselessly "o'erleaps itself." Her predicament, as the author specifically declared, was that of "an entire generation" — by which was meant the post-

Napoleonic generation which had been weaned on grandiose imperial dreams that could not be reconciled with the moneygrubbing mediocrity of Louis-Philippe's regime. As it was in politics, so it was in love. The dream had been too dazzling, the vision too intoxicating, for reality to be anything more than a cruel disappointment.

In the normal course of human development, as a French proverb has it: "At eighteen one adores, at twenty one loves, at thirty one desires, at forty one thinks it over." But in the case of Aurore Dudevant the tendency to mystic adoration, characteristic of teenage adolescence, had been so strong that its effects had adversely affected her capacity to love. The first man she had truly loved she had consequently adored — as Lélia confesses in a passage almost certainly inspired by the memory of Aurélien de Sèze: "I loved with the same love with which I loved God and the heavens, the sun and the sea . . . Alas! This man had not lived according to the same ideas. He had known other pleasures, other ecstasies; he would have liked to share them with me. But . . . my dreams had been too sublime; I could no longer descend to the gross appetites of matter. A complete divorce was thus unwittingly effected between my body and my mind . . ." And when the easygoing Pulchérie suggests that her sister should spend less time in exalted reverie and content herself with living and loving, Lélia wretchedly admits that what is relatively easy for another is virtually impossible for her. "The coldness of my senses placed me below the most abject of women, the exaltation of my thoughts raised me higher than the most passionate of men."

Vainly does Pulchérie observe that while men are brutal and stupid, women are fickle, and that there is as much hatred as affection in the love that unites them. The idea that the union of man and woman was intended to be transient in the designs of Providence, that everything is opposed to their association, and that "change is a necessity of their nature" strikes Lélia as too irrelevant to her particular problem to merit comment. For what continues to obsess her is her lover's lack of recognition for the "sacrifices" she must make to his carnal passion. "He took for marks of bliss my groans of suffering and impatience. He laughed at my tears; at times his outrageous selfishness feasted off them with pride. And when he had shattered me with his fierce embraces, he fell carelessly and rudely asleep next to me, while I stifled my sobs so as not to wake him. O misery and slavery of womankind! . . .

"What made me love him for a long time (long enough to wear out my soul) was doubtless the feverish irritation wrought on my faculties by the absence of personal satisfaction. With him I experienced a kind of strange, delirious avidity which, originating in the most exquisite powers of my mind, could not be satisfied by any carnal embrace. I felt my breast devoured by an inextinguishable fire and his kisses brought me no relief. I hugged him in my arms with a superhuman strength and I fell back exhausted and discouraged because I had no possible way of expressing my enthusiasm. With me desire was an ardor of the soul which paralyzed the power of the senses before arousing them; it was a wild fury which seized hold of my brain and was there exclusively concentrated . . .

"When he was drowsy, satisfied and glutted, I remained motionless and dismayed by his side. I thus spent hours watching him sleep. He seemed so handsome, this man! There was so much strength and grandeur in his peaceful brow! Next to him my heart beat wildly; the blood mounted to my face in agitated waves, then my limbs were seized with unbearable shudders. I seemed to feel the turmoil of physical love and the mounting tumult of material desire. I was wildly tempted to wake him, to fold my arms about him and to elicit the caresses from which I had not yet been able to profit. But I held out against these deceitful solicitations of my suffering, for I knew that he did not have it in him to calm me. God alone could have done it . . .

"Sometimes in my sleep, a prey to those rich ecstasies which devour ascetic brains, I felt myself being borne aloft with *him* on clouds and sweet-scented breezes. I then swam in floods of voluptuous delight; and passing my indolent arms around his neck, I collapsed onto his chest with a faint murmur. But he then woke up and that was the end of my rapture. Instead of this airy being, this angel who had rocked me in his wing beat, I found the man, the brutal man, as voracious as a wild beast, and I fled in horror. But he pursued me, he claimed not to have been vainly disturbed in his sleep, and he savored his fierce pleasure on the breast of a swooning, half-dead woman.

"One day I felt so tired of loving that I suddenly stopped. There was no other drama in my passion. When I saw with what ease this fatal link was broken, I was amazed at having so long believed in its eternal duration."

This long quotation from the most intimate and tortured of her books is enough to show up the hollowness of the charge that was later made by Stéphane Ajasson de Grandsagne's son, who claimed, on the basis of 123 impassioned letters which Aurore had written to his father, that she was a nymphomaniac. George Sand's real trouble was nympholepsy — a frenzied pursuit of ecstatic rapture, a mystic yearning for the unattainably sublime, a desperate craving for the ineffably tender, for what James Joyce so beautifully termed "the soft, sweet swoon of sin."

Incredible as it may seem in someone who was the mother of two children and who had had at least two lovers as well as a husband, Aurore Dudevant at twenty-eight was psychologically still something of a virgin — as she was later to confess quite frankly. Behind the somewhat austere, laconic reserve which had first convinced Charles Didier that she was cold and incapable of passion, there was concealed the ardent Saint Aurore, still craving to recapture the sense of mystic rapture religion had once given her. Casimir, though he had tried to be a tender husband, had killed what little love she may have felt for him the day he had slapped her at Le Plessis Picard; and Aurore, as is true of most sensitive women, could derive little pleasure from being pawed and panted over by someone she no longer loved. Stéphane Ajasson de Grandsagne may not have been much more delicate in the heat of fornication — which would explain why, for three deliciously tense months, Aurore had resisted the amorous advances of the young Jules Sandeau, preferring to stroke his hair, to hold his plaintive head in her lap, and to retain the ravishing illusion of a pure, chaste, unblemished passion. But finally she had yielded, as much to her own desire as to his pleadings and caresses. The relief it brought her may at first have looked like bliss, but as the months went by, her instinctive apprehensions had been confirmed. The "hummingbird of the savannas" had revealed himself to be a disappointingly ordinary mortal. Once again her capacity for total rapture had frozen before it could find its climactic release. Like Lélia, she had thus found herself experiencing "the isolation of the heart . . . in the purest of intimacies . . . ," and like Lélia she could say: "I have never reached those complete effusions, that embrace of twin souls, the happiness I used to dream of and of which I have never grasped but the shadow!"

It would, nevertheless, be a gross oversimplification to see in *Lélia* nothing more than an unhappy woman's veiled confession of her troubling erotic problems. For if Lélia was of course herself, she was also above all a generic type: the symbol of a being condemned to suffer, love, and seek the unattainable. For the gospel of unlimited fornication preached by Pulchérie is shown by Lélia to be as deceptive and misleading as its opposite. It can only be practiced totally and absolutely by beings without hearts or minds, or what in the crude language of the twentieth century are sometimes called sense and sex machines. But the ordinary woman is not so constituted, and as George Sand had Lélia say, in a sentence that must have thrilled Dostoevski when he read it: "I shall perhaps refuse the carefree and mad life of my sister; for thought too has its raptures, its ecstasies and soft celestial bliss, one hour of which is worth an entire youth, a whole lifetime."

16. From Celebrity to Scandal

One year had now elapsed since that April Fool's Day when Aurore Dudevant had packed up her things and, bundling the plump Solange on to the stagecoach, had come up to Paris, bringing with her the manuscript that was to make her famous overnight. Now, in looking back over the preceding twelvemonth, George Sand was almost seized with dizziness. In the space of a few weeks her circle of friends, admirers, and acquaintances had expanded to include Sainte-Beuve, Gustave Planche, François Buloz, Charles Didier, and Marie Dorval. Madame Récamier, France's most celebrated, if fading, beauty, had more than once expressed an interest in meeting her. France's most celebrated, if aging, writer, René de Chateaubriand, had even written to his friend (and fellow viscount) Sosthènes de la Rochefoucauld to say that George Sand's two novels made him feel "jealous" — a far-fetched compliment, which the author of *Indiana* dismissed as insincere.

Nor was she taken in by the rapturous homage paid her by another of the writer's famous "conquests" — the altogether too garrulous Hortense Allart, who was very proud of her literary salon but whom George Sand found annoyingly pedantic, opinionated, and even "mannish" in the judgments she was pleased to dispense as an established *woman author*. "She pretends to admire me, I think, so as not to appear jealous, which would be poor taste," George Sand wrote to Laure Decerfz on the first of April 1833, the anniversary of her departure from Nohant. "I no longer see Balzac, he bores me. Besides, we are good friends and growl at each other from a distance," she continued, glossing over the fact that Balzac, who felt sorry for Jules Sandeau, was even less prepared to forgive her increasingly close association with Gustave Planche, who had dared dismiss his books as styleless. "Latouche is sick, odd, grumpy, he can't forgive me for being successful . . . He considers it a veritable crime and claims that I'm abandoning my old friends, when it is he who avoids and flees me." Here too she was being a little less than honest, for neither could the "recluse" of Aulnay condone her friendship with the intellectual upstart who, in the very first article he had contributed to the *Revue des Deux Mondes,* had called Latouche a corrupting worm "hidden in the depths of maturing fruit," a literary Judas Iscariot who had been glad to befriend Lamartine, Victor Hugo, and Alfred de Vigny so long as they were obscure but who had developed a ferocious hatred against them once they had won the recognition that had been denied to himself.

The literary dinners to which she was now frequently invited but rarely attended had permitted her to meet Alfred de Vigny, Alexandre Dumas, the poet Auguste Barbier, the philosopher-psychologist Théodore Jouffroy, and intellectuals such as Loeve-Veimars (Hoffmann's French translator), Eugène Lerminier, and Jean-Jacques Ampère (son of the famous founder of the science of electrodynamics) — three Germanophiles who were busy opening up France's cultural horizons with importations from beyond the Rhine.

"Such is my situation," she went on, in the same long letter to her La Châtre friend. "In addition to which there's Boucoiran, who comes in every morning with a doctoral air, kisses me on the forehead and closes his eyes while I slip on a chemise, before going in to the next room to give Solange her reading lesson and eating six pounds of bread and two turkey drumsticks out of lovesick despair. Add to that four or five publishers who come at least three times a week to pester me . . . some curious and idle gentlemen who hover around me and whom I politely usher out the moment they appear on the horizon . . . and two or three literary mediocrities whom one esteems and puts up with, and you'll have some idea of the entourage of a woman of letters, the least interesting and most unkempt animal on earth."

Boucoiran's lovesick despair was not, as might at first be supposed, caused by the fascinating dark-eyed temptress who so unceremoniously disrobed and robed herself in his presence; its object was a farmer's daughter at Nohant whom the frustrated Jules had considered marrying. Though the social distance separating the young tutor from the farmer's daughter was considerably less than that which, in the novel, had separated the nobly born Raymon de Ramière from Indiana's creole maid Noun, Aurore would hear none of it. Fiction was one thing, real life another. Boucoiran was accordingly invited up to Paris posthaste and offered a room in Hippolyte's house on the Rue de Seine, after which, his two-year term of service being now terminated, he was talked into tutoring Solange.

Boucoiran was followed a few weeks later by Maurice, whom Casimir escorted up to Paris in mid-April. Having no idea of just what awaited him, the nine-year-old boy had been looking forward joyfully to the "manly" change of life involved in his entering a boarding-school. But the sight of the treeless quadrangle, with its neo-Gothic windows, and of shouting schoolboys who rushed back and forth in a kind of artificial "recreation," watched over by solemn, black-robed teachers, was more than this pampered child of the Berry countryside could face. Afraid of angering his father, he tried to hold back his tears, but when he saw his mother turn and start hurrying away, trying to conceal her own emotion, he broke down completely. Tearing himself from the arms of a housemaster who was trying to console him, he ran sobbing after her, pleading to be taken home. Had Casimir not stepped in and brought the weeping child back to his teachers, Aurore might well have given in to her son's wailing entreaties.

When she returned to see him a couple of days later, the emotional wrench it caused her was almost worse. For Maurice had been forced to don a previously worn uniform, which was old and soiled. The money that should normally have gone to buy him a new uniform had been spent instead on buying cakes and candies. She was further outraged to discover that there were no chamber pots beneath the iron-post beds and that the inmates were not allowed to leave their dormitories in the middle of the night. But her indignant complaints were powerless against time-hardened rules and practices. Once again her son wailed and wept when the moment of parting came, and so did she as the coachman trotted her home in the fiacre. Nor could she stem her tears when Gustave Planche, hoping it would offer her relief, took her to the Conservatoire to listen to Beethoven's Pastoral Symphony; the alternately serene and stormy music failed to calm her, and she sat through the performance wretchedly trying to stifle her sobs.

Altogether, it was as miserable a springtime as she could remember. Though only twenty-eight, she felt emotionally worn out and prematurely aged. She couldn't help wondering, as she later expressed it in her novel *Jacques,* if it wasn't "the fault of my impotence . . . I saw the years floating by like dreams, and I said to myself that there was no time to lose if I wanted to be happy once again."

A chance for happiness now presented itself in the urbane person of Prosper Mérimée, now officially serving as private secretary to the minister of finance, Comte d'Argout. An unusually versatile individual who was at once archeologist, historian, linguist, folklore scholar, dramatist, short story writer, public servant, and accomplished seducer, Mérimée had first made his mark in 1825, at the age of twenty-one, with a collection of one-act plays, which he claimed to be the work of a gifted Spanish poetess and actress named Clara Gazul. This anthology established him at one stroke as a master of brisk, incisive dialogue. He had followed up this first triumph with an even bolder hoax — a long tale entitled *La Guzla* (an anagram for Gazul), which had supposedly been translated from the original Illyrian by an unknown Slavic author with the totally implausible name of Hyacinthe Maglanovich. As a consummate piece of literary fakery it could stand comparison with Latouche's finest experiments in the genre, exhibiting such a mastery of style and such a sure knowledge of Croatian folklore that the story took in Britain's leading Slavonic scholar, Sir John Bowring, a number of German "authorities," and even Pushkin, who undertook to translate the French "translation" into Russian!

A typical Romantic in his love for the Gothic, Mérimée shared the general taste for local color and rich pageantry, mixed with occasional glimpses of the "horrible" and macabre (scenes from the Spanish Inquisition, the Saint Bartholomew massacre, etc.). But where writers like Hugo tended to be long-winded and rhetorical, Mérimée, in his historical novels and short stories, was admirably concise and his characters spoke like human beings. No less remarkable were the travel articles he had been contributing for some time to the *Revue de Paris* and which had greatly impressed Aurore. But when several editors and critics, including Gustave Planche, sought to arrange a meeting between Mérimée and his feminine admirer, she was dismayed to discover that he had not even bothered to read one of her novels.

They finally met, however, some time in April 1833, at a time when George Sand was more than halfway through *Lélia*. Though on her guard at first, she soon found herself fascinated by this enthralling conversationalist and salon charmer. Here was someone who shared her own love of Spain and the Pyrenees. Unlike the lackadaisical Aurélien de Sèze who had toyed for a while with a Spanish grammar, Mérimée had really mastered the language of Cervantes, studied gypsy mores, and was full of spellbinding stories about the curious customs and practices of Basque smugglers. A good friend of Rossini's, whom both he and Balzac regarded as the wittiest man they had ever met, he was also a fervent admirer of Giuditta Pasta and a lover of the Italian music Aurore liked to play on her piano. Indeed, if the somewhat suspect memoirs of the Parisian music lover Armand de Pontmartin are to be trusted, it was at the Opéra that Mérimée finally won George Sand's heart, scandalizing the capital's high society by boldly walking down the grand staircase at the end of Meyerbeer's *Robert le Diable* carrying the sleeping Solange on his shoulder.

Later legend though this may be, what followed was no myth. For a week or two, perhaps even three, Mérimée made assiduous advances, clearly intimating that he would not be satisfied with a purely platonic friendship; he wanted a full-blooded union of body as well as mind. Profoundly disspirited by her break with Jules Sandeau, desperately anxious to prove to herself that she was still capable of love, secretly ashamed of her "puerile susceptibilities" (as she later termed them), she finally gave in. "I was not sufficiently convinced that I was absolutely and completely Lélia," George Sand later confessed to Sainte-Beuve. "I wanted to persuade myself that No, I could abjure this cold, odious role. Next to me I saw an unbridled woman" — Marie Dorval — "and she was sublime. I, austere and almost virginal, was hideous in my selfishness and isolation. I sought to overcome my nature, to forget the disappointments of the past . . . In a word, at thirty I behaved like a girl of fifteen . . ."

Mérimée's own account of what followed, dictated years later to his friend Comte Paul d'Haussonville, sounds reasonably authentic, even if he was led in retrospect to place it on a summer rather than a glorious spring evening. After strolling along the embankments of the Seine for some time, George Sand finally yielded to her companion's eloquent entreaties, remarking in a tone of deep resignation: "Very well, I am disposed. Let it be as you wish, since it gives you such pleasure. But for my part I must tell you that I am sure it will give me none whatsoever."

They accordingly went upstairs to her Quai Malaquais apartment, where they ate a light supper. George Sand, her dark hair tightly wound into a Spanish hairnet, had for the occasion put on a man's shirt, a black cravat, and a yellow silk wrapper concealing everything save two Turkish babouches of a garish blood-red hue. Just what she hoped to achieve with this extraordinary get-up is not clear, but she may have intended it as a manifestation of an almost defiant indifference. After all, it was Mérimée who was requesting the favor of her body; why should she try to behave like a flirt with an experienced Don Juan whose numerous conquests included any number of Opéra dancers and chorus girls? It was up to him to prove himself, it was not up to her to make the advances.

Unaccustomed to this total lack of coquetry, Mérimée was further amazed, as the decisive moment approached, to see George Sand calmly prepare the bed with her maid and then proceed to disrobe, while he sat in an armchair, as though they were an old couple who had lived together for forty years. Whatever erotic appetite might have been aroused by the champagne consumed at supper had completely evaporated by the time he had undressed in his turn and climbed in under the sheet. Mérimée, though a skilled seducer, was also, it seems, a somewhat fastidious lover, having already once been thrown off his erotic stride by the sight of two wrinkled stockings being unrolled down the veiny shanks of a lady with the celestial name of Madame Azur. Contact under the sheet with Madame Sand's strangely immobile limbs proved equally chilling — with the result that the would-be Don Juan suffered what Stendhal, in *De l'amour,* had described as the "fiasco of imagination." It was so complete that the impassive Madame Sand refused to lend a "helping hand." According to another account, which sounds like an apocryphal embellishment, she bit Monsieur Mérimée in the shoulder in a desperate effort to arouse him.

Was it after this disappointing first night that she wrote the following note, as pathetically eager as a schoolgirl to be allowed another chance? "I would like to see you tonight . . . Would you have the courage to come to my door at 9 o'clock, to know if I am here? If this bores you, don't do so. I am more resigned than you think. I have made a great deal of progress since yesterday. No, I'm not mad, believe me. I wouldn't blush at being so, but I feel that I'm not even very exalted."

No wonder. The whole carefully contrived business was about as appetizing to both parties as a piece of stone-cold turkey. Wounded in his masculine self-esteem Mérimée avenged himself by ridiculing her pathetic desire to please. Terribly upset by this sudden cruelty — so unlike his earlier advances — George Sand rushed over and made a clean breast of everything to Marie Dorval. Unable to keep a secret, the actress lightheadedly told her lover about it the next morning. Before the day was over Alfred de Vigney could note in his diary: "This monstrous woman" — he meant of course George Sand — "suddenly told her new friend yesterday: 'Well, it's over, I gave myself yesterday to — . . .' " — the name was later erased, but it was obvious who it was. "She had this man who scorned her and said so to her face . . . She added: 'He treated me like a little girl. He said to me: "It's not worth deceiving you one day in order to have you for one night." He said to me: "You have the tone of a young girl without having her advantages, and the pride of a marquise with none of her graces." ' "

This brief affair left George Sand absolutely shattered. "I wept out of suffering, disgust and discouragement," as she later wrote to her chosen "confessor" and fellow sufferer, the concupiscent and largely impotent Sainte-Beuve. "Instead of finding an affection capable of feeling sorry for me and helping me, all I encountered was a bitter and frivolous mockery . . . . If P[rosper] M[érimée] had understood me, he might perhaps have loved me, and if he had loved me he would have subjugated me, and if I could have submitted to a man I would be saved, for my freedom preys on me and kills me. But he did not get to know me enough, and instead of giving him the time to do so, which might have been the best way out of this folly, I was immediately discouraged and rejected the sole condition that could have attached him to me."

Once again she was tempted to drown herself in the Seine, and only the thought of Solange and Maurice kept her from doing so. Her anguish was aggravated by the discovery that Marie Dorval, in whom she had trustingly confided, had been indiscreet enough to mention the Mérimée fiasco not only to Alfred de Vigny but to Alexandre Dumas as well. Dumas, with his Gargantuan appetite for the salacious, had lost no time spreading the news of Don Prosper's misadventure, adding a bon mot to the effect that "*Mérimée a cinq pieds, cinq pouces* . . ." (Mérimée is five feet, five inches . . .) — the two final words, unstated, indicating a further degree of descending magnitude. It was a cruel quip and spread like wildfire through Paris' literary salons.

Feeling abandoned and betrayed by everyone, George Sand wrote several pathetic letters to Sainte-Beuve, complaining bitterly of "the baseness and infamy of men" in general, and more specifically of the *écriveurs* — as Solange called them — "those vain liars I particularly hate . . ." Fearful of compromising himself too openly by frequenting a woman with such a scandalous reputation, Sainte-Beuve let a month go by without replying and prudently avoided the Quai Malaquais apartment.

All those who knew George Sand were now convinced that Gustave Planche was her new lover, and her own careless and distraught behavior only helped confirm this impression. Having had trouble with her Nohant maid during the last stormy weeks with Jules Sandeau, she had Casimir take her back to the country. But the new maid, Julie Dorville, proved equally indiscreet. Baron Dudevant thus learned that Madame la Baronne had more than once shamelessly invited her daughter, Solange, who had developed a fierce dislike for Gustave Planche, to crawl in next to her, while she was in bed with her lover.

At a literary luncheon to which she was invited on June 21, Dumas made a mocking reference to this liaison in the presence of George Sand. Feeling herself insulted, she had Gustave Planche accompany her a day or two later to the offices of the *Revue des Deux Mondes,* on the Rue des Beaux-Arts, at a time when she knew that Dumas would be there. She demanded an apology, which Dumas flatly refused to give her. Instead, he went downstairs to the garden and there scribbled a note to say that inasmuch as she had seen fit to have herself accompanied by a man, it was natural that her companion should accept the consequences. Anything but eager to see two of his contributors killing themselves in a duel, François Buloz forcibly prevented Planche from going down into the garden to have it out with Dumas. A duel, nonetheless, seemed unavoidable — particularly since Buloz at this critical moment had to rush off to England on a business trip. Seconds were chosen, the choice of weapons discussed. But in his ponderous desire to obtain a prior "explanation," Planche wrote Dumas a note in which he explained that he would gladly shoot it out with him on his *own* behalf, since he was not Madame Sand's lover and could only speak for himself.

This was all Dumas needed to make Planche look like a good-natured ass. "My dear Planche," he wrote back. "Public rumor has it that you are Madame Sand's present lover. You gave credence to this rumor by accompanying this lady when she came to demand an explanation. Being unable to have an affair with her" — he meant of course a duel — "I sincerely wanted to have one with you.

"Today you tell me that not being her lover, you cannot and should not answer for her past or future remarks, and that the arm you offered her was not given in the capacity either of defensor or respondent. This being the case, you understand that the remark which wounded you is only an absurdity on my part. Consider it as such and, I beg you, say that I am a fool in the first article you will write about me. I shall have amply proved it by picking a quarrel with you over such a silly matter. Alex Dumas."

To Buloz's great relief, the pistols remained silent. But this pacific conclusion to an acrimonious quarrel offered George Sand scant relief. All of literary Paris was now abuzz with gossip about Madame Dudevant's "turpitudes." Feeling she had little more to lose, she penned a short note in early July to the Italian poet Alessandro Poerio, who had expressed an interest in meeting her. "Sir, I do not find your overture impertinent, I don't even find it singular, but I do find it naive. You must be much lacking in experience to like to see close at hand what pleased you from afar. I think you are in for a disappointment. Nevertheless, as a woman who is bored and who enjoys having her curiosity aroused, I will receive you on Monday at nine o'clock. But only on condition that if I displease you, you will say so on leaving, and that if you displease me, you will allow me to say the same, so that we should impose no mutual constraint upon each other for the future. You see, sir, that I place great confidence in the frankness you show me. George Sand"

Just what happened the next Monday after nine o'clock remains a tantalizing mystery — like so much else in this extraordinary woman's life. A handsome Neapolitan who for some time past had been one of the ornaments of the beautiful Princess Cristina Belgiojoso's salon, Alessandro Poerio had more than one attribute made to appeal to George Sand. Aside from being a poet of some distinction, he shared her libertarian and republican enthusiasms, had preferred exile from his native Italy to life under the Austrian yoke, and he had twice signed up for action under General Guglielmo Pepe, a pre-Garibaldi "rebel" for whom Aurore Dupin had named one of her horses.

Half a century later, when this and two other of George Sand's letters to Peorio were finally published in a Neapolitan paper, the accompanying editorial note claimed that during the poet's first visit to the Quai Malaquais apartment, "la George, on some pretext or other, whether to get ready to go out or to climb into a dressing gown or for some other reason, after asking permission — 'Allow me, sir, without formality?' — undressed and even changed her chemise, then dressed again, alone with the young man . . ." The story might be dismissed as a typical piece of Neapolitan braggadocio, but for the fact that it curiously resembles George Sand's matter-of-fact behavior in front of Boucoiran and Mérimée.

George Sand, at this singularly low ebb in her life, seems to have been ready to try anything. Having long sought but failed to be an ardent young Sténio, she was now ready to follow her brain child into a career of mild debauch — even though she knew that for a person of her exalted mystic temperament, it was likely to be hard, uphill work. (As she had had Pulchérie remark in *Lélia,* apropos of Sténio, but it was equally applicable to herself, "in the life of men like him, the intoxication of the senses should be a diversion and could not be an occupation.")

In her distress she again turned instinctively to her friend Marie, only to discover that *la grande Dorval* had left without a word of warning for a theater tour in northern France. "Your departure without saying goodbye caused me great pain," she wrote in a plaintive letter. "I fancied you did not love me. I wept like a donkey. Since you left, I don't know what hasn't been said" — doubtless by Gustave Planche and others — "to persuade me not to love you . . . People I hardly know and who don't know you at all have told and written me that you were betraying me! . . . I didn't listen or retain a word of it, and their foolishness gave me back my common sense."

It was six days before she could find out Marie's exact whereabouts in the north, and then only by sending the dutiful Gustave Planche to Alfred de Vigny's house with the request that he send her letter on. "I've forbidden Marie to reply to this Sappho who bores her," was the poet's irritated comment penciled in on the front page opposite the date.

The same despair echoed through a long, pathetic letter George Sand wrote at about the same time to her "dear confessor," Sainte-Beauve. "Oh my friends, a little help, a little pity," she pleaded. "I am in a dangerous pass and although I keep advancing, I still often stumble."

PART IV

Alfred de Musset

17. A Young Dandy of Genius

"Why wasn't it you I so loved?" George Sand had plaintively written to Emile Regnault in a letter asking him to help her find a new tenant for the Rue de l'Université flat (on which she still owed six months' rent). "I wouldn't have such bitter tears to shed today, but this error" — her three-year romance with Jules Sandeau — "will be the last of my life."

Doubtless she meant it, little realizing the surprise that life's perennial prodigality was soon to throw her way. "You must give your nerves time to calm themselves, your brain time to receive new impressions," she had had Trenmor, in *Lélia,* say to the despairing young Sténio. The words may have been her own invention, but they echoed the advice she had received in the early spring from Sainte-Beuve.

That one of these "new impressions" would soon turn into another tempestuous romance neither she nor her spiritual "confessor" could have foreseen in early March, when Sainte-Beuve volunteered to introduce her to the young poet Alfred de Musset. The enfant terrible of the French Romantic movement had, in the brief space of five years, made a dazzling ascension in the literary firmament, but he had also established a dubious reputation as a fast-living rake accustomed to living it up on punch and easy women. He was one of the better known *fashionables* (as they were called) who were often to be seen, in their fancy silk waistcoats, velvet revers, and saucy toppers, sampling aftertheater ices at the smart Café Tortoni or crowding around the gambling tables of the even smarter Café de Paris.

Though momentarily tempted by the idea of such an encounter,

George Sand quickly changed her mind. "He is very much the dandy, we would not get on, and it was more out of curiosity than interest that I wanted to see him," she wrote to Sainte-Beuve. "I think it imprudent to satisfy all of one's curiosities and better to obey one's sympathies."

Sainte-Beuve was not present, three months later, when chance finally satisfied her reluctant curiosity by bringing the authoress and the poet prodigy together in the apartment of Florestan Bonnaire, one of the *Revue des Deux Mondes'* financial backers. At a dinner party given for François Buloz and a number of his authors, she found herself seated next to a tall, trim-waisted young man whose blond hair was curiously parted, billowing into a wave which foamed and tumbled over his right ear, while a gentler cataract of curls descended over his left. His long, sharp nose, continuing the almost unbroken line of the forehead, his pinched nostrils, and a faintly jutting upper lip gave him the racy look of a thoroughbred. But most arresting of all were his eyes, bright blue, sparkling, and almost insolently direct when he spoke, heavy-lidded and dreamy when he listened.

As an accomplished lady-killer whose eclectic tastes ran all the way from bejeweled marquises to musk-scented sluts, Alfred de Musset had known many different types of women. But even he was startled by his first glimpse of George Sand, who turned up for this dinner in an unusual bolero, with a little gem-studded dagger provocatively dangling from her waist belt. He was struck even more by her faintly Oriental look, the deep olive complexion, the bronze luster of her skin, and most of all, the enormous, dark, almost Indian eyes.

Just what they discussed at this dinner we do not know for sure, but according to Musset's elder brother, Paul (who later wrote it up in an exasperating mixture of fact and fiction), the twenty-two-year-old Alfred broke the ice by asking, in a tone of playful banter, what Madame did with the "plaything" — the dagger — with which she had come armed.

"I often travel," she is reported to have answered. "Sometimes I dress like a man, but when I don't I need protection. This little plaything is always at my beck and call, and advantageously replaces a *cavalier servant,* who would only bore me."

"I would be curious to know how you handle this marine weapon at the moment of boarding," the skilled skirt-prober continued, only to have his neighbor reply, with perfect sang-froid: "That is up to you."

When the company broke up, after coffee, Alfred de Musset noticed that the ornamental dagger had disappeared into some hidden recess of George Sand's exotic vestment. Was this a discreet intimation that she had lowered her defenses, at least so far as he was concerned? It must have flattered his ego to think so. Bowing over the gloved hand she daintily extended toward him, the golden-haired dandy went off to amuse himself at the Opéra. But once back in his room in the town house where he lived with his family, on the Rue de Grenelle Saint-Germain, he copied out a few verses from a new poem, entitled *Rolla,* he was then engaged in writing, and sent them to George Sand.

The hero, or more exactly antihero, of these verses was the kind of pampered, life-weary rebel whom Byron had made so fashionable. A carefree rake and gambler, even though described as "great, loyal, intrepid and superb," Jacques Rolla has chosen to turn his back on the tedium of daily life and to dissipate his family savings in three years of riotous debauch. With the same reckless abandon he spends his last remaining pistole on a pretty fille de joie and refuses her kind offer of a necklace to pay his gambling debts, preferring to put an immediate end to his pointless existence. Though there was, to be sure, quite a bit of the young Musset in this imaginary character, George Sand must have been struck by his resemblance to her Sténio and even more startled by the note of philosophical despair sounded by a poet who was generally regarded as saucy, lighthearted, and irreverent. It was the protesting cry of a genuine *enfant du siècle,* the child of a doubting, disillusioned age which, suddenly bereft of its ancient faith and gods, had taken refuge in self-indulgence and frivolity: the cry of a postrevolutionary generation appalled to discover, as Charles Nodier had put it (long before Nietzsche), that GOD WAS DEAD.

Returning the compliment, George Sand sent Musset a copy of *Indiana* which, like Mérimée earlier in the year, the young poet-dandy had apparently not read. A couple of days later — June 24 — he replied with a thirty-eight-verse poem inspired by the scene in the novel where the punch-drunk Raymon loses his head and makes love to the voluptuous dark-haired Noun on the "narrow, virginal" bed of her mistress, Indiana, whom the intoxicated Lothario imagines he is embracing while feverishly caressing the body of her maid.

Sand, quand tu l'écrivais, où donc l'avais-tu vue,
Cette scène terrible où Noun, à demi nue,
Sur le lit d'Indiana s'enivre avec Raimond? . . .
Ah! malheur à celui qui lui livre son âme!
Qui couvre de baisers, sur le corps d'une femme,
Le fantôme d'une autre, et qui sur la beauté
Veut boire l'idéal dans la réalité!

(Sand, when you wrote it, where had you glimpsed
That terrible scene where a half-naked Noun
Gets drunk with Raimond on Indiana's bed?
Ah, woe betide the man who on a woman's body
Seeks to smother with his kisses
The phantom of another; who embracing beauty
Seeks the taste of the ideal on the lip of reality.

Musset's use of the familiar, second-person *tu* (instead of the normal *vous*) in addressing George Sand was deliberately intimate and provocative. It was as much intended to flatter the recipient as the accompanying note, which explained that these verses, though "of little value," gave their author the opportunity to express "the sincere and deep feeling of admiration which inspired them." No wonder! What George Sand had delicately portrayed in that intoxicating scene was precisely what the young Musset had so often experienced in his lovemaking, the almost schizophrenic divorce between carnal reality and mental illusion, what the cynical aphorist Chamfort, in his famous definition of love, had once described as "the exchange of two fantasies and the contact of two epidermises."

To Musset's poetic homage George Sand replied that very night, with a three-paragraph letter in which she remarked on the curious similarities between certain characters in her novels and those in Musset's poem *Namouna* (which he had completed at about the time she was starting to work on *Lélia*). She added that his creations were "in themselves far more beautiful than mine . . . My figures are of a grosser and more down-to-earth reality. They have traversed these times of pose and pettiness . . . Your portrayals belong to the youth of the soul."

She also promised to send him the proofs of *Lélia,* which would be available in a few days, though she had to admit that the novel's central theme was "entirely summed up" in a stanza of *Namouna,* and "I would tremble to give further instruction to a soul at once so young and knowing." (How could she fail to be receptive to a young poet who had devoted the second part of *Namouna* to describing Don Juan, not as a cynical self-indulgent sensualist, but as a frustrated lover forever pursuing an ideal perfection he can never find in any individual woman? Even if he had borrowed this idea from E. T. A. Hoffmann, was it not an echo of her own romantic quest? Clearly there was more depth to this young man than his nonchalant air, dandified attire, and dubious repute might lead one to suppose.) She concluded her letter by saying that she had not dared, when they had met at dinner, to ask him to call on her. "I still fear that the seriousness of my interior" — she doubtless meant her inner being — "might appall and bore you. However, if in a day of weariness and disgust with active life" — a reference to Musset's part-time duty with the National Guard — "you were tempted to enter a recluse's cell, you would be received with gratitude and cordiality."

The young poet-dandy lost little time climbing the three flights of stairs to visit George Sand's apartment, only to find that she was out. Capricious as ever, he refused to give his name to her maid, who could only report to her mistress, when she returned, that she had opened the door to a "handsome young man" who had a swagger stick in his hand.

The next time he called, Alfred de Musset was more fortunate. He found George Sand alone, dressed in a colorful negligee which seemed as charmingly bohemian as the blue-walled apartment with its flowers and cages full of twittering birds. He was offered some excellent Egyptian tobacco, while she sat crossed-legged on a cushion, puffing at a long-stemmed pipe made of Bosnian cherrywood. Her gallant visitor sank to one knee, ostensibly to admire the Oriental tracery in the Arab babouches she was wearing. He even ventured to touch one of them with his finger. She did not withdraw her foot, remarking instead with a smile that the liberties he was taking with her slippers made up for the bad impression her jeweled dagger had made on him at the *Revue des deux Mondes* dinner.

The delicate intimacy of this first call, if Paul de Musset is to be believed, was interrupted by the arrival of George Sand's friends Papet and Gustave Planche, whose distinctly offhand behavior — Planche's first act was to sprawl almost full-length across the couch — irked Alfred de Musset's aristocratic sensibilities. The poet had other reasons for disliking this intrusion. Planche had once seen him bend his head, during a dance, to kiss his partner's bare shoulder, in the fashionable salon of the lithographer Achille Devéria, and being as much of a "wallflower" as Musset was an impassioned waltzer, the caustic critic had immediately spread the word about this "scandalous" behavior.

Planche must instinctively have sensed the fascination which the dark-haired author of *Lélia* already exercised on the young author of the *Ballade à la lune* — the mocking poem that had so shocked the traditionalists of Victor Hugo's Cénacle when that most sacred of Romantic objects, the moon, was likened among other things to a drunkard knocking himself eyeless against a pointed tree. The next time Musset called at the Quai Malaquais apartment, Planche offered him some chocolates with an air of deceptive affability. They were, as it happened, laxative chocolates — specially doctored with ingredients which the critic had obtained from his father's pharmaceutical establishment. Seized with violent stomach cramps, the ashen-faced poet had to stretch out on the couch to keep from fainting dead away and had barely strength enough to drag himself home.

George Sand sent him a sympathetic note, which gave great pleasure to the "idiot wrapped up in flannel, like a burgermeister's sword," as Musset described himself in his letter of reply. His dearest wish, he added, was that she would soon have "the fantasy to lose an evening with him." The next day, Saturday, would suit her admirably, she immediately answered, provided he could call on her not later than nine o'clock. For after nine she would open her inkwell, take out her quills, and start writing. Nothing would then be allowed to disturb her *auguste permanence* — her studious confinement — as Gustave Planche and her Berrichon friends called her devotion to literature.

Each meeting seemed to enhance the feeling that they were two kindred souls, two love-racked sufferers. He had been the victim of an unrequited passion for an older woman; she had experienced an unhappy marriage, a disastrous liaison (with Jules Sandeau), to which had been added the recent humiliations of Vigny's scorn and Mérimée's sardonic mockery. No man had yet given her what she wanted and she had begun to doubt if such a man existed. Yet here was a young Prince Charming suddenly irrupting into her gloomy life with a refreshing gust of inspiration, poetic prankishness, and the tender homage Lélia's wounded sensibility so desperately craved. The gold buttons and the sky blue frock coat, the pale silk waistcoat and the tight, pearl gray trousers, the twirling swagger stick and the top hat tilted at a saucy angle were all, she recognized, part of the elaborate deceit of a sensitive Childe Harold, masking his sentimental and philosophical misgivings behind a mask of Byronic indifference.

In many areas, furthermore, they shared the same tastes and enthusiasms. Both were nostaligic Bonapartists who considered the mediocre present a lamentable comedown from the thrilling days of the Empire. Both had adopted a marked reserve toward the rhetorical excesses of the Victor Hugo school of literature, the young Musset having even been bold enough to make public sport of the "bearded Romantics" who wanted to relegate Racine and Aeschylus to the attic and "delve into the Middle Ages with a bloody dagger." Both were libertarians and had wept to see a rebellious Poland mercilessly ground to dust beneath the Cossack boot — the tragic Warsaw uprising of 1831 having moved Musset to cry with indignant scorn: *"Battez-vous et mourez, car nous sommes blasés!"* (Fight on and die, for we are blasé!). Both adored music, and though here George Sand was much his superior in knowledge and keyboard ability, it was he who had proclaimed that of all the arts music was the one that had caused him to believe in God.

Even the apparent differences in their respective characters added to the mutual attraction. Fanciful, teasing, and disarmingly outspoken, he gave her a feeling of joie de vivre she felt she had lost forever, while he found in her a depth he had never known in any other woman. "Your malady," he informed her with mock pomposity in mid-July, "has nothing pleasant about it; it would be easier to cut off one of your legs than to cure you; unfortunately nobody has yet found a cataplasm for the wounds of the heart. I beg you, do not stare too much at the moon," he added with a touch of Byronic irony, "and do not die before we have carried out that lovely project of a trip we spoke about. You see what an egotist I am. You say you narrowly missed departing for the other world; I'm really not too sure what I'm doing in this one."

Two days later Musset received the two printed volumes of *Lélia* that George Sand had promised him. The first was playfully autographed "To my *gamin,* Alfred," and signed "George"; the second with mock pomp to "Monsieur le vicomte Alfred de Musset, with the respectful homage of his devoted servant — George Sand." Twenty-four hours later he sent her a note to say that "to experience joy on reading a lovely thing written by another is the privilege of an ancient friendship. I do not have these rights with you, Madame, but I must however say that this is what has happened to me on reading *Lélia* . . ."

Though his praise was limited to twenty pages of *Lélia,* it was satisfying for George Sand's self-esteem to hear him comparing her to Chateaubriand and Byron. Realizing that what had begun as a literary flirtation was rapidly turning into something more serious, Paul de Musset vainly sought to warn his younger brother of the risks he was running in courting a woman who was "mysterious and complex: now soft, outgoing and generous, now hard, proud and susceptible." But Alfred was no longer prepared to listen. Indeed, the more dangerous such a courtship was made to seem, the more exhilarating it became. There was in him, as in many other Romantics, a gambler's instinct, an overpowering desire to live recklessly, a vertiginous desire to throw oneself into an abyss of emotional excess. Four years earlier, when he was only eighteen, he had fallen in love with a married lady of unusual intelligence, who was both musically inclined and "consumptive" — enough, at any rate, to add to the pathos of a melancholy passion — only to discover that she had been using his advances to distract attention from another, and for her, more precious lover. This shattering discovery had induced a raging fit, at the end of which Musset's tense body became "as rigid as a skeleton," as he later described it in *La Confession d'un enfant du siècle.* "I had a kind of brooding desire to possess her once again, to drink all those bitter tears on that magnificent body, and then to kill both of us." Fortunately for poetry and the history of romance, he had been thwarted in this destructive enterprise and had later worked off his mortification on the more or less willing bodies of ladies of both high and low repute.

Four years of feverish indulgence in gambling, "fermented liquors, courtesans and sleepless nights" had not been able to satisfy the delicate artist and sentimental lover who also inhabited the same tormented body. But now, confronted by a brilliant woman who commanded his respect, he felt himself "transported" and a being of a higher sort. The former art student who had once spent days copying the masterpieces of the Louvre pulled out his pencils and went to work again. "Dear George," he wrote to her the next day, at last dropping the stiff "Madame" he had used until then, "your beautiful black eyes . . . have been trotting in my head this morning — I send you this sketch, ugly though it is, out of curiosity, to see if your friends will recognize it, and if you will recognize it yourself.

"Good night," he concluded in English, "I am gloomy today."

This was no Romantic pose. Musset was smitten and knew it. In his next missive, composed after an afternoon walk, in the Jardin du Roi (as the Tuileries Gardens was then known), he dropped the ironic mask altogether. The tone was almost apologetic. This was the letter of a suppliant, on his knees before his beloved.

"Dear George, I have something foolish and ridiculous to tell you. I am foolishly writing it, Heaven knows why, when I should have said it to you, on coming back from this walk . . . I am in love with you. I have been in love ever since the first day I called on you . . . I have no hopes in saying this to you. I can only lose a friend and the only agreeable hours I have spent in the last month . . ."

To this declaration of love George Sand responded by letting Musset read her impressions of him, as recorded in a private album. Just what these impressions were we do not know, for the pages were later ripped from the album and disappeared, along with many of the letters she had written to him. But in his next letter to her, written in the solitude of his bedroom, Musset pleaded: "Feel sorry for me, but do not despise me. Since I could not speak up in front of you, I shall die in silence. If my name is inscribed in some corner of your heart, no matter how faint or faded its imprint may be, do not efface it. I can kiss a scurvy and dead-drunk girl, but I cannot kiss my mother.

"Love those who know how to love, I only know how to suffer. There are days when I could kill myself; but I cry, or I burst into laughter — but not today for example. Farewell, George, I love you like a child."

This was no Aurélien de Sèze, more or less devotedly accepting a platonic idyll. Five years older than Aurore Dudevant, Aurélien had never asked to be mothered. But the twenty-two-year-old Alfred de Musset could not forget that the object of his passion was six and a half years older than himself — as had been the case with the Madame Beaulieu who had so deeply hurt and humiliated him four years previously. If he instinctively sought a pure, unsullied, even "angelic" mother figure to keep from relapsing into his periodic debauches, he also needed to pour out his heart upon her breast, in a kind of incestuous intimacy — regardless of the disclaimers he might make to the contrary. The "consoling angel" he craved was one whose bed he had to share.

Had she been in a mood for moderation, George Sand would not have bothered to answer this extraordinary outburst. Instead, she replied at eight o'clock the next morning, though she normally rose around noon. That evening, she said, she had arranged to take Maurice and Solange to the top of the towers of Notre-Dame to watch the fireworks celebrating the third anniversary of the "Three Glorious Days" of revolutionary turmoil that had toppled the reactionary regime of Charles X. But by midnight the children would be home and in bed, and then her gamin Alfred was welcome to call on her.

Call on her he did. "It was the most beautiful night on earth; the moon was sinking, and the stars were shining more brightly in a dark azure sky." Musset, a year or two later, may have been indulging in poetic license in evoking its wonder as they gazed out over the leafy garden and listened to the soft tinkle of the fountain below.

Still, she did not yield easily to his advances — the memory of her disastrous experience with Mérimée was still too vivid. But Musset was no casual armchair spectator waiting for Madame to warm the sheets. He was on his knees before her. He was passion and poetry combined, smothering her in a shower of intoxicating words and tearful pleading. How could she resist this young Adonis who was beseeching her to save him from his past dissipations? Toward dawn she finally gave in. "Softly she turned her head; her eyes were full of tears. Her body bent like a reed, her half-opened lips fell on mine, and the universe was forgotten."

"Eternal angel of joyous nights, who will sing of your silence?" Musset was later inspired to write by the memory of this blessed night. "Oh kiss! Mysterious beverage which the lips pour out like cups exchanged! Oh, voluptuous swoon of the senses! Yes, like God, you are immortal! . . . Oh love, principle of the world . . . I am not surprised that your name should be blasphemed; for they know not who you are, those who think they have seen you face to face, because they have opened their eyes; and when you find your real apostles, united on earth by a kiss, you order their eyelids to close like veils, so that they may not see their happiness."

Six days later, the two ecstatic lovers decided to leave Paris, now stewing in a heat wave, to enjoy a bohemian "honeymoon" in the forest of Fontainebleau. The decision was taken so suddenly that George Sand, who on August 3 had sent a note to Alessandro Poerio, complaining because the Neapolitan poet had "dropped" her, had to send him a second letter to cancel her dinner invitation.

Gustave Planche agreed to keep a watchful eye on the children, left to the care of Julie Dorville, the maid, and on August 5 the two lovers traveled up the Seine by riverboat as far as Fontainebleau, where they put up at a country inn. After the five o'clock dinner they hired a couple of horses and set out with a guide toward the rock formations of Franchard, which Alfred de Musset had visited more than once (and which are still used for practice training by Paris *alpinistes*). Irked by the guide's pretentious chatter, they sent him back with the horses once they had reached the famous gorges, saying they would return to the inn on foot.

It was a radiant night, even though the August moon was somewhat beyond its prime. Clambering to the top of one of the cliffs, they rested for a while on the dry moss, gazing upward at the stars. Suddenly Musset stood up. George Sand asked him what was the matter.

"There's an extraordinary echo over there," he answered, indicating the other side of the ravine. "The last time I was here with the little . . . but you would rather not know her name, I imagine? . . . I derived great pleasure from listening to her voice, while she sang over there on that rocky ledge just opposite us."

George Sand winced. That her beloved Alfred should so casually and cruelly evoke the memory of some young girl with whom he had previously dallied on this very spot caused her more pain than she dared admit.

"I can see you don't believe in my echo," Musset said gaily. "I want you to hear it. Stay here. I'm going to climb up to the other side . . . You won't be frightened, will you, remaining five minutes by yourself?"

"No, not at all," she answered. Was she not after all the disciple of Rousseau, Chateaubriand, and Ossian?

Prête-moi la lueur de ton pâle flambeau
Lune, mélancolique amante du tombeau.
Combien j'aime le soir et ta clarté douteuse
Favorable au penchant de mon âme rêveuse.

Why should she be frightened by the "doubtful clearness" of a moon she had once described, while at the Couvent des Anglaises, as the "melancholy lover of the tomb"? So she sat on the dry moss and waited for Alfred to reappear on the other side of the dark gully. Halfway down the slope, she heard him call to ask if she was all right; she replied that she was. Then there was silence. She began to feel a vague malaise. Getting to her feet, she was about to call out when she heard Musset utter a desperate, hoarse cry from somewhere down below. Heedless of the bushes, which tore at her clothes, she half ran, half slid down the steep slope until she came upon a haggard, wild-eyed Alfred who was trembling convulsively.

It was some minutes before he could sufficiently recover his composure to be able to explain just what had happened, and even then it sounded too strange to be believed. Troubled by the feeling that he had unwittingly hurt her by mentioning his previous visits to this spot with dissolute companions and wanton women, he had lost interest in climbing the opposite slope to demonstrate the reverberating echo. Instead, feeling tired and a bit dizzy, he had sat down for a moment on a patch of grass. Suddenly, without his opening his mouth, he was amazed to hear an echo mocking him with an obscene refrain. Scrambling to his feet, he had seen a pale, disheveled figure come running toward him through the heather. Thinking it was some poor fellow who had been set upon by thieves, Musset groped wildly for his cane, but as the stranger passed him, staggering like a drunkard, he turned and scowled at him, a hideous scowl of scorn and hate. Convulsively Musset had thrown himself on the ground, so as not to see that awful, spectral face, a face he recognized with chilling horror as his own!

This brief seizure, in the Fontainebleau forest, was George Sand's first experience of Musset's latent schizophrenia. He had made no secret of his past debauches, and she naturally assumed that this moonlight hallucination was the spectral creation of a guilty conscience, stimulated by the fatigue of this outing and the wine he had drunk at dinner.

The next day all trace of his fit had disappeared, and Alfred de Musset was once again his gay, carefree, imaginative self. They spent the next week riding through the sandy forest or going on long hikes, George Sand clad in a blue blouse, man's trousers, and nailed boots. The upsetting incident of the first night would have been happily forgotten had Alfred not insisted — much to her dismay — on making a comic sketch of them wandering through the moonlit heather, he with a distraught and haggard air, she with a sadly torn dress.

The lovers' return to Paris coincided with the appearance of the August 15 issue of the *Revue des Deux Mondes,* twenty-five pages of which were devoted to the publication of Alfred de Musset's long poem *Rolla.* Its alternately profound and facile verses had already been warmly praised by Sainte-Beuve and several other literary connoisseurs. But now the private praise turned into public acclaim. No one was more surprised and moved than Musset himself when one evening, as he was walking up the stone steps of the Opéra, he threw away his still unfinished cigar only to see a young admirer hastily retrieve and wrap it up in a piece of paper, as though it were some precious relic.

The August 15 issue of the *Revue des Deux Mondes* also contained the critical essay that Gustave Planche had written about *Lélia.* This, he proclaimed, was no "ingenious adventure tale nor the dramatic development of a passion. It is the thought of the century upon itself, it is the complaint of a society in its death throes which, after denying God and the truth, abandoning the churches and the schools, attacks the heart and says that its dreams are follies."

As pathetically anxious to please as ever, Planche had already written to George Sand at Fontainebleau to suggest that she write to Chateaubriand and Béranger to draw their attention to her new novel. An incisive pamphleteer and the composer of patriotic ditties which enjoyed an immense vogue, particularly with the tens of thousands of French men and women who had remained nostalgically liberal and Bonapartist, Pierre-Jean de Béranger was universally regarded as one of the great poets of the day. Béranger immediately replied with a friendly note in which he expressed the admiration he already felt for the author of *Indiana* and *Valentine.* Chateaubriand went further; he read the novel almost at a single sitting, then wrote with typical Romantic flourish: "You will live, Madame, and you will be the Lord Byron of France." Then comparing himself to an aged convict chained to the galley ships of life, he concluded with exalted humility: "For you, Madame, youth and glory; for me nothing" — but feeling that this might sound too negative, not to say subversive, for a defender of the Christian faith, he changed "nothing" to "God."

Charles Didier, from whom a hard-pressed George Sand had just borrowed 100 francs, felt crushed by "this masterpiece of poetry, feeling, nature, and strength." It was enough to make the humble novel he himself was working on look utterly ridiculous in comparison — though, as he noted in his diary, "I shall not say all of this to Madame Dudevant, who is apt to pay little heed to those who admire her." His admiration left him so tongue-tied that when he next called on her, shortly after her return from Fontainebleau, he was afraid to admit that he had read *Lélia* and been swept off his feet by it. He found her already hard at work on a new short story — *Metella Doria* — destined for Buloz and the *Revue des Deux Mondes* (which was about to publish another, *Aldo le Rimeur*). "Spent an hour with her," the Swiss poet noted in his diary, "after which she threw me out. Was very friendly, very gay, saying she was 15 years old. We spoke of *Lélia,* then of Stoicism. On her head she was wearing a kind of *flammeum* such as is worn by the Italo-Albanians. Smoked a cigarette . . ." After which he added, with a passing reference to the intense jealousy now felt by Hortense Allart for the more famous George Sand: "Would it still be possible for her to love?"

The answer to this question was unequivocally provided in a long letter George Sand wrote to Sainte-Beuve on August 25. Yes, she had to admit to her chosen "confessor" that the impossible had happened and that she had fallen in love again and "this time very seriously with Alfred de Musset" — in whom she had found "a candor, a loyalty, a tenderness" which thrilled her.

"Now that I have told you what lies on my heart," she went on, "I shall tell you how I intend to behave. Planche has been considered my lover, not that I care, I haven't denied it. I have only told my friends the strict truth: *he is not* my lover. I very much want people to know now that he is not my lover, just as it is a matter of supreme indifference to me if people believe that he was. I cannot, you understand, live in intimacy with two men who would be considered to enjoy the same relations with me, that would not be fitting for any of the three of us."

Paradoxically, it was just when the faithful Gustave Planche was being shown the door that he rushed most gallantly to her defense. In a blistering attack published in *L'Europe littéraire,* a journalist named Capo de Feuillide opened fire on *Lélia,* urging readers misguided enough to purchase or to rent such a book from a *cabinet de lecture* (a kind of nineteenth-century lending library) to lock it up in their desks "so as to contaminate no one. If you have a daughter whose soul you would like to remain virgin and naive, send her out to play in the fields . . ." For the truth, he roundly declared, was that this novel was in places as perverse as the books of the infamous

Marquis de Sade, its depraved heroine stank of "mud and prostitution" — a prostitution of the soul as well as of the body — and as for the author's name, George Sand, it could not possibly be a woman writer's pseudonym, as was generally supposed.

Having gone out of his way to hail this controversial novel as destined to "start a blazing revolution in contemporary literature," Planche felt personally insulted and challenged Capo de Feuillide to a duel. Pistols were procured and a meeting place agreed upon. François Buloz and Emile Regnault acted as Planche's seconds, accompanying the suddenly heroic Gustave out to a secluded corner of the Bois de Boulogne. There several fortunately wild shots were innocuously exchanged between the two duelers.

George Sand was more than a little annoyed to find her honor being defended by a gentleman who no longer enjoyed the favor of her intimacy, while Musset was nettled to discover that he had been beaten to the draw by the man he had supplanted. He avenged himself by composing a ninety-six-line poem relating the "epic" encounter between two "very unknown" *hommes de plume,* who were satirically described as shooting it out from a murderous distance of 600 paces!

Toward the end of August Solange was dispatched to Nohant to join her brother, Maurice, while Alfred de Musset left his parents' house and took up residence at 19 Quai Malaquais. Here he amused himself composing humorous doggerel about his amiable "hostess" and her friends:

Pâle et mélancolique,
D'un air mystérieux,
Papet, pris de colique,
Demande où sont les lieux.

(Pale and melancholic
And with an air of mystery,
Papet, seized with colic,
Asks the way to the toilet.)

In honor of the canaries and waxbills chirping and twittering in their cages, he called George his *oisillon* — his "little bird" or fledgling. Since this too made for an easy rhyme, he changed his own name to Mussaillon, writing on the first page of her red-cloth-bound drawing book that "I, the undersigned, Mussaillon Ist, declare that my album is not as obscene" — the word he actually used was *pig-like* — "as all that . . . It is vexing to be accused of George Sand's turpitudes." This was a reference to her penciled sketches, most of which revealed a remarkable gift for incisive caricature. His own pencil drawings — at any rate of her — were kinder, even though there was no disguising her worst feature, the disappearing chin. He also added a couple of sketches of himself — deliberately exaggerating the wild hair, the horsy features, the sidelong-glancing almond eyes, the floppy cravat, and the dandified nonchalance with which he kept his coattails back and his hands in his pockets.

Stimulated by her new lover's effervescent presence, George Sand sang Spanish and Italian romances and played the piano. Everyone talked and laughed. Paul de Musset, who was a frequent visitor, later admitted that he had never known such an atmosphere of carefree merriment. Alfred and his sweetheart would climb into some theatrical disguise to surprise themselves, their friends, and the more or less serious contributors to the *Revue des Deux Mondes.* One such, Professor Eugène Lerminier, a huge, red-faced Alsatian who could outtalk, outdrink, and outeat them all, was invited one day to meet a distinguished member of the British House of Commons who was reported to be bound for Vienna on some mysterious mission. Dressed in an impeccable black frock coat, complete with flowering cravat, a frilled jabot and gloves, Deburau, the famous acrobatic clown whose acquaintance Aurore had made several years earlier with Gustave Papet, proved an admirably phlegmatic Briton, eating and drinking his way through the meal with monosyllabic concentration, while Alfred de Musset, his blond mustaches shaved for the occasion, capered around the table, upsetting dishes, removing forks, displacing knives, and provoking a maximum of chaos, disguised as a clumsy provincial maid. When Lerminier, in a supreme effort to pierce the English parliamentarian's baffling taciturnity, asked him what he thought of the European balance of power, Deburau lifted a plate and spun it round and round on the tip of his knife, while the clumsy maid gave naive expression to her glee by "accidentally" emptying a water pitcher over the bewildered professor's head.

In another letter to Sainte-Beuve, written in mid-September,

George Sand confessed that she was "happy, very happy . . . each day I grow fonder of him, each day I see the little things that made me suffer disappear, each day I see the fine things I admire shine and glitter. And then, above all else, he is a *good sport,* and his intimacy is as sweet as the preference he has shown for me is precious."

The fact that they were now living openly, not to say brazenly, in sin, added to the sweetness of their liaison. They were romantic rebels and only too happy to thumb their noses at convention. Financially hard-pressed to maintain a household whose upkeep was about double the meager allowance she received from her husband, George Sand maintained her exacting schedule as best she could, working till three, four, or even later in the morning. Musset, having slept while she burned the midnight oil, would concentrate on his own poetic creations in the morning, while his mistress slept off her weariness till one or two o'clock in the afternoon.

By mid-September she had a short story ready for Urbain Canel, a publisher who made a specialty of printing books written by the young Romantics. The price she demanded was 500 francs — "for I must confess with the ingenuousness of pure souls that I have the most pressing need of it." Entitled *Garnier,* it was a rather farfetched piece of fantasy which included passages obviously inspired by Musset as well as E. T. A. Hoffmann, whose fantastic tales they both enjoyed reading. But the flow of inspiration was anything but one-sided, for in a moment of amorous generosity she tore some twenty pages from the red notebook she had begun filling two years earlier and gave them to Musset to do with as he pleased. These notes for a historical story about the Florentine "Conspiracy of 1537" were completely transformed by the young poet's genius. And thus was born *Lorenzaccio,* which has been called the only Shakespearean comedy ever authored by a Frenchman.

"My dear Buloz, *Métella* is finished," she could announce with a sigh of relief on October 2. "We now have 60 pages of my scribblings. Come and pick them up this evening, I'm not sending them to you because I want to reread them to A" — her darling Alfred — "who is sleeping like a top at this hour" — the moment being seven o'clock in the morning. A hardheaded bargainer when it came to defending her interests, she sold this novelette to Buloz for 1000 francs.

To escape from the storm of outraged gossiping which *Lélia* had unleashed, George Sand and Alfred de Musset treated themselves to another riding and hiking holiday in the Fontainebleau forest in early November. On her return to Paris she was charmed to discover that her friend Achille Ricourt had come out with a ringing defense of her novel in his lavishly illustrated review *L'Artiste,* saying among other things that "this book will leave deep and lasting traces in our literature . . . This is not a book made to be read by boarding-school girls, any more than is Byron's *Don Juan,* which is a masterpiece. There are no libertine ideas in *Lélia.*"

What, after this, remained to be said? To be compared once again to Byron must have been sweet music to George Sand's troubled soul. Chateaubriand, Sainte-Beuve, Gustave Planche, the hard-headed François Buloz, her darling Alfred de Musset, normally so difficult to please — all were agreed that *Lélia* was a major literary event. Balzac, to be sure, had turned his back on her, persuaded that she was responsible for the breakup of her liaison with Jules Sandeau, while the hypochondriac Latouche had angrily rebuffed the reconciliation she had attempted between himself and Gustave Planche and indignantly insisted that any future editons of *Lélia* no longer be dedicated to him.

Of the persons whose opinion she valued, only one, Béranger, the pamphleteer and poet, had not expressed his opinion in print. But he had made no secret of the high regard in which he held her on the one occasion on which they had met. "I would much like to see Béranger again and to cultivate an acquaintance which seems to me precious," she wrote to Sainte-Beuve shortly after her return from the second trip to Fontainebleau in a letter which revealed how hurt she still was by the disastrous fling with Mérimée. "I have no desire to make new friends, I have everything I need in this world, the life of my heart is arranged and I am not looking for anything more. But to talk from time to time with such a good and distinguished man would be most agreeable to me. I wrote to him and invited him to dinner, asking his permission to introduce Musset to him. He replied with a charming letter, and several days later he came to see me, to say that he was leaving for the country for eight or ten days and that he would come to dine on his return. He said this to my maid, for as it was only two in the afternoon I was not yet up" — an interesting glimpse of her nocturnal mode of life. "I would like to write to him, but cannot bring myself to do so. I am very proud, my friend, and the more people speak ill of me, the more haughty and concentrated do I grow . . . I am now apprehensive and distrustful, and I no longer dare take a step even when my heart bids me to do so."

In this case her fears were unfounded. Far from making fun of George Sand, Béranger went out of his way to berate a friend who had dared speak with "too little reverence" of her. "Do you realize that we know each other and that she recently honored me with her visit?" he wrote to him on November 20. "That *Lélia* should not have satisfied you as regards the content I understand, but I am surprised that you should not admire the pen of this woman of genius. She seems to me the queen of our new literary generation . . ."

18. Winter in Italy

"Do NOT GAZE too much at the moon, I beg you, and do not die before we have carried out that lovely project for a trip of which we've spoken," Alfred de Musset had written to George Sand in one of his first letters. And where could a romantic couple like themselves dream of spending a belated honeymoon more than in "fair Italy" — as Byron had called it — "the garden of the world, the home of all Art yields, and Nature can decree"? Her adolescence had been charmed by the haunting verses of Petrach and Metastasio; her youthful soul had thrilled to the celestial harmonies of Porpora, Leo, Pergolesi and Durante; she had been taught to speak the language of Dante almost as well as that of Milton. His first poems had been published under the title, *Contes d'Espagne et d'Italie,* and if Spain, for the young poet-genius, was the country of Don Juan, Italy was the birthplace of Boccaccio and Casanova — that "terrible musketeer" and Prince of Adventurers, as he had written in an article praising the Venetian seducer's recently published *Memoirs.* It was Italy which had inspired the names of Lélia and Sténio, provided George Sand with the background to some of her first short stories, and had given Musset the Florentine intrigue he needed for his five-act play *Lorenzaccio.* Italy was the land of carnival carouse and madcap fantasy — the opposite of the classical restraint which had tied French culture into knots.

It was more than mere sentiment, however, which made George Sand feel sympathetic to the idea of a trip to Italy. Unlike Balzac, an earthy writer who was quite happy to compose social novels about the Paris he knew and lived in, she was instinctively drawn to the fanciful and exotic. Alfred de Musset's poetic inclinations undoubtedly encouraged this penchant, as much as their common admiration for E. T. A. Hoffmann, the creator of a new genre of literary fantasy which, on a more philosophical and sophisticated level, continued what the Grimm Brothers had done for Germanic folklore and fairy tales. The heroine of her latest tale, Princess Quintilia Cavalcanti, had an Italian name, but the setting of her magnificently unbridled life ("the entire day given over to business, the entire night to love. You barely sleep four hours in the morning," one of her admirers expostulates!) was an "Illyrian" principality located in what we would now call Dalmatia. Quintilia, of course, was a heroic magnification of George Sand, boldly brandishing the flag of feminine defiance. ("I shall have opened the way for other women," Quintilia says to her male secretary. "Other women will succeed, other women will be frank, and without stripping themselves of the softness of their sex, they will perhaps assume the firmness of your own.") But though the other characters were thinly disguised transpositions from real life, *Le Secrétaire intime* was a fundamentally frivolous work, as the author candidly admitted to Sainte-Beuve in mid-November. Originally intended to be a short story, she developed it into a novelette in order to obtain a larger advance from Buloz, who set his rates according to the number of pages delivered, but the result, she feared, was "a pastiche of Hoffmann and myself."

If there was one lesson to be drawn from this fiasco, it was that she had to be more familiar with the exotic settings she felt she needed for her romantic stories. She had failed where Hyacinthe de Latouche had succeeded with his novel *Fragoletta,* because unlike him, she had not spent three years in Italy and knew even less about Dalmatia. A trip to Italy was what she needed to provide her with invaluable local color, particularly for a novel she was planning about her father and his adventures during Napoleon's Lombardy campaigns.

Though her romance with Musset had proved a balm to her troubled heart, it had done nothing to solve her pressing financial problems. Living in Paris now cost her close to 2000 francs a month, or more than six times as much as the meager allowance of 300 francs her husband had been talked into granting her. The 5000 francs her publisher Dupuy had finally agreed to pay for *Lélia* had long since been spent, while Musset's long poem *Rolla,* though it had filled twenty-five pages of the *Revue des Deux Mondes,* had netted him only 500 francs. *Fantasio,* a two-act prose play which had kept Alfred busy for part of this autumn of 1833, had brought in the same, an amount all too quickly spent.

By late November they were both so short of funds that George Sand had to write François Buloz an urgent note to say that she was in dire need of fifty francs. Three days later — November 25 — she signed a contract with him providing for the eventual publication in book form of *Métella,* the still unfinished story about Quintilia Cavalcanti, and a new short story still to be written. In exchange, she received the final installment on a 5000-franc advance, most of which had already been spent.

Since it would have been sheer madness to set off for Italy on a mere 1000 francs, there was only one solution: persuade Buloz to give her a new advance on the "Italian" novel she was already ruminating. On the thirtieth she wrote to Casimir to say that she was going to spend the winter in Italy "to cure myself of the rheumatism which has affected me this year." She was going to bring Solange down to Nohant, dropping her off on the way south. Maurice, being at boarding school, was no longer a problem.

On December 4 she wrote a brief note to Buloz, who had given his provisional agreement to her project, asking him if he would accompany her to the police station to act as a witness for the issuance of a passport. The next day, Thursday, she wrote him a long and far more urgent letter, saying that she had finished the story about Quintilia Cavalcanti, which was now ready for him. But Alfred de Musset had just informed her that there were only two steamboats a week between Lyon and Marseille, and this being the case, they would have to leave Paris the following Monday — in exactly four days — if they were to reach Marseille in time to catch the monthly packet, which was due to sail for Genoa on December 15. "So you must give me my 5000 francs on Sunday, or I shall give up this trip; for if I stay on another month here, I shall already have spent almost half of it." In fact, she needed 200 francs right away to reserve two seats on the Lyon stagecoach and to settle a couple of small debts.

The final days in Paris were spent in a fever of activity. On December 6 Aurore wrote to Casimir to say that she no longer had time to make the detour via Châteauroux, and that Julie Dorville, the maid, would instead be bringing Solange down to Nohant. Buloz, hesitating to give her the large advance she was demanding in one lump payment, when she had not yet fulfilled her previous contract, kept her on tenterhooks until the very last moment. Sunday came and went with no sign of money, and on Monday, December 9, Aurore had to write a second letter to her husband, asking him to pay Julie 160 francs for wages that had gone unpaid for six full months. That afternoon she signed a new contract with Buloz, who finally agreed to advance her 4000 francs on a new "Italian" novel, to be called *Jacques,* which she pledged herself to deliver to him in finished form by June 1. The remaining 1000 francs were to be forwarded to her at Genoa or elsewhere during the month of January.

Musset had meanwhile discovered that there were no stagecoach seats to be had before Thursday, the twelfth. It would now be nip and tuck getting to Marseille in time, but they decided to chance it. Solange's bed and blankets were hastily transported to Sophie Dupin's apartment, to be used by Maurice on his free days out of boarding school, while the keys to the Quai Malaquais flat and wine cellar were entrusted to Boucoiran — in case *Monsieur le Baron* took it into his head to journey up to Paris during his wife's absence and to go through her belongings.

Alfred de Musset, meanwhile, had been having troubles of his own. Though he was no longer a minor — having celebrated his twenty-third birthday the previous day, December 11 — his family and friends were unanimous in considering it an act of folly to rush off to Italy like this with an older woman of such dubious repute. The young Musset could only laugh when he heard his fast-living friend Alfred Tattet join the chorus of protests. "What! Coming from you, who want to go there with an actress!" To which Tattet, a well-heeled banker's son, replied, with exquisite hypocrisy: "Oh, for me it's different. I'm not a poet, and then an actress isn't a woman novelist."

Musset's mother was not so easily silenced. Of the five children she had given the Chevalier Victor-Donatien de Musset-Pathay — an authentic aristocrat who had broken with the family's noble traditions by espousing the cause of the Republic and Napoleon — two had died in infancy; she had lost her husband in the cholera epidemic of 1832, and the fragile health of her third and in some ways favorite child, Alfred, had been a frequent source of worry. Reluctant to upset her once again, Alfred waited till the very last moment before breaking the news. The reaction was predictably negative. What! A trip to Italy with Madame Sand? Certainly not. Moving into the Quai Malaquais apartment was scandalous enough, but this was worse.

Anything but impressed by this maternal veto which seemed to have reduced her lover to a state of meek subservience, George Sand hurried downstairs, hailed a cab, and had herself driven to No. 59 Rue de Grenelle. The town-house porter was requested to inform Madame de Musset that Madame Sand, who was waiting downstairs in a fiacre, wished to have a few words with her. With her old-fashioned bonnet, her dark hair curled into ringlets, and her sharp black eyes, Madame de Musset must have reminded Aurore a bit of her own mother, while the aging widow must have been even more impressed by the austere but intense young woman who so imperiously demanded to see her. She finally gave her consent to the trip, knowing that her headstrong Alfred would in any case do as he pleased and that the likely alternative to Madame Sand was a relapse into debauch.

That evening, shortly before six o'clock, Paul de Musset, who had preceded them to the Messageries — the mail-coach terminal — saw his brother, Alfred, and George Sand climb out of a hackney cab, followed by a retinue of trunks and bonnet boxes. Huddled around a stove in the smoky, low-ceilinged waiting room, they watched as the mail-coaches were driven out, one by one, from the dark inner courtyard, their destinations announced and the waiting passengers bundled aboard. Theirs was the thirteenth — as the superstitious Alfred was quick to note. "What a child you are, to believe in nonsense like that!" exclaimed George Sand gaily, as they climbed in. The coachman cracked his whip, and as the waving figure of Paul de Musset disappeared from the carriage window, they felt a violent lurch. Frightened by the whiplash, one of the four Percheron horses had shied, dragging the coach so far to the left that as it passed out through the vaulted entrance, the rear wheel ran up over the stone hitching post. A little farther on, as they were clop clopping down a narrow street, one of their horses accidentally knocked over a man who was pushing along a water barrel mounted on a cart. The incident was trifling, but again it was hardly auspicious.

They reached Lyon some thirty-six hours later and spent a day and a night there before climbing onto the paddle-wheel steamer at seven o'clock in the morning. By an extraordinary coincidence they found themselves on the same riverboat with Henri Beyle, alias Stendhal, who was returning to his post as French consul at Civita Vecchia. George Sand spent a good part of the day listening to him make witty fun of her naive illusions about Italy, while Alfred de Musset sketched her tight-waisted dress and traveling bonnet, depicting himself in a long fur-collared coat, stovepipe trousers, and with an extraordinary gusset cap on his head. Dusk had fallen by the time they reached Pont Saint-Esprit, where the riverboat pilot decided to stop for the night. In the small country inn where they went for supper, Stendhal felt so inspired by the heady Provençal wine and the distinguished company that he got up from the table and pranced around on the rough floorboards in his top hat and fur-lined boots, gripping a napkin in his left fist, in a grotesque imitation of the fandango.

The next day at Avignon, where there was another long halt, Stendhal dragged them out to visit the main church and got all worked up at the sight of a life-size woodcarving of an almost naked Christ, claiming that the Latin people's addiction to such painted ugliness was as "barbarous" as their love of nudity was cynical. A poor sailor, Stendhal had decided to proceed overland to Genoa, and when the time came to say goodbye, George Sand found herself not unhappy to see the last of him. His brilliant wit and flow of conversation were reminiscent of Latouche's, having, however, more depth, if less elegance of phrase. But she was dismayed by his penchant for dazzling paradox and a taste for the obscene which shocked her romantic sensibility. To Stendhal she felt like saying what she was to write the next day to Alphonse Fleury (who had just announced his engagement to her La Châtre friend Laure Decerfz): "Faith alone makes for love, and he who lacks the first will be denied the second."

In Marseille she was overjoyed by the Mediterranean warmth and sunshine, but curiously unimpressed by the magnificently decorated bedroom, full of carved paneling and painted mirrors, which Paganini had occupied before them at the Hôtel Beauvau. She even went so far as to write to Boucoiran that its balcony view over the picturesque *Vieux Port* reminded her of nothing so much as the "duck pond at Nohant."

On December 20 the two lovers boarded a large paddle-wheel steamer bound for Genoa, which they reached the next morning. So eager was Alfred de Musset to take in everything he could in the relatively brief time allowed them that he dragged George from one splendid palace and church to the next, only noticing her, as well as his own, fatigue when he stopped to bathe his perspiring forehead in the cool waters of a grotto fountain in the gardens of the Villa Pallavicini. Later he succumbed to a violent nosebleed, serious enough to force them to seek out a local doctor.

George Sand also felt a bit worn out and feverish when the time came to continue southward toward Leghorn on the same paddle-wheel steamer. However, she endured the voyage far better than Musset. For like Byron's Don Juan, the amorous Alfred was overcome by seasickness. The sea was rough and most of the passengers locked themselves into their cabins. George, however, insisted on pacing the deck, while her green-faced companion sat huddled on a bench, his teeth chattering. Later he drew a sketch of the ridiculous scene, making deliberate fun of his wild, windblown hair, billowing out from under the top hat, while he vomits over the rail. George Sand, on the other hand, is shown with her little boots planted firmly on the deck, a flowered hat perched jauntily over her dark hair, puffing on a thin cigar while her gloved hands dig into the pockets of her high-buttoned, ankle-length traveling dress.

From Leghorn, where they disembarked, they had themselves driven inland to Pisa. George Sand now felt feverish, intermittently wracked by fits of shivering which the warm winter sunshine of Italy seemed unable to dispel. She saw the Campo Santo and the leaning tower in a kind of daze, and even Musset, normally so impressed by architectural beauty, had to admit that the town was like a "desert."

That evening, at the *albergo,* she felt so weak and drowsy that she no longer cared which was to be the next city they visited. Their original intention had been to head for Rome and Naples, but Musset now suggested that they go instead to Venice. This way they could spend Christmas in Florence, the setting for the 1537 Conspiracy he had, on the basis of George's helpful notes, just turned into the play *Lorenzaccio*. They finally decided to toss for it. Venice, to their surprise, came up ten times in succession.

Her romantic imagination having led her to expect something more grandiose and "sublime," George Sand was not impressed by the first glimpses of the rolling Tuscan hills, with their yew- and cypress-studded gardens and charmingly tiled villas. Their four days in Florence were equally disappointing. Musset, who had expected something gayer, was oppressed by the sight of so many dark-stoned palaces, while George, still feverish, was worn out by the number of chapels and museums she was made to visit by her art-loving companion.

On December 28 they set out again, headed for Ferrara. The night was clear and frosty as they crossed the Apennines, accompanied by two mounted constables dressed in canary yellow costumes who rode on so casually ahead or fell so far behind as to make their mail-coach an easy prey for mountain brigands. Still plunged in a state of feverish apathy, George nodded her way through Bologna, saw nothing of Padua, and was only vaguely aroused by the crossing of the Po and its desolate sandy plains.

It was ten o'clock at night when they finally reached Mestre and the Adriatic. Trying not to shiver, George Sand watched their luggage being moved from the carriage in which they had bumped for hours over the frozen roads to a narrow, black-hooded gondola tied to the bank. The causeway that now links Venice to the mainland did not then exist, and it was in this closed, coffinlike conveyance that they were to make the rest of the trip.

Propelled by three black-clad gondoliers, they set out across the calm lagoon. Inside the tent the two lovers could at first see nothing. The movement of the gondola was so gentle that at times they had the impression they were not moving. Finally Alfred managed to pull back a curtain, and there through the protective pane of glass was Venice.

Forgotten in an instant were all the fevers, fatigues, and disappointments. Suspended like a lantern over the twinkling lights of the Giudecca waterway up which they were gliding, the moon now came into view with an almost theatrical sense of timing: a sultry, heavy-lidded moon, against whose huge, bloodshot disk the sculptured fretwork of domes and terraces was magnificently silhouetted. Slowly, as it rose through its shredded bank of cloud, the disk shrank and silvered, until the cornices of the Ducal Palace and the cupolas of San Marco shone like pieces of alabaster.

"How lucky we are!" Musset cried. "This is as beautiful as the most beautiful of dreams! This is the Venice I knew existed, this is as I wanted it, as I imagined it in my verses! And this moon rising specially for us, to be seen in all her poetry! I feel this is a joyous omen and that here my Muse will speak to me."

They were finally deposited on the stone wharf of the Riva dei Schiavoni, in front of the Albergo Reale, as the Hotel Danieli was then officially called in sycophantic homage to the "royal" Habsburgs who were now the overlords of the once proud and arrogant Venetian Republic. Here George Sand was informed that the available accommodations were limited. Was it discretion and an exaggerated fear of the strait-laced Austrian police which prompted Musset to take another gondola over to the Hotel Europa, where foreign diplomats were normally lodged and where Chateaubriand had put up the previous September? Like the Europa, the Danieli had originally been a palazzo, and while its ornate balconies, Venetian Gothic windows, and lavish furnishings — often including a piano — made for magnificent apartments, they were necessarily limited in number. The two lovers were, however, reunited the second night and their names quaintly inscribed in the hotel's registry as "Mr. Musset" and "M. Dudesiant." The suite given to them on the first floor bore the unlucky number 13, but the superstitious Alfred was prepared to swallow his misgivings at the prospect of occupying a sumptuous apartment with two bedrooms and a splendid blue-damask drawing room whose tall windows looked out over the quay and the lagoon.

The first days in Venice were a sheer delight. The pastel subtlety of its changings skies, the Turneresque beauty of its morning mists, the distant thunder of the Adriatic rolling its invisible breakers against the Lido's farther shore, the serenades of its round-hatted gondoliers, the quarter-deck cries of the state frigate anchored at the entrance to the San Giorgio canal, the early-morning cannon shot fired to herald the ritual start of a new day and answered by the sudden, simultaneous tolling of innumerable church bells for the Angelus, the faint voices of fishermen and sailors singing to each other across the echoing water as they scrubbed their wooden decks and repaired their nets — everything was an enchantment to eye and ear.

The enchantment, however, was of brief duration. After the first gondola excursions, George Sand began complaining of persistent headaches, so violent that they finally forced her to keep to her room. Already irked by the apathy she had shown for so much of their Italian trip, Musset now lost patience. It was no fun, he told her, traveling with a perpetually sick woman. George took refuge in an offended silence which exasperated the petulant Alfred even more.

While she stayed indoors, he went out for strolls around the animated Piazza San Marco, took solitary trips to the Lido, sitting at the same tavern near the old Venetian fort where Byron before him had sampled the sweet Samos wine. Alone, he also visited the convent of San Lazzaro, where Byron had taken lessons in Armenian. So obsessive was the memory of the noble Scottish bard that he even visited the Mocenigo Palace, which Byron had inhabited in 1817 — as was indicated by a signboard nailed to a gondola hitching post in the Grand Canal. Here an aged footman scornfully informed him that *"Avea tutto il palazzo, Lord Byron!"* — Byron had rented the entire palace, and not simply one floor, as Musset was proposing. (The rent, according to Musset's later claim, would not have been exorbitantly high, but he was troubled by the palace's unfortunate exposure, its Moorish windows receiving all too little of the winter sun.)

With each passing day it became more distressingly evident to the young French poet what a mistake it was to have come to Venice *accompanied.* Byron had not brought his amorous provisions with him; he had preferred to live robustly off the land. Free to bestow his favors as he pleased, he had had several delightful adventures with ladies whose expertise in passionate osculation (he believed) put them above the women of any other country. Though Musset didn't like to admit it — for he was still in love with her, sick and ailing though she was — George Sand was now less a companion than an obstacle between himself and the city, whose sensuous temptations he was burning to savor.

Even his most innocent desires were countered with an intransigence which drove him wild. He proposed that they go to the Fenice; she replied that the operas being given in this most fabulous of theaters had been better sung in Paris. He suggested that they call on the French consul, a friend of his father's who could introduce them to the city's aristocratic salons. She had not come to Venice, she retorted, to hobnob with the city's high society; she had come, like himself, in search of poetic inspiration. So let him get to work, as she was trying to do, to earn something for both of them to live on. For though life in Italy was less expensive than in France, they had already gone through several thousand francs, and at a minimum of twenty francs a day (six francs for their three-room suite, three francs for each meal, a daily fee for the gondolier and other incidentals), life at the Danieli was not exactly cheap.

The simmering misunderstanding between them finally frothed over one evening during a visit made to the hotel's *casino* — a kind of pleasure dome and gambling pavilion located on the Lido. "George," Musset said to her, in a moment of pique, "I was mistaken, I ask your forgiveness, but I *don't love you.*" If he had lifted his hand and struck her in the face, the effect could not have been more brutal. She felt stunned and angry: angry enough to want to leave Venice immediately.

The one thing that stopped her was the realization that she was in no condition to travel. Nor was she sure that Musset, who had his moments of hurt pride, would accept the money she would have to leave him. She was also worried at the idea of leaving him to his own devices in a foreign country whose language he spoke far less fluently than she did.

The next day a doctor came in to bleed her. He was an aging physician whose eyesight was so poor and whose hand trembled so much that he kept missing the vein in her arm. This first attempt to find relief from her blinding headaches and intermittent fever having failed, she asked the hotel manager if he couldn't find someone a little more competent. Another doctor was accordingly summoned — an assistant surgeon from the Hospital of San Giovanni e Paolo named Pagello. The previous evening he had, in fact, been strolling along the Riva dei Schiavoni with a friend when he had noticed a young lady seated next to a blond-haired young man on a first-floor balcony of the Danieli. He had been struck by the scarlet turban she had wound around her dark hair, by the "soldierlike unconcern" with which she was smoking a cigar, but most of all by her "melancholy physiognomy" and the "decisive and virile expression" of her two dark eyes — little realizing that he would be called in the very next day to bleed her. Now he found her seated on a low settee, her head wearily propped against one cupped hand. The blond young man of the previous evening — Alfred de Musset — explained to him that the signora was suffering from headaches and felt that a bleeding might relieve the pain. The young doctor Pagello bled her properly and George Sand experienced a feeling of almost instant relief. She thanked him, saying she would let him know if she needed his services again, but to make doubly sure that she felt better, he called on her again the next day.

This improvement in her physical condition did nothing, however, to heal the breach that was widening between herself and Musset. To some extent it only aggravated the quarrel. For now that she felt better, George Sand went to work with a vengeance. Over a month had gone by since they had left Paris, and neither of them had yet written more than a few lines. She had promised Buloz a short story to complete the trilogy for which he had advanced her 5000 francs, and now she had to make up for lost time. At night she locked herself into her bedroom, working by oil lamp and candlelight. The sight of this nocturnal industry drove Alfred de Musset wild. What kind of honeymoon was this? Byron, sixteen years earlier, had had Teresa Guiccioli to console and inspire him. But what did he have? A kind of prim, purse-lipped chaperon, a *dueña* whose glum silence was full of mute reproach. And she was right, as he knew, which only made it worse! On two cups of milk she could find the energy to stay up half the night and fill twenty pages of closely spaced writing, only needing to scratch out or change a word every now and then, whereas all he could wring from a full bottle of Samos wine was a meager verse or two!

The luxurious Danieli now seemed to him a prison. Ah, Venice! The city of Lord Byron, yes . . . but also the city of the resourceful Giacomo Casanova, who had written up his amorous conquests in such an entertaining way. Byron had written a long poem about Don Juan; he, Alfred de Musset, wanted to write an epic poem about the prince of eighteenth-century seducers, the superlative adventurer he had once boldly likened to "sublime artists" (like himself). But how could he write about the exemplary lecher locked up in this pseudo-Moorish palace when there was so much to see and experience?

"I'm not like you, with a steel spring in the brain, released by a button through a mere act of will," he one day complained to a silently reproachful George Sand, adding, "I'm a creator!" In another outburst he called her "boredom personified" and even "stupid!" On yet another occasion he undertook to explain, with airy sophistry, that "Change is perhaps the secret of life. To change is to renew; to be able to change is to be free. Is the artist born for slavery . . . and isn't a pledged fidelity slavery?"

"All right," George Sand finally told him, out of sheer weariness with such disputes, "go out, enjoy yourself, take in a ball or two, indulge in a few *conversazioni*!" — with members of Venice's high society. The one thing she specifically requested was that he stay away from the gambling table. In Paris he had left a 360 franc gambling debt unpaid, and it was a source of considerable embarrassment to both himself and George to have to write to François Buloz and ask him to take care of it — against future poems which Musset would be sending him.

Though he was even ready to find fault with the permission thus granted to enjoy himself ("So you are abandoning me to my fate? You are already weary of the struggle? So it's you, my dear, who no longer love me!" . . . etc., etc.), Musset now began to disappear for increasingly long stretches of time. He called on the French consul, he was taken backstage to meet the singers and dancing girls of the Fenice, he may even have been invited to a masked ball in Baron Gina's magnificent Venetian palace. Now that the communicating door between their bedrooms was firmly closed, George Sand could only guess what he did with his nights. But one day, at lunchtime, a crestfallen Alfred confessed to her that he was afraid he had contracted a "nasty disease."

This news, coming on top of so much else, could no longer anger George Sand, but it did fill her with a sense of infinite distress. She who had prided herself on her maternal ability to rescue this young man from his licentious past, who had thought she could subdue the demon and release the angel within him, making him a nobler, more virtuous, hardworking and responsible human being, had clearly failed.

"Let's leave," she suggested wearily. "I'll take you back as far as Marseille."

"That would be the best thing to do," he agreed. "But I would like to work a little, now that we are here."

This belated show, or at least announcement, of industry left her speechless. She didn't quite know what to make of it. Was his wish seriously meant, or was it one more caprice on the part of a spoiled child who, having enjoyed a few Casanovan nights making love *à la vénitienne* in a conveniently hooded gondola, was now more reconciled to staying on?

She herself was in no particular hurry to leave now that she felt better and with the annual carnival season just two weeks away from its Mardi Gras climax. "Every Sunday we have masks on the quay and on the piazza," she wrote to Jules Boucoiran on January 28. "There are companies of savages, Neapolitan fishermen, Venetians, etc. Their costumes are quite pretty. They arrive in the lagoon in beflagged boats with musicians." In the same letter she asked the faithful tutor to call on Buloz and to reassure him that the third story she had promised him for the trilogy was well on the way to completion; also, could he send her the 1000 francs he still owed her as quickly as possible?

Two days after writing this letter she succumbed to a violent attack of dysentery, which virtually paralyzed her for five days. Musset, just to complicate matters, came down with typhoid fever soon after. She now found herself having to be a nurse as well as a bread-provider. The money from Buloz had not arrived; instead, Buloz had sent her a letter complaining that he had not received the third story she had promised him for the trilogy. The *Revue des Deux Mondes'* financial backers, he added, were giving him trouble over the lavishness of his advances.

For George Sand this was the last straw! "He deserves to be kicked in the arse," she wrote in a second, angry letter to Boucoiran. "I don't see why I should let myself die of hunger, or fatigue, or fever here, while Buloz sleeps soundly on his two good ears . . . He'll have to wait another month at least."

Instead of finishing *André,* the novelette she had been slaving over "like a dog" for Buloz's trilogy, she decided to start work on a novel to be called *Everard* for Ernest Dupuy (who had published *Indiana, Valentine,* and *Lélia*). According to the terms of the proposed contract, which Boucoiran was instructed to present to the publisher (keeping it a careful secret from Buloz), Monsieur Dupuy was to pay Madame Dudevant 1600 francs immediately *after* receipt of the completed manuscript, eventual publication to be postponed until three months after the publication of *Jacques* (the "Italian" novel for which Buloz had already paid her a 4000 franc advance).

That this desperate proposition offered no solution for her present predicament George Sand was not long in realizing, for in her furious desire to punish Buloz she was only punishing herself. Meanwhile, there was an urgent problem to be attended to: she and Alfred had to move out of the ruinously expensive Danieli to some cheaper abode. But before new lodgings could be found, Musset's "nervous and inflammatory fever" (as she described it in another letter to Buloz) took a sharp turn for the worse.

"Today" — February 4 — "he is very ill and the doctor declares he doesn't know what to make of it . . . How do you expect me to busy myself with literature or anything else at a moment like this?" she went on plaintively. "The only thing I know is that we have just six hundred francs left, that we are going to have huge expenses to bear in medicines, sick-watchers, doctors, etc., that we are living in a very expensive hotel. Alfred is not in a transportable condition and may not be so for another month, at best . . . If my misfortune is carried to extremes and Alfred should die, I admit that what happens to me thereafter matters but little to me. If, God willing,

Alfred should recover, I don't know with what we shall pay the expenses of his illness and return journey. The thousand francs you are due to send me won't suffice and I don't know how we'll manage. At least don't delay the dispatch of this sum, it will be needed more than ever when it arrives. I'm sorry for the inconvenience that has been caused you in having to wait for your manuscript. But is it really my fault? If Alfred had several calm days, I could quickly finish my work. But he is in a state of dreadful agitation and delirium. I can't leave him for an instant, it's taken me 9 hours to write you this letter.

"Farewell, my friend. Feel sorry for me. George."

In a postscript she begged Buloz not to breathe a word about all this to anyone — "two people are enough to spread a secret all over Paris" — for should Musset's mother hear of it, she would go out of her mind! During his delirious ravings of the previous night, she went on, Alfred had several times mentioned his gambling debt of 360 francs, which if unacquitted might well lead to a duel, and she accordingly asked Buloz to take care of that immediately. "Should I have the misfortune to lose him, you may be sure that I will pay back all the advances you may have made him, and this one is not enormous."

She followed this up with an urgent note to Boucoiran asking him to do nothing about the proposed contract with Dupuy — now that she had taken the bull by the horns and explained the full gravity of her and Alfred's situation to Buloz. Next she dashed off a letter in intelligible, even if in somewhat incorrect, Italian to Signor Paiello, as she spelled his name. Could he return to the Albergo Reale to see the young *signor francese* he had already treated, and bring a good doctor with him? "He is a poet much admired in France. But the exaltation of cerebral work, wine, fetes, women, gambling have greatly wearied him and excited his nerves . . . He spends his time crying, lamenting an ill that has neither name nor cause, he keeps asking for his country, says he's about to die or go mad!"

No wonder she felt lost and in desperate need of assistance! Byron, when likewise afflicted by a mysterious Venetian fever, had been nursed back to health by a captivating *amorosa,* Marianna Segati, who though married to a draper had not hesitated to console the noble lord with long, breathtaking kisses exchanged both above and below the sheets. But though Alfred demanded the same amorous attention, this was one thing George could not bring herself to give him. This fretful craving and her persistent refusal only exasperated his delirious outbursts — with the result that he now lost all control, called her vile names, accused her of being a prude, a puritan, a blue-stockinged bigot who nursed and watched him out of a sense of duty only, and who when it came to it, was so inexpert in bed that she had never been able to give him "the joys of love." The language was probably cruder, but this cruel commentary on her feminine inadequacies, coming on the top of so many other humiliations, reduced her in her turn to almost hysterical sobbing. Sandeau in his wildest moments of despair had simply been an importunate young lover; Musset in his was nothing less than a sadist.

When Dr. Pagello reappeared, he was accompanied by a second physician named Zuanon, who also worked at the Hospital of San Giovanni e Paolo. Thinking he was simply an expert bleeder, George Sand had taken the handsome young man with the caressing eyes and the dashing sideburns and mustache for some kind of medical assistant, not realizing that Pagello was a full-fledged surgeon. The mistake turned out to be a blessing in disguise. For two days later Musset was seized with a violent fit which it took the combined strength of the two doctors to master. Leaping out of bed stark naked, he raced around the drawing room, shouting and screaming to the doctors to get out, then seized hold of a terrified George Sand in a determined effort to kiss her. The fit lasted for six hours, six hours of wild singing, shouting, and convulsions. "Oh my God, my God, what a spectacle!" George wrote the next morning to Boucoiran. "He came near to strangling me while kissing me. The two men could not get him to let go of the collar of my dress. The doctors announce another fit of the same kind for the next night, and more perhaps thereafter, for there is no telling what may happen for the next six days . . . Fortunately" she concluded, "I have found an excellent doctor" — Pagello — "who doesn't leave him day or night, and who gives him remedies of very good effect."

Realizing that she was in no condition to start work on a new novel, George Sand enclosed a second letter to be personally delivered by Boucoiran. This one was addressed to Vicomte Sosthènes de la Rochefoucauld, a friend of Chateaubriand's whom she had met at Hyacinthe de Latouche's. Apologetically she wrote to ask if he could lend her 1000 francs. A legitimist who had served under Charles X as head of the Direction des Beaux-Arts, Sosthènes de la Rochefoucauld had made himself a laughingstock by the puritanical zeal he had displayed in forcing Opéra ballerinas into long skirts and covering nude statues with fig leaves. But the viscount was also a perfect gentleman and apparently not ungallant, for an insanely jealous Sandeau had once made a terrible scene with Aurore, claiming that she had been unnecessarily coquettish in encouraging his compliments — which had not prevented Jules from later trying to borrow some money from him. To find herself now reduced to the same pass must have embarrassed George Sand — but then, she wasn't requesting the money for her own selfish benefit; it was on behalf of "a companion whom you know and who is dearer to me than my own life."

For eight days George Sand did not undress, stretching out when she could on the drawing room sofa. What had begun as typhoid fever was aggravated by a bronchial inflammation — it may even have been pneumonia — which caused Musset to cough blood. By applying suction cups the doctors managed to overcome this additional complication. But throughout, Musset proved a troublesome and refractory invalid. He was reluctant to take the sedatives Pagello prescribed to calm his agitated nerves; he kept rejecting the different tonics and syrups offered him, spitting them out on to the floor after a few sips and shouting hoarsely for wine and champagne. Each time a cold compress was placed on his burning forehead, he raved and moaned that his tormentors were trying to bury him alive, for obsessed as ever with the theme of death, he was hysterically convinced that the cold wet weight he could feel just above his nose was a wad of graveyard earth shoveled into his open tomb.

On February 13 George Sand could at last write to Buloz to say that the worst was over — though she shuddered at the thought that she had been spending twenty francs a day on drugs and medicines, along with the doctors' bills still to be paid.

It was during these long vigils at Alfred's bedside that George

Sand found herself drifting into an ever more intimate friendship with the broad-shouldered, strong-handed young doctor, whose medical proficiency and calmness of manner were so reassuring. With his beautifully chiseled nose, a pair of seductive eyes, soft chestnut curls and sideburns, a sensuous mouth and "teeth like fresh almonds" — as Paul de Musset was later to describe him — Pietro Pagello was considerably more than a surgeon. His beautiful mother had been tutored by an associate of the famous Venetian dramatist Gasparo Gozzi, while his silk merchant father had spent a small fortune maintaining a noteworthy literary salon. Mad about Byron, like so many others of his generation, the young Pietro spent his evenings in the company of a happy band of bon-vivant artists, poets, verse-loving lawyers, and dilettantish aristocrats who met regularly at the Trattoria del Capello, on the Piazza San Marco, or at the Café Florian, where they came to read the papers and exchanged the latest news about revolutionary plots and the cause of Italian liberty.

Even in his condition Musset soon realized that something was afoot between the handsome surgeon and George Sand. One night, after the cold compress had been removed from his forehead, he became aware of two voices discussing his desperate condition. His field of vision was limited by a curtained canopy, so that he had only a partial view of the two forms that were seated not far from his bed. But gradually, he perceived that the two forms were not seated separately, but that one of them, a woman, was seated on the other's knees. The two heads slowly merged in a kiss. Uttering a faint moan, Musset managed to turn his head on the pillow. A moment later he saw Pagello lean over him and heard him say: "He's better. If he continues like this, he will be saved!"

That same night, or it may have been the next — for Musset could not clearly recall — he saw Pagello getting ready to leave when George Sand invited him to have a cup of tea with her. The surgeon sat down and they chatted gaily for a few minutes, then spoke to each other in whispers. The word "Murano" kept returning; they were apparently discussing the possibility of making a gondola trip to the island of Murano. "Once I'm dead and buried!" the young Alfred thought to himself. Making an effort, he focused his gaze in their direction and had the distinct impression that they were drinking from the same cup. Later, when Pagello rose to leave, George Sand accompanied him out. They passed behind a screen placed in front of the door, and though Musset could see nothing, he had the impression that they were kissing. George Sand came back for a candle, accompanying the surgeon out on to the landing, where they remained for an unusually long time. Summoning up all of his strength, Musset propped himself up on one elbow, then heaved himself toward the end of his bed. The room was plunged in semidarkness, save for the warm glow of the fireplace reflected on the polished floor; but by the light of the single remaining candle he could see the table, and on it was just one tea cup.

Though it was now mid-February, this was no northern winter: it was already the Adriatic spring, with soft, sensuous gusts of flower-scented air floating in each time the windows were opened. In her emotionally distraught and sleepless state George Sand found herself more than usually affected by nature's annual rebirth, made all the more intoxicating by the sounds of carnival revelry outside. "Oh be quiet, you harmonies of the night!" she wrote in her notebook, her pen racing over the paper in a burst of frustrated inspiration. "Cease racing along the dark walls, you quivering guitars! . . . Sink behind the alabaster minarets, voluptuous moon, you who pour out love and languor with the floods of your soft light; hide yourself in the dark clouds, leave those silvery vapors in which you veil yourself like a courtesan beneath her transparent mantilla. Oh Venice, thus seen you are too beautiful, and to die under your skies is to die twice over."

But it was not for death that she was pining, as her soul thrilled to the sound of guitars and mandolins and her senses swooned beneath the moon's insidious caress. It was for an amorous communion with this joyous life she could feel pulsing about her, with these poetic mysteries which seemed so beautifully reflected in Dr. Pagello's liquid eyes; it was for a rapturous surrender to that aphrodisiac enchantment which Venice seemed to breathe in every ripple of her mermaid body.

One night as they were softly conversing together, Musset, whose fits and fevers had abated, asked if she and the doctor would mind moving to the other part of the living room (where his bed was now located), so that he could get some sleep. Seated at the round table in front of the glowing fireplace, they continued their whispered discussion — about the contemporary French novel, which Pagello roundly condemned as being "a school of immorality." Leaping to her feet, George Sand gave him a long, penetrating look. Then, brusquely sitting down again, she seized a quill pen and by the light of two sputtering candles, began furiously writing. After an hour — or so it seemed to the doctor — she laid down the pen and without looking at him, she buried her head in her hands. Rising at last from her chair, she folded the three pages she had written into an envelope and handed them to the doctor. He asked to whom he was to deliver this missive. Tearing the letter out of his hands, she wrote on the cover, "To the stupid Pagello," and handed it back to him.

On returning home, Pagello must have been more than a little surprised by the epistle he had just inspired — one of the most astounding love letters ever penned, and one which shows how much Musset's ravings had opened all of Lélia's old wounds.

"Born under different skies, we have neither the same thoughts nor the same language; do we at least have similar hearts?

"The warm and foggy climate from which I come has left me full of soft and melancholy impressions. What passions have you been given by the generous sun which has tanned your forehead? I know how to love and suffer, but what is your way of loving?

"The ardor of your gaze, the violent hug of your arms, the audacity of your desires tempt and frighten me. I know neither how to combat nor how to share your passion. In my country one does not love like this. Next to you I am like a pale statue; I look at you with astonishment, with desire, with anxiety.

"I do not know if you really love me. I shall never know it. You speak only a few words of my language, and I do not know enough of yours to be able to ask such subtle questions . . . You have perhaps been brought up in the conviction that women have no souls . . . Shall I be your companion or your slave? Do you desire or love me? When your passion is satisfied, will you know how to thank me? . . .

"Am I for you something unknown which makes you seek and

dream, or am I in your eyes no more than a woman similar to those that grow fat in the harems? . . . Do you know what is that desire of the soul which the senses cannot satisfy, which no human caress can put to sleep or weary? When your mistress falls asleep in your arms, do you stay awake to look at her, to pray to God and to weep?

"Do the pleasures of love leave you panting and besotted, or do they plunge you into a divine ecstasy? Does your soul survive your body, when you leave the bosom of the one you love? . . .

"What I have vainly sought in others I shall perhaps not find in you, but I can always believe that you possess it. You will let love's looks and caresses, which have always lied to me, explain themselves to me according to my fancy, without the addition of deceitful words. I shall be able to interpret your daydreaming and have your silence speak eloquently . . .

"Let us then remain like this. Do not learn my language, I don't want to find in yours the words which would tell you of my doubts and fears. I don't wish to know what you do with your life and what role you play among men. I would like not to know your name; hide your soul from me that I may forever find it beautiful."

This extraordinary confession threw the twenty-seven-year-old doctor into a dither. He knew French well enough to appreciate the lyrical intensity of its expression. *Questa donna me fa paura,* he noted in his diary. "This woman frightens me. She seduces me with the irresistible fascination of her genius, but this genius is already the slave of a religion I do not recognize."

The next morning, when Pagello returned to the Danieli for his ten o'clock visit, he found Alfred de Musset much calmer and improved. George Sand, in the bedroom next door, was getting dressed. Normally she used these brief morning hours, while Musset slumbered, to try to do a bit of writing. But this morning was different. When she finally appeared, she was elegantly dressed and asked the bewitched doctor to accompany her while she went out to do some shopping. They spent the rest of the morning strolling around the Piazza San Marco, with its picturesque cafés full of Turkish and Armenian merchants, talking about one thing and the other and exchanging variations on the phrase "I love."

The shoe was now on the other foot. The frustrated roué, whose dreams of being a French Lord Byron had been reduced to a few nights of Casanovan dissipation, was now the cuckolded poet-lover, and it was Madame Sand who was playing the role of Lord Byron. As self-indulgent in his misfortune as he had been in his happiness, Musset now yielded with masochistic frenzy to the wild torments of jealousy. Once again Aurore found herself leading a complicated double life. For a moment she was tempted to leave the Danieli and to rent a small room where she could receive Pagello's visits without arousing Alfred's sickly suspicions. But it was the good-natured doctor who insisted that she stay on, feeling that she could afford to show compassion to a young man who had been so close to death.

She finally did as he suggested, probably realizing that her sudden disappearance would have driven Musset out of his mind once again. But George Sand had been too deeply hurt by his insulting words and deeds to be prepared to forgive him overnight. As she wrote to Pagello, in another letter of tortured soul-searching: "My conduct may be magnanimous, but my heart cannot be compassionate. I'm too bilious, it's not my fault. I can still serve Alfred out of duty and honor, but to forgive him out of love is impossible for me . . .

"I am getting old and my heart is wearing itself out, but I can turn to ice toward you from one day to the next," she continued, in a strange mixture of threat and apprehension. "Beware, beware for me! To conserve my love and my esteem, one must keep very close to perfection . . . I forgive my friends everything, there are some among them I love without being able to esteem them. But love, for me, is a veneration, a cult. And if my god lets himself suddenly sink into the dung, it is impossible for me to lift him up again and adore him . . .

"Alas, I have suffered so much, I have sought this perfection so much without finding it! Is it you, is it you at last, my Pietro, who will realize my dream? I think so, and so far I see you as great as God. Excuse me for sometimes being afraid. It's when I am alone and think of my past woes that doubt and discouragement seize hold of me.

"Yes, I love you, you are the one I should always have loved. Why did I meet you so late — when all I can bring you is a beauty withered by the years and a heart worn out by disappointments?" she sighed, as once she had sighed to Emile Regnault about his friend Jules Sandeau. "But no, my heart is not worn out. It is severe, it is distrustful, it is inexorable, but it is strong, this passionate one. Never have I felt its vigor and its youth more strongly than the last time you covered me with your caresses . . . ."

Did she really believe all this, or was she simply trying to work herself into the proper romantic mood? To have to confess, even secretly, that she had yielded to a wild springtime urge, or had flung herself into Pagello's willing arms in a spirit of revenge to restore her shattered self-esteem and to forget the humiliations Musset had heaped upon her would have been too galling for a person of her exalted temperament. It was God, no less, who had decreed that she should fall in love again, and as she put it — "I feel that He has not withdrawn the fire of heaven from me." Let Pagello remain as he was, then — reassuringly simple, solid, unaffected, such a relaxing change from the high-strung, hysterical, foul-mouthed Musset. "I find nothing in you that does not please or satisfy me," she added humbly. "It is the first time I have loved without suffering at the end of three days. . . . So go on being my Pagello, with his big kisses, his simple air, his girlish smile, his caresses . . . his ample waistcoat, his soft gaze . . ." — and a couple of other qualities which were later deleted by a literary censor for reasons of propriety.

No wonder the well-meaning surgeon had been frightened by this fascinating, dark-eyed woman! Whatever her religion was — Gothic? neo-Gothic? — it was certainly not his, which was considerably more pagan, uninhibited, and less complex. But now that he had tasted of this strange, forbidden fruit, he was not going to turn back. Besides, he was honest enough to realize that he had helped George Sand get herself into this infernal mess.

For a hellish triangle it was, and one of their own making. "Curiosity about evil is an infamous malady which is born of impure contacts," Musset was later to diagnose his predicament in *La Confession d'un enfant du siècle*. "It is the roving instinct of ghosts who pry up tombstones by night; it is the inexplicable torture with which God punishes those who have gone astray." Knowing from his own experience to what depths of depravity he himself could descend, he now spent his waking hours searching George Sand's face and gestures for tiny telltale symptoms of intimacy between *his* George, as he still confidently thought her, and this not unsympathetic doctor to whom — much as he hated to admit it — he owed so much.

Had he known for sure, had he possessed absolute proof that she had become Pagello's mistress, his torment would have been ended there and then. It would have been a shattering blow to his male vanity, it might have provoked one last terrible scene, but it would have hastened the eventual cure. The crestfallen young poet would have concluded that George Sand was like Madame Beaulieu, whose dainty foot he had one day seen, under the table, softly reposing on her secret lover's — that she was as wanton as the rest of womankind. But of what went on outside this luxurious hotel room, he knew nothing — even though his feverish brain was ready to imagine the worst and his sharp tongue ever-ready to give vent to the vilest imprecations. "You're no better than a slut!" he one day shouted at her, after intercepting an exchange of tender glances between George Sand and Pagello, adding as he fell back weakly on his pillow: "My one regret is not to have put twenty francs on your mantelpiece the first time I had you."

"The patience which Brigitte," i.e., George Sand, "opposed to these aberrations only went to excite my sinister gaiety. How strange the sufferer's wish to make the loved one suffer!" Musset later described these scenes in *La Confession d'un enfant du siécle,* thus anticipating Oscar Wilde's masochistic dictum: "Each man kills the thing he loves."

"We are suffering, my friend, we are suffering," she again wrote to Pagello after one more of these nerve-racking scenes. "My life with Alfred is awful. We have suffered so much together that we can no longer be calm. All of our conversations are full of bitterness and we can speak neither of past, present, or future without directly or indirectly reproaching ourselves for the harm we do to each other . . . I am impatient to give him back his freedom and to reclaim my own. Oh, my freedom, my holy freedom — which I had such trouble conquering and which I had sworn so much to keep!"

A few days later she wrote again to her beloved Pagello to report that Musset had been "very sad and good. I see that he no longer dares get angry at our intimacy, but that it makes him suffer. I would be cruel were I not to spare him the woes I can spare him. I know that far from complaining, you will approve . . . Keep coming to see us in the evening; but I think you would do well to stop coming every morning. I shall write to you when I can escape and give you a rendezvous in a gondola; it won't be for two or three days. I must have Alfred get used to seeing me go out alone without suspecting me . . ."

In early March Musset's wealthy friend, the dark-whiskered and somewhat saturnine Alfred Tattet, reached Venice with the actress Virginie Déjazet and established residence at the Hotel Europa. His arrival offered George Sand a badly needed respite, for Tattet's presence tended to have a soothing effect on the restive Musset. It also permitted her to leave the Danieli more frequently, without Musset's flying into fits of jealous rage. Though he did not particularly care for George Sand, Tattet was full of gentlemanly solicitude; he took her to the Fenice, he treated her to ices, cakes, cups of tea, and glasses of punch at the Café Florian, he took her on gondola excursions up and down the Grand Canal, he even accompanied her to the Manfrini Gallery, where the sight of a Giorgione painting of a woman playing a guitar so overwhelmed her that there and then she offered him a carnation to stick in his buttonhole.

Musset was still not sufficiently recovered to accompany them. Besides, he had come to hate Venice with a passion, and his one desire was to clear out as soon as possible and head for Rome with George. Where the money was to come from for such a trip he did not bother to ask, just as it did not occur to him that his companion might have other plans. For she now had but one desire: to stay on in *Venezia la bella,* which she had found to be "the most beautiful city in the universe," and also one of the cheapest. Or so at least she fancied. In Venice, as she wrote rhapsodically to her half brother, Hippolyte, one could live better on 300 francs a month than in Paris on 900. A gondola complete with gondolier could be hired for sixty francs a month — the equivalent in Paris being "a carriage, a pair of horses, a coachman and a footman, which is to say from twelve to fifteen thousand francs a year." Firewood, wine, food, and clothes all cost half of what they did in Paris — like the pair of Moroccan leather shoes she had just bought for four francs. "If my son weren't tied down at the Collège Henri IV, I would certainly take my daughter with me and settle down here for several years. I would work as I'm used to doing and I would return to France when I had had my fill, having amassed a small hoard."

Not all of this was lagoon-fed fancy. For when it came to work, George Sand found Venice an extraordinary inspiration. "The love of work is a remedy for everything," as she wrote in the same letter to Hippolyte. "I bless my grandmother who forced me to acquire the habit of it. This habit has become a faculty, and this faculty a need. I have sometimes been able to work for thirteen hours at a stretch without falling ill, and on the average without wearing myself out, seven or eight hours a day."

The first fruit of this incredible industry was a novelette entitled *Leone Leoni,* which she dashed off in exactly fourteen days. Shortly before leaving Paris she had read the Abbé Prévost's *Manon Lescaut,* and this tale of a young man's hopeless passion for a beautiful but fickle young lady had given George Sand the idea of reversing the situation — by telling the story of a young woman's desperate passion for a hopelessly unstable and inconstant man. Named Leone Leoni — in homage no doubt to the Venetian Republic's heraldic lions — this larger-than-life adventurer ("a robust body animated by an immense soul") owed as much, and indeed more, to Alfred de Musset than to Casanova. The resulting portrait — which Buloz was to hail as "the strongest and most vigorous" George Sand had yet achieved — was that of a strangely schizophrenic personality, a generous, noble, and tenderhearted lover as well as a cynical and unscrupulous seducer, a man relentlessly pursued by his abject past, a picaresque hero-villain with a "soul of bronze, fire, gold and mud which I have received from heaven and hell united" — as the hapless heroine (Juliette Ruyter) laments to her temporary savior, Aleo Bustamente, an honest, upright, uncomplicated Venetian, who was just as obviously inspired by the benevolent, pipe-smoking Pietro Pagello.

The dramatic vicissitudes of her life had, once again, left their indelible imprint on George Sand's literary output. Her original intention had been to satisfy Buloz's request for a third short story (to complete the projected trilogy) by describing a lowly flower girl's pathetic romance with a young noble named André. This was in effect a new variation on an old George Sand theme: society's hypocritical refusal to condone marriage between the high and humbly born. But in the electrically charged atmosphere of Venice this "tranquil and pastoral" subject, with the Berry countryside as a setting, seemed altogether too tame, and it was accordingly shunted aside for *Leone Leoni.* The immediate result was to complicate George Sand's financial predicament. For in the meantime Buloz, despairing of ever receiving the promised third story, had decided to fill the gap by republishing several of George Sand's earlier short stories — an expedient which (according to her calculations) reduced the value of the collection to 3500 francs, when the advance she had received on it totaled 5000 francs. She thus found herself owing Buloz 1500 more francs, in addition to the 5000 francs he had advanced to her for the "Italian" novel *Jacques* — for a total debt of 6500 francs.

A woman of less fortitude and intense determination might at this point have buckled under the strain. But not George Sand. On March 7 she wrote another urgent note to Jules Boucoiran, telling him that she was in desperate need of the 1000 francs Buloz still owed her for *Jacques.* Even with the 1000 francs she was expecting from Sosthènes de la Rochefoucauld, she would still need another 500 francs at least, and *"tout de suite, tout de suite,"* for the return trip to Paris. However, *Leone Leoni,* which she valued at 2000 francs, and the first half of *André,* which she valued at 1250 francs, would by themselves wipe out almost half her debt to Buloz.

That same day she wrote a thank-you note to Sosthènes de la Rochefoucauld who, unlike the tightfisted Buloz, had immediately sent her the 1000 francs she had requested, even though he was at the moment financially hard-pressed. "I intend to travel and to live alone for two or three years," she added. "You know of my old projects for retiring to Switzerland. I shall go and accomplish them in the Orient, even farther if I can. I would like to push my voyage as far as that other world from which one doesn't return," she concluded, with melodramatic flourish, and she may even have meant it.

One thing by now was certain: she wanted to be rid of Musset as soon as possible. He had become a burden and an encumbrance, and in the "poisonous" atmosphere of Venice — as it had proved to be for him — he had hardly written one line of verse, whereas she had already penned a full volume's worth of prose. Musset must have sensed her feelings, for at some point prior to Alfred Tattet's departure from Venice in mid-March, he flew into another jealous rage, seized a table knife, and made for George Sand and Pagello, shouting that he was going to kill them both unless they told him why they were looking so glum! Tattet promptly intervened, disarming and managing to calm his hysterical friend, who finally contented himself with challenging Pagello to a duel.

No one took the challenge seriously, and the incident was soon forgotten in the commotion of their moving from the expensive Danieli to a small, three-room apartment located on a narrow alleyway perpendicular to the Grand Canal. Satisfied that his friend Musset was out of danger, Alfred Tattet moved on to Florence with his mistress. No sooner had he left than the old quarrels were revived. Each time George slipped away for a clandestine meeting with Pagello, there would be a frightful scene which went on for hours when she returned. At night, Musset would get up and come into her room to see if she was really working, and even after she had blown out the candle, she could hear his furtive footsteps creeping round her bed.

As his strength returned, Musset renewed his amorous advances, to which she was in no mood to respond. In a rage he would stagger down the stairs and out of the house, disappearing for hours at a time. On returning he would explain that he had been out for a ride in a gondola, but she could tell by his state of nervous excitement that he had stopped at a tavern and emptied a bottle of Cypriot wine. She was haunted by the memory of another Alfred — named Périgois — a young La Châtre lad who had suffered delirious fits like Musset's before dying of consumption at the age of twenty; and while she may not have thought that Musset was also a consumptive, despite his bronchial coughing, she was gripped by the same fear that had paralyzed her with Sandeau, of seeing her lover die in her arms through an excess of erotic indulgence. As she wrote to Tattet, in answer to a kind letter he had sent to her from Florence: "It seems very much his desire that we should not part and he shows me much affection. But there are days when he has as little faith in his desire as I in my power, and then I am between two shoals: that of being too much loved and of being dangerous in one respect" — sexual overindulgence — "and that of not being loved enough, in another respect, to fulfill his happiness" — a reference to the frigidity of which Musset had complained.

There was another reason she could not mention to Tattet, though he had seen enough of Pagello to entertain his own suspicions, and that was that she was in love with another man. Suspicious as ever, Musset got up one night after seeing a crack of light under George's door. He pushed it open and saw her seated on the bed, writing on a sheet of paper resting on her knees. He heard a crinkle of paper as the candle was blown out.

"What are you doing?" he asked.

"I'm reading."

"Then why did you blow out the candle?"

"It went out by itself. Light it again."

Musset relit the candle, as she had suggested.

"So you're reading!" he cried. "And yet you don't have a book! Why don't you say instead, you infamous slut, that you are writing to your lover?"

Enraged in her turn, George Sand told him that if he persisted in carrying on like this, she would see to it that he never left Venice by having him locked up in a lunatic asylum.

This was no idle threat. Next door to the Armenian convent he had visited was an asylum for the insane run by the Hospital Fathers of San Giovanni di Dio — the sight of which had so affected Musset that he had jotted down some notes for a poem to be called *Le Fou*. Cowed by George Sand's threatening words, he withdrew to his bedroom. Later, he heard George get out of bed, open the window, and then shut it again. Convinced that she had torn up the letter she had been writing and tossed the bits into the street, he rose at dawn and crept downstairs in his dressing gown. To his surprise he found the front door open. Farther down the narrow, windswept alley he saw a woman in a petticoat wrapped in a shawl. She was bent over, searching the ground. He walked up and tapped her lightly on the shoulder:

"George, George, what are you doing here at this hour? You won't find the pieces of your letter. The wind has swept them away. But your presence here proves that you were writing to Pagello."

George Sand's reply — according to a literary "testament" which Musset dictated twenty years later — was again to threaten to have him locked up. She started running, with Musset following as fast as he could on his unsteady legs. Reaching the Grand Canal, she leapt into a gondola, telling the gondolier to take her to the Lido. But before the gondolier could unhitch and push away from the bank, Musset had jumped in beside her. Not a word was spoken as they crossed the lagoon. On the other side she jumped out and ran toward the Jewish cemetery, finally collapsing, exhausted and weeping, onto a tombstone.

"If I were you," Musset said to her, "I would give up this impossible enterprise. You won't succeed in meeting Pagello without me and in having me locked up with the madmen. Admit that you're a fool" — the word actually used was considerably stronger. "Yes, I'm a fool," she agreed, letting herself be tamely brought home.

Poetic fiction? Possibly. But Musset's account of this crazy night (which his brother Paul also reproduced in his novel *Lui et Elle*) is no more unbelievable than are some of George Sand's letters to Pagello. If Musset triumphed in this particular quarrel, it was a pyrrhic victory at best. He could not keep George Sand from seeing Pagello again, any more than he could prevent the strong, handsome doctor from helping him home, tottering and tipsy, after another of his wild "binges." Refusing to envenom their quarrels, Pagello now announced that he wouldn't again embarrass them with his presence.

This was, to a curious degree, a repetition of the gesture Aurélien de Sèze had made years earlier in undertaking to calm a suspicious Casimir by pledging a pure, sublime, unsullied "friendship" in lieu of an adulterous relationship, and it affected Musset in much the same way. Pagello's magnanimity made him feel suddenly ashamed. "Next to you two," he remarked wistfully to George, "I am a dwarf. I am ashamed of myself. I feel I ought to put your hand in his, and go off on my own to weep over the happiness I did not know how to deserve. Pagello is the man you needed, my poor George, he would have known how to respect you."

There were no more jealous scenes, no more angry recriminations. There was not even a violent protest against George Sand's decision to stay on in Venice and send Musset back to Paris via

Milan, the Alpine passes, and Geneva, with a barber's assistant named Antonio who had been running errands for them. Musset seemed ready to accept everything without a word. Not to be outdone by Pagello, he even offered, in a goodbye note scribbled in a gondola moored to the San Marco piazzetta, to leave Venice without seeing her again, if she would but send him the money for the journey. "If it matters little to you to know if your memory remains with me or not, it matters to me, now that your ghost is already receding and growing dim before me, to say that nothing impure will remain in the furrow of my life over which you have passed, and that he who did not know how to honor you when he possessed you, can still see clearly through his tears, and honor you in his heart, where your image will never die." To which he added, with that patronizing impertinence which made him so endearing: "Farewell, my child."

George was moved to tears by this pathetic note. This was *her* Alfred speaking, the better sunlit half she had sought to save from its dark and shadowy companion, the Alfred for whom she still felt a passionate compassion. There could be no question of his leaving Venice like this. The final evening was spent *à trois,* and in such an atmosphere of exalted emotion that Musset finally placed George Sand's tiny hand in Pagello's, saying: "You love each other, and yet you love me, you who saved my body and my soul!"

As a farewell gift she gave Musset a new album in which to jot down his travel notes and poetic inspirations, writing on the first page: "To her good comrade, brother and friend Alfred, his mistress George." On the last page Pagello insisted on writing down the names of several Italian friends working for the Austrian administration who might be of assistance on the way. Together George and Alfred took a last nostalgic walk in the public gardens, now swept by a wet March wind. The final gondola trip to Mestre was equally cold and dispiriting. George gave Alfred a tender farewell kiss, almost proud to feel that she had contributed to his salvation. "But after I had deposited you on dry land," as she was soon to write, "and when I found myself alone in that black, coffinlike gondola, I felt that my soul was leaving with you. All that was left for the wind to rock on the ruffled lagoons was a sick and stupid body."

19. Pietro Pagello's Venice

WEEKS OF UNREMITTING TENSION, sleepless vigils, and bitter quarreling had left George Sand so utterly worn out that on her way back into Venice she could no longer properly distinguish material objects from their watery reflections: she saw everything upside-down, as though her gondola were gliding *over* a long enfilade of white marble bridges underarching the canal. Pietro Pagello, who was waiting for her on the wharf, put her up for a night with his Genoese friend Lazzaro Rebizzo, a gentleman poet who dreamed and talked of liberating Italy from the Austrian yoke. After which, Pietro suggested that she accompany him on a trip to Treviso, in the Dolomites — a proposal she welcomed with enthusiasm.

The six-day tour, much of it spent hiking, proved a badly needed tonic. At Castelfranco Pagello introduced her to his father, who seemed to enjoy discussing literature, art, and flowers with his French visitor, while hardly addressing a word to his son — a tacit reproof of this unorthodox liaison. At Bassano they visited the famous Parolini grotto, where with the tip of her parasol George romantically inscribed her name and Piero's in the mossy bank. The springtime fragrance of the Brenta valley, the envigorating smell of verdant slopes dotted with scented cyclamen, the sight of a snow-crowned rampart of ridged rock, eating into "the solid blue of the sky," thrilled her almost as much as had the Pyrenees. Clad in a cap, blue cotton blouse, and cloth trousers, she whistled gaily as they tramped over mountain paths and goat tracks. Each time the handsome doctor took her by the hand, she felt as though it were going to be crushed inside his powerful paw, and next to his tall figure her five feet three inches were almost dwarflike. Stimulated by the brisk mountain air, the fresh butter and anise-flavored bread she devoured with gusto, the hot coffee she drank with relish, she kept up with him so well that one day she actually hiked twenty-four miles.

She returned to Venice with exactly seven centimes in her pocket — or so she claimed in a letter to Boucoiran. Yet she was already making plans for an even more extensive journey into the Austrian Tyrol — that mysterious region she had dreamed of visiting ever since she had heard the Austrian prisoners at Nohant sing their jolly yodels with such instinctive harmony. While visiting the grottoes of Oliero, magically illumined by the golden rays of the western sun, it had suddenly occurred to her that she should write up this journey into the mountains as a kind of letter, interspersed with meditations and addressed, spiritually if not explicitly, to Alfred de Musset — in order, as she later explained to him, "to shut the traps of those who are certain to say that you ruined and abandoned me."

She was also seriously tempted by the idea of making a quick trip to Constantinople — the mysterious Venice of the Orient whose praises had been sung by Casanova, Lamartine, and not least of all Byron. But this heady daydream finally dissolved like a mirage — for lack of money. George Sand's search for local color and novelistic inspiration was thus limited to Venice and the hundred islands and islets of its archipelago.

These turned out to be richer than expected. Wonderfully picturesque, to begin with, was the Ca' Mezzani boarding house, in the tumble-down quarter of San Fantino, into which she moved so as to be close to Piero, who was already housed there with his brother, Roberto. Roberto, a gay, happy-go-lucky Venetian who was employed in the city's marine administration, was an Italian version of Hippolyte Chatiron, whom he resembled in his inexhaustible fund of jokes and witticisms, made all the quainter for George Sand's foreign ear by the local dialect in which they were reeled off. Though he couldn't understand what his brother saw in *questa sardella* — this sardine, as he unflatteringly called the emaciated Aurore (for it took her a long time to recover from the ten tempestuous weeks with Musset) — Roberto refused to play the puritan and lecture Piero on his "sinful" association with a foreign lady when he himself was happily carrying on an affair with a plump, languorous, and talkative housemaid named Cattina.

George Sand's arrival in the Ca' Mezzani — which seems to have been a rather ramshackle house three or four stories high — was not long in provoking a typically Venetian uproar. Try as she might to lead an unobtrusive existence, she could not pass completely unnoticed, and her unconventional mode of life and manners soon had local tongues wagging. Her insistence on smoking Pietro Pagello's long-stemmed carob-wood pipes, her strange nocturnal hours, the casual way in which she clung to Pagello's arm whenever they went out for a stroll (something even married women rarely did with their Venetian husbands), and not least of all the fact that she was a writer aroused endless curiosity. Here, even more than in Paris, a double standard was used to judge the behavior of her sex, and what was regarded as normal masculine behavior for a Lord Byron was deemed a scandalous offense for her. Many of Pagello's acquaintances, on meeting the couple on the Piazza San Marco or the Riva dei Schiavoni, would purse their lips, look away, and pass by without returning his salutation, even when he doffed his top hat.

Her deliberately antisocial behavior merely aggravated the situation. Lazzaro Rebizzo, who dropped in every morning to see her, sought in vain to lure her to Countess Soranzo's salon, where her stubborn refusal to appear was considered odd, not to say boorish. "I have to put up with a siege from the curious who are already flocking around my cell," she wrote to Alfred de Musset in mid-April. "I don't know why it's always like this when one wants to be alone." A number of local "shrews," as she called them, had apparently read her novels and were eager to invite her to their *conversazioni* — ritual afternoons or evenings when literary or "philosophical" themes were discussed and poetry occasionally read. But as George Sand wrote, "I wouldn't hear of it. I lock myself into my room and like a divinity in its cloud, I envelope myself in the smoke of my pipe. I have an intimate friend who would delight you," she went on, faithful to the bird-loving traditions of her Delaborde grandfather. "He's a friendly little starling which Pagello one day pulled from his pocket and placed on my shoulder. He's the most insolent, cowardly, playful, greedy, extravagant being you can imagine . . . He sits on my knee or on my foot when I'm working, he snatches everything I eat out of my hands, he shits on Pagello's *bel vestito* . . ."

Pagello's elegant frock coat, as it happened, was soon to be subjected to sterner tests. Fatally attractive to members of the fair sex, the handsome surgeon was already credited with two mistresses when George Sand appeared on the scene. One of them was a pale-faced Veronese beauty named Arpalice, whose patrician blood waxed singularly hot at the intrusion into Pagello's life of this black-eyed foreigner. She put on terrible scenes, quite unnerving the normally placid doctor. "He is so kind and tender that he hasn't the heart to tell her he no longer loves her," George reported to Musset, adding that the jealous ex-mistress had even solicited *her* aid in attempting a reconciliation. "I can't do otherwise, though I feel I am doing both of them a rather poor service," she went on, calmly glossing over the fact that she was now Pietro's bedmate. "Pagello is an angel of virtue and deserves to be happy. This is why I shouldn't reconcile him with the Arpalice. But it's also why I shall leave."

This was eventually what happened, though George Sand did not leave Venice, as Musset was led to expect; she merely moved out of the storm-ridden Ca' Mezzani, taking the two Pagellos with her. The move was prompted by the arrival of yet another female in this turbulently bohemian household. This was a twenty-eight-year-old girl with the sweet, doll-like name of Giulia Puppati. An illegitimate half sister of the Pagellos and the deceptively angelic product of a love affair between their father and an itinerant Englishwoman, she had come clandestinely to Venice from her home at Castelfranco in order to see her music teacher and lover, the composer Nicoló Vaccaj. But local rumor soon had it that she was the mistress of *both* Pagellos "and that she and I are the doctor's lovers," as George wrote in another letter to Musset toward the end of April.

The arrival of this blue-eyed *amorosa* shook the Ca' Mezzani to its foundations. The actors living on the top floor, who already looked askance at George Sand, began talking about "orgies" and wondering how many more women were going to be admitted to the Pagellos' burgeoning harem. The hot-blooded Arpalice stormed up the stairs, forced her way into Pietro's room, and flinging her patrician upbringing to the Adriatic winds, she put on a scene worthy of a Neapolitan fishwife, tearing out whole clumps of the doctor's hair and ruining his *bel vestito* — as George Sand gleefully reported to Musset. The hysterical shrieking was such that she at first thought the handsome surgeon was "operating on thirty cats at once, but the door was noisily opened and I heard the doctor shout: *'Carogna, io ti ammazzo!'* [I'll kill you, you offal!] But for me he would have killed her, reason enough for her to detest me even more."

The owner of the Ca' Mezzani having indicated that the "carnival" had to stop, the two Pagello brothers decided to move with George Sand and Giulia Puppati to a smaller house where they could be on their own. Located on a narrow alleyway bordered by a canal, it had just two floors, linked by an inner staircase. George Sand and Giulia Puppati occupied the first, Pietro and Roberto the second. While the poorly paid doctor used up his savings buying necessary furniture, George spent a few busy days upholstering the chairs in new materials and sewing the curtains — particularly needed by Roberto Pagello, who discovered that he could not undress without becoming an intriguing spectacle for the *popolo,* who would shamelessly gather on the bridge beyond his window to admire his classic nudity.

Altogether it seems to have been a merry household which was thus established near the Ponte dei Barcarolli. Though Roberto likened it to a *palazzo* and said that he was going to have it entered in the *Traveler's Guide to Venice,* the atmosphere was so bohemian that George Sand called the upstairs living room — a kind of minstrels' gallery — Pagello's "pandemonium." Littered with music scores on which Vespasiano, the cat, regularly planted his furry bulk, it was decorated by four gaudy landscapes, into whose green skies, blue trees, and reddish waters Pietro Pagello would gaze for inspiration while improvising on the upright piano. He also amused himself composing verses which, though not up to Musset's, had all the naive charm of the Venetian dialect. His brother Roberto could also play the guitar, which was seldom missing from their gondola excursions. The romantic Giulia sang, her throaty voice suddenly rising to a crystalline purity of tone when hitting a high note, while George provided her share of entertainment by doing comic sketches — a few strokes of her skillful pen or pencil sufficing to "fix" the caricatural profile of someone she might have seen only once.

Though she occasionally smoked one of Pagello's long-stemmed *pipettas,* George Sand usually preferred to roll her own cigarettes, which she did with a dexterity which never ceased to amaze the good-natured surgeon. He was no less amazed by her diligence, for the joyous distractions were seldom allowed to interrupt her writing — six to eight hours at a stretch, spent in front of a card table, from which she would look up every now and then, as though seeking a new metaphor in the coils of cigarette smoke around her.

Pagello was also agreeably surprised by her proficiency in the confection of French sauces, increasingly needed to disguise the fish dishes which became their daily fare. For as the weeks dragged on, with no sign of money from Paris, drastic economies had to be made in their day-to-day existence. They went out less frequently and had to content themselves with the part-time services of an aged gondolier named Catullo, who for a modest fee of fifteen francs a month made himself and his hooded craft available for three hours each evening. The generous Lazzaro Rebizzo offered George Sand an unlimited run on his purse, but she proudly refused to borrow more than 200 francs. As for Pagello, he was so strapped for funds that he had to pawn some of his belongings and get up at dawn and walk for miles through a maze of narrow alleyways, linked by stone and marble bridges, to cull a bouquet of flowers (which he was too poor to buy for his beloved) from one of the city's outlying gardens.

George Sand's first *Lettre d'un voyageur* (*Letter from a Traveler*) was finally completed and sent off to Paris in the latter part of April. Subtitled "To a Poet," it was sent to Alfred de Musset, who was given carte blanche to commit the manuscript to the flames if he didn't like it. Instead, he went into raptures, calling it "sublime . . . Never have you written anything so beautiful and so divine, never has your genius found a better place in your heart." François Buloz, who published the first of its two installments in the May 15 issue of the *Revue des Deux Mondes,* was no less enthusiastic: "Really, George, you are making progress. How poetically and vigorously all this is written!" He asked her to send him more of the same, and even suggested that she prolong her stay in Italy until September, since it had proved such a stimulus to her imagination.

His "dear George" would have been more receptive to his flattery had the payments made for these *Letters from a Traveler* exceeded the niggardly 300 francs which he finally granted for each. Partly inspired by the ceaseless chatter which the two talkative maids, Loredana and Cattina, carried on in the room next to hers, and which, as she became more familiar with Venetian speech, she found to be astonishingly reminiscent of the provincial gossip of La Châtre, her novel *André* was completed and sent off in late May. It was accompanied by a second *Lettre d'un voyageur* which was quite simply a minor masterpiece. Still the money failed to arrive. She dispatched letter after letter to Jules Boucoiran, imploring him to collect the 2000 francs Buloz owed her, using half to pay off her debt to Sosthènes de la Rochefoucauld and forwarding the balance to Venice. Her letters went unanswered. By now reduced to a diet of shellfish and sardines, she imagined Boucoiran dead of some disease or dying of a broken heart; anxiously she wrote to Gustave Papet and even to her son, Maurice, to find out what had happened. No one in Venice had heard of the *Revue des Deux Mondes,* and there was not a copy to be found in any of the city's reading rooms or libraries which might have told her if the material she was so industriously dispatching was finding its way into print.

She was finally bailed out by a French acquaintance — the same Joseph-Sulpice Blavoyer who had ridden over the moutains of Auvergne and paid her such outlandish court during her trip to the Mont-Dore in 1827. Happening to meet him one day in the Public Gardens — to which she had repaired with the premonitory feeling that she would there meet some providential soul — she broke down and admitted her financial plight. But proud as ever, she refused to borrow more than 400 francs (which she repaid before the summer was over).

The financial crisis was resolved a few days later, when an envelope which Boucoiran had sent her in mid-May containing a letter of credit for 1100 francs was found at the Venice post office; it had been misplaced in the box reserved for mail from London. Relieved at last of the financial worries which had weighed on her more or less incessantly since her arrival, George Sand could now relax and enjoy the city's ineffable beauties.

They were wondrously described in her second *Lettre d'un*

voyageur, which merits a place next to the Fourth Canto of *Childe Harold* for containing some of the most inspired pages that have ever been written about Venice. Though what she wrote was prose, it had the ring of poetry, as Buloz noted: a poetry no less touching for being more humble than Byron's epic stanzas and applied to the simplest sights and objects — such as the café candles planted in iris-petaled or seaweed-crystal holders of Murano glass. Though she too could depict the sea-girt city in flaming colors — at times it reminded her of a proudly returning fleet, with dark sunset sails and pennants still ablaze against the cherry red and smalt blue of the heavens, at others of a New Jerusalem magically floating on a giant mirror of red bronze — her own descriptions were more subtly attuned to the chromatic metamorphosis occasioned by the change of seasons.

Now gone was the wintry whiteness which had prompted the death-obsessed Musset to liken this city of marble columns to a graveyard full of bones. Everything was overlaid with a soft emerald patina. The gray marshlands of February had turned into aquatic meadows, verdant with watercress and rushes, gladiolas and strange mosses, on which herring gulls, bustards, and petrels made their nests. The canals were now tapestried with leaves, the ornate pillars wreathed in white-blossomed creepers, the arched balconies draped with giant campanulas, honeysuckle clusters, Greek roses, and potted tulips from Persia whose red-and-white corollas recalled the carnival cloth worn by the eighteenth-century contemporaries of Canaletto and Guardi. The sensuous Venetian spring could be heard as well as inhaled, for an astonishing number of these leafy balconies housed cages full of nightingales, which sang both day and night, as they would have in the country. Calling and answering each other across the sonorous canals, they would lapse into silence at the approach of a gondola full of serenaders, resuming their flutelike warbling with redoubled zest only when the sound of human voices and mandolins had dwindled away.

The absence of carriage wheels, horses' hoofs, and jingle bells made this sonically the most entrancing of cities. Here too the second *Lettre d'un voyageur* (and the third which followed somewhat later) paid homage to Venice's bewitching spell in terms that have perhaps never been equaled. Nor could this have been accomplished by a transient sightseer, unfamiliar with the local dialect and mores of its inhabitants. Only an "insider" — such as George Sand, under Pagello's tutelage, was rapidly becoming — could have guessed what brought together the *facchini* (porters) and the boatmen, as they lolled on their gondolas or gossiped in a circle under the trellised vine leaves of a *traghetto.* For the fellow with the upturned cap perched on his flowing locks whose gesticulating figure was outlined against the pink wall of a *palazzo* was in fact boasting of his latest adventure in the nighttime smuggling of tobacco, brought in under the snoring noses of Austrian customs officials.

And who but a musical connoisseur could have disentangled the harmonic combinations which were revealed whenever one of these "conspiratorial" gatherings burst into song? The melodic theme would first be sung in a nasal falsetto voice by some portly tenor, followed a moment later by the hoarse-voiced basso. Thematic elements borrowed from operas old and new and even from church music were indiscriminately used in the improvisation of these potpourris, with the result, as George Sand wrote, that "a Bellini cavatina becomes a four-part chorus. A Rossini chorus is adapted to two voices in the midst of a Mercadante duet, and the refrain from some ancient barcarolle from an unknown master, slowed down to the grave tempo of a church chant, quietly terminates a theme borrowed from a psalm by Marcello."

Without going as far as to declare that these choruses of *facchini* and gondoliers were superior to those of the Paris Opera — as more than one enthusiast had sought to convince her — George Sand had to admit that heard from afar under the moon-blanched arches of a Moorish palace, they afforded greater pleasure than better music "performed in front of the painted canvas of a stage-set colonnade." Thanks to a "magic of acoustical effects" provided by the unique conjunction of echoing water, sound-channeling marble, and the gliding motion of one's gondola, the humblest song on these enchanted nights is "listened to with indulgence, not to say gratitude . . . as it approaches, passes, and loses itself in the distance."

To be sure, the plain cloth garments and round hats now worn by most gondoliers were a far cry from the splendid silk tunics, floating scarfs, and plumed headgear the older of them had worn in the glorious days of the Republic. But George Sand found that these boatmen had lost none of their legendary wit. A few random cries, unintelligible to someone not versed in the Venetian dialect, were thus revealed to be an elaborate exchange of insults, proferred with a scrupulous regard to form. When two gondolas collided around the blind corner of a *canaletto,* not a word was uttered by either boatman until both had backed off and ascertained the usually negligible "damage." Whereupon one of them would frowningly berate the other: "Why did you not cry *Siastali?*" (a word of Turkish origin meaning "To the left").

"I did," the other would protest.

"I say you didn't."

"That I did, I tell you."

"Corpo di Bacco, but I wager you didn't!"

"Sangue di Diana, but I swear I did!"

"But with what a wretched voice!"

"And what unwashed ears have you to hear with?"

"In what tavern, tell me, did you learn to croak?"

"What ass was it your mother dreamed of when she carried you in her belly?"

"The cow which conceived you should have taught you to moo."

"The ass which bore you should have given you its family ears."

"What was that you said, you dog?"

"What did you say, you son of a she-ape?"

And so the quarrel was continued, the insults growing ever more terrible as the distance between the adversaries grew, until one of them would shout, when they were already two bridges apart: "Just come back here and I'll show you what kind of wood my oar is made of."

"Wait, you sea hog, till I sink your eggshell by spitting on it!" etc.

And thus, as George Sand noted, insulting metaphor was heaped on insulting metaphor, until the most hideous, throat-cutting oaths could no longer be heard save as distant cries echoing unintelligibly over the intervening waters.

Yes, all these varied sights and sounds were wondrously recorded and the descriptive passages enlivened by snatches of dialogue taken from her own experience. For this and the succeeding *Lettre d'un voyageur* made no claim to objectivity; they were highly personal impressions and all the more scintillating for it. Pietro Pagello and his "forty-yard-long" *pipetta,* the jovial, guitar-strumming Roberto, the romantic Giulia Pupatti with her "sirenlike" voice and the mysterious rose which the hand of her lover has tucked beneath her dark mantilla, Catullo, the stout-waisted gondolier who likes to compare his arthritic limp to Lord Byron's — all flit through these enchanting pages under slightly altered names, like figures in a Watteau painting. But they are as recognizable as the two-story house near the Ponte dei Barcarolli and the threatened *coltellata* (knifing) which the furious Arpalice has promised for her foreign rival: a threat which the doctor and Giulia Puppati did not lightly dismiss, alarmed as they sometimes were by George Sand's predilection for solitary nighttime strolls.

20. A Tense Homecoming

YET ANOTHER VENICE was revealed to George Sand during the last weeks of her Adriatic sojourn. A stifling Venice, stewing in its midsummer heat, in which the gondoliers, like the nightingales, seemed to have lost their voices. A city of daytime corpses lethargically stretched out on sofas or the cushioned bottoms of their boats, who slowly fanned themselves to life at dusk on the cooling marble of their balconies or beneath the sun-scorched awnings of their cafés. A city of thunder-charged nights, punctuated by the short shrill cries of scurrying water rats and eerily illumined by distant flashes of lightning and the phosphorescent glimmer of seaweed and tiny shellfish sparkling like quicksilver in the shadowy waters of the canals.

This, and much else besides, was again vividly portrayed in the third *Lettre d'un voyageur,* which was begun in Venice shortly before she left. A mosaic of scintillating vignettes, like its predecessor, this deliberately rambling essay was less fancifully composed than at first appeared. For it carried a social message that was to make itself increasingly heard in George Sand's novels. Thus her elaborate description of the Feast of the *Redentore* (the Redeemer) — celebrated on the canal of La Giudecca by scores of gondolas glowing with streamers and Japanese lanterns — served to emphasize the virtues of Venetian democracy, implicitly contrasted with the plutocratic inequalities to be found elsewhere in Europe. The absence of coachmen and horses, which in Paris contributed so much to distinguish the rich and nobly-wheeled from the mud- and dung-splattered pedestrian, had here a beneficially leveling effect. For in Venice even the poorest family could boast a punt, if not a lacquered gondola with a dragon-headed prow. Just as in the outdoor cafés of this aquatic city the aristocrat would not take offense at the proximity of a Chioggia fisherman leaning his tattered elbows on the same table, so the closed gondola of the aged nobleman, the banker's dazzling craft, or the vegetable vendor's crude punt would jostle and rub up against each other with festive fraternity, while rich and poor alike supped on the candle- and lantern-lit canal.

Here indeed was a city made to appeal to her democratic inclinations. "The beauty of the spot, the cheapness of vital commodities, the absence of etiquette," as George Sand was to write twenty years later in *The Story of My Life,* "the proximity of sea and mountains, the admirable climate — save for one winter and two summer months — the cordiality of human relations which my mode of living enabled me to restrict to two or three friends, everything would have attached me to Venice if my children had been with me; and I often dreamed of one day buying one of those old deserted palaces which were then being sold for ten or twelve thousand francs, and of returning with them to settle down in some habitable corner and to live and work amid the poetry of splendid ruins."

While this might have proved beneficial in terms of literary and even financial productivity, it would almost certainly have left her emotionally dissatisfied. As it was, the six momentous months George Sand spent in Venice saw her compose two novels (*André* and *Jacques*), a long short story (*Leone Leoni*), and two *Lettres d'un voyageur,* soon followed by a third — an astonishing creative output which she herself valued at 14,000 francs. But these months also left her sentimentally divided between two men, one of whom could claim to possess her body, while the other claimed her soul.

She had begun to feel the tidal force of these contrary attractions almost from the day she had said goodbye to Alfred de Musset. His first letter to her, sent from Geneva on April 4, had struck a responsive chord. How, he asked, could he forget that pale, haggard face which had bent over his bedside for eighteen sleepless nights "in that sinister room where so many tears flowed. Poor George! Poor, dear child! You were wrong: you thought you were my mistress, you were only my mother. Heaven made us for each other; and our minds, in their lofty spheres, recognized each other like two mountain birds and flew one toward the other. But the embrace was too strong; we were committing incest . . . ."

"Don't, Alfred, don't believe that I can be happy at the thought of having lost your heart . . . ," she had hastened to reply. "You are right, our embrace was incestuous, but we did not know it. We threw ourselves innocently and sincerely into each other's arms. Well, do we have a single memory of those embraces that is not chaste and holy? One day, in a fit of fever and delirium, you reproached me with being unable to give you the pleasures of love. I wept over it then, but now I am happy to think there is some truth in this reproach. I am happy to think that those pleasures were more austere, more veiled than those you will find elsewhere. At least you won't be reminded of me in the arms of other women. But when you are alone, when you need to pray and cry, you will think of your George, of your true comrade, your nurse, your friend, and something better than all that."

Musset too found it as impossible to forget her as she did him. From Paris, shortly after his arrival, he wrote to say that he was safely back, though suffering from a ridiculously sunburned face and a skin inflammation on the legs which made him feel slightly feverish at night. In a determined effort to forget her, he had sought to resume his past dissipations with his notorious dandy friend, Comte Edmond d'Alton-Shée, but had found it more difficult than he imagined. "They had seated a poor opera dancer next to me, she felt foolish, but far less foolish than I. I couldn't find a word to say to her and went to bed at eight o'clock. I've been back to all the salons to which my habitual rudeness has not yet denied me access. What do you want me to do? The longer I live the more attached to you I feel, and though I'm calm, I'm devoured by a grief that accompanies me everywhere."

"Your furniture" he reported, after a visit to the Quai Malaquais apartment, "is covered with large woolen blankets. Your bed has nothing but its mattresses, the windows are curtainless. I can't stay there. The only thing left for me to do is lock myself up, but I can't yet work, and as soon as the imbecile" — he meant himself — "begins to reflect for a quarter of an hour, the tears come to his eyes."

Buloz had told him that Gustave Planche, Jules Sandeau, and Emile Regnault were all up in arms against him, but he didn't care. Madame Hennequin, the wife of the lawyer who owned the Quai Malaquais apartment, had said the most frightful things about George Sand to Musset's mother, but Alfred had nipped this particular piece of gossip in the bud by telling his mother of the long nights Madame Sand had spent by his bedside in Venice. For the rest, nobody had dared attack her, and all he had found was admiration — "as at the time of *Indiana*" — a reference to the enthusiasm which had greeted the recent appearance of the first half of *Leone Leoni* in the *Revue des Deux Mondes.*

Thus, over a distance of a thousand miles, was established a strange spiritual partnership — with Musset telling his George to love her Pagello, and George recommending to her Alfred a moderate indulgence in wine and women. She had to admit, for her part, that she was in a "singular moral state, between an existence that is not yet completely finished and another that is not yet started. I wait, I let myself drift, I work, I keep my brain occupied, and I let my heart rest a bit." For the truth, which emerged more clearly with each successive letter, was that she loved her good, kind Pagello with deep gratitude, with heartfelt affection — with everything but the kind of passion that Alfred de Musset had been able to inspire.

This was the poisoned cup Musset had given her to drink and she could no longer get it out of her system. As she wrote to him again, in a candid avowal of her sentimental masochism: "I have next to me a friend, my mainstay, he does not suffer; he is not weak, he is not suspicious . . . He doesn't need my strength . . . he is happy without . . . my having to work for his happiness. Well, I have to suffer for somebody, I have to use up this excess of energy and sensibility that are within me. I have to nourish this maternal solicitude which has grown accustomed to watching over a suffering and tired soul. Oh, why couldn't I have lived between the two of you, and have made you happy without belonging to one or the other? I could easily have lived ten years like that, for I truly needed a father" — presumably Pagello — "but why couldn't I keep my child near to me?" — by which she must have meant Alfred.

This was about as close as George Sand ever came to defining her conception of the perfect lover of her romantic dreams — a doubly incestuous father-son figure: a father-protector who could provide her with the paternal care and affection she had so tragically lost at the age of four, a dependent son on whom she could lavish an infinitely fretful solicitude. But since the two could hardly coexist in the same human being, her soaring hopes were foredoomed to founder in recurring fits of nympholeptic despair. What she termed her *spleen* and her frequent suicidal moods were thus more than a fashionable romantic ailment; they were the product of an inner contradiction, of an irreconcilable clash between two conflicting inclinations which left her almost as schizophrenically divided as Musset himself.

Determined to be back in Paris by mid-August, in time for the prize-distributing ceremonies at Maurice's boarding school, George Sand now made ready to leave Venice in her turn. Encouraged by Musset, who did not like the idea of his beloved George making the trip alone, the good Pagello agreed to accompany her, even though he knew it would cause a lot of critical eyebrow raising among his fellow Venetians. More scrupulous than Musset, who had let George finance his return journey to Paris without displaying undue haste to reimburse her, the doctor insisted on footing his share of the bills and took the precaution of unhooking the four Zuccarelli landscapes which graced (or disgraced) the living room and having them sent to Paris, to be sold there if necessary.

On July 24 the two lovers said goodbye to a steaming Venice and headed for Milan. George Sand, who detested stagecoaches, insisted that the trip be made by *vetturino* — which is to say, with hired coachman and carriage — so that they could stop and rest whenever and wherever they chose. The cap, cloth trousers, and blue blouse were once again pulled from her trunk and much of the distance covered on foot. At Verona they visited the old Roman arena (later described in George Sand's novel *La Comtesse de Rudolstadt*) and admired the house where a legendary Romeo was reported to have wooed a legendary Juliet. The two lakes of Garda and Iseo offered welcome relief from the stifling heat of the rich Lombardy plain, but the *alberghi* at which they had to stop were sometimes distressingly primitive.

From Milan, which impressed her as far more luxurious a city than Paris, Aurore wrote to Maurice and Casimir to announce her return in mid-August. Pagello wrote at last to his father, who had accused him of dissipating his youth, ruining his career, and publicly renouncing "the principles of Christian morality" in which he had been brought up by his mother: "I am in the last stage of my folly, and I must run through this one, as I have run through the others, with closed eyes. Tomorrow I leave for Paris, where I shall leave *la* Sand, and I shall return to embrace you, being worthy of you again. I am young and can remake my career. Don't cease to love me and write to me in Paris."

Proceeding northward, they climbed the Simplon pass into Switzerland, agreeably surprised by the successive changes of temperature — from the torrid heat of Italy to the chill of the Alps, followed by the vernal warmth of the Rhone valley into which they descended.

On the way up they ran into Antonio, the Venetian barber who had accompanied Alfred de Musset back to Paris and who was now homeward bound. *"Per il sangue di Diana!"* he exclaimed, when he finally recognized Pietro Pagello's dust-dovered companion. The sight of this equally dusty hiker, hurrying up in his kid gloves and tight-fitting suit to bow his pomaded head over the hand of an urchin (which is how she looked in her cap, shirt, and trousers), and this in the middle of the mountains, amused George Sand no end. But generous as ever, she would not let the homesick and almost penniless Antonio continue on his way without giving him the several hundred francs Musset had vainly tried to obtain from Buloz for his return trip to Venice.

Exhilarated by the fresh Swiss air and the view of so many waterfalls and snowy peaks — even more numerous and awe-inspiring than the Pyrenees — George Sand insisted on climbing back into the mountains above Martigny for a glimpse of Mont Blanc. There was also a literary motive behind this sightseeing detour. In her novel *Jacques* — inspired as usual by real life — the husband (a transmogrified Musset) bows out of his wife's life and leaves her with her lover, Octave, much as George had been left in Venice in the tender care of Pagello. She had been wondering just how to have the husband disappear from her novel, and the solution now came to her in a flash: she would have him vanish into a crevasse while crossing an Alpine glacier, like the famous *mer de Glace* which rests against one of Mont Blanc's snowy flanks. Most of this detour had to be made on muleback to spare George Sand the violent heart-pounding brought on by the altitude, but on the way down she slipped from her dawdling mount and ran joyfully down the grassy slopes into the little village of Chamonix, closely pursued by a dramatic storm which rolled its rippling and cracking thunder up against the peaks and down the echoing valleys.

Geneva, where they tarried for a week, provided them with a few final moments of felicity. For the closer they came to Paris, in the cramped, smelly stagecoach which carried them across the dusty roads of Burgundy and Champagne, the more anxious and withdrawn George became. She clearly dreaded this homecoming which, though it would reunite her with her children, promised to be harshly judged. In Venice Pagello had been her guide, mentor, and protector, and though many people had disapproved of their liaison, she had been able to live more or less incognita and thumb her nose at convention. But in Paris, where she was now a celebrity, she had no need of a protector and her companion would be less a pillar of strength than an embarrassment.

The faithful Jules Boucoiran, who was waiting for them at the stagecoach terminus, took her back to her Quai Malaquais apartment, while Pagello was lodged in a cheap third-floor room at the Hôtel d'Orléans on the nearby Rue des Petits Augustins. George Sand immediately took to her bed, the physical exhaustion of the trip compounded by her psychological malaise. Long exposure to the burning sun of Lombardy and the Alps had turned her normally olive-hued features brick red, and she had no desire to see anyone in this condition. (Sun tans were then anything but the fashion.) The only exception was Gustave Papet, to whom she wrote an anguished note, saying that she was suffering terribly and was in desperate need of his friendly advice.

The advice, whatever it was, does not seem to have calmed her troubled spirit, made all the more agitated by the news that Alfred de Musset had postponed his departure from Paris to see her. Feeling too unwell to move, she had Boucoiran and Pagello take the concluding part of *Jacques* to Buloz, even though his office was just around the corner. The result was an almost comic encounter, which began with Buloz expressing his surprise when informed by Boucoiran that George Sand had reached Paris two days before.

"This she-devil of a woman is driving me out of my mind!" he exclaimed. "Here's a volume for which I've been waiting for a whole month! But I hear she's got herself involved in a new love affair with an Italian Count!"

Boucoiran smiled but said nothing, Pagello blushed, while Buloz remained frozen-faced, stubbornly refusing to admit that he might have been tactlessly slow-witted.

On Sunday, August 17, George finally consented to see Alfred de Musset. It was a painful meeting for both of them. She told him that she was happy with Pagello and that it would be better for both of them if they no longer saw each other. Only once did she betray the emotion it cost her to utter these words — when through the open window came the sound of a waltz that was particularly dear to both of them and tears came into her eyes.

Musset went home feeling utterly crushed. For months he had lived only for this moment, his despondent hopes encouraged by George's letters. But she had made a point of receiving him with Pagello, in whose embarrassing presence he could do no more than kiss her hand.

Returning home, Alfred called on his mother and asked her to lend him enough money to go stay with an uncle in the Pyrenees. Then locking himself into his room, he wrote his beloved "Georgette" a letter at once pathetic and romantically exalted, in which he depicted himself as the victim of an implacable destiny and reiterated his intention of writing up their story, even though his fate might not be of profit to anyone: "But those who follow the same road as I will see whither it leads; those who walk on the edge of the abyss will perhaps turn pale when they hear me fall."

The idea of leaving Paris without seeing her again was, however, more than he could endure. "The day I left Venice you gave me an entire day," he went on plaintively. "Today I'm leaving forever, I'm leaving alone, without a companion, without a dog. All I ask is one hour and one last kiss. If you fear a moment of sadness, if my request importunes Pierre [Pagello], do not hesitate to refuse. It will be hard, but I won't complain. But if you are courageous, receive me alone, either at your place or elsewhere, wherever you wish. Why would you be afraid to listen to the solemn voice of Destiny? . . . Let ours not be the farewell of a Mr. or a Mrs. So-and-so. Let it be two souls who have suffered, two suffering minds, two wounded eagles who meet in the sky and who exchange a cry of pain before parting forever. May it be an embrace, as chaste as celestial love, as profound as human suffering. Oh, my fiancée," he concluded, repeating a poetic image George had used in a letter written from Venice, "place the crown of thorns upon me gently; and farewell! It will be the last memory retained by your old age, that of a child who is no more."

This was the exalted language her romantic nature craved. This was the language Alfred would always use, but which Pagello could never give her, and this realization filled her with despair. More undecided than ever, she wrote to Sainte-Beuve, asking him to call on her, for she was "mortally sad" and did not know how to extricate herself from this dreadful pass. In a few days she would be leaving for Nohant, but the idea of returning to Paris in October and of not finding her "child" Alfred there left her singularly depressed.

There was a further exchange of letters between the two tormented lovers. But not until the following Thursday, August 21, would George Sand grant Alfred his request for a second meeting. Musset by this time had changed his plans, having been persuaded by his friend Tattet to remove himself to the elegant spa of Baden-Baden, near the Rhine, rather than to the Pyrenees and Portugal. Their meeting this time lasted two tense, dramatic hours. George Sand, who only four days before had seemed to him so contented and serene, made no secret of her sadness, saying she had reached the conclusion that happiness on earth was an illusion. There were times, she confessed, when there was nothing she looked forward to more than the peace of eternity. But Alfred could rest assured: whatever happened, her love for him would never die. She would forever treasure it, she would carry it with her to the grave. But for this love to endure, it must henceforth remain unsullied, pure, and absolutely chaste. Though physically they would be parted, perhaps even by great distances, spiritually they would always remain as one, prior to their eventual reunion in heaven. Thus their love would become a radiant example for others and provide an inspiration for future generations, when the world was purged at last of its materialistic crassness and a new Golden Age — of the Mind and of the Spirit — was born. And so that each could give strength to the other, in their moments of discouragement and despair, let them swear a solemn oath that whatever happened, one of them would not die without the other.

Swept off his feet by the rhapsodic nobility of these sentiments, Musset rushed home and penned another letter to his beloved, imploring her not to leave this sorry world before he had finished the book he was writing about their exemplary romance. "No, my beautiful one, my holy fiancée," he declared, "you will not lie in this cold earth without its knowing who trod it. No, no, I swear by my youth and genius, nothing but spotless lilies will grow on your tomb. With my own hands will I place over it your epitaph in a marble purer than the statues of our one-day glories. Posterity will repeat our names like those of those immortal lovers . . . like Romeo and Juliet, like Héloyse and Abeylard. Never will one be spoken of without the other. It will be a holier wedding than those that are celebrated by priests: the chaste and imperishable marriage of Intelligence . . . I will end your story with my hymn of love. I will appeal from the depths of my twenty-year-old heart to all the children of the earth. Into the ears of this blasé and corrupt, godless and dissolute century I will blow the trumpet of human resurrections which Christ left at the foot of his cross . . . ," etc.

Made giddy in her turn by these effusions, George wrote Alfred a short note saying: "I must be yours, it is my destiny." The note was left on the couch next to the cane which Musset, in his poetic exaltation, had absent-mindedly forgotten in her apartment, and the maid was instructed to deliver it the next morning to the Rue de Grenelle. Instead, the letter was delivered to Musset by Pagello, who probably read it on the way over. That single, thrilling sentence — "I must be yours, it is my destiny" — was enough to bring Alfred back to the Quai Malaquais apartment, where there was a last passionate embrace before the final parting. George promised that one day — she didn't know when — she would be his again, physically as well as spiritually, for a blissful twenty-four hours!

On August 24 a sad but no longer desperate Alfred de Musset left for Baden-Baden. The same day George Sand left for Nohant, taking with her the four Zuccarelli landscapes which she told Pagello she could easily sell to a La Châtre "connoisseur" for a good price. Pietro, lonely and increasingly upset, was entrusted to the care of Jules Boucoiran.

Feeling the need of moral support, in anticipation of the critical reception Casimir was likely to give her, Aurore brought along her mother as well as her son, Maurice. On reaching Nohant she sent word to all her friends to come to see her, anxious as she was not to be left alone with her husband. She found Solange plumper and healthier than ever, but so unnaturally subdued that she dismissed the maid who, she decided, had been making excessive use of the switch. Casimir, out of deference to her mother, did not once raise his voice during Madame Dupin's three-week stay, and he even expressed his readiness to receive Pagello — an invitation the handsome doctor prudently declined, realizing that if he was out of his element in Paris, he would be even more so at Nohant.

George, who had made him promise that he would write her every two days from Paris, informed Pietro shortly after her arrival at Nohant, that she had sold the four Zuccarelli paintings for 1500 francs. Overjoyed by these glad tidings, which made him feel "like a Rothschild," the doctor went on a scientific splurge, buying himself a box of surgical instruments and a number of French medical books. In his letters, however, he was unable to conceal the jealousy aroused by her renewed interest in Musset, and this infuriated her. That was perhaps a mad letter to have written to Musset — the one in which she had declared: "I must be yours, it is my destiny" — but Pagello had no business reading it. He who had hitherto been a model of loving consideration was now acting like a husband who had claims upon her.

Though the 1500 francs were in fact a present George was making to Pagello — for the Zuccarelli paintings were never sold — she felt more than a little guilty at having left him to fend for himself in Paris. "I am of an ever growing sadness and disgust," she wrote to Boucoiran around the tenth of September. "I enjoy myself and seek distraction with my friends, whom I see every day. But at night I fall back on myself, and sometimes my thoughts are so black that I am tempted to write to you to say that we won't be seeing each other again."

Musset's first letter, written from Baden-Baden on September 1, did nothing to alleviate her somber mood. It was a delirious letter, full of the amorous ravings of a madman. "Never has a man loved as I love you. I am lost . . . I am drowned, I am flooded in love; I no longer know if I'm alive, if I'm eating, walking, breathing, or talking; all I know is that I love you . . ." Had she any idea what it was like to wait five months for a kiss? For five long months he had tried to forget her, he had felt the "coldness of the tomb" penetrate his solitude, and oblivion descend on him "drop by drop like snow"; and then suddenly, just as his heart had almost ceased to beat, like a dying flower, it had been revived, as though by a "drop of vivifying dew . . . Oh, my God, I felt it, I knew it, we should not have seen each other again." For this revivifying kiss had undone all his earlier resolutions aimed at finding solace in the arms of other women. And, he clearly implied, it was *she* who had thus fatally encouraged him. So let her now send him a letter, a letter containing nothing but the expression of her love. "And tell me that you give me your lips, your teeth, your hair, everything, and that head I have held in my hands, and that you kiss me, you, me! Oh God, oh God, when I think of it, I have a lump in my throat, my eyes grow blurred, my knees shake. Ah, it's horrible to die, it's horrible to love like this. How I thirst, George, how I thirst for you! I beg you, let me have that letter. I am dying, farewell!"

This crazy, incoherent letter provoked a chilling reply. Here was Alfred forgetting once again that they had pledged themselves to a "sacred" relationship. "It's passion you're expressing, but it's no longer the holy enthusiasm of your good moments. It's no longer that pure friendship from which I had hoped the too vivid expressions would gradually disappear." Once again she was ensnared in an impossible situation, torn between two stubbornly uncomprehending men — one of whom spent his time *desiring* her, while the other smothered her with jealous reproaches.

For Pagello too had now proved a dismal disappointment. "He who in Venice understood everything no longer understood anything from the moment he set foot in France, and now he is desperate. Everything about me hurts and irritates him, and must I say it?

he is leaving, he has perhaps already left, and I won't retain him, for I am deeply offended by what he has written me, and I feel he no longer has faith, consequently," she added with a curious twist of logic, "he no longer loves . . . Oh, how unhappy I am, I'm not loved, I don't love! Here I am, an insensitive, sterile and cursed soul! And you come and talk to me of transports of delight, of desires. What have I done to you, you madman, that you should thus shatter everything in my soul, my confidence in you and my confidence in myself?"

The realization that her love for Pagello had suddenly disintegrated left her emotionally shattered. Once again she felt like the frozen-hearted Lélia at the time of her break with Jules Sandeau. In a note sent to François Rollinat (who lived at Châteauroux), she described her "hundred-year-old skeleton" as "sleeping, smoking, taking snuff, scribbling on paper, and crying its eyes out." To Saint-Beuve a few days later she wrote that she was ill enough to think she had not much longer to live.

In desperate need of distraction, she persuaded Charles Duvernet and his plump wife, Alphonse Fleury and his newlywed Laure Decerfz, the jovial Alexis Duteil, and the pensive François Rollinat to accompany her on a visit to Talleyrand's château at Valençay, some fifty miles to the north. Talleyrand's niece, the beautiful Duchesse de Dino, graciously opened her apartments to them, leading them personally to the monumental drawing room, where George Sand complimented her on the magnificent portrait Prud'hon had painted of her. The duchess, for her part, found George Sand distinctly small and "of insignificant appearance," though with "rather lovely eyes," as she noted in her diary, but she was put off by her "pretentious hairdo, known in the language of the stage as *classic.* She [Sand] has a dry, trenchant tone and definite opinions on the arts" — whether in passing judgment on Canova's marble busts of Paris and Napoleon, or on the Annibale Carracci copy of Raphael which she innocently took for the original. The duchess did, however, find George Sand's speech recherché, adding: "All in all, little grace." As for the rest of the company, they were dismissed as "utterly common, in appearance at any rate, for not one of them said a word."

This visit had two immediate consequences. The first was another essay for Buloz's *Revue des Deux Mondes* entitled "The Prince." The Prince, of course, was Talleyrand, savagely portrayed as "the greatest knave in the universe," an aristocratic fop waited on by countless servants and one of the finest chefs in France, a heartless diplomatic spider who for years had spun a web of elaborate intrigue high above the heads of the hoodwinked and uncomprehending people. Though she later regretted having written this *boutade* — as she charitably termed a diatribe which revealed Sand in her bitchiest and blackest mood — it was another significant expression of her fundamentally democratic inclinations. Almost certainly too, it was an attempt to work off her inner frustrations against an appealingly aristocratic target. For George's Berrichon friends were for the most part liberals, when not avowed republicans like the massive "Gaul" (Alphonse Fleury), who was ready to declare at the dinner table that Louis-Philippe should be assassinated. If their opinions had been solicited, their personal preferences would probably have gone to the "good," honest, relatively uncomplicated Pagello — a bourgeois like themselves — rather than toward that complicated, flighty, obnoxiously dandified aristocrat, Alfred de Musset.

The second consequence of the visit to Valençay was a furious scene with her husband, the kind Aurore had dreaded from the start. Though she had left with his permission, and though he had even let her travel in the Nohant calèche, Casimir was resentful of the pleasure she had derived from this three-day outing and mortified by the thought that his wife had friends who were more attached to her than to him. On her return Casimir exploded, as he had seven years earlier at Châteaubrun, calling her "in Rabelaisian language" (as she later described it) a whore, a harlot, a strumpet.

This outburst precipitated her return to Paris. She was accompanied this time not only by Maurice, but also by Solange, who stayed with her at the Quai Malaquais apartment for the first few weeks before being placed in a boarding school in mid-November. Her daughter's presence was one more inhibiting factor (or pretext) in George Sand's increasingly cool behavior toward Pagello. During her absence at Nohant the handsome surgeon had lived modestly in the same cheap hotel, eating at a restaurant run by a former Venetian and visiting a number of Paris hospitals. He had made some friends in the French medical world, but this was not the world of George Sand. It was not the world of Alfred de Musset, nor even that of François Buloz, who is reported to have invited Pagello to a *Revue des Deux Mondes* dinner at which Delacroix ridiculed his ideas on art, Sainte-Beuve made mincemeat of his literary prejudices, and Mérimée crushed him beneath the weight of his archeological erudition. Pagello needed no urging to return to Venice. Alfred de Musset was back in Paris on October 13, and though the young poet's relations with George Sand were anything but clear, the doctor realized full well that he was now what Musset had been in Venice — a *terzo incómodo,* an embarrassing third party.

After receiving the final 500 francs George had promised to bring him from Nohant for the paintings she had supposedly sold, Pagello returned to his humble hotel room and packed his bags. Early the next morning he walked over to the Quai Malaquais, where he found Boucoiran waiting to take him to the stagecoach terminus. Not a word was exchanged during the final parting. "I shook her hand without being able to look her in the eyes," Pagello later wrote in his diary. "She seemed perplexed; I don't know if she was suffering; my presence embarrassed her. He annoyed her, this Italian who with his simple common sense knocked down the uncomprehended sublimity with which she was wont to surround the lassitude of her loves. I had already let her know that I had deeply sounded her heart, full of excellent qualities but shadowed by many vices, and this knowledge of mine could only cause her displeasure, which made me shorten the visit as much as I could."

After kissing the children, who may well have wondered who this strange man was, Pagello took Boucoiran by the arm and they went out together. On the way to the stagecoach terminus Maurice's erstwhile tutor chatted away in his high-pitched voice in an effort to hide his emotion. But unlike George Sand, there were tears in his eyes when the moment came for him to shake the doctor's hand as he climbed into the coach. He had developed a genuine affection for this handsome, simple, uncomplicated foreigner who had behaved honorably throughout, even if, like Jules Sandeau, he had been tried and found wanting.

21. Two Wounded Eagles

Alfred de Musset had returned to Paris more than ever burning to see his Georgeot, the masculine nickname he had coined for her in Germany. The six weeks he had spent distractedly ogling the ladies and losing money at the gambling tables of Baden-Baden had not helped him to forget her. Dutifully he had sent back the letter she had asked him to return — the one in which she had breathlessly declared, "I must be yours, it is my destiny" — along with a letter of his own in which he gave free rein to his angry bewilderment. He couldn't understand how, on the eve of his departure, she could have written him such an impassioned missive, only to write another two weeks later which poured cold water on the passion she had deliberately inflamed. The abominable cruelty of this treatment made him want to have it out with her. What did he care if his return to Paris upset Pagello? "I confess I'm no longer in a mood to spare anyone. If he must suffer, well, let him suffer, this Venetian who taught me to suffer! I'm paying him back in kind, he who taught me a lesson in such a masterly fashion. As for you, you are now forewarned, and I reply with your own words: *I write you this so that, if you should learn of my return, you should have no idea of a rapprochement with me.* Is this harsh? Perhaps. There is a region of the soul, you see, which pity leaves when suffering enters. Let him suffer! He possesses you . . . Farewell."

Just how George Sand replied to this confused and angry letter, we do not know. Like the August letter ("I must be yours, it is my destiny") which had aroused Pagello's jealous suspicions, this one later disappeared and was probably destroyed by her. But she must have been sufficiently alarmed by Musset's threatening tone in the final paragraph to write him a "sad letter" (as he himself described it) which prompted him to return forthwith.

From his room in the family town house at 59 Rue de Grenelle, he dashed off a note to George to say that he was hers "body and soul," and that whenever she had an hour or even "an instant to lose," she should write to him and he would come running. To this characteristically impulsive note George took her time replying. Torn between her desire to see Alfred and a fear of the consequences, she let several days go by in an agony of indecision. Each time Musset called at 19 Quai Malaquais, he was denied admission, and as he complained to Sainte-Beuve, "she is well guarded" — by the maid Sophie Cramer, Jules Boucoiran, and one or more of her Berrichon friends. But in the end desire got the better of her caution. She may also have been frightened by the harsh things a desperate Musset might begin to say about her if she showed herself too obdurate. One evening, in any case, she wrapped herself in a mantle and hurried over to the town house on the Rue de Grenelle. When the door was opened — by Alfred — she flung herself with a moan into his arms.

Buloz, who called on her at the Quai Malaquais a day or two later, was escorted down the stairs by Boucoiran. Mystified by this extraordinary George-Alfred-Pietro triangle, he began questioning the young tutor as they strolled along the banks of the Seine. They tarried for a long time by the Pont des Arts, which links the Louvre to the beautifully domed Institut de France, while Boucoiran a bit too candidly told him everything he knew. Back in his office on the Rue des Beaux-Arts, Buloz noted on the back of a letter Musset had sent him: "One can't be a great writer, it seems, without renouncing all the qualities of a simple, good man, without renouncing heart and virtue. G. Sand — Catherine II, feeble and trembling before A. de M. who threatens to unmask her." This comparison with the strong-willed Russian Empress was followed by a vertical list of George Sand's lovers, interspersed by gaps probably denoting periods of amorous inactivity:

Aurélien de Sèze

Ajasson de Grandsagne

Jules Sandeau
Mérimée
Planche
A de Musset
Pagello } Abandonment and resumption
A. de M.

No wonder Buloz was intrigued by this curiously split personality, by this ostensibly strong and virile woman who could be made to tremble like a leaf by a young man who was six years her junior. Even after his departure (around the twenty-fifth of October) the shadow of Pagello continued to fall between them and to poison their passionate romance. The past refused to be buried, and even if Musset had wanted to wipe the slate clean and to take up again where they had left off the previous December, prior to the fateful Venetian honeymoon, he had friends who were determined to keep it vividly in mind. Pained to see his friend succumbing once again, Alfred Tattet undertook to enlighten him as to what had really happened in Venice. One evening, while Musset was in Baden-Baden and Aurore at Nohant, Tattet had invited Pagello to dinner; over several bottles of good wine he had plied him with questions, until the naive doctor had told him everything about the start of his affair with George. Tattet now repeated the particulars to his friend. "Nonsense!" Musset interrupted him, refusing to believe that she had become Pagello's mistress while he was still in his sickbed at the Danieli. "All right," said Tattet, irked by his friend's violent reaction. "See her if you will. But you won't see any more of me . . . because I don't wish you to be made to look like a fool." And on that cold note they parted.

When Alfred told George that he had had a row with his friend Tattet and explained why, she was left speechless with dismay. Any lingering fondness she may have felt for the handsome surgeon was now destroyed at one stroke. So Pagello, in a moment of drunken stupor, had betrayed her. Or had he? How much had he really told Tattet?

Anxious to know more, she wrote a brief letter to Tattet, asking him to call on her when he returned to Paris from his country house northwest of Paris. The tone was noncommittal and intended to convey the impression that what distressed her was the idea that she could have caused a row between two old friends. Musset, however, was quick to sense the nervous flutter into which this news had thrown her. Instantly all his old suspicions were revived, along with those haunting visions of George seated on Pagello's lap, drinking tea from the same cup, bending her head down over his, etc. Lightheartedly at first and then more insistently, he began plying her with questions in a determined effort to ascertain the truth: at what moment, exactly, had she become Pagello's mistress?

This questioning drove her wild. How dare he ask such questions? He who hadn't hesitated to leave her alone at the Danieli, when she was sick and bedridden, and to go out and frolic with the dancing girls of the Fenice! What was the point of his declaring in one breath that he was desperate, that he couldn't live without her, and subjecting her in the next to a humiliating interrogation? "In Venice I didn't allow you to question me on the slightest detail, whether it was on such and such a day that we kissed each other on the eyes or on the forehead, and . . . now that I am once again your mistress, you haven't the right to tear away these veils with which I am duty-bound, toward Pietro and myself, to remain enveloped. Do you think I would have answered, if he had questioned me about our pillowcase secrets? . . . Didn't I foresee that you would be made to suffer by this past which exalted you like a beautiful poem, so long as I refused to give myself to you, but which only seems like a nightmare to you now that you have seized me again like a prey? Let me go, we are only going to be unhappier than ever . . ."

Exactly what was said we shall never know. For the plaintive letter she sent to Musset after the first of these jealous scenes was rewritten, years later, for posterity, doubtless to soften the disagreeable acerbity of their mutual recriminations. In early November there was a momentary reconciliation. Alfred stopped needling her, ready to give her the benefit of the doubt and to believe that she had not become Pagello's mistress until after he had left Venice.

Once again he moved into the Quai Malaquais apartment, displacing George's Berrichon friends and introducing new acquaintances from the world of the arts — such as Franz Liszt and later, Heinrich Heine. Liszt, who came to dinner in early November, was even younger than Musset, having just turned twenty-three. Already recognized as the greatest keyboard virtuoso of his time — being for the piano what Paganini was for the violin — this narrow-shouldered, delicate-featured, golden-haired musician was almost as dazzling when he spoke as when he played. His bright-eyed curiosity seemed boundless and the energy with which he discussed the latest ideas and trends was inexhaustible. Almost uneducated in everything but music when his father had first brought him to Paris in 1827, he had later steeped himself in Homer, Plato, Locke, Kant, Byron, Hugo, Chateaubriand, Lamartine, to name but those, and had deliberately cultivated the company of the foremost French writers of the day — from Charles Nodier to Dumas, Balzac, and Vigny.

Liszt's latest intellectual passion was the fifty-two-year-old Abbé de Lamennais, a once ultramontane royalist who had created a sensation by publishing a little book openly challenging the Vatican as a stronghold of shortsighted reactionaries and calling for the drastic regeneration of the Catholic faith to favor the poor, downtrodden and oppressed against the selfish rich. At La Chennaie, in Brittany, Lamennais maintained a kind of open country house for young men who shared his doubts about official Catholicism and who wanted to improve their minds. Liszt, who had only recently returned from a two-week visit there, painted such a sympathetic picture of the loquacious abbé, tramping around the countryside in his huge unpolished shoes, blue peasant stockings, and worn straw hat, tirelessly discoursing on religion, philosophy and art, that George Sand, who had been deeply stirred by Lamennais' *Paroles d'un Croyant,* felt an urge to leave for Brittany in her turn.

This urge was singularly encouraged by the new crisis which now engulfed herself and Musset. Their reconciliation had lasted barely a week when Musset heard that Gustave Planche had been making public fun of George Sand's amorous exploits and his own cuckolded misadventures in Venice. Alfred promptly sent off a letter demanding an explanation. Planche assured him in an answering note that he never spoke, whether favorably or unfavorably, of Musset with others, and that there was not a word of truth in these malicious allegations. For forty-eight hours, however, it looked as though a duel would be fought between them. This news alarmed Alfred Tattet, who feared the publicity such an event would inevitably attract and who had no desire to see Musset become the laughingstock of the Paris literary world. The two friends met again, but this time Tattet pulled no punches. He repeated in detail everything Pagello had told him: how it was George Sand who had taken the initiative with an incredible, amorous confession, penned only a few feet away from Alfred's bedside at the Danieli, etc.

The realization that he had been brazenly cuckolded in Venice by a woman who had revealed herself a master, not to say a mistress, of deception, threw Musset into a cold rage. He wrote to Planche to say he accepted his denial of the gossip he had been accused of spreading. Then he called on George Sand, determined to know the truth once and for all. This time he was implacable, sparing her nothing. Crushed by the precision of his accusations, she finally broke down and confessed everything. Throwing herself on her knees, she implored his forgiveness.

But Musset was not in a forgiving mood. He told her he was through with her, that he did not wish to see her ever again. His declaration threw George into a paroxysm of despair. She had given him back all the letters he had written to her over the past few months to help him write the novel he wanted to weave around their ill-fated romance (the novel which became *La Confession d'un enfant du siècle*). All she had left was one letter, the latest he had written.

In a moment of hysteria she cut her long black hair, then went out and bought a skull, in which she lovingly placed both locks and letter. Nature once again was trying to imitate art. The heroine of *Indiana* had likewise cut her hair in a desperate moment. But the skull added a new, grotesque twist that was missing from the novel. Just what it was supposed to symbolize is not clear. The death she felt in her heart? Her suicidal despair? Or was it that she had read too many novels by Ann Ward Radcliffe, Charles Nodier, and other masters of the macabre?

That night, when at last she sank into a feverish, fitful sleep, she dreamed that her darling Alfred was next to her in bed, that he was kissing her, . . . that she was in a state of swooning bliss! She woke up with a start to find herself in an empty bed, in a darkened room, with no one to console her but a staring skull! She let out a nervous scream, which once again woke the poor maid (whose nights were now frequently disturbed by the sound of anguished cries and hysterical weeping).

Just what happened next is not clear. According to Paul de Musset's novel *Lui et Elle,* which was published twenty-five years later, George Sand had her shorn hair delivered in a parcel to Alfred, who happened to be entertaining guests in his room. He half opened the package, then hastily thrust it into a drawer. His friends, realizing that something was weighing on his mind, soon withdrew. Opening the drawer, Alfred undid the package with a beating heart, ran his hands through the locks he had so often stroked, then buried his face in them with a groan.

In her novel *Lui,* Musset's later mistress Louise Colet provided a more dramatic but not necessarily less accurate version of what happened. According to this account, George Sand went in person to the town house to deliver her parcel, sinking to her knees as Alfred opened the door — as though she were Mary Magdalene throwing herself at the feet of Christ. In her outstretched hands was a skull. "Her face was livid," Louise Colet had the narrator (Musset) explain, "and her eyes seemed deep and hollow, like the empty sockets of the skull she was presenting to me. She did not utter a word but moved toward me on her knees and soon touched me with her sinister offering. I brushed it aside and it rolled onto the floor at my feet. Out of it flowed a long black tress of hair . . ." After escorting her out in silence, Musset came back to the skull, which he kicked to one side. Then, bending down, he picked up the dark, familiarly scented locks and "buried his burning forehead in them with frenzy."

This skull was no invention of Louise Colet's. George Sand herself told François Buloz about it on November 13, when she broke down in front of him and tearfully implored him to put in a good word for her with Alfred. We also know, from the intimate journal which George began writing at this time, that this skull spent a number of days on a table in her bedroom, which had a portrait of some unidentified person on one wall and a crucifix on another.

This intimate journal is an extraordinary document, every bit as extraordinary as the day-by-day account of her life, thoughts, and feelings she had once penned for Aurélien de Sèze. She was driven to writing it by the realization that Musset no longer wished to see her or even to receive letters from her. To it, since his door was now closed, she accordingly poured out her heart.

The first entry, simply marked "Saturday midnight," was probably written on November 15, 1834, after an evening spent at the Théâtre Italien, where she had gone to see Bellini's *La Straniera.* With her hair cut short, she had had to hide herself in the pit, disguised as a man. As she described herself: "My hair is cut, there are circles round my eyes, my cheeks are hollow, I look old and stupid, while up there" — in the rows of boxes — "there are all those pale, blond women, dressed in white and pink, with feathers, rolling curls, bouquets, bare shoulders; and I, where am I, poor George?" Banished to the pit, while Alfred was up there, exercising his charms on one of those tempting beauties. "Ah, you madman, you leave me at the finest moment of my life, in the truest, most passionate, most heart-rending day of my life! Do you think it's nothing to have mastered a woman's pride and to have flung it at your feet?"

At times she was tempted to put an end to her days, at others to make the pilgrimage to Brittany in the hope that she could find solace in the Abbé de Lamennais' country retreat. The thought of her children kept her from throwing herself into the Seine, and she gave up all idea of leaving Paris, realizing that the hyperjealous Musset would immediately suspect her of having eloped with some new lover. Buloz, Marie Dorval, Sainte-Beuve, and even Liszt, who came to call on her several times, witnessed her uncontrollable grief — with the result that the literary salons of the capital were soon abuzz with gossip about her: gossip which portrayed her as disguising herself as a man in order to pay clandestine visits to Musset's lodgings, where she crawled on her knees before him.

"What is this fire which devours my entrails?" she confided to her journal. "I have the impression that a volcano is rumbling inside me, and that I am going to erupt like a crater. Oh God, have pity on this being who suffers so! . . . Lovely head, I shall no longer see you bend over me and wrap me in a soft languor! You will not again stretch yourself out on my little, warm, supple body, like Elijah on the dead infant, to revive me. You will no longer touch my hand, as Jesus did with the daughter of Jair, saying: 'Little girl, arise!' Farewell, my blond hair, farewell my white shoulders, farewell to everything I loved, to everything that was mine. Now in my ardent nights I will embrace the trunks of pine trees and the rocks in the woods, while shouting your name, and after dreaming of pleasure, I shall fall fainting on the damp earth."

"Cruel child," she complained, "why did you love me after hating me? What mysterious change goes on inside you with each passing week? Why this crescendo of displeasure, disgust, aversion, fury, cold and scornful mockery, and then suddenly these tears, this softness, this ineffable love that returns! Torment of my life! Fateful love! I would give everything I have lived through for one day of your effusions" — by which she meant his lyrical, and doubtless amorous, enthusiasm. "But never, never! It's too awful!" — the idea that she would *never* see Musset again. "I can't believe it. I'm going to go. I'm going — No, cry, howl, but you mustn't go. Sainte-Beuve doesn't want it."

But go she did, that much is certain. This time, if Paul de Musset's novelistic account is to be trusted, there was no response when she knocked on Alfred's ground-floor door. She then called up to Paul, saying she *had* to see Alfred. Lighting an oil lamp, Paul came downstairs and opened the door into his brother's room with a key which he retrieved from a secret hiding place. Unwilling to leave her alone in such an obviously distraught condition, he lit the fire and engaged her in casual conversation until Alfred finally turned up, gaily jingling some coins he had won at the card table. Paul then left them alone, but was able to follow the ensuing scene in pantomime, as George's gesticulating shadow crossed and recrossed the pale windowpanes of Alfred's room.

Later, hearing a woman's light step on the courtyard's stony cobbles followed by a rap on the lodge window, Paul came down to join his brother, whom he found deeply moved.

Alfred confessed with a sigh that never had he seen her more beautiful and touching! This wasn't the demon of Venice, nor the angel of Fontainebleau. "It was another sublime creature, lit by the divine fire of passion, and all the more charming in that she wasn't trying to please, but simply to persuade. And with her cut hair! . . . Ah, my friend, is it possible that I am the cause of this mutilation? . . . But Heavens! What am I doing, rattling on like this when she's out there in the dark, empty streets with no arm to lean on and nobody to defend her?" Seizing his top hat and his cane, he hurried across the courtyard, rapped loudly on the porter's window, waited for the latch to be released, then disappeared into the street, closing the massive oak door with a dull boom behind him.

George, as it happened, had not left the town house, having rapped too timidly on the lodge window to arouse the sleeping porter. Paul de Musset found her on the stairs leading to his room, in tears. Feeling pity for her sobs — for this was the end, she said, Alfred was through with her! — he agreed to lead her back to Alfred's room and to let her stretch out on his couch.

Back in his room, Paul de Musset sank into a chair and finally dozed off. He was brusquely woken by his younger brother, now in a state of high alarm.

"Get up, come, we must go look for her!" cried Alfred. "While you're sleeping there, she's probably dead or dying! I wasn't able to find her! The maid said she hadn't seen her! . . . Oh, to think she may have drowned herself! With the river out there in front of her!"

"Nobody has died!" Paul hastened to reassure him. Rushing down to his room, Alfred threw himself down in front of the couch, took George's head in his two hands and tearfully kissed her.

Something of the sort may well have taken place — even if this account crammed different days or moments into one momentous night. Alfred, in any case, was deeply stirred. He also knew, he who was so death-obsessed, to what extremes of suicidal despair she could be driven. So he forgave her. Once again they were united in a moment of wild, erotic abandon, and with a fury of carnal passion surpassing everything she had ever known before. Indeed, so exhausted was George by these emotional upheavals and the amorous frenzy which followed that for two successive days she had to put off going to Delacroix's studio for the portrait Buloz had commissioned for the *Revue des Deux Mondes.*

This reconciliation had barely lasted a couple of days when a new storm broke over their tormented heads. The cause this time was Franz Liszt, whom Musset had lured over to the Quai Malaquais apartment and who had returned to see George Sand several times after her first break with Alfred. It is difficult to judge from what remains of the intimate journal (for parts of it were later ripped away) just what impression the twenty-three-year-old virtuoso made on the thirty-year-old novelist and vice versa. Almost certainly there was a mutual attraction. But the young Franz, after one platonic and several less platonic romances, was going through an inner crisis of his own, torn between a desire to remain celibately independent and austerely faithful to his muse and a yearning for the romantic soulmate he fancied he had found in Marie d'Agoult, a tall aristocratic lady with flaxen hair and sea green eyes who in certain respects bore an astonishing likeness to himself.

This explains the caustic nature of George Sand's comments after hearing Buloz make some casual reference to her growing sympathy for Liszt. In love with Liszt? The idea struck her as absurd. So Musset was jealous of Liszt? If only it were true rather than a cruel excuse on Musset's part to get rid of her! For she felt about as capable of loving Liszt as of liking spinach. So why should she close her door to Liszt, she asked. "For what reason? Because of whom? For the space of one or two encounters I fancied he was in love with me, or disposed to fall in love with me. Perhaps if I could have done so, I would have gratified him; but . . . I felt obliged to make him understand that he was not to think of it — when suddenly, after the charming reception I gave him in your presence, Buloz, I became clearly convinced during the third visit that I had made a lot of foolish fuss over an unnecessary virtue and that Liszt had nothing on his mind but God and the Holy Virgin, who does not absolutely resemble me. Good, happy young man! If it's so, then I esteem and like him very much; and if it's an affectation, it matters little to me, since I don't know him."

It was not in fact an affectation with Liszt, who was given to moments of mystic exaltation, in which he spoke rhapsodically of God and the Holy Virgin. Nor was Musset's jealousy feigned. With Pagello his worst suspicions, after countless denials, had been dramatically confirmed. How could be believe George now, when she protested that she felt nothing more than a vague sympathy for the intense green-eyed musician?

On November 21 Musset left her early in the evening, saying he was tired. George was feeling a bit feverish, but Alfred showed no inclination to sit by his bedside to comfort her. The next day he did not call, nor did he bother to find out if she was feeling better. She wrote him a note; he did not answer it.

Nor did he bother to call on her the next day, a Sunday. On Monday she could bear it no longer. Hurrying over to the Rue de Grenelle, she tugged at his bell rope in vain. The porter informed her that Monsieur Alfred had gone out — where to he did not know.

The following morning she went to sit for Delacroix, at his studio near Saint-Germain-des-Prés. He gave her some straw cigarettes to smoke and then remarked, of a copy of a Goya drawing which Alfred had done in his studio, that Musset could have been a great painter if he had wanted to be. Thus encouraged, George poured out her woes, as she had done with so many others, while he sketched and painted, seeking to capture her rapt expression. And thus she was portrayed, with a loose cravat about her neck and above the open spencer, with her short boyish hair and her eyes raised heavenward as though, like Joan of Arc, she were listening to voices.

"Let yourself go," Delacroix advised her. "When I'm like that, I don't try to be proud, *I wasn't born a Roman.* I abandon myself to my despair, it gnaws at me, crushes and kills me. When it's had its fill, it tires in its turn and leaves me."

Charming advice, she couldn't help thinking. But her own gnawing despair had not had its fill and would not leave her alone. To all who came to see her or on whom she called — and they included the mystically tormented Liszt, the frivolous Hortense Allart, and the cynical Heinrich Heine (who was already spreading the word that his friend Franz was George Sand's latest lover) — she poured out her woes with reckless abandon. "Liszt said to me this evening that only God deserved to be loved," she again confided to her journal on November 28. "Possibly, but when one has loved a man it is very hard to love God, it's so different. Liszt, it is true, added that he had never in his life felt a lively sympathy for anyone but Mr. de Lamennais, and that never would an earthly love possess him. Lucky little Christian, he is. Heine, whom I saw this morning, told me that one loves only with one's head and one's senses and that the heart plays but a feeble role in love. I saw Madame Allart at 2 o'clock, she said one must *employ cunning* with men, and pretend to be angry in order to win them back. Sainte-Beuve is the only one who hasn't hurt me and who hasn't talked nonsense. I asked him what love was and he replied: 'Tears. You weep, you love.' "

Ten feverish days later George Sand finally left for Nohant. Shortly before her departure she had her friend Alexis Duteil journey up from La Châtre to act as her legal adviser in the drafting of a new agreement with Buloz. Crawl though she might in the presence of Alfred de Musset, she could still display the imperious will power of a Catherine the Great in dealing with her publisher. For by the terms of this astonishing contract Buloz was browbeaten into offering her and her heirs a total sum of 40,000 francs. Of these, 10,000 francs were to be paid to her in monthly installments of 500 francs for the right to publish a Complete Edition of her Works, while the remaining 30,000 were to be paid in annual sums of 3000 francs to her literary executor for the right to publish her "posthumous works" — a four or five-volume edition of her Memoirs.

It was with "death in her soul," as the French say, that she returned to Nohant, more than ever convinced that she had not much longer to live and that the time had come for her to fulfill the ambitious literary project she had first conceived at the Mont-Dore in 1827. Overcome with belated remorse, Alfred de Musset sent her a kind note, begging her to forgive him for his recurring fits of anger. She sent him a leaf plucked from the Nohant garden; he followed up with a lock of blond hair she had vainly implored him in Paris to cut off and give to her as a memento. "I no longer wish to see him, it hurts me too much," she wrote to her "Director of Conscience," Sainte-Beuve. "But I shall need strength to refuse him admission, for he will certainly ask to see me. He no longer loves me, but he is always tender and repentant after being angry, he will want to efface the sad memory of our parting; he will think he's doing the right thing and he will be mistaken, for I shall find myself loving him all over again and having worked in vain to detach myself from him."

At Nohant, however, she felt herself gradually revive in the company of her Berrichon friends, and she would have been quite happy to bury herself in the country she loved so much, but for the presence of Casimir, who lost his temper once again at the lunch table and, in the presence of a dozen guests, bawled his wife out like a serving girl when some champagne she was trying to pass to Duteil was carelessly spilled. He seemed more than usually grumpy and even took to his bed, saying he was ill and that she was costing him too much. But when she finally went into his bedroom to determine the cause of his moaning and groaning, a dejected Casimir admitted that he had indebted himself to the tune of 22,000 francs by buying poor quality land sold to him at a ridiculously high price.

In early January George Sand returned to Paris. She brought with her another highly personal essay — a long meditation on life, suicide, and boredom which she gave to Buloz for the mid-January issue of the *Revue des Deux Mondes.* Written in a flowing, elegiac style, this poetic lamentation made a frank confession of her unhappiness. She was depressed by the thought that she was "no one's other half. I don't mind growing old, but I would mind a lot growing old alone. But I haven't found the being with whom I would have liked to live and die, or if I met him, I didn't know how to keep him." To which she added, even more pathetically: "The winter of my soul has come, eternal winter!"

Franz Liszt and Heinrich Heine were again invited to the Quai Malaquais apartment in a vain effort to provide solace and distraction. The moment the impassioned Musset heard she was back, he invited her to dinner. George displayed a certain reluctance to get involved once more to judge by the tone of her next letter: "I feel I'm going to love you as I did before, if I don't flee. Remember, I shall perhaps kill you and myself with you," she added melodramatically, without specifying how this erotic holocaust was to be consummated.

"Happiness, happiness, and after it death, and with it death!" Musset replied ecstatically, eager to immolate himself on the rekindled pyre of their old passion. "Yes, you forgive me, you love me! . . . Yes, I'm twenty-three years old, and why am I so young and in the prime of manhood if not to pour out my life so that you may drink it on my lips? Tonight at ten o'clock, and you may be sure I'll be there ahead of time. Come as soon as you can. Come so that I can get down on my knees, so that I can ask you to live, to love, to forgive!"

George having been accompanied to Paris by her Berrichon friend Rozanne Bourgoing, who was now installed in the Quai Malaquais apartment, the lovers had to arrange their trysts elsewhere — probably in some uninhabited pavilion lent them by a friend. For after the tumultuous scenes of the previous November, which had scandalized the porter no less than Musset's family (his mother, sister, and two brothers all lived under the same roof), there was no question of George's making clandestine visits to Alfred's room in the town house on the Rue de Grenelle. But no sooner had they fallen into each other's arms and become lovers again than the old doubts and quarrels were revived, more poignantly than ever.

One afternoon, as he accompanied her home, she asked if he wouldn't like to stay for dinner. They wouldn't be alone, she added, for Liszt would also be there. Abruptly Musset stopped, then turned on his heel with a hollow laugh, hailed a cab, and disappeared. Scenes like this, and there were many of them, reduced her repeatedly to hysterical despair. In vain she wrote to him that "Love is the happiness people give to each other." For a complicated sadomasochist like Alfred, for a pampered child who both craved and resented her motherly solicitude, this was altogether too simple, too placid, too bourgeois a prescription for felicity. Love for him meant suffering: the torment one inflicted on the loved one first, followed by the remorse one felt at having behaved so abominably.

"My knees are on the floor, my back is broken," she wrote to her tormentor after another terrible scene. "I want to kiss the ground and weep. I no longer love you, but I adore you forever. I no longer want to have anything to do with you, but I can't get on without you. Only a bolt of lightning from on high could cure me in annihilating me. Farewell, stay, leave, only don't say I'm not suffering . . . ; my one and only love, my life, my entrails, my brother, my blood, go away but kill me as you leave."

Half hoping to pacify her lover, George Sand wrote to Liszt, who was about to leave Paris, asking him not to call on her again when he returned to the capital. For one desperate moment she thought of seeking refuge with her bachelor friend Charles Meure, the King's Prosecutor, who had been shifted to a new post at Château-Chinon, not far from the rolling hills of Burgundy. But she abandoned this mad idea, which would only have aggravated the hostile gossip. She was also tied down by the arrival on business matters of her husband, who had agreed in December that the time had come for a legal separation. It had tentatively been agreed between them that he would obtain the rental income derived from the Hôtel de Narbonne in Paris and be granted the custody of Maurice, while she would keep Nohant and her daughter, Solange.

The idea that she would soon be leaving Paris to bury herself in the country, where she would be virtually inaccessible, upset Musset so much that he had to take to his bed. Gustave Papet, being a doctor, was sent to see him, and George was smuggled in to his bedside, disguised as a kind of assistant nurse, in a bonnet and apron. But once recovered, the capricious Alfred provoked new rows, and, not content with that, resumed his drinking with his dandy friends and flirting with their petticoated companions.

On February 22 there was another scene in the presence of Maurice and Solange, who had been let out of boarding school to spend this Sunday with their mother. Picking up a letter George had written to Alexis Duteil, Alfred angrily accused her of infidelity once again, as though Duteil too were now her lover because of the intimate tone she used in writing to him. "Sainte-Beuve is right. Your behavior is deplorable, impossible," she wrote in a half-angry, half-pitying letter. "My God, to what a life am I going to abandon you! The intoxication of wine! Girls, again and forever! But since I can no longer do anything to keep you from them, must I prolong this shame for me, and this torture for you? My tears irritate you. And with it all, this insane jealousy of yours! The less right you have to be jealous, the more jealous you become!"

There was a final flare-up when Musset returned to the Quai Malaquais apartment and made cruel fun of her hypocritical mode of speech, as when she spoke of the "chaste" nature of friendship. Chaste, indeed! He'd drunk of that cup too — and found that hers contained arsenic! In a rage George picked up an ornamental dagger lying on the bookcase, but was immediately disarmed by Alfred who, holding it above her bosom, cried: "It's you who are going to die! Now be quick and say your prayers!"

This time both of them had passed the point of no return. After he had left, she sent him a short note, saying her mind was made up and that she was leaving Paris. Musset, who had also decided to leave Paris, replied with a short note of his own, saying he would like to see her for one final instant. "Don't be frightened; I haven't the strength to kill anyone this morning."

When he called later that same day, he invited her to dinner, adding with calculated cruelty: "I would like you to meet my new mistress." After which he said he was going on to the Masked Ball at the Paris Opera — that is, if he wasn't too drunk!

George Sand declined the invitation and was almost relieved to see him go. What a strange farewell! But later that same evening a messenger brought her another letter, accompanied by a small parcel. It was from Alfred and written in Italian: "*Senza veder, e senza parlar, toccar la mano d'un pazzo chi parte domani.*" (Without seeing and without talking, to touch the hand of a madman who is leaving tomorrow.) Inside the parcel was a domino and a black satin mask.

Was this a final challenge? A final humiliation, intended to show her to what depths of cynical depravity he could descend on this Mardi Gras evening? Her curiosity balefully aroused, she procured herself a mask made of a coarser material so as not to be recognized and hid her hair and neck in differently colored ribbons. Then she had herself driven to the Opéra through flakes of softly falling snow.

Inside, though an orchestra kept striking up with new quadrilles, no one was dancing, and the aimless rambling to and fro of so many people disguised in black masks and dominoes made this carnival ball more like a *danse macabre* — which reached its appropriate crescendo with a vast hubbub of voices and an eerie pistol shot. Never had George felt more lonely than in the midst of this unreal, sinister, pointless phantasmagoria.

She finally came upon Alfred in the lobby, where he was seated unmasked between two masked girls. She overheard one of them making fun of his affair with George Sand: "It seems you were cuckolded there in Italy, but wouldn't believe it." Horrified to hear her name thus taken in vain, she hastily withdrew, but so awkwardly that she was recognized by Musset.

So, at least, George Sand later tried to make the world believe, in the novel she wrote about their tempestuous romance. Alfred de Musset did not leave Paris, as he had said he would, managing to miss his stagecoach, probably on purpose. For he now redoubled his visits to the Quai Malaquais apartment, as though anxious to ward off the inevitable.

On March 6 George sent Alfred's mother a goodbye note, along with a little caged bird "which is utterly blameless," as she put it. "You have doubtless suffered a great deal because of me, and instead of harboring a grudge against me, I know that you treat me with indulgence. I thank you for it and ask your forgiveness from the bottom of my heart for all the sorrows and anxieties I have caused you."

To make sure that Alfred would not frustrate her stern resolve by putting on a painful, last-minute scene, she sent Boucoiran out to reserve her a place on the Orléans mail coach and had him smuggle out her night bag in advance. If Musset turned up at five o'clock that afternoon, Boucoiran was to tell him that George's mother had just returned to Paris, was quite ill, and needed to see her daughter immediately. Putting on her bonnet, George would then leave, as though running to her mother's bedside — when her real destination was the mail-coach terminus and Nohant.

The stratagem worked so well that not until a day or two later did Alfred de Musset learn that his Georgeot had left Paris. Her departure was so precipitate that she had to write to Boucoiran from Nohant, asking him to wrap up and send on all sorts of things she had left behind — like her houkah with its porcelain vase and amber mouthpiece. Boucoiran had already been instructed to deliver a package to Alfred de Musset, a package containing the intimate journal she had started writing the previous November.

Thus ended one of the most extraordinary love affairs of the nineteenth century, and indeed of all time. From the strictly literary point of view — the fateful trip to Venice excluded — it brought George Sand little, for the novel she later wrote about this particular romance, *Elle et Lui,* would better have remained unwritten. She, on the other hand, had brought a great deal to Musset: it was her historical material which had provided the plot for *Lorenzaccio;* extracts from the letters she had sent to him from Venice had gone into the dialogue of another play, *On ne badine pas avec l'amour* (*There's no Trifling with Love*); and their romance was to inspire that beautiful prose poem, *La Confession d'un enfant du siècle,* in which she became the heroine, Brigitte. And this is not to mention the dozen poems she had inspired or was to inspire in the future.

Musset himself was sufficiently attached to life to resist the temptation to blow out his brains with a pistol. After all, he was a famous poet and had better things to do than to imitate Goethe's Young Werther (whose baleful example he later denounced in *La Confession d'un enfant du siècle*). Life was one thing, literature another. He went on to have a number of other mistresses. None of them, however, affected him as deeply as had George Sand. He was even prepared to admit that she had changed him from a boy into a man. As he wrote to Alfred Tattet some four months after the final parting, in August of 1835: "If you see Madame Sand, tell her I love her with all my heart, and that she is still the most womanly woman I have ever known."

PART V

Storm & Stress

22. The Firebrand of Bourges

Never had Aurore felt a greater need to turn over a new leaf than now, in this month of March 1835, as she went for pensive strolls around her garden. The pastel yellow shiver of the daffodils and the deepening blush of the hyacinths told her that spring was around the corner, but the season of her heart was more like autumn. In four years she had had as many love affairs, all of which had ended dismally. She had been no more successful as a mistress than as a wife, and with both of her children in boarding school, she was beginning to wonder if she was not also fated to be a failure as a mother.

Even her literary triumphs left her singularly dissatisfied; while they had made her famous, not to say infamous, in the eyes of the reading public, there was not one of her novels that could really be considered "positive" or optimistic in its message. Like her love affairs, they had been self-centered and nonsocial in being almost exclusively concerned with the romantic torments of individual lovers. Certain of them — for example *Jacques* or *Mattea,* the long short story she was now finishing for Buloz — even struck her as frivolous compared to the kind of novel she felt she should be writing. As she had written to Sainte-Beuve the previous September, thanking him for the autographed copy of his novel *Volupté:* "Let others do as they will, but you, my friend, must write a book that changes and improves men . . . Ah, if only I could, I would lift my head again and I would no longer be brokenhearted; but in vain do I seek a religion — will it be God, love, friendship, or the common weal?"

Her troubled state of anguished doubt and indecision affected both her health and her work. She suffered a severe attack of liver trouble and for more than a week was covered all over with hepatic sores. In November she had committed herself to finishing a new novel for Buloz by the end of May 1835, the contract even providing for a deductable "penalty" of 250 francs for each month's delay in delivery. But instead of tackling this novel, she embarked on a new short story called *Mauprat.* The first part of it had hardly been sent off when she abruptly demanded it back, explaining that the subject was "too strong" and needed full-length-novel treatment. Though she apologized for making him wait — "it's not my fault, there's not a night I haven't spent working from eight to ten hours" — Buloz must have been dismayed to be asked to pay her debts and to provide her money for a trip to Switzerland.

Jules Boucoiran sent her the volumes of Greek drama and of Shakespeare plays she had forgotten in Paris, and Buloz sent her Plato's *Dialogues,* but they brought her scant relief. Casimir, who some weeks before had promised to turn Nohant over to her in the autumn, now seemed increasingly peeved at the prospect. His moodiness and irritability got under her skin, and as she wrote to Buloz in early April, she had to get away from Nohant so long as "Monsieur le Baron exercises his authority here."

Her feeling of frustration was aggravated by a row with her Paris landlord, who wanted to take back the Quai Malaquais apartment, and by the contradictory advice and attitudes of her Berrichon friends. Alexis Duteil, like Casimir a heavy drinker, cynically suggested that the best way of humoring her husband would be to "become his mistress" — that is, go back to sleeping with him — a prospect which aroused her indignation. She was no less dismayed to learn that the gossips of La Châtre — with the unexpected encouragement of her friend Rozanne Bourgoing — were already passing severe judgment on her "heartlessness" in wanting to throw "poor Baron Dudevant into the street." This was the last straw. As she wrote to Alexis Duteil: "I'm not prepared to take this kind of nonsense seriously. My profession is to be free, and my taste to receive favors and grace from nobody, even when I'm offered charity with my own money." Whereupon she tore up the written agreement she had signed in February with Casimir, and which would have made her the mistress of Nohant in six months' time. It was an act of proud folly she soon had cause to regret.

The one friend who, in all these discussions, seems to have given her the soundest advice was Gabriel Planet, the young law student who had founded the little Berrichon club in Paris where Aurore and Jules Sandeau used to go to warm their frozen selves by the stove and to read the newpapers in the cold winter of 1831. Planet had since returned to Bourges where, aided by a famous lawyer named Louis Chrysostome Michel, he had founded a local paper for the propagation of liberal — which is to say republican — opinions. A frequent visitor to Nohant, he had been distressed to see how brutally Casimir often behaved toward his wife. But feeling that Aurore had a tendency to spoil her children to compensate for Casimir's fits of irascibility, Planet had quite rightly urged her to place both Maurice and Solange in boarding schools.

To get her away from the depressing atmosphere of Nohant, Alphonse Fleury volunteered in early April to drive her over to Bourges, some forty-five miles to the northeast, for another long conversation with Planet. At the inn where they were to spend the night, the discussion soon veered away from Aurore's family problems to the broader question of the kind of books she should be writing at a time when France was seething with social discontent and revolutionary ferment. "You should hear Michel on the subject!" said Planet. It was what all her Berrichon friends had been saying for some time, for this Michel de Bourges, as he called himself, was a forensic prodigy who could reduce the most stony-faced jury to tears.

A stable boy was sent to fetch Michel, but when he turned up a little later at the inn, George Sand had difficulty believing that this stoop-shouldered, balding little man could be the oratorical firebrand he was reported to be. The huge, overhanging forehead, deeply furrowed by vertical as well as horizontal wrinkles, the short, bushy brows, and the gimlet eyes which seemed to be imprisoned behind a pair of ungainly spectacles would have made him look forbidding but for the soft smile which played nervously about his lips and the dazzling white teeth which were occasionally exposed. There was, as the poet Lamartine was to note, something cenobitic about the pale, hollow cheeks: he seemed to have been prematurely aged by life's vicissitudes, and, though only thirty-seven, he looked at times as if he were sixty. His head seemed to have sunk into his shoulders, and the impression of an invisible but incessant intellectual ferment at work beneath that massive dome was enhanced by the cavernous tone of his voice.

No one could have differed more from the aristocratic Alfred de Musset than this son of a poor Provençal woodcutter who had been murdered in the last years of the eighteenth century by a band of Royalist fanatics. Brought up by his illiterate peasant mother and a local priest, the young Michel had mastered Greek and Latin well enough to serve as a tutorial assistant at a Paris boarding school while studying at night to obtain his law degree. He was a born orator, with a genius for improvisation and a Provençal fieriness of speech which swept everything before it. During his term of service in the army he had persuaded a military court to acquit a fellow soldier who had been accused of "deserting" — in those days a capital offense — when in fact the man had only stolen off to pay a visit to his dying mother. Later, during the burial ceremonies for a French deputy who had been killed by a member of the Royal Guard, he had delivered a thundering funeral oration which had almost touched off a prorepublican riot, forcing him to go underground to avoid arrest.

Like Fleury, Planet, and virtually all of Aurore's Berrichon friends, Michel had hailed the July Revolution with enthusiasm, and even helped to avert a bloodbath at Bourges by boldly persuading the Royalist general to surrender without a shot being fired. But his greatest triumph, one which had given him a national reputation, had come one year later, during a mass trial of Paris students accused of starting a riot near the Pont des Arts. What none of the better-known lawyers had been able to achieve, he did — defending the accused with such ringing passion and rhetorical brilliance that all were acquitted in an atmosphere of frenzied jubilation.

Egged on by the ardently republican Alphonse Fleury, Michel de Bourges grew increasingly eloquent as the dinner progressed, inspired not by wine — he drank nothing but barley water — but by the presence of the author of *Lélia,* which had left him "goggledeyed," as he candidly confessed, when he had read it. Silent at first, George soon found herself unwittingly playing the role of devil's advocate against him. Yes, it was true, she had been "socially atheistic"; she had lived for herself and written novels that were less educative or instructive than designed to entertain. But she couldn't help protesting against the idea that works of art were to be judged only in terms of their instructive value and that the writer's primary obligation was to educate or "elevate" the public to which his books were addressed rather than to heed the inner voice or ideal to which he strove to give expression in the name of Art. Stimulated by this unexpected opposition, Michel de Bourges outdid himself, pouring out his ideas with irresistible fervor and enthusiasm.

At midnight, when they should normally have parted, Michel proposed that they all take a brief walk through the moonlit streets of the old cathedral town. But the brief walk lasted four hours, as they strolled back and forth over the echoing cobbles, past the ghostly lampposts and the shadowy façade of Jacques Coeur's Renaissance palace. Michel talked about life, death, equality, justice and its dread instrument, the guillotine — and in the end it was not less than nine times that they accompanied him to his door, only to have him insist on accompanying them back to theirs.

The next morning Fleury insisted on leaving Bourges immediately, as though frightened by the prospect of a second encounter with Michel. Ardently republican though he was, even he had been a bit appalled by Michel's truculent insistence that "the enemies of the people" had to be eliminated, no matter what. He had refused to spare anyone. No, not even George Sand. Should she decide to oppose the people's will, when the republic was established, she too would have to be guillotined! He hadn't meant it seriously, of course, as George Sand realized when she called him "dear executioner" and "beheader."

Amazed to find that they had left when he returned to their inn later that same day, Michel dashed off an impassioned letter which George had some trouble reading so illegible was the handwriting — the hurried scrawl of an indefatigable talker whose cramped wrist could not keep up with the impetuous torrent of his thoughts. Here was a noble soul which the torments and temptations of romantic love had clearly led astray, and it was up to him to save her: "Love is a selfish passion. Extend this burning and devoted love, which will never find its recompense in this world, to all of suffering humanity. Devote less solicitude to one sole person! None is sufficiently deserving, while all crave it in the name of the Almighty Author of creation!"

The peremptory tone of this injunction would normally have raised her hackles but for the solicitude which shone through every line — much as the myopic softness of his gaze tempered the peasant brusqueness of his manners. For this humble woodcutter's son who (in Bourges at any rate) walked around in rough wooden shoes and a shapeless padded cloak, concealed beneath the ruggedness of his exterior a sensitivity as delicate as the fine white shirts he wore beneath his waistcoat and the multiple cravats he wound round his neck or even tied incongruously around his ears and almost hairless pate, when not wearing a top hat, as a protection against draughts. The awareness that he was something of an invalid, with a body which seemed unable to keep pace with his nervous temperament, made him all the more attractive to George, stirring as it did the maternal fiber within her.

"I feel myself being reborn and I see a new destiny opening before me," she wrote on April 21 to Liszt, who had written her a sad letter in which he had expressed the sorrow he had felt each time he had passed in front of the newly whitewashed façade of 19 Quai Malaquais at the thought that, because of Musset's jealousy, George's door was now closed to him. After which she added, a bit too confidently, speaking of her destiny: "I can't yet really tell you what it will be, but it is no longer the bondage of love. It's something like a faith to which I will devote everything that is in me; God has not yet descended upon me, but I am building a temple, that is, purifying my heart and my life."

That it was to be a temple of physical as well as spiritual love did not at this moment occur to her. Under the impact of Michel's fervent letters, which followed in rapid succession without waiting for the answers, she felt her energies being galvanized for an intensely intellectual battle. Her new novel, *Engelwald,* was left to gather dust, *Mauprat* momentarily forgotten. Instead, she spent the rest of April composing a sixth *Lettre d'un voyageur,* which she dedicated to "Everard" — a pseudonym for Michel de Bourges. This letter bore eloquent witness to her struggle to hold out against his intransigent republicanism. It wasn't only that she could not accept the naive notion of absolute equality, which he defied in his own person: "You don't like men, you're not their brother, for you are not their equal. You are an exception among them, you were born a *king* . . . Ah, here you are getting angry again; yet basically you know it well, there is a royalty of divine institution. God would have granted equal doses of intelligence and virtue if he had wished to found the principle of equality among us as you understand it. But great men are needed to command small men, just as it takes a cedar to shelter a hyssop." What bothered her even more, she who was an artist or, as she termed herself, a "poet," was the idea that everything should be subordinated to political considerations. To the *great* of this world she would always prefer the *good,* even though, like Michel, she believed that "the great law of equality . . . is the first and only invariable law of morals and equity." But there are other things that count as much as "greatness and strength; there is kindness. A tear often does more good than the victories of Spartacus."

As for herself, she was ready to admit it: she was resolutely apolitical. "I am of a poetic, not of a legislative nature; if need be a warrior, but never a parliamentarian." Why this Roman severity? As though Taglioni, the dancer, should be forced to walk around in clogs and Liszt's hands be put to work turning a winepress! Why should the minstrels be silenced in the republican utopia he was bent on establishing and no longer allowed to sing romances to women, while Michel and his like busied themselves devising laws for the rest of mankind?

Outside, the nightingale was filling the darkness with such a "lovely modulation" that she had to interrupt her writing and go out to listen to it. What a melancholy night! "A gray sky, faint veiled stars, not a breath among the plants, an impenetrable obscurity on earth. The large pine trees lift their vague black masses in the gray air . . . Oh, Lord! Not so long ago I still loved, and such a night would have been delightful. Each sigh of the nightingale fills my breast with an electrical commotion. Oh God, Oh God, I am still so young!"

Buloz, to whom she turned over the sixth *Lettre d'un voyageur* when she returned to Paris in early May, must have recognized the old mating call when he read these pulsating lines. Spring was in the air again and she was in no mood to resist it. Nor was Michel de Bourges, who had to hurry up to Paris at about the same time to act as one of the defense lawyers in the biggest political trial Louis-Philippe's regime had yet witnessed. Though he had left his wife in Bourges and spoke constantly of virtue, he was more than ready to forget both in George Sand's arms.

The tense weeks which followed were among the most hectic George had ever known. She who only a few weeks before seemed resigned to leading a hermit's quiet life now found herself propelled into the center of a swirling storm. Michel de Bourges, who had rented a room on the nearby Quai Voltaire, was constantly tramping up the stairs to see her, usually accompanied by three or four lawyer friends. Sometimes he would be so exhausted from hours of intense debate with his colleagues that he would practically have to be carried up and stretched out on the couch before dinner.

The trial which had brought them all to Paris was known as *le procès monstre* (the mammoth trial), because it involved more than a hundred defendants. In January of the previous year, at a time when George Sand was in Venice, the silk workers of Lyon had gone on strike to protest a forced reduction of wages. The subsequent passage of a law banning labor unions and the arrest of six strike leaders had fanned unrest into a desperate movement of revolt. Ten thousand soldiers, supported by artillery, had finally been ordered to "restore order" in the tense city, unleashing three days of savage street fighting and touching off mutinies and uprisings in other parts of France. Accused of deliberately conspiring to overthrow the July monarchy, two thousand republican sympathizers were rounded up and held in several Paris prisons. Most of them were later released. But 121 of the "ringleaders" were retained and summoned to appear for trial before the House of Peers, thus transformed by governmental fiat into an extraordinary court of law.

In addition to Michel de Bourges, this trial had mobilized most of the leading republicans in France. They included the septuagenarian Filippo Michele Buonarotti, a descendant of Michelangelo and a French Revolutionary veteran famed for his preaching of the gospel of total equality; Armand Carrel, publisher of *Le National* (for which Sainte-Beuve had long written articles of criticism); Hippolyte Carnot, one of the leaders of the Saint-Simonians (of whom more will be said shortly); and the celebrated chemist François Vincent Raspail. But the chorus of sympathy and protest was not simply limited to republicans, it even included the heretical priest Abbé de Lamennais, who journeyed up specially from Brittany to put in a good word for the accused.

The immense prestige enjoyed, not only in France, but in much of Europe by this soon-to-be-defrocked clergyman requires some explanation. Alfred de Musset called him "our modern Luther," and for George Sand, even before she met him in this momentous month of May 1835, he was "Christ's only apostle on earth." A thorn in the sore flank of the Establishment, he was for the 1830s what Jean-Paul Sartre has become in our own time. Yet this eloquent iconoclast had started out in life as an ardent defender of the faith. Born in 1782, the son of a well-to-do Saint-Malo shipowner and merchant, he had been brought up in a strictly Catholic tradition and had learned to detest the Republic, which had brought ruin to his family. With reluctance, he had been talked into taking orders, but he had gone on to make a name for himself by the extremism with which he advocated papal supremacy. After the fall of Napoleon, to whom this particular doctrine was anathema, Lamennais had made a frontal assault on eighteenth-century agnosticism in a four-volume *Essay on Indifference in Matters of Religion,* which argued that no society can exist without religion and that without faith nothing truly great or significant can be accomplished on earth. This was exactly what the Vatican, still reeling from the earthshaking upheavals of the French Revolution and the Bonapartist empire, wanted to hear. Lamennais, almost overnight, became France's most celebrated priest. His incisive style was compared to Pascal's. Pope Leo XII had his portrait hung in his bedroom next to an ivory crucifix, and not content with that, he invited him to Rome and sought to make him a cardinal.

All in vain! For this inordinately diffident little man with the incandescent soul felt more kinship for Savonarola than for the worldly heirs of the Medicis. Not a man to compromise his beliefs, he wanted all or nothing, and what he could no longer love, he was quite prepared to hate. He wanted Rome to dominate the monarchies of Europe as it had done in the Middle Ages, and he wanted the kings to humble their noblemen and financiers and to show more concern for the poor. When each failed to act as he wished, he turned against both, deriving an almost satanic satisfaction from his predictions of their impending doom and destruction. He now became — of all things — a Catholic liberal, not to say a revolutionary. For daring to predict the disappearance of hereditary monarchy and the triumph of universal suffrage — both heresies in the Europe of Metternich — and for venturing to demand freedom of expression and workingmen's associations, his liberal paper *L'Avenir* (*The Future*) was suspended by Rome prior to the explicit condemnation of freedom of expression in the papal encyclical *Mirari vos.*

Lamennais' riposte, delivered after eighteen months of somber meditation, was an onslaught on the very notion of kingship and hierarchical order. Entitled *Paroles d'un croyant* (*Words of a Believer*), this little book was charged with political dynamite. Its thesis, succinctly stated, was that all men being fundamentally brothers, the domination of man by man was an invention of the Devil. Kings, princes, potentates, were thus implicitly condemned as agents and instruments of Satan. "You have but one father, who is God, and one master, who is Christ. When you are told of those who wield power on earth: 'These be your masters,' do not believe them. If they be just, then are you their servants; if they be unjust, then are they your tyrants . . . ." But the reign of tyrannical darkness, Lamennais confidently predicted, was drawing to a close, and a cleansing storm was soon due to purge the earth. "And the kings will howl with fear on their thrones; with their two hands will they seek to hold on to their crowns, but the winds will tear them from their grasp and likewise sweep them away."

This "lyrical version of the *Communist Manifesto,*" as Harold Laski was to call it, eventually ran through one hundred editions and was translated into most of the languages of Europe. George Sand was smitten by the apocalyptic beauty of its prose, as was Franz Liszt, who told the abbé after reading it: "It is quite evident that nineteenth-century Christianity, that is, the entire religious and political future of mankind is in you! . . . Yours is an appallingly glorious vocation!"

It was in fact through Liszt (once again persona grata at 19 Quai Malaquais) that George Sand finally met Lamennais. The occasion was an extraordinary musico-philosophical dinner party which the young Franz gave in the lamp and candlelit splendor of his apartment on the Rue de Provence. To understand the stir aroused by this event, we would have to imagine a party given in our own century by Béla Bartók and attended by Jean-Paul Sartre, Simone de Beauvoir, Gottfried Benn, Emmanuel Mounier, Jacques Prévert, Beniamino Gigli, Lily Pons, Monsignor Daniélou, and Mischa Elman. "The three rooms in which Mr. Liszt receives were literally crowded," to quote a contemporary account. "On a couch the author of *Indiana* and *André* was listening charmingly to the author of *Paroles d'un croyant.* In a dark corner several gentlemen were indulging in a serious exchange of views: they were Mr. Ballanche, this antique philosopher, . . . Baron d'Eckstein, the illustrious publisher of *Le Catholique,* and Mr. de Guerry, the eloquent preacher . . . Elsewhere Mr. Emile Deschamps" — the poet and playwright — "was pouring out the treasures and inexhaustible youth of his wit. Heinrich Heine was getting off some sparkling criticism . . . Leaning against a door Mr. Barrault, the Saint-Simonian, with his long oriental beard . . . was telling some Asian stories, perhaps inspired by the lovely black eyes of Mademoiselle Falcon" — the famous Opéra singer. "Adolphe Nourrit sang, as he does each time the subject of his songs is religious, with the inspiration and voice of an angel. Kreissler" — which is to say Liszt — "was at the piano."

George Sand seems to have been so overwhelmed by the eclectic brilliance of the company that later, when Sainte-Beuve asked her what they had talked about, she replied that she didn't know, but that Lamennais must have talked to Ballanche, Liszt with Nourrit, and she herself with the cat — by which she probably meant Liszt's fourteen-year-old pupil Hermann Cohen, more generally known as "Puzzi" (the funny one), the nickname that had once been given to Franz in his days as a child prodigy.

A few days after this strange party Liszt, again accompanied by his protégé, "Puzzi," led Lamennais over to the Quai Malaquais apartment to meet Michel de Bourges. This too must have been a singular encounter — between the one-time defender of the faith who had so long anathematized the Revolution and the ardent republican who dreamed of overthrowing church and state. But for the sharp, sword-blade nose jutting from the narrow, ascetic face, Lamennais might almost have looked handsome, notwithstanding his frail physique. Like Liszt he had green eyes, though of a paler hue, eyes which flashed fire and which, combined with an almost angelic smile and simplicity of manner, gave him a singularly magnetic personality. In each other's presence the lawyer and the priest were as uncommunicative as two prima donnas, the abbé concentrating his soft-spoken charm on the child prodigy seated at his feet, while Michel de Bourges watched Liszt perform wonders on the piano. Unleashing somber storms of sound, which subsided just as suddenly into soft, silvery shimmers, the keyboard magician managed to combine the same passion and tenderness, fury and compassion that were to be found in Lamennais' apocalyptic prose. Deeply moved, Michel de Bourges finally stood up and declared in his deep, truculent voice: "Young man, you are great!"

No doubt he meant it. But later he may have suffered from a feeling of remorse at the idea that he, the self-appointed guardian of republican virtue, could let himself be mollified by this quick-fingered genius. For several evenings later, after taking in a play at the Comédie Française, George Sand, Gabriel Planet, and another friend were strolling along the banks of the Seine, as was their wont, when Michel de Bourges suddenly exploded. Above their heads they could hear the sound of instrumental music and see the trees of the Tuileries Gardens lit by the brilliance of a court ball which Louis-Philippe was giving in the Royal Palace. George, who had been listening with but half an ear to her companions' energetic discussion of the *social question,* being more receptive to the moonlight playing on the still waters of the Seine and to the strains of music reaching them on soft gusts of linden-scented air, was aroused from her reverie by the name of Buonarotti, the old revolutionary prophet of a ruthlessly egalitarian society. What! exclaimed George Sand. They were trying to revive the idea of an absolutely propertyless society!

This was sheer madness! It was not along that particular road that a civilized epoch could be expected to advance.

"Civilization!" cried Michel de Bourges, striking his cane against the bridge's stone balustrade. "Ah yes, the big word with artists! Civilization! Well, I'll tell you that to rejuvenate and renew your corrupt society, this fine river will have to turn red with blood, this accursed palace be reduced to ashes, and this vast city turned into a wilderness over which the poor man's family will steer the plow and build its cottage!" George Sand listened in silent awe to these apocalyptic fulminations, and when the breathless Michel finally paused to ask her opinion on the matter, she encouraged him to continue, saying that this apologia for universal death and destruction reminded her pleasantly of Dante "just returned from hell. I'm beginning to enjoy your pastoral symphony: why interrupt it so soon?"

Michel de Bourges was now beside himself with fury. "All that interests you is my poor eloquence, my phrases, words and images! As though you were listening to a poem or an orchestra!" And with that he launched into another, even more vehement diatribe against society and its corruptions, finally breaking his cane against the stone rampart of the Louvre. Realizing the futility of further argument, George Sand turned on her heel and had Planet escort her back across the Seine to the Quai Malaquais, while an angry but crestfallen Michel followed lamely behind, still trying to convince her that the new Golden Age of liberated man (and woman) could not be ushered in without a revolutionary holocaust.

They had another, though less serious, disagreement over the line which the lawyers for the defense were to take in the mammoth trial which now opened at the Luxembourg Palace. Some of the defendants, and particularly those from Lyon, wanted to fight a straightforward judicial battle in order to expose the provocations to which the workingmen of Lyon had been subjected and the calculated ruthlessness of the military repression. Others, like Michel de Bourges, wanted to turn it into a frankly political battle, challenging the government's right to subvert the normal judicial process by turning the House of Peers into an extraordinary court of law. At Michel's request, George Sand drafted a preliminary statement which she felt all the defending lawyers could adhere to. Michel, however, found its tone too sentimental, too full of humanitarian pleading. He accordingly toughened it, adding a number of incendiary phrases such as "The infamy of the judge makes for the glory of the accused." Few of the defending lawyers, as George had predicted, were willing to endorse this truculent manifesto. Undeterred, Michel de Bourges arranged to have it published over his own signature with the cooperation of a fellow lawyer.

Women being denied admission to the visitors' gallery of the House of Peers, George Sand once again donned trousers, and when challenged by the ushers, brazenly declared that she was a friend of Duc Decazes, the House of Peers' Chief Referendary. Her presence in the gallery did not go unnoticed, for she unabashedly waved encouragement to those of the defendants whom she knew. But she was not present the day Michel de Bourges had to defend his manifesto against the charge of "contempt of court." He made a surprisingly deferential speech, limiting himself to a single anathema: a somber prediction that, for having been transformed into a kind of Hangman's Court, the Luxembourg Palace would within ten years go the way of the Bastille.

Exhausted by the weeks of tense discussion which had preceded this climax, Michel de Bourges came home ill and was put to bed with a fever. While George Sand nursed him, the mammoth trial degenerated into a judicial farce, the defendants finally refusing to testify on their own behalf. In early June Michel himself was condemned to one month of imprisonment and a 10,000 franc fine for having drafted the seditious manifesto attacking the judicial competence of the House of Peers. He took his time complying with the relatively mild sentence, and instead of giving himself up to the Paris jailers, he calmly left for Bourges in mid-June.

Leaving her two children in boarding school, George Sand left Paris at about the same time and journeyed down to Nohant. She talked of soon leaving for Switzerland, and even of making a special trip to Brittany to see Lamennais, who had replaced Sainte-Beuve as her spiritual "confessor" and adviser. But she was by now too spiritually and physically attached to Michel de Bourges to be able to contemplate a prolonged separation. In the latter part of June she even invited him over to Nohant, thus making it clear to her husband that she intended to lead her life as she chose. While Casimir rode into La Châtre to attend the funeral of Charles Duvernet's father, George and Michel went for romantic walks in the grove and clung to each other passionately under the sweet-smelling acacias. The realization that he, who had cynically disported himself for years with various maids and village damsels, was now being paid back in his own coin threw Casimir into a dark dudgeon. Returning from the funeral he took to his bed, while his wife unconcernedly accompanied Michel back to Bourges.

In early July George returned to Paris, where she was soon joined by her new lover. Here she led an almost clandestine existence, holed up in a dusty, ground-floor "nest" while the Quai Malaquais house underwent repairs. Michel being forced to return to Bourges in early August, she preferred to accompany him as far as Châteauroux with Solange rather than spend one more week in Paris waiting for the beginning of Maurice's summer vacation. It thus fell to a surly Casimir to journey up to Paris and to bring his son back to Nohant.

George took advantage of the Baron's four-day absence to invite Michel over for a secret visit to Nohant. Once again she was eager to play the romantic heroine, boldly defying convention and receiving her lover in her bedroom as she had done four years before with Jules Sandeau. And for two blissful days she succeeded. Michel was smuggled into the house under cover of darkness, the shutters were closed tight, as though Monsieur and Madame were absent — which is what the servants were instructed to inform any unwanted callers — and only at night did the lovers venture forth, watching the moon rise through the leaves above them as they dallied in the grove. The secret eventually leaked out, as was bound to happen in a house full of servants, and when he learned the truth, the doubly cuckolded Master of Nohant completely lost his head.

23. Baron Dudevant's Blind Rage

Leaving her children at Nohant with Casimir, George Sand returned to Paris in September in order to be near Michel de Bourges, who was supposed to spend this month in prison. She found him ill and feverish, afflicted with a severe bronchial cough which worsened progressively. A doctor who was summoned to the Quai Malaquais apartment to make an official diagnosis reported that it would be three weeks before the invalid would be in a condition to start his jail term at the Sainte Pélagie prison (then used for the incarceration of political offenders). Michel was accordingly granted a delay and permitted by the President of the House of Peers to serve his prison term at Bourges.

Having made little attempt to hide the fact that she was now Michel's mistress, and having taken even fewer pains to conceal her aversion for France's monarchical plutocracy, even going as far (in her sixth *Lettre d'un voyageur*) as to refer to Louis-Philippe as a "crowned log," George Sand now found herself under police surveillance. The idea that she and her long-haired and long-bearded republican friends were officially blacklisted as members of an "anarchist committee" made her laugh, but it was not altogether a joking matter. In late July a Corsican crackpot named Fieschi had tried to blow up the Citizen King's carriage with an "infernal machine." *Engelwald*, the novel which George Sand had rashly pledged herself to deliver to Buloz by the end of May, was to have been the story of an Austrian plotter whose reasons for wishing to indulge in tyrannicide were to have been elaborately described. Though the tyrant involved was Napoleon, there were passages in the manuscript which, in the existing circumstances, might have been considered seditious and have got not only herself but Buloz into trouble.

She accordingly shunted this story to one side and began work on a novelette which she decided to call *Simon* — in honor of Simon Peter, the disciple of whom Christ had said: "On this rock shall I build my church." Simon's real-life model was the rock-ribbed republican Michel de Bourges, here transformed into a twenty-year-old lawyer of peasant extraction. The hero's age was closer to Liszt's than to the thirty-seven-year-old Michel's, and this too was no accident. The novel, though set in the hill country of La Marche (south and west of Nohant), was clearly inspired by the young Franz's "shocking" liaison with Marie d'Agoult, an aristocratic adulteress who had dared to flout convention by abandoning her husband, a count, and her noble children to go live in brazen sin with her humbly born lover. Likewise in *Simon,* the aristocratic heroine, Fiamma, was portrayed as ready to renounce her titles in order to marry a gifted plebeian.

In early October George accompanied Michel back to Bourges, proceeding on alone to Nohant. Business matters, as she later wrote to Liszt, had forced her to abandon the idea of spending part of the winter with him and Marie d'Agoult in Geneva. "I am taking possession of my poor old house which the powerful and noble Baron Dudevant is at last willing to give back to me and where I am going to bury myself with my books and my pigs, determined to live agriculturally."

This hope too was destined to be frustrated. The previous May, Alexis Duteil, who, like Hippolyte, had long been one of Casimir's drinking chums and an occasional partner in his bedroom orgies with Nohant maids or village girls, had persuaded the "powerful and noble Baron" to sign a redrafted agreement for a separation. This agreement assured him an annual income of 7000 francs (the rent derived from the Paris town house, l'Hôtel de Narbonne) and the guardianship of Maurice, while Aurore was granted the income from Nohant and the tutelage of Solange. To sugar the bitter pill he was asked to swallow, Aurore informed her husband that his bedroom would be left unchanged, that he would be free to occupy it whenever he wished, and particularly during the summer vacations when the children were at Nohant. Casimir's response to this reiterated offer was one of sullen irritation, accompanied by the remark that never would he set foot in a house of which he was not the master.

The separation was to have taken legal effect on November 11, but the closer they came to this crucial date the surlier and more intemperate in his language Casimir became. More than ever he seemed determined to prove to his wife and everybody else that at Nohant his word alone was law. Aurore, who hated domestic scenes, had long since adopted an attitude of passive resistance, withdrawing into dignified silence at the dinner table each time her husband told her to shut up, and even refusing to be provoked when he got drunk and called her a "slut."

By mid-October the atmosphere had grown so tense that not a day passed without some disagreeable incident. On the seventeenth Casimir again tried to provoke her into a dinner-table discussion of their settlement, a matter Aurore proudly refused to discuss in the presence of the children. The next day there was another flare-up when he walked into her bedroom and told her that she had no business sending the gardener, who should have been working at the winepress, to La Châtre, and that she should have ridden in and picked up the mail herself. A number of guests were present at the dinner table when the gardener finally appeared with the mail, which did not keep Casimir from angrily berating him: "You will take your orders from me, do you hear? From me and no one else! If this happens again, I'll dismiss you!"

The next morning Casimir went hunting with Alphonse Fleury and Gustave Papet. On his return he seemed furious to find Rozanne Bourgoing and Aurore enjoying a good laugh in her bedroom — as though they were mocking him behind his back. The dinner passed off smoothly enough — so George Sand claimed in the detailed report she later drafted for her lawyer. But after dinner, when they had all moved into the drawing room next door, Casimir suddenly lost patience with his son, Maurice, who had asked if he could have some cream with his coffee.

"There's none left," he declared irritably. "Go to the kitchen, get out and stop bothering us!"

Instead of leaving, Maurice clung to his mother's armchair.

"Go to my room," Aurore said to her son, taking him gently by the arm. "I'll be along in a moment to work with you at your lesson. You're irritating your father, and he doesn't know — " she stopped short, but it was already too late.

"Why don't you finish the sentence?" her husband demanded after Maurice had walked out sobbing. " 'Your father doesn't know what he's saying.' "

"Perhaps so . . . but I didn't say it," his wife replied.

"But it's what you were thinking. So don't hesitate, say it!"

"I think you don't know why you're scolding him. For the past hour you've been picking on him for no reason at all."

"You want to make me look like a fool."

"Not at all, but I do think you're a bit tipsy."

"That may be, but you're going to shut up."

"Even if you so order me, I won't shut up, for I've not said a word too many."

"You're going to leave this room!" Casimir commanded.

"I won't. You forget, my friend, that I'm as much at home here as you are."

"You're going to leave this room, or I'm going to slap you!" he shouted.

"You won't."

"No . . . because I despise you too much to do it!"

"You don't despise me, you're just drunk."

"I'm not drunk and I'm going to slap you."

"You wouldn't dare!"

Rising to his feet, his red face flushed, Casimir lurched toward his wife, who was now standing with her back to the fireplace. Alphonse Fleury, Gustave Papet, and Joseph Bourgoing, a La Châtre tax collector, all sprang from their chairs and formed a rampart to protect her. The only one who remained seated was Alexis Duteil, who had buried his face in his hands.

"And you're going to let him do it?" Aurore cried to Duteil, irked by her friend's impassivity.

Rising in his turn, Duteil gripped Casimir by the arm and forced him to let go of Aurore's wrist, which he had managed to seize. A wild slap aimed at Aurore hit poor Rozanne Bourgoing in the chest. Together Dutheil, Bourgoing, and the towering Alphonse Fleury forced him back, while Gustave Papet protected Aurore in case the irate husband managed to break loose and come at her again.

"Let go of me!" he bellowed. "Get your hands off me! Stop meddling in my affairs, damnit! This has been going on long enough! We're going to see who's the master around here!"

With that he ran from the salon and, crossing the dining room, made for the vestibule. Here he picked up a hunting gun, which Duteil, aided by Fleury, immediately wrested from him. For a moment it looked as though Casimir were going to take a swing at his best friend, Duteil. But a moment later he calmed down and returned to the drawing room with the others.

Aurore walked out without saying a word, taking Solange with her. Duteil, who followed them, brought Maurice back to his father in an effort at reconciliation. Casimir gave his son a paternal kiss, saying: "It's not you I'm annoyed with." And with that he probably thought the incident was closed.

Later that same evening, after Maurice had gone to bed, Alexis Duteil came to see George in her study, anxious to see if he couldn't patch things up. But George was no longer in a mood to compromise. Up until now she had been prepared to grant Casimir full custody over her son, but she now had second thoughts.

Early the next morning she learned from the servants that Monsieur le Baron was preparing to ride into La Châtre. Alarmed by the idea that he might try to intercept her letters, she sent a hasty note over to Gustave Papet, in the nearby Château d'Ars, asking him to gallop into La Châtre at top speed and bring her mail back before Casimir could lay his hands upon it. She also asked him for the loan of a horse to hitch up to the Nohant cabriolet.

Later, after Casimir had ridden off, she drove out through the front gate and across the elm-shaded church square with Maurice and Solange. She took them to a nearby wood, overlooking the Vallée Noire, and here they spent the rest of the day picnicking and filling baskets with mushrooms and moss. Aurore wanted to spend the last hours of the vacation with her children and at the same time avoid her husband, who was to accompany Maurice and Solange up to Paris the next day. But that evening, when she returned to Nohant, she learned with relief that Casimir was not yet back. In fact, he spent the night in La Châtre and left the next morning with the children without asking to see her.

George now had Gustave Papet drive her to Châteauroux to consult François Rollinat — like Duteil a lawyer, but unlike Duteil, no friend of Casimir's. After hearing their account of what had happened, Rollinat agreed that things had gone too far; an amicable arrangement was no longer possible, given Casimir's instability of mood and character, and a legal separation would have to be officially obtained from the district court of La Châtre. The local magistrates being exceedingly loath to sanction marital separations, George might have to make a subsequent appeal to the higher jurisdiction at Bourges, where she was more certain to win the day. But for this reason Rollinat felt that they had to consult Michel, more experienced in the subtleties of legal procedure and more familiar with the temper of the magistrates at Bourges.

The three of them drove back to Nohant, where they ate a hasty dinner, before driving on posthaste to Bourges. It was two o'clock in the morning when they finally clattered through the empty streets of the old cathedral town and drew up beneath the somber prison walls. Michel had been given a cell in what had once been a fortress-castle of the dukes of Burgundy. The surveillance seems to have been lax, for they had little trouble bribing a jailer, who led them through a maze of damp corridors and winding staircases to Michel's furnished cell.

George's high-strung lover wholeheartedly approved of a legal separation. A short letter addressed to the presiding magistrate of the district court would be enough to start the procedure, but until the court had handed down its judgment she had to stay away from Nohant in order to give full weight to her rights as a plaintiff.

Creeping out of the prison with the first faint streaks of dawn, they drove back to La Châtre in the ramshackle cabriolet. On reaching the town, Aurore and Papet could congratulate themselves on having covered 150 miles in less than thirty hours. Alexis Duteil, at whose door they knocked, immediately agreed to put Aurore up for as long as she wanted, even though he was a friend of Casimir's; and after giving her dinner — for she was famished — he drove her to Nohant to pick up her nightgown, slippers, and personal belongings, including her precious pens and manuscripts.

For the rest of October and the first weeks of November Aurore lived at La Châtre, where the inveterate town gossips were as much surprised as she was to find her in their midst. The Duteils' was a gay household, with fourteen people (including seven children) at the dinner table, when they weren't joined by old friends like Fleury, Charles Duvernet, and Gabriel Planet, who had recently transferred his legal practice to La Châtre. George would often have to chase the talkative Planet and Duteil from her room at midnight, when she opened her inkwell, sharpened her quills, and began covering sheets of paper with that even handwriting which she so seldom needed to correct or cross out.

When Casimir returned to Nohant from Paris in late October, he was informed by the servants that Madame la Baronne had left for La Châtre. Still unwilling to believe that his wife meant business, he ignored the official summons and failed to appear for a preliminary hearing before the district court of La Châtre. But ten days later, on November 12, he was talked into signing an interim agreement with Aurore whereby he was assured of an annual revenue of 3800 francs from her holdings; added to the 1200 francs he received from his own properties, he could thus count on an annual income of 5000 francs a year. Aurore was granted custody of the two children, with the responsibility for their upkeep and education. Casimir was authorized to have Maurice spend half of his holiday time with him; he was also granted the right to see Solange as often as he wished, though he was denied any future say in what boarding schools she should be sent to.

Having signed this agreement, Casimir resigned his post as mayor of Nohant and returned to Paris. He seems to have thought that his wife would not pursue the matter further. But she had suffered too much from his previous backslidings and repeated bad faith to be willing to take chances. On November 21 the district court of La Châtre accordingly filed an official demand for a legal separation, and on December 1 Madame Dudevant was called upon to back up her request through the testimony of witnesses.

For a moment it looked as though George Sand was going to have two lawsuits on her hands. In late November she wrote to Buloz to say that she was determined to break the catastrophic contract she had signed just one year earlier (December 5, 1834) while in a suicidal mood. That contract had granted Buloz an exclusive right to publish everything she had so far written in an edition of Complete Works, this right to extend up to ten years after her death. Buloz had thus acquired the right to publish twelve volumes for the ridiculously low sum of 10,000 francs (or about 800 francs a volume), volumes he could reedit as often as he wished to, without having to pay an extra franc in royalties. Agreeing to let her off the cruel hook, Buloz even honored the distraught authoress with a lightning visit to Nohant, where a new contract for a sixteen-volume edition of her Complete Works was drawn up and signed by both parties. George Sand was granted a royalty of one franc fifty centimes on each volume sold, while Buloz was given a six-year period (ending in November 1841) in which to publish all sixteen volumes. The final three, in this projected edition, were to be composed of *Simon,* the one-volume novelette with the provincial La Marche setting which was now virtually finished, and *Engelwald,* the two-volume novel which was already six months overdue.

Again overestimating her capacities, George rashly pledged herself to deliver this latter work in three weeks' time (January 1, 1836), even though she still had a full volume to write. Her mind once again must have been on other matters, for in a moment of distraction she allowed the canny Buloz to maintain the provisions of the original *Engelwald* contract, according to which she was liable to a 250 franc "fine" for each month's delay in delivery. (Strictly adhered to, this meant that by the end of this December she already owed Buloz 1750 francs.) Michel de Bourges also provided the inspiration for this novel's hero, a balding mountaineer of some sixty years who, so far as one can judge from the surviving evidence (for the manuscript was later destroyed), was of Tyrolean stock. He may also have been a Protestant as well as an anti-Bonapartist plotter — to judge by George's extensive background reading at this time, which included the Bible as well as books about Napoleon and the nationalist movement in Italy.

Though she slaved daily from midnight till dawn in the little room overlooking one of La Châtre's busy streets, George Sand seems to have found it heavy going. By late January of 1836 she had to write to Buloz to say that *Engelwald* might end up being three, instead of two volumes long. The distractions, culminating in the annual Carnival frolics, were multiple. She had considerable difficulty in persuading the Nohant servants to testify about the goings-on they had witnessed, most of them being fearful of reprisals should Monsieur le Baron win this legal battle. Of the seventeen witnesses interrogated, the most devastating was Jules Boucoiran, who journeyed up from his mother's home in Nîmes to tell the judges what he had seen and heard as Maurice's tutor at Nohant. He painted a scathing picture of Baron Dudevant taking the edge off his lust with Pepita, getting the maid Claire with child, indulging in bedroom orgies with village girls when his wife was away from Nohant, generally behaving like a drunken brute, silencing his wife at table, and never losing an opportunity to call Solange, for whom he never showed the tenderness he felt for his son, Maurice, "You harlot's daughter!"

Aurore's greatest disappointment in these proceedings was her half brother, Hippolyte. Reluctant to answer questions about his own erotic exploits with his wife's maid Claire, he flatly refused to journey down to La Châtre in answer to a formal arraignment. The mere idea that he should be asked to testify against his old drinking chum so incensed him that he even sided with Casimir against his half sister, quietly encouraging the baron to contest the decision which the district court of La Châtre handed down in mid-February of 1836. By the terms of that decision Madame Dudevant's request for a legal separation was granted. Condemning him by default for again failing to appear, the court found Baron Dudevant guilty of abusive misconduct toward his wife, upheld her request for a legal separation, gave her the custody of both children, and enjoined them to proceed to a formal division of property along the lines of what had been agreed upon the previous November.

Hippolyte's hope all along had been that Aurore and Casimir would reach an amicable settlement which would obviate a public trial. But Casimir's pigheaded decision to appeal the district court's verdict to the Royal Court of Bourges now forced into the open what had hitherto been exclusively reserved for the eyes and ears of magistrates. It turned what had been a relatively discreet affair into a public scandal.

Increasingly impatient with her husband's legal maneuverings, Aurore had the notary impound the furniture at Nohant and place a moratorium on all income derived from the estate. In mid-March she made an incognito trip to Châteauroux to see Michel, who had come there to plead a lawsuit, and from there she journeyed on to Paris to be reunited with her children, whom she had not seen in four months.

In Paris, as at Nohant, George Sand had gradually gathered around her a small circle of male friends, all of whom were more or less in love with her and from one to ten years younger. Of the three who turned up at the Quai Malaquais apartment on the first evening of her return, the youngest, Emmanuel Arago, son of a famous French astronomer, was a lawyer and part-time vaudeville writer who had once collaborated with Balzac and Jules Sandeau. The next, Adolphe Guéroult, was a journalist who had worked for *Le Globe,* while the third, the thirty-year-old Charles Didier, was the same melancholy Swiss poet whom George Sand had first met in Hortense Allart's literary salon at the time she was writing *Lélia.*

A would-be novelist who had felt utterly crushed after reading *Indiana* and *Lélia* — the kind of novels he would have liked to write himself, had he but George Sand's talent — Charles Didier had achieved a succès d'estime with a book entitled *Rome souterraine* (*Underground Rome*), which though it claimed to be fiction was in reality an "inside" account of life in the patriotic and other political movements in Italy. An unhappy childhood in Geneva, aggravated by an eye injury which forced him to wear dark glasses, had tied this illegitimate son of a Geneva lawyer into psychological knots. George Sand, in the *Story of My Life,* later described him as a man whose genius was so bottled up inside him that it could never find adequate expression. "I called him my bear, and even my white bear, because along with a face that was young and handsome, he was distinguished by a handsome head of hair which had whitened before its time. It was the image of his soul, which was fundamentally full of life and strength, but whose outpouring had been paralyzed by some mysterious crisis."

Didier was by now morbidly jealous of the other young men who hovered about her, his latent Puritanism being frequently shocked by the excessive familiarity of her behavior with admirers like Emmanuel Arago and Adolphe Guéroult, whom he considered "bad company." Less offensive, to judge by Didier's fascinating though annoyingly laconic diary, was the twenty-four-year-old Charles d'Aragon, a young civil servant whom George had met at Buloz's house on the Rue des Beaux-Arts and whom she occasionally used, when short of funds, for the free-franchise transmission of her manuscripts. (Mail costs at this time were prohibitive — except for administrative officials, who did not have to pay any postage.) Yet the young aristocrat — d'Aragon being a count — was as much a cause of jealousy as the others, as can be judged by this Didier entry for March 26 describing a midnight supper shared with Emmanuel Arago and Charles d'Aragon: "A fantastic night. We only left her at five o'clock in the morning. It was broad daylight. Arago was tipsy. I had to take him . . . and put him in a cab. They are both of them (Arago and d'Aragon) in love with her. I was there, watching, with my head in the cushions of the couch, while she, somewhat sad and not too sharp-tongued, ran her fingers through my hair, calling me her old philosopher."

Increasingly agitated by these marks of favor, the "old philosopher" returned to the Quai Malaquais apartment the next evening armed with three bottles of champagne. The company this time included a second woman authoress in the person of Madame Jal. The bottles were soon emptied and everyone grew pleasantly high, though in his diary Didier claimed that he was less so than the others. "George was gay and laughing. I don't like her free and easy tone, but I forgive her. She grows tender when she drinks, so do I. She kept kissing me, I kept kissing her, and when we parted at eight o'clock in the morning, in the midst of a dreadful thunderstorm, she gave me her cashmere shawl in exchange for my white muffler."

Was the onset of spring once again affecting George Sand? Charles Didier's diary is here bafflingly vague. Had George wanted to seduce him, she could easily have done so in a tête-à-tête. But she seems to have preferred the company of several young admirers, as though fearing what might happen if she were left alone with one of them. Didier came away from another "fantastic" evening at the Quai Malaquais apartment jealously persuaded that George Sand was starting an affair with Charles d'Aragon. Didier's rivals were no less persuaded that she wanted *him* for a lover. Two nights later — a night which lasted until six in the morning — she made cruel fun of Emmanuel Arago after deliberately provoking him with one of her garters. When the scandalized but fatally bewitched Didier called on her the next day, she scoffed at his prudery and then gave him a "maternal" kiss on the forehead which was so soft and protracted as to seem positively incestuous.

A curious woman, this Sand, at once frank and impenetrable! Which is doubtless why Didier found her so enthralling.

On April 13 her Three Musketeers were joined by a fourth — Luigi Calamatta, a talented Italian painter and disciple of Ingres whom Buloz had commissioned to do an engraving of George Sand. "We got tipsy, particularly d'Aragon and I," Charles Didier recorded in his diary, adding with exasperating brevity: "A fantastic, delirious night" — presumably by virtue of what was said rather than what was done. For in dealing with these ardent young wooers George Sand behaved more like a Penelope than a Messalina.

Two days later Didier called on her at one o'clock, stayed all afternoon, had dinner with her, and spent the night at the Quai Malaquais apartment. Doing what? Didier's diary is singularly reticent on the subject, but it was probably not what one would logically expect. The next morning he took her for a walk in the Jardin des Plantes (already a zoo as well as a botanical garden), then led her to his apartment on the Rue du Regard for breakfast. "She was feeling a bit ill," he recorded in his diary. "I took care of her and cured her through magnetism. I took her home at six o'clock, after having been with her uninterruptedly for thirty hours, twelve of them spent with her alone. We are more and more friendly, bound by a close intimacy."

After sitting through another night with her at the Quai Malaquais apartment, Didier brought her to dine with his friend David Richard, a Genevan of Huguenot extraction like himself with whom he shared the Rue du Regard apartment. "I was happy but silent, she serious. She was ravishingly beautiful," the inhibited Didier recorded in his diary. At midnight he took her home, but the following afternoon she returned for dinner with a painter friend of hers named Mercier. David Richard, who was among other things a doctor, treated George Sand to a lesson in phrenology, a subject for which she had developed a recent passion. The would-be teacher was smitten in his turn, and as Didier noted: "He was a bit taken by her, and I a bit jealous." In the early hours of the morning Mercier left, David Richard went off to bed, and Didier found himself alone at last with George. But, as he noted in his diary, nothing happened. "I made a bed for her in my study and withdrew to my room. What a life! If people only knew!"

At eleven o'clock he was on his feet again, helping her with her "toilet" — by which he probably meant that in addition to the soap and warm water he brought to her in a china basin, he was allowed to comb her dark hair. After a late breakfast he accompanied her to Maurice's boarding school. "She talked a lot about Michel [de Bourges] and described the intellectual nature of their relations. She swore to me she had not had a lover since she broke with Musset."

Did Didier believe her? If so, he was being singularly naive. Three years earlier, in August of 1833, she had written him a note asking him for an urgent loan of 100 francs, and when he had brought the money to the Quai Malaquais apartment, she had told him that she was just back from Fontainebleau, where she had spent a week riding through the forest *alone.* Several weeks later he had learned the truth from Sainte-Beuve, who had even volunteered the information that George Sand had written him a long letter telling him that she was now in love with Alfred de Musset.

In another respect too George Sand had not changed, for in this hectic spring of 1836 she was as penniless as in the summer of 1833. On April 4 she wrote to Buloz, asking him to expedite payment for the articles on Spain which Charles Didier had written for the *Revue des Deux Mondes.* Shortly afterward she herself asked Buloz for 300 francs, needed to pay some urgent bill. Ten days later she had to write to him again, saying she needed 500 francs to pay for her return trip to La Châtre. The legal costs involved in her protracted litigation with Casimir were ruining her — at a time when she was forced to hold up the publication of *Engelwald* (now virtually completed), because its outspokenly republican sentiments were certain to make a bad impression on the judges at La Châtre and Bourges.

Her legal battle with her husband had meanwhile entered a critical new phase. In mid-April Casimir had had his La Châtre lawyer formally contest the verdict which the district court had handed down two months earlier by producing his own list of grievances against his wife. All her infidelities — from her first encounters with Aurélien de Sèze in the Pyrenees in 1825 down to her trip to Italy with Alfred de Musset — were systematically catalogued; and as though these weren't damning enough, Casimir had added, for the year 1832: "M. Gus[tave] P[lanche]. Julie Dorville [the maid] testifies that Mad[ame] A. D[udevant] slept with the above named, having her four-year-old daughter climb into the same bed. Antipathy felt by Solange for Mr. Plan[che]." Casimir's lawyer was so shocked by this list of grievances — presented by a man who was not demanding but *contesting* a legal separation — that he refused to read them in court, contenting himself with officially filing the list of grievances in Casimir's own hand.

Casimir was in fact resorting to a kind of blackmail operation. By threatening to make a public exposé of her numerous infidelities, he was hoping to break down his wife's determination and to force her to an out-of-court settlement on his terms: full custody over Maurice and the continued ownership of Nohant, his wife being left to get along on whatever revenue was forthcoming from the Hôtel de Narbonne and her books. The maneuver came very near to succeeding, for when Casimir's Paris lawyer confronted her with his list of grievances, Aurore was ready to abandon everything rather than see her daughter's name dragged in mud. Her friends, however, talked her out of it, and none of them more forthrightly than the outraged Alexis Duteil, who broke off all further relations with his former drinking and wenching companion.

To bring added pressure to bear on his wife, Casimir had also prepared a list of grievances against Michel de Bourges, implicitly accusing him of having committed adultery with Aurore, not only in Paris but also at Nohant. This too threw George Sand into a momentary panic. Afraid that she might have to find someone else to defend her, she called on several Paris lawyers and asked them for a professional opinion on Casimir's list of grievances. The resultant brief, which seven of them signed and dispatched to the district court of La Châtre, declared that the insulting charges which Baron Dudevant had accumulated against his wife were "perhaps without an example in judicial annals"; they declared themselves "penetrated by a feeling of horror on seeing a father, in his need for vengeance and hatred, not respecting his daughter's future" and added that inasmuch as the husband had now defamed his wife and given her new grounds for complaint, a separation *had* to be granted.

Originally scheduled for April 19, the judicial hearing accorded to Casimir's contestation had to be postponed for several weeks to allow Michel de Bourges time to acquaint himself with the new elements in the case. George Sand was simultaneously faced with another dilemma. To cut down on her expenses, she had decided to give up the Quai Malaquais apartment. There was also a danger that her vindictive spouse might have her furniture impounded. On April 25 she accordingly had most of her furniture moved to the flat which Charles d'Aragon occupied in Buloz's house on the Rue des Beaux-Arts, while she herself moved into Charles Didier's lodgings on the Rue du Regard. The melancholy Swiss poet gave up his bedroom for her, contenting himself with the living room couch.

The first evening George and he spent long hours reading *Engelwald* and then indulged in an all-night tête-à-tête. "Her moving in here has aroused a huge amount of gossip, first of all in the house, and then outside," he noted soon afterward. But like a faithful dog, he accompanied her everywhere and was only happy at her side. "When David R[ichard] goes to bed, we remain alone and our intimacy is renewed. I study myself, I observe her, anxious, troubled, doubting. This complicated being is still incomprehensible to me in more ways than one; and I'm afraid of her impetuous mobility. I keep studying her, I don't understand. Is she loyal? Is she putting on an act? Is her heart dead? Puzzles still unsolved."

A few days later he added another entry which showed him as perplexed as ever. "In the evening she goes out and doesn't return till midnight. She finishes the beginning of the sixth *Lettre d'un voyageur,* then becomes tender and caressing. She lies down at my feet, her head on my knees, her hands in mine . . . Oh Siren, what do you want of me?"

It wasn't sex, that much seems certain. Not at least with him — though in his masculine innocence and vanity he liked to think he attracted her, forgetting that whereas she was the focus and center of his thoughts, he was for her a purely peripheral attraction. Poet though he was, Charles Didier seems to have been singularly insensitive to the tremendous tensions under which George Sand was now laboring. It had been a shock for her to discover to what depths of ignominy her husband could descend, just as it had been a shock to learn that Casimir's widowed mother-in-law, Baroness Dudevant, had told Maurice about her demand for a separation (something she had tried to conceal from him) and had even tried to poison his mind against his mother by saying the most horrible things about her — causing the twelve-year-old boy to return to boarding school in tears! Her demand for a legal separation now threatened to become a public scandal. Buloz seemed reluctant to launch the publication of her Complete Works, which could bring her some badly needed earnings, and in Paris she did not have a single female friend to whom she could turn for sympathy — with the exception of Marie Dorval, whom she could only frequent at the risk of being called a lesbian!

Sentimentally she felt herself once again adrift on an ocean of uncertainty. Married like herself and with two stepchildren, Michel de Bourges was not a free agent and had shown no eagerness to abandon his wife for George. She had no right to ask such a sacrifice of him; and she may even not have wanted it, realizing how difficult it was to accommodate herself to his argumentative and despotic character. Life with Michel was not unlike her life with Musset — subject to frequent storms that were at once exhilarating and exhausting, and only stilled when Michel fell sick. With her "white bear," on the other hand, she could enjoy the kind of soothing calm she had once known with Pagello. Unlike Pagello, who was not an Italian for nothing, Didier could be counted on not to importune her with his amorous advances — which probably explains why she chose to inhabit his lodgings, rather than go stay with Charles d'Aragon or Emmanuel Arago, who could probably not have restrained their youthful lust.

The simplest way of avoiding this new entanglement would, of course, have been to return to La Châtre. But George Sand shrank from returning to this hornets' nest of hostile gossip. To anybody willing to listen, Casimir now openly proclaimed Michel to be Aurore's lover, promising to box the scoundrel's ears and to run him through with a sword should he dare take up the cudgels for his wife in court. So fearful, indeed, was she of an adverse decision — which would have forced her to resume married life with her husband — that she made secret plans to defy the verdict, if necessary, by borrowing 10,000 francs and fleeing with her children to America!

These fears, as it happened, were totally unwarranted. Still, it took a special trip on the part of her La Châtre lawyer to persuade her to leave Paris and to accompany him back to the country. At La Châtre she was received with open arms by all her friends, more than ever outraged by Casimir's abominable behavior. On May 11 Michel de Bourges turned up for the official court session and proceeded to lecture a stony-faced Casimir, seated only a few feet away in the crowded courtroom, on how a civilized husband should behave toward his wife, without the Master of Nohant's daring to open his mouth. The district court confirmed the earlier judgment, granting Aurore's request for a legal separation.

Instead of heeding this verdict, Casimir returned to Nohant, as though it had always been his by birthright. Shortly afterward he let it be known that he was appealing the decision to the Royal Court of Bourges. The scandal of an open court session now being unavoidable, George Sand decided it was time she made clear just what she really thought of marriage and adultery. To the Royal judges of Bourges, whom she wanted to impress, her arguments may well have sounded like the specious products of circumstance. In fact, they were anything but new, though what they revealed was a new and unknown George Sand: a George Sand who was opposed to the revolutionary gospel of "free love" and who still continued to believe, in spite of everything, in the ideal virtues of monogamy and marriage.

24. The Misconduct of Woman or the Infamy of Man?

THE CHIEF PROPONENTS of the gospel of "free love" were to be found at this time among those who had undertaken to develop the ideas of one of the most seminal thinkers of modern times — Count Henri de Saint-Simon, who had died in 1825. Of his disciples the most influential — and also the most disruptive — was a tall, handsome, persuasive engineer named Prosper Enfantin, who in little more than half a dozen years had virtually made himself the uncrowned Pope of a new religious cult. Among other things this cult proclaimed the equality of the sexes, the "rehabilitation of the flesh," and the need for a Woman Messiah who, like some nineteenth-century Empress Theodora of Byzantium, would share supreme power and authority with her husband-Pope. Thus sublimely joined in a physical as well as spiritual union, the two reigning autocrats would draft a new code of sexual behavior aimed to determine where man's (and woman's) "ardent mobility" ends and rank immorality begins.

A typically Romantic product of France's postrevolutionary and post-Napoleonic "morning after," the "doctrine" preached by Saint-Simon had sought to fill the vacuum left by the wholesale collapse of established values. Its central thesis was the idea that work, industry, and commerce were to replace war and predatory spoliation as the primary activities of mankind. Titled aristocracies, essentially based on the profession of arms, would give way to what we would now call "meritocracies" of talent, composed of artists and scientists, businessmen and bankers, inventors, artisans, and engineers. War would cease to be the dominant factor in relations between sovereign states and would be replaced by the rational exploitation of the globe through the "material, intellectual, and moral activity of mankind in association." Likewise, within each country, class antagonisms would yield to a condition of social harmony once production and the distribution of wealth were determined according to the fundamental principle: "To each according to his capacity, to each capacity according to its works."

In keeping with the Romantic notion that rational doctrines need a religious sanction, Prosper Enfantin and his fellow Saint-Simonians proceeded to organize themselves into a hierarchical theocracy whose task it was to exemplify, and thus to propagate, the new gospel of collective love and universal fraternity. They formed themselves into "families" of forty to fifty members, including women as well as men, who met once or twice a week to discuss the "doctrine" and to stage experiments in communal living. Martial hymns were sung before and after meals, and the same "Onward, Christian soldiers" spirit was evident in the blue tunics they wore (with a vest buttoned at the back to remind them that the individual is helpless without the cooperation of his fellow men). The senior members even formed themselves into a College, not unlike that of the cardinals in Rome, and went on to elect two Popes, or "Supreme Fathers." One of them was Enfantin. The other was a converted revolutionary named Saint-Amand Bazard, who finally died of apoplexy brought on by his emotional distress at seeing the Saint-Simonian movement headed in an increasingly mystical, pantheistic, and promiscuous direction.

At the heart of this first schismatic conflict was the feminist problem. Saint-Simon himself had said relatively little about the status of women in the new social order he prophesied — beyond advancing the idea that the fundamental social unit is the couple. He had also suggested that Christianity had made itself unpopular and contributed to its own undoing by attributing exaggerated importance to the virtues of chastity and monastic celibacy. In the hands of his less cautious disciple Enfantin, a robust bachelor who (as one French historian has put it) "was not afraid of wine," this idea of the necessary "rehabilitation of the flesh" ceased to be a doctrinal offshoot and was elevated to the rank of central dogma. Refusing to condone this apologia for free divorce and "divine promiscuity," Bazard, a happily married man of middle age, and a number of other Saint-Simonians protested, and for weeks the feminist problem was heatedly debated in an atmosphere of wild mystic fervor — with certain of the more susceptible disciples undergoing prophetic "seizures," ecstatic trances, and convulsions, as though the Holy Ghost had descended on them and given them the gift of tongues. From this schismatic turmoil Enfantin emerged the victor, and from then on at official functions an empty seat was placed alongside of his own papal "throne" to signify the need for a High Priestess, for a Woman Messiah, to preside over the movement in intimate association with himself.

Like Rasputin or Gurdjeiev, whom he faintly resembles, Enfantin seems to have been endowed with a magnetic gaze which had a powerful impact on women. One of its early victims was Hortense Allart, who after visiting the Saint-Simonian community which he had set up in his suburban house outside of Paris, spent weeks raving about LE PÈRE and announcing her intention of becoming LA MÈRE.

It wasn't long before a far more celebrated authoress was being suggested for the empty seat. The novel which more than any other had persuaded George Sand's feminine contemporaries that she was a believer in "free love" was *Jacques* — a book which today goes unknown and unread but which at the time seemed positively explosive in its implications, being the story of a husband who, to assure his wife's happiness, sacrifices himself in favor of her lover. At the time she wrote this novel, which she began in Venice, George Sand was laboring under the triangular stress of her two affairs with Pagello and Musset, and it did not occur to her that the fictional transposition of her own dilemma would be interpreted as a forthright denunciation of marriage. Whence her surprise, one day at a provincial dinner organized by a group of ladies who had resolutely excluded their husbands from the feast, to find herself being asked to draft a petition favoring the abolition of marriage. "My Lord, how stupid women are when they want to talk about things they know nothing about!" was George Sand's immediate reaction.

In November 1834 she was asked to become one of the "mothers" of the Saint-Simonian "family." George Sand replied that she felt sympathy for what the Saint-Simon doctrine offered men but was uncertain as to what it offered women. *Lélia,* contrary to what many readers had been led to believe, did not contain a general message or a moral code, being essentially one woman's "cry of pain." Those of her women readers who had "so far managed to practice the ancient morality" were advised to go on practicing it. "This moral code, being the most difficult, is certainly the finest, and women who are able to observe it can only lose by abjuring it."

Not content with this plea for marital fidelity, she added: "I hope that the fathers of Saint-Simonism will not undermine the great belief that the love of *one* man for *one* woman is the holiest element of human greatness . . . . Let women correct themselves by taking the purest for examples, let them suffer and pray, while they wait for marriage to cease being a degrading tyranny, albeit remaining a sacred link. What will women achieve through revolt? When the male world has been converted, woman will also be converted without one's having had to bother oneself about her."

Infidelity, for George Sand, was thus no intrinsic virtue; it was a kind of in extremis expedient to which a woman has recourse to protest a state of marital enslavement. As she had written to her friend François Rollinat, in a remarkable letter warning him against the pitfalls of an extramarital affair, the ideal of romantic love — "a mixture of enthusiasm and selfishness" — which had inspired her generation had done nothing to alleviate the lot of contemporary women. "Deprived of the salutary prejudices of devotion, exposed to the intellectual ferments which have seeped into the nooks and crannies of their education, they are no less rigorously chastised by public opinion. Public opinion is made up, on the one hand, of intolerance for cold, ugly, cowardly women, and on the other, of the mocking and insulting criticism of men who don't want devout wives, who don't yet want well-educated wives, and who still want faithful wives. But it is not easy for a woman to be philosophically perplexed and faithful at the same time . . . The women of our time are thus neither well-educated, nor devout, nor chaste, and the moral revolution which should have transformed them to the liking of the male generation has been wrongly undertaken. No attempt was made to raise woman in her own eyes, and to place her on a footing of equality which would have made her capable of virile virtues. Chastity would have been glorious on the part of free women. For women slaves it is a tyranny which wounds them and whose yoke they boldly shake off. I can't blame them for it."

George Sand's intimate conviction was that no satisfactory reform of marriage could be carried through without a simultaneous transformation of society. But she was by now sufficiently imbued with Michel de Bourges' militant republicanism to doubt that such a transformation could be peaceably brought about, as the Saint-Simonians seemed to think, by the contagious success of their experiments in communal living. This was what she had to explain to them in April of 1836, during her last weeks at the Quai Malaquais apartment, when she was agreeably surprised one day by the arrival of a huge collective gift, presented to her by members of the Saint-Simon "family." The gift was composed of fifty-nine different items, most of them handmade or wrought by the "brothers" and "sisters" of the order, and included shoes, trousers, a waistcoat, a hat, cuffs and collars, earrings and necklaces, a brooch, a locket, a purse, a water color, and a riding crop!

Embarrassed to be thus singled out and honored, George Sand, in her letter of grateful acknowledgement, could not conceal the reservations she felt about the idealistic naiveté of these new evangelists, who seemed to think that society could be magically transformed without a shot being fired. "I believe that my old brothers" — she was thinking of Michel de Bourges and his like — "must strike some mighty blows; and that you who are vested with the priestly ministry of innocence and peace, cannot soak your levitic robes in the blood of battle. You are the priests, we are the soldiers . . . ," she went on, only to admit, a little further on, that she herself was too much of a bohemian bard and outsider to be either soldier, priest, master, disciple, prophet, or apostle. "In my poet's head I dream of homeric combats . . . I also dream of the new day after the storm, of a magnificent sunrise, altars strewn with flowers, lawgivers crowned with olive wreaths, the dignity of man rehabilitated, man freed from the tyranny of man, woman from that of woman" — for she had not forgotten the sufferings of her childhood and adolescence, still less the maternal pressures which had pushed her into a disastrous marriage — "a guardianship of love exercised by the priest over man, a guardianship of love exercised by man over woman, a government which will be called *council* and not *domination, persuasion* and not *power* . . ." etc.

Up till now George Sand's views on the problem of woman's position in society had either been privately expressed in salon talk and letters, or indirectly (and often equivocally) transmitted through her fiction. But now, with her lawsuit against her husband due to be debated in public session before the Royal Court of Bourges, she felt the time had come to set the record straight. The opportunity for doing so was conveniently provided by a critical article which appeared, shortly after her return to La Châtre, in the May 15 issue of the *Revue de Paris.* Its author, an obscure pedant named Nisard, while praising the stylistic elegance of George Sand's novels, denounced them as perverse for condemning marriage and championing adultery. "The ruin of husbands, or at least their unpopularity, is the aim of George Sand's works," he roundly declared. To which she proudly retorted, in the following issue of the same fortnightly: "Yes, Monsieur, the ruin of *husbands* would have been the object of my ambition if I had felt imbued with the strength of a reformer. I was much surprised when certain conscientious Saint-Simonian philanthropists . . . in their sincere and estimable search for truth, asked me what I would put in the place of husbands. I replied naively that it would be marriage, just as I believe that it is religion one must put in the place of priests who have done so much to compromise religion."

She went on to point out that "The misconduct of women is often provoked by the ferocity or infamy of men . . . A husband who willfully scorns his duties by laughing, swearing and drinking, *is sometimes* less excusable than the wife who betrays her loved ones by weeping, suffering, and expiating." Marriage would remain an intolerable institution so long as society maintained a hypocritical double standard for judging the behavior of men and women — with an "unlimited indulgence" accorded to male peccadilloes, while the ancient standards of Christian chastity were implacably imposed on the female sex.

*

Soon after she had delivered herself of this ringing rebuttal, George Sand decided to move from the little room she occupied in Duteil's crowded house at La Châtre. By late May it had grown uncomfortably hot and stuffy, while the early morning cries of the children were disturbing for someone who went to bed at about the time the rest of the household came to life. She accordingly moved to the house of her friend Rozanne Bourgoing. Built into the town's ramparts, next to the old fortress-castle (which today houses a George Sand museum), the house commanded a sweeping view over the green meadows of the Indre valley and the pale poplars bordering the river. Directly beneath her window was a tiny garden full of fragrant honeysuckle and roses and beyond it a terrace built out over the cliff, where the family dined and her friends joined them for coffee. "My bedroom is quite vast," George wrote to Marie d'Agoult. "It is decorated with a bed which has red cotton curtains, a real hard, flat peasant bed, two straw chairs and a white wooden table . . . Sometimes at dusk I ride out alone on horseback and return around midnight. My coat, straw hat, and the melancholy trot of my mount make me look in the dark like an itinerant salesman or farm hand."

Charles Didier had meanwhile been growing increasingly fretful. The eight days George Sand had spent in his and David Richard's lodgings had aroused endless gossip about the new "lover" she was reported to have taken. The news had even spread to Didier's hometown of Geneva, from which Liszt had written to his "brother" George to ask if it was true. She answered that there was as much truth in this report as there was in the rumor that Liszt was now living in Geneva with George Sand — though she did admit that she had "relegated Didier to an upstairs garret" while occupying his bedroom, where she had spent several agreeably "patriarchal" days, a statement which Franz, and even more his golden-haired mistress Marie, must have greeted skeptically.

What galled Didier even more than these rumors, which he was too much of a puritan to appreciate, was the cavalier manner in which George let ten days go by after leaving Paris before bothering to write to him. The increasing intimacy of their relations in Paris had led him to believe that they were both on the verge of a sublime romantic passion. Instead, he now realized, or at any rate suspected, that for her he was no more than a passing whim. He answered her first letter with one of his that was full of reproaches, following up a day or two later with another in which he asked her to give up any idea of moving back into his lodgings the next time she came up to Paris. "Her staying with me places me in a false position, and imposes a dangerous test to which I would rather not be exposed," he noted in his diary. "I don't want to play the role she would like to assign to me."

Taking on a new lover, at this delicate moment in her life, was not the kind of action likely to make a favorable impression on the Royal judges of Bourges. George Sand thus had no interest in playing up a friendship which up till now had been "patriarchally" platonic. But this was precisely what the hypersensitive Didier could not accept. He wanted to be a lover, he didn't want to be a friend; and when she wrote to ask if he could get hold of a copy of the *Revue britannique,* which had recently published an unflattering article about a number of French authors, including herself, Didier answered with a tactless letter in which he complained that he was tired of being treated like an errand boy. Why should he, who was not her lover, now be expected publicly to take up the cudgels for her?

George Sand's reply to this ungallant epistle was sharp, long, and furious. "You don't know me at all and you will never know me," she told Didier bluntly. "We are two contrary natures: *you don't love, all I can do is love.* Friendship for you is a contract with clauses for the well-combined advantage of both parties; for me it's sympathy, embrace, identity, it's the complete adoption of the qualities and faults of the person one feels to be one's friend . . . You claim to love me a great deal, yet you attribute to me . . . a calculated dryness, how shall I put it? — something worse, a kind of prostitution of the heart, full of baseness, egotism, falseness, you make me out to be a kind of platonic slut. Heavens! My old friends are right, I should never try to make a new friend . . . My misfortune is to throw myself wholeheartedly at each fine soul I encounter. I imagine that he will open up for me and understand me, as I understand him, that he will be able to see into me with sympathy, just as I do with him — but I'm mistaken. What I took for a noble soul is a gloomy, sickly, suspicious soul that has lost the ability to believe and thus to love. That's what has happened with you and me. It has caused me more pain than I can tell you, and I've had to go back to bed with the fever which had left me and which has suddenly returned . . .

"One doesn't make a henchman of the first fellow who happens along; one would rather be defended by a friend than by a stranger . . . Only, when my friend is there, he doesn't wait for somebody else to seize the passing drunkard who's insulted me and to fling him in the mud. Above all, he doesn't ask whether, having not slept with me, he won't look ridiculous in taking up the cudgels . . ."

By the time she had finished, George Sand must have been exhausted. It was the second such letter she had had to address to Didier in one day. He, as it happened, never received it. For the letter which had immediately preceded it was so shattering that it spurred him to match George's earlier madness in moving into his lodgings with a piece of madness of his own. "If it were only a whim of pride, it would be nothing," he noted in his diary. "But there is a depth of mournful tenderness and of tears which completely disarms me. She breaks with me, but cries. I make no reply; what is there to answer? But I leave for La Châtre . . ."

It must have been, as he noted, an uncomfortable journey, full of nerve-racking doubts and perplexities. He had no idea how he would be received, and he must have realized that his arrival in the little provincial beehive of La Châtre could hardly fail to unleash a buzzing swarm of gossip. What the Bourgoings must have thought when they opened the door to this tall, white-haired stranger with the tinted spectacles, Charles Didier in his diary unfortunately neglected to mention. Rozanne, who had stayed several times at the Quai Malaquais apartment, may already have met him in Paris. It was she presumably who led him into George's room on this dramatic eighteenth of June. She was in bed and even asleep, but she reacted to this surprise visit much as she had in September of 1831, when Jules Sandeau had defied the dog and Casimir's shotgun and climbed into her bedroom at Nohant. "I wake her up and throw myself without a word into her arms," Didier recorded in his diary. "She hugged me in her arms, and a complete reconciliation was made in this long and mute embrace."

That evening she took him to Nohant, which Casimir had fortunately vacated. The five days that followed were, as Didier noted ecstatically, among the loveliest of his life. "I yielded to the charm and abandoned myself to my destiny" — which was apparently to become the latest of George's lovers. Or was it? The laconic language of Didier's diary makes it impossible to say. "The dart sank ever deeper, I made no attempt to pull it out. Horseback rides through the fields, in the bridle paths of *Valentine*. Rustic solitude, the world forgotten. Evenings under the leafy trees of Nohant. Moonlit nights. Always alone, alone for fifteen or twenty hours at a stretch. Nights spent on the terrace, talking beneath the twinkle of the stars, my arm around her and her head resting on my breast. I would have been absolutely happy had the name of M[ichel de Bourges] not been pronounced; but it was and cast a shadow."

Hypocrisy not being one of her virtues, George Sand made no effort to hide the newcomer's presence at Nohant. "I see all her Vallée Noire friends," Didier later noted in his diary, ". . . All good fellows who adore her and whom she poeticizes with an incredible power of imagination . . . She is rewriting *Lélia* according to my ideas, and reads some lovely pages. Charmed, intoxicated, happy, I forget myself in a delightful intimacy. We drive back from Nohant at midnight in the cabriolet, my hand in hers, my arm about her waist. Oh peaceful night! Oh calm days! I abandoned myself without resistance to the charm of living and loving. She had written me a second letter to Paris" — the one quoted from earlier — "after my departure. I burn mine in front of her. The storm has not even left the shadow of a cloud between us. We love each other a thousand times more than before. M[ichel de Bourges] is very jealous of me; he speaks of me in all his letters."

No wonder. The news of this new "friendship" had not only spread to Geneva, it had reached Bourges as well — and had thrown the irascible Michel into a rage. That he could be unfaithful to George any time he wished by sleeping with his wife was one thing, but that his mistress could be unfaithful to him, and at a time when she needed all his eloquence to obtain her separation from her husband, was more than he could endure. Or was it all part of a deliberate act intended to shield her intimate relations with her lawyer behind the smokescreen of a new affair? Didier may have had his

A George Sand Album

GEORGE SAND

by Delacroix

Maurice de Saxe
by Quentin de la Tour

Aurora of Koenigsmark
by unknown painter

The front court of Nohant

Louis-Claude Dupin de Francueil
anonymous pastel

Aurore de Saxe
anonymous pastel

Drawing room at Nohant

Maurice Dupin
by unknown painter

Sophie Dupin
pencil sketch by George Sand

Hippolyte Chatiron
pastel by Aurore de Saxe

Aurore Dupin
pastel by Aurore de Saxe

Aurore and Casimir Dudevant

by François Biard

Maurice Dudevant in 1837

by Luigi Calamatta

Solange

by Mercier

Aurélien de Sèze

by unknown artist

Stéphane Ajasson de Grandsagne

lithograph by Achille Devéria

Jules Sandeau

drawing by Aurore Dudevant

Marie Dorval

lithograph by Jean Gigoux

Sainte-Beuve

by Bornemann

Notre-Dame and the Pont Saint-Michel

by Corot, showing corner house on the right where Aurore and Jules Sandeau lived in mansard flat

Alfred de Musset smoking a cigar

by himself

George Sand with a fan

colored drawing by Alfred de Musset

Pietro Pagello

by Bevilacqua

George Sand and Marie d'Agoult at the theater
by Mme. Edouard Odier

Franz Liszt
by Ary Scheffer

Marie d'Agoult
by Henri Lehmann

Château de Montgivray
home of Hippolyte Chatiron

Michel de Bourges
anonymous lithograph

George Sand
by Julien Boilly

George Sand's writing desk
at Nohant

Lamennais
engraving by Luigi Calamatta

Pierre Leroux
lithograph by Marin Lavigne

Louis Blanc
by Geoffroy

Franz Liszt
caricature by George Sand

Pierre Bocage
in costume for
Les Beaux Messieurs de Bois-Doré

George Sand in 1838

by Delacroix

Chopin

sketch by George Sand

The Charterhouse of Valldemosa in 1840

by J. B. Laurens

Auguste Clésinger

lithograph by Lafosse

Solange

drawing by Clésinger

Chopin in 1838

by Delacroix

Marionettes at Nohant

George Sand and Ledru-Rollin

by unknown artist

Pauline García Viardot

by Maurice Sand

Charles Marchal
photographed by Bingham

Alexandre Manceau
photographed by Nadar

Gustave Flaubert
photographed by Nadar

Alexandre Dumas *fils*
by Edouard Dubufe

Maurice Sand
photographed by Nadar

Lina Calamatta Sand
photographed by Nadar

George Sand
photographed by Nadar

doubts. Though he received several letters from George after his return to Paris — one of which he could describe as "adorable . . . full of tenderness and sweetness, affectionate, caressing . . ." — in July she let three weeks go by without writing him a word.

One may well wonder if, even in their tenderest moments together, when she curled up at his knees or let her head repose on his chest, Didier wasn't a sentimental ersatz for the ardent lover she would secretly have liked to have been hugging. From the amorous point of view this July was a singularly frustrating month. It was so hot that she could not concentrate on her writing. Instead, she wore herself out in long, early morning walks — sometimes she even rose at three — and plunged into the cool waters of the Indre full-clothed or in a slip (after hanging her dress on a bush) when the sun's rays became too burning. Her feeling of frustrated solitude was further exacerbated by Michel de Bourges' furious letters, which moved her to write to Marie d'Agoult: "Of *great men* I have had my fill . . . As long as they live, they are nasty, persecuting, crotchety, despotic, bitter, suspicious. They are worse for their friends than for their enemies."

These angry words were soon forgotten when, in the fourth week of July, she finally left for Bourges with Alexis Duteil and his wife. George was put up by her friend Eliza Tourangin, the daughter of a wealthy cloth merchant related to Duteil, in whose spacious house and garden she led a conspicuously demure life. For here, as in Paris, she had to face a constant stream of visitors. At Michel's suggestion, Solange was let out of boarding school and brought down to Bourges by the obliging Gustave Papet to enhance Madame Dudevant's image as a dutiful mother. Those who had expected to see her stride around in red trousers and a pistol belt were sorely disappointed, and many an innocent burgher must have failed to realize that the small, simply dressed woman with the shawl and bonnet whom he had just passed in the street was that paragon of female sinfulness, George Sand.

Casimir's appeal had attracted so much attention that special seating arrangements had to be made for the unusually large number of ladies who wanted to attend the two-day trial session, which began on July 25. Madame Dudevant appeared in a simple white dress and cape, with a falling collar and a flowered shawl. Though the Royal judges were regarded as generally hostile to her, most of the onlookers were on her side. Casimir's lawyer, Thiot-Varennes, did his best to portray Baron Dudevant as a model husband who had had the misfortune to marry an unbridled wife, but his conclusion — that Madame Dudevant should tamely ask her husband's forgiveness and agree to return under the marital roof — inevitably fell flat.

Michel de Bourges, who followed, had little difficulty depicting the ignominy of a husband who had been living for years off the income provided by his wife's property. If this case had attracted so much attention, he said, it was because it was a case of persecuted genius. In an effort to make her sound adulterous, Casimir's lawyer had read an extract from the long "Confession" Aurore had addressed to her husband in 1825. Using the same "Confession," Michel read Aurore's account of how at Lourdes she had said goodbye to her youthful passion (Aurélien de Sèze, unnamed), and as it was reported in the press: "This passage, written at the age of twenty with a magic style and a brilliance of coloration worthy of the finest pages penned by the author of *Jacques,* produced an impression impossible to describe."

The most telling argument of all was a quotation from D'Aguesseau, the famous lawgiver and magistrate who had served as Minister of Justice under Louis XV: "It is folly as well as impiety to wish to keep an adulterous woman in one's house." Addressing Casimir directly in his deep, stentorian voice, Michel added dramatically: "And you wish to be allowed to prove your wife's ill conduct and to gather testimonials for the facts advanced in your request; with one hand you claim her, with the other you sink a dagger in her breast!"

At the conclusion of the two-day session, the ten judges split five to five in an inconclusive decision. The announcement was greeted with a storm of boos and whistling from the spectators, who were manifestly favorable to Madame Dudevant. Without waiting for a later hearing, in which his marital misdemeanors would have been even more brutally denounced, Casimir now accepted the settlement he had first signed and then refused to honor. He was granted the income from the town house in Paris on condition that he pay the expenses of his son's boarding-school education and guarantee him an annual allowance of 2400 francs beginning in his twentieth year. Aurore, who was authorized to see Maurice whenever he was let out of boarding school, was granted exclusive custody over Solange and the ownership of Nohant.

When two days later she returned from Bourges, she found the villagers gaily dancing under the elms in front of the mossy church to the raucous wheeze of a bagpipe. It was Sunday, and they were celebrating the feast day of Saint Anne, the village's patron saint. Never had the rustic music or the joyous cries of the dancers sounded sweeter to her ears than now, as she drove in through the stone gateway. Nohant at last was hers.

25. Dr. Piffoël and the Humanitarians

FROM NOHANT, where she spent the first days of August dismissing servants who had been too sympathetic to Casimir, George wrote to Charles Didier in Paris, asking him to remove Maurice from his boarding school and to bring him down to the country. It was apparently a friendly invitation — to judge by a letter she simultaneously dispatched to Gustave Papet (who had meanwhile returned to Paris from Bourges) — in which she wrote: "I hope that he [Didier] will soon visit me, and my joy would be perfect if you could come at the same time." But, she added, she would have to limit her invitation to several weeks; for toward the end of August she would be leaving for a month-long trip to Switzerland with Michel de Bourges. This news hit the melancholy Charles Didier like a mace stroke. Too much in love with George to be able to consider sharing her affections with another man, he preferred to stay in Paris sulking; and the thirteen-year-old Maurice finally had to make the stagecoach trip to Châteauroux alone.

Ever since she had broken with Musset, some sixteen months before, George Sand had dreamed of going on a hiking tour of Switzerland, inevitably linked in her imagination with Childe Harold and the Castle of Chillon. Later she had even hoped to spend part of a winter in Geneva, to which Franz Liszt and Marie d'Agoult had moved to get away from the critical "high society" of the Faubourg Saint-Germain, where their "unprincipled" liaison was harshly judged. That the flaxen-haired Marie should dare flout convention by abandoning her aristocratic husband to live in sin with a pianist-composer whose father had served as bailiff for a Prince Esterházy in Hungary was already considered shocking; and that she should follow this up by giving birth to an illegitimate daughter was regarded as the height of scandal. For George Sand, too, Geneva beckoned like a haven, and not simply because it was surrounded by snow-capped mountains which exalted her romantic craving for the sublime. At his boarding school Maurice had been subjected to cruel teasing by other students who had read in the *Gazette des Tribunaux* (which specialized in reporting court proceedings) that in Bordeaux Madame Dudevant had made the acquaintance of young men with whom she had done things an honest woman does not do, and that later in Italy she had done the same. Aurore was understandably anxious to remove her children beyond the range of gossip, which was as rampant at La Châtre as in Paris. A trip into the mountains, which Franz and Marie were planning, thus afforded a welcome diversion and the possibility of an Alpine honeymoon with Michel de Bourges.

Michel, however, did not accompany her to Geneva — causing her to remark bitterly in a letter sent to Charles d'Aragon that "Man is nastier in love than in a state of indifference or even hatred." Though the documentary evidence is missing — his letters to George Sand having later been destroyed — the reasons for his failure to join her in Switzerland are not hard to guess. Michel's wife had not taken kindly to her husband's liaison with France's most famous woman writer, while he was enraged by the "affair" he was convinced she was carrying on with Charles Didier. There was presumably some sort of explanation between them when George passed through Bourges on August 28, but that was the last she saw of *her* Michel. Hers proved to be a kind of widowed honeymoon, as accompanied by Maurice, Solange, her childhood friend Ursule, and a maid, she journeyed on to Autun. Here an affluent young Royalist she happened to meet at a stage-post inn, Gustave de Gévaudan, was so taken by her provocative dark eyes and unceremonious speech that he insisted on accompanying them over the rough roads of the Jura mountains to Geneva.

A note left at the hotel where they were to meet informed her that Liszt and Marie d'Agoult had already left for Chamounix (as it was then spelled) in the Haute-Savoie and that a Geneva friend named

Adolphe Pictet had stayed behind to keep her and the children company. The "Major," as he was called (for his pioneering work on percussion shells in the Swiss artillery), turned out to be a walking encyclopedia of scientific, linguistic, and philosophical information, and they had not been together five minutes before they were engaged in a heated argument over the democratic merits of the Swiss republics. His roguish bearded face reminded her curiously of Mephistopheles "in a custom official's hood," while George, in a beltless blouse floating loosely over a black silk cravat and a gold-buttoned waistcoat, reminded him at first of a bell . . . and then . . . but he was soon too confused to say. For the first thing she did was to hand the Major a "poetic cigar," as she termed it in her husky, contralto voice — a cigar wrapped in trumpet lily instead of tobacco leaves which gave off an extraordinarily sweet-scented smoke and made him feel a trifle dizzy.

George Sand's subsequent arrival at the Hôtel de l'Union — to her ear it sounded more like *onion* — at Chamounix, seems to have created the same kind of bewilderment. The hotel was full of impeccably top-hatted English gentlemen accompanied by their demurely veiled spouses whom the short, trousered newcomer did not in the least resemble. The hotel manager first took her for a dark-haired page in the service of the young Gustave de Gévaudan, who had volunteered to accompany her into the mountains.

Escorted upstairs to room number 13, she could hardly see anything as the door was pushed open by the candle-holding maid. The first object she almost tripped over in the flickering light was Liszt's pupil Puzzi, seated astride a sleeping bag. The pandemonium which followed — with the statuesque Marie d'Agoult being embraced by the "page," who was simultaneously being hugged by the equally long-haired Liszt — so bewildered the maid that she went downstairs to report to the kitchen staff that the hotel had been invaded by a troupe of gypsies.

When Adolphe Pictet joined them a little later, he found the fair-haired Marie d'Agoult seated at one end of the sofa holding a scent bottle in her hand, while the dark-haired George, seated at the other end, was quietly puffing on a long Turkish pipe. Liszt, at her feet, was seated on the floor. The atmosphere was charmingly informal but a bit perplexing for the academic Major. After George had taken a candle and retired to her room, he had to admit that in all his years of traveling and studying — and he had gone as far as Berlin to be taught philosophy by Hegel, no less — he had never encountered a creature quite like this one. Liszt insisted that there was nothing mysterious abut her; she was like a piece of rock crystal, containing streaks and bubbles, which would "never hide any of its faults." Pictet remained unconvinced. She reminded him of a Sphinx whose impenetrable gaze seemed to say: "Guess what I am, or tumble into the abyss!"

The argument was interrupted by some loud swearing from down below. Liszt opened the window and saw three Englishmen pointing indignantly upward. They had been enjoying the crisp evening air when some unspeakable bounder, up there, yes, in the room next to his, had poured water on their heads! Liszt went downstairs in an effort to placate them and later persuaded George Sand to lean out over the flower box in her window to apologize for her "absent-mindedness."

The next morning they rose before dawn for the long trek up to the Mer de Glace. Elegant as ever, Marie d'Agoult led the way in a neat traveling dress and floating veil, holding a dainty parasol over the mule, which the guide led with a halter. Next came Ursule and then the two children mounted on the same donkey and uttering joyful squeals. George Sand, with a broad-brimmed straw hat on her head, sat crossed-saddled smoking cigarettes, while Liszt, dressed in a blouse and velvet beret, followed behind with Gévaudan, and finally the Major, in his military cloak and cap. The rising sun, burning away the valley mists, revealed a brilliant panorama of dark pines and snowy peaks which Marie d'Agoult kept stopping to admire.

"All these stops are fine," George finally shouted. "But they are lazy excuses for remaining majestically seated on your mules!"

Sliding off her own, she gaily challenged the Major to a slope-climbing race — up to a dark gray rock perched some distance above them. With that she was off, like a mountain goat, scrambling up a rocky gulley and following a zigzag course, while Pictet, choosing a steeper path, sought in vain to catch up. She was there to give him a helping hand, up the last few feet. There were cheers from down below, as George came laughing down the mountainside and triumphantly remounted her mule.

When they reached the Bossons glacier, she was much amused to hear her daughter remark in the imperious tone she confidently assumed now that she was turning eight: "Don't worry, George, when I become Queen I'll give you all of the Mont Blanc."

That night the crowded dining room was full of candles and they had to content themselves with one end of a table opposite a plump Briton who kept eyeing them suspiciously.

"Who are those people?" he asked his neighbor, who had to confess he didn't know.

"Monsieur, qui est ce peuple?" he repeated to a Frenchman seated nearby.

The Frenchman told him that the man in the military gear (Pictet) was fluent in Sanskrit and any other language he could name. The pale young fellow (Liszt) could play any instrument with equal ease, while the young boy with the dark hair (George Sand) was an incomparable juggler! The Englishman adjusted his pince-nez with curiosity. George Sand pulled out a lorgnette and subjected him to equally sharp scrutiny.

"My Lord, but he's ugly!" she exclaimed, while the red-faced Briton hastily removed his bifocals.

Liszt was so amused to hear himself referred to as "that fellow" that he decided to adopt it as a pseudonym. From then on he and Marie d'Agoult were regularly referred to as Mr. and Mrs. Fellows, or more simply "the Fellows," for the benefit of British travelers, whose sedate slumbers might have been disturbed by the knowledge that they had had to share a table or a corridor with a pair of unmarried sinners. George, who invariably gave herself a huge proboscis when she drew herself in caricature, assumed the name of "Piffoëls" — giving a ludicrous Helvetian twist to the French slang term *pif* (distantly related to the English "sniff"), which designates a big nose.

Liszt ordered a bowl of hot punch brought upstairs. It came in flaming and made a most impressive sight. George, who had privately agreed with Franz that they must get the Major drunk, pulled several of her datura-leaf cigars from a cedarwood box and had Liszt hand them to the intended victim. These "poetic cigars," which a friend had sent her from some Middle Eastern country, may well have contained a touch of opium. In the euphoria of the moment the donors forgot themselves and began smoking them too. No one could recall the next morning just what had happened next — save for the abstemious Marie d'Agoult, who reported that when last seen (for she had finally walked out in disgust) Liszt had been angrily silencing the chairs that were singing out of tune with a candle snuffer, the Major was carrying on a learned discourse with some invisible partners lodged somewhere in the ceiling, while Piffoëls skipped around the room uttering wild hoots of laughter.

As though to belie any idea that she might have been a bit "high" the previous evening, George Sand appeared the next day dressed in a smart black riding coat, a sky blue cravat (which contrasted sharply with the piece of twisted silk Liszt habitually wound around his neck), and a pair of immaculate white trousers. A round Spanish-style hat and a pair of suede leather boots completed the attire. Marie d'Agoult could not conceal her surprise, asking her friend if she thought she was in Paris and about to go to the Opéra. This, George explained, was her "indoor costume" — for rainy weather.

They were pursued by downpours for the rest of the trip. At Lucerne Marie and George were almost poisoned after eating some indigestible dish. But while Marie found consolation in Franz Liszt's arms, George spent a more than usually painful night, pining for her absent Michel. There was another stop at Fribourg to visit the cathedral. No one seeing them could have guessed that the urchin in the dripping blouse and mud-splattered gaiters was Europe's most famous woman writer or that the long-haired young man was the Continent's foremost piano virtuoso.

George Sand's stay in Geneva, which lasted ten days, was less anonymous, arousing as much curious (and not always friendly) gossip as had Liszt's and Marie d'Agoult's arrival in the Protestant city. Everywhere she went — whether to listen to a Calvinist preacher, go to the theater, dine in a well-known restaurant, or attend a concert given by the young Puzzi — she was the focus of all eyes. But it was not only the staid burghers of Geneva she shocked, for Madame Cohen, the mother of the piano-playing prodigy who came from Hamburg, could not forgive her for casually strolling through the streets — on the arm of her son, furthermore — dressed in man's clothes and smoking a cigar.

While they were shunned by the prim aristocracy inhabiting Geneva's hill-climbing *vieille ville,* all of Liszt's less conventional friends — such as the composer Franz Grast, the ardently republican James Fazy (founder of the *Journal de Genève*), and the painter Nancy Mérienne, who did at least one protrait of George Sand during her stay — came to call on her in Marie d'Agoult's salon on the Rue de Tabazan. In the evening Liszt would play the piano, while George stretched out unceremoniously under it — this being, she stubbornly maintained, the only place she could really feel "enveloped" by his music. Inspired by a rondo Franz had just completed, George spent one particularly fertile night writing *Le Contrebandier,* a charming piece of nonsense about a Basque outlaw who could improvise the strangest verses to a familiar village tune. Berlioz later claimed (with pardonable exaggeration) that the finest technical analysis of Liszt's work would never "approach this lovely transposition into poetic prose."

Accompanied once again by Gustave de Gévaudan, George Sand left Geneva in late September and headed back for Nohant. Her one regret throughout had been that Michel de Bourges could not have been with them to share in their bohemian pranks and merriment, and incidentally to make fun of the indolent Legitimist who had dutifully (and platonically) tagged along. But at Lyon, where she had looked forward to a passionate reunion, there was no sign of Michel. Here she spent four frustrating days cooped up in a hotel room, where she tried to absorb herself in her writing while her self-appointed bodyguard and swain took the children out for walks along the banks of the Rhone. She found herself again without a centime, and though it hurt her pride to do so, she had to borrow money from one of Liszt's Lyon friends as well as from her traveling companion and Frédéric Girerd, a lawyer friend of Michel's whom she sought out when they reached Nevers. Gustave's family chateau being located nearby, he now took leave of George Sand, who traveled on to Bourges with her children and Ursule — only to discover that Michel had in the meantime left for Lyon, in the hope of meeting her there!

The upshot of these crossed paths and purposes was a furious exchange of letters between Bourges and Nohant. Michel accused her of infidelity with Gustave de Gévaudan — a charge she angrily denied, saying that she was neither a *femme galante* nor a coquette, that she could have had twenty lovers during her Swiss tour if she had wanted to, but that in this respect she was as pure as the piece of rock crystal she had specially brought back for him.

"Love with you is a form of sickness, with me it's a sentiment. You think you can spit in my face when the taste of bile is on your lips. This, according to you, is a right, an attribute, an inevitable consequence of the love which the strong feel for the weak. You know I have never accepted such conditions . . .

"Save for Liszt, who is like a brother to me and whom I kiss every evening and morning in the presence of his mistress and *coram populo*" — in public — "I neither gave nor received a single masculine kiss from Bourges to Geneva, and from Geneva to Bourges . . . I won't hide the fact that my chastity caused me great suffering. I had very troubling dreams. The blood came rushing to my head a hundred times, and under the hot sun, in the midst of lovely mountains, listening to the birds sing and inhaling the soft scents of woods and valleys, I often had to go sit apart, my soul brimful of love and my knees trembling with voluptuous desire. I am still young and though I tell other men that I have an ancient's calm, my blood is hot and in the presence of an intoxicatingly beautiful nature love boils inside me like the sap of life in the universe."

Nothing could have been easier for her than to indulge in a secret tryst or two, enjoying "a moment of brutality which Catherine the Great would hardly have turned down. What kept me from this sullying misdeed, trifling in itself but ineffaceable for those who love, is not what women call their virtue, a word which for me is meaningless. It's the love I harbor in my heart and which causes me to feel an insurmountable disgust at the idea of being amorously hugged in the arms of any other man but you. It's of you I dream when I wake up drenched in sweat, you I call when sublime nature sings her passionate hymns and the mountain air penetrates my pores with a thousand pinpricks of enthusiasm and desire."

In short, the last thing she had expected to find on her return was a letter such as "an aged banker might write to a kept girl . . . Try to calm and cure yourself, try to see clearly and to abdicate your despotic ideas, and to understand that I too have just as much right in the eyes of God to walk and breathe and to sit down next to persons of the other sex and to exchange human words with creatures of my species . . ."

Skilled though she was in the ways of amorous deception, there is good reason to believe that George Sand was here speaking the truth. It is unfortunate that only a handful of the many letters she wrote to Michel de Bourges have so far been published, for the others would probably have told us a lot about the real nature of her relations with Charles Didier. Almost certainly those relations were more platonic than the five days of "sweet intimacy" they had spent together at Nohant might lead one to suspect; and if she had become Didier's mistress, it was but briefly and reluctantly.

In mid-October, when the time came to reenter Maurice and Solange in their respective boarding schools, she wrote to Didier to say she would be staying with him for a few days. But she promptly changed her mind when Marie d'Agoult, who had left Geneva with Liszt a week or two before, wrote to say that Franz had found a suite, with a "somewhat pompous salon," in the Hôtel de France on the Rue Neuve-Laffitte (not far from where the Paris Opera now stands). George was invited to join them in the same hotel. "Get me a room with a big bed for Solange and myself, and a sofa or folding cot for Maurice," Piffoëls immediately replied. "We'll share the salon, as we shall our friends. Those of mine you don't like will be received on the landing."

George's room was on the second floor above the entresol, while the suite occupied by Marie d'Agoult and Liszt was one floor further up. She could thus have lived a relatively independent life if she had wished to — something she showed few signs of wanting to do. When Charles Didier called on her shortly after her arrival, she complained of his disgruntled air and coldness of manner, but insisted on treating him as a friend, no more. Two evenings later she let him take her to the theater, but when at last they were alone, she seemed so profoundly unhappy that she stretched out at his feet and would not let him touch her.

Originally she had only intended staying a week or two in Paris — the time needed to put Solange and Maurice in school. The fees she had had to pay to various lawyers during the legal tug of war with her husband had bled her white, and according to Buloz's calculations, she now owed her publisher 10,000 francs (considerably more than $10,000 in terms of today's purchasing power). Living in Paris had now become a luxury she could ill afford, but she could not leave the city because of Maurice's ill health. Though his ailment was diagnosed as "hypertrophy of the heart," there is no doubt that Maurice's troubles were primarily psychological and that the hypersensitive young boy dreaded the prospect of returning to school and of having to face the cruel taunting of his fellow boarders.

Often accused by her friends of hopelessly spoiling her only son, Aurore tried for once to be frozen-hearted: Maurice *had* to return to school like the other young boys of his age. The Abbé de Lamennais, a frequent caller at the Hôtel de France, lectured him gently in the same sense: his father (who was in Paris at this time) was already annoyed with him for being so late, and Maurice owed him a minimum of filial obedience. Dutifully Maurice returned to school. His mother came to see him the first two days and found him looking dreadfully peaked and haggard. The third day, afraid that her maternal feelings would get the better of her self-control, she sent the maid, who returned with a message from the school doctor: Maurice was in the infirmary and would she please come to pick him up. The mere suggestion that he would have to return to the classroom, the doctor later explained to her, was enough to touch off a violent acceleration of the heartbeat, which only abated when Maurice was told he could return home to his mother.

Casimir, who came to see Maurice at the Hôtel de France — at Aurore's specific request — and who took him back to his Paris apartment several times, only made matters worse by accusing his son of cowardice. He was a pampered mama's boy, deliberately feigning to be ill to avoid having to go back to school! But by God, he was going to make a man of him, even if it meant shipping him to the Indies as a cabin boy! Though there was an element of truth in these brutal accusations, the threats that accompanied them turned the poor boy into a nervous wreck. He lost his appetite, was subject to fainting fits and to prolonged spells of trembling; the little sleep he got at night was punctuated by agitated dreams. Three other physicians were called in for consultation, and all agreed with the school doctor that Maurice was too ill to be readmitted.

In the midst of these maternal, financial, and sentimental cares — torn as she was between a choleric, unstable, and despotic Michel de Bourges and a morbidly possessive Charles Didier, whose gloomy disposition was now getting on her nerves — George Sand had to face the ceaseless commotion of the Hôtel de France. In the staid backwaters of Geneva Marie d'Agoult had felt a bit like a "carp tossed out on the lawn," as she liked to put it. But in Paris she was back in her element, even though she had now completely broken with the aristocratic Left Bank and the titled snobs of the Faubourg Saint-Germain. The persons invited to her "pompous" salon comprised a characteristically eclectic mélange of poets — Didier, Heinrich Heine, the Polish mystic Adam Mickiewicz; composers — Meyerbeer, Berlioz, and on rare occasions Chopin; musicians — the Belgian violinist Joseph Massart and the operatic tenor Adolphe Nourrit; conformist and nonconformist Christians — the militantly Catholic Baron Ferdinand d'Eckstein (a converted Jew who had become the editor of an important religious weekly) and the heretical Abbé de Lamennais; "liberal" intellectuals and journalists — Victor Schoelcher, an anti-slave-trade pamphleteer, the Saint-Simonian Emile Barrault, and the former Saint-Simonian Pierre Leroux, who was now trying to develop a new philosophy of his own.

Many of them, including Liszt, had been seriously attracted by the ideas of Saint-Simon, and virtually all of them were convinced that in the brave, new world of tomorrow which they were intent on preparing, the artist was destined to fill a special, God-ordained role. Typical in this respect was Heinrich Heine, who had left Germany and established himself in Paris in 1831, not only because of the July Revolution but because Saint-Simonism seemed to him the religion of the future. No longer was society to be hamstrung by antiquated notions or absurd prejudices — like the one that had forced Heine to abjure his Jewish faith and to be baptized a Christian in order to obtain a law degree, or the unwritten code that had so angered the young Liszt when he had first come to Paris, according to which musicians were only admitted to the finest Paris salons by way of the servant staircase and for the duration of their performances. In the new organization of the world which they were determined to promote, artists were to be placed alongside of, if not above scientists and engineers in the hierarchical organization of society.

Thus was born the idea that the artist had a socially useful role and that his mission was to work for the education and advancement of the whole of society and not for the private delectation of a privileged minority. Though George Sand had taken a dim view of the Saint Simonians' fumbling efforts to found a new church headed by a self-proclaimed Messiah, she could not but be sympathetic to this conception of the artist's sacred mission. No one had proclaimed it more emphatically than Liszt's friend, the bearded Emile Barrault: "One art alone has preserved real power — music. The most popular artist of our time is probably a musician." He meant, of course, Liszt. "This vague and mysterious language which appeals to all souls . . . should be the only common language among men."

This belief in the educative value of music was no empty slogan for Franz Liszt and his friends, any more than was their denunciation of art for art's sake and their conviction that art must not only be beautiful but socially *useful* — an idea which George Sand was to do much to propagate in her novels. A German priest named Mainzer, who like Heine had been more or less forced to leave his homeland for daring to express dangerously "liberal" opinions, was already organizing classes of musical instruction for workingmen, while Adolphe Nourrit, though a fashionable Opéra tenor, was training choirs of four hundred workingmen to sing cantatas with French librettos written by Lamartine, another Saint-Simon enthusiast.

Because they spoke incessantly of the need to civilize and educate humanity — an idea which made the dandified Alfred de Musset laugh and caused the sceptical Sainte-Beuve (a disillusioned Saint-Simonian) to shake his head — Franz Liszt, George Sand, and their friends were commonly known as the *humanitarians.* They were, inevitably, the butt of much joking — as in this contemporary newspaper account of a typical philosophico-musical evening at the Hôtel de France:

You climb fifty-seven steps and then ring at the gate of Paradise. The bell rope is an ancient belt which would formerly have graced a lady of the Court. It's not Saint Peter who comes to open; it's a maid who opens the gate of Heaven. She is red-haired and from Picardy.

For we are at the Humanitarians'. You introduce yourself as an Apostle, you come recommended by two or three saints, and you are admitted. The blond and very well behaved Divinity [Marie d'Agoult] *greets you charmingly.*

All the Gods are reunited . . . Four old Gods play a hand of whist in one corner . . . Here is one who deigns to be famous in our gangrenous society; he is fat and well fed, a strong and melodious divinity [Adolphe Nourrit]. *Another God approaches him. What a contrast! This latter God is as thin as a matchstick: it's the God Franz!*

"What if we had a little music? Puzzi, open the piano!" . . .

The God Franz seats himself; his hair falls in waves to the floor. Inspiration comes, the God's eye catches fire, his hair shudders, his fingers grow tense and furiously pound the keys; he plays with his hands, his elbows, his chin, his nose. Everything that can pound pounds away . . .

There are cries of "Sublime!"

"It will cost me twenty francs in repairs," remarks the Divinity of the House.

The Puzzi God says nothing, but faints away.

"Franz! You are yourself!" says a deep-throated male voice.

The God thus named is clad in a Turkish costume. A floss silk shawl is wound round his head like a turban, he wears white pantaloons and boiled leather babouches. He is smoking cheap tobacco in a porcelain-bowl pipe. The Turkish God's posture is very oriental; enveloped in clouds of smoke, he is the center of conversation. Some greet him with a: "Bonjour, George!", *others ask: "How are you, Madame?"*

"Well Major [Pictet]," *says the God George to another God, "how do you like this costume?"*

"You look like a camel merchant."

"Our good Major! Always frank . . . and primitive!"

Then a small, dapper weasel-faced God whom everyone calls Monsieur l'Abbé [Lamennais] *bobs up and down, unrolling a sheet of paper. People gather around him; it's a speech against the Pope, they whisper, you'll see how the Abbé has treated him! The Abbé reads, everyone applauds, midnight strikes, it's time to retire . . . The evening was charming — with plenty of talk, card games, music, smoking, drinking, and reading . . . Delighted, you pick up your hat and withdraw from the humanitarian Olympus.*

The role of Jupiter on this bohemian Olympus inevitably fell to Liszt. For as Heinrich Heine was to write, when Liszt began working up a storm on the piano, "we would see the flashes of lightning dart across his face, his limbs shook as though buffeted by the tempest, and his long floating hair seemed to drip from the downpour thus rendered."

If Liszt was the keyboard's Michelangelo, Frédéric Chopin (to quote Heine again) was the "Raphael of the pianoforte." A refugee from the Cossack butchery of Warsaw, he had been living since the autumn of 1831 in Paris, where his fame as a performer, as well as a composer, had soon spread beyond the small circle of salons he frequented. But when his friend Liszt informed him that George Sand would like to meet him, Chopin replied that he did not know how to talk to a "bluestocking" — which is what he apparently thought a woman author must be.

Early in November of this same year (1836) Chopin gave in to his friend's eloquent entreaties and let Franz bring George, as well as Marie d'Agoult (whom he already knew), to his Chaussée d'Antin apartment. It was a memorable evening — and not only because it brought Chopin and George Sand together for the first time. Liszt (though he spared his friend's piano) was at his apocalyptic best, while Chopin dazzled everyone with a keyboard takeoff on Meyerbeer's *Les Huguenots,* which was so delicately executed that his listeners did not quite know whether to laugh or cry.

Chopin seems to have been more repelled than attracted by George Sand's mannish mode of dress. "Is it really a woman? I am inclined to doubt it," he is reported to have remarked to Ferdinand Hiller, the German pianist and composer. He was in any case rarely present at the musical soirees held in Marie d'Agoult's salon. Unlike his fellow Pole, Mickiewicz, whose poem *Dziady* (*The Forefathers*) had inspired Lamennais, Chopin had little taste for Romantic mysticism and preferred to leave theological discussions to others. He was above all else a Polish patriot, with a deep detestation of Russian imperialism, and he was too skeptically and esthetically inclined to share Liszt's humanitarian hopes for the transformation of society.

There is no record of George Sand having seen Chopin again until December 13, when she was invited to his apartment to meet the music-loving Marquis de Custine and the novelist Eugène Sue. The heavily curtained apartment had been specially decorated for the occasion, with bowls and low vases full of violets — Chopin's favorite flower — and a cluster of flickering candles on the piano. George made a spectacular entry, dressed in white pantaloons, a scarlet sash, and a frogged jacket with crimson buttons — thus sporting the red and white colors of the Polish flag. Far more diffident in public than her "scandalous" attire led strangers to believe, she quickly withdrew to the fireplace, and after sitting down on a settee, she enveloped herself in a defensive cloud of cigar smoke while conversing with the slender, pale-faced Eugène Sue.

The company included a number of musicians — including the Czech pianist and composer Johann Peter Pixis and Joseph Brzowski, a composer of religious music recently arrived from Warsaw. Present too were Antoine Berryer, an arch-Royalist deputy and lawyer who was generally regarded as the finest orator France had produced since Mirabeau, the ardently republican journalist Victor Schoelcher, and a number of Polish exiles, led by the massive Albert Grzymala, a bitter enemy of the Russians who had fought under Napoleon during the winter campaign of 1812, been wounded, and spent three years as a prisoner at Poltava.

Liszt, as usual, dominated the evening, telling stories and fencing verbally with Chopin before sitting down next to him at the piano (Chopin on the left, Liszt on the right) to execute a dazzling performance of Moscheles' E-Flat Sonata for four hands which left Brzowski absolutely spellbound. After ices had been passed around and tea served by Marie d'Agoult, Adolphe Nourrit sang several Schubert lieder, accompanied by Liszt — who ended the evening, typically enough, not at the keyboard, but involved in a long philosophical discussion with one of his Polish friends.

Neither George Sand nor Chopin could have guessed at this point what was to grow out of these first two encounters. We do not even know if they saw each other again before the year 1836 was out. In all probability they did; for by the early spring of 1837 George was imploring Liszt and Marie d'Agoult to bring Chopin and his friend Grzymala down with them to Nohant. She was still desperately in love with Michel de Bourges, who was now blowing hot and cold, and sensing that her own passion was increasingly unrequited, she not unnaturally looked to music for spiritual consolation.

26. Twelve Months of Drama

SHORTLY BEFORE the New Year of 1837 Liszt and Marie d'Agoult moved from the Hôtel de France into a nearby apartment. George Sand had intended to leave directly for Nohant with Maurice (whom Casimir had finally relinquished to her custody), while the robust Solange was entrusted to the care of a Paris boarding school. But heavy snowfalls and a last-minute quarrel with Buloz, accused of needlessly holding up the sixteen-volume edition of her Complete Works, delayed her departure. Too poor to afford another week at the hotel, she fell back once again on Charles Didier's hospitality.

This renewed proximity did nothing to improve their increasingly tense relations. What Didier took to be a mark of favor was for George no more than a temporary expedient. In the end she was obliged to stay ten days with the lovesick poet, whose fumbling attempts at intimacy were pitilessly rebuffed. A night or two after New Year's there was a particularly painful scene between them. She accused him of being a sensuous materialist, only interested in physically possessing her; he accused her of being an amorous coquette who liked to "try out" new lovers as they came along. She withdrew to her room in a huff, and when a contrite Didier came in a little later to apologize, she pushed him out, preferring to spend the night next to her son. For the next three days they hardly spoke to each other. Didier went down on his knees, begged her to forgive his verbal brutality, and reluctantly she let him kiss her hand. But when the time came for her to leave, the farewells exchanged were (as Didier noted in his diary) "cold and furtive."

Instead of taking the stagecoach, George Sand had decided to return to Nohant in the cabriolet she had borrowed from her friends in Bourges. Having no coachman to drive the horses, she had enlisted the services of another *cavalier servant* — a twenty-eight-year-old baron named Antoine Scipion du Roure, who was a friend of François Rollinat's musically gifted brother, Charles. It was a slow journey, with short relays to spare the frail Maurice. Even so, Scipion du Roure must have been surprised by the length of their stopover at Bourges. It lasted the better part of two days — much of them spent by George Sand in tearful tête-à-têtes with Michel de Bourges. He accused her once again of having slept with Gustave de Gévaudan during the four-week Swiss tour and asked her to return all the letters he had written to her. What he had to say about her latest "flirt" — Scipion du Roure — we do not know, but it was probably in the same truculent vein.

This brutal rebuff plunged her yet again into depths of suicidal gloom. From Nohant she wrote Michel a pathetic letter: ". . . The stars are veiled, the snow is falling, the earth is silently covered with its shroud. My soul is as sad as the night, as sad as winter. My hopes are vanished; my life drags on indifferently toward a haphazard goal . . . For me there is only one certainty, one certitude: it's that I love you, Michel."

In late January the arrival of a new tutor for Maurice — an aspiring young journalist with a marked taste for poetry named Eugène Pelletan — helped to pull George from her amorous despondency. He was followed in early February by Marie d'Agoult, who arrived with a magnificent portrait which Luigi Calamatta had painted of Liszt. Marie was installed downstairs in what had once been Madame Dupin de Francueil's bedroom. George had already moved upstairs, next to Maurice, occupying a bedroom which had also been redecorated for the occasion with a white and blue wallpaper which visitors to Nohant can admire to this day.

Though the houseguest was tall and blond, the hostess small and dark, they shared many similarities of background and experience. Both were of mixed ancestry, Marie's being in some ways more mixed than Aurore's, since her father, Count Alexandre de Flavigny, was a French nobleman, while her mother came from a wealthy Frankfurt banking family. Both had been brought up in a strictly Catholic tradition from which they had gradually drifted on discovering how intellectually crippling convent life could be. Both had been unhappily married to military men, and though Marie could not lay claim to royal blood, her marriage to Count Charles d'Agoult (who was also a cavalry colonel) in 1827 had been attended by the King and Queen of France. Both were ardent Romantics, brought up on Chateaubriand, Byron, and — in Marie's case — Goethe, which she could read in the original. Both harbored literary ambitions, and though Marie's had yet to blossom, her husband had more than once complained of her "graphomania" and of the trunkfuls of written paper which accompanied her on their travels. Finally, both had chosen men younger than themselves for lovers. One year younger than George Sand, Marie d'Agoult was six years older than Franz Liszt.

The two women also shared a marked taste for nature which took them out on long horseback rides and botanical excursions. The long winter evenings were spent in pleasant fireside chats, discussing art, life and death, Shakespeare, women's rights and marriage, "the republic of the future," and the latest volumes of the *Encyclopédie nouvelle,* which Pierre Leroux and Jean Reynaud had made into a vehicle for the propagation of a socialistic Christianity.

Out of these discussions came a series of six "Letters" which George Sand wrote for her friend, the Abbé de Lamennais, recently become the editor of an anti-Establishment daily called *Le Monde.* Addressed to an imaginary unwed girl of twenty-five, these *Lettres à Marcie* presented a comprehensive exposition of George Sand's views on the "feminine question." Once again she condemned the gospel of free love and the "dangerous attempts" which certain female adherents of the Saint-Simonian philosophy had made to "taste pleasure in liberty." To "open wide the gates of license" struck her as a strange remedy for the contemporary "corruption of society." For the ideal she was preaching, a romantic ideal which seems hopelessly old-fashioned in an age as resolutely antiheroic and "realistic" as our own, was antipermissive, aimed at making women purer and thus "greater."

In the third and longest *Lettre à Marcie* she explicitly decried the "clamor" of the feminist movement as trivial compared to the deeper ills of mankind. "The people are hungry; let our leading lights allow us to think of providing bread for the people before thinking of building temples for them. Women cry out against slavery; let them wait till man is free, for slavery cannot engender liberty."

Thus, she condemned those of her female contemporaries who felt that the first duty of "emancipated" women was the proclamation of their rights. "Too proud of their recently acquired education, certain women have shown signs of personal ambition . . . The smug daydreams of modern philosophies have encouraged them, and these women have given sad proof of the powerlessness of their reasoning. It is much to be feared that vain attempts of this kind and these ill-founded claims will do much harm to what is today called the cause of women . . . If women were rightly guided and possessed of sane ideas, they would be better placed to complain of the rigidity of certain laws and the barbarism of certain prejudices. But let them enlarge their souls and elevate their minds before hoping to bend the iron shackles of custom. In vain do they gather into clubs, in vain do they engage in polemics, if the expression of their discontent proves that they are incapable of properly managing their affairs and of governing their affections."

A moral revolution capable of regenerating a corrupt society was thus needed to pave the way for the social revolution which would "liberate" men as well as women. But by itself violence — whether verbal or otherwise — was not enough, and she had little faith in the militancy of embattled womanhood, as historically exemplified by heroines like Joan of Arc, Héloise, and Madame Roland. Women were made to be "artists" — by which George Sand meant poets, painters, actresses, and musicians — they were not made to be politicians. Indeed, she could not think of a single woman in contemporary Europe capable of imposing her point of view in a parliamentary debate, so that a law admitting a handful of women to the French or any other legislature would be pointless. The elevation of women to high office would in the existing circumstances be an "act of madness. Women are not suited to the posts which the laws have hitherto denied them. Which in no wise proves the inferiority of their intelligence, but only the difference of their education and character. The first of these obstacles will cease with time; the second is, I think, eternal." But, she insisted, "I am very far from thinking that woman is inferior to man. She is his equal in the sight of God, and nothing in the designs of Providence destines her to slavery. But she is not like man, and her nature and temperament assign to her another role, no less fine, no less noble, and of which I do not think she can complain unless mentally depraved."

There can be no doubt that George Sand, were she alive today, would regard the militant crusaders of Women's Liberation as "mentally depraved" — if only because, like Simone de Beauvoir, they consider household chores to be inherently degrading. Nor would she have welcomed the idea that motherhood is an unfortunate calamity, a burden Nature has imposed on the members of her sex. "Is not man's life difficult and rough, in nature as in society? . . . The wife has the fatigues of housekeeping, the husband those of the *establishment* — two diverse yet equally necessary and thus equally noble ways of working for the family."

Because the woman-mother (as opposed to the woman-lover, described as "passionate, unstable, flighty") is "all calm, kindness, serenity," moved by "an angelic sentiment," and made to transmit, protect, and preserve life, she is less concerned by the future of ideas and of "the great human family" than she is by the material welfare of her own brood. Thus, George Sand concluded, "the role of each sex is traced, its task is assigned, and Providence gives to each the instruments and resources which befit it. Why should society upset this admirable order . . . by . . . giving women the same attributes as men? Women complain of being brutally enslaved, of being badly educated, badly advised, badly directed, badly loved, badly defended. All this is unfortunately true. But what confidence would women inspire if they were to demand by way of compensation, not household peace nor the freedom of maternal affections, but the right to parade in the forum with sword and helmet, the right to condemn people to death?"

These arguments, which would rank George Sand as a feminine reactionary, not to say an outright enemy of Women's Liberation if voiced today, did not appear conservative enough to Lamennais. Though he preached a gospel of equality for men, the heretical abbé was less ready to see the same gospel extended to women, having remained at heart a misogynous bachelor whose one great passion in the past had been reserved for a young Englishman. When George Sand read the printed text of her third *Lettre à Marcie* (published in the February 19, 1837, issue of *Le Monde*), she was dismayed to find that several crucial passages had been arbitrarily cut out. She wrote Lamennais a letter of protest, saying that at his urging she had undertaken to write about the "feminine question" and that having done so she could not sidestep the central problem of divorce and separation — even though for her part she would sooner spend the rest of her life in a prison cell than remarry. "How can one write about women without debating a question which is of primordial importance and which occupies the first place in their lives? Believe me, I know this better than you; this is one time when the disciple dares to say: 'Master, there are paths over which you have not trodden, abysses into which my eyes have plunged while yours remained fixed on the heavens. You have lived with the angels; I have lived with men and women. . . .' "

Three weeks passed before the next *Lettre à Marcie* was published. In Paris these "Letters" were already the talk of the town, the subject of heated debate in the salons and cafés. But after writing two more "Letters," George Sand decided to terminate her collaboration with *Le Monde,* since Lamennais had in effect denied her the right to express her opinions freely. She did not allow this passing tiff to affect her veneration for "Christ's sole apostle on earth," as she had once called him, but this particular god having failed her, she was more than ever ready to look around for another.

Liszt, who reached Nohant in the middle of this altercation, could only stay one week. He had to hurry back to Paris to face a sudden challenge to his piano-playing supremacy posed by his Austrian rival, Sigismund Thalberg, whose aristocratic mode of playing made him the darling of the Faubourg Saint-Germain. In mid-March Marie d'Agoult left in her turn, after promising to come back as soon as possible with Chopin, Mickiewicz, and Grzymala. George was left alone with Maurice and his twenty-three-year-old tutor, Eugène Pelletan.

Mauprat, the "short story" she had begun writing for Buloz after her break with Musset in the spring of 1835, had since turned into a novel which, as usual, occupied her nights. Though originally inspired by a number of local landmarks — like the Vallée Noire, the ruined tower of Gazeau, and the fountain of Fougères, which were used in the description of the Mauprat family's feudal castle — this too had turned into a didactic tale, but one aimed at extolling rather than condemning marriage. More enterprising, persevering, and resourceful than the long-suffering Indiana, who stoically endures the numbing vicissitudes of an unhappy wedlock, the dashing Edmée of *Mauprat* sets out to save, succor, and transform her brutish lord and master into a superior, civilized, and even cultured being. The theme, thus baldly stated, sounds a bit exalted and naive, which was undoubtedly the case. For it was precisely such a task of educative transformation which the young Aurore Dudevant had boldly undertaken with her husband in 1825 and 1826. In real life the endeavor had proved a disastrous failure. In the novel, on the other hand, the indomitable heroine manages to surmount all obstacles and attain her exalted goal. Her novel, *Simon,* had had a happy ending, too, but in *Mauprat* the emphasis was even more marked. It showed how much in the space of six years George Sand had changed — from the stoic passivity of *Indiana* (1832), through the negative despair of *Lélia* (1833), to the positive, forward-looking, and "progressive" *humanitarian* of 1837.

Mauprat thus became a novel of redemption, designed to illustrate the author's Rousseauistic conviction that man is naturally good, that social conditions alone are responsible for corrupting his fundamental virtue and honesty, and that even the most bestial and brutish individual can be saved. Idealized though Edmée de Mauprat so obviously was — and indeed, with her broad-brimmed hat and feather, her silver gray riding jacket and her crop, she was an idealized George Sand — she was the first of those heroine-redeemers who were to make such an impression on the young Dostoevski and indirectly to inspire his curiously saintly sinners. For the Liza of *Notes from Underground,* the Sonia of *Crime and Punishment,* the Grushenka of *The Brothers Karamazov* — those Mary Magdalenes of Russian fiction — all exemplified the truth George Sand had enunciated in her third *Lettre à Marcie:* that it was women, not men, who through the centuries had observed and thus preserved the fundamental teachings of the Gospel.

In *Mauprat* the name she gave to the rustic poacher-philosopher who prophesies the brave, new world of tomorrow was Patience. This could be interpreted as a tacit reproach to Michel's revolutionary impatience to destroy everything and to start again from scratch. Indeed, no matter how hard she tried to concentrate on *Mauprat,* she found Michel's face and voice and gestures forever interposing themselves between herself, her ink, and her paper. In mid-March she was thrown completely off her stride by the discovery that he was now having an affair with someone George had actually seen at Bourges — a fat woman of "repulsive obesity" who sang off-key, notwithstanding her musical pretensions, and who was insufferably affected in her manners.

In a long letter which read in parts like an ultimatum George insisted on knowing what Michel could see in such an "infamous" creature and how he could bring himself to spend all of his free hours with her. "Does this woman help you to relieve your loins, as would a public tart? Alas, I am younger than you are, I have more blood, more muscle, more nerves than you do, I have a health of iron and a surfeit of energy which I do not know what to do with; yet the handsomest of men could not make me unfaithful to you, despite your forgetfulness, your scorn, your infidelity. When I am bothered by fever, I have the doctor drain off a pound of blood. The doctor says it is a *crime,* a form of suicide, that . . . I must have a lover or my life will be threatened by its sheer excess. Well . . . I can't do it. I can't even bear the thought of it."

It had not been easy, she continued, to master her desires. Having "led a life almost entirely devoted to passion up until the prime of life," she had suddenly been forced to endure an "anchoretic chastity . . . But perhaps all this is pride on my part, perhaps your needs are more imperious than mine, perhaps before yielding you had to fight more than I had to fight to triumph over them.

"Well, if you have done this, I can forgive you for it. If you are sincere, if you confess it frankly, without false pride, without hypocrisy, or if at least . . . Oh, to what lengths my love, my humiliation go! If you swear to me that you prefer me to all others, that none other can give you the voluptuous delights you say you have found in my arms, tell me whatever you like if it is true, for in that case you must suffer," she went on, growing increasingly furious and incoherent at the thought of what Michel might have felt in someone else's arms. "It is hateful to think that this lovely body, so adored, so impregnated by my kisses, several times worn out by our delirious embraces, several times healed and revived by my lips, my hair, my burning breath — Alas, whither am I wandering with my memories? Once, when I had revived your senses with my breath, I thought I was going to die, so deliriously, so ardently had I sought to transmit to your suffering entrails the life and love which filled my breasts. Oh, how sweet it would have been thus to have died, giving you my life, infusing in you the sap of robust years which I felt weighing lightly on my shoulders. My God, to think that this adored body has been sullied by contact with an infamous stomach, of a vainglorious slug! To think that your mouth has inhaled the breath of a mouth which is said to be prostituted by self-adoration and the cult of social puerilities . . . ," etc.

This was the first in a number of tortured, love-crazed letters which all sounded the same note of hysterical despair. In one letter she humbly begged him to grant her twenty-four hours of his precious time; in the next she asked him to forget her ridiculous request, written in a moment of weakness, saying she did not want to see him until she could show him a gay rather than a somber, tearful face. In yet another letter she implored him to meet her anywhere — at Châteauroux, Saint-Amand, Lignières — anywhere but Bourges . . . Bourges which was her hell, because it was there she had met one of Michel's mistresses. But in the end, even this resolution was forgotten.

April Fool's Day was celebrated with the usual jokes and horseplay, but for George Sand the gaiety this year was forced and even bitter. Not realizing the pain it would cause her, François Rollinat appeared disguised as Michel de Bourges, and she had to go out into the vestibule, not knowing whether to cry or to keep up the pretense of laughter. But six days later, just as she was beginning to give up all hope of getting more than short, cold replies to her incandescent letters, Michel de Bourges paid a surprise visit to Nohant. In an instant all doubts and protests were forgotten, and "three months of suffering erased by one hour of happiness."

Three days later she took the cabriolet and using post-horses, she galloped them to Bourges for a fleeting glimpse of Michel, returning twenty-four hours later with a streaming cold caught from driving through the frosty night. Was he really in love with her again, as he had seemed to be on that blissful evening of April 7 when he had taken her into his arms and kissed her beneath the pale crescent of a new moon, or had she once again succumbed to her capacity for wishful thinking?

Their encounter in Bourges seems to have left the question open. The letters she wrote to him after her return to Nohant — at the rate of one a day — kept wavering from hope to doubt and back again. She begged him to make another visit to Nohant to prove that this sudden return of passion, after months of wintry coldness, was genuine and stable. She made him wild promises, saying that if he did not stop loving her, he would find her in twenty years as faithful and attached to him as she was now. She even mixed in a little sentimental blackmail: "If you stop loving me, your soul will die, for no other flame will be able to revive it and dissipate the cold of the eternal night. I defy anyone, man or woman, to love you as I love you." But groan, plead, and threaten as she might, Michel de Bourges showed no haste to return.

Maurice's tutor Pelletan had meanwhile been sent to Paris to bring Solange back from her boarding school. When he returned, the "Pelican" — as he was nicknamed — found himself confronted at the Nohant dinner table by a talkative newcomer, an aggressive, loudmouthed veterinary who engaged everyone in argument and got gloriously drunk, or at least pretended to do so, for he turned out to be Gustave de Gévaudan disguised as a rustic horse dealer. The young chevalier's visit provided an excuse for more than the usual number of practical jokes — beds lined with horsehairs, "ghosts" pursued in the attic, water pitchers emptied on unsuspecting heads, and a superb impersonation put on by George's maid, Sophie Cramer, who "received" an importunate Châteauroux lawyer with such aplomb that he went away charmed by his "memorable meeting" with France's foremost woman writer (who watched the scene from behind the curtains of her four-poster).

Gustave de Gévaudan was persuaded to stay on — to meet Michel de Bourges! George, still hoping that her lover would soon return to Nohant, felt that a meeting between the forty-year-old republican and the twenty-year-old monarchist would help to convince the irascible Michel of the absurdity of his suspicions regarding her "love affair" with the young Gustave. But her "old husband" (as she often called him in writing to others) being too busy to leave Bourges — or so at least he claimed — she found herself once again going more than halfway to meet him. This four-day trip to Bourges, which she undertook between May 2 and 5, could not have been more ill-timed. Liszt and Marie d'Agoult were due to arrive at any moment, and on the eve of her departure she had a major row with the Pelican, who chose this most inopportune of moments for declaring his love for her! The maladroit wooer, who had imprudently "advised" the mistress of Nohant as to how her son should be brought up, was told to pack his bags, while Gustave de Gévaudan stayed on at Nohant to play the host to Marie d'Agoult and Liszt.

This time, instead of taking the cabriolet, George Sand galloped to Bourges on a spirited black horse which Gévaudan had brought her. She reached Bourges so exhausted that at the inn where she again registered under a false name, she slept twelve hours at a stretch. These were followed by as many hours of intense lovemaking with Michel; after which she climbed back on to her horse, galloping back so fast that she covered twenty-one miles in two hours. Liszt, preceded by an Erard piano he had had sent down from Paris, was by this time installed in the downstairs bedroom with Marie d'Agoult; Maurice, whose ill health remained a constant source of concern to his mother, had recovered from a cold; while the golden-haired Solange seemed more radiant, though as headstrong as ever, under the watchful eye of François Rollinat's sister, Marie-Louise, who had agreed to serve for a while as her governess.

To make up for lost time, George Sand had to devote a number of almost sleepless nights to the final chapters of *Mauprat,* which Buloz was anxiously awaiting for the next serial installment in the *Revue des Deux Mondes.* "Cigars and coffee alone have enabled me to maintain my sorry verve at 200 francs a folio" — a sheaf of sixteen printed pages. "My body is also exhausted by another terrible but delightful fatigue, of which I bear the stigmata in a thousand places," she wrote to Michel de Bourges, deliberately mixing the sacred and profane, as was her wont. "The coming night I shall have to work another fourteen hours, like this one, and the next night the same, for six days running. My word is at stake. Shall I die of it? Already I am worn out, and I have hardly started. My weary eyelids can hardly stand the brightness of the rising sun. I am cold at the hour when everything is warming up, I'm hungry and can't eat; for appetite is the result of good health and hunger that of exhaustion. But just appear, my lover, and revived like the earth by the return of the May sun, I will throw off my icy shroud and tremble with love; the wrinkles of suffering will vanish from my brow, and I shall seem young and beautiful, because I shall leap with joy in your arms."

But her pleading fell again on deaf ears. Michel wrote her an "adorable" letter which she hid for a full day in her bodice and went to read alone, seated on the flower-studded moss in the grove. But as the days passed his letters grew rarer and finally ceased altogether. She sought to lure him with the music of Franz Liszt, but the "old lion" of Bourges turned a deaf ear to that too. Yet he was neither ill nor had he succumbed from the aftereffects of intense lovemaking, as George seems for a moment to have feared. Gustave de Gévaudan, on his way home, wrote from Bourges to say that Michel (who had earlier sworn to kill the young whippersnapper if ever he laid eyes on him!) had received him graciously and fascinated him with the "magnetic" power of his personality.

By mid-May George was writing Michel furious letters of reproach, saying it was clear he no longer loved her. The advent of another full moon, which Michel stubbornly refused to share with her, brought on a new fit of spleen, which even Liszt's music could only partially allay. To relieve her frustration she taught her black horse to jump over bales of hay, injuring one of its legs and almost killing herself in the process. But as she wrote to Michel, "I would have made it jump over a precipice" had there been one nearby, so black was her mood.

Her one consolation was provided by her friends Marie d'Agoult and Liszt, with whom she spent the evenings reading or discussing Byron, E. T. A. Hoffmann, and Dante. Liszt, who only needed to wind a maroon-colored scarf around his head to resemble the Florentine poet, felt so inspired by Dante that he began work on a fantasia-sonata in his honor. He had brought along the scores of a number of Beethoven sonatas (all too little known at the time), as well as of symphonies which he spent hours transposing for the piano. Seated upstairs in her study, George would listen in silent fascination as the first notes of some strange new theme were struck and often left incomplete, "with one leg in the air, dancing in space like clubfooted imps," as she noted in the intimate journal she now started keeping. "The leaves of the linden trees undertake to complete the melody with a soft, mysterious whispering, as though sharing the mystery of nature with each other. It's perhaps a work of composition he's trying out by fragments on the piano. Next to him are his pipe, his ruled paper and his quills . . . As he pauses in front of his piano, he must unconsciously jot down these whimsical phrases, obeying instincts of feeling rather than a work of the mind. But these quick, impetuous melodies remind me of a vessel battered by the tempest . . ."

"Powerful artist," she noted the same day, "sublime in great things, always superior in petty things, yet sad and devoured by a secret sore." What this sore was it was not difficult to guess. Though Marie d'Agoult was the mother of his child and was to give him two more (one of whom, Cosima, became Richard Wagner's wife), they were fundamentally an ill-matched couple. Hers was too calculating a temperament, too analytical a mind to suit Franz's generous, outgoing, essentially spontaneous disposition. What he had thought was love was really admiration for an aristocratic lady of uncommon beauty and intelligence who had sacrificed her reputation to live with him in sin; it wasn't the wild, adolescent passion he had felt for his first love — the young Caroline de Saint-Cricq he had vainly sought to marry. His liaison with Marie was thus to some extent a *pis-aller,* satisfying a deep-seated psychological need to avenge himself against the social conventions which had kept him, a mere commoner and music teacher, from marrying the daughter of a count who was also a cabinet minister of Charles X. Up until now he had displayed an almost heroic fidelity toward Marie, but the time would come when, like any full-blooded Romantic, he would demand his freedom. This Marie d'Agoult sensed, and it made her, behind her mask of affable serenity, wretchedly unhappy. Indeed, there were times when she couldn't help wondering if the woman Franz Liszt needed wasn't the poetic and imaginative George Sand rather than her own hypercritical self.

George, for her part, was much too preoccupied by Michel de Bourges to harbor any such designs. When she thought of Princess Arabella — as she had dubbed Marie in her seventh *Lettre d'un voyageur* — she thought of a white lily whose flexible stem sways with the breeze. But George herself was more like a sunflower "whose proud corolla, without paling, drinks in the ardent rays of daylight. Piffoël," she asked herself in her intimate journal, "why in the devil don't you lower your head when the storm passes? Why are your tears so acrid, and why must you break without having bent? Like the sunflower, you want to turn toward your master and salute him willingly in all his glory; but if your master hides his face and hurls a thunderbolt at you, you dry up and break, for you don't want to yield."

The bitter truth of course was that if the statuesque Marie d'Agoult could display the gracious flexibility of a lily in her relations with Liszt, it was because Franz was less despotically inclined than the tyrannical Michel de Bourges. With the latter love was a form of contest, of struggle, as was life in general. He had to dominate, and once he had overcome and triumphed, he expected an attitude of slavish submission. Like a Turkish sultan, he would make love or pay visits when it suited him.

"Spring is here at last!" George wrote to him again toward the end of May. "Won't you come to lay your head on my breast and to go to sleep with your hands in mine? You promised me only a few days ago that the month of flowers would not go by without your coming to live with me for a few hours. Do you recall? Do you think of it?"

The answer was: Yes, but that it irked him immensely. It irked him because of this colossal claim she was imposing on him — as the only person in the world who was capable of loving him as he needed to be loved. "Come," she wrote, "you who do not know love and can never know it except with me."

Even a less irascible individual might have been provoked by this kind of bland assertion. Michel de Bourges blew up. "Damnation!" he wrote back. "At home I have to wage a daily, and even hourly war on your behalf. So be it. That's only fair. Nothing here below is given to man without struggle and combat. But at least in your arms I found a shelter against those woes, a secure refuge against these omnipresent worries. But no, you demand, you want me to fight you . . ."

To this blast George Sand replied with one of her own: "Poor fellow! What childish words! This is what the ungrateful child does when, to be rid of a tender reproach, he beats the stomach that conceived him and bites the breast that fed him. This is what the embryo does when it wriggles like a worm inside the entrails which bear it . . ."

Once again her maternal solicitude had got the better of her language, and this time with definitely negative effect. Having been cared for when he was ill by France's foremost woman author had flattered Michel's masculine ego in the early months of their liaison, but he was less overjoyed at the prospect of being treated like an infant whenever he failed to reciprocate her love. Determined to have it out with her mulish lover, George decided to make one more trip to Bourges. Her departure was delayed at the last moment by the unexpected arrival of Pierre Bocage, a well-known French actor who had played on the same stage with Marie Dorval and for a while enjoyed the favor of her bed. A tall, striking, though somewhat stoop-shouldered man, Bocage was on his way to Lyon, but promised to make a longer stopover on his way back in July.

The next day George was in such a hurry to be off that she forgot the key to her night bag and had to get a locksmith to open it on reaching Bourges. Once again she put up at an inn under an assumed name. Exactly what ensued we do not know, but the encounter must have produced a lot of sparks. George must have realized that they had reached a parting of the ways. As she wrote to Michel's friend and fellow lawyer Frédéric Girerd some two months later: "I have suffered from Michel everything you foresaw . . . Tired of being so devoted, having fought my pride with all the strength of love and finding only ingratitude by way of recompense, I felt my soul break and my love die out. I am cured . . . The wound, from sheer excess of bleeding, finally closed, and this time I am sure of the fact that I no longer love."

*

Those lines were written in early August. But in the second week of June she was still too close to this dispiriting dénouement to take such a philosophic view. And it was precisely at this moment that Charles Didier chose to turn up unexpectedly at Nohant. Even worse, he managed to arrive when everyone was seated round the dinner table. George, without rising from her seat, kissed him on both cheeks, but she was visibly as much embarrassed by his awkward appearance as he was.

Didier's arrival created a general malaise. Liszt, who a night or two before had charmed his hostess by playing Schubert's *Erlkönig*, while Marie flitted between the trees and white lilac bushes in a sylphlike dance, deliberately neglected his piano. He was eager to hear the latest gossip from Paris and to know why Lamennais had abandoned the editorship of *Le Monde* (for which Didier had also worked). Seated outside on the small stone terrace — for it was another hot summer night — Marie d'Agoult watched in fascination as the flaming punch was brought out and placed on the table. The flickering blue flames cast eerie lights and shadows over George Sand's scarlet dress, and the scene struck her as worthy of the witches in *Macbeth*. But what intrigued her most was the transparent play of feelings reflected on Charles Didier's face. She had already been struck by his touchiness over trifles. As she noted in her diary: "At the slightest word his forehead would suddenly flush; entrenched behind his gold-rimmed glasses, his eye attentively scrutinized the expression of our faces, and often his smile would die on his lips, frozen by a passing thought of mistrust or doubt."

The next day — June 16 — Didier fancied he and George were about to renew their old intimacy when he came upon her after dinner arranging the flowers in his bedroom. But the illusion was of short duration. From then on she carefully avoided his pathetic attempts to corner her in an intimate tête-à-tête. She affected a lighthearted air and even teased him in public, to his intense mortification. By the nineteenth he had to admit to his diary that he had made a terrible mistake in coming to Nohant. To console himself he went out riding with the fair Marie d'Agoult. They rode through fields bright with red poppies, white daisies, blue cornflowers and forget-me-nots, they paused to admire the ruminating cows and indifferent oxen in the pastures; but his thoughts were elsewhere and it pained him to recall the delightful ride he had made one year earlier along the same banks of the Indre with Her (*Elle,* as she is invariably referred to in his diary).

The longer he stayed, the more miserable Didier came to feel. He found himself increasingly drawn to Liszt — a "noble heart," as he noted in his diary. Whenever Solange was dispatched to her bedroom for repeated disobedience, Liszt would creep upstairs and talk her into coming down and apologizing to her mother. One night he sat down in front of his piano and began singing some Schubert lieder. One of them, entitled "You no longer love me," made Didier more than usually morose. Liszt caught his mournful eye and quickly moved on to another.

In a moment of distraction — or was it deliberate? — George offered Didier a privileged glimpse at her intimate journal, which she had facetiously entitled: "Daily Talks with the very knowing and very skillful Doctor Piffoël, Professor of Botany and Psychology." Between the twelfth and the twentieth of June she had made no entries, followed by: "Nothing. Two fine thunderstorms, weather less hot. Admirable *clair de lune,* evening horseback rides with my sister" — by which she meant Marie d'Agoult. Not a word about Didier, who had reached Nohant on June 15, but whole paragraphs were devoted to Liszt, Marie d'Agoult, Michel de Bourges, and a baby warbler George had picked up from the ground. For Didier this was the last straw; unable to control his grief, he broke down and cried.

Yet still he stayed on. Marie d'Agoult undertook to explain to him that George was now incapable of love and friendship and unable to harbor serene affections. While George in her Piffoëlesque journal aired her own spleen and feeling of despair, Didier in his bedroom was plagued by nightmarish specters and insomnia, and even a sudden savage urge to murder George as the root cause of his misery.

To keep from going mad, he left Nohant for a few days. When he returned on July 14, he found that three new guests had arrived during his absence — François Rollinat, the lawyer, Pierre Bocage, the actor, and Félicien Mallefille, a young wall-eyed dramatist who had also frequented Marie d'Agoult's Paris salon. George, who had just got up — at ten o'clock in the morning — kissed Didier tenderly, and as he noted in his diary: "The rest of the day was good. But I have no illusions: she is busy with B[ocage]. This rivalry with an actor wounds and disgusts me. Liszt approves of my leaving."

Marie d'Agoult speeded his departure by uncharitably intimating that George had "entered the world of gallantry" — which is to say, promiscuity. Didier was so upset that he almost left without saying goodbye to his hostess. She called him at the last moment, expressed surprise that he should be leaving, and seemed singularly moved at the idea that her "white bear" would soon be gone. "She hugs me in her arms and I kiss her large, dry, impenetrable eyes," as Didier noted in his diary. She then accompanied him to the door of the pavilion — the one opening directly onto the La Châtre–Châteauroux highway — there was a final kiss and he was off.

Didier's departure caused few regrets at Nohant. Bocage, who wanted George Sand to write a play he could act in, redoubled his advances and was soon flirting with her openly. Deeply wounded in her self-esteem by Michel de Bourges' cruel treatment, she allowed herself to be charmed by the actor's dark blue eyes and tall romantic figure — the same which had aroused such a flutter of nervous hearts, in May 1831, on the memorable first night of Alexandre Dumas' *Antony,* when using a real dagger, Bocage had inadvertently cut Marie Dorval, the martyred heroine, causing her to utter a death cry that was anything but feigned. Aurore had missed that dramatic première but had been present for another, in February of 1833, when Victor Hugo's play, *Lucrèce Borgia,* was staged. Her neighbor was the thirty-three-year-old Bocage, who was as enthusiastic in his applause as she was. As George was to write years later to Victor Hugo himself, their hands, after clapping, were joined that night in friendship and were to remain so thereafter.

Bocage's arrival at Nohant at a moment when George's spirits were at a particularly low ebb seemed providential — at any rate to her. It had been heralded most curiously by a dream Marie d'Agoult had had the previous night: she had dreamed she had suddenly fallen in love with Bocage and had hied herself to a secret rendezvous masked like the grandes dames of the early eighteenth century. "We commented on the strangeness of this dream, for we never talk about Bocage," Marie d'Agoult recorded in her diary. "It's been more than a year since I saw him on the stage, where, I might add, he has always struck me as a very mediocre actor, completely led astray by our contemporary bourgeoisie. Toward the end of dinner George was informed that a gentleman wished to see her. She went out and brought back Bocage! Franz and I were dumfounded, as though we'd seen a ghost."

They were subsequently almost as surprised by the speed with which George could forget Michel de Bourges. For it was soon clear that her four-year-old friendship with the "mediocre actor" was now at last turning into something hotter. Liszt couldn't help joking about it to Bocage, saying it was too bad George had to be bled so often by her doctor. The intimation was presumably that she was in midsummer heat and that Bocage might do well to replace Gustave Papet's lancet. When Bocage rather imprudently repeated the joke to George, she pretended not to understand its meaning. But she was privately so vexed that she sent a note down to "Mirabelle" (another of Marie d'Agoult's nicknames) asking her to tell the *crétin* — the "dolt," as Franz Liszt was called, in mock homage to his quick-wittedness — to stop making jokes about herself and Bocage.

On the eve of their departure for Geneva, where Marie d'Agoult and Liszt had left their eighteen-month-old daughter Blandine in the hands of a Swiss governess, another newcomer suddenly drove up. A friend and protégé of Liszt's, Alexandre Rey was a typically romantic young man, a would-be poet with a head full of dreams. "These two young men suffer from the malady of their generation," as Marie d'Agoult noted in her diary, apropos Mallefille and the latest arrival, "an overexcited ambition at grips with a poverty which is all the more cruel for being in daily contact with a whole class of people who are not a superior class by virtue of a recognized right, but superior by reason of wealth, with all it entails in power and privileges. Mallefille, who was dreaming of reforming the French stage, is fed up with plays and wants to go to Circassia . . . Rey dreams of nothing less than a humanitarian poem which should be finished in six months. This poem, which he has been ruminating in his head for years, is to be the psychological history of microcosmic man, as far as I can gather . . . His conversation, which is usually one long platitude, augurs ill of his becming a new Dante or a new Milton."

In late July, after her summer guests had left, George had to hurry up to Paris to see her ailing mother. She left Solange to the care of François Rollinat's sister Marie-Louise. A local pedagogue had been brought to Nohant to act as temporary tutor for Maurice, and fearing what the spiteful gossips of La Châtre might say when they learned that governess and tutor had been left alone in the manor house, George Sand asked Gustave Papet to house Maurice at the nearby Château d'Ars.

No longer having an apartment of her own in Paris, George Sand now established residence at Fontainebleau — in the same Hôtel Britannique where she and Alfred de Musset had celebrated their August honeymoon three years before. Here Madame Gratiot — as she was officially listed in the registry — was joined by Bocage for another ardent honeymoon, which was brief but singularly felicitous and destined to remain a pleasant memory for both of them. When, some days later, he left on a theater tour in Belgium, the actor offered her free use of his calèche during his absence to supplement the weather-beaten cabriolet in which she had driven up from Nohant.

This proved an unexpected windfall in view of the dramatic events that were to follow. Aurore now had a choice of carriages with which to drive in to see her mother, which she did daily. Reluctant to remain alone in her tiny fourth-floor flat — she was too highstrung to be able to keep a maid for more than a week — Madame Dupin had moved to a rest home on the Rue du Faubourg-Poissonnière, where her daughter found her stretched out on a hideous wooden bed in a small airless room and looking a hundred years old. Aurore was shocked by her forced, wrinkled smile, and even more by the den she was inhabiting. Her half sister, Caroline, explained to her in a whisper that their mother had personally chosen this extraordinary habitat. She had come to the rest home with a small bag of gold coins which she kept hidden under her pillow, and fearful of attracting the attention of the robbers she kept seeing in her feverish hallucinations, she had insisted on occupying the smallest room available.

Twenty-four hours later Aurore had talked Sophie-Victoire out of her latest caprice, and she was comfortably installed in a large, sunny room overlooking a spacious garden. Dr. Gaubert, one of the four physicians who had earlier examined Maurice, was now called in to look at Madame Dupin. He told Aurore, after taking her out into the garden, that her mother had not much longer to live. Her liver was hideously swollen, the worst pains were fortunately over, and she would die in peace. While the two daughters waited for the inevitable end — taking Madame Dupin out for brief carriage rides and sitting next to her in the garden — Aurore received an urgent message from her half brother, Hippolyte. The previous February Casimir's stepmother, Baroness Dudevant, had died, and he had inherited the country house at Guillery along with a certain amount of land. These lands, which presently brought in an annual income from tenant farmers of from 5000 to 6000 francs, could, according to Casimir's reckoning, bring in twice that sum once cleared of debts. He had accordingly written to Aurore asking her for a special loan of 30,000 francs. Coming from somebody who had proved himself a wretched businessman and who had dissipated three quarters of his father's inheritance, this was a preposterous request. It seemed doubly outrageous to George Sand, on the part of a man who had been granted the annual income of *her* town house in Paris and who spent his time, hunting, fishing, and drinking while she stayed up at night writing novels to maintain her family and her estate.

Aurore would have been better advised to leave matters as they were. But encouraged by her Berrichon friends, who were as shocked as she was by this crude attempt at uxorial exploitation, she rashly undertook to bring legal action against her former husband. Since she in fact was now caring for Maurice, with all the educational and other expenses this entailed, she demanded that the settlement they had signed at Bourges the previous July be revised in her favor, making her rather than Casimir the beneficiary of the 7000 francs of rental income that were brought in by the town house in Paris.

Hippolyte, who was still in Aurore's bad books for having failed to support her during the long separation wrangle, was anything but happy about these new legal proceedings. But he was even more alarmed by the violence of Casimir's reaction. Since Madame Sand wanted war, war was what she was going to get, by God! Let her give him 30,000 francs by way of compensation, and he would relinquish his claim to the income from the Hôtel de Narbonne. As for her claiming exclusive responsibility for Maurice's education, this was sheer impertinence on her part and contrary to the terms of their separation settlement. It was high time he put an end to this nonsense! In fact, he was going to go down to Nohant and remove Maurice from her clutches!

Hippolyte felt it to be his fraternal duty to warn his half sister about Casimir's thundering threats. After all, it was up to her to decide if the delicate Maurice was strong enough to reenter boarding school. The message did not fall on deaf ears. Aurore hurried over to Félicien Mallefille's house and beseeched the young dramatist to take the cabriolet and to drive it posthaste to Nohant. Maurice must be removed and brought to Fontainebleau before his father could lay hands on him.

The adventurous young playwright, who had begun life as a sailor in faraway Mauritius, leaped at the challenge. This was better than the stage, which he had been hoping to reform. Forgotten in a trice was his intended trip to the Caucasus. Caressing his dark beard and hidalgo mustache, while his two walleyes flashed fire, he declared himself her man.

Arming himself with two pistols, Mallefille climbed into the cabriolet and was off at a gallop. Twenty-four hours later he reached Nohant — at two-thirty in the morning. He woke the sleeping household — after all, Baron Dudevant might arrive at any moment! — and then hied himself over to the nearby Château d'Ars, where Gustave Papet was aroused in his turn at four. Papet promised to keep a sharp eye on Solange, moving her if necessary from Nohant to his parents' home; and with Maurice comfortably installed beside him, Mallefille drove off into the dawn. They spent the night at Bourges, where the rickety carriage was returned to its owners, and early the next morning they proceeded north by stagecoach to Fontainebleau.

On August 17 Maurice was happily reunited with his mother. Two days later Madame Dupin died. At her mother's funeral, which followed on the twenty-first, Aurore was startled to see a solemn, gray-haired gentleman step up to pay his last respects — her former husband, Casimir. So it had all been a false alarm. Maurice was not in danger and she could breathe more freely.

Several weeks were needed to attend to the financial arrangements necessitated by her mother's death. Aurore insisted that the annual pension — some 2500 francs — which her mother had received from the Dupin de Francueil estate now go to her half sister, Caroline, to help pay for her son Oscar's education. It was an unusually generous action, for neither of the recipients had a drop of Dupin blood in their veins, nor was Aurore on particularly close terms with her half sister.

Her return to Nohant was also delayed by the urgent need to finish another novel for Buloz — the third in some eight months! *Mauprat,* which she had completed in mid-May, had been followed almost immediately by *Les Maîtres Mosaïstes,* a story inspired by the historic rivalry between two Venetian clans skilled in the making of mosaics. The Venetian background, though well and accurately described, provided a convenient frame for the exposition of Liszt's and Lamennais' ideas on social art, the cult of the Beautiful, and the insidious temptations to which artists are exposed in pandering to the tastes of an uneducated public. Thus the unscrupulous Bianchini brothers, corrupted by a love of fame and "filthy lucre" — the same which had become the be-all and end-all of Louis-Philippe's get-rich-quick regime — were contrasted to the altruistic Zuccati brothers, genuine artists who preferred to remain faithful to a noble ideal of craftsmanship and creative integrity. The noted musicologist and Sand scholar, Thérèse Marix-Spire, has suggested that the younger of the two Zuccati brothers, was pointedly given the name of Francesco — the Italian form of Franz — while his elder brother, the doubt-ridden Valerio, described as "frail of body, like a reed of the lagoons," was strangely reminiscent of Frédéric Chopin.

The third novel, *La Dernière Aldini,* which George Sand began writing in Fontainebleau in late July and completed in mid-September, was written in a minimum of time for money — of which she was once again in dire need. She herself called it a "Piffoëlade" and even (in a letter to Marie d'Agoult and Liszt) a *cochonnerie* — mere trash. It was yet another variation on the by now familiar Sand theme — a noblewoman's unhappy love for a commoner.

Shortly before finishing this novel, George Sand invited Dr. Gaubert out to Fontainebleau for a look at Maurice. The doctor declared that the boy's heartbeat was still too irregular to permit his returning to boarding school. He prescribed a regimen of plentiful fresh air and exercise, which Aurore and her son followed by getting up at dawn and riding through the sandy forest on small ponies, which they frequently dismounted to chase butterflies and pick flowers. Bocage, delayed by illness in Belgium, finally joined her on September 16. They were due to leave the next morning for Nohant when George received an urgent letter from Solange's governess, Marie-Louise Rollinat, telling her that a dreadful thing had happened: Baron Dudevant had turned up unexpectedly and forcibly dragged Solange away. Her mother, Madame Rollinat, who had come to stay with her in the empty manor house, had vainly tried to stop him. She herself had been pushed against a table, which had been overturned in the struggle, almost crushing the poor Solange.

Casimir's presence at Madame Dupin's funeral had thus only been a feint. Unable to lay hands on Maurice, safely hidden at Fontainebleau under his mother's assumed name of Gratiot, the irate baron had taken out his wrath on Solange. George Sand immediately raced into Paris and began pounding on different office doors. The Minister of the Interior, no less, was talked into using the semaphoric telegraph to determine whether Baron Dudevant had taken the child to Guillery, as she suspected. He had. A judge was talked into issuing a court injunction calling on the father to return the child to her mother. Maurice was entrusted to the care of the liberal journalist Louis Viardot and Charlotte Marliani, the wife of the Spanish consul in Paris whom George had met and befriended in Marie d'Agoult's salon. Bocage offered George his carriage and a robust manservant. He could not, however, accompany her himself — his presence at such a ticklish moment would have been too compromising and a serious faux pas.

The intrepid Mallefille was accordingly picked for the job. At ten o'clock at night the carriage drew up in front of his door, and Mallefille's brother Léonce was told to get hold of him at once — there wasn't a moment to be lost! Once again the pistols were packed into the carriage, and, accompanied by Bocage's manservant and a lawyer's clerk, George Sand and her latest *cavalier servant* clattered out of Paris.

Driving night and day, as fast as the post-horses could pull them, they reached Nérac some seventy hours later. Here George Sand called on the sous-préfet, a young and still relatively little known man called Eugène Georges Haussmann, who was later to make a name for himself carving tree-lined boulevards through the medieval labyrinth of Paris' narrow streets. The young official was only too glad to oblige. He ordered a constable and two mounted policemen to accompany Madame Sand, and not content with that, he took his place inside the carriage with her.

Mallefille in the end did not have to use his pistols. But the sight of the mounted policemen taking up positions around his country house reduced Baron Dudevant to such a state of spluttering rage that he almost burst a blood vessel. Trying to look calm, he came to the door and politely invited his former spouse to step inside, an honor she no less courteously declined. Solange was brought out and entrusted to her mother "like a princess at the limit between two states," as George Sand later described it. Casimir vowed that he would get Maurice back "by authority of justice," the sous-préfet looked questioningly at Madame Sand, Madame Sand shrugged her shoulders, and the encounter ended with a frigid exchange of bows.

Back at Nérac the gallant sous-préfet insisted that the famous authoress stay on a day or two to recover from the exertions of the trip. Having come this far, George now took it into her head to go even farther south — for another look at her beloved Pyrenees. Mallefille and the lawyer's clerk were accordingly offered a free trip to Lourdes — where Solange gaped at the quantity of marble houses and bridges — and to other sentimental landmarks the young Aurore Dudevant had once visited with Aurélien de Sèze. There was fog, snow, and drizzle, but nothing could dampen the party's enthusiasm.

This mad excursion — costing in all 2000 francs — did nothing to improve George Sand's shaky finances. Nor did it appease Casimir's chronic irascibility. He now swore to an increasingly dismayed and disapproving Hippolyte that he was going to get even with his former wife if it was the last thing he ever did. Yes, by God, he was going to prove that at Nohant not only Marie d'Agoult but George Sand as well had shared Liszt's bed! Hippolyte was careful not to pass on this news to Aurore, not wishing to cause her undue alarm, but he wrote an urgent note to Casimir's business factotum in Paris, imploring him in Heaven's name to try to keep the impulsive baron from this supreme piece of folly.

In early October Mallefille was dispatched from Nohant to Paris with the first part of *La Dernière Aldini,* for which he was instructed to obtain several thousand francs from the penny-pinching Buloz. Maurice was brought back to Nohant by Charlotte Marliani and a distinctly disheveled "philosopher" named Pierre Leroux, who had become a major attraction of her Paris salon. Even more hard-pressed than his hostess — for he had nine children and a wife to feed— Leroux could only stay five days, but Charlotte Marliani stayed on long enough to meet Michel de Bourges, who found her "absolutely charming." He had turned up at Nohant while George was headed for the Pyrenees, his masculine vanity obviously nettled by her determination to put an end to their affair. The news that he had wanted to see her again was enough to rekindle the dying embers of her passion. Hearing that Michel was due to pass through Châteauroux on October 18, George borrowed a saddle horse from Gustave Papet, to whose care Maurice was entrusted *just in case.* Galloping madly through the cold night, she managed to catch a brief glimpse of Michel, who swore he would never set foot inside Nohant again. But on his way back from Niort, where he was campaigning for election to the Chamber of Deputies, he suddenly yielded to temptation and surprised George by turning up late one night at Nohant and staying on for two days.

"The tenderness and kindness he has shown me are inconceivable, after all the cruel things that happened between us," George reported to their mutual friend Girerd a few days later. "Besides, our respective positions have greatly changed, and there are such strange complications that I can only tell you about them verbally, it would be too long . . ."

Michel does not seem to have appreciated these "strange complications" — by which George obviously meant her new adventure with Bocage. In early November he wrote to several La Châtre friends to tell them that he had been successfully elected to the Chamber as a deputy from Niort, but he pointedly refrained from sharing the good news with George. She wrote him two letters, which went unanswered. She took this new rebuff philosophically — after all, she had another lover — and as she wrote again to Girerd: "I am softly vegetating. I fancy myself as being a bit like a green cypress standing guard over a cadaver."

Thus her love for Michel died, killed by the disinterest of the man who had inspired it. Bocage, who had succeeded (but not replaced) him in her affections, discreetly withdrew from the scene, lacking the time to make another visit to Nohant. His place was taken — not immediately, but gradually — by the black-bearded and mustachioed Mallefille, after George Sand had given up all hope of having a protégé of Lamennais' (and thus a distinctly heretical priest) installed at Nohant as combination tutor and resident curé. Mallefille, to her delight, proved an excellent tutor. Maurice, under his guidance, began making astonishing progress in history and philosophy, and as the doting mother wrote to Buloz, "he governs my Solange lioness as though she were a lamb."

The hot-blooded Mauritian was not a man to miss such an opportunity, and, unlike the unfortunate Pelletan, he knew how to press his amorous advances. Before the year was up he was unofficially installed as resident lover, as well as resident tutor, thus inaugurating a new office which from now on was seldom to be vacant for long. George — "the great poet, the untamed child, a woman weak to the point of audacity, mobile in her sentiments and opinions, illogical in a life always influenced by the haphazard," as Marie d'Agoult had summed her up in her diary — thus once again surprised her friends. Not the least astonished was the fair-haired Marie, who couldn't help recalling how physically repelled George had felt the first time she had been introduced to the dark, wall-eyed dramatist. But all this was now happily forgotten, the magic of voluptuous nights effacing the blemishes of the day. "Decidedly Mallefille reigns," François Buloz noted on a letter from George, in which she asked him to accept two articles Mallefille had written for the *Revue des Deux Mondes.* But this reign, as we shall see, was to be of short duration.

PART VI

The Years with Chopin

27. Less Malleable than Wax

To ADD TO her sentimental woes, the winter of 1837–1838 was one long season of physical hardship. Still plagued by liver trouble, George Sand was further crippled by rheumatism, so severely that by mid-January her right hand and arm were almost completely paralyzed. *Les Maîtres Mosaïstes* had been followed by another Venetian tale entitled *L'Uscoque,* the title of which (obviously inspired by Byron's *Corsair*) was derived from the word *uscocco,* designating one of those lawless Dalmatian sea captains whom the Habsburg emperors had employed in the seventeenth century to protect their Adriatic ports against Turkish pirates. But the muscular action of writing finally became so painful that she was reduced to dictating the final pages to Mallefille or occasionally Maurice.

Dictated too were the first pages of a new novel called *Spiridion,* which marked a new departure in George Sand's literary efforts in being less dramatic and more philosophical, inspired as it obviously was by the Abbé de Lamennais and Pierre Leroux's syncretic socio-Christian humanitarianism. Now at last convinced that an expanded, twenty-volume edition of her Complete Works would prove a good investment, Buloz came to the rescue with the offer of a 6000 franc advance for this and later novels. The initial payment was to be followed, from February on, by monthly installments of 1000 francs to enable her to make another trip to Italy in search of that Mediterranean warmth she and her ailing son so badly needed. Eager though she was to leave, she decided it would be wiser to finish her new novel first — something she rashly thought she could accomplish in a couple of weeks. She also wanted to have her second lawsuit with Casimir over and done with before heading for Rome, where she intended to enroll the artistically inclined Maurice in an art school for two years of intensive training with pencil and palette.

The end of February thus found her still at Nohant when Balzac, who had been visiting a friend in the nearby town of Issoudun, wrote to ask if he could pay a call on "the lioness of Berry" — or perhaps he should say the "nightingale in her nest" — without fear of breaking his nose against her closed door. Though she was suffering at this moment from a dreadful toothache, this was one visit the self-styled "recluse" of Nohant could not refuse. During the week he spent here she took pleasure in introducing her celebrated guest to the soothing pleasures of the water pipe. As Balzac was to write in his *Traité des excitants modernes:* "I owe the key to this treasure to Georges Sand" — the treasure, elaborately described, being the hookah she had taught him to suck on at Nohant.

In private, however, he was far less charitable, noting in a long letter written to a friend, that having reached Nohant around seven-thirty in the evening, he had found *le camarade* George Sand "in her dressing gown, smoking an after-dinner cigar by the fire in a huge, empty room. She was wearing a pretty pair of yellow, fringed slippers, coquettish stockings, and red trousers . . . Physically, she had developed a double chin, like a Church canon. She hasn't a single white hair, notwithstanding her dreadful misfortunes. Her dark complexion hasn't changed; her lovely eyes are as lustrous as ever. She still looks stupid when sunk in thought, for, as I told her after studying her for a while, her expression is concentrated in her eyes. She has been at Nohant for the past year, very despondent, and working her head off. She leads much the same life as I do. She goes to bed at six in the morning and gets up at noon; I go to bed at six in the evening and get up at midnight. But naturally I conformed myself to her habits, and for three days we talked from five in the evening . . . until five in the morning, with the result that I learned more about her, and vice versa, in those three long conversations than in the four preceding years, when she loved Sandeau and was involved with Musset . . .

"Her type of man is a rare bird, that's all. He will be all the rarer in that she isn't amiable, and consequently she will find it hard to be loved. She is boyish, an artist, she is great-hearted, generous, devout and *chaste;* she has the main characteristics of a man; *ergo* she is not a woman. No more than in the past did I, during those three days of frank talk, find myself affected by the epidermal gallantry one is expected . . . to deploy with every sort of woman. I found myself talking with a friend. She has fine virtues, virtues which society misinterprets. It was with a seriousness, honesty, candor and conscientiousness worthy of the great shepherds who lead the human herd that we discussed the great questions of marriage and freedom. For, as she said with immense pride (I wouldn't have dared think of it myself): 'Inasmuch as we are preparing a revolution in future living habits through our writings, I am as much struck by the inconveniences of the one [marriage] as of the other [freedom].' . . .

"She is an excellent mother, adored by her children, but she dresses her daughter Solange like a little boy, which is not a good thing . . .

"As regards Liszt and Madame d'Agoult, she gave me the subject for *Les Galériens* [*The Galley Slaves*] or *Amours Forcés,* which I am going to write, because she herself can't do it. Keep this a close secret. All in all, she's a man, all the more so for wanting to be one, she has abandoned a woman's role, and is not a woman. A woman attracts, she repels; and as I am very much a man," the proud seducer added, puffing out his portly chest, "and as she has this effect on me, she must have the same effect on others like me. She will thus always be unhappy. She now loves a man who is inferior to her, and in that kind of relationship there is only disenchantment and disappointment for a noble-hearted woman. A woman must always love someone who is superior to her, or be deceived into believing that such he is."

Balzac's impressions, filtered through the prism of his personal tastes and prejudices, differed strikingly from those of Auguste Charpentier, who was invited to Nohant in early April to paint portraits of the mistress of Nohant and her children. "I am still spellbound by this famous Madame Sand," the twenty-three-year-old painter wrote to his aunt shortly after his arrival. "The public doesn't know her and all the things that are said about her are abominable calumnies. Madame Sand is the best mother and the finest woman one can imagine. Hers is as admirable a head as one can see, and I'm still not over my first impression. I won't start her portrait until tomorrow, I wanted to spend a day studying her admirable person . . .

"Here one leads the happiest and freest existence possible. Everyone gets up when he feels like it. At 7 or 8 o'clock in the morning a servant comes to light a huge wood fire and asks what you would like for breakfast. Each is served in his room.

"After breakfast one works, goes visiting or plays billiards for relaxation. During the day Madame Sand stays in her room and receives no one.

"At five o'clock the bell rings, one gets dressed and all gather for dinner. From this moment on everyone lives *en famille,* one moves on into the drawing room and anyone who wishes to may smoke a cigarette. Madame Sand sets the example. But as nobly as can be. I have spent two evenings admiring this woman, so remarkable and lovely that one would not think her more than 28 years old . . ."

The result of this admiration was at least one, and more likely three portraits — the finest of which portrayed George Sand at her most seductive, dressed in a black, slightly décolleté dress, sharply brought in at the waist. Her thick black hair is loosely enveloped in a black mantilla, falling over her shoulders, her neck encircled by a nooselike chain, made of gold, to which is attached, below the waistline, a cameo engraving. The short-sleeved arms are bare, the wrists half covered by embroidered lacework mittens, and her right hand holds a closed fan. The ungainly double chin, of which Balzac spoke, has dissolved into shadow, and the strikingly oval face — not for nothing was Charpentier a follower of Ingres — is full of brooding sensuality, dominated by the prim, pursed, assertive mouth and the serpentlike fixity of the two dark, devouring eyes.

Urgent business forced an interruption in her poses. Leaving Charpentier at Nohant to complete his portraits of Maurice and Solange, George Sand traveled up to Paris in mid-April with Alexis Duteil, who was now acting as her lawyer in the continuing wrangle with Casimir. Financially, the four weeks she spent in the capital were ruinously expensive, for while they permitted her to regain ownership of the Hôtel de Narbonne, she had to sell 40,000 francs' worth of government bonds to provide Casimir with compensation.

The material loss, however, was offset by an unexpected spiritual gain. No longer having a place of her own to stay in, George was generously put up by her friend Charlotte Marliani at 15 Rue de la Grange-Batelière — not far from the spot where Maurice Dupin used to bounce his black-eyed daughter on his knee. The Marlianis were then living in an elegant town house owned by Musset's friend Alfred Tattet, and though their apartments were less grand in size and furnishings than the affluent banker's, they could hold their own in the choiceness of their guests. For it was here, at a dinner offered for Marie Dorval after a theater performance at the Odéon, that Chopin put on one of his unforgettable impromptus, improvising on the piano with that air of rapt concentration which was so uniquely his.

"On vous adore" (We adore you) — George Sand scribbled on a sheet of her own stationery by way of thanks. To which Marie Dorval added the breathless words: *"Et moi aussi! et moi aussi! et moi aussi!"*

Was this the first time George Sand had dared write a note to Frédéric Chopin? Unfortunately there is no way of answering this question, for most of their correspondence was later destroyed. But this note was regarded as so precious by its recipient that he carefully glued it into the album in which he kept his most treasured mementos.

Chopin's visit to the Marlianis' home was followed by others. On May 8 they saw each other again, when George Sand, dressed in a tight-sleeved, flowered dress decorated with a lace jabot and her dark hair tied into a flaming red hairnet, made a noteworthy appearance alongside Victor Hugo, Charles Nodier, the novelist Sophie Gay, and Balzac's former mistress, the flamboyant Duchesse d'Abrantès, at a concert-dinner given by Astolphe de Custine (a literary esthete whose novels and whose even more fascinating *Lettres de Russie* were to become one of the great inspirations of the equally effeminate and esthetic Marcel Proust). The high point of the evening, once again, was provided by Chopin's dazzling improvisations on the piano. If Chopin occasionally submitted to such "public" demonstrations of his genius, it was only with the greatest reluctance — as George Sand made clear in the note she sent to Delacroix just four days later. "To persuade you to come this evening, I shall tell you that Chopin is going to play the piano for us in limited company, with his elbows on the piano, which is when he is truly sublime. Come at midnight, if you are not an early sleeper, and if you meet any of my acquaintances, say nothing to them about it, for Chopin has a dreadful fear of *Welches*" — by which she meant "barbarians."

That this strange, cigar-smoking woman was anything but a philistine in her appreciation of good music Chopin was quick to realize. Liszt, who had gone to such pains to bring them together, had long since told Chopin of her impressive musical knowledge. She was not herself a piano virtuoso, like the Clara Wieck who had so charmed Chopin several years before in Leipzig and who was to become Robert Schumann's wife. She may not even have played the piano as well as the Maria Wodzinska he had wanted to marry and whose lukewarm postscripts (added to her mother's letters) had proved such a cruel disappointment to him. But George Sand had something which that inhibited, emotionally undeveloped fiancée (if such Maria could be called) had lacked: a deep intensity of feeling and understanding which made her almost tongue-tied in public or semipublic gatherings. For this pensive quality, in such marked contrast to the iconoclastic audacity of her attire, was anything but a pose. Behind the would-be extrovert who smoked cigars and sheathed her olive-hued legs in mannish trousers there was, Chopin realized, a more diffident, secretive person in whom he recognized the dark mirror image of his own intensely private self. And this intimate realization was obviously reciprocal.

If the talkative and uninhibited Franz Liszt, with his pronounced humanitarian sympathies, had been made to appeal to George Sand's extrovertial self (the one-time "devil" turned "author" of the Couvent des Anglaises), Chopin, behind his laconic mask, appealed to something deeper — reaching down, or perhaps one should say up, to those wordless realms of feeling which are impervious to logic and where the very act of speech seems a frivolous intrusion. Born in 1810, the same year as Musset, he was five and a half years younger than she was. Like Musset and indeed like herself, Chopin was essentially a romantic anti-Romantic, detesting those facile rhetorical excesses which had marred Victor Hugo's plays and played havoc with the orchestral compositions of Berlioz and Liszt. But unlike Musset, too much a slapdash artist relying on the punch-fed inspiration of the moment, Chopin was a perfectionist who was never satisfied with approximations. Though George Sand in this respect was different — never having the time nor, one suspects, the inclination to polish her gushing prose — she felt boundless admiration for the seriousness with which Chopin approached the problems of his art. A Romantic in his desire to capture and render different moods, he was nonetheless a classicist who sought an absolute clarity of form. Bach was his god, and Mozart, that master of orchestral economy, his favorite composer: preferences which likewise commended themselves to Aurore, drilled by her grandmother in the "celestial" music of the eighteenth century.

Nothing could have seemed less predestined than this sudden burgeoning romance between the hypersensitive pianist and this somewhat mannish woman who had at first repelled him. But by mid-May of 1838 the ice had completely melted and they were exchanging their first hesitant embraces in a mood of startled rapture.

News that Maurice was ill brought George Sand racing back to Nohant, from where she wrote to Albert Grzymala, who seems to have feared the disruptive effect which too intimate a friendship could have on the high-strung Chopin. This "monument of duplicity and hypocrisy," as this long and tortuous epistle has been called, was in reality a laborious effort to envisage the kind of relationship between herself and Chopin that would be best suited to his artistic temperament. She had no desire to play the role of "evil angel" in his life by tearing him away from his "youthful love" — Maria Wodzinska — *if* he was still genuinely in love with her. What George wanted to know was which of the two — herself or Maria Wodzinska — he had to forget or abandon to preserve his happiness and peace of mind, indeed his very life, "which seems to me too frail and tottering to undergo great sufferings." For, she protested with a bit too much insistence, "if I had known that there was a bond in the life of our child" — by which she meant Chopin — "I would never have bent down to inhale the scent reserved for another altar. He too would doubtless have withdrawn from our first kiss if he had known that I was, as it were, *married*" — to Mallefille, presumably. But no, she went on: "We did not deceive each other, we abandoned ourselves to the passing wind which for several instants carried us up to another region." But alas, after this "celestial firing" of their winged souls, they had had to return, like birds, to their earthly nests and humdrum family life. She, because of Maurice's ill health, could not settle down in Paris, etc.

There was another consideration she felt obliged to mention: the presence in her life of another man (Mallefille) — "an excellent, indeed a *perfect* human being from the point of view of heart and honor whom I will never leave, because he is the only man who, having been with me for almost a year, has not once, even for a *single minute,* made me suffer through his fault. He is also the only man who has given himself entirely and absolutely to me, without regret for the past, without reservations for the future. And then, he is of such a good and wise nature that there is nothing I cannot get him to understand with time; he is a malleable wax on which I have imposed my seal, and when I want to change its imprint, I'll manage it with a little patience and precaution. But today this wouldn't be possible, and his happiness is sacred to me."

Such being her partially shackled condition — for a number of years at least — she would feel more than a little frightened were Chopin to place his fate in her hands. She could try to remain remote, avoiding all personal contact so that Chopin could free his mind of her obsessive image. Or she could move as closely as possible to him — "without compromising Mallefille's security" she hastened to interject — by softly recalling her presence to the Master in his "hours of repose and beatitude" and by "sometimes chastely hugging him in my arms when the celestial wind will agree to carry us up for a ride through the air."

It was an astonishing proposition, and one which bore an odd resemblance to the proposal she had once made to Casimir apropos of Aurélien de Sèze. For though she was now George Sand, she was still the same Aurore Dudevant who was ready to render to Caesar that which is Caesar's and to God that which is God's. To Mallefille she would continue to pay the carnal tribute she had once paid to her husband, while to Chopin would go the spiritual homage, the pure, unsullied transports of "celestial" delight she had once reserved for Aurélien de Sèze. Or so at least it sounded up to this point in her letter. For now, having climbed out so far on this precariously platonic limb, she hastened to crawl back, as though suddenly conscious of the puerility of her proposal. She had to admit that on returning to Nohant she had no longer felt the same tenderness for "poor" Mallefille. Indeed, she had even experienced a depressing feeling of embarrassment under the fire of his caresses, and this lukewarmness on her part, which she had needed considerable courage to hide, was clearly a warning that she was still very impressionable "and weaker than I thought."

Having already been *spiritually* unfaithful to Mallefille, she went on, she might as well surrender the rest, "for he who has lost the heart has lost everything." Thus, *in principle,* she felt that a "complete consecration" of her friendship with Chopin would not really aggravate the fault already committed by her wayward heart, it would simply make their attachment to each other "more human, more violent, more dominant, after possession . . . This is why, when one wants to live together, one must not outrage nature and truth by recoiling from a complete union . . ." Indeed, if Chopin had asked her to go to bed with him in Paris, she would have given in, "as a result of that straightforwardness which makes me hate precautions, restrictions, false distinctions and subtleties of every kind."

This was followed by several long paragraphs in which she expressed her frank dismay at a certain prudishness she had encountered in Chopin, who "in the manner of the devout" seemed ashamed of the temptations of the flesh that had assailed him and "to be afraid to sully our love through one additional transport. This manner of envisaging the final embrace of love has always been repugnant to me. If this final embrace is not a thing as holy, pure and devout as the rest, there is no virtue in abstaining . . . Can such a thing as love exist without a single kiss, and a loving kiss without voluptuousness? To *despise the flesh* can only be wise and useful for those who are only *flesh;* but with those one loves, it is not the word despise but the word *respect* which one must use when one abstains."

But far from wishing to *respect* Chopin, she seemed to feel it her duty to teach him the "sacred" joys of physical union, which some gross predecessor had clumsily spoiled for him. "Who then is the unfortunate woman who has left him with such impressions of physical love? So he had a mistress who was unworthy of him? Poor angel! One should hang all the women who villify in men's eyes the most respectable and holiest thing in creation, the divine mystery, the most serious of living acts, the most sublime in the universe . . . From this way of separating the spirit from the flesh has sprung convents and houses of ill fame."

Having thus appointed herself a kind of *doctoresse d'amour* whose duty it clearly was to complete the half-bungled process of Chopin's devirgination, she invited Grzymala to bring him down to Nohant, giving her due warning in advance so that she could arrange to have Mallefille sent off to Paris or Geneva on some conveniently trumped up mission.

Less than a week later she wrote a second, this time very brief note to Grzymala to say that "business matters" necessitated her rapid return to Paris; he was to keep it secret so that "the little one" — Chopin — would be given a charming surprise. But Chopin, who seems to have been as anxious to see her again as she was to see him, was given advance warning by Charlotte Marliani, whom he had taken to visiting in George Sand's absence. "I shall stay at home until five o'clock and shall not stop giving lessons (I am finishing my second)," Chopin hastily scribbled to his friend Grzymala on the day of George's expected arrival in the city. "What is going to happen? God only knows, I don't feel well."

A later note, likewise dispatched to Grzymala, complained that Aurore — the Roman goddess of dawn — "was yesterday drowned in fog. Today I hope there will be sunshine." George Sand may have been troubled by Mallefille's presence in Paris — he had been sent up a week or two before to attend to certain financial problems involving the Hôtel de Narbonne — and postponed the "complete consecration" of her romance with Chopin until his predecessor had been sent back to Nohant. But with Grzymala's paternal blessing they were soon physically united in Chopin's daintily furnished apartment on the Chaussée d'Antin.

Not content with having herself "immortalized" by Auguste Charpentier, George persuaded Delacroix to paint a joint portrait — an idea Chopin accepted only with reluctance, being temperamentally more drawn to the classical serenity of Ingres than to Delacroix's fiery use of color. To overcome his hesitations, a Pleyel piano was carted over to the Left Bank and installed in Delacroix's second-story studio on the Rue des Marais Saint-Germain. And here it was that the two lovers were painted — Chopin seated at the piano, a shock of romantic hair overshadowing his knit brows, his brooding eyes staring off into space in search of melodic inspiration; George Sand standing by him, her eyelids devoutly lowered and her mouth partly open, as though left breathless by the virtuoso's quick-fingered modulations.

Her new liaison notwithstanding, George Sand's life soon regained much of its unorthodox regularity. After the five o'clock dinner, which she usually shared with Charlotte and Manuel Marliani and their friends — which now included Chopin and Grzymala — she would often retire around midnight to a small mansard room she rented (under the pseudonym of Madame Dupin) in a hotel on the nearby Rue Laffitte. The tiny dormer window gave her a pocket handkerchief spread of sky, "with just twelve stars" (as she wrote to Delacroix). Here, on the nights she did not spend with Chopin, she would work with her customary intensity until 8:00 or 9:00 A.M., and occasionally even until noon, before lying down for a few hours of sleep.

She had finally decided not to leave for Italy or even Switzerland, as she had originally intended, before settling her troublesome marital and financial problems. An agreement signed with her husband in early July granted her custody over her two children for eleven months in the year, Casimir being allowed to have them with him for the remaining month. Three weeks later she signed a new contract with Buloz, which guaranteed her a sum of 5000 francs for each new volume published, the *Revue des Deux Mondes* retaining a virtual monopoly in serial publication rights through to the end of 1840. While the terms were relatively generous — roughly twice as high as those she had first negotiated with Buloz five years earlier — only by turning out enough prose to fill three volumes a year could she hope to assure herself a comfortable income of 15,000 francs. And in the meantime she had to finish at least one new book in order to leave Buloz with a maximum of manuscript material before she pushed off toward the south with Maurice and Solange.

"I am still in the state of bliss in which you left me," she wrote ecstatically to Delacroix in early September, after the painter had retired for a few weeks to the country. "There is not the tiniest cloud in this pure sky, not a grain of sand in our lake. I'm beginning to believe that there are angels disguised as men who pass themselves off as such and who inhabit the earth for a while to console and lift up with them toward heaven the poor, exhausted and saddened souls who were ready to perish here below."

This amorous euphoria also affected her literary output. Under the influence of Chopin's daily presence and genius, she found herself curiously unable to finish *Spiridion,* a religious novel based on Lamennais' and Pierre Leroux's ideas of a debased and perverted Christianity. The novel's solemn, monastic setting seemed too melancholy for her present, sunlit mood. *Spiridion* was accordingly shunted aside for something written in a less ponderous vein. Or so George Sand originally intended. Entitled *Les Sept cordes de la lyre* (*The Seven Strings of the Lyre*), this new opus became a musico-philosophical dialogue presented in the form of a play, like *Faust.* A century later André Maurois termed it a "detestable pastiche" of Goethe, but he could with equal justice have called it a pastiche of Hoffmann's *The Violin of Cremona.* It was nonetheless pure Sand, a new version of her youthful epic *Corambé* overlain with the mystic pantheism of Ballanche and Pierre Leroux. This *drame fantastique,* as the author called it, was if anything even more rhetorical and didactic than *Spiridion,* exalting the educative value of art and echoing the Saint-Simonian ideas ("music is the language of the infinite") that had been so eloquently and passionately discussed in those long sessions at the Hôtel de France two years before, the only difference being — and what a difference it was! — that here the well-meaning sage Albertus (a composite Liszt-Lamennais-Leroux philosopher) was reduced to silence by the naive, mystically inclined Hélène, who finds in music a far surer key to the understanding of the secrets of the human heart than the most rigorous dialectic. "Listen to the voice that sings of love and not the voice that explains it," declares the Spirit of the Lyre, a kind of chained-up Ariel and at the same time a disembodied personification of Chopin. For those who had keen ears this meant that Chopin, the aristocratic esthete who believed in art for art's sake, had at last triumphed over Liszt, the champion of a utilitarian art, or as André Malraux would say today, of an "art for the masses."

The serenity of this idyllic summer was brusquely shattered in mid-September, when the unfortunate Mallefille finally awoke to what was going on. To keep him occupied and out of Paris, George Sand had had him take Maurice on a two-week excursion by riverboat down the Seine as far as Rouen and Le Havre. But on his return to the capital he was made to understand that their love affair was over and that he could no longer enjoy the favor of George's bed.

Wall-eyed though he was, the dark-bearded playwright could still see well enough to realize that Madame Sand was hiding something from him. Having recently been encouraged to write a highly laudatory article about Chopin, he was more than a little mortified to discover that it was the pianist and composer he had just lavishly praised who was the cause of his misfortunes. Posting himself one night in front of Chopin's house, he surprised George Sand as she emerged and would — according to one account — have laid violent hands on her had a passing carriage not placed itself between them and allowed her to make a precipitate escape. According to another version, he began furiously pounding on Chopin's door, shouting bloody murder, and had to be forcibly restrained by Albert Grzymala from seizing the frail pianist and strangling him on the spot when the door was finally opened.

When another of Maurice's tutors, Alexandre Rey, took him to task for his "scandalous" behavior, Mallefille angrily challenged him to a duel, which was apparently fought without excessive loss of blood or life. As George Sand explained in a letter addressed to the homespun "philosopher" Pierre Leroux, who was asked to calm the cuckolded ex-lover: "His love which was calm (too calm for my liking when mine was ready for everything) has flared up in the face of obstacles and objections which have wounded his self-esteem and vanity. Now he is persuaded that he is experiencing a deep, tragic, unbridled passion, and by dint of declamation, he has managed to feel all of its fury and suffering."

The excellent, *perfect* being whom she had sworn she would never leave the previous May thus turned out to be imperfect, and this specimen of human wax considerably less malleable than she had hopefully supposed.

28. The Solitude of Valldemosa

THE IDEA OF GOING to Italy for the winter had by this time been abandoned in favor of Mallorca. The main reason for the change seems to have been financial, for as Manuel Marliani pointed out to his friend George, Mallorca could be reached more easily and cheaply than Calabria or Sicily, which alone offered a corresponding mildness of temperature in the coldest winter months. Chopin, who had (or so he thought) at last found a soul mate in the tender, dark-eyed, and maternally solicitous George Sand, needed little persuading to be included in the trip. Certain of his friends, alarmed by his persistent coughing, had long been pressing him to spend the next winter in some sun-filled Mediterranean city rather than in a gray and sunless Paris; and though Grzymala was frankly apprehensive about his ability to endure the rigors of such a journey, the same Dr. Gaubert who had examined Maurice the previous April was of a contrary opinion, declaring that Chopin's chronic cough was not, so far as he could determine, the product of consumption. As for the piano which was so vital to his life and well-being, this ceased to be an obstacle when his friend the publisher and piano-maker Camille Pleyel assured him that he would have one shipped to him by boat to Palma de Mallorca.

To help finance the trip, Chopin agreed to sell Pleyel a series of twenty-four preludes (one in each major and minor key) for a total sum of 2000 francs. Five hundred francs were given to him in advance, it being agreed that the remaining 1500 would be paid when the half-dozen still unfinished preludes were finally completed. An additional 1000 francs were lent to him by a Jewish banker. George

Sand, being accompanied by two children and a maid, needed more. Buloz once again was asked to make the necessary advance, which once again he did: 6000 francs — as compared to the 4000 francs which had sped George Sand and Alfred de Musset on their fateful way to Italy almost five years before. Though he was still waiting for the finished manuscript of *Spiridion,* which she had been promising him for weeks, Buloz consented to act as her witness for the passport-issuing formalities, and he even prevailed on the French foreign minister, Comte Molé, to give her a precious letter of introduction to the French consul in Barcelona.

As the fifteen-year-old Maurice was too delicate to stand overnight stagecoach trips, his mother decided to cover as much of the distance as possible by riverboat and to allow twelve days for the journey to Perpignan, where Chopin was to join them at the end of the month. Accompanied by her two children, a maid, three large trunks (one of them filled with textbooks), and half a dozen smaller packages and bonnet boxes, George Sand left Paris on the morning of October 18, proceeding up the Seine as far as Melun, where a carriage was waiting to drive them over to the country house of her friends, the Roëttierses du Plessis. She found her "foster father" sadly aged and so gout-ridden that he was reduced to hobbling around on crutches. While the Roëttierses kept the children entertained in the spacious grounds, George Sand locked herself into her bedroom and, writing furiously, managed to finish the third part of *Spiridion,* leaving the manuscript pages in an envelope to be forwarded to Buloz in Paris.

From Melun they traveled on to Chalons-sur-Saône. Here they took another riverboat to Lyon, where there was another leisurely stopover to see friends. Proceeding down the Rhone as far as Avignon, they continued overland to Nîmes, where Jules Boucoiran outdid himself to keep them entertained. One of his painter friends was so struck by Madame Sand's unusual garb at the breakfast table — a magnificent white cashmere wrapper, which brought out the dark luster of her thick ebony hair, held in place by a tiny gold dagger — that he hurried home to paint her portrait from memory. That same evening he rounded up a few youths, and giving them pitch-smeared torches, he had them run through the shadowy arcades of the old Roman arena in a ghostly pageant that was much enjoyed by George and her children.

There were more spectacles and entertainments at Perpignan, where they were joined by Chopin, looking "fresh as a rose and pink as a turnip" (as George Sand later put it) and not at all like somebody worn out by a four-day stagecoach journey. Tipped off by Manuel Marliani, the Spanish consul had them serenaded with guitars, jew's-harps, and ophicleides. And it was with the sound of this gay music still ringing in their ears that they boarded the paddle-wheel steamer at Port Vendres, from which they sailed round the promontory of Cadaqués and down the Costa Brava under a radiant blue sky and a hot Mediterranean sun which thrilled them all.

At Barcelona, where they spent five days waiting for the next departure of the weekly packet to Mallorca, the sky was even bluer. Behind the city's massive ramparts, with their bristling cannon, redoubts, portcullises, and drawbridges, the great Mediterranean port seemed strangely tranquil and unconcerned by the turmoil prevailing in the rest of Catalonia, where bands of Carlist marauders roamed the countryside, raiding villages and farms, occupying isolated villas and country houses, pillaging and ransoming travelers rash enough to venture out on the unguarded highways. At night, when the guitars at last fell silent and the empty streets echoed only to the plodding tramp of the *serenos* making the rounds with their lanterns, clubs, and keys, the stillness was periodically broken by the distant cries of sentinels and the feverish chatter of gunfire.

On November 7 they were finally able to embark on a paddle-wheel steamer equipped with a single tall funnel, two masts complete with mainsails, and even a flying jib (in case the coal-powered steam engine broke down). Recently purchased from its British manufacturers, *El Mallorquín,* as it had been christened, was anything but a luxurious vessel, its chief purpose being to transport pigs from Mallorca to the mainland. As they were now traveling in the opposite direction, the passengers had the steamer pretty much to themselves. The eighteen-hour voyage was relatively calm, and rather than retire below, George Sand and Chopin preferred to remain on deck, admiring the steamer's phosphorescent wake and listening to the steersman's melancholy chant as he sang to keep himself from dozing off. The midnight swell was strong enough to upset the normally ebullient Solange, who vomited everything she had eaten on shore. But as the sun rose the next morning over Mallorca's silhouetted mass, she forgot all about her uneasy stomach, running up and down the deck and clapping her little hands in excitement at the sight of the slowly approaching coastline. Finally the port of Palma crept into view, its impressive ramparts dominated by the rectangular mass of its spireless cathedral, the fortress tower of the Almudaina Palace, and a spectacular row of bone white, Don Quixote windmills.

In Barcelona they had found rooms easily enough in a "nasty inn" pompously named the Cuatro Naciones. But in Palma, to their dismay, there was not even an inn to which the word "nasty" could have been applied. Totally unequipped for tourism and unaccustomed to foreign travelers, the small port had recently absorbed a considerable number of Spaniards, who had crossed the waters to find refuge from the war-stricken mainland. But for the help of the French consul, for whom they had a letter of introduction, George Sand and Chopin might have been reduced to camping out on the wharf or returning to Barcelona with the next shipment of hogs. He found them two rooms in a wretched pension situated near one of the town's nine fortress gates, in a quarter teeming with gypsies, seamen, and the usual port parasites, and smelling heavily of rancid olive oil. Here, for one uncomfortable week, they slept on crude bedsteads covered with ill-stuffed mattresses and were driven wild by a buzzing armada of mosquitoes and the ear-splitting hammer blows of a barrel maker housed next door.

Finally, after four days of weary searching, they were fortunate enough to find a sparsely furnished villa in a little hamlet situated a short distance beyond Palma's ocher walls. Unlike the majority of houses they had visited, this one was equipped with windowpanes — an almost unheard of luxury in Mallorca! — as well as shutters, though as usual, there was no sign of a fireplace. There were camp beds to sleep on, the chairs had rush seats, the tables were made of rough white wood, and the only mural decorations, in what was supposed to be the "living room," were some cheap tiles which the owner had decided to have framed, as though they were valuable portraits. But what did it matter when outside there were flowered terraces, a little garden, fragrant lemon trees — with a backdrop of silver green olive groves and pine-covered mountains on one side and a view, over the blue Mediterranean on the other?

"What a sky! What a countryside! We're in raptures," George wrote to Charlotte Marliani. The house and garden cost just fifty francs a month. To say nothing of the monastic "cell" — in fact a three-room apartment — which had been promised them (for the astronomic sum of thirty-five francs a year!) in the charterhouse of Valldemosa, which she had visited the previous day with Chopin and the children.

Chopin was equally enthusiastic, writing to his friend Julian Fontana, one of the rare Paris friends who had been let into the secret of this trip: "I am in Palma, among palms, cedars, cacti, olive trees, pomegranates, etc. Everything the Jardin des Plantes has in its greenhouses. A sky like turquoise, a sea like lapis lazuli, mountains like emeralds, air like heaven. Sun all day, and hot; everyone in summer clothing; at night guitars and singing for hours. Huge balconies with grapevines overhead; Moorish walls. Everything looks toward Africa, as the town does. In a word, a glorious life!"

The first week in this new abode was blissful. The delicate Maurice throve, his pale cheeks were flushed with color, and he put on weight. Solange, grown gentle as a lamb since her seasick crossing from Barcelona ("She vomited up all the venom inside her," as her brother remarked to their mother), applied herself dutifully to her studies, when she was not roaming the countryside in search of quartz and other mineral stones. Chopin, who also went out for long walks, was at last able to resume work on his unfinished Preludes, using an ill-tuned piano they had managed to rent from a family in Palma. Ever the night owl, George could sit outside until five in the morning without feeling a shiver, listening in fascination to the faint tinkle of the collar bells worn by cows and donkeys, the distant sound of a bolero played by an invisible guitar — and nearer, the plaintive grunts of stabled hogs and the hoarse cries of a peasant shouting at them through the window to keep quiet so that he could go back to the recitation of his rosary.

Their good fortune, however, did not last long. A bare week after their move to *So'n Vent* (Wind House, as the low, tile-roofed villa was called in the Mallorquín dialect), Chopin caught cold during a long excursion into the mountains, when they were overtaken by a piercing sea wind blowing at almost gale force. Chilled to the bone and utterly exhausted by the struggle not to be bowled over by the furious gusts or to lose his balance on the stony mule track, he had trouble making it back to the villa, where he was hastily put to bed with a wracking cough. George Sand, who had had to buy everything from sheets and towels to saucepans and mattresses to equip the ill-furnished house, now had to get a local locksmith to *make* her a Prussian stove — an unknown commodity in a land where fireplaces did not exist. The locksmith being, like most Mallorcan artisans, as slow as he was unskilled, it was weeks before the stove was ready. An open *brasero* was accordingly installed in a makeshift effort to warm the unheated house, but its thick charcoal smoke so aggravated Chopin's bronchitis that he was soon spitting blood.

George Sand appealed again to the French consul, who sent Palma's foremost doctor out to see the invalid. True to the standard practice of the day, the physician ordered the invalid to be bled — a remedy which might have put an end to his days then and there. Fortunately, both Chopin and George Sand refused to heed this prescription; whereupon the doctor shrugged his shoulders, said there was really nothing wrong with the gentleman so far as he could see, and would they mind paying him forty-five francs! A second physician was summoned, but his hands were so filthy and stank so dreadfully that the fastidious Chopin would not let him feel his pulse. The third, who seems to have been slightly less pernicious, contented himself with prescribing medicines that could not be found in the one woefully understocked pharmacy in Palma. Preferring her own remedies and methods to those of dubious "professionals," George Sand applied poultices, and to such good effect that by early December Chopin could write to his friend Fontana in a facetious vein to say that the first doctor "sniffed at what I spat up, the second tapped where I spat from, the third poked about and listened how I spat it. One said I had already expired, the second that I was expiring and the third that I would expire. And today I'm the same as ever."

In this last respect he was unfortunately exaggerating. For before Chopin could fully recover from his bronchial attack, the little household was smitten by two additional misfortunes. The clear skies and warm weather they had enjoyed until then abruptly vanished one night, and when they woke the next morning, the lemon trees had been stripped of their blossoms, the dirt road leading up to their villa was a river of mud, and along with the moan of the wind, which kept pelting their windowpanes with raindrops, they could hear the sound of gushing water. The stony brook nearby, under whose graceful poplars and willows the peasant women had come every day to water their thirsty goats in pools of placid water, was now a raging torrent.

Within forty-eight hours the tile-roofed villa of *So'n Vent* became virtually uninhabitable. The moisture seeped through the thin walls, causing the plaster inside to bulge like a sponge. "Never have I suffered so much from the cold," George Sand was later to recall, though it was less a wintry chill than the universal, penetrating damp and the absence of a warm fireplace or stove that caused her to shiver whenever she stopped bustling around — which was not often, since she now had to attend to the cooking, with the help of her French maid — Chopin's delicate stomach being unable to digest the usual Mallorcan dishes, cooked in pork grease or rancid olive oil.

The second misfortune they owed to their landlord. Word had reached him that someone in the villa was coughing and even spitting blood, which could only mean that he was consumptive. They were accordingly invited to evacuate the premises forthwith, before the disease had infected the entire neighborhood and spread to his own family. Nor was that all: tuberculosis being considered a contagious disease, they were required to reimburse Señor Gomez for the cost of replastering and whitewashing *So'n Vent*'s contaminated walls and replacing beds and bedding, which had to be burned in accordance with the provisions of Spanish law.

They were saved once again by the affable French consul, Pierre-Hippolyte Flury, who put them up for five days in his Palma house until the final arrangements could be made for transporting them and their belongings — including the rented piano — up the narrow mountain road to the charterhouse of Valldemosa.

Had George Sand or Chopin been better acquainted with the island of Mallorca, they would have realized what an act of folly it was to move up to the mountains with the onset of winter. But they had come to Mallorca persuaded that it was a sun-blessed paradise, and the first weeks had confirmed this impression. Almost from the moment they had set foot on the Palma dockside, their eyes had been drawn to the mountains of Valldemosa a few miles to the north, which took on a rosy flush as the sun began to sink, gradually fading to a silvery lilac, and then a darkening violet, before subsiding, as night fell, into a deep, mysterious blue. Their first visit to the now abandoned monastery merely confirmed this attraction. For George Sand this was a dream come true — the Camaldulite monastery whose moon- and storm-lit ruins she had described in *Lélia,* the Benedictine monastery of *Spiridion* after it had been sacked by French revolutionaries. If anything, reality here outdid the dream — for nothing could have been more dramatic than this cradle of wild mountains, with its twisted, gesticulating olive trunks and its statuesque cypresses lined up like halberdiers.. Overwhelmed by the splendor of the view over gorges, terraced gardens, and the silver sea barely visible beyond the golden plain, neither George Sand nor Chopin bothered to inquire why certain inhabitants of Palma gratefully withdrew to these cooler heights during the hot summer months, but why none of them chose to remain here in winter. To their soaring poetic spirits this abandoned monastery was a gift from heaven, as was the cell which three Spanish refugees from the mainland — a well-mannered husband, his beautiful, melancholy wife, and a nondescript nephew — were glad to relinquish to them, along with a few, badly needed pieces of rustic furniture, for the rough equivalent of 1000 francs.

On December 15 their belongings, including the rented piano, were piled on to a mule cart, while George Sand, Chopin, the two children, and the French maid Amélie fitted themselves into a horse-drawn *birlocho* or cabriolet. The nine miles up to the charterhouse led them at first across untended slopes of prairie grass, dotted with bright asphodels, after which they began to climb steeply up a sinuous and rocky gorge. The road, which was more like a riverbed strewn with clumps of weed and scrub brush, small landslides of earth, and random rocks, became increasingly steep and difficult to climb. Finally, just beyond the village of Valldemosa — a tiny swallow's nest of houses perched on a hillside — they dismounted opposite an opening in a wall, on both sides of which were carved the arms of the royal house of Aragon.

Beyond this relatively humble gateway a terraced walk of gently inclined flagstones led up past gardens full of cypresses and orange trees to a squat watchtower, one of three originally built to protect the sanctuary from the incursions of Saracen pirates. Large enough "to house an army corps," as George Sand was to describe it, the charterhouse of Valldemosa was in fact a vast, semifortified enclosure embracing the area once occupied by a palace belonging to the kings of Aragon and Mallorca. It was so vast that it included three cloisters, the second large enough to encompass a graveyard where the Carthusian friars were buried, in a deliberate rejection of terrestrial vanity, under mounds of unmarked earth.

The third and most recent cloister, dating from the eighteenth century, was flanked by a vaulted walk more than 150 yards long. Twelve tall doors opened into twelve "cells," each of which had once been occupied by a friar. The appellation is misleading, for these cells — one of which Chopin and George Sand were now to inhabit — were composed of three high-ceilinged chambers, vaulted over with dusty timberwork and lit by Moorish rosettes. The central chamber, which had once been used for prayer, reading, and meditation, was still furnished with a kind of high-backed stall, set into the wall. The chamber to the right contained a hollowed-out alcove for the bed; while the chamber to the left, which had once served as dining room and workshop, was connected to the walk by a hollowed-out tunnel through which it had been the custom to pass in the friar's meals.

Austere these vaulted "cells" would certainly have been but for their one redeeming feature: a kind of vaulted porch giving on to a private south-facing garden. Large enough to contain a few lemon and pomegranate trees, this garden was equipped with a rainwater cistern, and its brick walks were shaded from sun and rain by an arched trelliswork of grape leaves and rambling roses. Beyond a tilework balustrade, there was a short drop down to the first of a series of graded gardens, planted with oranges and grapevines, almonds, and palm trees, which descended down the slope in carefully terraced tiers.

"We are living in an immense, abandoned and half ruined charterhouse, but I have neatly arranged a cell," George Sand wrote to François Buloz shortly after Christmas. "We are perched on the mountains, and the vultures chase the sparrows, swooping as low as the orange trees in the garden. On both sides of the horizon, beyond sublime scenery we can glimpse the sea, which is equally sublime. The Charterhouse, with its large cloisters, its cemetery, its arcades, its chapels, its bubbling fountains, its big laurel bushes, its clipped yew hedges, and above all its silence and abandonment, fulfills all the dreams that could ever have crossed poetic minds. I find myself so unworthy of inhabiting an abode which would have been on Byron's level that I don't think I will ever be able to write about it."

Though this was the way she felt every time she paused to admire the landscape, the picture was a bit too rosy. For the troubles they had already encountered trying to heat the chimneyless villa of *So'n Vent* were if anything multiplied by their move into the mountains. The primitive metal stove, complete with elbow pipe, which they had ordered from Palma's foremost ironmonger, at first smoked so badly and then grew so red-hot that the doors would have to be opened to air out the cell and reopened later to let out the excessive heat. The ironmonger, to make matters worse, had lined the stove with a foul-smelling cement, which reeked so abominably that they had to buy benzoin from the pharmacist to alleviate the stench.

An 1835 decree had ordered the dissolution of all monasteries and convents housing less than twelve monks or nuns. This being the case with Valldemosa, the charterhouse had been emptied of all but one of its inmates but left otherwise unmolested. One of its present "guardians" was a portly sacristan who was reported to have seduced a visiting *señorita* — being only employed by the state, as he put it, to protect *paintings* of saints and virgins. The other was a kind of "housekeeper" named María Antonia, who occupied the cell next to that inhabited by Chopin and George Sand. Deceptively soft-spoken and well mannered — she even claimed to be nobly born — she had come from the mainland to escape the ravages of the Carlist wars and had hired one of the charterhouse's cells, ostensibly to assist visitors to Valldemosa, but in reality to live off them like a leech. Proudly refusing tips and any direct payment — for any services she rendered were accomplished *por el amor de Dios* — she calmly helped herself to the food she was asked to prepare for others, rapaciously assisted by a bony hag named Catalina, who took care of the pots and pans, and a little barefoot girl who was known as *la niña.*

The installation of Chopin's hired piano, added to the chairs and beds needed for a party of five and the wooden tables George Sand needed for her writing and the children for their lessons, left no room inside the cell for cooking. Their meals were consequently prepared next door, in the kitchen which María Antonia "generously" made available to them. Here, aided by the maid and the quick-fingered *niña,* María Antonia would pick chicken drumsticks, cutlets, or an entire fish from the earthenware saucepan on her *brasero* and even invite the sacristan to help them empty the pot when her robust appetite failed her. Outraged by the exorbitant prices the nearby villagers made her pay for scrawny chickens and fleshless fish, George Sand was doubly incensed to find herself thus forced to feed a family of eight. To limit the petty thievery, she had their two *braseros* set up on the brick porch looking out on to the garden, where the flames were buffeted and the hot dishes quickly cooled by the wintry winds.

With each passing day the housekeeping problems grew more burdensome. The witchlike Catalina was denied access to the cell when it was found that she was spreading lice, and unable to find someone to replace her, George Sand had to lend a hand with the broom and help her grumbling maid Amélie make the beds. The simplest vegetables — tomatoes, peppers, or potatoes — were sold to her for four or five times their normal price by villagers who realized they had these foreigners at their mercy. The urchin paid to bring the goat milk so badly needed by Chopin would drink most of it on the way up from the village, calmly refilling the half empty vase with water from a monastery fountain. The goat and later the sheep which George Sand bought out of sheer desperation had to be locked into a special court near the belfry tower to keep Catalina and the *niña* from milking them on the sly. Even then, the daily yield was so meager and had such a sharp taste that it had to be laboriously mixed with ground almonds to be drinkable. Their provisions of biscuits and dried fruit were regularly pilfered, and there were days when they had to do without bread, the loaves brought up by muleback being too rain-soaked to be edible.

For the rains, and diluvial rains at that, were now far more frequent than the intermittent bursts of sun- or moonshine. Often Valldemosa was blanketed by low-flying clouds, when not buffeted by howling winds, which moaned and whined down the draughty gallery outside. Occasionally there was a distant shudder, made by falling masonry, as another tottering arch gave way and crumbled into ruin. The mountains which viewed from a distance had seemed so rosily serene were now the seat of elemental storm and strife. The constant thunder of the surf, monotonously pounding at the base of the cliffs to the north and west, the plaintive cry of sea gulls driven inland by furious gusts of wind, and worst of all, the macabre sight of eagles and buzzards swooping low in the fog to snatch some unsuspecting sparrow from the branch of a pomegranate tree — all began to prey on Chopin's high-strung nerves.

Plagued by his recurring fits of coughing, he was tormented by the depressing feeling that he would never emerge from this monastery alive. He saw himself being buried, like one of the old Carthusian friars, in a nameless grave, condemned to an anonymous burial by a hostile populace which was not prepared to waste pity on someone who was suffering from contagious consumption. Like Musset, he began to be haunted by visions of death and was subject to weird hallucinations. Often at night the charterhouse was visited by an aged drunkard who would stagger down the long gallery, enter María Antonia's cell, frightening the life out of her with his wild, bloodshot eye, his somber, oath-punctuated sermons, his pilgrim's stave and peasant knife. Finally talked into leaving by the sacristan, he would totter up to the next door — that of George Sand and her brood — and begin hammering on the heavy oak and shouting hoarsely for "Father Nicolas." Chopin would start up in superstitious terror at the sound of the name, as though the sepulchral voice echoing in the gallery were a voice from beyond the grave announcing his own father Nicolas' death.

Several times, after taking the children out on nocturnal explorations of the charterhouse's ivy-covered ruins — for it was when viewed by moon or lantern light that they were at their most romantic — George Sand returned to the cell to find Chopin seated before his piano with haggard eyes, his hair almost literally standing on end. Though he said nothing, he looked as though he had just seen a ghost or a whole family of specters.

Shortly before Christmas word reached them that the Pleyel piano had at last reached Mallorca. George Sand and Maurice had themselves driven down to Palma to argue with the customs officials, who wanted to charge them 700 francs (almost as much as the instrument was worth) for the right to "import" this dangerous piece of contraband. The sky, which had been exceptionally clear in the morning, suddenly clouded over in the afternoon, and on their way home they were overtaken by a cloudburst. Unable to make further headway against the torrents of mud and water that were soon cascading down the mountainside, the driver decided to turn back with his mule and rickety *birlocho,* leaving George Sand and Maurice to continue on alone in the darkness. Leaping over raging torrents and moving from bush to bush and tree to tree — the only landmarks left in the pelting rain — they dragged themselves uphill through knee-high streams of water. Three hours later, when they finally staggered into the monastery, dripping, mud-splattered, and their shoes torn to ribbons, they found Chopin bent over the piano, playing one of his recently completed Preludes with tearful desperation. He stood up with a wild cry, looking utterly distraught, then said in a strange, broken voice: "Ah! I knew you were dead!"

After recovering his wits, he told George that in his feverish imagination he had seen them dead, or rather drowned, like himself. He had sat down at the piano in an effort to calm himself and had begun playing in a kind of waking dream, persuaded that he was slowly drowning in a lake, while icy drops of water kept falling on his chest. "Listen!" said George Sand, pointing to the ceiling. Overhead the insistent patter of the rain could be distinctly heard beating down on the monastery's curved tiles. Chopin, as though only now waking from his trance, denied having heard it, and even displayed annoyance at the idea that the insistent repetition of the same note in his music could have been inspired by a conscious effort at "imitative harmony."

George Sand later claimed that certain of the beautiful preludes he completed during their two-month stay at Valldemosa were directly inspired by visions of dead monks and the haunting sound of funeral chants, while the laughter of the children playing in the garden, the remote sound of a guitar, the piping of little birds beneath the dripping leaves, or the chance sight of a pale rose bravely holding out against an unexpected snowfall inspired the rippling gaiety of other passages. But she was also quick to note that Chopin was more easily and deeply upset by the plaintive cry of a famished eagle, the bitter whine of the wind, or the mournful desolation of snow-covered yews than he was elated by the scent of orange trees, the charm of a trellised bower, or the Moorish chanting of the peasants working in the fields. Even more curiously, a genuine misfortune was less shattering in its impact upon him than a trifling mishap.

Nothing oppressed Chopin more than the feeling that he was hopelessly cut off from friends and "civilization" by the unpredictable vagaries of the mail. For when the north wind blew, the skipper of the paddle-wheel *Mallorquín* preferred to remain tied up at the dockside, for weeks at a time if necessary. The rare letters they received from Paris took six weeks or more to reach them. Battered by the elements, the old charterhouse came more and more to seem like a fortress under siege, surrounded by a howling nature as hostile and ill-disposed as the villagers of Valldemosa.

For this unfriendly human climate they were themselves mostly to blame. Feeling that it was not up to her to adapt herself to the backward customs and traditions of ignorant fishermen and peasants, George Sand here displayed the same devil-may-care insouciance which had once shocked the staid burghers of La Châtre. The midnight walks she liked to take through the ruins with her children, beneath a scudding moon, were more than a little disquieting to the superstitious villagers, while they were frankly shocked by the trousers Solange was allowed to run around in and by the reports that reached them of George Sand smoking homemade cigars in the privacy of her cell.

These eccentricities might well have been forgiven had she but consented to attend Sunday Mass with her children. But this she made not the slightest effort to do. When Charles Dembowski, a fellow countryman of Chopin's as well as a distant kinsman of the Marlianis, turned up at Valldemosa one day armed with a letter for George Sand, he found the villagers dressed up in carnival masks for a local fiesta. A long procession of squealing pigs and mules was being driven past a statue of Saint Anthony (Mallorca's patron saint), while a priest standing on the town-hall porch sprinkled the beasts with holy water. Anxious to deliver the letters that had been entrusted to him, Dembowski continued on up to the charterhouse and was invited to stay for supper. Later that same evening he returned to the tavern, where the villagers were still dancing. He was introduced to the *alcalde,* which is to say the mayor, and also to the local priest, who had been informed of his visit to the monastery. The priest, who had spent the morning sprinkling holy water on the hogs and donkeys, seemed particularly annoyed that George Sand should not have bothered to attend the festivities. *"Por cierto que esta señora francesa tiene que ser una mujer muy particular"* (This French lady must certainly be a very special woman), he complained. "She speaks to nobody, never leaves the charterhouse, never appears at church, not even on Sundays, thus accumulating Lord knows how many mortal sins on her soul. I have been told by the apothecary who also lives at the charterhouse, that the *señora* rolls her own cigarettes, drinks coffee at all hours of the day, sleeps in daytime and spends her nights writing and smoking. You who know her, dear Sir, pray tell us what she has come to do here in the middle of winter." It was a question Dembowski was hard put to answer, being much mystified himself by this stubborn search for seclusion.

An evening or two later George Sand and Chopin were startled by an extraordinary noise, as though thousands of nuts were being rolled by the sackful across a marble floor. They hurried out into the dark, deserted cloister, but at first could see nothing. The brittle sound of rolling nuts kept growing closer and soon a trembling glow illumined the resounding vaults and arches. Finally a number of flaming torches came into view, followed in the reddish smoke by an unholy throng of devils with pointed beaks instead of noses, shaggy ears, and horses' manes and tails, who seemed to be egging on a flock of captive shepherdesses. Barely able to hold up the lantern she held in her hand, George Sand watched in apprehensive fascination as the unsightly horde advanced upon them solemnly to the wooden click of castanets. Disguised in carnival masks, the villagers of Valldemosa had come up to celebrate the recent wedding of a well-to-do farmer in María Antonia's cell. One of them, a lawyer, stopped to address the dark-haired stranger in Spanish, then asked her in awkward French how she liked the *cartouche* — the equivalent, he must have thought, of the Spanish *cartuja* (charterhouse), not realizing that it actually means "cartridge." George Sand was apparently not amused by the slip. She and Chopin did, however, consent to go next door for a while to watch the perspiring husband dance jotas and fandangos with all the village girls in a cell gaily decorated with paper lanterns and ivy wreaths though reeking more strongly than ever of rancid oil and garlic.

This festive event seems to have been the only occasion on which they deigned to mingle with the natives — the "monkeys," as George Sand and Maurice referred to these sly, suspicious, thieving country folk, who avenged themselves on these pagan "sinners" by charging exorbitant prices for everything, while the urchins threw stones at Maurice and Solange each time they saw her appear in trousers.

Neither the belated installation of the little Pleyel piano (an upright with two strings per note, as was then the fashion) which they finally argued away from the Mallorcan customs for the sum of 300 francs, nor the early advent of spring in late January — when the orange trees broke into blossom and Maurice sat outside in his shirt-sleeves studying Thucydides — could alleviate the curse which seemed to have descended on them. While Maurice seemed to thrive on the invigorating mountain air, the omnipresent damp brought out all of George Sand's old rheumatic pains and did nothing to help Chopin's wracking cough. Like Musset in Venice, he felt trapped and had but one desire — to escape from this tomblike cell and these echoing vaults before death claimed his emaciated body. Fearful of leaving him for more than a brief instant, George remained, as though chained to his bedside, unable to accompany the children when they went out on excursions.

By early February she could stand the strain no longer. Working far into each night, she hastened to finish a new, three-volume version of *Lélia,* which she was intent on delivering to Buloz as soon as possible so that he could reimburse the 3000 francs she had been forced to borrow from a Spanish banker in Paris. The banker's correspondent in Mallorca, a Señor Ernest Choussat de Canut, was willing to relieve them of the Pleyel piano for 1200 francs. But when it came to transporting their trunks and, above all, the sick Chopin down from Valldemosa, not one of the relatively affluent persons to whom they had been introduced in Palma was ready to lend them a carriage, doubtless fearing that the contaminated vehicle would subsequently have to be burned. They were finally reduced to hiring a two-wheel cart. The terrible jolting Chopin underwent in this springless vehicle as it lurched and scraped its way downhill unleashed another frightful spasm of coughing and the spitting up of quantities of blood-flecked phlegm.

The French consul offered them shelter once again, but Chopin was still coughing convulsively the next day when he was helped aboard the *Mallorquín.* The upper deck was entirely occupied by pigs and they were forced to go below, where the heat was intense and the stench unbearable. The captain asked them not to stretch Chopin out on the cabin's best bed (since it too would have to be burned the next day), but no heed was taken of his request. Though the heat abated during the night, they were kept awake by the heart-rending squeals of one hundred hogs, regularly beaten into submission with whips, clubs, and crowbars, and forced to lie on their sides in the hope that this would keep them from being sick.

By the time they reached Barcelona the next morning, the hypersensitive Chopin was a nervous wreck. He kept coughing up blood and phlegm "by the bowlful" (as George Sand later wrote) and was as white as a sheet. The captain, however, insisted that all of his hogs had to be disembarked first inasmuch as they were his principal cargo. Afraid that Chopin was going to cough himself to death before they could get off this cursed craft, George Sand scribbled out a note and tossed it with a coin to a nearby boatman, asking him to row over to a French brig anchored across the way. The note had a magical effect on the French captain, who had himself rowed over in his cutter to pick them up. The children were so relieved that on climbing onto the French warship's deck, they shouted: *"Vive la France!"* The ship's physician went to work on Chopin, calming his convulsive cough and easing his hemorrhage. The French consul sent over his personal carriage and had them driven to the Cuatro Naciones hotel, where Chopin was given eight days to recover from the rigors of the trip. Here too they had trouble with the owner, who forced them before leaving to pay for both bed and sheets, which he was required by Spanish law to burn.

The *Phénicien,* which they were finally able to board, seemed a floating paradise after the hot, cramped, stinking *Mallorquín.* More than anxious to please, the captain had his own mattress carried over to Chopin's cabin to improve the softness of his bunk. Thus cared for and comforted, Chopin was able to endure the thirty-six-hour voyage to Marseille without too much pain or suffering. In Marseille he was delivered into the competent hands of Dr. François Cauvière, a friend of the Marlianis whom they had met in Paris the previous September and who had already been helpful in getting the Pleyel piano shipped over to Mallorca. He prescribed a month of absolute rest before they moved on to Nice or Genoa, as was their intention. As George Sand could write on February 26 to Charlotte Marliani, "He no longer spits up blood, sleeps well, coughs little, and above all is in France!"

29. The Tigress of Armenia and Her Little One

AFTER SEVERAL DAYS spent in the house of the hospitable Dr. Cauvière, Chopin, George Sand, and the children moved to the Hôtel de la Darse, the owner of which was Manuel Marliani's brother Joseph. From here George Sand sent Buloz an urgent letter saying that once again she was penniless and in desperate need of money. The manuscript of the profoundly overhauled *Lélia* (now become a novel of faith and hope rather than a novel of feminine despair) had been posted in Barcelona but had not got beyond the customs and post office of Marseille, where she retrieved it. She now sent it on to Charlotte Marliani, who had already been instructed to demand a total of 7500 francs for this three-volume work. The 6000 franc advance Buloz had made to her the previous October had by now been paid back with *Les Sept cordes de la lyre* (worth 5000 francs) and a second printing (in the series of her Complete Works) of *Simon* (worth 1500 francs), leaving her with a credit of 500 francs. Added to what Buloz owed her for the overhauled *Lélia,* this made for a credit of 8000 francs — more than enough to reimburse the Spanish banker in Paris (from whom she had borrowed 3000 francs) and to have a few thousand francs left over.

Buloz, who was anything but happy about *Les Sept cordes de la lyre* — finding this five-act dialogue painfully full of windy mysticism and pseudo-philosophical rhetoric — sent her a preliminary payment of 500 francs, tartly reminding her that *she* still owed him 4500 francs for an advance he had made to her four years earlier for the undelivered *Engelwald.* Never more outraged than when she was in the wrong, George Sand now hit the roof, calling Buloz a "Jewish tightwad," a literary Shylock — like the music dealer, Probst, and even more Pleyel, who had offhandedly sent poor Chopin 500 francs, instead of 1500, for the twenty-four Preludes that had been mailed to Paris from Mallorca.

Rant and rave though she might in her letters, George Sand was privately forced to admit that Buloz had a case. Though she was personally convinced that *Spiridion* and *Les Sept cordes de la lyre* were among the most "profound" things she had written, and infinitely superior to "little novels like *André*" — the kind of light stuff her editors were clamoring for — she could not honestly ask Buloz and his financial backer and associate Félix Bonnaire to make the increasingly conservative *Revue des Deux Mondes* into an organ for the propagation of Pierre Leroux's Christian messianism, even though, as she wrote to Charlotte Marliani, she felt "that the readers of the *Revue* [*des Deux Mondes*] should grow a little less stupid, since I for my part am growing less stupid."

Realizing that there were times when she had to compromise with her exalted expectations, George Sand now set out to write a Renaissance melodrama. Though Balzac, when he later read it, was charitable enough to speak well of *Gabriel* and to suggest that it would make a real thriller if staged, there was something painfully implausible in this story of a Florentine duke who has his granddaughter, Gabrielle, brought up as a boy in order to keep his title and possessions from passing to the male descendants of his younger son. But since Shakespeare had more than once indulged in this kind of sex-changing travesty, why shouldn't she, particularly since it offered a convenient vehicle for airing feminist convictions and for showing how the conventions of male dominance, in matters of inheritance and other material interests, can vitiate paternal instinct and affection.

For George Sand, at any rate, the ten weeks spent in Marseille thus proved as laborious and tiring, if not as nerve-racking, as the fourteen weeks spent in Mallorca. Dr. Cauvière having prescribed a period of complete rest for Chopin, she had to postpone the projected trip to Italy until he was well enough to travel. From the Hôtel de la Darse they moved to the more pleasant Hôtel Beauvau, where George had already stayed with Alfred de Musset five years earlier. Here nothing was allowed to interrupt the simple routine of their family life. "I don't cough much, only in the morning," Chopin could write to his friend Julian Fontana in early March. "I drink no coffee, nor wine, only milk; I dress warmly and look like a girl." A piano was duly installed in his room, while George had a room of her own in which to work at her desk, far into each night.

The problem of educating the children, which had so plagued her in Mallorca, was happily resolved with the help of Alexandre Rey, Maurice's former tutor, who had fought the duel with Mallefille the previous September and who now providentially reappeared in Marseille — so providentially that one wonders if it was altogether fortuitous.

More difficult to satisfy was the desire to live privately in a public hotel. As George Sand wrote to Charlotte Marliani in early March: "I am besieged here as in Paris. From morning till nightfall the idle and curious, as well as literary beggars, keep hammering at my door in person or with their letters. I maintain myself inflexibly on the defensive, neither reply nor receive, and give it out that I am ill. Don't be surprised if you receive news from here that I am dying . . . The literary mob persecutes me, just as the musical mob is hot on Chopin's heels. I am giving it out that he is ill, and if this goes on we shall be issuing death notices for both of us."

Though neither of them liked Marseille — "this city of merchants and greengrocers, where the life of the mind is perfectly unknown" — they were unable to rent a house in the vicinity of Aix or Avignon, as they had originally hoped. Nor was Chopin's recovery as rapid as she would have wished, even though he was soon well enough to drink a glass of diluted champagne, and by early April to go out on sunny days for carriage rides. "He's so nervous that the slightest thing fatigues him," George wrote to Charlotte Marliani in mid-April, adding later in the month: "This Chopin is an angel. His kindness, his tenderness, his patience sometimes make me anxious. I imagine that his is too delicate, exquisite and perfect a nature to live for long off our fat, heavy terrestrial existence. In Mallorca while deathly ill he wrote music that reeked of paradise. But I have grown so used to seeing him in heaven that it doesn't seem to me that his death or life prove anything as far as he is concerned. He doesn't know himself in what planet he is living. He is not at all aware of life as we conceive and feel it."

Chopin would probably have been annoyed had he read these last lines — not so much for what they stated as for what they left unsaid. He was not all that anxious to be treated as an angel. But for the moment he had to admit that he was being cared for with touching devotion by someone whose industry, compared to his own fitful inspirations, was awe-inspiring. "My lady has just finished a magnificent article on Goethe, Byron and Mickiewicz," he could write to Grzymala on March 27. "One must read it; it gladdens the heart."

Two weeks later he wrote again to say: "My Angel is finishing a new novel: Gabriel. Today she will be writing in bed all day. You know, you would love her even more if you knew her as I know her now." To which the Angel in question added, in a French postscript: "I'm all fired up. I don't even take the time to get up. I'm giving birth to a new novel which could do with a pair of forceps. I kiss you and we love you."

Prolix as ever, George Sand had written a long essay in which Mickiewicz was hailed as the prophet of an indomitable Poland, and a martyred Poland, in accordance with the teachings of Pierre Leroux, was depicted as the birthplace of a new, revivified, and purified Christianity. For this she now demanded a fee of 2000 francs from Buloz, while Charlotte Marliani, acting as a kind of benevolent literary agent, was instructed to obtain another 5000 francs for *Gabriel* — money George urgently needed to undertake a brief trip to Italy before returning to Nohant with Chopin.

Their stay in Marseille was unexpectedly saddened by the news that their old friend Adolphe Nourrit, once the star tenor of the Paris Opera, had committed suicide in Naples. His body reached Marseille on April 19, to be buried five days later. At the request of his widow, Chopin agreed to play the organ for the funeral elevation and exodus, but he almost lived to regret it. For the choir sang off-key, while the organ wheezed terribly. Outwitting the local gossips who flocked into the church expecting to see her "seated on the catafalque" (as she wrote to Charlotte Marliani), George hid away in the organ loft, where her "little one" (Chopin) valiantly strove to limit the sonic damage by avoiding the high-pitched tubes and concentrating on the deeper notes.

A few days later, having received a first installment of 2000 francs from Buloz, she, Chopin, and the two children could at last board the paddle-wheel steamer for Genoa. Here they enjoyed ten days of sightseeing during which Chopin did a lot of walking without getting overly tired. On the return trip they were tossed and heaved about for forty hours; everyone, including George Sand, was sick, but Chopin, though exhausted by the ordeal, managed to survive this too without undue harm.

But their difficulties were by no means over. In Marseille George Sand found a letter from Charlotte Marliani informing her that Buloz was dragging his feet on paying what he owed her. Unwilling to tarry any longer in a city which had begun to "stink horribly" in the hot May sun, George borrowed 1000 francs from Dr. Cauvière to pay for the hotel and the expenses of the journey to Nohant. It began with a ferryboat trip up the Rhone as far as Arles, there they disembarked with their carriage. Proceeding by short stages so as not to tire Chopin, they spent a week traveling up the Rhone as far as Tournon, after which they climbed over the mountains to Saint-Etienne and Aubusson, finally reaching Nohant on the first day of June.

"Here we are at last after a week of travel," Chopin promptly wrote to Grzymala. "We are all feeling fine. Lovely countryside: skylarks, nightingales. You are the only missing bird . . . Come, if only for a few minutes. Choose a moment when they [Grzymala's friends] are all in good health and will resign themselves for several days out of charity for others. Let us embrace you. In return you will receive pills and excellent milk. My piano will be at your disposal. You will lack nothing."

"Yes, my dear friend," George Sand wrote to Charlotte Marliani the next day, "I am home and delighted to be able to rest at last from this life of packages and inns which I've been leading for six months on land and sea. We all arrived safe and sound and Chopin was not too worn out by the journey. He is in good health, save that he is thinner, more delicate and nervous than he was prior to this long illness and convalescence, which is not yet over. I set great hopes by a couple of months at Nohant, and he would like to stay as long as possible . . . For my part, I badly need a season of calm . . ."

A season of calm, however, was one thing that was not to be granted to George Sand. The repairs on the Hôtel de Narbonne, she was now informed by Hippolyte (to whom she had entrusted the task of overall supervision), were certain to be double and might even be three times as much as the original estimate of 20,000 francs. By the terms of her final separation settlement, she still owed Casimir 10,000 francs, and to this had to be added another 10,000 franc debt he had passed on to her on a piece of half-paid property. All told, these various liabilities amounted to 80,000 francs, which she was required by law to pay off over a period of ten years: that is, at a rate of 8000 francs a year when the annual income from Nohant barely totaled 7000.

Though Hippolyte generously lent her 14,000 francs, it was more than ever clear that only through writing could George keep herself and her two children alive and provide for their proper education. She accordingly sat down and wrote a long letter to Buloz to explain why she was in such critical need of money. Unlike him, she had neither "post nor subsidies" to maintain her — a reference to Buloz's recent nomination as Royal Commissioner to the Comédie Française; if he was unwilling to accept her essay on Goethe, Byron, and Mickiewicz (the *Revue des Deux Mondes* having just published one on Goethe, written by Buloz's brother-in-law), she would have to find a place for it elsewhere, and if her writings no longer found favor with him, there was no point in maintaining their existing contract. As for *Engelwald,* since there seemed no chance of publishing a novel which might appear to vindicate the designs of an assassin in the France of Louis-Philippe, she suggested that she be allowed to repay the outstanding debt of 4500 francs by deductions from her future book earnings. "Good night, my dear Buloz," she concluded this frank letter. "Reply to me at Nohant, where I have been for five days with a perfectly cured Maurice, a Solange as beautiful and strong as ever, and myself neither beautiful nor rich but still strong enough to kiss Christine" — Buloz's wife — "and to deal you a few punches."

Stung to the quick, the "petty, penny-pinching merchant" — as she had termed him — replied with a furious letter in which he justified his decision to publish another article on Goethe, prior to hers, on the grounds that his brother-in-law had spent two years studying and translating the second volume of *Faust,* which he had read in the *original German.* He concluded his epistolary reprimand with a few blunt words of his own: "Farewell, you have woken the slumbering cat. Goodbye, tigress of Armenia."

The "tigress of Armenia" took her time answering this angry outburst, wishing to obtain the professional advice of her two lawyer friends, François Rollinat and Emmanuel Arago. But the reply was no less stinging for having been delayed. Buloz, she pointed out, could not have his cake and eat it too. Having signed a contract which obligated him to publish everything she wrote, first in the *Revue des Deux Mondes* and then, if it was fiction, in book form, he had no right to delay payment for the things she sent him on the grounds that they were unpalatable to his readers. If what she was sending him was too metaphysical or "phantasmagorical" for his particularly limited and uneducated taste, there was only one honest thing to do: break the contract and let each go his way. She would start writing plays for the Comédie Française only after he, Buloz, had lost his job, "for you are too difficult." No one had ever seen a tigress, or even a tiger, in Armenia — the proper, classical word (for an ancient Persian province) being Hyrcania. After which she added, in a final whiplash: "Kiss Christine for me. I feel sorry for her being the wife of an Etuvian jackal" — the land of Etuvia (a pun on the word *étuve,* or stove) being as much of an invention as the tigresses of Armenia.

The upshot of this exchange of insults, which was continued through several more letters, was a tentative peace settlement. Insisting that she was still "Queen of the *Revue,*" Buloz agreed to publish her essay on Goethe, Byron, and Mickiewicz and urged her to write up her Mallorcan experience, as she had done for Venice.

Buloz's new post with the Comédie Française and his eventual readiness to publish both of her dialogue plays — *Les Sept cordes de la lyre* and *Gabriel* — were enough to persuade George Sand that she had a vocation as a dramatist. *Gabriel* being more like the old, pre–Leroux George Sand, Buloz chose to encourage this illusion in the hope that it might give birth to a truly gripping piece of melodrama, a theatrical equivalent of the *Leone Leoni* (a kind of reverse *Manon*

Lescaut) she had been inspired to write in Venice. The result, pointedly named after the second daughter Marie d'Agoult had borne to Liszt, was a five-act play called *Cosima* ("or Hatred in Love," as it was subtitled). It was finished in mid-September, in time to be discussed with Buloz during a brief visit he made to Nohant with his wife. Determined to prove that the "penny-pinching merchant" of yesterday was in reality an enlightened patron of the arts, Buloz accepted the text, which he had great difficulty imposing on the reluctant actors of the Comédie Française.

Altogether it was a busy summer — with George Sand having to refresh her memory of Greek or Roman history in preparation for the next day's lessons with Maurice and Solange. For Chopin, on the other hand, it was more like a holiday, pleasantly reminiscent of the summers he had once enjoyed with Countess Skarbek at Zelazowa Wola or on Prince Valentin Radziwill's estate near Poznan. He was given an upstairs bedroom gaily decorated with red and blue Chinese wallpaper and warmed by the midday sun since it overlooked the garden. George Sand's room, to the right, was separated from his by a small, book-lined study with communicating doors, while the little antechamber to the left eventually became a kind of music room where he could work on his compositions.

Life at Nohant was delightfully free from organized constraint. Like the others, Chopin could get up when he chose and breakfast on the morning cup of chocolate that was brought to his room, after which he could do as he pleased. At five o'clock in the afternoon a bell summoned everyone to dinner. Often this was his first glimpse of George Sand, who usually rose at midday and tutored her children in the early afternoon. The after-dinner hours were traditionally given over to evening entertainment. Sometimes Chopin would have Solange sit down at the piano and accompany him in some small composition for four hands. When, as often happened, there were guests, he would be asked to put on one of his celebrated imitations. Turning toward the mirror, he would try to pull his neatly curled hair down over his ears, loosen his impeccable cravat, and imitate Liszt's dramatic keyboard flourishes. A moment later, the cravat rearranged, he would sit as stiffly as a ramrod and let his mobile fingers ripple over the keys with the detached perfection of the German virtuoso Kalkbrenner. These sketches, as George Sand was later to write, were sad rather than cruel and "so perfectly understood and delicately translated that one never tired of admiring them."

Amused though he was by Hippolyte's unflagging wit and the comic inventions of Alexis Duteil, ever ready to entertain the company with a hideously off-key chanting of the Mass, Chopin soon began to show signs of restlessness. In early July George Sand wrote to Grzymala, beseeching him once again to make his long-promised visit to Nohant. She couldn't help feeling that Chopin, who enjoyed the social life of Paris, needed a less placid and rustically uneventful existence. She was even willing to have him make a short trip to Paris. "I am ready for any sacrifice rather than to see him waste away in melancholy. Come and feel the pulse of his morale. Who can fix the dividing line between physical illness and intellectual languor? It's not to me he would wish to admit that he is bored. But I guess it. He was not accustomed to such an austere life, and I am turning to an alarming degree into a *mère de famille* and a pedagogue. I have been forced to. Come to see us. The *father* and the *son* really need the cooperation of the Holy Spirit to maintain themselves in the heights of the Empyreum. Heartfully yours, dear old husband."

This was an old joke between them: for a long time George Sand had been calling Grzymala her "husband" and he had been calling her "Dear Wife" in the letters they wrote to each other, while the "son" or "little one" they watched over with motherly or fatherly solicitude was the all too fragile Frédéric, or Frycek, as he was called in Polish. But what was the nature of this Empyreum, to which she was here alluding in such curious language? Three weeks before writing to Grzymala, George Sand had taken a knife and inscribed the date — "19 June 1839" — on the wall of her bedroom. Was it meant to commemorate the first anniversary of their liaison, the night on which their love had received its "complete consecration"? Or did it symbolize some solemn vow she now took, forever closing this particular chapter in her relations with Chopin?

There is no ready way of answering this question. But one is led to suspect that the chastity which George Sand imposed on Chopin during the most critical phases of his illness in Mallorca was either maintained or reimposed at Nohant. The insistence did not come from Chopin, that much seems reasonably certain; it came from her and was maintained (in later years, if not already in 1839) with austere intransigence.

Years later, in writing up *The Story of My Life,* George Sand described this odd relationship in singularly cryptic terms. After mentioning the prolonged anxiety caused her by Maurice's frail health, she frankly admitted that with Chopin she was not "under the illusions of a passion. I had for the artist a sort of very lively, very real maternal adoration, but which could not for a moment struggle against the love born of the entrails . . ." — by which she meant her love for her own children. "One more duty in my life, already so full and crushed by weariness, seemed to provide one more chance for practicing that austerity toward which I felt drawn with a kind of religious enthusiasm."

That her relations with Chopin were influenced by the same mystical élan, à la Pierre Leroux, which now echoed through her writing, is certain, but it is probably not the whole truth. One year before, in her long letter to Grzymala, she had declared that nothing in her view was more sacred than a total union of body and soul. But this was what she was now determined to separate. What had happened in the interim? We can only surmise — for the documentary evidence is lacking — that she had found the physical act of lovemaking with Chopin considerably less exalting than his music. This in itself is not surprising — given her lusty appetite, the coughing to which he could be reduced by the slightest exertion, and his cadaverous physique. Chopin, on his return from Mallorca, was so thin that he weighed less than 95 pounds. No matter how reassuring Gustave Papet, like Dr. Cauvière, might sound in stating that there was no sign of a lesion and that Chopin was not consumptive, she knew better than anyone just how delicate he was, and she was not going to hasten his death by allowing him to indulge in amorous excess. The same fear that had once paralyzed her with Jules Sandeau and with Alfred de Musset in Venice — the fear of seeing her lover die of erotic pleasure in her arms — now seems to have crippled her with Chopin. This time, however, it was easier to disguise this self-imposed restraint beneath a cloak of religious self-sacrifice.

Presumably this ticklish question was thoroughly discussed between herself and Albert Grzymala in early September when the latter came for a two-week visit to Nohant, and presumably Grzymala once again gave his approval, as earlier he had grudgingly consented to her incestuous union with their "little one." This ascetic regime may not have been to Chopin's liking, but in terms of art it was singularly rewarding. For by early summer Chopin had completed the Sonata in B-Flat Minor (including the Funeral March, which had been finished long before), a lively Impromptu in F-Sharp Minor, and two lovely Nocturnes. They were followed by a Waltz, a Scherzo, a second Ballade (in F-Major), two Polonaises, two Etudes, and three new Mazurkas.

30. The Capucin Philosopher's Disciple

In September of this same year, 1839, Chopin's friends Julian Fontana and Albert Grzymala were recruited, along with Emmanuel Arago, to find new apartments in Paris. For Chopin a small bachelor's flat was found on the Rue Tronchet, just behind the Madeleine; for George, Maurice, and Solange two twin-story apartments overlooking the coach houses and sheltered garden of a town house on the Rue Pigalle, then a relatively sedate residential street leading uphill toward the field- and vineyard-surrounded village of Montmartre. The pavilion to the left was inhabited by Maurice, who was given a workroom in which to spread out his drawing boards, easels, and plaster statuary. Next to it was the salon, essentially reserved for evening entertainment. Here a Pleyel piano was installed, in a charming décor of Chinese vases, green-upholstered armchairs and couches, a flower stand full of plants, a cabinet full of dainty bric-a-brac, paintings by Delacroix and Calamatta, and a copy of a magnificent Giorgione nude. The dining room, with its tables, chairs, and sideboards in sculpted oak, was located in the other (right-hand) pavilion. Two paneled doors, which George Sand had specially made to reduce the drafts, opened into a coffee-colored living room, which she also used as a study. Next to this was her brown-walled bedroom, with the bed — two superimposed mattresses reposing on the floor, *à la turque,* as Balzac was later to describe them.

For the next two years in Paris Chopin and George Sand thus led semiseparate lives — in the sense that they did not live under the same roof. Often they did not see each other before the five o'clock dinner, by which time he had finished his afternoon music lessons —

three or four, at twenty francs an hour, which assured him a steady revenue of from sixty to eighty francs a day. George, having spent half the night writing and risen late, as usual, would have had time to attend to business and domestic chores. Dinner was usually spent *en famille,* "between four candles," when the company was limited to a few choice friends — like Grzymala, Delacroix, Charlotte and Manuel Marliani, and *la Divine,* as Marie Dorval was called. Often George and Chopin were invited out together. But he was always free to accept invitations alone when they were issued by strait-laced hostesses or aristocratic music lovers who could not officially condone the presence of a mistress, even when she was France's foremost *femme de lettres.* Such was the case on October 29, when Chopin was invited out to the Château de Saint-Cloud, on the western periphery of Paris, with his friend Ignaz Moscheles, the pianist-composer, to entertain Louis-Philippe and his red-cheeked Queen (who only stopped her sewing to applaud Chopin's Nocturnes and Etudes and Moscheles' four-hand sonata). Knowing how George felt about France's pear-faced monarch and his stuffy, bourgeois court, Chopin had the coachman drive him back to Paris in a hurry to say good night to the Lady of his Heart.

This latitude, given their different temperaments and obligations, was vital to their continued cohabitation, as both instinctively realized. And never was it more vital than during this autumn and winter of 1839, when Chopin and Moscheles were so often together, while George Sand struggled to meet the bills — more than 5000 francs — she had run up with antique dealers and *tapissiers* during the three hectic weeks she had spent furnishing the two Rue Pigalle apartments. Desperately short of money once again — "I don't have 20 francs with me," as she wrote to Buloz in mid-December — she dashed off another long short story (*Pauline*), which was published shortly afterward in two successive issues of the *Revue des Deux Mondes.*

Her play *Cosima,* on the other hand, caused her endless trouble. Lockroy, one of the Comédie Française's foremost actors, first accepted a lead role and then brusquely bowed out. Marie Dorval agreed to play the role of Cosima, but as she was not a Comédie Française actress, George Sand had first to win over Buloz by bringing them together at a dinner and then obtain the authorization of Count Charles Duchâtel, the Minister of the Interior (who had the right to decide which plays could or could not be staged in France's subsidized state theater). None of the actors particularly liked the text — all too obviously the work of an amateur — and Marie had to ask her friend George to make all sorts of corrections and improvements. Buloz, who had glibly assured her at Nohant that he could have the play staged in fifteen days — proof that he knew as little about the theater as she did — kept postponing the date of the first rehearsals, which he finally told her would have to last two months.

By late January of 1840 the harassed author was so worn out by endless wrangling with peevish actors — something new in her literary experience — that she was more than ready to have Buloz withdraw the play altogether. But determined to bring this unruly troupe of actors to heel, Buloz stubbornly insisted on maintaining the play on the agenda. Chopin, understandably lost in the welter of debate, gave George contradictory advice, first encouraging her — in the hope that the box-office earnings would solve her critical financial problems — then discouraging her when the obstacles began to loom, and then encouraging her anew in unison with Buloz. The play, portraying a virtuous husband's long-suffering attempt to save his beautiful wife from a fatal infatuation with a vain and callous lover, must have struck him as a welcome change from George Sand's previous works, most of which had condemned marriage as a form of slavery and exalted unbridled passion. But if, as seems likely, Chopin thought that this would disarm her French critics, he was sadly mistaken.

George herself was under no such illusion, being already persuaded by late February that her play would meet with a "first-class whistling" and a barrage of "more or less cooked potatoes." Sainte-Beuve, with whom she affably shook hands across the table at a dinner given by Buloz — thus ending the four-year breach in their friendship — was amazed by her philosophical detachment, her one desire now being to get the "*grande soirée des pommes cuites*" (the boiled apple session) over with as soon as possible. "I've been so advised and disadvised, readvised and redisadvised," she wrote to Balzac, that she had to turn down his generous offer to attend a rehearsal and to give her the benefit of his advice (for, as he humbly put it "a donkey can give advice to a Bishop"). With Alexandre Dumas, who also wrote to ask for a ticket, she was equally frank in warning him not to expect a play, but only "a dialogued novel of the most monotonous kind."

Prepared for the worst, she did not even try to pack the pit with an enthusiastic claque, as Victor Hugo had shamelessly done in 1830 to ensure the success of *Hernani*. Not that this precaution could by itself have won the day. For by late April it was clear that France's foremost theater had been sold out to George Sand's bitterest enemies. The opening shot was fired even before the curtain went up by Charles Lassailly, a curiously bohemian dandy (he habitually wore *one* glove) who had authored a grotesque novel in which the demonic hero tortures and kills his mistress by the protracted tickling of the soles of her feet. He now vented his epileptic rage on Lélia — this "woman of double sex," this "hermaphroditic being," this "modern Sappho," whose son, made to dress up like a girl, would rue the day he had been born, and whose daughter, forced to dress like a boy, would one day be universally mocked as an abominable coquette for being "impure like her mother," etc. This violent abuse was no more spiteful than the storm of hostile whistling and jeering which greeted *Cosima* on the opening night. Marie Dorval, though a veteran of almost forty years of stage experience, was put off her acting, while Pierre-François Beauvallet, in the role of the Don Juanish seducer Ordonio Elisei, played so poorly that Heinrich Heine, who also attended the première (along with Chopin, Marie d'Agoult, and a host of other celebrities), compared him to a "pig with a gold ring in his snout."

Altogether, it was a disastrous first night, and the subsequent performances were no more successful. Charles Didier, who attended the fourth one in early May, found the play even worse than he had been led to expect by the adverse comments he had heard, noting in his diary: "It has neither passion, style, nor interest." George Sand, who was now prepared to admit as much, begged Buloz to put a quick end to the fiasco, but pigheaded as ever, he let *Cosima* drag on for three more performances.

This resounding flop plunged George Sand even further into

debt. Once again she was plagued by the liver trouble her doctors had traced back to nervous strain and overwork. "It cost me more trouble, time, and health to put on this platitude than it would have taken to write four volumes," she complained to a sympathetic critic. This was only a slight exaggeration. Living in Paris and providing for the education of her children cost her, on an average, more than 1000 francs a month. The ten months she had devoted to the writing and staging of *Cosima* had cost her a good deal more than 10,000 francs, given the expense of furnishing the Rue Pigalle apartments; and all she was eventually able to recoup was 5000 francs from the publication of the play in volume form.

Chopin, fortunately, cost her nothing. He could more than pay for his own clothes and manservant, and even hire a carriage and coachman on the 400 to 500 francs a week he earned from his music lessons. At Nohant, on the other hand, he could no longer give lessons — a monthly loss of almost 2000 francs — while there was little hope that the Ballades, Nocturnes, or Mazurkas he might be inspired to compose there would bring in half as much, given the niggardly disposition of the "sharks," "cutthroats," and "Jews" he had to deal with and whom he was constantly denouncing in his letters. Regretfully George Sand concluded that they would have to forego the pleasure of returning to Nohant during the summer of 1840.

Anxious to find some way of doubling her income from the same (already excessive) quantity of work, she was tempted for a while by the idea of writing a novel in French and of having it simultaneously translated into English, for publication on both sides of the Channel. This idea may have been suggested to her by Henry Bulwer, the First Secretary of the British Embassy in Paris, who had been Hortense Allart's lover for a number of years and who was later rumored to have become George Sand's as well.

But the new novel on which George Sand now began working seemed hardly likely to appeal to middle-class English readers. Entitled *Le Compagnon du Tour de France,* it was inspired by a journeyman carpenter named Agricol Perdiguier, who had been trying to unite the strife-torn factions of the French working class movement by reviving the communal spirit of the medieval guilds. To this end he and his friends had been traveling around France setting up workingmen's centers — known under the curious name of *devoirs* (duties) — which were to serve as communal inns for itinerant journeymen and as "lodges" (in the masonic sense) for the propagation of a kind of Christian socialism. In George Sand's novel the hero, Pierre Huguenin, is also a carpenter, but one of a curious sort, for he inspires a fateful passion in Iseut de Villepreux, the daughter of a count who, though himself a former *carbonaro* liberal, cannot accept the idea of his daughter's marrying a proletarian.

The deliberate complication of the plot — with two workingmen arousing the love of two noblewomen — could not disguise the fact that this was essentially a new variation of an already familiar theme: established society's unwillingness to condone marriages between persons from different social strata. Victor Hugo, in *Ruy Blas,* had already shocked convention by portraying a queen's love for a lackey, but in *Le Compagnon du Tour de France* the idea that wealth and titles have a corrupting influence on honest artisans was more directly and didactically expressed. Chopin found the portrayal of the honest, upright hero just too good to be true, while Buloz was frankly dismayed by the novel's forthright apologia for all sorts of radical and socialistic ideas. He had found the mysticism of Ballanche difficult enough to swallow in works like *Spiridion* and *Les Sept cordes de la lyre,* but the guild socialism and evangelical egalitarianism of the philosopher Pierre Leroux was even more unpalatable to his solidly middle-class taste. George Sand, however, refused to make the alterations and cuts he demanded. *Le Compagnon du Tour de France* was accordingly declared unpublishable in the staid *Revue des Deux Mondes,* and its author was allowed to give the manuscript to another publisher.

The subsequent appearance of the novel — in December of 1840 — aroused an unusual stir, even in the already controversial career of George Sand. She was torn to pieces in the conservative press and even accused (in one arch-Catholic publication) of going out to the Paris suburbs on Sundays and of getting drunk with Pierre Leroux in her industrious effort to acquaint herself with the conditions of working-class existence. Though this was one more example of the innumerable legends that were woven about her, it was nonetheless true that this novel, like several others which were to follow, owed a great deal to Leroux, who had by now supplanted Michel de Bourges and Lamennais as George's intellectual inspirer.

Heinrich Heine had already had occasion to regret the ascendancy of this "Capucin philosopher," who "unfortunately exercises a rather unfavorable influence on the talent of the penitent, drawing her into obscure dissertations of half-developed ideas." A squat, broad-shouldered man with a bumpy forehead, a mass of tousled hair, and heavy rings of flesh under his deep-sunk eyes, Pierre Leroux looked more like a Breton barge skipper than the "sublime philosopher" George Sand took him to be. Heine, who had made his acquaintance at the Saint-Simonian gatherings he had attended in the early 1830s, was struck by the fact that Leroux never wore gloves, which he evidently considered an aristocratic affectation.

Forced by his father's death to interrupt his university studies at the Ecole Polytechnique (which specialized in science and mathematics), Pierre Leroux had first worked as a stonecutter and mason before becoming a typesetter and compositor. His experience in the printing business had helped to make him, in 1824, one of the founders of *Le Globe,* a newspaper which later became a vehicle for the propagation of Saint-Simon's ideas. It was here that Sainte-Beuve, who worked for the same newspaper in the early 1830s, first got to know him, being sufficiently impressed by his idealism to recommend his articles and essays to George Sand. Dubiously at first and then with more attention the spiritually tormented author of *Lélia* had followed his encyclopedic labors until her growing admiration had turned into outright hero worship.

The reasons for this are not hard to find. This homespun "philosopher" who had never finished university was essentially a social prophet who cared less for abstract thought than for the welfare of his fellow men. He was a seer rather than a thinker, less violent than Michel de Bourges in his egalitarian sentiments, more sanguine than Lamennais in his vision of the future. His philosophy, if such it can be called, was a strange amalgam of borrowed ideas. Like Rousseau, Leroux was persuaded that man is fundamentally good and well-meaning and, like Condorcet, convinced that he is capable of infinite improvement. He believed, like Socrates and Leibnitz, that lack of virtue is ultimately traceable to ignorance and lack of knowledge and, like George Bernard Shaw, whom he anticipated in this respect, he felt that poverty is the mother of immorality and vice. An evolutionist rather than a revolutionary, he regarded mankind as one vast human family — in time as well as space. For if the soul of each human being is immortal, as he believed, it was not in the orthodox Christian sense of an eternal heaven and an everlasting hell. Death, in his view, is but a temporary return to God, accompanied by a Lethelike purification of the memory, prior to a new reincarnation — each reincarnation being higher and better than the last. A romantic utopian, he looked forward to a world in which *socialism* and universal *solidarity* — two words he helped to popularize — would replace personal egotism and competitive individualism as the dominant ideals of mankind.

Buloz, who had once refused an article by Leroux, saying: "God is not a topical subject," would not have taken violent exception to these exalted speculations had the "Capucin philosopher" been content to stop there. But in the autumn of 1840 he brought out a major opus entitled *De l'humanité,* in which the forthcoming golden age of universal concord and brotherhood was portrayed in unmistakably communistic terms. Since nothing is more divisive than property rights, Leroux argued, they should be replaced by a new organization of society, in which land, like everything else, is communally owned and managed.

That this utopian philosophy posed problems for the mistress of Nohant George Sand was too intelligent not to realize. But then, she was not exclusively a landowner who lived off the labor of those who actually tilled the soil; she was a self-sustaining author, and as she wrote to Hippolyte, "If I had only Nohant to live on, I would not know on which nail to hang myself." Still, there was an undeniable contradiction between literature and fact, between what she professed and what she practiced, as the normally reticent Chopin felt obliged to point out. For kindly though she was to her tenants, George showed no readiness to do away with the periodic rents they owed her. She justified this refusal on the grounds that many of her wealthier peasants were richer than she was. "As for the philosophical question of property which has made us battle so strongly against Chopin," she added a bit smugly in a letter written to Hippolyte in mid-December of 1840, "it is a principle to be conserved in the heart and clarified and sorted out as much as possible by the reasoning and reflection of each of us . . . In truth the savage love of property dominates men, great and small. But what we may perhaps be destined to see, if the people are educated, is a new management of property and a succession of forms whereby we shall make it pass away, prior to the advent of a more enlightened century, when laws will regulate heritage and restrain the rights of individuality . . . Let us believe in the beautiful *ideal,* and let us do everything we can to realize it, for it would be pointless to try to oppose it. It will take place despite us, and we shall be swept away by God's justice, which is nothing ought in this world than the suffering of the people, like geese striving to battle a torrent."

This idea — that there is no use trying to resist the wave of the future, or what Marx and his followers were to call "the locomotive of history" — also found expression in the elaborate account of the trip to Mallorca, which George Sand finally wrote up for the *Revue des Deux Mondes* in this same December of 1840. Entitled "Winter in the South of Europe," it even included an apologia for the work of revolutionary destruction when applied to monasteries which had once housed the instruments of the Catholic Inquisition.

But it was in her next novel, *Horace,* written in the spring and summer of 1841, that her new faith in the messianic mission of the masses was most forthrightly and dramatically exposed. Far from regretting the first bold plunge she had taken in this direction with *Le Compagnon du Tour de France,* George Sand was now tempted by the idea of doing for the proletariat what Balzac had been doing for the bourgeoisie, but in an entirely contrary spirit. For the realistic portrayals of Balzac, sardonically content to depict his bourgeois "heroes" and "heroines" in all their grasping, unscrupulous, and selfish splendor, she wished to substitute a loftier, frankly idealistic description of proletarian existence in order to demonstrate the new truth she had stumbled on: that the sentiments and ideas of proletarians could be as poetic and "sublime" as those of pampered aristocrats.

Ostensibly *Horace* was the story of a clever, indolent, and flighty student who, a bit like Jules Sandeau, chooses to turn his back on the serious study of medicine or law in an effort to make a name for himself in literature. Facility hastens his undoing; for giving himself up to a life of pleasure and amusement, he squanders his parents' hard-earned savings and callously abandons his proletarian mistress for an aristocratic vicomtesse. Had she been willing to leave it at that, George Sand would have produced a perfectly good social novel of the kind that Balzac, or after him, Maupassant or Emile Zola, could have written. But more than ever obsessed by the evangelical egalitarianism of Pierre Leroux — "whom I revere as a new Plato, a new Christ," as she wrote to Charlotte Marliani — she contrasted the flighty student Horace Dumontet's iniquitously bourgeois life with the honest labors of a hardworking jeweler named Paul Arsène. In the process she all but openly justified the assault on the Paris archbishopric, which she herself had witnessed in 1832, as part of a universal, revolutionary struggle to do away with the iniquities of private property.

The result was a new row with Buloz, who accused her of using her fiction for the propagation of Pierre Leroux's communistic philosophy, while she accused Buloz of sycophantic docility toward the Louis-Philippe regime and the opportunistic abandonment of his old liberal sympathies. Buloz countered by declaring that the *Revue des Deux Mondes* would always combat "tendencies of social disorganization," adding: "You are not a communist, I hope; at least, up until *Horace* I've never seen a trace of it in your writing." He requested changes and eliminations in the text of the novel which George Sand, after consulting Leroux, refused to make.

The publication of *Horace* marked another turning point in George Sand's eventful life. It put an end to her eight-year association with François Buloz — "that Shylock who would sell my hide if it were fit for making shoes," as she wrote. It cast a passing shadow over her friendship with Liszt and, as will presently be shown, transformed her brittle amity with Marie d'Agoult into solid animosity. It also helped distend her once cordial relations with Lamennais, who had disappointed her again in the spring of 1841 by bringing out a pamphlet in which he made no secret of his conviction that women are intellectually inferior to men. Unlike most of her previous novels, *Horace* did not find favor with the apocalyptic abbé, who had already indicated in *Paroles d'un croyant* that there were limits to the cause of absolute equality. "There will always be poor people, for man will never destroy evil itself . . . It is not in taking that which belongs to another that poverty can be destroyed; for how in making people poor would one diminish the number of the impoverished? . . . Each has the right to keep what he has, for otherwise nobody would own anything."

It was an ingenious argument, but one which cut little ice with a new generation of hotheads and dreamers who were more inclined to agree with the anarchist philosopher Proudhon that "Property is theft." Though George Sand was not prepared to go quite that far, she was not afraid from now on to consider herself, theoretically at any rate, a communist. *Horace,* coming after *Le Compagnon du Tour de France,* sufficed to persuade thousands — and they included men such as Giuseppe Mazzini, Alexander Herzen, and Mikhail Bakunin — that George Sand was France's leading social prophet. Nor were they entirely wrong when it is recalled that as late as 1840 Sainte-Beuve could still consider her a greater novelist than Balzac.

But for George Sand the ideas of Pierre Leroux would have been rapidly forgotten. Her novels, being exempt from the strict censorship and seizure which Austrian, Prussian, and Russian customs officials practiced on the import of all doctrinal material, carried his and other subversive French ideas to the farthest corners of Europe. They were all the more difficult to outlaw in that the socialism they proclaimed was emphatically Christian. As she had had one character in *Horace* suggest: democratic societies can only thrive if they have a divine sanction for their theories. This is what she sought to give them. In so doing, she became what the British historian David Owen Evans has called "the mythologist of social democracy," assuming "a Wagnerian role . . . of trumpet for the democratic idea and the cause of the people."

31. Pauline García and *Consuelo*

On the twenty-fifth of April 1841, less than a week after George Sand had begun writing *Horace,* Franz Liszt put on a special Beethoven concert at the Paris Conservatoire. Having generously volunteered to raise 60,000 francs for a commemorative marble statue which a group of German music lovers wished to put up in the composer's hometown of Bonn, he treated the audience to a "sublime" rendition of the Overture in C, *Consecration of the House,* previously unplayed in Paris, a sparkling transposition of Beethoven's *Adelaide,* and a difficult piano and violin sonata before his friend Hector Berlioz took over with an electrifying orchestral performance of the *Pastoral* Symphony. The applause, as usual, was deafening and the response delirious, as bouquets of flowers and endless *"Bravos!"* rained down on the stage from crammed balconies and boxes.

No less choice, though less flamboyant, was the piano recital which, by an extraordinary coincidence, was staged the very next evening in Camille Pleyel's brilliantly candlelit salons. Unlike Liszt, who had been traveling all over the continent giving concerts, Chopin was making his first public appearance in eight years. "Like those flowers which only open their soft-scented calyces in the evening," as Liszt was to say of him, Chopin had been reluctant to make a public demonstration of his virtuosity, insisting for months on the difficulties of organizing such an event, only to let himself be talked into it at the last moment by a number of Parisian friends.

"Things have gone faster than expected," George Sand could write a week before the event to the mezzo-soprano Pauline Viardot, who was off in London giving recitals of her own. "No sooner had he got off the fatal *Yes* than everything was arranged as though by miracle, three quarters of the tickets were bought up even before the announcement had been made, and then he woke up as from a dream and nothing could have been funnier than the meticulous and irresolute Chip-Chip obliged no longer to change his mind. He hoped that you would come and sing for him, with him accompanying. When I received your letter and he lost all hope, he wanted to cancel his concert. It was no longer possible; he was too much involved. He then went and threw himself into the arms, I mean at the feet of Madame Damoreau" — a forty-year-old soprano whose almost "insolently" pure tone Chopin had from the very first preferred to María Malibran's more dramatic inflections. "This Chopinesque nightmare," George Sand went on, in the same ebullient vein, "will take place in Pleyel's salons on the 26th. He doesn't want posters, he doesn't want programs, he doesn't want a numerous public, he doesn't want it talked about. He is so frightened by so many things that I am proposing that he play without candles and listeners on a mute piano."

Though the seats were relatively expensive — fifteen and twenty francs — not one of them was empty when the performance began at eight o'clock. To make the concert-shy Chopin feel more at home, Camille Pleyel had seated a few guests on the platform not far from the piano, while in the front rows he could see nothing but smiling friends: George Sand, Delacroix, Heinrich Heine, Franz Liszt, the Polish poets Witwicki and Mickiewicz, the French cellist Auguste Franchomme, and the playwright-musicologist Ernest Legouvé. The Ballade in F Major which Chopin played, along with several Mazurkas, two Polonaises, and a Scherzo, was so enthusiastically applauded that he was forced to repeat it as an encore.

It was a dazzling and well-deserved triumph, not least of all financially. For as Aurore wrote soon afterward to Hippolyte, "Chopin can now twiddle his thumbs for the entire summer. By giving a two-hour concert and batting out a few chords he has put 6000 and a few hundred more francs in his pocket, amid the Bravos, the *encores,* and the flutterings of the loveliest women in Paris. The scoundrel!" she added, with a touch of envy. To earn as much she had to slave through six straight weeks and sometimes burn the midnight oil for three months at a stretch.

Liszt was so enthusiastic that at Legouvé's request he wrote up his impressions of the evening in the *Revue et Gazette musicale,* declaring that what Chopin had done — to allow years to pass without giving a concert — would have condemned any other artist to certain obscurity and oblivion, but that this "exquisite, exalted, eminently aristocratic celebrity" being surrounded by "faithful disciples, enthusiastic pupils, and ardent friends," had been spared annoying quarrels, painful vexations, and carping attacks. "Every criticism of him has been silenced, as though posterity had already rendered its judgment. And in the brilliant audience that hastened to be with the poet who had been silent for so long, there was not a single hesitant response, not one reservation: one paen of praise was on the lips of all."

This, of course, was poetic license. For the truth, as nobody was better placed to know than Franz, was that his own generous admiration was not unreservedly shared by his hypercritical mistress. The same Marie d'Agoult who in February of 1837 had noted in her diary: "George is the only woman I could live with for a long time without growing tired" had by the spring of 1841 become a bitter enemy of the woman writer she had once so admired. So bitter that it had even warped her friendly feelings toward Chopin. Just five days before the April 26 concert she had written to her friend, the painter Henri Lehmann, that "a small malevolent coterie is trying to resuscitate Chopin, who is going to play at Pleyel's place. Madame Sand hates me, we no longer see each other . . ." To which she later added, after the concert was over: "Madame Sand, infuriated by all these triumphs" — Liszt's Paris recitals and the scores of others he had given in various European cities — "has pushed Chopin into giving a private concert, among friends."

That George Sand had to push her concert-shy Chip-Chip into giving a public recital is certain. But that she acted out of jealousy toward Liszt was malicious nonsense. George's friendly feelings toward Franz had not substantially changed any more than had his toward her — as he pointedly made clear by calling at the Rue Pigalle apartment and leaving her a long-stemmed pipe he had thoughtfully bought for her in Central Europe. The person who did have reason to be jealous of Liszt's concert triumphs was Marie, the mother of his three children, who knew that as Franz went from city to city, and from one ovation to the next, he was the pampered darling not only of kings and princes but even more of music-loving hostesses dying to swoon into the slender virtuoso's welcoming arms. There had been too many harsh words and stormy scenes between them for her not to realize that their "epic" romance was all but over. "Dante! Beatrice! It's the Dantes who make the Beatrices, and the real ones die at eighteen!" he had one day told Marie, driven wild by her relentless predilection for sublime comparisons. The realization that she was increasingly unwanted had gradually soured her to everything. She had already found it difficult to forgive George Sand her literary successes and the fascination she had once exercised on Franz, but the thought that George might succeed with Chopin where she had failed with Liszt was more than she could endure.

This is not to say that all the wrongs were on Marie d'Agoult's side. Had George been a truly loyal friend, she would not have carved up Princess Arabella for the psychophagic pleasure of Balzac during his brief stay at Nohant in February of 1838. She had every reason to fear what might result, even if the final product exceeded her expectations. But Marie d'Agoult was no less bitchy in writing to Charlotte Marliani from Pisa the following November: "The journey to the Balearic islands amuses me. I regret it didn't take place one year earlier. When G. used to have herself bled, I always used to say to her: *In your place I would rather have Chopin.* How many lancet pricks that would have spared her! . . . Knowing them as I do, they should get on each other's nerves after one month of cohabitation; they are two *antipodic* natures, but never mind, it's as pretty as could be and you don't know how happy I am for both of them . . ."

Feeling that this was a spiteful way of talking about a friend, Charlotte Marliani had written to George in Mallorca, urging her to break off all further relations with Marie. Later, after consulting the Abbé de Lamennais, who declared himself shocked by the "jealous, nasty irony" in Marie d'Agoult's letters, she had shown them to George, who decided from then on to limit her appearances at Marie d'Agoult's exotic Moorish salon on the Rue Neuve des Mathurins, close though it was to the Rue Pigalle.

Balzac's novel *Béatrix,* which first appeared in serial form in the spring of 1839, had in any case envenomed their relations beyond the point of reconciliation. In this novel George Sand was transformed into a talented, self-effacing heroine, Félicité des Touches (even better known under her nom de plume of Camille Maupin), while Marie d'Agoult received a literary comeuppance as the envious, vain, and socially ambitious Béatrix de Rochegude, a predatory marquise who seeks to mask her shallowness of intellect and character behind the rich elegance of her dresses, the exquisite artistry of her make-up and hairdo, the calculated grace of her poses, the vaporous undulations of her shawls and veils. Whereas the first is capable of genuine passion, the second is only capable of self-esteem. The world being what it is — fundamentally frivolous — this monument of social artifice manages to hook the Italian singer Gennaro Conti, but this and other amorous triumphs turn out to be singularly hollow compared to the happiness Félicité des Touches finds in convent life, where her genius flowers more splendidly than ever.

In the preface Balzac wrote for the novel, Marie d'Agoult's vain efforts to hold on to Liszt were thus pointedly referred to: "When certain women of high rank have sacrificed their position to some violent passion; when they have flouted the laws, do they not find in their pride of race, in the value they bestow upon themselves, and even in their own superiority, barriers as difficult to surmount as those already overcome? . . . All has not been said when a noble and generous woman has resigned her social and aristocratic sovereignty. She remains forever attached to the author of her ruin, like a convict to his chained companion." Marie d'Agoult was understandably outraged by this unflattering portrayal of her haughty failings, so dramatically contrasted to her rival's unassuming genius, and not unnaturally she laid the guilt at George's door. Liszt, who for months had been begging Marie to avoid a total break with their former friend, now found himself fighting a losing battle. As for Balzac, he seems to have derived a childish satisfaction from the havoc thus wreaked.

From then on all of George Sand's "misdemeanors" and misfortunes became occasions for rejoicing for Marie d'Agoult, who had long since decided that "One never thinks ill enough of people." In

January of 1840 the embittered Charles Didier noted in his diary: "G[eorge] S[and] is said to be pregnant, by whom?" — the intimation being that it could be by anyone except Chopin. Marie d'Agoult was only slightly less charitable in passing on this latest piece of gossip to Liszt, adding that George, in her opinion, had merely grown fat — "which does not become her."

"I think it won't be long before the Chopin household breaks up," Marie was happy to inform Liszt two months later. "Some of our mutual friends say he is morbidly jealous, that passion is killing him, that he tortures himself and others. She" — George Sand — "is at the end of her patience, and is only afraid he might die if she left him."

Already bored to tears by the "metaphysical repetitiveness" of *Les Sept cordes de la lyre,* Marie d'Agoult could hardly conceal her relish over the spectacular failure of *Cosima.* The publication of *Le Compagnon du Tour de France* reinforced her conviction that George Sand's talent was sliding inexorably downhill. "I haven't seen Madame Sand. She has written a novel that isn't selling. This doesn't make her any more gracious," she reported to Henri Lehmann on New Year's Day of 1841. She followed this up with a distinctly critical review which Emile de Girardin published in *La Presse* over the hypocritical signature of *"L'inconnu"* — the supposedly "Unknown One."

It only remained for George Sand to apply the coup de grâce to a moribund friendship. This she did in her novel *Horace* by painting a cruel portrait of the Vicomtesse de Chailly, a society lady and aspiring "patroness of the Arts" who contributes to the undoing of the frivolous Horace Dumontet. Recalling Marie Dorval's sarcastic query, after meeting the tall, angular Marie d'Agoult — "Who is that shellfish?" — George now dipped her pen in acid to produce this scathing caricature:

"The Vicomtesse de Chailly had never been beautiful, but she was determined to seem so, and by dint of artifice she passed herself off as a pretty woman. She had, at any rate, the airs and the aplomb, all the necessary mannerisms and privileges. She had fine green eyes of a changing expression which could upset and intimidate, but not charm. Her skinniness was frightening and her teeth were problematical, but she had a superb head of hair, always arranged with remarkable care and taste" — a transparent reference to the painstaking attention which Marie d'Agoult's personal maid lavished on her mistress' golden locks.

"The Vicomtesse de Chailly had never had much wit, but she was determined to have some and to make people believe it. She uttered the most abject platitudes with perfect distinction and the most absurd paradoxes with stupefying calm . . . she was impudently toadyish with all those she wanted to attract, pitilessly caustic with those she wanted to sacrifice. Cold and mocking, she feigned enthusiasm and sympathy with sufficient art to flatter the vanity of simple souls. She prided herself on her knowledge, her erudition, her eccentricity. She had read a bit of everything, even of politics and philosophy; and it was curious indeed to hear her repeating to some solemn-faced gentleman, as though it were hers, what she had read in the morning or heard the previous evening. In short, she had what one can call an artificial intelligence."

The intention was too obvious, the ink too black for a truly effective piece of satire. For how such a graceless creature could attract the flighty hero the author was not really able to explain. It was one of many implausibilities in one of George Sand's most interesting and controversial, though uneven, novels. If one person saw herself brutally caricatured in the Vicomtesse de Chailly, there were half a dozen young men (and probably many more) who recognized themselves in the shallow, unstable, and erratic Horace Dumontet — the literary forerunner, be it said in passing, of that equally dilettantish student, Frédéric Moreau, whom Gustave Flaubert, with infinitely greater mastery, was to immortalize in *L'Education sentimentale*.

Altogether different from the pretentious Marie d'Agoult was the person who was to inspire George Sand's most ambitious novel, the person whom Clara Schumann was to consider "the woman of greatest genius it has been given me to meet." Like Liszt and Chopin, Pauline García was a child prodigy but with a parental background even more conducive to musical development. Her Catalan mother and her Sevillian father had both been opera stars. Her brother, Manuel, was also a singer of distinction. As for her elder sister

María, she was none other than the "sublime" Malibran who had inspired the future George Sand's first literary efforts—*Rose et Blanche* and *La Prima Donna.*

Unlike her pretty elder sister, Pauline García was almost ugly, with bulging black eyes, a horsy, pinch-nostriled nose, an olive complexion, and a thick lower lip which made her mouth seem oversize—until she smiled, when the white Andalusian teeth completely transformed her grave, heavy-lidded face. When she made her Paris debut in 1838, at the age of seventeen, certain French critics found her studied reserve a bit cold for their taste, but none of them questioned her ability. "There is a child who will efface and eclipse us all: my sister, who is ten years old," María Malibran had predicted in 1831, and she was not mistaken. Berlioz, after hearing Pauline García sing the role of Desdemona in Rossini's *Otello,* marveled at the "virginal purity" of her voice, noting that her two-and-a-half-octave range, which was already "immense," was all the more remarkable for uniting "three kinds of voices which are almost never found together: the contralto, mezzo-soprano and soprano." Alfred de Musset was so impressed that he wrote two dithyrambic articles in the *Revue des Deux Mondes,* boldly declaring that "Mademoiselle García begins as others would like to finish." Afraid that the seventeen-year-old diva might be tempted to leave France if the Parisian public failed to recognize her genius, Musset and his music-loving friends showered the young Pauline with flattering compliments and invitations. Indeed, Musset was so enthralled by her many-sided genius—for she could draw as well as he could, sing in five languages, compose, and play the piano like a virtuoso—that he finally proposed to her. Though dismayed by the arrogance of his look and the red eyelids which had lost their lashes—the physical consequence of years of alcoholic debauch—she found it hard to refuse a famous poet who wrote so sympathetically about her.

From a catastrophic marriage with Musset Pauline was saved in the nick of time by George Sand, to whom she had been introduced in Charlotte Marliani's salon and who lost no time warning the innocent young singer and her more experienced mother of the risks she was running. George also seems to have had a hand in encouraging Pauline's later marriage to Louis Viardot, a liberal-minded art critic and Hispanophile who had energetically revived the fire-gutted Théâtre des Italiens in 1838. Pauline was already singing for Viardot's opera company in the autumn of 1839, when George Sand invited them to dine with Chopin at the Rue Pigalle apartment. The singer was as overawed by the composer's keyboard virtuosity as Chopin was by Pauline's astounding gifts, and from then on hardly a week passed without their seeing each other at their respective homes or at Charlotte Marliani's.

To judge by a kind of comic strip, composed of seventeen cartoons, which Alfred de Musset drew to illustrate its multiple vicissitudes, Louis Viardot's courtship of Pauline was a long and tortuous affair. George Sand was portrayed smoking a cigarette while lecturing Pauline, or solemnly seated with a cane while conversing with Madame García, who was not overly thrilled by the idea of her daughter marrying a man who was twenty-one years older. But marry him she finally did in April of 1840. George Sand may also have been influential in persuading Louis Viardot to give up his management of the Théâtre des Italiens in order to devote himself exclusively to promoting his wife's career. While he thus became a second father to Pauline, George Sand became a kind of foster mother. In her letters she called her friend *fifille,* while her "little daughter" addressed her with the endearing "Ninoune."

If the passion George Sand had conceived for Marie Dorval some eight years earlier smacked of the profane, this one was entirely sacred. "She is the only woman I have loved so tenderly over the past ten years," George confided to her Piffoëlesque journal in mid-February of 1841, on the eve of Pauline's departure for a concert tour in England. "She is the first woman since Alicia the nun whom I have loved with unmitigated enthusiasm . . . Still, she is a child of 19 years, and I don't know if the abyss which age opens between us can one day be filled." The answer was that it could. Four months later she wrote to Pauline again, in the hope that she and her husband Louis would soon pay a visit to Nohant: "I can say that you are the most perfect being I know and have ever known. When I see you even for an hour, the weight of my existence disappears, as though I had been born yesterday, like yourself . . ."

The summer of 1841, like that of 1839, was again spent at Nohant. The 6000 francs Chopin had earned from his February concert, added to a 7500 franc advance which George Sand received from a new publisher, Aristide Perrotin, for a popular edition of her Complete Works as well as the 5000 francs which Buloz had rashly advanced her for *Horace* (not realizing what he was in for), enabled them to leave Paris in mid-June and not to return until November. The summer, though, was ruined by gale winds and incessant rains which turned roads and fields into quagmires. George had to limit herself to brief gallops round her garden after breakfast and dinner, while Maurice, Chopin, and eventually Solange (after she was let out of boarding school in late August) spent an inordinate amount of time indoors around the newly installed billiard table. To keep Chopin happy a new Pleyel piano was sent down from Paris, but the ill-tuned (and possibly ill-made) instrument pleased him as little as its predecessor. Its tone was probably not improved by the resounding first blows he dealt to the plaintive keyboard each time the unsatisfactory piano "acted up."

The one bright moment in an otherwise wet and dispiriting summer was provided by the two-week visit made to Nohant by the Viardots in early August. Accompanied by Papet and Hippolyte Chatiron, Louis Viardot, an ardent hunter, tramped around the dripping countryside in search of game, while his now pregnant wife spent hours poring over music scores with Chopin in preparation for the joint recital they gave for the benefit of Aurore's closest friends shortly before the Viardots returned to Paris.

This brief visit did more than consolidate a budding friendship, it also helped to involve George Sand in a momentous new venture which was to keep her occupied for much of the decade. Even before *Horace* was completed, her relations with Buloz had deteriorated to the point where her one desire was to say goodbye to the *Revue des Deux Mondes.* But furious though she was with this Savoyard "Shylock" for being so slow in publishing the complete edition of her Works (in twenty-three volumes) and for making a deal behind her back with a bookseller to be relieved of some 18,000 unsold copies of her novels, she knew that it was only because her novels were first serialized in Buloz's *Revue* that he was willing to pay her the exceptionally high price of 5000 francs a volume. At a royalty rate of 1 Fr. 25 centimes a volume from her new publisher, an edition of 2000 copies — which in those days was already substantial — could only bring her 3000 francs, or three fifths of what Buloz paid her, and this without the added advantage of magazine publicity. The prospect of earning less for the same quantity of effort did not exactly enchant a writer who already felt exhausted and prematurely aged from ten years of unrelenting labor, and with no hope of letup in the future. "If ever I manage to live without wearing myself out," she wrote to a Paris friend in early August, "I shall believe in the divinity of Louis-Philippe and in the holiness of the Pope" — the same Pope Gregory XVI who in May of this same year had approved the new Vatican Index on which not less than eight of George Sand's novels were blacklisted as "pernicious" and "corrupting" for good Catholic readers!

The obvious way out of this dilemma — or so it seemed to George Sand and Louis Viardot, with whom she discussed the problem at length — was to found a new magazine. Balzac had suggested it to her more than a year before, even going so far as to recommend Victor Hugo as the third member of the editorial triumvirate needed to launch such an "independent review"! Nothing had come of this suggestion, which the chronically hard-pressed Balzac had probably put out as one more moneymaking scheme. But the idea was now revived and Viardot was commissioned to enroll Pierre Leroux as editor-in-chief and to round up the 50,000 francs which would be needed to finance the first year of publication.

Thus was created the *Revue indépendante,* which George so named as a further snub to François Buloz, whose *Revue des Deux Mondes* was by implication stigmatized as not independent — of government control. Its birth coincided with Buloz's rejection of *Horace,* which may have freed George Sand of a burdensome association but did nothing to improve her financial situation. Her Paris lawyer had to pay back the 5000 franc advance, and to help her meet this new debt, Alphonse Fleury, Charles Duvernet, and the well-to-do Gustave Papet generously volunteered to underwrite a 10,000 franc loan which was obtained from a La Châtre banker. The manuscript of *Horace* was then turned over to Leroux and Viardot to be used in the first numbers of the *Revue indépendante.*

Though George Sand had proudly defied Buloz, saying: "I am quite willing to ruin myself, provided I can speak my mind," she had no wish to sell Nohant for the simple privilege of free expression. But the need for retrenchment was obvious. She accordingly dismissed an old couple who had served them in Paris, and announced her intention of making do with a single maid who could also cook. Chopin, who made a brief trip to Paris in late September to see if he could find quarters that were warmer and quieter than his Rue Tronchet apartment, was informed on his return that he could occupy the lower floor of the second pavilion on the Rue Pigalle. This would simplify his life considerably while relieving George Sand of part of the rent. Maurice's drawings, plaster statuary, and assorted bric-a-brac were accordingly moved upstairs, along with his bed, books, and other belongings, while the copy of the Giorgione nude which graced the drawing-room was moved out, lest the sight of those voluptuous curves upset the tender sensibilities of the young ladies who would now come to the Rue Pigalle for their piano lessons. In this way Chopin could be spared the cost and discomfort of having to take a hackney cab from the Rue Tronchet to the Rue Pigalle for the five o'clock dinner, and the even greater discomfort of having to return home later in an often freezing cab, from which he emerged shivering and coughing.

The inaugural issue of the *Revue indépendante,* containing a first installment of *Horace,* appeared in early November. Chopin, though he felt a personal distaste for Pierre Leroux's disheveled hair and slovenly appearance, had allowed his skepticism to be disarmed by Louis Viardot's contagious optimism and the prospect of Adam Mickiewicz's becoming a regular contributor now that he had left Lausanne and accepted a Chair in Slavonic Literature at the Collège de France. But this being no more than a hope for the future, George plugged the gap with an essay on proletarian poets — like the Toulon mason Charles Poncy, Savinien Lapointe the cobbler-bard, and Jean Reboul, a verse-loving baker whom she had met at Nîmes in October of 1838 while on her way to Mallorca. In all, her personal contribution to the first issue amounted to ninety-six pages, or almost a third of the monthly's total content. Her contribution to the second (December) issue was only slightly less: eighty-four pages, including a second *Horace* installment and an article "Lamartine, the Utopian." "Our review is doing very well," she wrote ecstatically to Hippolyte in early December. "Not a day passes without our receiving twenty more subscriptions. The success is greater than we expected, and the most serious minds have been struck and convinced by Leroux's deductions and conclusions." The proof of it, she claimed, was a statement recently made by a Collège de France professor to the effect that Pierre Leroux had accomplished what neither Montesquieu nor Rousseau had been able to achieve: he had come up with an adequate definition of the notion of the *right* of sovereignty!

Not a few of George Sand's friends, however, were dismayed by this new passion for a kind of communistic Christianity in which all proprietary rights (and not least of all the husband's right to "own" his wife) were resolutely trampled under foot as being deplorably bourgeois. "If you have read the two numbers of the *Revue indépendante,*" Sainte-Beuve wrote to a Swiss friend, "you will have seen just how far pathos and promiscuity can be carried. This Leroux fellow writes philosophy like a buffalo wading through a swamp." Charles Duvernet, whose sensibilities had been so thrilled by Chopin's heavenly music, had to admit that he was considerable less thrilled by Leroux's unorthodox speculations. Most scathing of all was the Abbé de Lamennais, whose doctrine of evangelical equality could not be stretched to the point of admitting that "Jesus Christ formally authorized adultery."

This new radicalism on George Sand's part did not keep Chopin from being asked to give a second concert for Louis-Philippe and his court in early December. Nor did it affect her friendship with Delacroix or the even more conservative Marquis de Custine, who considered it a rare privilege to be invited to the Rue Pigalle to listen to Pauline Viardot sing sad Mexican songs to Chopin's exquisite accompaniment. But the need to put in an afternoon appearance at the Left Bank offices of the *Revue indépendante* and to spend a good part of each night writing (to provide new "copy") meant that more than ever she only saw her Chip-Chip at dinnertime and in the evenings, which were consumed by a new passion for billiards.

In marked contrast to George's overly active life, Pauline Viardot's was now at a virtual standstill — for reasons which had nothing to do with the birth of a daughter in mid-December. Since her husband's resignation from the Théâtre des Italiens in 1840, the new manager had not dared to renew Pauline's contract for fear of angering the company's prima donna, the thirty-three-year-old Giulia Grisi, who was now at the peak of her career. The Paris Opera was similarly closed to her, its director being completely under the thumb of the tyrannical diva Rosine Stoltz, who was even more determined to eliminate all potential rivals. The tumultuous ovations her recitals had unleashed the previous February in London, comparable to the earlier triumphs of Henriette Sontag or her own sister María Malibran, seemed to have made no impression on the other side of the Channel; and Pauline García-Viardot found herself effectively barred from Paris' two opera stages for the duration of the 1841–1842 season.

In this welter of feminine intrigue George Sand found a subject ready-made for literature. Thus was born *Consuelo.* Originally planned as a novelette, it gradually developed into her longest and most ambitious work of fiction. Like Pauline García, the heroine of this new novel was Spanish, had gypsy blood, and was described as being almost ugly, with a round "insignificant face"; but she was gifted with a "good, sweet, obliging and gay" disposition that was positively disarming. Like Pauline García, too, Consuelo had a "heavenly voice" which, under the musical guidance of the composer Porpora, she tirelessly strives to improve. Into the Venice of the mid-eighteenth century, George Sand introduced the jealous cabals and rivalries of Paris opera singers, once again freely drawing on elements of her own experience. Venice's reigning prima donna, la Corinna, who is rabidly jealous of the young Consuelo's triumphs as a singer, was modeled on the plump Giulia Grisi — a "fat goose" whose stage mannerisms struck George Sand as worthy of an onion-smelling cook. La Corinna's patron and lover, Count Zustiniani, was a caricature of Léon Pillet, the weak-willed director of the Paris Opera who was so much under the spell of his despotic mistress, Rosine Stoltz. There was a good bit of Marie d'Agoult in another rival, the blond Clorinda, whose beautiful shoulders are so tempting to the eye, but who becomes positively ugly when jealous — as ugly "as even Venus would have become, stirred by a low and nasty sentiment." As for Consuelo's evil genius, the handsome but indolent Anzoleto, he owed even more to the conscience-stricken but self-indulgent Alfred de Musset, unable to limit his recurring infidelities to his "beloved."

Interwoven into this fairly standard plot was an artistic theme which made this novel something more than a sprightly account of feminine intrigue in a picturesque Venetian setting. This was the idea of musical "purity" as opposed to musical effect. Explaining that he is not opposed in principle to difficult trills and other vocal embellishments, the old maestro Porpora goes on to point out why he is emphatically opposed to their abuse. "There is that which amuses and that which moves the heart; there is that which surprises and that which delights. I know full well that *tours de force* are in favor; but for my part, if I have taught them to my students as useful accessories, I almost regret it when I see most of them make excessive use of them, sacrificing the necessary to the superfluous, and an enduring delight on the part of the audience to shouts of surprise and feverish acclamations."

For George Sand these sentiments were anything but new. They had led her as far back as 1835 (in the *Lettre d'un voyageur* dedicated to Michel de Bourges) to praise the conscientious violinist Pierre Baillot, who had deliberately eschewed Paganini's free-fiddling acrobatics. The same sentiments had led her, in an article on Pauline García, to regret that the audiences of the Théâtre des Italiens could remain indifferent to a beautifully sung phrase only to break into wild applause at the artificial prolongation of a high note "which does no more than imitate the whistle of a teakettle, and which sacrifices the sense of the melody to a piece of silliness which is not agreeable to the ear." A deep-seated abhorrence of ornamental ostentation had also led her to prefer Chopin's extraordinary subtlety in melodic invention and variation to the flamboyant pyrotechnics of Franz Liszt. Virtuosity, as Liszt himself now realized with increasing bitterness, is inevitably degrading when it becomes an end in itself. It panders to the uneducated tastes of an ignorant public; it reduces the musician, as he would often say, to the status of a "performing bear."

*

On the twenty-first of February 1842, just three weeks after the first published installment of *Consuelo,* its real-life model, Pauline Viardot, gave a recital with Chopin and the cellist Auguste Franchomme. Camille Pleyel's glittering salons were once again filled to overflowing with a choice audience of aristocrats and sympathetic connoisseurs, among whom George Sand moved with smiling ease. Chopin played several Mazurkas, three Etudes, and a Ballade. Pauline sang several pieces by Handel, a melody written by their hypochondriac friend Joseph Dessauer, and last but by no means least, a lyrical rendition of La Fontaine's fable *Le Chêne et le Roseau* (*The Oak and the Reed*) for which she had herself composed the music. The evening was once again a triumph, and perhaps even more dazzling than Chopin's recital of the previous April. "*Petite fifille* and great woman that you are," George wrote to Pauline, "you were superb today and my hands are all swollen, as are those of my young ones." To her half brother she wrote a few days later to report that "the great Chopin's concert was as beautiful, brilliant and lucrative as last year's (5000 francs in receipts, a unique achievement in Paris and which proves how desirous people are to hear the most perfect and exquisite of musicians)."

Unique though it may have been as a musical achievement, this dazzling success did nothing to advance Pauline Viardot's operatic fortunes. A few weeks later Louis Viardot decided to take his wife to Spain in the hope that her compatriots might prove more receptive to her genius than the blasé and cabal-crippled Parisians. The editing of the *Revue indépendante* was left to Pierre Leroux. More than ever the task of keeping readers entertained — and not simply indoctrinated by Leroux's utopian speculations about the irresistibly forward march of "humanity" — fell on the tiny shoulders of George Sand.

By mid-March the review could boast some 600 subscribers — "which is enormous for a monthly review which has only had three months of existence," as George could proudly report. That she was as responsible as Leroux for this happy result there can be no doubt: while certain readers found the final chapters of *Horace* a bit difficult to swallow, the first installments of *Consuelo* were greeted with unanimous delight. The description of the Venetian embroglio into which the humbly born Consuelo was plunged was one of the liveliest things George Sand had ever written: so lively indeed that Leroux kept clamoring for new installments. Delacroix was only voicing the general opinion when he congratulated Consuelo's creator: "It is your purest type, the amiable girl of your finest inspirations."

The very saintliness of this heroine, in a city that was as corrupt and intrigue-ridden as Paris, posed a problem which the author finally resolved with an extraordinary piece of literary hocus-pocus — by brusquely shifting the scene of action from the Adriatic to Bohemia. When a disappointed Consuelo reaches the Hoffmannesque Riesenburg ("Castle of the Giants"), where she is to become the music teacher of the Comte de Rudolstadt's niece, she finds herself in the presence of a musician of genius. Named Albert — like Grzymala — Count Rudolstadt's son was less a Czech than a Polish creation, being like Adam Mickiewicz an exalted visionary and mystically inclined. His delicate health and frequent moodiness, on the other hand, were obviously inspired by Chopin. Like Chopin, too, Albert de Rudolstadt is subject to the temptations of the flesh and to fits of amorous passion which the virtuous Consuelo (like the severe but less virtuous George Sand) feels herself duty-bound to rebuff.

Fiction, once again, was so closely linked to fact that Albert de Rudolstadt's mysterious disappearance into the subterranean labyrinth of caves adjoining the castle, where he is mystically united to his pro-Hussite forebears by a strange process of spiritual palingenesis, was little more than a literary transposition of the terrible crisis through which Chopin passed in April of 1842, when Jan Matuszynski died of hemorrhages caused by pulmonary tuberculosis. Ever since their schoolboy days in Warsaw Chopin had considered Jan to be "made of the same clay" as himself. Having to sit by his bedside and watch his doctor friend literally coughing himself to death, in the room he had invited him to occupy in the Rue Pigalle pavilion, was a nerve-racking experience for the high-strung Frédéric, who went completely to pieces when the final convulsions were over. George Sand had to spend two nights and days trying to calm him, as his melancholy imagination was once again seized, as at Valldemosa, by nightmarish visions of corpses and specters calling to him from beyond the grave.

Six weeks later George Sand and Chopin left for Nohant with

Maurice and Solange, who was removed from her boarding school on the grounds of poor health. Yet another Pleyel piano was sent down to supplement the unsatisfactory instrument of the previous year so that Chopin could practice in his upstairs "music room" as well as in the ground-floor salon. Save for the two hours a day that he devoted to Solange's piano lessons, he could spend the rest of his time composing, which he apparently did to good effect. For on May 28 George could write to Delacroix that Chopin had composed "two adorable Mazurkas which are worth more than forty novels and are more meaningful than the century's entire literary output."

Delacroix, only recently recovered from a five-month bout of laryngitis which had forced him to interrupt his studio teaching and the painting of frescoes for the library of the Luxembourg Palace, came down in early June and stayed a month. To spare his vocal chords, George Sand was careful not to engage him in arguments on political and social questions, as she had so often done in the past. For much of each day he was invisible, working in the upstairs attic, where a space had been cleared for his easel and brushes. He gave instruction to Maurice, who had developed a positive hero worship for his teacher, did a profile sketch of Chopin, and as a token of his gratitude he presented his hostess with a little painting of Saint Anne giving lessons to the Virgin; she liked it so much that she decided to keep the original, asking Maurice to make a copy for the tiny Nohant church for which it had originally been intended. "This place is most agreeable and the hosts could not be more amiable," Delacroix wrote to a Paris friend. "When we are not gathered for dinner, breakfast or billiards, or out on a walk, each of us stays in his room reading or lolling on his couch. At times through the window opening on to the garden there waft in gusts of Chopin's music, for he too is working; they mingle with the singing of the nightingales and the scent of the rose bushes."

The friendship which had sprung up in Paris between these two creative souls was in many ways a strange one. Though both were romantics in their work, they were classicists in their tastes. Delacroix, who was something of a musical connoisseur, harboring a passion for Rossini and Cimarosa and knowing many of Mozart's operas by heart, was enchanted by Chopin's subtle compositions, which strove for *nuance* rather than strident effect. Chopin, on the other hand, was always pained when asked to comment on his friend's paintings. "He has an infinite amount of wit, finesse, and malice," as George Sand was to write of her "Chopinet," "but he is unable to understand anything of painting and statuary. Michelangelo frightens him. Rubens repels him. Everything that seems eccentric scandalizes him." That necessarily included Delacroix's pulsating tableaux and fiery use of color. Which did not keep Delacroix from writing to the same Paris friend to say that he had had "endless" tête-à-têtes with Chopin, "whom I like very much and who is a man of rare distinction; indeed, the truest artist I have met."

Though this summer, unlike the preceding one, was hot and sunny, it was anything but an enjoyable vacation for George Sand. Months of overwork, occasioned by her break with Buloz, accumulating debts, and the need to keep the *Revue indépendante* supplied with fiction, had caused an irritation of the optic nerve. The slightest exposure to sunlight was enough to induce a blinding headache. For most of the summer she had to wear dark glasses or sit indoors behind tightly drawn curtains. Sometimes, when the pain was too acute, she would have to lie down with a cold compress on her forehead. Yet there was no respite. Leroux kept demanding new installments of *Consuelo,* which she had to send to Paris around the twentieth of each month for inclusion in the monthly's next issue. It was the kind of forced labor to which Dickens, Dostoevski, and so many other nineteenth-century writers were to be condemned, and it drew forth the same despairing sighs and protests.

The problem was compounded in the case of *Consuelo* by the novel's sudden shift of setting. George Sand had lived in Venice, and the old crumbling houses of the Corte Minelli, where Consuelo had spent her humble youth, were ones she had personally known with Pietro Pagello and his friends. But the Bohemia to which Consuelo was almost magically transported in the second volume was as unknown to the author as the "Illyrian" principality in which she had once described the adventures of the imperious Quintilia Cavalcanti. This time, however, George Sand was determined to do her homework, and this necessarily involved much background reading in Czech history.

In this second volume of *Consuelo* the focus had also shifted from music to religion by an association of ideas which might have seemed strange to someone unacquainted with the author's intellectual development. The quest for purity and a dislike of ornamental frills in music was linked in George Sand's mind to a search for a similar purity in religion. The same love of power, pomp, and riches which had corrupted the French monarchy and the ancien régime had, in her and Pierre Leroux's opinion, corrupted the Catholic Church as well.

In this sense George Sand at thirty-eight was not radically different from the fifteen-year-old Aurore Dupin who had sought a direct, mystical communion with God, unhampered by the distractions of the liturgy and purely external manifestations of devotion. As she wrote to Ferdinand Bascans, the director of the Paris boarding school to which Solange had been sent: "It does not suit me that she should accustom herself to the hypocrisy of genuflexions and signs of the Cross, nor to the idol worship wherewith the holy figure of Christ is dishonored. Solange is far more skeptical than I would like. I therefore believe that the sight of all these ceremonies whose primitive sense has been lost and which no orthodox priest of our times could properly explain to her, has a bad effect on her . . . You would even oblige me greatly by suppressing the Mass entirely for her, as a waste of time, since she employs it above all to mock the devotion of others.

"If, as I requested last year, it has been given to you to explain Christ's philosophy, to impress her with the narrative of this beautiful poem about the life and death of this divine man, to present the Gospel to her as the doctrine of equality, and to explain the Gospels so scandalously distorted in Catholic translations and so admirably rehabilitated in Pierre Leroux's *De l'humanité,* it would provide her with true religious instruction of a kind I would be happy to have her profit from during Holy Week and every day of her life. But this instruction can only come from you, not from the holy comedians . . ."

This scathing indictment of the Catholic clergy in effect made George Sand a Protestant — but a Protestant who wanted to see the Church, like human society, totally transformed and the Gospel applied in all its egalitarian ferocity. "Progress," she boldly proclaimed to the poetess Louise Colet, "would be accomplished in spite of God, had God chosen to make of this century a Sunday rest day." "I have always had a certain respect for fanatics," she wrote to her in another letter, "for the latter are always logical, because they act in accordance with their faith." She was even prepared to condone the excesses of the French Revolution, the "fierce and pure-hearted" Saint Matthew being the "ancestor" of Robespierre and his consorts!

What appealed to her in the Prague reformer Jan Hus and his fifteenth-century disciples was not simply their desire to cleanse a corrupted Catholic Church, it was, as she had learned from an article on the subject published in Pierre Leroux's *Encyclopédie nouvelle,* their revolt against an unjust and hierarchical society. They had been authentic Christian revolutionaries as well as Czech nationalists struggling to establish an independent Protestant Bohemia against the oppressive tyranny of the Catholic Habsburgs. Albert de Rudolstadt was not only a descendant but, he himself was convinced, a "reincarnation" of one of the fifteenth-century Czech martyrs who had vainly fought to purify their faith and assert their ethnic independence. In him the quest for musical purity, religious simplicity, and ethnic integrity were thematically combined. The character who emerged was thus one of the most complex and bizarre of all of George Sand's creations: a three-fold personality, combining the musical genius of Chopin with the mystical patriotism of Mickiewicz and the revolutionary Christianity of Pierre Leroux.

While Chopin worked fitfully on a new Scherzo, a new Polonaise, and a new Ballade, George Sand ended this summer of 1842 in a positive frenzy of work, having to complete two installments of *Consuelo* in a fortnight to make up for the time she knew she would lose on her return to Paris. There was a brief respite in mid-September when Pauline and Louis Viardot came down for a two-week visit, bringing their nine-month-old daughter Louise. Their arrival coincided with Solange's twelfth birthday, which was celebrated with a gay champagne dinner and candlelit dancing. But no music could have been sweeter to George's ear than Pauline's dramatic account of her triumphal tour of Spain. It had reached its climax in Granada, where ten thousand men, women, and children had pushed their way through the gates or climbed over the brick walls of the Alhambra to listen to her sing the Andalusian *vitos* and *peteneras* in an Arabian Nights decor of Moorish arches and fountained patios.

In late September hosts and guests traveled back to Paris together. By common accord Chopin and George Sand had decided to give up the two pavilions of the Rue Pigalle, for Chip-Chip could not face the prospect of returning to the apartment where Jan Matuszynski had died. He had also found it too difficult of access, by an unprepossessing servants' staircase, to suit the aristocratic tastes of certain of his clients.

Chopin solved the problem by finding himself a comfortable ground-floor flat on the Square d'Orléans, where Charlotte Marliani had already established residence. Facing the sandy quadrangle on one side and looking out on to a garden full of greenery on the other, it consisted of a small bedroom and a spacious salon where the maestro could receive his "magnificent countesses and his delightful marquises" — for the relatively modest rent of 600 francs a year. George Sand was able to rent a larger apartment (for 3000 francs a year) on the first floor of a newly built house overlooking the same sandy quadrangle, with its central flowerpots and fountain. One entered via a vestibule where visitors could divest themselves of hats, coats, and canes before moving on into a spacious billiard room. Here they were likely to be offered a pipe or a cigar from the well-stocked mantelpiece — which is why Arsène Houssaye could later write that Madame Sand in Paris had never had a salon but only a *fumoir*. Beyond this "smoking room" were several smaller living rooms furnished with couches, where those who were tired of the stony clink of cues and balls could retire to converse or listen to Chopin performing on the piano. Three flights up was a studio, where the nineteen-year-old Maurice could spread his brushes and decorate the walls with plaster casts. Marie-Sophie Taglioni, the dancer, Kalkbrenner, the composer, the pianists Valentin Alkan and Pierre Zimmerman, the sculptor Jean-Pierre Dantan, the painter Claude Dubufe and his equally gifted son Edouard were already living within, or were soon to move to, this quiet enclave of the arts.

The daily five o'clock dinner, after the first few weeks, was prepared by Madame Marliani's cook and eaten in Charlotte's large dining room, adjoining an equally large salon, full of beautifully lamplit paintings, which was also used for musical soirees. George contributed her maid and her share of expenses to this common gastronomic effort. Thanks to this arrangement the semimarital existence shared by two such "antipodal" characters as George Sand and Chopin outlived all of the envious Marie d'Agoult's darkest predictions. In his entirely separate living room Chopin could entertain his Polish friends or anyone else he chose to. He hired an irascible Polish valet in whom he developed great confidence, since the loyal Jan hardly spoke a word of French and could be counted on not to exchange malicious gossip with the neighbors' domestics. Chip-Chip did not even have to answer the five o'clock summons to dinner, habitually announced by an outdoor bell rung by an Italian political refugee named Enrico whom Charlotte Marliani had adopted and who cut a distinctly comic figure in his checkered trousers and shabby topcoat. Far more worldly than George Sand, Chopin needed the stimulus of drawing room conversation and the hospitality he was always sure of receiving in the houses of his friends, the Platers, or at Princess Czartoryska's, whose palatial residence on the Ile Saint-Louis was shortly to become a permanent "open house" for Polish exiles. At these fashionable soirees George Sand almost always felt out of place and ill at ease. Far shyer than her forthright manners might lead one to suppose, she had never much enjoyed superficial salon conversations, which a growing deafness in one ear made it increasingly difficult for her to follow; and she was never more loquacious than in a private tête-à-tête.

Her new radicalism, furthermore, kept her from frequenting the drawing rooms of the great and wealthy whose traditional selfishness and unconcern for the downtrodden proletariat she and Pierre Leroux were tirelessly denouncing. But her very militancy in this respect made hers a curiously "open house" for a motley crew of humanitarian enthusiasts, gesticulating revolutionaries, and proletarian poets, whose casual behavior and attire were not exactly to the taste of the delicate Chopin and the fastidious Delacroix, both of whom were very particular about their dress and speech.

These distractions notwithstanding, the winter of 1842–1843 was a relatively calm one for the Sand-Chopin household. She was still too crippled by debts and by her feeling of social and intellectual obligation to Pierre Leroux to have much time for romance or sensuous indulgence. "I have resumed *Consuelo,*" as she put it in a letter to Charles Duvernet, "like a dog that is whipped." The chastity she had so long imposed on the heroine of her novel reflected her conviction that she herself had become, if not the bride of Christ (a convent expression she abhorred), then a kind of Mary Magdalenish disciple of Pierre Leroux. This was on the whole a Lenten season for the senses, in which all her energies were channeled into keeping the *Revue indépendante* well supplied with fiction.

Her protracted quarrel with Buloz was at last settled, after a lawsuit which he appealed, in November of 1842. But it cost her 11,700 francs, which she had to pay off once again with the products of her pen. Long delayed by this troublesome litigation, the popular edition of her Complete Works, on which she had been counting, could not even be started until the end of this year, and in view of the substantial advance, 10,000 francs, she had already received, it would be months and indeed years before she could expect to have it bring in any money.

Nor did this legal settlement terminate her troubles with Buloz. Weakened by the departure of the great tenor Rubini, who had been one of its mainstays, the Théâtre des Italiens made overtures to Pauline Viardot. But the jealous Giulia Grisi would only let her have secondary roles in several Rossini operas. Pauline's first appearances, in October and November, met with friendly reviews in the Paris press — whereupon she was violently criticized in the *Revue des Deux Mondes* and the *Revue de Paris,* now controlled by Buloz's associate Florestan Bonnaire. Giulia Grisi was lauded to the skies, Pauline Viardot Garcia's "immature, languishing, almost dying" voice was dragged in the mud. The nadir in this campaign of systematic denigration was reached in an article written by Buloz's brother-in-law, Henri Blaze, who wondered why Madame Pauline Viardot did not seek instruction from her rivals and betters: "The counsels of a tragedian like la Grisi . . . would be worth more to her than all the more or less psychological inspirations derived from contemporary novels, and which end up becoming as nebulous as the vaporous nuances of Monsieur Chopin's microscopic mode of playing the piano."

Unable to forgive George Sand for her "desertion" from the *Revue des Deux Mondes* and for the abuse she had heaped on his Caesarean head, François Buloz worked off his rage by attacks against her friends. Louis Viardot took up the cudgels for his vilified wife by taking over the music column of the *Revue indépendante* — an action which did nothing to endear either of them to the jealous Giulia Grisi. Long before the end of the 1842–1843 season, it was clear that her word at the Théâtre des Italiens was law and that Pauline Viardot would have to look elsewhere for the recognition she deserved. With George Sand's vigorous blessing, negotiations were opened with the Austrians and in April of 1843 Pauline and Louis Viardot left for Vienna, leaving their sixteen-month-old daughter in George's care. Pauline's first appearance in *The Barber of Seville* touched off such ovations that Metternich's haughty wife was moved to comment: "She must have an extraordinary talent to make everyone forget her lack of beauty." The first report to reach Paris, published in the *Revue et Gazette musicale,* declared that her triumph had been "colossal." Pauline's first letter from Vienna, written in early May, informed her Ninoune that she had been invited to the Hofburg to sing before the Emperor — an honor Louis-Philippe had never thought of paying her. Vienna, to which George Sand had transported Consuelo some months earlier in her novel, had offered her real-life model the same rapturous homage. Nature, even before Oscar Wilde, was imitating Art.

In late May of 1843 George Sand, accompanied by Louise Viardot and her nurse, as well as by Chopin and his Polish manservant, returned to Nohant. The trip, as far as Orléans, was made for the first time by train, a new experience which Chopin bore quite well, though the rumble of the wheels on the iron rails left him with a headache. The piano arrived a few days later, along with a number of mislaid trunks. In the absence of Solange, who had been left at her Paris boarding school, and of Maurice and Hippolyte, who had left for Guillery to visit Casimir, Chopin rode around the countryside on a donkey — which dutifully followed George Sand everywhere she went, its sniffing nostrils pressed against the jacket pocket in which she kept crusts of bread.

Though persistent rains soon put an end to these outings, forcing him to retire to his piano, Chopin spent this summer in even better health than during the previous year's heat. George Sand, for her part, felt more than ever at home. As she wrote to Charlotte Marliani: "Just to be able to see the clouds racing across the sky, the trees bending under the wind, the rain whipping the windowpanes, gives me a country feeling. I see a broad horizon, I stay in my dressing gown all day, I don't hear the bell ringing in my antechamber, nobody comes to *compliment me on my writings.* In short, I forget completely that I am Madame Sand."

This was not strictly true, for at Nohant, no less than in Paris, she could not escape from her relentless literary pressures. As Conan Doyle was to be stuck with Sherlock Holmes, so George Sand was now stuck with her excessively popular heroine. Fortunately for her, she had let Albert de Rudolstadt die but had preserved his bride, who, unlike Holmes, needed no dexterous hocus-pocus to be resuscitated.

Thus *Consuelo,* after 105 chapters, was curiously prolonged in the no less extraordinary sequel, *La Comtesse de Rudolstadt.* George Sand now plunged into the history of the Rosicrucians, the Freemasons, the Invisibles, the Illuminism of Weishaupt and Knigge, and even the mystical divagations of Swedenborg. Like her intellectual mentor, Pierre Leroux, she was more than ready to believe that these occult societies and philosophies were fundamentally egalitarian as well as libertarian in inspiration, and thus forerunners of the *carbonaro* groups that were battling for Italy's independence and of the more or less secret Society for the Rights of Man which Godefroy Cavaignac had founded in France. Indeed, the deeper she delved into the "occult history" of mankind — by which of course she meant Europe — the more convinced she became that the incendiary ideals of Liberty, Equality, Fraternity were not eighteenth-century inventions, but almost cabalistic products of the barbarous fifteenth century.

Delacroix, who came down to spend ten days with them in July, was as charmed by Chopin's company and as skeptically amused as ever by George Sand's evangelical fervor. As she wrote to Pierre Bocage, the actor, in mid-July: "If I were selfish I would feel right happy, but as my heart hasn't yet been dried up by old age, I often suffer from spleen at the thought that the welfare of my house and family give neither peace, nor affluence, nor freedom to millions of needy human beings. It is a grave question to know if we have the right to be happy to the detriment of the downtrodden, and if I were not deterred by domestic affections, I know what I would do with *my château* and *my lands.* Yet I submit to the common law, I grow cravenly fat, and I pretend to feel myself justified because I slave to give the joys of life to my children and my servants. And yet there are people who call me a *fanatic,* a *communist,* and a romantic, because I occasionally express remorse or regret for my paucity of virtue. Staying here right now is my friend Delacroix, who is a charming and excellent man, but who thinks me totally mad when I happen to remark that we are all scoundrels."

She also had to admit (in the same letter) that there were times when she missed the self-indulgent aberrations of her romantic past. "In losing my youth I have lost that thirst for personal happiness which constitutes the strength, the torments, and the bliss of that egotistical age." But he should not conclude from this that she was always in a *state of grace* — that is, relieved of the torments of physical desire. Nor had the morbid jealousy of a "certain young man" (Chopin) for a "certain old woman" (herself) completely withered away for "lack of nourishment." Chopin having somehow managed to read a letter which Bocage had written to her, she had frankly admitted that he had once been her lover. He had taken it very badly, doubtless persuaded that Bocage had enjoyed the pleasure of her bed longer than he had, and as she wrote sorrowfully of herself: "The old woman was mistaken in believing that sincerity and straightforwardness are the best remedies."

The end of the summer holidays was once again enlivened by the arrival of Louis Viardot and his wife, Pauline, who brought along her mother. George Sand, Chopin, and not least of all Maurice, who had conceived an adolescent infatuation for the twenty-two-year-old diva, listened enthralled as she related her extraordinary triumphs, first in Vienna and later in Berlin. Meyerbeer, the director of the Royal Prussian Conservatory of Music, had pointedly called her "my dear little Consuelo" and told her that he wanted to write an opera inspired by George Sand's description of the Rudolstadt family and their castle at Riesenburg. Franz Liszt, equally taken by the novel, was reported to have expressed a similar desire.

In late October Chopin and Maurice returned to Paris: the first to resume his piano lessons, the second his instruction in painting in Delacroix's atelier. George Sand preferred to remain behind for another month. By spending one more month at Nohant in the autumn, and one less in Paris in the spring, she calculated that she could save between 4000 and 5000 francs a year. She also wanted to finish the final chapters in Consuelo's curious odyssey, which had eventually led the wandering singer from Haydn's Vienna to the Berlin of Frederick the Great. But slave though she did each night, she was still more than three months from the conclusion, which she only reached in mid-February of 1844.

This marathon literary effort was all the more remarkable in being simultaneously accompanied by articles which she wrote to denounce the local mistreatment of a half-wit orphan. She also found the time and energy to help her Berrichon friends Charles Duvernet, Alphonse Fleury, and Alexis Duteil found an opposition weekly. In doing so, she was not entirely disinterested, for her secret hope was that *L'Eclaireur de l'Indre et du Cher*, as it was called, could be turned into a vehicle for the propagation of Pierre Leroux's communistic philosophy. At this even the stoutly republican Alphonse Fleury began to balk, being less convinced than she that the "new gospel" (of absolute, propertyless equality) had already "been formulated by the people." "Dig in the arid field of your bourgeoisie," she heatedly berated him. "Perhaps you will give up when you have broken your picks. There is none of the bourgeois in my blood. I am the daughter of a patrician and a bohemian, like the young Zdenko of my novel."

Thus fact and fiction, in her exalted imaginings, were to march forward hand in hand toward a triumphant apotheosis which she felt was just around the corner: this being, as she had one of her characters (a "philosopher" like Leroux) explain in the epilogue of *La Comtesse de Rudolstadt*, "the unity of life in humanity, the unity of dogma in religion." Today such utterances sound quaint, not to say absurd. But at this time, the pre-Marxist springtime of communism, there were not a few who believed that class conflicts could be peaceably resolved, national quarrels patched up, and religious doctrines eventually harmonized within the compass of a new, purified, and rejuvenated Christianity. As she wrote to one acquaintance: "George Sand is no more than a pale reflection of P. Leroux, a fanatical disciple of the same Ideal, but a mute and charmed disciple in the presence of his word, ever ready to throw away all her works to write, speak, think and pray under his inspiration. Have you read *Consuelo?* It has some very boring chapters which are mine. It also has some magnificent pages, which are his."

While the serialization of *Consuelo* and *La Comtesse de Rudolstadt* had helped to launch Pierre Leroux's *Revue indépendante,* it had proved anything but a financial boon to their author. George Sand accordingly welcomed the overtures made to her by Louis Véron, the former editor of the *Revue de Paris,* who had recently taken over the running of the daily *Constitutionnel.* In Balzac's France, as in the England of Charles Dickens, the novel had become a public fad. The telegraph did not yet exist to provide "hot" news, so that newspaper and periodical editors were as anxious to fill their columns with serialized fiction as the novelists were to supply them with space-filling "copy." The kind of cheap editions which the British were beginning to produce had not yet become the fashion in France; and at a time when half or two thirds of a publisher's proceeds might comes from sales made to *cabinets de lecture* (reading rooms which functioned like lending libraries), the profits an author could expect from the laborious sale of an edition of 1000 to 1500 copies were apt to be considerably less than what he could expect to derive from serialization. With 20,000 subscribers, the middle-of-the-road *Constitutionnel* was a well-established daily which could offer George Sand 10,000 francs for the right to serialize a novel which she could later publish in book form elsewhere. As this was almost twice what Buloz had once paid her for both serial and publication rights, George let herself be talked into signing two contracts. The first was for a novel called *Jeanne,* partly inspired by the historical figure of Joan of Arc and a continuation of George's psychological probing into mystical and ecstatic states of mind which was already so marked in *Consuelo* and *La Comtesse de Rudolstadt.* The second was for a *roman de moeurs* — a novel about contemporary French society along the lines of what Balzac was writing — which she pledged herself to deliver by the following September.

Jeanne, which Balzac later hailed as a "masterpiece" — for the psychological finesse with which the central figure of the heroine (a humble serving girl of peasant origin) was treated — kept George Sand occupied from March till late May of 1844. She finished the novel shortly before leaving for Nohant — an extraordinary achievement when one thinks that this was a particularly busy spring, marked by her tireless efforts to help launch *L'Eclaireur de l'Indre et du Cher,* a laborious correspondence with various proletarian poets whom she felt it her duty to advise, tortuous negotiations with several Paris publishers, and a couple of severe crises during which it looked as though Chopin were going to cough himself to death. (During one of them, in mid-February, he insisted on dragging himself to the funeral of Camille Pleyel's mother, and fell weeping into the piano maker's arms when they met next to the open grave.)

Liszt, after completing another triumphal tour in Germany — which had seen him add the Irish-Andalusian dancer Lola Montez to his long list of feminine conquests — returned to Paris in mid-April to give two new concerts. His nine-year romance with Marie d'Agoult having ended, he did not have to fear her displeasure in sending Madame Sand a magnificent bouquet of flowers and then calling on her in person. Delighted to renew a friendship she had always cherished, George invited Franz to spend a few weeks at Nohant in July or August. She was understandably thrilled by the prospect of playing summer hostess not only to Europe's greatest piano virtuoso but also to Pauline Viardot, whose operatic triumphs in Saint Petersburg that winter had been such that Rubini was already declaring that he had never encountered a finer female voice. George also looked forward to the visit of her old mentor, Hyacinthe de Latouche, with whom she had recently been reconciled after a breach which had lasted a full decade.

All these high hopes were dashed, however, by a series of mishaps and disappointments. Latouche suffered an apoplectic stroke. The portly Albert Grzymala, on whose friendly presence she had also counted, almost broke his back tumbling down a flight of stairs.

Pauline Viardot had to devote all of July and August to furnishing the new country house which her husband had recently acquired in the Brie country east of Paris. Liszt, unexpectedly distracted by some new love affair, could not make it.

The cruelest mishap was suffered by Chopin, who on the eve of their departure for the country learned that his father Nicolas had died in Warsaw at the age of seventy-three. The news left him paralyzed. For forty-eight hours he locked himself in his room and would see no one but George and the French doctor she summoned to take care of him. Another link with his native Poland had been severed, this time irrevocably. For the first time in their six-year liaison George Sand wrote to his mother Justyna, saying that there was no need for alarm over her son's "external situation" and that she (George) would continue to look after his health and "surround him with as much care and affection as you would do yourself."

A few weeks later, at Nohant, Chopin received a letter from his sister Ludwika, informing him that she and her husband Kalasanty Jedrzejewicz, a professor of agronomy, were undertaking the long overland journey to Paris to see him. George Sand answered immediately, inviting them to use her Square d'Orléans apartment before coming on to Nohant. "Do not be unduly alarmed about his health," she added, realizing what a shock it might be for Ludwika to see how thin her brother had become. "It has varied little over the past six years, during which I have seen him every day. A spell of heavy coughing every morning, two or three more serious crises every winter, but which only last two or three days each, now and then some neuralgic pains — such is his regular condition. For the rest his chest is in a healthy state and his delicate constitution shows no trace of lesion. I hope that with time it will be strengthened, but I am certain at least that with a regular life and plenty of care it will last as long as another."

To be on hand for his sister's arrival in mid-July, Chopin hastened up to Paris in a stagecoach which was so crowded that Manuel Marliani (who had stopped off at Nohant, on his way back from Spain) had to find a seat on the roof. The next ten days were spent in a giddy round of sightseeing, visits to Polish friends, evenings at the Opéra, and musical soirees which left the delicate Frycek utterly exhausted — so exhausted that to George Sand's considerable surprise he reappeared at Nohant on July 25 accompanied only by his old Polish servant, Jan. Unable to face the prospect of more sightseeing and evening entertainment, he had left his sister and brother-in-law to the care of Charlotte Marliani and Grzymala.

Not until August 9 did Ludwika and her husband finally reach Nohant after vainly waiting for a week in Paris for Pauline Viardot to accompany them. For George Sand, at any rate, this unfortunate contretemps proved a blessing in disguise. For once again she was faced with a formidable deadline. *Jeanne,* which had been serialized in Louis Véron's *Constitutionnel* from April 25 to June 2, had been followed almost immediately by a novel of Eugène Sue's called *Le Juif errant* (*The Wandering Jew*), which proved to be almost as rambling as its title. Sue, who kept inventing new adventures as he went along, soon began showing signs of strain and asked Véron for a respite. Véron accordingly asked George Sand if she could not advance the delivery date by one month so that he could have the new novel by August 15 instead of mid-September, as had been foreseen in the contract. Spurred on by the substantial increase in payment promised if she could meet this new target date, George gave up all physical exercise — not once during this summer did she go riding — and devoted her sleepless nights to blackening the paper. "I have neither time to eat or sleep," she wrote to a Paris friend on August 12, and exactly two weeks later she could write again to announce: "I finished my novel yesterday" — August 26 — "I'm dead."

The extraordinary strain imposed by this literary challenge did not keep George Sand from acting the perfect hostess to her Polish guests. To Chopin's intense relief the two ladies hit it off, and there was not a tense moment. George found the discreet Ludwika to be an "angel like her brother," while Ludwika was full of admiration for the maternal solicitude shown to her brother, Frycek, by the industrious authoress. Kalasanty enjoyed the long rides through the countryside, examining fields and flora with an experienced eye; Chopin entertained them in the evening with extracts from his still unfinished Sonata in B Minor or by playing four-hand compositions with Solange; George read passages from her new novel. Here too she was agreeably surprised. For in the conversations which ensued

Ludwika approved of the plot of *Le Meunier d'Angibault* — the complicated story of a get-rich-quick scoundrel who drives his two daughters wild by refusing to allow them to marry the men they love — and showed herself far more advanced in her political and social views than her conservative brother, who treated Leroux's communistic aspirations with the skepticism they deserved.

Genuinely sad to see her visitors leave after three short weeks, George gave Ludwika a pencil sketch she had drawn of Frycek to take home, along with a rosary for her mother. She begged them to return for a longer stay next year. Maurice, in an unusual show of courtesy, insisted on accompanying them back to Paris, promising that he would return immediately with Chopin. But the final leave-taking with the Jedrzejewiczes completed, he let Chopin return alone, preferring to hie himself out to the Viardots' country house east of Paris.

The truth, which George Sand had hitherto only vaguely suspected, was that the twenty-one-year-old boy was head over heels in love with the twenty-three-year-old diva. And even more astounding — one is tempted to add, more astounding than fiction — was the fact that this youthful infatuation was apparently reciprocated. As Pauline Viardot wrote to her "dear Ninoune" from Brussels on September 20: "How is Maurice after his little trip? We promised each other to be brave . . . I can't say more about it at this moment. I love him very seriously. Write me soon — *à double entente,* if it's possible" — the "double meanings" being clearly intended to circumvent the suspicions of her impresario husband — "by addressing your letter to the Imperial Management of Petersburg Theaters."

The gifted though ugly "daughter" George Sand had "adopted" years before and who had inspired *Consuelo* had thus fallen in love with her own son.

32. The Death Throes of a Romance

EXACTLY WHAT took place between the ardent young wooer and his responsive "flame" at the Viardots' country place at Courtavenel is anybody's guess, for the evidence is missing. So far as we know, it was the first such "passion" the dark-eyed Maurice had managed to inspire, even though — to judge by certain of his mother's scolding letters — it was not the first amorous adventure in which the carnival-loving student-artist had been involved. A long letter which Pauline is thought to have written to her Ninoune from Petersburg in November has not been found and may later have been destroyed as too compromising.

What is certain is that this burgeoning romance found little favor at Nohant, where it was regarded as a passing infatuation. Chopin, at any rate, was not deceived by Maurice's ceremonious insistence on escorting the Jedrzejewiczes back to Paris. As he wrote to his sister from Nohant on September 18: "Maurice has not yet returned, but he'll be here tomorrow or the day after. You may recall how on leaving here I predicted that I would come back alone on the stagecoach and that all of this journey by post chaise was designed to save appearances."

Though Maurice's adolescent infatuation for Pauline Viardot was to prove more than a passing fancy, upsetting (as we shall see) his mother's hopeful plans for a different kind of match, George had more urgent problems to worry about during this troublesome autumn of 1844. In eagerly contracting for a second George Sand novel, the "odiously bourgeois" Louis Véron (as Hyacinthe de Latouche liked to call him) had expected to receive another story with a pastoral setting like *Jeanne*. Instead, he was given a work packed with more social dynamite than anything she had yet written. Entitled *Le Meunier d'Angibault* (*The Miller of Angibault*), it was full of incendiary phrases certain to raise the hackles of Véron's middle-class readers. "The rich man's money has not been earned by the poor man's work: it's *money that's been stolen* . . . It's the inheritance of his father's feudal rapines . . . it's been extorted by pillage, violence and tyranny . . ." etc. Phrases all too obviously inspired by Pierre-Joseph Proudhon's celebrated maxim: *"La propriété, c'est le vol!"* — Property is Theft!

Véron refused to publish *Le Meunier d'Angibault* in the *Constitutionnel.* Weeks of laborious wrangling ensued. George Sand claimed that her frankly communistic sympathies were fully justified in a novel of *contemporary* life: "It is impossible that creative artists should not be impressed by the approach of the future, and my novel takes place today." Unconvinced by this dubious argument, Véron finally agreed to pay her an "indemnity" of 5000 francs, leaving her free to find another editor. Though this was a far cry from the 50,000 francs she claimed she would have earned had the novel been serialized, she could consider herself lucky to have obtained that much.

Her stubborn refusal to compromise with her extreme opinions precipitated a new financial crisis — not only for herself, but also for her favorite "philosopher," Pierre Leroux. It had been her intention to turn over part of the proceeds from her new novel to Leroux, who was in dire need of money to develop a printing machine of his own design. Though he had been tinkering with this machine for years — with absolutely nothing to show for it — he had managed to persuade George Sand that it was going to revolutionize the printing industry, much as his egalitarian gospel was going to revolutionize mankind. Certain of her friends who had been asked to contribute to this magnificently "progressive" cause had begun to have second thoughts. One was Charlotte Marliani, who had come to the conclusion that to finance Pierre Leroux was to pour money down the drain. Another was Charles Veyret, an engineer friend of Chopin's who was even better qualified to judge the real worth of Leroux's "inventive genius."

It was months, however, before George Sand could bring herself to face the unpleasant truth: Leroux was something of a sponger, and a charlatan to boot. She made no complaint when he casually helped himself to the 6000 francs which one of her publishers offered her for a second edition of *Consuelo* and *La Comtesse de Rudolstadt.* She voiced no objection when he decided to move to Boussac, a picturesque Auvergne town in the hill country of La Marche, in order to take over the printing of *L'Eclaireur de l'Indre et du Cher,* which up until then had been produced in Orléans. She was even happy to write a preface for a "new" translation of Goethe's *Werther,* which Leroux (who knew no German) had quietly passed off as his own, though it was in fact the work of another Frenchman who had died a dozen years before! But by June of 1845 even she had to admit to a growing impatience over Leroux's ceaseless appeals for money — made not only for himself and his nine children, but on behalf of his two brothers and their concubines (for as full-fledged "progressives" they disdained anything as stupidly middle-class as marriage).

Le Meunier d'Angibault, which Louis Véron had rejected, was finally serialized in the *Réforme,* a liberal newspaper which had recently been launched by a number of republicans. They included Alexandre Ledru-Rollin, a lawyer who had taken part in the mass trial of 1835 alongside of Michel de Bourges; Etienne Arago, a brother of the famous astronomer François Arago and the uncle of George's friend Emmanuel; and not least of all the young social historian Louis Blanc.

Born in 1811, the same year as Jules Sandeau, Louis Blanc seems to have aroused maternal feelings of a particularly tender kind. George was soon calling him "my child," "dear child of my heart," and finally "my dear angel." Two of the scant letters which have survived make it clear that they became lovers during the first months of 1845. But their liaison does not seem to have lasted very long. George confessed to the pint-sized Louis that though her heart was "very healthy," she was declining physically: "For months now I've been feverish, I've had a terrible fever every night. Don't say anything about it here" — she meant in the presence of Chopin and the children — "it would frighten them. I don't have one foot in the grave, like Chateaubriand, and I have no desire to be buried for another ten years . . . But I am afraid of not being able to complete my task and of bursting like an overfilled bottle. I feel myself slowly dying. I no longer sleep at all. It's perhaps and probably due to insomnia and the illusion of suffering that I have been so affected by these ideas of death which have been so tastelessly paraded before the public by litter-bearing poets" — one of them being her old friend Musset.

Prolonged overwork and relentless financial pressures, as much as the sexual abstinence she had imposed on herself and Chopin, were responsible for reducing her to this fretful pass. Though ideologically satisfying, George Sand's brief association with the *Réforme* proved both financially and artistically frustrating, its editors being slow to pay and feeling free to chop up her novel into installments which blithely disregarded chapter endings.

Lack of funds and a typhus epidemic in the Berry countryside delayed the return to Nohant in the late spring of 1845. But by dashing off a novelette named *Teverino* (a light-hearted fantasy, partly inspired by the composer Rossini, about a horse-taming minstrel who brings song, merriment, and novelty into the unadventurous life of a staid Italian couple), George Sand was able to scrape up enough money to make the journey possible in early June.

This time the trip was made in a calèche which Chopin had recently purchased. With Pauline Viardot and Chopin's manservant, Jan, also accompanying them, it was a crowded carriage which finally drew up under the venerable elms in the little church square at Nohant. On the way they were surprised by a drenching cloudburst, the first of a long series of downpours which soon had the entire countryside under water. The Indre broke its banks, bridges and millwheels were swept away, Hippolyte's garden and country house were flooded in a deluge worse than anything the oldest inhabitants of the province could remember. Louis Viardot, who had come down to fetch his wife, finally returned to Paris alone, after they had made an abortive effort to cross a flooded weir. Delighted by this contretemps, which kept Pauline at Nohant for an additional week, Maurice painted two portraits of his "beloved," while she charmed Chopin by singing some exquisite Spanish romances she had composed the year before in Vienna.

The wet weather, which continued into July and August, forced George Sand to spend her time indoors, where she suffered from severe rheumatic pains. Adopting a new work schedule, she locked herself into her study from noon to six o'clock each day to work on a new novel, which she finally called *Le Péché de Monsieur Antoine.* The somewhat arbitrary title referred to the secret "sin" which Antoine de Châteaubrun had committed in fathering a daughter with another man's wife (an exploit curiously reminiscent of Aurore Dudevant's secret sinning with Stéphane Ajasson de Grandsagne). But this "mishap" was incidental to the main plot or purpose of the novel, intended to illustrate a conflict between generations — in the persons of an energetic industrialist named Cardonnet, who has brought progress to a rural village, and his son Emile. Considering his father's fortune to have been obtained through the exploitation of his millworkers, Emile refuses to carry on the family business, preferring to marry the daughter of a humble carpenter. (As Frances Winwar once remarked, in George Sand's social novels there is always a carpenter!) Fortunately for his (and for George Sand's) progressive dreams, the son inherits four and a half million francs from a philanthropic marquis of communistic inclinations, and with these he can establish a rural commune sufficiently grandiose to satisfy Pierre Leroux's most exalted expectations. The plot was eminently implausible and the novel full of tiresome speechmaking.

This summer of 1845 was not a happy one for Chopin either. The bad weather got on his nerves, making him more than usually irritable and withdrawn. He was dissatisfied with his piano, which was again out of tune, and he seemed unable to develop and perfect his compositions, repeating the same theme over and over with an obsessive insistence which George Sand listened to dismayed. For, as she had to point out to him more than once, his first spontaneous statement of a new melodic line was often the best, each attempted improvement merely weighing down or muddying the ingenuous purity of the initial inspiration.

Gustave Papet, who examined him carefully, found nothing physically wrong. But he told George privately that Chopin was subject to hypochondria and would probably remain so until well into his forties, when his nerves would have lost their "excessive sensibility." "I'm not made for life in the country," Chopin admitted in a letter to his sister, "but the pure air is a joy to me." George, who knew this better than anyone, thus found herself confronted with a cruel choice: between the good air of Nohant, such a tonic to his lungs, and the stimulation of Paris, so badly needed by his nerves. To make matters worse, the choice was no longer entirely hers. "I would gladly sacrifice my love of the country for him," as she wrote to Marie de Rozières, a former student of Chopin's who had given piano lessons to Solange, "but Maurice is not of this opinion, and if I listened to Chopin more than to Maurice, there would be an uproar. This is how it is in even the most close-knit families. All cannot have the same tastes, and all are not happy at the same time."

This latent conflict was aggravated by Chopin's Polish manservant, Jan, who rang the dinner bell too loudly and was constantly quarreling with George Sand's personal maid, Suzanne. George, who knew how attached Chopin was to his old valet, did not take these domestic incidents too tragically. But Maurice and Solange were less kindly disposed, teasing the aged manservant so mercilessly that Chopin was finally obliged to dismiss him.

In early September Maurice was sent up to Paris with the first part of *Le Péché de Monsieur Antoine* which, stuffed with communistic rhetoric though it was, had been unintentionally presold to the archconservative newspaper *L'Epoque*. After paying a brief visit to Pauline Viardot's country house east of Paris, Maurice returned to Nohant with his third cousin, Augustine Brault, who was descended from Sophie Dupin's grandfather. A pretty brunette whom George had helped to get admitted to the prestigious Conservatoire for instruction in singing and piano playing, Augustine had spent an unhappy youth under the domination of a mother who had led a rather disreputable life (among other things giving birth to an illegitimate daughter) before marrying a humble tailor named Joseph Brault. George Sand, who had taken pity on their plight at a time when Brault was unemployed, had tided them over several crises with periodic gifts of money and had ended up virtually adopting Augustine. The mother, who was very much a scheming hussy, had long been trying to persuade her daughter to try her luck on the stage. But as Augustine, though pretty, had neither a good voice nor dramatic talent, George Sand and others had vigorously advised against it, knowing that the young girl would be given only minor parts and would be quickly forced to choose between prostitution and starvation. Adèle Brault then decided she would have to find her daughter a rich husband. Under the illusion that her famous relative must be rolling in money, she was delighted by the prospect of Augustine's marrying Maurice. Nothing could have been more pleasing to George Sand, who liked this idea of her son "ennobling" and enriching the life of a virtuous young girl who had had the misfortune to be born poor. But Maurice, now a proudly whiskered twenty-two, was still too fatally smitten by his adolescent passion for Pauline Viardot to be much affected by Augustine's modest charm.

During Maurice's absence George took Chopin and Solange on a visit to the old fortified town of Boussac, with its high castle perched on a precipitous rock overlooking the Creuse River. Pierre Leroux, with whom they spent a few hours, told them that he was going to use his printing press to launch a new magazine, the *Revue sociale*, thereby implying that the *Revue indépendante*, which he had in the meantime abandoned, had outlived its prime. Two years earlier George Sand would have greeted this news with enthusiasm, being then persuaded that the founding of progressive reviews all over France would accelerate the country's conversion to Leroux's communistic Christianity. But the hypnotic spell had begun to wear off, and she was not surprised, when the first two numbers appeared, to find that they were worthless.

This four-day outing, the last which she and Chopin were to undertake together, seems to have inspired her. In late October she sat down and in just four days she wrote *La Mare au diable* (*The Devil's Pond*), a kind of pastoral idyll which was mercifully devoid of revolutionary predication. It could easily have been mistaken for the work of a conservative author, for George did not conceal her regret over how many ancient customs, legends, and traditions, going back to medieval and even Celtic times, had disappeared "from our deep valleys . . . with the rapidity of lightning" — victims of the railway and other instruments of "progress": a progress too exclusively industrial and materialistic to be the romantic kind she still dreamed of.

In late November she let Chopin return to Paris without her — one more sign of the gradual estrangement that was more or less unconsciously taking place between them. She explained that she wanted to start another novel in the tranquillity of the country, but the real reason was a desire to renew her long-interrupted friendship with her cousin René de Villeneuve, the owner of the Château de Chenonceaux. She was apparently afraid that her cousin's strait-laced wife, already scandalized by her radical extremism, would be doubly shocked if she appeared with her well-known lover. Nor was this her only fear. As she wrote to her cousin René: "I have an abominable failing. I smoke cigarettes! Very small and tasteless, compared to those which certain *lionesses* consume today. I smoke almost continually, and as much as possible in hiding. But I still smell of cigars no matter how careful I am about it . . . And yet, if I remain three hours without smoking, I fall into a state of stupor, I yawn, I chew my fingernails, I suffer the torments of hell, and this suffering is such that it is one of the main reasons which keep me from going out and frequenting high society, which I must admit is not to my taste."

Momentarily overcoming her aristocratic prejudices, Madame de Villeneuve proved an amiable hostess to her cigar-smoking cousin-in-law, who was overawed by the magnificent scale of the ceilings, impressed by the stiff splendor of the antique furniture and hangings, and charmed by the soft ripple of river water flowing under the arches of this most exquisite of Renaissance chateaux. Even the lack of plumbing, which obliged them to empty their chamber pots into the Cher — to the vast delight of Solange and Maurice! — seemed to add to the primitive enchantment of this garden-girt jewel of Touraine.

Shortly before Christmas George Sand returned to the Square d'Orléans apartment in Paris. One month later she offered generous asylum to Augustine Brault — to save her from the repeated insults and beatings to which the poor girl was subjected by her mother, incensed to learn that Maurice was not interested in marrying her. In thus admitting a new member to the family, George had no idea of what trouble she was piling up for the future. A fond mother who had long pampered her children, she had always leaned over backward, or so she thought, to keep the younger Solange from feeling that she was being slighted or less favored than her older brother. At seventeen, Solange was already a full-bosomed young woman, and there had even been some talk of marrying her off to Louis Blanc. As robust and strong-willed as she had been as a child, when her mother had dubbed her her "Lioness," she seemed, under Chopin's musical spell, to have been tamed; and George was thus lulled into believing that she had sheathed her young claws forever.

For the first few months there were no overt signs of tension. Solange continued to receive lessons from Marie de Rozières, while Augustine, who was four years older, was given free musical instruction by Pauline Viardot's brother, Manuel García, now the senior singing instructor at the Paris Conservatoire. For the traditional Mardi Gras supper the golden-haired "Sol" — as Chopin had nicknamed her — appeared in the heavily bewigged disguise of Louis XIV, the "Sun King," while the modest Augustine played the petticoated part of Charlotte Corday. Any jealousy Solange may have felt over the intrusion of this pretty, vivacious, and even-tempered cousin was at this point well disguised. The two girls were even inseparable companions, racing up and down the stairs between Madame Sand's apartment and Maurice's fourth-floor studio.

In early May, after signing a 12,000 franc contract for a two-volume novel to be called *Lucrezia* (8000 francs for newspaper serialization, 4000 francs for a book edition), George again left for Nohant, traveling as far as Blois by train. She was accompanied by Solange and Augustine, whom she now called "my daughters" and took everywhere she went. Maurice had been sent off to Guillery to spend a month with his father, while Chopin stayed on in Paris, absorbed by his piano lessons and social obligations. When he finally joined them three weeks later, bringing with him a small machine for making ices, neither he nor George Sand could guess that it was to be his last visit to Nohant.

This summer of 1846 — as gloriously hot as the previous one had been wet and dispiriting — began with a four-day excursion which took George and her "two daughters" to the marshlands of

Mézières-en-Brenne, some twenty-five miles to the west of Châteauroux, whither they had been invited by an affable country squire to watch some horse races. Chopin, who was anything but a riding and hunting outdoorsman, preferred to remain at Nohant, basking in the bright June sunlight. When the ladies returned, they went bathing every day in the Indre. It was so hot that they even went for moonlight dips; George would lie on her back on the wet sand with the shallow water covering her slip, while she smoked a cigar and watched Solange and Augustine frolicking like naiads with the splashing dogs.

"Chopin" as she wrote to Marie de Rozières, "is astonished to find himself sweating. He is mortified by it; he claims that wash as he may, he *reeks*. We laugh till the tears come into our eyes to see such an ethereal being refusing to sweat like everyone else; but don't breathe a word about this to him, it would only make him furious . . ."

Early in July the music-loving Charles Duvernet, who admired Chopin as much as he had disliked Liszt (whose political arguments he could not stand), brought over a young lady from La Rochelle named Eliza Fournier. Her account of the evening she spent at Nohant is as vivid a description as exists of these memorable soirees. Obliging as ever, Chopin played on for hours until it was almost midnight, switching without warning from the gay and lilting to the sad and melancholic, and back again as the mood possessed him. "Never have I heard a talent such as his: prodigious in its simplicity, softness, kindness, and wit. In this last genre he played us a takeoff on a Bellini opera which had us in stitches, such was the finesse of observation and the witty mocking of Bellini's musical style and habits. Then he played a prayer, for Poles in distress, which brought tears to our eyes; then an Etude on the sound of the tocsin which made us shiver; then a funeral march, so grave, somber, and sorrowful that our hearts swelled, our chests contracted, and all one could hear in the silence were a few ill-contained sighs caused by an emotion too deep to be dominated. Emerging from this sorrowful inspiration and recalled to himself after a moment of rest by several notes sung by Madame Sand, he had us listen to the jolly airs of a dance called the *bourrée* which is common to this part of the country . . ."

Chopin concluded his performance with an astounding tour de force: a piano imitation of a defective music box, executed with such exquisite mastery that, as his rapt listener later noted, "if we hadn't been in the same room, we could never have believed that it was a piano which was tinkling under his fingers. All the rippling finesse and rapidity of the little steel struts which cause the invisible cylinder to vibrate were rendered with matchless delicacy, and then suddenly a faint, barely audible cadence was repeatedly heard, only to be interrupted by the machine, which had something wrong with it. He played us one of those airs, a Tyrolean one I think, in which a note is missing from the cylinder, and which got stuck each time the moment came to play this note."

Just five days after this memorable evening Nohant was visited by Matthew Arnold. The twenty-four-year-old poet, who had only graduated from Oxford two years earlier, was returning from Boussac and the rocky heights of Toulx-Sainte-Croix, which he had wanted to visit because they had provided the dramatic setting for George Sand's novel *Jeanne,* which he was then reading. "The midday breakfast at Nohant was not yet over when I reached the house, and I found a large party assembled," he later recalled. "I entered with some trepidation . . . but the simplicity of Madame Sand's manner put me at ease in a moment. She named some of those present; amongst them were her son and daughter . . . Maurice and Solange . . . and Chopin with his wonderful eyes. There was at that time nothing astonishing in Madame Sand's appearance. She was not in man's clothes, she wore a sort of costume not impossible . . . to members of the fair sex at this hour amongst ourselves, as an out-door dress for the country or for Scotland. She made me sit by her and poured out for me the insipid and depressing beverage, *boisson fade et mélancolique,* as Balzac called it, for which English people are thought abroad to be always thirsting — tea. She conversed of the country through which I had been wandering, of the Berry peasants and their mode of life, of Switzerland whither I was going; she touched politely, by a few questions and remarks, upon England and things and persons English — upon Oxford and Cambridge, Byron, Bulwer. As she spoke, her eyes, head, bearing, were all of them striking; but the main impression she made was an impression . . . of *simplicity,* frank, cordial simplicity."

Neither of these two visitors could have realized that at the very moment they were recording these impressions, the fragile harmony of family life at Nohant was quietly disintegrating. In early July Albert Grzymala came down to Nohant, accompanied by a Countess Czosnowska whom Chopin had insisted on inviting because she was a good friend of his sister Ludwika. The newcomer found scant favor with the "Lady of the House" (Chopin's prudish way of referring to George Sand in his letters to his sister), and her dog Lili even less. Both were found guilty of "reeking" — the French term coined for the occasion being *empester,* which carries the additional connotation of "infecting." "I say nothing about it to Ch[opin]," George reported in a letter to Marie de Rozières. "I welcome those he likes even when they don't suit me, and in this respect I do the contrary of what he does with regard to me" — a pointed reference to Chopin's acute jealousy, which had forced her to keep not only Bocage and Louis Blanc, but the innocent young publisher, Pierre-Jules Hetzel, from coming to visit her at the Cité d'Orléans apartment. "I did well to get angry one day and to have the courage to tell him some home truths and to threaten him with being fed up. Since that moment he has been reasonable . . ."

Chopin was distinctly unhappy over the less than cordial welcome extended to Laura Czosnowska. "The cousin did not like her, nor consequently did the son," he wrote to his sister. "There were therefore jokes, from which they moved on to crude pleasantries . . . One must have a soul of the quality of Ludwika's to be able to leave a pleasant memory for everybody here." After which he added, pathetically: "The Lady of the House repeated to me several times in Lorka's presence: 'Your sister is worth a hundred times more than you,' and each time I answered: 'You are pefectly right.' "

Nohant was no longer the country home to which Chopin could invite the Polish friends whose company he cherished in the absence of his distant family. Joseph Dessauer, the Czech pianist and composer, had been warmly welcomed a year or two before, melancholy hypochondriac though he was. But this summer George refused to extend her hospitality to the Polish composer Josef Nowakowski, an old Warsaw friend who was visiting France. The reason given was that there was no free bedroom available. For in addition to Augustine, the "family" at Nohant had acquired one more member —

Eugène Lambert, a young art student whom Maurice had befriended in Delacroix's atelier. This precedence given to a friend of Maurice's was more than a mere pinprick for someone as hypersensitive as Chopin.

No less indicative of the ever-growing discord was the new novel George Sand had spent her early mornings writing for the past three months — for she now rose at 6:00 A.M. and was usually in bed by midnight. Unlike *Le Compagnon du Tour de France, Horace,* and other didactic novels, *Lucrezia Floriani* was a straight-forward pyschological piece of fiction in which the political and social overtones were muted. Its subject was the death agony of a romance, killed not only by the disparity between two lovers but by the ferocious exclusivity of one of the two partners, almost as jealous of the past as he is of the present. It was thus, though George Sand later tried to deny it, her own love affair with Chopin that she was portraying.

The plot of this new novel was basically simple. Lucrezia Floriani, a famous actress, has withdrawn to a luxurious villa on the shores of Lake Iseo (the same which the author had once visited with Pietro Pagello, in 1834). She who has had many love affairs in the past — not casual affairs of the flesh, but deep, passionate affairs of the heart (even when they only lasted eight days!) — is persuaded (again like George Sand) that her sensual life is finished. But chance brings to her villa a young Prince, Karol de Roswald, who (like Chopin) is six years younger than herself and practically a virgin. He falls ill, she takes care of him, and from his bedside she soon moves into his bed. They enjoy several weeks of undiluted bliss, during which she fancies once again that this is to be a deathless romance. But the illusion is short-lived. Appalled by what he learns about her licentious past, the Prince grows morbidly jealous, irritable, and possessive. He becomes intolerant and thus intolerable, finally poisoning his mistress' domestic happiness through his querulous suspicions and needling insinuations. What had first seemed an enchantment comes increasingly to be a burden. She loses her beauty and her zest for life, convinced that she is prematurely old and done for. One day she dies.

If Albert de Rudolstadt was in part a fictitious idealization of Chopin the artist, the Prince Karol of *Lucrezia Floriani* was a cruel portrait

trait of Chopin the man — depicted with all of his exquisite virtues and insufferable vices. Lucrezia Floriani is not long in realizing that their characters are (as Marie d'Agoult would have said) "antipodal." The Prince is an aristocrat by birth and instinct; she is a plebeian. He is virtuous; she is a sinner. She is full of compassion for human weaknesses; he demands an absolute perfection in everyone. "Karol did not have minor faults. He had one major one, great, involuntary, fatal: intolerance of mind. He did not have it in him to open himself to a feeling of general charity in order to enlarge his judgment of human affairs," etc.

But all this was but a mild preamble to the author's devastating portrayal of Prince Karol's obsessive jealousy, so reminiscent of Chopin's own behavior:

"One day Karol was jealous of the Curé who had come to collect money. Another day he was jealous of a beggar whom he mistook for a wooer in disguise. Yet another day he was jealous of a servant who, being much spoiled like all the servants of the house, answered with a boldness which struck him as unnatural. After which it was a hawker, then a doctor . . . Things reached such a pass that the poor woman [Lucrezia] no longer dared notice the face of a passer-by, the skill of a poacher, the withers of a horse. Karol was even jealous of the children. What am I saying — *even?* He was that above all. They were indeed the only rivals he had, the only beings whom Lucrezia thought about as much as himself . . . He soon took a dislike to the children . . . He noticed at last that they were spoiled, noisy, exuberant, and flighty, and he fancied that not all children are like that. He was annoyed to find them almost constantly between their mother and himself. He felt that she gave in to them too often, that she was becoming their slave. At other moments he was scandalized when she punished them."

In mid-August, when Delacroix came down to Nohant for a two-week stay, George Sand spent a long evening reading *Lucrezia Floriani* to the assembled company. Delacroix listened appalled, as this experiment in literary vivisection unfolded itself relentlessly. He kept looking from George Sand to Chopin and back, expecting to intercept a telltale frown or a meaningful glance. "Executioner and victim both amazed me," he later recalled. "Madame Sand seemed absolutely at her ease, and Chopin never stopped admiring the story. At midnight we retired together. Chopin wanted to accompany me, and I seized the opportunity to sound out his impressions. Was he putting up a front for my benefit? Not at all. He had really not understood, continuing to praise the novel."

Chopin's relations with the children at Nohant were not, of course, precisely the same as those between Prince Karol and Lucrezia Floriani's children. Nor was the mounting tension altogether Chopin's fault. George Sand had for some time been encouraging her son to become a "man," not realizing the storms this would lead to. The presence of Augustine was an aggravating factor. For adolescents being what they are — desirous above all of impressing others, and not least of all persons close to their own age — the young Maurice was tempted to assert his masculine authority as the future "Master of Nohant." Solange, for her part, though seemingly delighted to have a feminine companion, was increasingly jealous of her older cousin — which may partly explain her sullen mood and behavior through most of this summer, when she lost her appetite, complained of sleepless nights, and suffered an attack of jaundice, which was only made worse by her persistent refusal to heed her mother's prescriptions.

For Solange's unusually moody behavior there were also other reasons. During the four-day outing to Mézières-en-Brenne in early June it was the pretty and unassuming Augustine Brault who had first caught the eye of a young chevalier named Fernand de Preaulx. Only later, after perhaps being tipped off to the truth (that she was of very humble origin), did he begin to pay attention to the blond-haired Solange with her "duchesslike airs." From then on things went very fast: so fast that within ten days of their return to Nohant, George Sand was already talking of Fernand de Preaulx as a possible son-in-law. In a letter written to her lawyer friend Emmanuel Arago she described the twenty-four-year-old viscount as "tall, lean, strong, a superb head, long hair, long beard, blue eyes, black eyebrows, a fresh complexion, a gruff voice, an open, frank, naive and affectionate air, slightly better dressed than a peasant, riding a horse like a cossack, obliging, gentle as a lamb but always ready to break the jaw of the boor who would dare make fun of a lady; not rich, not very well educated, I think, nor very intelligent, but a good fine soul nonetheless."

The impecunious young squire was not long in paying a visit to Nohant. Though he was from a conservative and ultramonarchist family, he found the somewhat bohemian atmosphere of Nohant very much to his taste, while Solange's feminine vanity was flattered by his assiduous attentions. In September he accompanied George Sand and the family on two excursions to the hill country of the Creuse — the first to admire the old castles of Crozant and Châteaubrun, the second to try some salmon fishing. Chopin, however, did not accompany the others. As he wrote to his sister in October, "these things fatigue me more than they are worth. And when I'm tired I'm not gay, and then the young ones don't have fun."

While Chopin found Solange's new suitor "a handsome young man" and altogether acceptable, she herself seemed more reserved and anything but eager to rush into matrimony. Her mother, though generally approving her daughter's resolution to let six months pass before making up her mind, was a bit put off by Solange's rather cool response to the young man's wooing. "My opinion on the matter," she wrote to Charlotte Marliani, "is that she wouldn't be displeased to be called *Madame,* like all young girls, but that she doesn't yet know what love is. She never seems to take anything seriously when she's well, and when she's ill she spends her time crossing everybody."

Chopin's return to Paris in early November was delayed by diluvial rains and autumn floods which washed away a number of bridges and seriously impeded the crossing of the Loire. Not until mid-November would George let Chopin expose himself to the risks of such a crossing. But once he had left, she assumed — perhaps because he had enjoyed such a healthy summer — that he could get along without her. She continued to write regularly, but it was above all to keep him informed of what was going on at Nohant, which she finally decided not to leave until the following February.

The summer drought, followed by heavy autumn rains, had resulted in a catastrophic harvest, and by early December the pinch was cruelly felt in the poorer farmsteads of Berry and Touraine.

There were increasingly hostile incidents between starving peasants and well-to-do gentry, several chateaux were ransacked and their owners molested, and even at Nohant the front gate and door were solidly locked and bolted. "We barricade ourselves each night," as George wrote to Marie de Rozières, "and I hold myself ready, money in one hand and a pistol in the other, so as not to be forced to give up my life as well as my purse." This was, of course, a piece of romantic exaggeration. None of the neighboring peasants harbored ill feelings toward the Lady of Nohant, who went out of her way to succor the poorest neighbors, many of whom were finally reduced to living off chestnuts. Where in the past she had often found herself with as many as thirty persons to provide for, now suddenly she had sixty mouths to feed.

Circumstances being what they were, George Sand was glad to have three or four young men in the house to defend her: her son, Maurice, his artist friend Eugène Lambert, Fernand de Preaulx, and on occasion the twenty-eight-year-old Victor Borie, a friend of Pierre Leroux's whom George had lured to La Châtre to become the editor of *L'Eclaireur de l'Indre et du Cher*. Nor were the long winter evenings at Nohant as gloomy as the surrounding despair might have led one to fear. George Sand now decided to keep the company entertained with musical sketches and charades of her own invention. "Our consciences being at peace," as she wrote a trifle smugly to Emmanuel Arago, "this sad year does not keep us from being gay *en famille*. Say what one will, winter in the country is so lovely! The snow is so white, the cold so stimulating to the appetite, the fireside so pleasant! We began our carnival the day before yesterday with some magnificent travesties. Every evening I have a ballet to compose and write . . . I'm the orchestra, accompanying the pantomime on the piano . . . Solange, who doesn't want to stir her stumps, is the public, and I the orchestra, poet, prompter, stage manager, producer, etc. There is no cashier . . . Someone arriving in the midst of all this would think he were dreaming or imagine that he had stumbled into a madhouse."

So entertaining were these theatrical soirees that soon even Solange had thrown her petulant dignity to the winds, preferring to show off on an improvised stage rather than sulk in the audience.

The "plays," ceasing to be pantomimes, became increasingly ambitious and complex — so complex indeed that New Year's Eve was celebrated by a curious theatrical hodgepodge drawn from Molière's *Dom Juan* and Mozart's *Don Giovanni.* "With screens, old curtains, leafy branches, rags gathered in the attic, silver and gold paper, we manage to make costumes and portable décors, putting everything up in 10 minutes in the drawing room, where it is warm," George wrote to her publisher friend Pierre-Jules Hetzel. "With bits of thread we make the hairiest kinds of wigs, and out of paper the most extravagant ruffs, having all the *chic* of ancient portraits . . . I have no reason to complain of my troupe . . . Each takes the role which pleases him, the first or the last much as the mood takes him, and there are no disputes . . ."

The theatrics completed, long after the servants had retired for the night, the amateur actors would treat themselves to a midnight supper, play with the dogs and prowl through the house armed with shotguns, flintlocks, and medieval halberds in mock search of any "brigands" who might have broken in. Thus the curse was taken off the long winter nights in this ill-heated manor house, with its cold bedrooms (where the temperature was never more than 54°F.) and the freezing studio where Maurice and Eugène Lambert had to keep blowing on their bluish knuckles as they drew and painted.

Having spent much of the winter at Nohant, Fernand de Preaulx accompanied George Sand to Paris when she finally returned to the Square d'Orléans in early February of 1847. Chopin had been seriously ill during her absence (though she was only informed about it now), but he seemed to have recovered, for she found him virtually unchanged. Solange's young suitor found favor in his eyes, and he seemed pleased by the prospect of their forthcoming marriage, which was now planned for April at Nohant.

These hopes, however, were rudely dashed by the intended bride. Far too tolerant as usual, George let the young Fernand call on Solange every day, and even spend whole evenings together with her in her room — in defiance of the current norms of behavior. But the more Solange saw of her ardent young swain, the less she liked him. Tall and handsome though he was, he was too rustic and uncultured for her spoiled taste. He lacked Maurice's and Lambert's talents for witty improvisations, and at Nohant he had proved himself the poorest actor of the lot — which is why he had been chosen for the part of the Statue-Commander in George Sand's strange adaptation of *Don Giovanni.* He was so ill-read that George had to go to special pains to have him read certain French classics. But his most unpardonable fault, in the eyes of the hopelessly pampered Solange — who dreamed of a life of luxury, with expensive dresses, footmen to wait on her, and a coachman to drive her about in an elegant equipage — was the conspicuous modesty of his means. With Fernand de Preaulx, a typical product of France's impoverished nobility, she knew she was unlikely ever to enjoy such luxuries, while her title of vicomtesse would not spare her a life of rustic monotony in the country, far from the glittering excitements of the capital.

Having proved to her own satisfaction that she could make herself as desirable to the young man as her cousin Augustine, Solange had assuaged her wounded vanity. Fernand de Preaulx had served his purpose. She thus took to taunting him in every way she could, reducing the guileless squire to a state of pleading misery. Having made a slave of him, she withered him with her contempt, finally informing him that the marriage was off.

The crestfallen suitor returned to his family, where little effort was made to hide a general feeling of relief at the prospect of their no longer having to accept a daughter of the infamous Madame Sand. Chopin felt genuinely sorry for this good-natured young man, while George was considerably embarrassed by this unexpected dénouement — having boasted to far too many people of the forthcoming marriage.

This first suitor had hardly been eliminated when a second and far more dynamic one suddenly burst onto the scene. Not long after George Sand's arrival in Paris, one of the habitués of Charlotte Marliani's salon, a retired army captain named Stanislas d'Arpentigny, brought around a thirty-three-year-old sculptor who said he was "dying" to meet the writer. A robust, black-bearded fellow with the intense gaze of a young Mephisto, Auguste Clésinger had been a swashbuckling cuirassier before establishing a reputation as a highly talented sculptor. Introduced to George Sand, he lost no time inviting her and Solange, as well as Maurice and Lambert (since they too were artists, like himself) to his sculptor's studio, where he informed her that he *must* do a bust of her and another of her daughter.

In the course of this first visit George particularly admired the statue of a fawn which had been displayed at the previous autumn's salon. The following morning a messenger appeared at the Cité d'Orléans carrying the statue in his arms. The impetuous Auguste then let it be known that he would not charge a centime for the bust he proposed to do of George, not even for the bronze it would require! Visit followed visit, and soon both George Sand and her daughter were posing for their busts, while the sculptor was almost daily to be seen at Charlotte Marliani's salon or in George's modest living room. He sent George huge bouquets of flowers, and not content with that, he presented her with a couple of small dogs.

It was soon clear that these flattering gifts were motivated by the sculptor's keen interest in Solange. She for her part seemed to bask in this sudden sunburst of masculine attention, while her mother could not conceal her admiration for Clésinger's talent, apparently feeling that here was a forceful genius who was going to do for sculpture what Delacroix had done for painting — boldly liberate it from the classic conventions of the past. The bad taste he had recently displayed in exhibiting the statue of a well-known woman whose voluptuous contortions were brazenly linked to the serpent wound round one of her legs should have been warning enough. But for George Sand this was the kind of poetic license great artists need to be able to breathe.

Alarmed by this unexpected turn of events, Stanislas d'Arpentigny called on George and did his best to warn her. Talented though he might be, this Clésinger was a highly unstable and dissolute individual. He was a terrible spendthrift, he had had to flee Italy (where he had gone to study art) in order to escape his creditors, and he had been disowned by his outraged father — which hadn't kept him from running up massive debts in Paris. He drank to excess, as anyone could see, and in private he beat his mistresses. One of them was now in a family way, but this would not deter him from callously abandoning her, etc.

Though Chopin, Delacroix, Emmanuel Arago, Manuel and Charlotte Marliani were all equally distrustful of Clésinger, George Sand refused to heed their admonitions. Years of living with Chopin's morbid jealousy and conservative opinions had rashly led her to conclude that his was a hopelessly jaundiced eye and that he was incapable of viewing human beings and situations in their true light. And then, how often she had heard the most ridiculous rumors being spread about herself! Two fellow artists, Jules Dupré and Théodore Rousseau, whom she consulted, hastened to assure her that what she had heard was indeed unfounded and that Clésinger, though somewhat turbulent and loud-spoken, was a gifted artist with a shining future ahead of him.

Irked by her refusal to listen to his warnings, D'Arpentigny refused to return to Madame Sand's apartment, telling Charlotte Marliani that he could not risk meeting a person whose unruly mode of life he had felt duty-bound to condemn. George, however, refused to be impressed. D'Arpentigny, though a stout republican with a certain literary flair who had occasionally written for the *Revue indépendante,* was after all only an ex-soldier, even if he did happen to be a friend of Alfred de Musset's. But Dupré and Rousseau were painters; and who could judge Clésinger better than Rousseau, who had lived in the same house with him? Let Clésinger's enemies say what they would about him: she wasn't going to listen. It suited her romantic fancy to imagine that Clésinger was an artistic genius, and even more, a genius of *humble origin* — like Pierre Leroux. The comparison should have given her pause, if only because Leroux was so chronically impecunious. But she was convinced that Clésinger, being a genius, was bound to make a fortune! Without realizing it, she was reasoning like one of the revolutionary dreamers of her novels; but in real life there was unfortunately no philanthropic millionaire to bail her out.

In early April George left Paris with Solange and Augustine. Chopin remained behind, together with Maurice, who was planning to leave for Holland to visit the art galleries and museums. Hardly were they installed than bouquets of roses, specially brought down by stagecoach, began arriving for Solange — causing an embarrassing amount of local chatter. George Sand decided that the best way to put an end to these attentions was to invite Clésinger down to Nohant. She could have spared herself the trouble of writing to him. For the impulsive Auguste was already on his way. He turned up at Nohant "like Caesar" — as George wrote to Maurice — and immediately issued an ultimatum. He wanted a definite "Yes" or "No" answer from Solange, and he wanted it in twenty-four hours! To her mother's amazement she immediately answered "Yes." Gone was all trace of the reluctance she had displayed toward Fernand de Preaulx. If Clésinger's style was brusque, this was the way she liked it. At last she had found a man who was a match for her own willfulness.

The next forty-eight hours were spent in a frenzy of activity which left George Sand speechless with admiration. This Clésinger, she wrote to Maurice, "does everything he wants, at the very hour, at the very minute, without needing to sleep or eat. In the three days that he's been here he hasn't slept two hours. This tension of the will, without fatigue or letup, amazes and pleases me."

It would have pleased her less had she realized that this extraordinary dynamism was essentially an act put on to impress a "wealthy" woman author. For like his younger brother Xavier, a twenty-five-year-old opportunist who had vainly requested the hand of Augustine Brault, Clésinger was persuaded that George Sand was rolling in money. More prone to indolence than to unremitting toil, the sculptor was generously prepared to help her spend her fortune.

Solange having agreed and her mother being delighted at the prospect of having a dynamic genius for a son-in-law, it only remained to secure Casimir Dudevant's approval. Chopin, who disapproved of Clésinger, was not to be informed for the time being. For as George wrote to her son: "This is none of his business, and once the Rubicon is crossed, the *ifs* and *buts* only do harm."

Clésinger accordingly returned to Paris, while Maurice postponed his trip to Holland. For some months past the latter had been in an agony of indecision, unable to get over his hopeless passion for the unattainable Pauline García-Viardot, now triumphing again in distant Berlin. His mother, who did not relish the idea of her son's breaking up a match she had taken such pains to foster, had long been pressing him to forget the impossible and to concentrate on the readily available and not unwilling Augustine, but Maurice had found it difficult to effect this passionate transference.

Now, as they journeyed down to Guillery, Maurice told Clésinger that he had been thinking of proposing to Augustine, but for some reason hadn't yet done so. Clésinger boldly egged him on: Why, she was perfectly adorable, an angel, and devilishly pretty to boot! Indeed, if Solange had turned him down, he would have proposed to Augustine himself! Fired by his companion's facile bombast, Maurice threw his vacillation to the winds and on reaching Guillery, he told his father he wanted to marry Augustine. Casimir, who had readily consented to Solange's marriage with Clésinger, immediately blew up. What! Maurice marry Augustine? Never! Maurice had better get this insane idea out of his head and fast! Or risk seeing himself totally disinherited!

Having obtained what he wanted, Clésinger now changed his tune — to Maurice's bewildered surprise. No, the sculptor agreed with Baron Dudevant, Augustine wasn't the girl for Maurice! Besides, he added casually — and this was the first inkling Maurice had had of this new development — his painter friend Théodore Rousseau was much interested in Augustine and had probably already written to Maurice's mother on the subject.

If Maurice had been a more quick-witted and decisive personality, he would have realized at this point what a scheming opportunist Clésinger really was. Unfortunately, like his mother, he had succumbed to Auguste's torrential volubility. From Guillery he wrote a lame letter to Nohant, reporting his father's refusal to condone his marriage to Augustine; he added that all things considered, he was probably right, since he would make a "wretched husband."

Short of money once again, George Sand spent much of this hectic April writing a novel at top speed — so fast indeed that an entire volume was written in just twelve days. Entitled *Celio Floriani,* it had for a hero one of Lucrezia's sons and had a lot to do with amateur theatrics.

Not until early May was Chopin informed of what was afoot. On May 4 the first banns were published and news of the impending marriage was carried in the Paris newspapers, causing Delacroix to note in his diary: "This precipitation is incredible!" Incredible it was, no matter how one looked at it. But George Sand seems to have thought that this was a golden opportunity, a now-or-never chance to deliver her unmanageable daughter into the hands of a man capable of dominating her. As she wrote to Pierre-Jules Hetzel, the publisher, in a singularly lucid letter: "I don't know who will devour the other, or if two such similar natures, having the same virtues and failings, will mesh the teeth of their steel gears."

The news that Chopin had suffered a severe attack of asthma, coming on top of so much else, plunged George once again into a mood of suicidal despondency. With Maurice still at Guillery and Clésinger now installed at Nohant, she couldn't leave Solange alone under the same roof with her bridegroom-to-be without arousing gossip in the countryside. Her conscience was frankly troubled, and not simply because of her inability to help Chopin through his latest crisis. "I don't dare write to him," she wrote to Marie de Rozières, "I'm afraid of upsetting him; I fear that Solange's marriage has displeased him greatly and that each time I mention it he has a disagreeable shock. Yet I could not keep it secret from him, and I had to act as I did. I can't make Chopin the head of the family and a kind of guardian; my children would not accept it, and the dignity of my life would be lost."

She repeated the same argument in another letter, written to Albert Grzymala on May 12, in which she announced her intention of returning to Paris at the end of May (once the wedding was over) and of bringing Chopin back to the country. "I think Chopin must have suffered in his little corner not to know anything and to be unable to give advice. But in the problems of real life it is impossible to take his advice into consideration. He has never understood human nature nor had a proper view of facts. His soul is all poetry and music, and he cannot endure that which is different from himself . . . I see him wasting away without ever having been able to do him good, since it's the anxious, jealous and moody affection he harbors for me which is the main cause of his sadness. For seven years now I have lived like a virgin with him and *with the others*" — a sentence which might well have surprised Louis Blanc had he seen it. "I have aged before my time, and even without effort or sacrifice, so weary was I of passions and disillusioned beyond remedy. If one woman on earth should have inspired his absolute confidence, it was I, but this he has never understood . . .

"I think you know how it has really been! He complains that I have been killing him through privation, while I was convinced that I would kill him if I acted otherwise . . . In this respect I accomplished prodigies of patience of which I would not have believed myself capable . . . I have reached a state of martyrdom, but heaven is inexorable toward me, as though I had great crimes to expiate; for in the midst of all these efforts and sacrifices, he whom I love with an absolutely chaste and maternal love is dying of his insane attachment for me!"

While it appealed to her religious and artistic fancies to play the role of a long-suffering martyr, this was not simply a pious pose. For the same sentiments were expressed in another letter, perhaps written on the very same day to Pierre-Jules Hetzel: "He has hurt me so much, *with his malady*" — she meant of the mind as much as of the body — "that for a long time I hoped to die before him . . ." But having discovered since that she was as robust as a horse, this now seemed unlikely, and her one wish, before dying, was "to close his eyes and marry my two daughters!"

On May 19, a bare week after these two letters were dispatched, Solange and Clésinger were married in the little Nohant chapel, in a wedding ceremony so private that not one of George Sand's Berrichon neighbors was invited to attend. George later explained that she had not wished to expose them to the presence of Casimir Dudevant, who journeyed up from Guillery for the occasion. Having to put her former husband up at Nohant, as well as put up with him for two days and three nights, was in itself a strain she preferred to bear in private. To make matters worse, on the very eve of the wedding she pulled a tendon in her leg and had to be carried into the chapel.

Nor was this the last of her troubles. The realization that his younger sister was getting married while he had missed the boat with Augustine threw Maurice into a state of tearful agitation. It was aggravated by the news that she was receptive to the letters she had begun receiving from Théodore Rousseau. Augustine could not now take two steps without being pursued by the lachrymose Maurice, whose pathetic pleas for belated consideration she not unnaturally rebuffed, being more offended than pleased by this sudden flare-up of a passion he had hitherto reserved for Pauline Viardot. From her closed and bolted door he would stagger down the corridor to his mother's study, sobbing like a girl and asking her for help and consolation. At the wedding breakfast he tried to drown his grief in champagne, but his face was so long and his look so doleful that Casimir made crude sport of him, telling him he ought to be glad he was still a bachelor, that it was far better to enjoy the pleasures of sex without the inconveniences of marriage, and that the easiest way of curing himself of his ludicrous infatuation would be to surprise Augustine and bed her down in a hayloft: advice which merely fanned the despondent wooer's romantic despair.

At four o'clock the next morning Casimir left for Guillery, as happy to shake the dust of Nohant from his boots as its owner was to see him depart. George, accompanied by her son, son-in-law, and her two "daughters," had herself driven to the nearby Château de Culan, where she pulled her tendon once again by trying to walk too soon and had to be carried around in the arms of the robust Clésinger.

On May 23 Solange and her husband left for Paris, shortly before the arrival of the painter Théodore Rousseau, who had received his wedding invitation too late to attend the marriage. The thirty-five-year-old bachelor's tender letters had made a favorable impression on Augustine, and while Maurice sulked, George was overjoyed by the prospect of soon marrying off her second "daughter" to the man whom she, Théophile Gautier, and many others regarded as the foremost of living French landscape painters. Rousseau, being a friend of Delacroix's as well as of Clésinger's, was indeed an ideal choice for a son-in-law, and well placed to overcome Chopin's and Delacroix's misgivings about Solange's husband.

The matrimonial euphoria generated by these fond hopes lasted ten days. On May 31 George Sand traveled up to Paris, accompanied by Maurice, Augustine, Théodore Rousseau, and Victor Borie, whom George had installed at Nohant as a kind of private secretary. Expecting to stay one short week — the time needed to complete the wedding arrangements — she brought two light summer dresses and was not long in regretting it, as the torrid weather of late May was chilled by a harsh northern wind in early June. Her injured leg still caused her much pain, and for the first couple of days she had to be carried upstairs.

But these physical discomforts were as nothing compared to the spiritual torments to which she was now subjected. Solange, who took her time coming to call on her, finally appeared, looking anything but radiant and dragging her cashmere shawl behind her "like a broomstick." Her mother was dismayed to see how sloppily she was dressed, she who had always been so fussy and spoiled in this respect. Solange's premarital enthusiasm had completely disappeared, along with the bloom in her cheeks, and she seemed both pale and peevish.

George was not long in discovering the reason. At Nohant Clésinger had glibly assured her that his debts totaled no more than 2000 francs. This was what Solange had also been led to believe. In fact, he was already 12,000 francs in debt before going on a spending spree intended to dazzle his wife and everyone else through his largess. He had bought 5000 francs' worth of jewelry for his young bride, had spent even more on "wedding purchases," and had run up tailors' bills to the tune of almost 4000 francs! He had hired two liveried servants and placed a hired carriage at Solange's beck and call — all of which might have satisfied his young wife's expensive tastes had she not quickly realized, from the number of creditors who kept pounding on the door, that her husband did not have the wherewithal to pay them.

Suddenly revealed to be more of a Mephisto than a Michelangelo, the tempestuous Auguste lost stature in Solange's eyes. But having chosen to become his wife, she had to share the hazards of his existence. He had married her less for her blond looks than for the dowry she was to bring him. This consisted of the Hôtel de Narbonne — the town house on the Rue de la Harpe — which was officially valued at 200,000 francs. But one quarter of this sum was tied up in as yet unpaid arrears for previous repairs. The question of how the gap was to be filled, so that Solange could obtain the full amount of her 200,000 franc dowry, had been lengthily discussed before the marriage. Clésinger, cynically encouraged by Casimir Dudevant, had proposed that the 50,000 francs be raised by placing a mortgage on Nohant — a recommendation George Sand had wisely rejected. Instead, she had decided to give Solange a lump sum of 50,000 francs once she had successfully concluded a major new contract for an eighty-volume edition of her Complete Works. The income brought in from this edition was also to provide for a dowry of 100,000 francs for Augustine.

News of this last provision threw Clésinger and Solange into a towering rage. He was dismayed to realize that he might have to wait for months before being able to obtain the ready cash he desperately needed; she was incensed to learn that Augustine, though only a distant relative, was to get a dowry half as great as her own.

All of Solange's pent-up jealousy against her pretty, good-natured cousin now came boiling to the surface. When Augustine came forward joyfully to embrace her at the Cité d'Orléans apartment, Solange let herself be kissed on both cheeks with an air of frigid disdain. That same evening she and Clésinger invited Maurice to come to their studio apartment, where he was copiously plied with champagne and informed that Augustine was a scheming "leech" who had wormed her way into the bosom of the family for the sole purpose of getting her grasping hands on as much money as possible. She was a shameless coquette who had made advances not only to Maurice, but to Rousseau and Clésinger as well! Why, she was so determined to supplant Solange in Auguste's affections, in order to get the 200,000 francs for herself, that she had visited Clésinger in his bedroom at Nohant . . . and if he had wanted to, instead of being outraged by her brazenness, he could have had her there and then!

Maurice staggered home in a state of drunken disbelief. His mother, whom he insisted on waking up at two o'clock in the morning, had him sit down by her bed and tell her everything. The next day, accompanied by Augustine and Rousseau, they went to have lunch with Solange and Clésinger. Solange and her husband were deliberately rude to Augustine and even discourteous toward Rousseau, exchanging meaningful glances and whispered comments.

George Sand went home in high dudgeon, and that evening when Solange and her husband came to dinner, she told them off in sharp terms. If they refused to receive Augustine at their table, then she was not going to lunch with them anymore. Augustine was going to stay with her at the Square d'Orléans apartment, and if they didn't like it, they needn't come to dinner any more. Solange, seemingly surprised by her mother's sudden firmness, lapsed into a sullen silence, while Clésinger sought fumblingly to justify their new dislike, saying that Solange had "opened his eyes" to what Augustine was really up to.

Neither Augustine nor her foster mother returned to lunch at the Clésingers' again. But Solange, who still came to lunch regularly with her husband at the Cité d'Orléans apartment, seemed to grow more insolent with each passing day. She put on grand airs, spoke of buying horses and carriages, of building a country house, boasted of all the men who were mad about her, made shameless advances to Victor Borie, and even provoked some brutal reprimands from her irritated husband by making him believe that his fellow artist Jules Dupré had been writing love letters to her.

The first banns announcing Rousseau's impending marriage to Augustine were already out and the second were on the point of being published when the painter suddenly developed cold feet. An anonymous letter (probably drafted by Clésinger, with Solange's connivance) informed him that Augustine, far from being a virgin, had led a dissolute life before being admitted to the Sand household. Clésinger, whom he consulted, assured Rousseau of the truth of the letter's accusations, adding that Augustine had even had an illegitimate child with Maurice — though the scandal had been hushed up. As for the dowry George Sand had supposedly promised Augustine, it was no more likely to materialize than the 50,000 francs she had promised to Solange, but of which the latter had not seen a penny.

The painter let himself be convinced by these Iago-like insinuations. He wrote a fatuous letter to George Sand, saying that he who had hitherto refused to accept "the yoke of any human law" had reluctantly and against his fixed principles finally agreed to enter into matrimony with Augustine, in the honest belief that she was a pure girl and that she was to receive an adequate dowry. But he could no longer content himself with vague promises: he now wanted definite proof of purity "or the sincere and complete avowal of faults committed" from the person he was to marry, and "from you, who want to marry her off, I demand that material power of money necessary to fulfill the commitment which I am contracting to employ myself to her happiness."

George Sand's reply was razor sharp: "Your letter is an act of delirium. I feel sorry for you for having in one day taken leave of your reason, your kindness, delicacy and affection . . . It has never been my intention to make my daughters the mistresses of my friends, and if you thought I was in principle the enemy of marriage, you have never read one of my books, or else you haven't understood them . . . We are *women,* and for this reason we are not weak, and we do not reply as we could to men who believe themselves strong. You have doubts about the frankness of the mother and the purity of the daughter, who *want* the marriage. Beware, Rousseau, of being harmful and in the wrong in thus speaking to George Sand and Augustine. They will not humble themselves further, the one to prove her purity, the other her loyalty in questions of *money* and *ideas.* There are suspicions which are not forgiven and which kill love and friendship at one stroke."

Belatedly realizing what a fool he had been, Rousseau tried to make amends in a second, no less pathetic letter, which made not the slightest impression. It was too late; the damage by now was done. Augustine's fondness for the painter had been killed forever by his humiliating suspicions, and the mere thought of him now made her miserably unhappy.

Her expectations now doubly shattered by this even more conclusive fiasco, George Sand decided to return to Nohant in mid-June. Once again she was accompanied by Maurice, Augustine, Eugène Lambert, and Victor Borie. Chopin, whom she had seen (exactly how often we do not know) during her stay in Paris, was expected to come down later — or so at least George believed. For the truth, which he was too courteous to impart to her, was that he now felt little inclination to spend the summer at Nohant surrounded by "strange faces."

Shortly after her arrival at Nohant George Sand received a letter from Clésinger in which he admitted for the first time that he now owed a grand total of 24,000 francs. The sculptor had also discovered, to his considerable dismay, that Solange still being a minor, they could neither sell nor use the Hôtel de Narbonne to borrow money. He had therefore decided to come down to Nohant to see if he couldn't raise a loan to be backed by a *conseil de famille* — a kind of "family committee."

A day or two later Solange and her husband turned up at Nohant, preceded by a small mountain of trunks, packages, and crates containing pieces of Clésinger sculpture. George, to avoid a new row, had decided to treat them royally and to install them in her grandmother's old room on the ground floor, which she had taken special pains to decorate. At a council of war held on the eve of their arrival the other members of the household had pledged themselves not to make fun of Solange's grand airs and to ignore Clésinger's habitual bragging. A kind of sullen, makeshift truce was thus inaugurated, in an atmosphere of mounting tension. Unpunctual as usual in answering the summons of the dinner bell, Solange would casually saunter into the dining room when the others were finishing the meal, and her mother, who could not wait to go for a stroll in the garden or to withdraw to her upstairs study, was not exposed to her presence for more than five minutes every day.

But the inevitable explosion was not long in coming. One day Solange, who up till then had preferred to go out riding alone, took it into her head to invite Augustine out for a drive in the cabriolet. Pretexting a headache, Augustine politely declined. In a rage, Solange walked out into the driveway, seized a whip from the stable wall, and climbed into the cabriolet, ordering a servant to go up and tell Mademoiselle Augustine that she was to come downstairs, because *she* was waiting for her! Her mother, on hearing Solange issue these imperious instructions, leaned out of the window of Augustine's upstairs room and told her daughter that Augustine was *not* going with her.

From that moment on no holds were barred. Accompanied by her husband, Solange called on her Uncle Hippolyte, who invited them to stay for lunch at his country house of Montgivray. Augustine, they told him, was a scheming bitch, a wanton slut of a girl who had slept with Maurice, with his friend Eugène Lambert and Victor Borie as well — while the Mistress of Nohant happily closed her eyes and pretended not to notice what was going on under her own roof! Tipsy and featherbrained as ever, Hippolyte readily swallowed this story, which was also repeated — though with less success — to Théophile Simonnet (a La Châtre lawyer who had married Hippolyte's daughter, Léontine) and to the curé of Saint-Chartier, who listened to it all with shocked dismay.

George soon began receiving scribbled notes in which her wine-besotted half brother, who had not visited Nohant since Solange's marriage, implored her to stop *ruining herself* for Augustine. Solange and Clésinger now made daily trips to Montgivray, where they were sure of a hearty welcome.

One day, during the evening dinner at Nohant, a servant brought in a note for Solange, who opened it furtively and hastily scribbled a reply. George, who was not blind to what had been going on, expressed surprise that she should be so assiduously cultivating the company of Hippolyte (whom Solange had never particularly cared for in the past) now that her uncle had taken to criticizing her mother behind her back. How so? cried Clésinger, rushing to Solange's defense. Yes, they were good friends of Monsieur Chatiron, and what of it? Madame Sand had no business lecturing his wife on this or any other subject. For if anyone had a right to complain, it was he — about the way his wife was being treated at Nohant. She was isolated, ostracized in her own home; her legitimate place had been usurped by a "stranger"! And such being the case, he was of a mind to leave.

"Very well," George Sand replied. "You might have done better not to have come at all, being so ill disposed toward family life."

"Then we'll leave!" cried Clésinger. "And woe to the one who refuses to pay my wife the respect that is due her!"

George Sand asked him if it was she he had in mind. No, cried Clésinger, it was the *eel* (he meant of course Augustine), the *intriguer* "who has made it her job to please you."

"Not one word more!" George Sand cut him short. "Or I'll leave the table, and not come down from my room till you've left the house!"

At that both Solange and Clésinger withdrew to their room for the remainder of the evening. The next day Solange did not appear for the midday breakfast, but her husband did. He put on a furious scene in front of all the servants, claiming that at three o'clock in the morning somebody, in an effort to scare the wits out of them, had started throwing stones at their window and had broken a pane — a manifest impossibility, since the outside shutters were closed. Later, George Sand went into their bedroom to see her daughter, whom Clésinger had described as "very ill." She found her suffering from a mild recurrence of jaundice, apparently brought on — as had happened the previous summer — by Solange's stubborn insistence on halting her monthly period by plunging into ice-cold water.

Clésinger, who had begun to pack his belongings, declaring to anyone and everyone that he had had enough and was leaving, did not appear for dinner, any more than did Solange; and when Maurice, in a conciliatory move, went in to talk to them, they both began shouting at him — so loudly that their voices could be heard by the gardeners and the kitchen staff — calling him a "dolt" and Augustine a "thief" who was plundering Solange's wardrobe — their mother (so she claimed) having given Augustine a trousseau worth 6000 francs! Maurice finally lost patience, told them to go to the devil, and walked out.

When the time came for the usual after-dinner drive Maurice was still so worked up that his mother persuaded him to mount his white horse in the hope that this would calm him, while she and Victor Borie followed in the cabriolet. To get her out of harm's way, Augustine had been sent down to the river on some errand with Eugène Lambert. The two returned some time later and found Clésinger blowing noisily on a French horn in the garden under Solange's window. Passing through the dining room, they went on into the salon, where, after closing the door and the French windows, Augustine sat down and began playing the piano. Solange would not normally have been "disturbed" by her cousin's delicate tinkling had a servant not opened the drawing room door for a moment to bring Augustine and Lambert a carafe of water. Solange immediately rang for a maid, ordering her to go tell Mademoiselle Augustine that she was not to touch the piano, which *was not hers,* that she was ill and needed quiet, etc. Inasmuch as her own husband was making three times as much noise with his horn, Augustine paid no heed to this "order," and, quietly closing the door, she resumed her playing.

A minute or two later Clésinger burst into the drawing room and angrily repeated Solange's command: "My wife *orders* you to stop!" Lambert then rose to his feet: "Monsieur, would you kindly address yourself to me. It was I who asked Mademoiselle to play the piano. If you do not like it, it is to me you must say so." Thrown off his stride by this unexpected resistance, Clésinger stamped out, slamming the door behind him.

When George Sand walked into the house shortly afterward, Solange shouted to her from her bedroom that she wanted to see her.

"You must be feeling much better to be able to shout like that," remarked her mother as she came up to her bedside.

"No, I'm very sick," replied Solange. "Augustine is out to have me die. Forbid her to touch *my* piano. She has one in her room, let her go up and use it."

Her mother pointed out that if anybody's, the piano was *hers,* since she paid the rent on it, and that in any case it couldn't be heard through two closed doors and an intervening dining room.

"But I know she's playing and it upsets me!"

"My poor girl, you're mad! Good night, and stop bothering me!"

But before George Sand could leave the room, Clésinger seized her by the arm. "I *want* an explanation!" he demanded.

"I've already given it to you. You should not have come, and you would do well to leave as soon as possible!"

"Is that all? I want other explanations!"

"Leave me alone . . . and hurry up and get out!" cried George in a temper. "That's the only explanation I have to give you."

The next day Solange and her husband began packing in earnest, crating up the vases, clocks, and pieces of marble which Clésinger had had sent down from Paris to prepare for their "installation" at Nohant. Packed up with the rest was the bronze statue of the fawn he had offered to his future mother-in-law prior to the marriage, carefully inscribing her name on the pedestal. Packed up too was another statue representing Melancholy, which he had given to her on the occasion of the wedding. He had already accepted 500 francs from George Sand — a generous reimbursement for what the bronze had cost him — but this did not now keep him from reclaiming both "gifts."

Leaving the servants to attend to the packing and crating, Solange and her husband drove off to Montgivray to have lunch with Hippolyte. When George Sand walked in after they had left, she could hardly believe her eyes: her grandmother's former bedroom looked as though it had been ransacked by robbers. The bed had been stripped of its silk counterpane, the velvet covering unnailed from the mantelpiece, the candlesticks and snuffers stowed away in crates. The only things they hadn't yet removed were the curtains and several Sèvres and Japanese vases which George had brought down from her own room. They were hastily taken back upstairs.

Flushed with the wine they had been copiously offered by Hippolyte, Solange and Clésinger returned in the midafternoon and were outraged to discover that their bedroom had been "stripped" of *their* precious vases! Seizing a hammer, Clésinger began furiously pounding nails into the unclosed crates, while bawling out the servants and the sweating carpenter for their intolerable "sloth."

In the middle of this furious hammering the curé unexpectedly turned up and was taken on a stroll through the garden by Victor Borie. His arrival was not exactly fortuitous, for it had been reported to him that at the Montgivray lunch table an intoxicated Hippolyte had sworn to help Solange and Clésinger remove Augustine *by force*. Yes, by God, he would personally pack her on to the stagecoach and not leave her side until he had deposited her with her parents in Paris! Fearing the worst, the good curé had hastened over to Nohant to lend a friendly hand.

He was well advised in doing so, for shortly after his arrival the storm finally broke. It was precipitated by Solange, who happened to find Eugène Lambert placidly heating some paint on the kitchen stove. Thwarted in her desire to insult Augustine, who at George Sand's request had prudently locked herself into her room upstairs, she decided to vent her wrath on this young man who had dared stand up for her cousin the previous evening.

Before he could say a word to her, Solange hurried back to her husband and told him that Lambert had been deliberately discourteous. Walking into the kitchen in his turn, Clésinger ordered Lambert to pay his respects to his wife, now, on the spot. Though dwarfed by the sculptor's Herculean build, the young painter pluckily replied that he was unfailingly courteous to Solange and that he was not accustomed to being told how to display good manners. With Solange egging him on from behind, Clésinger grew increasingly vociferous, repeating his order and threatening Lambert with his raised fist. Finally he took a wild swing at the little painter, but unbalanced by the hammer he was carrying in one hand, he missed, while Lambert, darting nimbly to one side, gave him a sharp kick in the stomach.

Hurrying in from the vestibule, Maurice sought to pacify the frantic sculptor, who was bellowing like a wounded buffalo and wildly brandishing his hammer. But Maurice's soothing words only made him more furious. George Sand, who had left her study door open in order to follow what was going on below, now came rushing down the stairs. Without hesitating an instant, she walked up to Clésinger and gave him a sharp slap in the face, then tried to wrest the hammer from his hand. But the sculptor was too strong for her, and too strong for Maurice, who was also trying to twist the hammer from his grasp. Shouting that he was going to kill the *two of them,* Clésinger wrenched the hammer free, while his mother-in-law tugged desperately at his hair. For one tense moment it looked as though he was going to bring the hammer down on Maurice's head, but a second slap from George Sand, which hit him between the eyes, momentarily dazed him. Uttering a wild oath, he lunged at her, punching her in the chest with his free fist.

Maurice now completely lost his head. Darting off to fetch his pistols, he shouted that he was going to shoot Clésinger *like a dog!* But before he could carry out his threat, Clésinger had been tackled by a young manservant named Jean, who had only recently entered George's service. Pinning one of the sculptor's arms behind his back, he pushed him against a wall. The curé rushed in a moment later from the garden and immobilized the other arm. He was followed by a breathless Victor Borie, who disarmed the flushed Maurice when he finally appeared with his two pistols.

Solange, who had watched the fray in silence, now walked up to her husband and putting her two hands on his shoulders, she said: "My friend, go back to your room. You have hit my mother and have put yourself in the wrong."

That evening Solange and her husband dined alone in their bedroom. The next day, July 12, they left for Montgivray, proceeding from there to La Châtre, where they put up at a local inn. Solange did not even bother to say goodbye to her mother. But from La Châtre she wrote a short note, asking if she could take away *her* white horse. The horse was in reality Maurice's, but ever since her own black mare had died several years before, Solange had taken to claiming that the white one was hers. This absurd request was accordingly refused, as was the "loan" of Chopin's calèche.

Solange avenged herself by immediately writing to Chopin in Paris, saying that she had left Nohant "forever" as a result of the most frightful scenes her mother had put on. She asked Chopin not to leave for Nohant until she had seen him, said she was too ill to travel by stagecoach, and asked him if she could borrow the carriage which her mother had refused her. Chopin immediately replied with two letters: the first (addressed to her) to say how sorry he was to hear about her health and that the carriage was at her disposal, the second (addressed to George Sand) to say that Solange and her husband could take his calèche to Blois (where they were due to board the train).

During the several days they spent at La Châtre, waiting for Chopin's answer, Solange and her husband broadcast their own account of these happenings, telling the maids, cooks, random stagecoach passengers, and anyone within earshot that they had been driven from Nohant by a heartless mother, whose head had been turned by an infamous intriguing bitch who had seduced her son, helped herself to a lavish trousseau, and was bent on getting herself a dowry of 200,000 francs! Appalled by what he heard, Hippolyte's son-in-law Théophile Simonnet vainly sought to expedite their departure, even offering to take them in under his own roof in an effort to limit the damage. But neither he nor his wife, Léontine, could persuade them to hold their tongues. When they finally left in Chopin's calèche (which had been driven over by a servant), there were three hundred curious onlookers in the street to see them off, and there was not a soul in La Châtre who had not heard about the "scandalous doings at Nohant."

It took George Sand more than a week to recover from these tumultuous events. She was paralyzed by blinding headaches which made her wonder for a moment if she hadn't suffered a stroke. Afraid that she might give in once again to her daughter's wiles — for Solange was soon sending her honeyed missives from Paris, hypocritically trying to make up — she sat down and wrote the longest letter she had ever penned to Emmanuel Arago, giving him a blow-by-blow description of everything that had occurred. She also wrote, far more briefly, to Chopin, explaining that she had been punched in the chest by her son-in-law, and that she would soon be coming up to Paris "to bring Chopin back to Nohant."

The day she was to leave — July 26 — she received a letter from Chopin which altered all her plans. "I don't have to speak about Mr. C[lésinger]," he wrote. "My mind only became familiar with the name of Mr. C[lésinger] at the moment when You gave him your daughter.

"As for the latter, I cannot be indifferent about her. You may recall that I used to intercede with You in favor of Your children, and this without preference, each time the occasion presented itself, certain as I was that You are destined to love them *always* — for those are the only affections that don't change. Misfortune can veil them, but not disfigure them.

"This misfortune must be singularly powerful today to be able to close Your heart to news about Your daughter, at the start of her definitive career, at a time when her physical state is particularly in need of maternal care.

"In the presence of so serious a fact concerning Your holiest affections, I shall say nothing as regards myself. Time will act. I shall wait — *forever the same*. Your devoted Ch[opin]."

The meaning of this letter was unmistakable. Chopin, in her quarrel with Solange, had chosen to side with the latter; he felt more sympathy for the misguided daughter than for the offended mother.

"So be it, my friend," George replied in her answering letter, one of the very few to have survived later destruction. "Do as your heart now dictates and take your instinct for the language of your conscience. I understand perfectly.

"As for my daughter, her illness is no more disquieting than last year's, and never have my zealous care, orders, and pleas been able to determine her not to govern herself like someone who wants to be sick.

"It ill behooves her to say she needs the love of a mother she detests and slanders, whose holiest actions and whose home she sullies with her dreadful remarks. It pleases you to listen to it all and perhaps to believe it. I won't engage in this kind of struggle; it is abhorrent to me. I would rather see you go over to the enemy than to defend myself against an enemy that has sprung from my bosom and been nourished with my milk.

"Take care of her, since it is to her you believe you must devote yourself. I won't hold it against you, but you understand that I am entrenching myself in my role of outraged mother and that nothing henceforth will make me disregard its authority and dignity. It is bad enough to be a dupe and a victim. I forgive you, and will make no reproaches from now on, since your confession is sincere. It surprises me, but if you feel freer and more at ease like this, I won't suffer from this bizarre about-face.

"Farewell, my friend, may you soon be cured of your troubles, and I now hope for it (I have my reasons for that); and I shall thank God for this bizarre dénouement to nine years of exclusive friendship. Give me news of yourself sometimes. There is no use again discussing the rest."

Reality, once again, had shown itself more unexpected than fiction. In the novel, Lucrezia Floriani had finally died of despair, leaving a bereaved Prince Karol and her children to bewail their loss. In real life no one had died. But George Sand, in rushing her daughter into marriage, had lost Solange — and Chopin as well.

PART VII

Revolution & Reaction

33. 1848

SUDDENLY it all made sense. What she had dimly felt in writing *Lucrezia Floriani* — that there was something "sickly" in Chopin's carping jealousy toward her — was now at last explained. Partially at any rate: that she might have been the ultimate cause of his growing disaffection, she could not bring herself to admit, wrapped as she was in her chaste mantle of mother-protectress. But one thing George Sand now clearly understood: the focus of Chopin's sentimental cravings had with the passage of the years gradually shifted to Solange. Thwarted in his desire to possess the mother physically, the frustrated composer had sought psychic compensation in the affections of the daughter — a disposition the golden-haired "Sol" had readily encouraged. Fellow "victims" of circumstance — Solange by virtue of her elder brother's "primacy" and Augustine's "odious" intrusion on the scene, Chopin by virtue of the countless lovers whom, in his sex-starved fancy, he imagined George to have had or to be having — both had come to feel emotionally dispossessed.

The cultivation of their respective grudges had thus established a growing complicity between them, manifested by private hobnobbing, shared secrets, and sudden petulant scenes which had the force of lovers' quarrels. Platonic their relations had certainly been throughout — for Chopin, as George Sand wrote to Emmanuel Arago, had never been more than "a kind of little Papa" for the headstrong and supercilious Solange. But the sight of a young man making advances to Solange had more than once sufficed to unleash a fit of jealous pique which Chopin had then vented on the perplexed and nettled mother. Thus was explained the terrible attack of asthma which for four tense days had confined the choking composer to his bed in early May; it was simply his nervous, or as the specialists would now say, his psychosomatic reaction to the news of Solange's impending marriage to Clésinger.

Curiously enough, neither George Sand nor Chopin seem to have realized that the breach between them was irreparable. For weeks each still expected the other to write and to beg forgiveness. But George could no more forgive Chopin for having sided with Solange than he could forgive her for being a hardhearted mother who had left her daughter in the lurch just when she was most needed. Chopin continued to enjoy free access to George's Paris apartment, even after her furniture and belongings had been transferred, in early August, from the first-floor apartment at Number 5 to a smaller third-floor flat at Number 3 Square d'Orléans. The moving, supervised by Marie de Rozières, was undertaken in the name of economy — George Sand, in the summer and autumn of 1847, being more hard-pressed than ever. This was, as it happened, the last service Marie de Rozières was ever to accomplish for her. When Marie wrote a disapproving letter, all but openly blaming her for what had happened, George concluded sadly that she too had gone over to the "enemy," and in December she relieved her of all responsibility and had the apartment keys entrusted to her Paris lawyer.

Nothing more graphically betrayed the intense distress which these painful happenings caused her than the marked scarcity of letters flowing from her normally industrious pen. She did not write to Albert Grzymala, the avuncular friend to whom she had originally confided her love for Frycek. Nor did she write to Delacroix, who was secretly appalled by the letter she had written to Chopin (briefly describing the climactic events of July 11) when it was shown to him by the composer. Both, George assumed, had become part of what she now called Chopin's "coterie." She did write to Charlotte Marliani, who having domestic problems of her own — her husband Emmanuel had started an affair with a Russian mistress — was more sympathetic to her plight. She also wrote to Pauline Viardot, who replied from Dresden (where she was under contract for the opera season), to assure her that Chopin, far from joining Solange's "faction," had shown himself concerned over the unhappiness all this had caused and was causing her.

While this may have been true enough in the midsummer of 1847, it had ceased to be true by the onset of winter. There being no one else in Paris to give him a different version of what had happened, Chopin naively chose to believe what Solange and her husband told him. Nohant, they reported, had become a hotbed of promiscuous vice; Victor Borie had become the latest of George Sand's lovers, while Maurice disported himself lecherously with Augustine. Repeated with relish by Marie de Rozières, these salacious reports were accepted by the impressionable Chopin as proof of his long festering suspicions.

In reality, the "proof" was little more than gossip. Augustine by this time was fed up with Maurice's shilly-shallying, while Victor Borie spent most of the summer of 1847 at Orléans, working for a local printer. He did, however, return to Nohant in September, by which time George may have decided she could do with a new and less ethereal lover. Gustave Papet had been remonstrating with her for years, telling her that her self-imposed chastity was a form of suicide and that she was killing herself for Chopin's benefit. Nicknamed *Le Pôtu* — "The Chum" — Borie was as plump and bonny as Chopin had been frail and cadaverous. Exactly when their affair began it is impossible to say, for the scornful references in George's letters to her "presumed lover" (Borie) may simply have been dust thrown in her correspondents' eyes. But sometime in the autumn of 1847, if not early in 1848, lovers they became — thus providing *ex post facto* "proof" of what had earlier been alleged.

George Sand's mood during these depressing autumn months may be judged from a letter she wrote to her publisher friend Pierre-Jules Hetzel in mid-October: "I was 43 years old when we last saw each other, now I'm 86." Too nervously upset to be able to work with her old speed and determination, she had to muster every ounce of her formidable determination to be able to finish her novel *Celio Floriani,* as well as a new pastoral idyll entitled *François le Champi.* Victor Borie, who was sent up to Paris on business, was unable to get the novel serialized in the *Journal des Débats.* George Sand's literary output, it seemed, was declining not only in quantity but in quality as well. Already 30,000 francs in debt, she decided to follow Hetzel's advice and, abandoning fiction for a moment, to write up the story of her extraordinary life. The enthusiastic response of

Maurice, Augustine, and Lambert, to whom she read the first experimental pages in October, encouraged her to persevere in this "enormous" enterprise which, as she wrote to Charlotte Marliani, would take her a solid year at least and be "my salvation or my death."

Hetzel, who made three trips to Nohant to discuss the project with her, was finally able to obtain a contract with a prosperous paper manufacturer who had recently teamed up with her old publisher Dupuy. The contract called for five volumes, each to be bought at a price of 26,000 francs — for a total of 130,000 francs. Copy was to be delivered at eight-week intervals, with a 1000 franc penalty for every fortnight of delay. Though the sums involved were considerable (the equivalent of several hundred thousand dollars in terms of today's purchasing power), George Sand did not expect them to bring her more than momentary respite. For generous as ever, she intended to give away one fifth of the total (25,000 francs) as a dowry for Augustine and to invest 50,000 francs of it to provide Solange with an annual pension. Most of the rest would have to go to the repayment of her debts.

Augustine, predictably enough, proved easier to satisfy and eventually to marry off than had Solange. Ignoring the timid advances of Eugène Lambert, who had fallen in love with her in his turn, she responded favorably to the overtures made by a Polish exile named Charles de Bertholdi, whom Borie one day brought over to Nohant. An artist who made a living by giving drawing lessons to boarding-school girls, Bertholdi would not hear of a dowry — this institution being contrary to his ideas of marriage. This made him congenial to George Sand, who had not forgotten the row with Théodore Rousseau. So did the fact that he was meticulous and orderly in his habits, without debts, and impervious to nasty gossip about Augustine — which is to say, the very opposite of Clésinger. Uninspiring he might be, but at least Charles de Bertholdi was honest and dependable.

What was good enough for George Sand was, however, insufficient for Augustine's father, Joseph Brault. Informed that his daughter wanted to marry a drawing master who could only boast a modest salary, he wrote to say he would not hear of it, that a girl as pretty as she deserved a "wealthy match," and that if she persisted in this "folly," he would come down to Nohant himself and give her the thrashing she merited. Augustine having more than once been pounded into submission by a rain of paternal fist blows, George Sand decided to take no chances. When the irate parent finally reached Nohant, he found himself confronted by Maurice, Borie, and Lambert, while two stalwart gendarmes who had been quietly summoned to the scene paced up and down outside. The frustrated tailor finally left "as meekly as a lamb," but inwardly seething at George Sand's refusal to assure Augustine a dowry *in writing* before a notary. The minimum he would accept, he later made it known, was 80,000 francs — about three times as much as George Sand could afford! This absurd demand could fortunately be ignored, for Augustine was no longer a minor. But her father's obstinate resistance effectively delayed her marriage by three months.

Solange and Clésinger, in the meantime, had continued their wild, spendthrift existence in Paris. Chopin generously lent them money, which quickly went the way of the rest, and by early autumn the creditors were threatening to seize the furniture in their already mortgaged house. Forced to dismiss their servants, they had their meals cooked for them by the concierge, from whom they also borrowed shamelessly. Solange, just to complicate matters, was now pregnant, while her husband was more furious than ever to discover that even if the Hôtel de Narbonne were sold, the 100,000 francs left over (after the payment of arrears and his personal debts) had to be *invested,* by virtue of a clause which Casimir Dudevant had wisely slipped into the marriage contract.

Not knowing where to turn next, Solange and Auguste journeyed down to Besançon in late September in an effort to borrow 8000 francs from Clésinger's father. The trip was not conspicuously successful to judge by a letter Solange sent to Chopin. A few weeks later George Sand wrote to Charlotte Marliani, explaining that she had had to put an end to Chopin's "occult tyranny" and the wild outbursts it had led to. His entourage would "make a martyr out of him, and rather than accept the truth, they will prefer to suppose that at my age I got rid of him in order to take a lover. I could not *care* less. But what I do care about and deeply, is the nastiness of my daughter, who is the center of all these nasty rumors. She will come back to me when she needs me, I know. But this return will be neither tender nor consoling."

Less than a week after these words were written — in early November — Solange and her husband turned up at La Châtre and persuaded Charles Duvernet to put them up. When the news was brought to George Sand by one of her servants, she sent word that she would be willing to receive her daughter. The meeting took place in the garden of Nohant. Solange shed a few crocodile tears while kissing her mother, whom she found "much changed, but as cold as ice, even hard," as she later described it to Chopin. George, for her part, was struck by Solange's icy air in submitting her rosy cheek to Maurice's fraternal kiss. The tears dried up almost as soon as they were shed, and with an insouciance which left her mother speechless, the pregnant Solange proceeded to romp with her dog, pick violets, and go for a stroll through the village, as though there had never been a cloud between them.

The next morning Clésinger sent word that he would like to drive over for a business chat, but George Sand flatly rejected the proposal. A little later Solange reappeared. This second meeting was no more successful than the first. George, in an effort at conciliation, offered Solange the use of her Square d'Orléans apartment, an offer which was haughtily refused.

The next day the importunate couple left La Châtre — to the intense relief of both George Sand and Charles Duvernet, who had found Clésinger's table-pounding tirades and fondness for the bottle difficult to take. Belatedly realizing that her mother was almost as debt-ridden as her husband, Solange now decided to appeal to the generosity of her official father, Casimir Dudevant. The dyspeptic baron was flattered by this attention unexpectedly bestowed on him by a girl he had in the past all but openly repudiated as a "harlot's daughter," and he let her make Guillery her home for the winter. But he prudently refrained from loosening his tight purse strings for his spendthrift son-in-law. A frustrated Clésinger was allowed to return to Paris more or less empty-handed, while his pregnant wife basked in the sunny warmth of Gascony, far from the offensive clamor of irate creditors.

To find her daughter and her former husband thus making common cause against her was not the least of the surprises George Sand had to face during this dismal autumn. To strangers and admirers, like the romantic Italian patriot Giuseppe Mazzini, who made a two-day visit to Nohant in late October, she put up a brave and even smiling face, but the effort it cost her was immense. Her headaches, though less frequent, were as shattering as ever, while she was plagued with renewed attacks of quinsy. "There are moments like this," as she wrote to Charlotte Marliani, "which seem to be the universal explosion of all the ills we have stored up in ourselves for years."

She was not unduly surprised to discover that Solange and her husband had managed to run up 8000 francs' worth of debts in and around La Châtre during the previous summer, debts which she personally assumed. When George sent her daughter a promissory note for 1250 francs in late December, Solange wrote back to say that this "scrap of paper" was so woefully insufficient in her present plight that it was like "a grain of sand in the sea." Her indignant mother had to reply with a sharp note, reminding her that her name was not Rothschild and that the "scrap of paper" she had received was the first half of an annual pension of 2500 francs which she was setting up for her and the rough equivalent of what she was now saving by moving into a cheaper apartment. But the prodigal daughter seems to have found it quite natural that her mother should go in for some belt-tightening, while her even more prodigal husband undertook a lightning trip to Guillery, six hundred miles away, in a private calèche pulled by relay-post horses which cost him 1000 francs, when he could have traveled at one tenth the cost in a public stagecoach.

In early February of 1848 Maurice and Eugène Lambert were sent up to Paris to empty the Square d'Orléans apartment of its furniture and to look for a new and smaller flat where George Sand and her son could stay during their visits to the capital. Lambert was instructed to get the banns for Augustine's impending marriage published in her father's municipal precinct, while Maurice badgered the Ministry of War into giving him certain service records concerning his grandfather, Maurice Dupin, which George Sand wanted for the early chapters of her autobiography. Lackadaisical as ever, he seems to have been in no rush to fulfill his mother's urgent request, preferring the giddy intoxication of carnival balls to the tedious buttonholing of administrative officials.

George Sand by this time was so absorbed by her father's exploits and adventures as an officer in the armies of Napoleon that she scoffed at Victor Borie's forecast that France once again was headed for a period of revolutionary turmoil. Borie's fervent republicanism for once had not led him astray, and George Sand could not have been more mistaken. But it is only fair to add that the three days of revolutionary upheavals which put an end to Louis-Philippe's bourgeois monarchy took not only Paris but all of Europe by surprise.

For the past eight years the nation had been governed by a man whose maxim *Enrichissez-vous!* — "Get rich" — had made France appear, superficially at least, a land of Law and Order, a country devoted to the ideals of Peace, Progress, and Prosperity. The Prime Minister, François Guizot, was a stern, unsmiling Protestant who had first made his name as a history professor and then as a parliamentary orator. He believed in the virtues of universal education, which he had done much to promote, but he was rigidly opposed to a universal franchise which, he was convinced, would once again expose France to mob rule and the wild excesses of the Robespierre terror of 1793. Granted a few decades of peace, after the military splurges of the Napoleonic era, France would grow prosperous, the average citizen richer, wealth would gradually seep down to the lowest levels of society, making the poor less wretched and the ignorant more literate. France, under the ancien régime, had been ruled by a titled aristocracy; under Louis-Phillippe and Guizot it had become a plutocracy, in which some 250,000 persons, with annual incomes of 500 francs or more, were allowed to vote and thus determine the fate of the remaining 35 million.

Though Guizot's prudence had much to commend it, his policies were too cautious to appeal to a generation of romantics whose imaginations had been stirred by the revolutionary ideals of 1789 — Liberty, Equality, Fraternity — and by the imperial panache of Napoleon. Lamartine had come closer to the general mood in a ringing speech made in 1843, when he had defiantly proclaimed:

"France is a country that is bored." At a time when Poland was gagged and partitioned by three conservative autocracies — Russia, Prussia, and Austria — Guizot's policy of "Peace at any Price" inevitably seemed pusillanimous, and at a time when the average French workingman earned less than two francs a day, his social policies seemed selfish and unjust, aimed at enriching the wealthy who had enough to speculate on the stock market and to purchase railway shares, while keeping the poor and downtrodden "in their place." The disastrous harvests of 1845 and 1846 had driven up the price of bread and other staples, and certain parts of France had been severely affected by the dreaded potato blight. The discontent was particularly pronounced in Paris, where unemployment and theft were rising and one third of its million inhabitants were now dependent on charity of one form or another.

In late December of 1847 Guizot stirred up a hornet's nest by stigmatizing the "blind or hostile passions" of the opposition parties in a Speech from the Throne which, as the head of the government, he had prepared for Louis-Philippe to read to a joint session of the upper and lower chambers of the French parliament. The opposition moderates, led by Odilon Barrot, a popular orator, and Louis Adolphe Thiers, the historian turned politician who had done as much as any man to place Louis-Philippe on the throne in 1830, retaliated by organizing provincial banquets marked by inflammatory speeches calling for an end to Guizot's ministry. The climax, in this campaign of a gastronomic castigation, was to have been a huge banquet staged in the pavilions of the Champs-Elysées. But at the last moment it was officially prohibited by a government decree issued shortly after Maurice and Eugène Lambert had reached Paris.

On February 22 throngs of workingmen, soon joined by students, began collecting in various squares and boulevards. Shouting "*A bas Guizot! Vive la reforme!*" — by which was meant a reform of the limited franchise — one such crowd surged across the Place de la Concorde bridge toward the Chamber of Deputies. The mob was routed easily enough by a squadron of dragoons, but feeling was now running so high that the next day barricades and red flags began springing up spontaneously.

In an effort to supplement the local contingents of regular troops, who were hopelessly outnumbered by hostile demonstrators, the Guizot government called out the National Guard, but most of its officers and men preferred to mingle with the mobs and to call for Guizot's resignation. Yielding to the public clamor, Guizot tendered his resignation, which an intimidated Louis-Philippe hastily accepted. But before a new government could be formed, there was a major clash in front of the Ministry of Foreign Affairs in which fifty demonstrators were mowed down by a regiment of riflemen. Within the next twenty-four hours more than a million paving stones were ripped up and four thousand trees chopped down for the erection of 1500 barricades. The July Monarchy was going down as it had begun — in an orgy of revolutionary turmoil. If George Sand once again was not on hand to watch the pandemonium, her son, Maurice, was, piling up paving stones and shattering streetlamps with wild Jacobin enthusiasm.

Events were by now moving so fast that even Thiers could no longer control the situation. Cowed by a hostile demonstration staged in front of the Tuileries Palace by a number of National Guardsmen, the seventy-four-year-old Louis Philippe abdicated in the early afternoon of February 24. A couple of hours later he and most of the royal family fled in two inconspicuous coupés and a cabriolet to the Château de Saint-Cloud, on Paris' western fringe, later making their way to England. That same evening the palace he had abandoned was occupied by a jubilant mob. Men and women took turns seating their bourgeois and proletarian posteriors on the gilt and velvet throne, after which it was tossed through a window and carried down to the Place de la Bastille to be publicly burned.

News of these tempestuous events, inevitably distorted and magnified, was not long in reaching Nohant, where George Sand was increasingly worried over the fate of Maurice. Every morning Victor Borie galloped dutifully into La Châtre to pick up her son's latest letter, to which she replied with urgent requests for his return. But Maurice was in no mood to comply. Delacroix, whose studio he visited, found him strangely "radiant," as he noted in his diary. "He walked out of here, as though drunk; I didn't believe him capable of such a degree of exaltation."

It was more than forty-eight hours before some kind of order began to reemerge through the confusing swirl of musketry, shouted slogans, and gunsmoke. When the Chamber of Deputies was invaded by "three hundred blood-stained insurgents . . . headed by a journeyman butcher, brandishing his carving-knife"— to quote from a report drafted by the British ambassador, Lord Normanby — a hard-pressed Lamartine suggested that the seat of power be transferred to the Hôtel de Ville, the tall-roofed and chimneyed town hall where eighteen years before an aging Lafayette had first presented Louis-Philippe to the Paris populace. Here, barricaded behind fixed bayonets and closed doors, Lamartine and his colleagues went through the motions of forming a provisional government, while outside on the steps George Sand's diminutive friend Louis Blanc whipped a noisy mob to fever pitch, with a demand for an immediate, unequivocal proclamation of a new republic.

The gradual realization that history was not repeating itself, that no new monarchy was going to rise phoenixlike from the ashes of the old, as Louis-Philippe's had risen from Charles X's, was the occasion for much rejoicing at Nohant. After eighteen years of weary waiting here at last was Aurore's dream come true. No time was lost forming a delegation of convinced republicans, who were to see to it that the new masters of France made the proper administrative changes for the department of the Indre. Augustine Brault, betrothed but not yet married, was entrusted to the care of Eugénie Duvernet, and on the last day of February George Sand left for Paris, at the head of a delegation composed of Gabriel Planet, Victor Borie, Charles Duvernet, and Alexis Duteil.

In Paris she found Maurice installed in a fifth-floor mansard flat, with a tiny balcony from which she could look out over the Odéon theater and the Luxembourg gardens. It was a birdcage compared to the elegant Square d'Orléans apartment, but the annual rent (300 francs) cost her one tenth as much, and during the day she could establish her headquarters *chez* Pinson, the cheap students' restaurant she had first frequented in the early 1830s with Jules Sandeau and her Berrichon friends. Now as then Paris was in a state of ferment, reliving a drama which was suddenly being restaged, and nothing could have seemed more quaintly and anachronistically revolutionary than the sight of the gentlemen who had suceeded the one-time sans-culottes ceremoniously doffing their toppers and calling each other *"Citoyen"* in the strictest Robespierre tradition.

That they were victims as much as the masters of events, more than one member of the new "ministry" would readily have admitted. For if ever there was a government which merited the title of provisional, it was the ad hoc administration which had established itself in the Hôtel de Ville under the general guidance of its foreign minister, the poet Lamartine. Anything but a revolutionary himself, he had been pushed by the more radical members of the Chamber and the demonstrators in the streets into accepting a republic in which he only half believed. Of this George Sand was well aware, and it explains her mingled admiration and distrust for a poet turned man-of-action who was at once a spellbinding orator and a vacillating liberal.

The government over which Lamartine presided was, like himself, divided, being composed of moderates who wanted to put an end to the prevailing anarchy by restoring orderly parliamentary rule and of radicals who wanted to use the Paris populace to impose their republican and socialist beliefs. George Sand had friends and acquaintances in both camps, though her sympathies naturally gravitated toward the radicals. Hippolyte Carnot, a well-known Saint-Simonian, had taken over the Ministry of Education, while the eminent astronomer François Arago, the uncle of her close friend Emmanuel, was now in charge of the navy. Both were moderates, as was Armand Marrast, the former editor of the *National* (the liberal newspaper to which Sainte-Beuve had long contributed) who had been appointed mayor of Paris. Marc Caussidière, the new prefect of police, was on the other hand a radical, a former *carbonaro* plotter whom George Sand had got to know at the time of the "monster trial" of 1835. The lawyer who had defended Caussidière in that extraordinary miscarriage of justice, Alexandre Ledru-Rollin, was Minister of the Interior, while George's former lover Louis Blanc, though thwarted in his desire to head a Ministry of Progress, had become an unofficial Minister of Labor, heading a commission which was supposed to improve the lot of Paris workingmen by limiting the hours of daily toil and giving work to the unemployed.

Though George Sand soon called on Louis Blanc, at the senatorial offices he occupied in the Luxembourg Palace, it was not with him but with Ledru-Rollin that she became most closely involved. In accompanying her Berrichon friends to Paris, George Sand did not intend to stay long. Her primary concern was to obtain a quick hearing from the Minister of the Interior for the delegation from the Indre. This she had no difficulty obtaining, the magic of her name being enough to carry her straight through the crowded antechambers into Ledru-Rollin's office.

A portly and rather pompous little man whose dark ring beard framed a pair of puffy cheeks, Alexandre Ledru-Rollin was a well-to-do middle-class demagogue who, as Maxime du Camp was later to write, made windy speeches "as a sound box makes music." His grandfather had been a famous conjuror known under the stage name of Comus, and something of his sleight-of-hand genius had been inherited by his glib grandson, who, when once asked where he and his fellow radicals were headed, had replied cynically enough: "I do not know. But since I am their leader, I must follow them." Whereas Louis Blanc was, like George Sand, a thoroughgoing socialist who had been brought up on Saint-Simon and other critics of laissez-faire capitalism, Ledru-Rollin was essentially a throwback to the French Revolution, a 1793 Jacobin whose ambition, as Minister of the Interior, was to dragoon France into becoming republican by reviving the old Committees of Public Safety and ruling the provincial departments through hand-picked commissars.

George Sand's staunch republicanism seems to have impressed Ledru-Rollin. He readily granted her request that Michel de Bourges's friend Frédéric Girerd be named commissaire de la république for the department of the Nièvre, and Charles Duvernet sous-commissaire (subcommissar) for the Indre, at La Châtre. He also agreed to endorse Alexis Duteil's nomination to the post of public prosecutor at Bourges. Nor was this all. He had intended to make Michel de Bourges commissaire de la république for the department of the Cher. But when he heard from George Sand and her friends that Michel had "betrayed" the republican cause (by undertaking to defend a prefect in a lawsuit against an opposition journalist), he changed his mind and appointed Gabriel Planet.

On the morning of March 4 an impressive funeral service was held at the Madeleine for all those who had perished on the barricades in the recent fighting. George Sand, who had gone to the Foreign Ministry to obtain a new passport for her Italian revolutionary friend Mazzini, was immediately ushered into the ornate office Guizot had once occupied; here Lamartine, who had replaced him, invited her to watch the mourners shuffle past and up the Boulevard des Capucines. "It was fine, simple and touching," she wrote ecstatically to Augustine, "four hundred thousand people pressed together from the Madeleine all the way to the Column of July" — by which she meant the commemorative column on the Place de la Bastille. "Not a constable, not a police sergeant to be seen, and yet such order, good behavior, reverence and mutual politeness that not a foot was trampled on nor a top hat dented. It was admirable. The people of Paris are the foremost in the world." As quickly mollified by the advent of the republic as they had been aroused by Guizot's intransigence, the Paris populace seemed remarkably pacific — for the moment at any rate.

Later that same day George Sand, accompanied by Eugène Lambert, went to call on Charlotte Marliani, who was still living on the Square d'Orléans. In the antechamber they bumped into Chopin, who was on the point of leaving with Edmond Combes, an author turned diplomat who had served as consul at Smyrna and Rabat and who had been dubbed "the Abyssinian" after publishing a travel book on the regions of the upper Nile. Chopin asked her if she had had any news from her daughter. George replied that she had heard from Solange a week before.

"You didn't hear from her yesterday, or the day before?"

"No."

"Then let me tell you that you are a grandmother. Solange has a little daughter, and I am very happy to be the first person to have brought you this news."

With that Chopin bowed and made his way downstairs. But there was one thing, it suddenly occurred to him, he had forgotten to add and which George Sand would certainly like to know. Feeling too exhausted to climb the stairs again — once was all his cough-racked lungs could take — he asked Combes to go back upstairs to tell Madame Sand that Solange and her baby daughter were both of them in good health.

George, on hearing the news, accompanied Combes downstairs and began plying Chopin with questions. She was intrigued to know how he had received the news. Through a penciled note which Solange had scribbled to him the day after her daughter's birth, Chopin replied. Was Solange's husband by her side, she asked. Presumably, answered Chopin, for the address on the letter seemed to be in his handwriting. "And yourself?" she asked, referring to his health. Chopin replied that his health was good. He held out his hand, signifying that the conversation was at an end. George took it reluctantly, not knowing what to say. The hand that had played so many immortal Etudes and Mazurkas was disturbingly cold and trembling. She felt tempted to say, "So it's you who no longer love me?" but she said nothing, not wishing to add to his sufferings. Chopin asked the concierge to release the door latch and walked out into the little square without another word.

She had made a gesture; it had been rebuffed. Moved as she was by this chance encounter, she had too many other things on her mind to imagine that this would be their last meeting. "I was never to see him again," she later wrote (in *The Story of My Life*). "There were evil-minded hearts between us. There were also some good ones who did not know how to go about it. There were some frivolous ones who preferred not to be involved in delicate matters."

If personal grievances had driven them apart, the public events of February 1848 were certainly not made to bring them together again. Appalled by the revolutionary turmoil which had overtaken Paris, Chopin left a few weeks later for London, while George Sand plunged boldly back into the fray. "I have spent many nights without sleeping, many days without sitting down," she wrote in dithyrambic tones to Charles Poncy, the proletarian poet. "People are mad, drunk, happy to have fallen asleep in the mud and to have woken up in the heavens . . . The republic has won through, it is assured, we will perish rather than abandon it. The provisional government is composed for the most part of excellent men, all of them incomplete and insufficient for a task which would demand the genius of Napoleon and the great-heartedness of Christ."

If anything, this was an understatement. With the sole exception of Lamartine, who had held diplomatic posts in Italy, not one of the ministers who had suddenly inherited the task of running the country, had had the slightest government experience. George Sand was just as inexperienced, which explains, though it does not justify, the lyrical quality of her enthusiasm. "You are great! You are by nature heroic; your boldness in combat, your sublime scorn of danger surprise no one," she crowed ecstatically in an eight-page manifesto entitled *To the People,* which she had printed up by her publisher friend Hetzel. "Once again you have proved to the world that you are the magnanimous race *par excellence.* As soft as strength, oh People! How strong you are, since you are so good!" etc.

She followed this up with a second manifesto, addressed this time to the traditional foes of the downtrodden and oppressed, that is *To the Rich.* It would be a crime, she wrote, were they to kill that "sacred brotherhood" which, for one glorious moment, had caused gentleman and pauper, employer, artisan, and employee to stand shoulder to shoulder at the barricades. What reason had they to fear the People who had just proved their heroic valor and determination? Because they were *communists* bent on destroying property and family life? Let them rest assured: she, who was a communist, had never met one who was so inclined. "No, alas! The People are not communist. Yet," she added in the next breath, *"France is destined to be communist before a century is up."* How so? She did not say. But that single sentence was enough to make a shambles of the rest. The historian Henri Martin, to whom she sent a preliminary draft, could only note with dismay that the words *communist* and *communism* — precisely the bogies she wished to lay to rest — had cropped up no less than fifteen times in a relatively short text. "What a weapon you have given to your adversaries!" he lamented.

By the time this second manifesto was published, George Sand had returned to Nohant, where her son Maurice was installed as mayor and the advent of the new republic celebrated with a fete, complete with bagpipes and a local contingent of National Guardsmen, incongruously arrayed in makeshift uniforms and wooden clogs. Once again she kept late hours while her restless quill scratched out new *Letters to the People* and other exhortations written for provincials in a kind of rustic dialect. "My heart and head are on fire," she wrote to Charles Poncy. "All my physical ills, all my personal sufferings are forgotten. I am alive, I am active, I'm only twenty years old." To which she added, significantly: "I've come back here to aid my friends as best I can to revolutionize Berry, which is asleep."

The rustic torpor of her province exasperated her. The smug burghers of La Châtre were suspicious if not hostile, the local artisans and workingmen on the whole indifferent, while the peasants scratched their heads, only dimly comprehending what was going on in Paris. Alphonse Fleury, who was busy launching a new newspaper — the *Républicain de l'Indre* — found it heavy going, and Charles Duvernet, the recently appointed sous-commissaire de la république, was greeted in the streets of La Châtre with cries of "*A bas Duvernet!*" and mocking shouts in favor of the reactionary mayor. The revolutionary fervor gripping Paris had clearly failed to stir these provincial backwaters, and as George Sand was forced to admit in a letter to Henri Martin: "Berry produces pure and patient men, but genius does not walk in our furrows."

That the provinces were nowhere near as radical as the capital the various members of the provisional government were well aware. But whereas the moderates, led by Lamartine, regarded this as a means of salvation from the local pressure of mob rule, the radicals, led by Ledru-Rollin and Louis Blanc, regarded the political "backwardness" of the provinces as a misfortune which had to be forcefully remedied. The extension of the franchise to all male citizens over twenty-one would, it was calculated, grant the right to vote to some eight million Frenchmen. Of these over three quarters were illiterate, yet it was they who in the forthcoming elections would have the decisive say through sheer force of numbers. The new electoral system, carefully tailored by the moderates, provided for the election of some seven deputies per department. Such being the case, it was a foregone conclusion that in most departments the uneducated voters would instinctively prefer to vote for some local "notable" with whom they were familiar than for some obscure revolutionary who had yet to make his mark.

For Ledru-Rollin and his friends the conclusion to be drawn was clear: the elections had to be postponed to give his hand-picked commissaires de la république time to "radicalize" the sleepy provinces. George Sand proposed that one peasant and one workingman be automatically chosen as candidates in each department to offset the crushing majority the bourgeoisie seemed likely to obtain and thus "to impose respect for the people" — by which she meant the lowest classes of society. She even wrote to Hippolyte Carnot, the Minister of Education, suggesting that authentic proletarians from Paris factories and workshops be dispatched to different departments to arouse the slumbering masses: a suggestion which seems to have fallen on deaf ears.

On March 20 George Sand returned to Paris with Borie, leaving Maurice and Lambert at Nohant, while Augustine was once again entrusted to the care of Eugénie Duvernet. The situation in the capital was more chaotic and confused than ever, and as Lamartine remarked to the British ambassador: "We are sitting on a volcano." A couple of days before, a massive demonstration, staged by radicals of every hue, should logically have culminated in the storming of the Hôtel de Ville had Ledru-Rollin and Louis Blanc not got cold feet at the last moment and refused to back the extremists. Though both were determined to postpone the elections by all means fair or foul, they were increasingly wary of each other and concerned by the ambitions of rival plotters. At his headquarters in the Luxembourg Palace Louis Blanc had established control over some 30,000 artisans and workingmen who could be mobilized for a march on the Hôtel de Ville. Ledru-Rollin, for his part, was hastily trying to recruit a Garde Mobile composed of young republicans, to neutralize the solidly bourgeois National Guard, still overwhelmingly favorable to Lamartine and his fellow moderates. But both Ledru-Rollin and Louis Blanc now felt the pressure of several hundred revolutionary clubs which had mushroomed all over Paris, composed for the most part of Jacobin extremists bent on imposing the "People's Will" through mob violence. The most sinister of these conspirators was Louis Auguste Blanqui, a small, haggard, thin-lipped individual who, to quote the modern historian Arnold Whitridge, "looked as though he had spent his life in a sewer." A tireless *carbonaro* plotter whom Guizot had had locked up for years in the fortress-prison of

Mont-Saint-Michel, he was persuaded that there was only one way of establishing a society of absolute equals — through force, or as we would say today, a putsch.

By agreeing to postpone the elections by several weeks, Lamartine managed to cool the revolutionary volcano on which he was uncomfortably seated. But the respite was necessarily brief. One of Louis Blanc's first acts, as an unofficial minister of labor, had been to issue a proclamation granting all workingmen the right to employment. It was an act of unquestionable magnanimity, but as revolutionaries quickly discover, decreeing the new utopia is one thing, putting it into effect and financing it another. In an effort to limit the damage, the Minister of Public Works, a moderate who had no use for Louis Blanc's socialistic theories, established a series of National Workshops which were supposed to keep the unemployed busy mending roads, terracing quays, and uprooting the stumps of tree trunks which had been cut down to bolster the February barricades. But the task of paying the tens of thousands who rushed to accept the state's largess soon outstripped the government's meager resources. Business, disrupted by the recent turmoil, was at a standstill, while the bankers, who had made Louis-Philippe's regime their own, were in no mood to bail out the makeshift crew of lawyers and journalists who had seized the reins of power. An effort to float a 250 million franc loan failed miserably, and in its desperate search for funds the government imposed a forty-five centime levy on every able-bodied man.

Whereas a graduated income tax and a policy of "Soak the rich!" would have been welcomed by George Sand as well as by the masses, this emergency levy unleashed a wave of discontent. Out of loyalty to Ledru-Rollin, for whom she was now working as a kind of "ghost writer," George undertook to justify it in the *Bulletins de la République* which the Ministry of the Interior had begun printing up for the edification of all "good citizens." But in Lyon, to which he had been sent as the government's all-powerful commissaire, Emmanuel Arago was almost shot down by a crew of musket-wielding ruffians who were outraged by his decision to raise the forced levy to one franc per head.

Dragged from one antechamber to the next, where he was often kept waiting till one o'clock in the morning, Victor Borie was soon complaining of the giddy tempo of his mistress' life. In addition to her new duties as the government's unofficial Minister of Propaganda, she somehow found time to work on her memoirs, launch a new weekly, and write a dramatic prologue for the theater. "I assure you I haven't time to sleep or breathe freely," she wrote to her son on April 7, and it was hardly an exaggeration. Exhausted by the 190 steps she had to climb each time she ascended to Maurice's mansard flat on the Rue de Condé, she rented a large room on the third floor, where Borie slept at night and where a copyist was installed in the daytime to work on her Memoirs. The new weekly she launched, with the help of Borie and Louis Viardot (who had returned from Berlin with Pauline), was called, typically enough, *La Cause du Peuple* (*The People's Cause*). Though fairly cheaply priced at twenty-five centimes, it lasted three short weeks — simply because people were too absorbed by the events of the moment to have time for another journal of opinion.

At the Comédie Française, from which the overly subservient Buloz had been removed in favor of a manager of stout republican fiber, the Marseillaise was now sung every night by Mademoiselle Rachel, between the concluding acts of the classic tragedies in which she starred. Like the Opéra, rechristened the Théâtre de la Nation, Molière's old theater was now known as the Théâtre de la République. It lived up to its new appellation by cutting prices for the cheaper seats to put them within the range of simple artisans and by offering an occasional free evening.

To mark this fortnightly innovation, Pauline Viardot composed the music for a new patriotic hymn, while George Sand wrote a dramatic dialogue in which Aeschylus, Sophocles, and Euripides (representing the Ancients), Shakespeare, Voltaire, and Beaumarchais (the "Moderns") undertake to harangue a dreaming Molière, who wakes to find himself the playwright laureate of a monarch more powerful and imposing then the Sun King himself — the Paris populace of 1848! The proletarians who were fortunate enough to obtain free tickets to this première displayed an impressive decorum, listening in almost religious silence to the epic tirades of Corneille and the witty dialogue of Molière. There was for once no supercilious whispering in the crowded boxes nor casual scattering of orange peels. When the time came for them to demonstrate their appreciation, they did not, like the well-heeled *fashionables* of yesterday, throw their flowers at the actresses' heads. Instead, a young worker climbed on to the stage, to present Mademoiselle Rachel with a bouquet which had been bought through an on-the-spot subscription. "The dandies cry *Encore!* in an imperious tone and accustom women to regard a brutal command as a form of homage," George Sand commented a bit too rapturously in *La Cause du Peuple.* "The people consider an actor a man, and a great actress not only as a woman but as a muse. The people are delicate and more gentlemanly than all of yesterday's gentlemen."

This attempt to bring culture to the masses coincided with another, less successful endeavor to have George Sand elected to the new National Assembly. In a gushing editorial published by *La Voix des Femmes,* a militant feminist named Eugénie Nibouyet insisted that because she was "male by virility" and a "woman by divine intent," George Sand merited the approbation of male voters and should logically become the first woman elected to the Constituent Assembly. George Sand's reaction to this effusive flattery was hostile. In an open letter sent to two Paris papers she scoffed at the proposal and expressed the hope that no one would be foolish enough to waste his vote on her, adding bluntly that she was totally unacquainted with "the ladies who form clubs and edit newspapers."

Outspokenly progressive though she was in her social views, George Sand realized that midnineteenth-century France was a man's world. Her name was entered on forty different lists of candidates, all to no avail. To involve women in politics even before they had secured their civil rights in marriage was, she felt, putting the cart before the horse. "Woman being under the tutelage and dependency of man by marriage," as she wrote in a long memorandum, "it is impossible that she present guarantees of political independence save by individually flouting laws and customs and breaking this tutelage, which has a legal consecration."

One of the first tasks of a truly socialist republic, she claimed, would be to bring about a radical reform in marriage laws, enabling women to retain the civil rights they enjoyed as spinsters but surrendered to their husbands on getting married — "a detestable error in our legislation which places a woman in the mercenary clutch of a man, and which makes marriage a condition of eternal minority." * What could be more ridiculous than the sight of a grandmother of eighty still being treated as a minor and as a kind of semiperson in the eyes of the law — a despotic law which gave a husband the exclusive right to determine the material conditions of his wife's and children's existence, granted him the final say in their children's education, allowed him to be unfaithful to his heart's content, and let him dissipate the family fortune on whores while beating or even killing his wife if she dared be unfaithful in her turn. As things now stood, there was no middle ground between "a slavery which exasperates her and a tyranny which vilifies her husband." Social customs had evolved to such an extent that in actual practice "a woman rules in most families." But this authority was not consecrated by the law, it had been gained through "cleverness, tenacity, and guile." Not to mention the classic resort to adultery, which made her lord and master the laughingstock of friends. For, she went on, there is "nothing vainer than the valet, no insolence like that of the woman who governs while pretending to obey. A man should not obey a woman, for this is monstrous. Nor should a man order his wife about, for this is cowardly . . . Man and woman should obey their vows, heeding honor, reason, and their love for their children. These are sacred ties, laws superior to the counsels of our pride and the urges of human passion."

Those women who wanted to begin by exercising political rights, she concluded, were amusing themselves with trifles. "What! Your husband will be seated on one bench, your lover perhaps on another, and you will claim to represent something when you are not even the representation of yourselves? An evil law makes of you the mere *half* of a man . . . and you think you can offer some kind of responsibility to other men? . . . But because you demand the immediate exercise of political rights, it is thought that you are also calling for freedom of passion" — the antimarital gospel of free love and promiscuity, as preached by Fourier and certain Saint-Simonians — "and from then on all idea of reform is rejected."

* A condition which, in France at least, lasted right up until 1970!

George Sand, as one can see, was not a suffragette — a term which, in fact, had not yet been invented. Her views on the feminist question had not varied significantly since 1837, when she had written her controversial *Lettres à Marcie.* Though her own had proved a catastrophic failure and though her daughter's seemed certain to be equally disastrous, she still believed that marriage — marriage between equals — was the cornerstone of individual happiness and social felicity. But the ideal had been vitiated by the doctrine and practice of male dominance. And it was because she was personally convinced that this doctrine, with all its fatuous duplicities, would continue to hold sway in a bourgeois republic, just as it had in a bourgeois monarchy, that she longed to see a new socialist order established.

That this would not be easy, she realized as well as anyone. From Guillery, where she had lost her baby daughter, Jeanne-Gabrielle, a mere week after her birth, a saddened Solange had written to say that she wondered "how people who could not get together against a common enemy when they were in the opposition . . . hope to act in concert to guide an entire nation. How do Louis Blanc, Ledru-Rollin, Flocon, Arago, etc., who had such bitter disputes in editing the newspaper *La Réforme,* think they can govern France of a common accord?" It was a good question, even if obviously inspired by Baron Dudevant's hostility to his former wife's radical friends and associates, and one which George Sand could not convincingly answer.

This, however, was no time for crippling doubts or craven-hearted misgivings. Whatever the odds against it, she was determined to do her bit for the establishment of a socialist republic. For her fellow radicals she drafted a confidential memorandum entitled "Governmental Plan for the Second Republic," in which she urged a wholesale reform of the electoral law (providing for national, as opposed to departmental elections, to limit the influence of provincial "notables") and the creation of a "homogenous" government from which all wishy-washy moderates were to be ruthlessly eliminated.

She followed this up with a blunt warning to "reactionaries," delivered in the sixteenth *Bulletin de la République,* which appeared on April 15 and which was entirely her handiwork. The pamphlet began by declaring that "eighteen years of falsehood and corruption" could not be erased overnight, though a new age had dawned. But if the forthcoming elections, instead of assuring the "triumph of social truth," were to restore the supremacy of a social "caste" — by which was meant the bourgeoisie — then these elections were certain to be the doom of the republic. "There would then be only one road of salvation for the people who built the barricades, and that would be to manifest their will a second time and to adjourn the decisions of a false national representation."

These inflammatory words created a sensation. Though George Sand did not sign her name to any of the *Bulletins* she helped write, and took pains to remain anonymous, it was soon common knowledge that she had authored this all but open call to revolutionary insurrection. It was in effect a simple restatement of the old Jacobin doctrine, ultimately derived from Rousseau, according to which the "will of the people," as expressed in an election, is not necessarily the same as the general will — which is to say, the enlightened course of action the electors would have chosen had they been sufficiently unprejudiced.

George Sand by this time was so deeply involved in conspiratorial plotting that she had to postpone her return to Nohant, thus missing the marriage which, on April 12, united Augustine Brault and Charles de Bertholdi. As the "Muse of the Republic" she had virtually ceased to have a private life, though she was beset as ever by private problems. Not the least of these was Solange, who had by now returned to Paris, looking "fat, red, and puffy" (as George wrote to Maurice) and peevishly discontent with a semibankrupt republic which had difficulty paying her husband for his monumental statues of *Liberty* and *Fraternity.*

The "Liberty Trees" which had been hopefully planted all over the capital could no longer disguise the fact that the tension between moderates and radicals was steadily mounting and that a showdown was unavoidable. The day George Sand's explosive editorial appeared, Lamartine was warned that Ledru-Rollin and Louis Blanc were preparing something against his provisional government. But this "naive Jesuit," as George called him, remained as usual indecisive. Toward noon, on April 16, some 30,000 workers began massing on the Champ de Mars, ostensibly to elect the officers of their union corporations, but in fact to stage a march on the Hôtel de Ville. The march would almost certainly have culminated in the overthrow of the Lamartine government had not Marrast, the moderate mayor of Paris, been fortuitously persuaded by General Changarnier (who had come to the town hall for other reasons) to have the drummers sound the *rappel général,* or call to arms. One hundred thousand National Guardsmen were thus mobilized at short notice to protect the approaches to the Hôtel de Ville.

Their revolutionary ardor already dampened by Louis Blanc's last-minute failure to show up, the 30,000 workers finally crossed the Seine, carrying banners urging the ORGANIZATION OF WORK and the CESSATION OF THE EXPLOITATION OF MAN BY MAN. On the other side of the river they found thousands of National Guardsmen, armed with bayonets and muskets, waiting to "escort" them to Paris' town hall. The workers, split into two single files, with a column of National Guardsmen between, were thus accompanied to the Hôtel de Ville.

"It was a beautiful, sad sight to see all those people walking proudly but unhappily in the midst of all those bayonets," George Sand, who accompanied them, later wrote to Maurice. "The bayonets shouted: *Long live the republic, Long live the provisional government, Long live Lamartine.* The workers replied: *Long live the good republic, Long live equality, Long live the true republic of Christ.* The crowds were massed on the pavements and parapets. I was with Rochery" — a young journalist who had been helping her to edit *La Cause du Peuple* — "and there was no way of walking otherwise than in the column of workers, who remained kind, polite and brotherly in spirit. Every five minutes a halt was called for the workers, so that the National Guard could advance a platoon's length or two ahead . . . They were thus trapped in the meshes of a huge net. They felt it and stifled their indignation."

On the square facing the Hôtel de Ville they were made to wait an hour, while Lamartine's National Guard and the teen-agers of Ledru-Rollin's Garde Mobile took up their positions. Finally the members of the provisional government appeared in the balconied windows of the town hall, "posing like Apollos." The workers who had gained access to the square were separated from the town hall by a thick cordon of National Guardsmen, through which a few chosen delegates were allowed to thread their way for the presentation of petitions and grievances. Lamartine appeared on the steps of the main entrance and improvised one more eloquent oration which George Sand, hemmed in like a sardine in this ocean of restless bodies, was too faraway to hear. Ten minutes later the frustrated workers melted into the side streets, while Lamartine began a pompous review of the victorious National Guard. "I disappeared at the same moment," George wrote that night to Maurice, "so as not to have the signal honor of also being passed in review, and I came back to dine at Pinson's, very sad and realizing that the *republican republic*" — she meant of course the socialist republic of her dreams — "was down and out for a long time perhaps."

Her gloomiest presentiments were fully justified. That same evening, when she and Victor Borie emerged from the restaurant, the workingmen had vanished and the streets were full of students, middle-class shopkeepers, and "belching loafers of every kind" who were ambling to and fro shouting "Down with the Communists!" and "Death to Cabet!" — this last being the visionary utopian who (half a century before Bernard Shaw and the Fabians) had been propounding the naive idea that Jesus Christ was a communist. Later, on the Pont des Arts, they heard the distant drums repeating the call to arms and saw flocks of National Guardsmen, their bayonets glinting in the flickering light of torches, heading for the Hôtel de Ville to the same hue and cry — *Mort à Cabet! Mort aux communistes!* Cabet, "a rather nasty imbecile" in George Sand's opinion, was a political innocent compared to revolutionary plotters like Blanqui and Raspail, but this had not kept him from becoming a universal bugbear.

The decisive moment, George Sand correctly sensed, had come and gone. The nervous middle class had triumphed, not because its cause was just, but because the radicals had shown themselves to be divided in the hour of crisis and more interested in furthering their personal ambitions than in the triumph of the proletarian cause.

Just as she had foreseen, the elections of April 23 were a decisive victory for the moderates. Lamartine, put up as a candidate in ten different departments, led the list of victors with 259,800 votes, followed by the astronomer François Arago, who obtained 243,640.

Ledru-Rollin lagged far behind with 131,000, while Louis Blanc was only able to obtain some 120,000. Provincial France had proved itself once again to be less radically inclined than the revolutionary capital. Of 900 deputies elected to the new Assembly only thirty-four were workingmen and sixteen peasants. The rest were lawyers, doctors, scientists, and engineers, men of letters like Alexis de Tocqueville or "notables" like Comte Molé — the same Molé who, as Louis-Philippe's Minister of Foreign Affairs, had facilitated George Sand's and Chopin's journey to Mallorca. The revolutionary clubs could only claim 200 deputies, the remaining 700 seats having been won by Royalists and moderate republicans. In the department of the Indre Alfred Fleury had barely managed to get himself elected, while a gang of La Châtre rowdies, worked up to fever pitch because of her *communist* affiliations, had invaded the village square of Nohant and rattled the front gates, threatening to sack Madame Sand's chateau.

When the new Assembly convened in early May the general sentiment was so hostile to the radicals that Lamartine had to exert the full weight of his prestige to have Ledru-Rollin elected to the Executive Committee. George Sand by this time was thoroughly disillusioned and had but one desire: to return as quickly as possible to the country. But her departure was postponed for a few days by Maurice's sudden arrival in Paris.

Before she left she was invited to a small literary luncheon by a British Member of Parliament, Richard Monckton Milnes, who had apparently taken it into his gentlemanly head to "fall for" Madame Sand. Having been more than once exposed to this kind of calamity, Madame Sand spent most of the meal conversing with her other neighbor — the celebrated author of *Democracy in America*, who had been reelected to the French Assembly by his Norman constituents. The company present, as Alexis de Tocqueville later recalled in his *Souvenirs*, was anything but "homogenous": there was George Sand, a "very modest and most agreeable young English lady," several "rather obscure writers," and Prosper Mérimée — who, seated across the table, had to ask his neighbor to identify the lady with the huge black eyes, so changed and unrecognizable did he find his former bedmate of the Quai Malaquais.

Tocqueville, however, had never seen George Sand before. He

had lived but little, as he later explained, "in the world of literary adventurers which she frequented. One of my friends having one day asked her what she thought of my book on America, 'Monsieur,' she told him, 'I am used to reading only the books that are offered to me by their authors.' I entertained great prejudices against Madame Sand, for I hate women who write, above all those who make a system of the weaknesses of their sex, rather than interesting us by showing them to us under their true guise. Nevertheless, she pleased me. I found her features rather massive, but her gaze quite admirable. All her wit seemed to have withdrawn into her eyes . . . But what most struck me was to encounter in her something of the naturalness of great minds. She had, indeed, a true simplicity of manners and language, which blended with the affected simplicity of her clothes. I confess that she would have seemed even simpler to me, more elaborately got up. We talked about public affairs for a whole hour — it was impossible at that time to talk of anything else. Besides, Madame Sand was then a manner of political man. What she had to say on the subject struck me greatly. It was the first time I had had any direct and familiar dealings with a person who could and was willing to tell me what was going on in the camp of our adversaries . . . Madame Sand gave me a singularly detailed and lively description of the workers of Paris, their organization, their weapons, preparations, thoughts, passions, and terrible determinations. I thought the picture overdone, but it was not; as was shown by what ensued . . . 'Monsieur,' she said to me, 'try to persuade your friends not to push the people into the street by worrying and irritating them, just as I would like to instill patience in my own. For if the battle is joined, you may be sure you will all perish.' "

Ten days later the sullen grievances she had so graphically described to Tocqueville exploded into violence. The spark of revolution had by now spread across Europe, igniting insurrections in Germany, Austria, and Italy, while Paris had become a rallying point for embattled Irishmen calling for the emancipation of their island from British rule, for German Democrats who wanted to march on Berlin, and for Belgian republicans who wished to topple the Saxe-Coburg-Gotha sovereign, Leopold I, from his Brussels throne. On May 13 news reached Paris that one more insurrection, this time in Poland, had broken out, only to be brutally suppressed by Prussian troops. Memories of Napoleon's Grande Armée were revived, as workingmen and students gathered in the streets shouting *"Vive la Pologne!"*

This was the chance the frustrated revolutionaries were waiting for. Two days later a huge mob of Polish sympathizers massed on the Place de la Bastille and then began a march toward the National Assembly. The demonstration was originally intended to pressure the Assembly into sending an army to Poland, but it soon got out of hand. Allowed to cross the Concorde bridge by the commander of the National Guard, the mob leaders clambered over the Assembly's grillwork bars, pushed past the sentinels, broke down the doors, and surged into the amphitheater. For two hours all was pandemonium, as even the most popular speakers were shouted down — like the fervently republican Armand Barbès, who sought in vain to have the Assembly vote a billion franc levy (to be imposed on the rich) to finance a Polish expeditionary force. Finally a Jacobin rabble-rouser named Huber, who had only recently been let out of a lunatic asylum, climbed on to the rostrum in his turn and declared the Chamber dissolved.

George Sand, who had joined the chanting crowd outside, was under the impression that the leaders of the demonstration had been welcomed with open arms by conservatives anxious to bury the social antagonisms of the past, not realizing that inside the Chamber all hell had broken loose. The solemn roll of drums and the arrival of the National Guard abruptly dispelled her illusions. Bayonets were used to clear the Assembly, and shortly afterward Paris' leading revolutionaries, led by Blanqui and Raspail ("the Marats of our day," as George Sand called them), were hauled off to prison. The quixotic Armand Barbès was also placed behind the bars. Pierre Leroux was locked up for a week; Théophile Thoré, the rabidly progressive editor of *La Vraie République* (to which George Sand had been contributing articles), had his offices and apartment ransacked, while George herself was threatened with arrest.

Though she had played no part in organizing this demonstration, George Sand's past associations with ringleaders like Thoré and Barbès made her naturally suspect. At the height of the uproar she had even seen a woman haranguing the crowd from the window of a café on the Rue de Bourgogne, not far from the Assembly. She had asked some bystanders who it was, only to be told: "George Sand."

"I am leaving in a couple of days, I need air and rest," she wrote to Etienne Arago, the editor of the radical newspaper *La Réforme,* who shared her socialist sympathies. "The spectacle of this bourgeois reaction makes me ill. Yesterday's events have put us back ten years. What deplorable folly!"

From Nohant, to which she and Maurice were only too happy to return, she wrote four days later to her conservative cousin René de Villeneuve: "God grant there be an end to the awful poverty and deep bitterness of the people of the industrial cities. Those of our countryside are calm, because the harvest is *fair and golden,* as they say; but it's not these people who now make revolutions. If the bourgeois assembly you have composed in a spirit of prudence and fear does not accomplish miracles in the near future, the upheaval of May 15th, which was in itself but a piece of foolish madness, will be the brief and awkward prologue to a long and serious drama."

Increasingly disillusioned, she wrote to Jules Boucoiran in Nîmes to say that she was now fed up with politics. "Revolutions arouse all the fine and evil passions, and I had the painful misfortune to find myself always better than the forced movement surrounding me. It is painful because passion, as such, intoxicates those who succumb to it, and nothing is sadder than to have the sole passion for the good . . ." To Charles Poncy she explained that there had arisen "storms in which reason and the heart" — by which she meant a sense of pity — "can do nothing against passion. But what is termed a political passion is something I shall never have. I have only passion for the idea."

To Théophile Thoré she was even more explicit in expressing her dismay. "I went home determined not to lose a single hair of my head on behalf of men like Raspail, Cabet and Blanqui. As long as these men enroll themselves under our banner, I will abstain. They are pedants and theocrats. I don't want to see the individual crushed, and I will go into exile the day we make the mistake of bringing them to power . . . They wanted to impose by surprise (and if they could have done so, by force) an idea which the people had not yet accepted. They would have established the reign of fraternity, not like the Christ but like Mahomet." And, she added, in three decisive sentences which showed how much already separated her from Karl Marx and those who were to espouse his revolutionary gospel: "Instead of a religion, we would have had a fanaticism. It is not thus that true ideas make their way in the world. At the end of three months of such a philosophical usurpation we would not have been republicans but Cossacks."

Those who have claimed that in later condemning the Paris Commune of 1871 George Sand proved herself a turncoat and a traitor to the radical ideas of her youth and middle age should reread these lines. For they show that progressive though she was in her social views, she was fundamentally opposed to revolutionary violence. Her ideal throughout had been a bloodless revolution: a revolution without bayonets and guillotines in which a reactionary government could be brought tumbling down, like the walls of Jericho, through a robust use of lung power, while the triumphant populace paraded joyfully through the streets, throwing their caps and bonnets in the air. But what she had witnessed close at hand had been substantially different. In revolutions, as in so much else, she remained a romantic.

34. Farewell to Politics

For weeks after her return to Nohant George Sand was the object of wild threats and rumors. It was commonly supposed that she had fled from Paris to escape arrest; in fact she had delayed her departure by two days lest people think she were trying to run away. Nohant, it was reported, had been turned into a fortress, bristling with muskets and diehard revolutionaries. Solange wrote to suggest that her mother stay put, for in Paris certain members of the National Guard were talking not simply of arresting her "but of doing worse than that." Etienne Arago advised her to leave for Italy, while Pauline Viardot, who had gone to London to compete in opera singing with Jenny Lind, offered her asylum in her country house east of Paris, where George was unknown.

For the smug burghers of La Châtre, of course, she was more than ever a bête noire. The woes of the republic were heaped wholesale on her head. Many held her responsible for the unpopular forty-five centime levy, which had touched off more than one hostile demonstration. Others roamed the countryside seeking to arouse the peasantry against this diabolical woman who was, they claimed, in league with a sinister troublemaker named *le Père Communisme* who wanted to have all children under three and adults over sixty ruthlessly exterminated! The braggarts spoke of arming themselves with flintlocks and torches and of making a bonfire of Nohant. "I would even find it rather funny," George wrote to Pauline "were the *conservatives* of La Châtre to come out here, out of sheer hatred of communism and to belie this alleged doctrine of doom and destruction, and to burn and pillage my home. What an example they would be giving; nor do I despair of seeing them undertake such an action against myself or another, thereby revealing their uprightness and love of order, their morality and *respect for property.*"

About the future of her country, as opposed to her own, she was less prepared to joke. "I fear the unintelligence of the rich and the despair of the poor," she wrote in a letter to Mazzini. "I fear a state of war which is not yet in people's minds but which can become a fact if the ruling class fails to pursue a democratic and frankly fraternal course . . . From one end of France to the other this caste issues orders and doesn't hesitate to condemn what it calls 'factious elements,' without thinking that these same people whom it provokes against itself could in a single day . . . become the terrible people of 1793 . . . In a word" — and here she was anticipating Dostoevski's "Legend of the Grand Inquisitor" — "what Christ preached to the men of his time — charity, brotherly love — has become incendiary predication, and if Jesus reappeared amongst us, he would be seized by the National Guard as a seditious anarchist."

In early June she was dismayed to learn that Augustine's father had brought out a scurrilous pamphlet entitled *A Contemporary: the Biography and Intrigues of George Sand.* Brault's "biography" turned out to be a confused and fanciful account of how George Sand had lured Augustine into her household to make her the mistress of her son, Maurice, though he was really in love with Pauline Viardot. Toward the end, it even insinuated that George Sand was a lesbian.

George reacted with her customary energy by mobilizing her influential friends. François Rollinat, whom the voters of the Indre had elected to the Constituent Assembly, was asked to take the matter up with the Minister of Justice. Though he first advised her simply to "ignore this piece of infamy," he finally yielded to her entreaties. Accompanied by his fellow deputy and friend, Alphonse Fleury, he called on the minister, who was talked into having the libelous pamphlet seized.

The actual seizure was delayed, however, by the bloodbath into which Paris was suddenly plunged by the government's decision to disband the National Workshops. Refused further payments unless they agreed to be conscripted into regular army units, the 100,000 workingmen who had been living off government charity began throwing up barricades all over Paris. The clash George Sand had long feared between a complacent bourgeoisie and a starving proletariat could no longer be avoided.

The task of restoring order fell to the new Minister of War, General Eugène Cavaignac, a stout republican whose brother Godefroy had once defied Louis-Philippe's police by founding a secret Society for the Rights of Man. George Sand had had dealings with both of them, she was on friendly terms with their mother, and she had even corresponded for a while with the general, at a time when her nephew, Oscar Cazamajou, was serving with the Zouaves in Algeria. Her friend Pierre-Jules Hetzel, furthermore, was now serving as the secretary general of Cavaignac's Ministry of War. She thus found herself torn between her instinctive sympathy for the impoverished workers of the Paris suburbs and her gratitude for services rendered in the past.

The ensuing carnage, which cost the life of the archbishop of Paris and of close to five thousand insurgents, soldiers, and teen-agers of the Garde Mobile, left her "crushed and appalled, one hundred years old," as George described herself in a letter to Eugénie Duvernet. Auguste Clésinger, the one-time cuirassier who had been boasting how, as a National Guardsman, he would make mincemeat of the rebels, hastily fled from Paris with Solange and their personal maid. But they returned just as quickly when it became clear that Cavaignac and his fellow conservatives had won the day.

"I no longer believe in the existence of a republic which begins by killing its proletarians," George wrote to Charlotte Marliani in mid-July, explaining that for the time being she could not risk returning to Paris, even incognito. She had to remain at Nohant "to instill some respect into a sizable band of imbeciles from La Châtre who threaten at any moment to come out and put my place to the torch. They are neither physically nor morally brave, and when they come out here, I sally forth among them and they doff their hats. But after moving on, they venture to shout: *A bas les communistes!*"

The witch hunt for "suspects" and the wave of mass arrests which marked this tense summer distressed George Sand almost as much as had the street slaughter of late June. So too did the closing down of radical organs of opinion, like Lamennais' *Le Peuple constituant.* In early July Karl Marx's *Neue Rheinische Zeitung* went the Parisians one better in reporting that George Sand was in possession of confidential papers proving that Mikhail Bakunin was in reality a secret agent of the Russian Tsar!

While George was kept busy disclaiming this and other imaginary reports about her "nefarious" activities, a search for scapegoats was being launched in Paris, where a parliamentary committee was appointed to determine the causes and "responsibilities" for the uprising of June 23 and the "events of May 15th." While she could not be blamed for the first, having left Paris some weeks earlier, many were quick to brand the sixteenth *Bulletin de la République* as a "call to insurrection." The charge was a bit fanciful inasmuch as a full month had elapsed between the publication of the *Bulletin* and the storming of the National Assembly, but for those who wished to believe so, it was the incendiary cause of mid-April which had brought about the revolutionary effect of May 15.

To have the "secret" of her authorship publicly betrayed by Ledru-Rollin's assistants at the Ministry of the Interior was bad enough, but it was no less galling to see the man she had so admired not unhappy to have the blame shifted onto her. Ledru-Rollin would not lift a finger to help her, thus proving himself anything but "a French chevalier in this circumstance," and had it not been for Etienne Arago, who took up the cudgels for her in *La Réforme,* George Sand would have been tempted to conclude that politicians are by nature slippery cowards, if not thoroughgoing scoundrels.

Nor were these the last of the many tribulations which the revolutionary upheavals of 1848 were to heap on her harassed head. The turmoil, which had paralyzed commerce and industry, had also played havoc with the arts, emptying theaters and forcing many actors, singers, and musicians to seek a livelihood abroad. The book trade was no less affected. In May, at the height of the uproar, George Sand's new publisher had informed her that there could be no question of bringing out the first volumes of her Memoirs at such an unfavorable moment; he would have to postpone publication, while putting her on a kind of pension, at 1000 francs a month. Given the unsettled circumstances, this was a fair proposal, but it effectively destroyed her fond hope of establishing dowries for her "two daughters."

Momentarily shelving her autobiography, George Sand began another pastoral novel, which she eventually entitled *La Petite Fadette.* This juvenile version of *The Taming of the Shrew,* to which Vladimir Karénine later compared it, was the story of an ungovernable young hellcat who is transformed by the miraculous alchemy of love from a village brat into a sweet, loving, and hardworking young woman. The village brat was quite obviously (though the author may not consciously have realized it) her own daughter, Solange, and the sweet, loving, and hardworking young woman, Augustine — or, to put it more precisely, the kind of young woman George would have liked her own daughter to become, if only Nature had been willing to conform to Jean-Jacques Rousseau's angelic prescriptions.

Getting this pastoral idyll published proved almost as laborious as writing it. George Sand was finally reduced to accepting 2000 francs for the serializing of a novel for which, a few years earlier (or so she fancied), "that tightwad" Buloz would gladly have paid her 5000. But even this paltry sum was welcome in this season of retrenchment. In 1841, when her fortunes had been at a very low ebb, she had borrowed 10,000 francs from a La Châtre merchant who had since died; she had paid interest on the debt for seven years, but the merchant's widow was now insisting on being repaid the full amount immediately. Charles de Bertholdi, just to complicate matters, was now virtually unemployed. His rash participation in several republican manifestations at Tulle, during the early days of the February revolution, had cost him the confidence of conservative parents, who were no longer willing to expose their boarding-school daughters to lessons in drawing from such a radical young "hothead." Once again mobilizing all her friends, in Paris as well as locally, George managed to get the luckless young drawing master appointed tax collector for the township of Ribérac, in the department of the Dordogne. But this ingenious piece of wire-pulling, involving a deposit of more than 11,000 francs, came near to bankrupting her as well as her friends Gabriel Planet and Charles Duvernet.

Far more nerve-racking was the financial plight of Solange. She and her husband had contrived a formal "separation of goods" which was meant to place the Hôtel de Narbonne beyond the grasp of Clésinger's impatient creditors. The maneuver had only partially succeeded, for the town house on the Rue de la Harpe was itself burdened by 50,000 francs' worth of unpaid arrears — which neither the sculptor nor Solange could possibly pay off in the immediate future. They could, however, have limited the damage by paying the accumulating interest (about 5000 francs), which had gone unpaid for a whole year. But as this would have involved some unpleasant belt-tightening, neither of them chose to give the matter further thought.

The irate creditors now demanded the complete and immediate repayment of what was owed them. While Solange casually hied herself from her father-in-law's home at Besançon to Casimir Dudevant's country house at Guillery — as though none of this were her concern — Victor Borie was sent up to Paris to look into the mess. He discovered that Solange and Clésinger had managed to run through 80,000 francs in one year. The money that should have gone to mollifying the creditors of the Hôtel de Narbonne had instead been used to rent a new apartment, finance all sorts of fancy repairs, and build a new coach house. Clésinger had added outrage to injury by brutally insulting their landlady. "Tell her [Solange]," the exasperated Borie exploded, "that if the furniture is now threatened, it's her fault, for she owes her landlady 900 francs and would have done better to pay it rather than make *three trips in a post chaise.*"

The outraged *Pôtu* was wasting his breath, as he must have suspected. There was now no arresting the inevitable dénouement. While Solange, pregnant once again, idled beneath the Gascon sun of Guillery, her Paris furniture was auctioned off. Crippled by debts herself, George Sand could only watch helplessly as the same fate overtook the Hôtel de Narbonne. A desperate, last-minute letter to Pauline Viardot, who had just returned to Paris, suggesting that she and her husband buy the contested property "for a song," was sent too late to avert the disaster. On December 6 the town house which Solange had received by way of dowry was sold for the bargain-basement price of 100,000 francs — roughly half of what it was really worth.

This blow was followed a few days later by a second, which was no less upsetting for George Sand, since it virtually sealed the fate of the republic. As the summer shriveled into autumn, it had become increasingly clear that the struggle for power had resolved itself into a duel between "the bloody saber of Algeria and the rusted sword of the Empire," as she wrote to Charles Poncy. By the first she meant General Cavaignac, who had won his military spurs in North Africa fighting Arab camel men; by the second she referred to Prince Louis Napoleon Bonaparte, who had been triumphantly elected to the Constituent Assembly by no less than five different departments in the by-elections of September.

At the time of this spectacular electoral triumph Napoleon's nephew — he was the son of Louis Bonaparte and of Hortense de Beauharnais — was still living in London as an exile. He was thus personally unknown to the French man in the street, save through the yard-high posters and the thousands of medals and lithographs marked HIM which had been lavishly distributed by his supporters. Unlike Cavaignac, whose hands were stained with proletarian blood, Prince Louis Napoleon was a glorious enigma, invested with the radiant glamor of an imperishable name. He was less the forger of a policy than the creature of a myth, an "imperial fetish" (as George Sand called him, in a letter to Etienne Arago) powerful enough to sweep all before it.

George found it difficult at first to take this new pretender seriously, but she was soon forced to change her mind. Some four years earlier — in 1844 and 1845 — while he was locked up in a prison-fortress near Boulogne for having tried to topple Louis-Philippe through an *opéra bouffe* "invasion," the prince had written several letters to George Sand, letters in which, while claiming to be a democrat of "advanced" social views, he had made it clear he was not a republican "because I believe a republic to be impossible in the presence of a monarchical Europe . . ." The conclusion George Sand had drawn from this short-lived correspondence was that Napoleon's ill-starred nephew was confused in his thinking and anything but bright. Brainless or not, who was there to oppose him in the impending elections to the highest office in the land? Lamartine was now a fading star, the orotund Ledru-Rollin a half-crippled balloon. The socialists were discredited, as well as feared, with many of their leaders behind the bars. There remained only "the disagreeable and hateful Cavaignac," as George Sand called him, that "massacrer of the suburbs" for whom she could feel neither "confidence nor esteem."

Disabused and disappointed, and thus psychologically ripe for something new, dramatic, and unsullied, the French people were now being asked by extraordinarily astute propagandists to vote for a myth, for a "phantom" reincarnation of the great Napoleon. The crowning touch in this campaign of deliberate mystification was a People's Almanac for the year 1849, which appeared in late November. It carried a portrait of the pretender framed by facsimiles of letters he had received from Chateaubriand, Béranger, Louis Blanc, and George Sand. The intention was obvious: to suggest to the public that Prince Louis Napoleon had been endorsed by these eminent gentlemen and ladies of letters.

George Sand lost no time responding to this trick of electoral hocus-pocus. In an open letter which she had published in three Paris papers, she denounced this breach of etiquette. At one time, she explained, she may vaguely have surmised that Louis Napoleon had an exalted destiny before him, but in all her letters to him she had stressed "not only the people's sacred right to work, but also France's sacred right to reject kings." Under a republic, she added, Mr. Louis Bonaparte — she refused to call him "Prince" — "who is by conviction a systematic enemy of the republican form of government, has no right to be a candidate to the presidency. Let him have the frankness to admit he is a pretender, and France will see if it wants to reestablish the monarchy for the benefit of the Bonaparte family."

This ringing challenge was naturally disregarded. In the elections of December 10, just as George Sand had foreseen, the peasants voted en masse for the Bonapartist pretender because (as she put it in a letter to Pauline Viardot) "they believe Napoleon isn't dead and that they are voting for him in voting for his nephew." Many monarchists voted for him out of dislike of the republic. The workers voted for him out of hatred for General Cavaignac. The result was a walkaway triumph, with Louis Napoleon winning close to five and a half million votes, to one and a half million for Cavaignac, 371,000 for Ledru-Rollin, 36,000 for the Jacobin Raspail, and a rock-bottom 18,000 for a totally discredited Lamartine. The result, as George Sand declared in a letter to Hortense Allart, was certain to be "unprecedented confusion." The forty-year-old adventurer would want to stride over all important problems in his seven-league boots. But "after profiting from a moment of stupor and infatuation at the outset, he will have a wretched end," she predicted to Charles Duvernet. "The people are a sovereign child. They have caprices and are not long amused by the same plaything."

All of which was true — save that the plaything, once enthroned, could not be so easily discarded. In fact, George Sand and her countrymen would have to wait for more than twenty years to see this particular adventure meet its wretched end.

Shortly before Christmas of 1848 Hippolyte Chatiron died in his nearby manor house of Montgivray. He had not seen his half sister since Solange's marriage, preferring to live in solitary retirement, or more exactly in a permanent tête-à-tête with the bottle. It was a sad end for a man whose jovial wit and disposition had for years enlivened the dinners at Nohant and even delighted the fastidious Chopin. "It's a suicide," Aurore wrote to Charles Duvernet. "He was fifty years old, he had a magnificent physique, intelligence, and a stout heart. But nothing can resist this passion for wine, and in combatting it for several years I only delayed the inevitable end."

The year 1849, like those immediately following, was almost entirely spent at Nohant — save for two brief visits to Paris in May and December. George continued to work on her autobiographical reminiscences while quietly encouraging Victor Borie and other friends in their progressive inclinations. The year was also marked by several deaths, which aggravated George Sand's feeling of having prematurely aged. The first, in May, was that of her old friend Marie Dorval. The great romantic actress, who had been so feted in the early years of Louis-Philippe's reign, had found it increasingly difficult to maintain her theatrical prestige during the later 1840s. In 1846 she had even been reduced to borrowing money from George to be able to undertake a health-restoring trip to southern France with her grandson, who had become the apple of her aging eye. But the little child had died, leaving Marie so paralyzed by grief that she had had to give up a major role offered to her in a new Balzac play. Her reputation as an actress, already threatened by her fifty years of age and by the revolutionary turmoil of 1848, which had emptied the theaters for weeks on end, never recovered from this blow. Rebuffed by the haughty manager of the Comédie Française (where her emotional style of acting had never been appreciated), she had finally accepted an engagement in Normandy, thanks to the intercession of the actor René Luguet, who had been her lover before marrying her daughter. She had fallen ill in the stagecoach which had brought her from Paris to Caen, where a doctor, called in for consultation, had diagnosed her malady as due to "pernicious fever" and an ulcerated liver. Her son-in-law had managed to get her back to Paris, in a stagecoach which had tipped over during a frightful storm, but several days later she had died — still smiling bravely. "Oh, that smile, it blazes still before my eyes," René Luguet wrote in a long letter to George Sand. "Adorable Marie! You were her last poet. I read *La Petite Fadette* at her bedside. Then we talked at length of all those lovely books whose touching scenes she related while crying. Then she spoke to me of you, of your heart. Ah, Madame Sand, how you loved Marie!"

No less painful was the news she received five months later of Frédéric Chopin's death. To escape the turmoil that had upset the music lessons which were his main source of income, he had left in April of 1848 for England. His seven months there had been disastrous for his health. In London he had met Pauline Viardot, and they had even appeared together in a musical matinee. But the diva's diplomatic efforts to patch up the breach between the hypersensitive composer and George Sand proved totally vain. "As I have just written, she particularly sang my mazurkas," Chopin wrote to his friend Grzymala in early July. "Tell de Rozières that Madame V[iardot] was very kind to me, for the news will get back here. Madame S[and], I know, wrote to Madame V[iardot], asking for news of me with much solicitude!!! How well she must play the role of a mother full of equity."

Under the nefarious influence of Solange and Marie de Rozières — the same "old frump" (as he had once called her) whose every word he now accepted as gospel truth — Chopin was ready to believe the worst of his former mistress and protector. "It's an infamy on the part of the father, but it's the truth," he reported to his family in Warsaw after being told of the libelous pamphlet which Augustine Brault's father had just published. It was Maurice, above all, who was responsible for what had happened, Chopin continued. It was he who had brought Augustine into the household, had made her his mistress, insisted that she be placed on the same footing of equality as Solange, that she be better dressed and better treated. Solange, however, had soon guessed the truth and thus become an embarrassment for everyone. Victor Borie, who was already George Sand's lover, needed Augustine to divert attention from his own amorous activities, while Maurice needed Borie to make it seem that the young Victor rather than himself was making advances to Augustine. "The mother [George Sand] found her daughter a nuisance because the latter had unfortunately guessed everything — whence lies, malaise, shame, and the rest."

The venom exhaled in this and other letters makes painful reading — particularly when compared to the quite different tone of voice employed by George Sand when asking for news of the composer. "Did you see Chopin in London, and can you give me news of him?" she wrote to Pauline Viardot in early December of 1848. "I keep asking people, and nobody gives me any news" — which was hardly surprising, since a very sick Chopin had only returned to Paris on November 23. "I still love him as my son, even though he was most ungrateful toward his mother, but I must get used to not being made happy by my children. There remain Maurice, you, and Augustine."

"You ask me for news of Chopin," Pauline Viardot replied to this and a second letter which repeated the same request. "His health is slowly declining, with fairly good days when he can go out in his carriage and others during which he coughs blood and suffers spells of coughing which choke him. He no longer goes out at night. He can still give a few lessons, and on his good days he can be gay . . . But it has been a long time since I last saw him . . . He always speaks of you with the highest respect, and I persist in affirming that he *never* speaks of you *otherwise*."

The good Pauline was indulging in wishful thinking. For the months passed without Chopin's showing the slightest trace of regret at having sided with Solange against her mother. George, being almost continuously at Nohant, was in any case ill placed to see him. In July of 1849 she received a letter from a Madame Grille de Beuzelin, who had befriended Solange, and who wondered if there might not be some way of repairing the regretable breach. George Sand, though touched by this overture, was forced to admit that she had little hope of reconciliation. She had had to choose between Chopin and her son, Maurice, and she had chosen her son. "As for Chopin, I have maintained on his score the silence of the tomb, and except to ask for news of him, I don't think I have uttered his name for the past year. Had he asked me to call on him during my brief sojourns in Paris, I would have gone; had he written or had someone write an affectionate note, I would have answered. But does he now really want a word of friendship, pardon or interest from me?" Her conclusion being that he didn't and that "his affection has long been dead."

When news reached her in early September that Chopin's sister Ludwika had come to Paris to see him, George wrote her a friendly letter saying: "Some write me that he is far more ill than usual, others that he is merely weak and crotchety, as I have always known him. Write me a note, I venture to ask you, for one can be misunderstood and abandoned by one's children without ceasing to love them . . ." Though her intention was good, this second sentence, with its strong maternal overtones, was unfortunately phrased, and as Georges Lubin has suggested, George Sand would probably have made a better impression on the kind Ludwika if she had written at greater length to explain what had happened. Her letter, in any case, remained unanswered.

On October 18 Charlotte Marliani wrote from Paris to say that Chopin had died the day before. The news had been brought to her at nine-thirty in the evening by Solange: a Solange so physically transformed that at first she had not recognized her. "She took my hand and asked me to give her your address in Paris, assuring me that she had met you 5 or 6 days before, alone, on foot, and that a daughter always recognizes her mother. I thought her mad, and asked her in what street she had met you. She answered, a bit embarrassed: '*On the quays,* and others besides me also met her.' Anyway, my dear, she said she wanted to go herself and tell you about Chopin's death, so that you should not learn of it from the newspapers. I told her that I had had the same thought and that I had written to you at Nohant, from which I was convinced you hadn't budged! She stayed 40 minutes. I think her husband was waiting at my door with a carriage . . . She told me that she had watched over Chopin and had closed his eyes. She claims that he asked to have an autopsy done on him for the utility of science. His heart will be carried to Warsaw. His sister is in despair . . . Solange seemed to me strangely calm. No feeling about Chopin despite her fine phrases. She complains of having been spoiled, without having been loved by you. 'It wasn't a horse or dresses I needed, it was affection, which I always lacked.' 'Do you have any yourself?' I asked her. She replied: 'I was capable of having some.' "

George Sand's reply has unfortunately not come down to us; it was destroyed one year later, after Charlotte Marliani's death, when this and a number of other priceless letters were burned at the insistence of an overly zealous notary. But we know from several other letters that have survived that George was so upset that she was unable to work for days. "I have lost my good health, I am ill," she wrote to Pierre-Jules Hetzel in early November. "This death has deeply affected me."

Any remorse Solange may have felt about her failure to keep her mother properly informed of Chopin's declining health was brief at best. The damage in any case was done, and Chopin died, as he had lived for the past two years, fatally enmeshed in the web of lies Solange had woven around him. A day or two before the impressive funeral service which was celebrated at the Madeleine, Charlotte Marliani ran into Princess Anna Czartoryska — that "saint," as George Sand liked to call her, for the solicitude she displayed toward her fellow Polish exiles. The princess, who was as credulous as she was charitable, tried to persuade Charlotte Marliani that Solange's hatred of her mother stemmed from a letter George was said to have sent to Clésinger and in which she had written: "Your wife is not legitimate, she is not Mr. Dudevant's daughter." Since George Sand could not conceivably have written such a letter, this was one more revealing symptom of Solange's warped psychology. The realization that she was not Casimir's child — dinned into her for years by his drunken outbursts ("You harlot's daughter, you!" etc.) — was one more grievance she held against her mother, and incidentally against

Maurice, who, as her mother's first-born child, had "unfairly" monopolized the maternal affection she would have liked to see exclusively concentrated on herself.

Chopin's disappearance from the scene inevitably affected the summers at Nohant. Delacroix, who had been as much appalled by Solange's hasty marriage as by *Lucrezia Floriani,* politely refused to be lured back to Nohant, even for a short visit. Though George Sand missed his thoughtful company, she was now free to invite other friends, the mere suspicion of whose presence would have been enough to arouse Chopin's sullen jealousy. Emmanuel Arago, who had returned to Paris after briefly serving as the Second Republic's ambassador to Berlin, was as welcome as ever, but so too was Pierre Bocage, who came down to Nohant for several weeks of this same year 1849. The handsome actor with whom George had had a brief fling twelve years before had recently been named director of the Odéon theater and was thus ideally placed to promote her dramatic productions. Unlike Buloz, who had failed so egregiously with *Cosima,* Bocage was a seasoned professional who could give her precious advice. With his help and guidance the pastoral idyll *François le Champi* was turned into a play and successfully staged at the Odéon in mid-November. Nobody was more delighted with the outcome than Emmanuel Arago, who frequently vacated his National Assembly seat to watch the rehearsals. Right up to the eve of the première he feared that the blasé Paris public might find the play too much like "rose water" for its cynical taste. It took a triumphal première to dispel his apprehensions. "A great, a huge success!" he wrote in an ecstatic letter to the author, who had remained at Nohand. "I'm more pleased, happier, and I might add, prouder than I can say."

This unexpected acclaim was all that was needed to push George Sand in this new direction, and there was hardly a theatrical season over the next half-dozen years which did not see a play of hers staged by some Paris theater. It also developed her interest in the amateur theater of Nohant, which became a kind of proving ground for the plays ultimately destined for the Paris stage.

George's sentimental life also underwent a change at about this time. Victor Borie, whom she had installed in Chopin's bedroom and who was her inseparable companion for most of 1849, losing gracefully at billiards and dominoes, accompanying her on visits to sick neighbors, and taking care of her when she fell ill, gradually fell out of favor when she discovered just how casual he was with her money. She had hoped he would strike out on his own by becoming a deputy from the department of the Corrèze, but he preferred to stay on at Nohant as her general factotum. In a belated effort to redeem himself in her eyes, he decided in late October to launch a new weekly called *Le Travailleur de l'Indre.* The first number, considered far too favorable to the working class, was seized by the authorities, and shortly before Christmas its editor was condemned to a year in prison and a 2000 franc fine.

Borie, who had taken refuge in Paris, did not have the courage to appeal this verdict. Instead, he fled to Brussels, where he found asylum with the painter Luigi Calamatta. This gave George Sand a ready-made excuse for breaking with him, though she was hardly happy about it. "What one regrets," she wrote to the publisher Pierre-Jules Hetzel, with whom Borie had often had to deal, "is not always the person who leaves, it's the faith one had in him, it's the habit one has contracted of esteeming him."

George Sand lost little time replacing her disappointing *Pôtu* with another resident lover. The new favorite was Hermann Müller-Strübing, a thirty-seven-year-old German scholar and musician. A radical who had had to flee Germany (where he had already spent seven years in a fortress prison) after the abortive uprisings of 1848, he had sought refuge in Paris and there renewed his acquaintance with Pauline Viardot, to whom he had been introduced by the Russian writer Turgenev during her triumphal opera season in Berlin in 1845. George Sand met Müller-Strübing during the brief trip she made to Paris in May of 1849, when she stayed with Pauline. The impression she made on the radical expatriate may be judged from the letter she wrote to Pauline Viardot shortly after her return to Nohant. "You told me that Dr. Müller was *in love* with me. I take that as I should, and I like him in the same manner, which is to say that he is altogether sympathetic to me, and that if he doesn't go to Germany and wants to come to see me at Nohant, I will receive him like a brother of yours and mine."

Six months later, during a second and longer trip to Paris in December, George reiterated the invitation, which was gratefully accepted. They traveled back to Nohant shortly before Christmas, accompanied by Alexandre Manceau, an already well-known engraver whom Maurice had befriended in Delacroix's studio. It was doubtless to forget Borie that she now started an affair with Müller-Strübing. "I am very happy to have had the courage, very happy with myself and the *other one,*" she wrote on New Year's Day of 1850 to Pierre-Jules Hetzel, who had now become what Sainte-Beuve had once been — a trusted adviser and confidant. "We embarked bravely and sincerely. God will do the rest. It's the first time I have associated myself with a robust man in the moral and physical sense. Hitherto I have, as it were, sought out weakness through a maternal instinct which merely turned me into a spoiler of children, a mother whose weakness was too well known. One is always dominated by weak beings. Perhaps I shall find equality with a strong heart. I feel myself calm despite the uncertainty of the future. I haven't felt the rapture or the terrors which are associated with all beginnings. Yet what I am doing is highly imprudent." She had known Borie for three years before going to bed with him, whereas she didn't know Müller-Strübing at all. But after all, what did it matter? "I don't believe in happiness, I'm not looking for it. I don't wish to live and I cannot live without loving. That is all I know."

The charm of novelty, however, was not long in wearing off this new adventure. Much as she valued Müller-Strübing's musical ability — which enabled him to replace her at the piano for the musical pantomimes that enlivened their evenings — she found this "real bar of gold" (as Pauline Viardot had described him) decidedly ponderous. He spoke French with a thick Teutonic accent and was a bit slow-witted. Though he meant well and strove hard to please, he was lacking in the little gallantries that meant so much to her.

A month had hardly passed when she was writing again to Hetzel to say that her German strong man was an excellent friend and a brother, but nothing more. As she explained more specifically in late March: "I have a serious esteem for him . . . but the mysterious entente of minds that resemble each other is just not there." There was a tense moment when she made it clear to her houseguest that their affair was over. The good Doctor first wanted to leave Nohant, but he was finally talked out of it by George, who said that it would be ridiculous for him to leave in a huff, when she would willingly have him stay on as a friend. "We are two friends, two men," she explained. "We are useful to each other, we esteem each other, we shouldn't part like this . . . ," etc.

Swallowing his pride, the scholar-musician stayed on and was soon hard at work translating the first volume of George Sand's *The Story of My Life* into German. He was asked by friends and neighbors — at La Châtre and elsewhere — to tutor their children in German and Greek, and in August he moved to the nearby Château du Coudray as a full-time tutor for Charles Duvernet's children.

To have lodged an ex-lover under her roof for months while she was taking on another was, admittedly, no mean feat of diplomacy. For by early April of 1850 it was clear that her new favorite was Maurice's friend Alexandre Manceau — the same Manceau who had traveled down with her from Paris with Müller-Strübing. Tall, thin, and frail where his predecessor had been plump and muscular, Manceau was a not unhandsome man of thirty-three with wistful gray eyes and a fine aquiline nose. Toward the mistress of Nohant he was invariably deferent, always calling her "Madame," but he soon made it clear that he had a mind of his own. For he had not been at Nohant two weeks before he was throwing the household into an uproar by insisting on changes in the amateur theatricals.

The *Grand Théâtre,* as it was pompously called — to distinguish it from the small portable theater of *petits acteurs* (or puppets) — had been temporarily established in the billiard room, at the eastern end of the ground floor. "Manceau came, saw, and criticized," George reported to Emmanuel Arago. The backstage area was declared to be too narrow, the backdrops badly hung, the changes of scenery too slow and unwieldy. The casual *laisser-aller* which had hitherto marked the theatrical evenings at Nohant — with the various participants improvising or deliberately altering their half-learned lines — now gave way to a new professionalism under the driving impulse of this deceptively soft-spoken newcomer, who revealed himself to be an amateur stage manager of considerable ability.

So indispensable did the new actor and stage manager rapidly become that a few weeks later, when business affairs called him back to Paris, George Sand wrote again to Augustine to report that the rehearsals had been interrupted by "the absence of Manceau, who won't be back for another couple of days. By that time I shall have redone the play I want to give to the Odéon, and we'll try it out as we tried out the first draft. As you see, this family theater is becoming a serious business. Maurice has been complaining that nothing can match the free improvisation of the *early days.* I don't want to eliminate it entirely from our theater; only I feel that since we have some excellent actors, we might as well try out my plays, since this is excellent training for me."

That Maurice was not particularly happy over this new development is certain. A cartoon he drew at about this time shows a determined Manceau leaning forward with his knuckles on the tabletop while he lectures the assembled company (nineteen in all, including five Duvernets and four Fleurys): "Those who miss rehearsals will be fined." But since he could not openly condemn his mother's dramatic experiments, which had become an important source of income, Maurice resigned himself to this new turn of events.

By mid-April George Sand and Manceau were lovers. To judge from a letter written shortly afterward to Pierre-Jules Hetzel, more than a little persuasion was needed to get the thirty-two-year-old engraver to climb into bed with the forty-five-year-old authoress. But the initial inhibitions overcome, neither regretted it. "Yes, I love him!" George wrote in an almost ecstatic letter to Hetzel. "He has never studied, he has always been an apprentice, because he can and wants to earn his livelihood. He has an extraordinarily artistic mind . . . He knows nothing but he guesses everything; and forever questioning, he proves to me how much his mind works internally . . ."

Here, in other words, was one more son she could educate and fashion into a more enlightened, nobler type of being. One who had no base "ambition of money or renown . . . He wants to grow in the eyes of God and of himself and of the few he loves . . . For" — and this was the great revelation which had changed everything — "he loves, he loves, you see, as I have never seen anybody love" — which for George Sand was saying a lot. "All the faults he has with others disappear in a *tête-à-tête.* There he is at once a caressing cat and a faithful dog; and all his calculations and intrigues are intended to obtain the approval of the person he loves. Very libertine in the past, he is chaste in real love, as chaste and ardent as the senses, the heart, and the mind can dream of being in love" — which again was saying a lot. Indeed, the more she thought of him, the more wonderful Manceau seemed. As sure-footed as he was skilled with his hands, he never broke anything — unlike "the 69 hundredths of men who mistake their noses for their feet, and whether from absent-mindedness, laziness or natural clumsiness, never accomplish what they want to do at the first stroke . . . He never gets on my nerves! He is punctual, he has a watch and he looks at it. I have never *waited* a minute for him at a rendezvous, yet he makes others wait out of sheer stubbornness. When on occasion he has been wrong in his dealings with me, I have never had to *wait* a minute for the glance and the word which set everything right" — unlike Chopin who nursed his grievances and grudges with impenitent intensity.

But all this, important though it was, was secondary compared to Manceau's most surprising talent: a wondrous capacity for nursing others, beginning with herself. So wondrous as to be positively feminine, the capacity of a "woman who is skilled, active and ingenious. When I'm sick, I'm cured by the mere sight of him preparing my pillow and bringing me my slippers. I who have never asked or accepted to be cared for, need his care, as though it were in my nature to be pampered." She who had spent so much of her time nursing others now surrendered to this new sensation with voluptuous abandon. The "featherless bird I have taken under my wing" (as she once described him) thus became her indispensable companion, to whom bit by bit she entrusted all of her personal affairs — from negotiations with publishers and theater directors to the administration of her finances and the running of Nohant.

In early August of 1850 Charlotte Marliani died, followed two weeks later by Balzac. The Square d'Orléans, which George had never really liked — her apartment being too dark and cramped to suit her — was now more than ever a memory, and the loss of these two further links with the capital fortified her resolution to reside as much as possible in the country. "I live at Nohant, often very ill in the depths of my soul, but resigned and gay on the surface, so as not to sadden those I love," as she put it in a letter to an old acquaintance. But she could not help regretting the intellectual excitement of the past, and though she would rather have died than admit it, she missed the melancholy enchantment of Chopin's music. Her own keyboard playing, on the fine piano Pauline Viardot had persuaded Camille Pleyel to send to her (at less than cost price) left much to be desired, and as she wrote to her foster daughter: "I am obliged to play music for myself; it's not at all gay when one can render nothing, either with one's throat or fingers, of what one sees written, feels and understands."

The installation of a furnace and a system of hot-air conduits took the curse off the long winters, and she might well have forgone the pleasure of ever returning to Paris but for the occasional need to visit publishers and to see how well her plays were doing. Thanks to her friend Pierre Bocage, who both stage-managed and acted the lead role in her next play, *Claudie* was a great success in the early months of 1851. It was followed in November by *Le Mariage de Victorine,* which got off to a brilliant start only to come a cropper one week later — for reasons which had nothing to do with the ability of author or actors.

George Sand, who had journeyed up with Manceau for the dress rehearsals and première, was still in Paris when Prince Louis Napoleon, not content to remain the ceremonial President of the Second French Republic, decided to stage a long-awaited coup d'état. On December 1 she spent the evening at the circus with Manceau and Solange, now the mother of a two-and-a-half-year-old daughter. As they escorted Solange home, they were trotted down the Faubourg Saint-Honoré past the Elysée Palace. "That's odd," Solange remarked as their carriage rolled by the entrance. "I thought there was going to be a gala ball tonight. For when I drove past at five o'clock to have dinner with you, I saw them laying out the carpets on the entrance steps. Is it this week that he's to be proclaimed emperor?"

The palace gate was closed, guarded by a single sentry. "There was no sign of illumination," as George later noted in the special diary she had begun keeping. "Not a carriage in the street. A deep silence, the dull glow of the gas lamps on the rough, shining cobble stones. It was one o'clock in the morning. Manceau and I came back via the Avenue Marbeuf and passed behind the garden of the Elysée. The same silence, the same obscurity, the same solitude. 'It's not for tomorrow,' I said to him with a laugh, and as I was tired, I slept soundly all night."

The next morning, when she woke up at ten o'clock, Manceau told her that the Assembly had been dissolved and the republican generals Cavaignac and Lamoricière imprisoned in the fortress-castle of Vincennes. The news made no impression on her whatsoever. The Second French Republic had long since ceased to be the republic of her dreams. Emmanuel Arago's wife, Lovely, whom she went to see after breakfast, was worried, but the people strolling up and down the boulevards seemed strangely unmoved, like George herself. Not until she reached the Gymnase theater, where *Le Mariage de Victorine* was playing, did she realize the full gravity of what had happened. The lead actress was in tears and there were not three hundred persons in the audience.

She spent the rest of the evening by the fireplace reading Edgar Quinet's *Révolutions d'Italie* with her eyes, while her ears kept listening for the tramp of marching feet, the clop-clop of horses' hoofs or gunfire. But there was not a sound outside. The Paris workers had learned their lesson in 1848 and were not going to build barricades or risk their lives for a republic that had betrayed them.

Two days later George Sand returned to Nohant, as a wave of repression began to sweep the country. In 1804 Napoleon I had proclaimed the Empire in an effort to reconcile republicans and monarchists and to establish a new aristocracy of merit. In 1852 his nephew Louis Napoleon, or more exactly the opportunists who had rallied to his cause, used the Empire as an excuse for crushing all republican opposition. Wholesale arrests, reminiscent of the Bourbon White Terror of 1815, were instituted. Victor Borie, Hermann-Müller-Strübing, Pierre-Jules Hetzel, Louis Blanc, Pierre Leroux, Luigi Calamatta, and Ledru-Rollin had already taken refuge in England or Belgium, but the many militant republicans who had remained in France now found themselves threatened with imprisonment and deportation to North Africa and the West Indies. The province of Berry was no more spared than any other. Jules Néraud's son-in-law, Ernest Périgois, was arrested, as was Alexandre Lambert, who had succeeded Victor Borie as the editor of *L'Eclaireur de l'Indre*. Also apprehended by the police was the young La Châtre lawyer Emile Aucante, along with his friend Luc Desages, a nephew of Alexis Duteil's who had married one of Pierre Leroux's daughters — a crime serious enough to warrant him a sentence to ten years of deportation. To escape a similar fate, Alphonse Fleury went into hiding. Even George Sand, it was soon being rumored, was not safe and likely to be banished at any moment.

Increasingly alarmed by this wholesale repression, George Sand finally decided to take the bull by the horns and to write to the President of the Republic — a republic which was now an autocracy in everything but name. She had not forgotten that the young Louis Napoleon had once professed to be a liberal of advanced social views whose pamphlet, *On the Extinction of Pauperism* — written during his imprisonment in the fortress of Ham — had so impressed Louis Blanc that he had made a special journey to the Channel coast to meet him. He had shamelessly exploited their correspondence during the presidential election campaign of November 1848, but though George Sand had taken umbrage at this breach of etiquette, the Prince-President could not honestly gainsay his earlier admiration for the author of *Mauprat* and *Consuelo*.

In appealing directly to the new ruler of France, George Sand also benefited from exceptionally favorable connections. Her cousin René de Villeneuve's wife, Apolline, had served as lady-in-waiting to Queen Hortense and even held the infant Louis Napoleon in her arms for the baptismal celebration. Armed with a *laissez-passer* issued by the Paris prefect of police, George Sand reached the capital on January 25, 1852, and was received by Louis Napoleon five days later. The former prisoner of Ham had not forgotten their bygone correspondence nor lost his admiration for George Sand. Taking her two small hands into his own, he listened sympathetically and even with a considerable show of emotion to her plea for a general amnesty and for a cessation of the wave of arbitrary arrests which had swept over the department of the Indre, arrests which were in many cases the simple settling of old scores. The prince, as Aurore reported to her cousin René de Villeneuve, "begged me to make any request I liked on behalf of my friends who had been the victims of these injustices, and he displayed the greatest esteem for my character, even though I told him that I was as much a republican as when he had known me and that I would never change."

Louis Napoleon granted her a second interview in early February, and for weeks thereafter she kept pounding on different ministerial doors to make sure that the Prince-President's expressions of clemency were translated into practical effect. Paris thus claimed her for several months, finally enabling her worshipful admirer Elizabeth Barrett to catch up with her. "I won't die, if I can help it, without seeing George Sand," the English poetess had fretfully insisted to her future husband, Robert Browning, after having tried but failed in early December to see the "strange, wild, wonderful woman" who had inspired her two sonnets — "A Desire," "A Recognition." With the help of a letter of introduction from Mazzini, she and Robert Browning were now invited to call on George Sand at Maurice's apartment on the Rue Racine. Overcome with emotion in the presence of her feminine idol, Elizabeth Barrett wanted to bend down and kiss her hand, but she was gently rebuked — "*Non, je ne veux pas*" — and, to her surprise, welcomed with a most un-British kiss on the lips. "She is somewhat large for her height — not tall — and was dressed with great nicety in a sort of gray serge gown and jacket, made after the ruling fashion just now, and fastened up to the throat, plain linen collarette and sleeves," the contented poetess reported shortly afterward to a friend. "Her hair was uncovered, divided on the forehead in black, glossy bandeaux, and twisted up behind. The eyes and brow are noble, and the nose is of a somewhat Jewish character; the chin a little recedes, and the mouth is not good, though mobile, flashing out a sudden smile with its white projecting teeth. There is no sweetness in the face, but great moral as well as intellectual capacities — only it never *could* have been a beautiful face, which a good deal surprised me . . . Her complexion is of a deep olive. I observed that her hands were small and well-shaped. We sat with her perhaps three quarters of an hour or more — in which time she gave advice and various directions to two or three young men who were there, showing her confidence in us by the freest use of names and allusions to facts. She seemed to be, in fact, *the man* in that company, and the profound respect with which she was listened to a good deal impressed us . . . Her voice is low and rapid, without emphasis or variety of modulation. Except one brilliant smile, she was grave — indeed, she was speaking of grave matters, and many of her friends are in adversity. But you could not help seeing (both Robert and I saw it) that in all she said, even in her kindness and pity, there was an under-current of scorn. A scorn of pleasing she evidently had; there never could have been a colour of coquetry in that woman. Her very freedom from affectation and consciousness had a touch of disdain. But I liked her. I did not love her, but I felt the burning soul through all that quietness, and was not disappointed in George Sand."

The Brownings were invited to call again the following Sunday, and did so. They even made a third call in March. In all, Robert Browning managed to see George Sand half a dozen times, once offering her his arm during a chance encounter in the Tuileries Gardens. "She was not on that occasion looking as well as usual," Elizabeth Barrett wrote a little later to another friend, "being very much 'endimanchée' in terrestrial lavenders and supercelestial blues — not, in fact, dressed with the remarkable taste which he has seen in her at other times. Her usual costume is both pretty and quiet, and the fashionable waistcoat and jacket (which are a spectacle in all the 'Ladies' Companions' of the day) make the only approach to masculine *wearings* to be observed in her. She has great nicety and refinement in her personal ways, I think, and the cigarette is really a feminine weapon if properly understood. Ah, but I didn't see her smoke. I was unfortunate. I could only go with Robert three times to her house, and once she was out. He was really very good and kind to let me go at all, after he found the sort of society rampant about her. He didn't like it extremely, but being the prince of husbands, he was lenient to my desires and yielded the point. She seems to live in the abomination of desolation, as far as regards society — crowds of ill-bred men who adore her *à genoux bas,* betwixt a puff of smoke and an ejection of saliva. Society of the ragged Red diluted with the lower theatrical. She herself so different, so apart, so alone in her melancholy disdain! I was deeply interested in that poor woman, I felt a profound compassion for her. I did not mind much the Greek in Greek costume who tutoyéd her, and kissed her, I believe, so Robert said: or the other vulgar man of the theatre who went down on his knees and called her 'sublime.' 'Caprice d'amitié,' said she, with her quiet, gentle scorn. A noble woman under the mud, be certain. *I* would kneel down to her, too, if she would leave it all, throw it off, and be herself as God made her. But she would not care for my kneeling . . ."

If George Sand struck her visitors as being a trifle aloof and distant, it was probably because she had never had much love for the English, far too smug and conservative for her own radical tastes. Besides, she had frankly not much cared for the poem in which Elizabeth Barrett, thinking to honor her, had called her a "large-brained woman and large-hearted man . . . whose soul, amid the lions of thy tumultuous senses, moans defiance, and answers roar for roar, as spirits can . . . ," feeling that this was really overdoing it — both as regards her roaring senses and her lion tamer's soul. Nor was the moment particularly conducive to the leisurely discussion of poetry when her thoughts were so much focused on the new calamities which had befallen her country.

Not until April could George Sand leave Paris. Thanks to her tireless efforts Emile Aucante and Ernest Périgois were released from prison, and from May 1852 on Aucante was housed at Nohant to preserve him from further molestation. The order for Fleury's arrest was finally rescinded, but only after the all too conspicuous Alphonse had accepted money and a passport (obtained by his friend George) and hied his towering bulk to Belgium. The most difficult to rescue was Pierre Leroux's son-in-law, Luc Desages. Unable to obtain the annulment of his deportation order, she managed at least to have the prisoner transferred from North Africa to Corsica. This is not to mention her countless intercessions on behalf of others both known and unknown to herself, who thus had their sentences commuted — from death to deportation and from forcible deportation in the colonies to exile in a foreign country. Marc Dufraisse, the radical republican who had served briefly in 1848 as prefect of the Indre, was allowed to leave for Brussels, from where he wrote to say that she was *Notre-Dame de Bon Secours* — Our Lady of Good Succor. Arnold, an outspoken communist, called her "the saint of Berry" in a letter written from London. And for the families of those she could not get released she tirelessly sought to raise money.

Her readiness to intercede for the condemned cost her not only time but trouble. The Bonapartist press played up her visits to the Elysée Palace and to high administrative officials, as though they had won a convert. Many rock-ribbed republicans who did not know her personally concluded from this that George Sand had sold out to the new regime. Some of them never forgave her, describing her savagely in articles and letters as a sycophant who had taken to haunting the antechambers of the presidential palace "cap in hand," when in fact she had only visited the Elysée Palace twice.

Long before Louis-Napoleon made himself Emperor of the French, George Sand had reached the melancholy conclusion that there was little more that she could do to make this regime change its autocratic ways, and after the proclamation of the Empire, in December of 1852, she refused to have anything more to do with politics and politicians.

PART VIII

From Empire to Republic

35. Indian Summer

More than ever George Sand now found herself thrown back on the resources of Nohant. These were considerable, given the household's interest in dramatics. Maurice's earliest experiments with marionettes were now a quaint memory, and even the portable Guignol frame which for several years had been used for these drawing room performances, was eventually discarded in favor of a fixed Punch and Judy stage. This was mounted on one side of what had hitherto been a kind of stage room for furniture, next to the former billiard room. The latter, after the removal of the billiard table and the raising of the floor, now became a stage thanks to the piercing of a proscenium arch in the intervening wall. On *Grand Théâtre* evenings the little puppet stage was hidden behind a screen and the remaining space filled with chairs facing toward the proscenium arch to form a tiny auditorium capable of accommodating as many as sixty spectators at one time. The chairs had only to be turned and the oil lamps and their reflectors redirected for the *petit théâtre* evenings reserved for marionette shows which, as the months and then the years went by, grew steadily more sophisticated, complex, and ingenious.

Oswald the Scotsman, The String-Bean Inn, Robert the Cursed, The Black Boars, The Dark Daughters of Ferrari, The Bald-Headed Ghost, The Blades of Toledo, The Hermit of the Rising Tide, A Tempest in a Heart of Bronze, The Recalcitrant Corpse — such are a few of the scores of puppet plays which Maurice and his friends, aided and encouraged by his theater-loving mother, dreamed up over the next few years. "The comic subjects," as she was later to write, "were often inspired by spur-of-the-moment impressions — some ridiculous adventure in the world of politics or art, an article in the local press, some amusing or singular tale, the visit of some absurd individual, an intruder who was caricatured without his realizing it . . ." Such, indeed, was Maurice's gift for improvisation — if we are to take his doting mother's word for it — that these new puppet plays could sometimes be readied in a matter of hours, with a minimum of necessary costume and scenic changes.

The "dramas" thus conceived inevitably demanded new puppet figures, whose expressive faces were carved out of linden wood and ingeniously painted by Maurice and Eugène Lambert. The costumes, covering the puppets' wooden limbs and covering the operator's hands, were all of them hand sewn at Nohant — by George Sand and anyone she could conscript for the task during the long evenings in the drawing room when one of the menfolk read aloud while the ladies stitched. She herself was particularly proud of a "green monster" she thus put together to "devour" the luckless Piero: the yawning jaws were made from two red-lined slippers and the scaly body from a piece of blue-satin sleeve which looked suitably green in the yellow light of the reflectors.

Décors and props were subject to ceaseless embellishment. Using horizontal sticks fitted out with pegs, Maurice was eventually able to simulate "crowd scenes" with as many as thirty figures on stage at the same time, each of which could deftly be animated with strings when speaking. Other strings, attached to colored lenses moving up and down in front of oil-lamp reflectors, permitted subtle lighting changes from garish red to wintry blue. Even more ingenious were the slowly rotating backdrops which Maurice was compelled to fashion to satisfy the ever more exacting connoisseurs, who complained because the sun was always at the meridian and the permanently stuck moon in the same corner of the firmament.

Nohant, in the absence of Solange and Augustine, was more than ever a masculine household, officially presided over by Maurice, who now slept downstairs in what had once been Madame Dupin de Francueil's bedroom. Manceau, like Chopin and Borie before him, had an upstairs bedroom, near George's, as well as a kind of studio, where he would work on his engravings. Emile Aucante was a permanent boarder until 1857, when he left for Paris to become an insurance broker and publisher. More readily available than François Rollinat, who lived at Châteauroux, and Alexis Duteil, who died of drink in 1852, he became his protectress' chief legal adviser, being paid for his services in negotiating new literary contracts. Eugène Lambert, whose predilection for still-life paintings of fowls and other wildlife had earned him the nickname "Cocoton" (derived from *cocotte,* the French word for a small hen), was often present for weeks at a time. But notwithstanding the remonstrances of his second "mother" — he had lost his first at a tender age — he was increasingly drawn to Paris by his professional obligations as a painter. As for Victor Borie, he had finally decided to follow his ex-mistress' advice, after a few poverty-stricken months in Brussels; returning to France, he gave himself up to the police and spent some months in prison. Released in the autumn of 1852, George's former lover was welcomed back to Nohant as a friend.

Fond as she was of her young "brood," not one of them gave George Sand as much unexpected joy as her little granddaughter, Jeanne-Gabrielle Clésinger, whom Solange had brought into the world at Casimir Dudevant's country house at Guillery in May of 1849. In January of 1851 Solange visited Nohant with her twenty-one-month-old daughter, whom George found "very pretty" but difficult to manage. "Sol[ange] came with the resolution of being amiable," as her mother wrote to Augustine de Bertholdi, "and she was most adroit in being amiable, like a society lady who is empty-hearted. That's all I can say about it, for the real motive of the visit and Solange's underlying intentions are things nobody can ever fathom. She talks of coming to spend a few summer months in the neighborhood, and has been casting around for a house to rent, but she won't find one, for the simple reason that there aren't any. I don't know if this is a way of getting herself invited to stay here. I told her frankly that I did not wish to receive her husband, nor her friends, nor her horses, nor her dogs, that I would only receive her and her daughter, and with a certain wariness at that, being on my guard against possible storms; to which she replied that she had had no intention of staying with me, inasmuch as she maintained a scale of living which my house could not offer. She says her husband earns a lot of money. I believe it. But it doesn't mean that the debts are paid. She still defends him stoutly, saying he has a bad character but a good heart. So much the better if she's happy . . ."

Having developed a taste for high society and the luxuries of the capital, Solange, who was as much a city girl as her mother was a country-lover, found the rustic calm of Nohant a bore and made little effort to conceal her feelings. Self-centered and indulgent as ever, she liked to contrast the "wealth" her mother had known in her youth to the "wretchedness" of her own condition, begrudging her mother's failure to leave her the handsome dowry she regarded as her due. Lacking the wherewithal to set herself up in style in some country mansion where she could show her mother what it was to "live" — with servants, hunt balls, and the rest — she fell back for a few months on her official father, Casimir Dudevant, who, now that he was living in sin with his housekeeper (who was to bear him a child), seems to have found Solange and her daughter increasingly irksome charges. Clésinger, taking advantage of his wife's absence, reverted to his old licentious ways. This was all the encouragement Solange needed, on her return to Paris, to take lovers of her own. Being as quick-witted as she was beautiful, and unlike her mother, an extrovert who throve on public flattery and adulation, she had little trouble finding admirers willing and rich enough to finance her extravagant whims. By 1852 her smoldering relations with her husband had grown so tense and heated that there was talk of a separation. Once again there were acrimonious arguments over questions of money. But to keep Clésinger — "a madman, if ever there was one," his wife, now called him — from laying hands on her three-year-old daughter, Solange gladly agreed to leave her little "Nini" at Nohant.

All the joys Aurore Dupin had known as a child were now relived, as it were, by proxy. The miniature grotto with its artificial spring, which her own mother had once built for her in the Nohant grove, was now duplicated on a more ambitious scale, thanks in no small part to Manceau's inventiveness and manual dexterity. Heaps of earth were moved to form small ivy- and flower-covered hills, and an old stone sarcophagus — a relic of Gallo-Roman times — filled with water to feed a tiny "spring." "I make the Grove of Bacchus,"

George Sand noted on the nineteenth of April 1853, in the long, narrow agenda book which she and Manceau now filled daily, with scrupulous regularity. "Emile [Aucante] is astounded; the nightingales too . . . I read the last volume of my memoirs, alone . . ." — by which she meant the bound manuscript. "The only funny one here is Nini," the doting grandmother wrote to Solange ten months later. "She's the joy of the household, with Manceau putting himself so much on her level that she often asks me: 'Grandma, am I still even more stupid than he?' "

Not content with flowered mounds and artificial springs, George Sand decided to have a wooden chalet built. She too would have a doll-like "refuge" to which she could withdraw, like Marie Antoinette from the fastidious grandeur of Versailles. Inevitably the chalet acquired the name of Trianon. "Superb weather," Manceau noted on the eleventh of March 1854, in his thin birdlike handwriting, so different from George's thick, round-lettered scrawl. "The garden is being cleaned up. The new gardener is obviously a spader. The *Chalet* is to be inaugurated Monday morning . . . Madame Sol[ange] goes to bed at 9 o'clock, *tant elle s'amuse*" — which can be roughly translated "so much fun is she having."

On Monday, March 13, it was George Sand's turn to record the day's happenings in their joint ledger. "Inauguration of the chalet, a dazzling cleaning up, fountain display, presentation of a bouquet, monumental inscription; Manceau verses, cannon fire. I lunch there to the sound of the cannon, presence of Monsieur le Maire" — the sympathetic *Père* Aulard, as he was commonly called. "Nini has her lesson there for the first time, and is proud to partake of such a glorious day. She reads very well. I do some gardening. Visit of Monsieur and Madame Périgois . . . The Simonnet ladies" — Hippolyte Chatiron's daughter and her mother-in-law — "come to dinner with the Père Aulard. Dominoes with Sol[ange], who goes to bed at 9 o'clock, *tant elle s'amuse!*"

This "*tant elle s'amuse*" had by this time become a standing joke with the other members of the household, obviously exasperated by Solange's supercilious refusal to be amused by these rustic entertainments. "Nini reads like an angel," Manceau recorded the next day, adding sarcastically: "The little mother [Solange] has finally covered the doll's crib. That makes 15 days she's been at it. Trianon . . . Madame Sol goes to bed at 9 o'clock. Manceau reads the new play . . . Sol is leaving on Thursday, *tant elle s'amuse*."

So fond of her Trianon did George Sand become that soon she was spending entire afternoons and evenings in her wooden chalet working on her latest brain child. Originally intended as a playlet for the amateur stage of Nohant, *Nello le Violoniste* was a Hoffmann-esque piece of drama woven around a Paganini-like virtuoso. But inspired by the sweet memory of Chopin's old friend Joseph Dessauer, the hypochondriac composer who was always grumbling about his fading eyesight, she turned it into a full-length tragicomedy, reentitled in the process *Maître Favilla*.

April, which had been graced by radiant sunshine and mid-June temperatures, went out on a wave of cold which was duly recorded by Manceau: "Despair on the part of Madame at seeing her Trianon covered with dead branches and young leaves." At least it was a despair she could share with her adored Nini. But not for long. In Paris Clésinger had just learned that Solange was carrying on an affair with her distant cousin, Gaston de Villeneuve, the grandson of René, who was now seventy-seven. The former cuirassier burst into his wife's room and after a furious scene, he made off with some compromising letters, turning them over to his lawyer. Now able to prove that he was saddled with an adulterous wife — enough to obtain a full-scale separation on his terms — he belatedly decided to prove himself a model father. Hurrying down to Nohant, where no one was expecting him, he demanded the custody of his child, which George Sand was forced to accord him. At one o'clock on Sunday, May 7, he was headed back for Paris, taking the little Nini with him. George, who had been preparing to celebrate the child's fifth birthday on the tenth, was heartbroken. "I slept badly," she confided to her agenda book. "I am still sad and angry."

Overcome with confusion and possibly remorse, Solange chose to retire to a convent, while Nini was entrusted to the care of Madame Bascans, the boarding-school mistress who had agreed to be the godmother of Solange's child. The news did little to cheer George Sand, whose fiftieth birthday, celebrated on July 5, came and went in a blaze of fireworks and painfully artificial merriment.

In October of this same year, 1854, the first extracts of George Sand's memoirs were serialized in a Paris newspaper. *The Story of My Life* which, as she had once written to Charlotte Marliani, would prove her salvation or her death, had by this time outstripped everything she had previously produced in length and minuteness of descriptive detail. The result was a fascinating though completely lopsided work, the first quarter of which was concerned with events occurring before Aurore Dupin's birth — from certain love affairs of the Maréchal de Saxe to extensive quotations from the letters her father had written to her grandmother while serving with Napoleon's armies in Germany and Italy. Some of the portraits which emerged — particularly those of Madame Dupin de Francueil, her mother and father, Deschartres, Hippolyte Chatiron, and for a later period, Marie Dorval — could stand comparison with the finest in the autobiographical genre. Hippolyte Taine, to name but one, felt that *L'Histoire de ma vie* was, by and large, a far more honest work than Chateaubriand's *Mémoires d'outre-tombe,* haunted though the latter are by the echoing wind of the poet's inexorable grandiloquence. But given the extraordinary circumstances of her life and the number of geniuses George Sand had come to know, one can only regret that certain of them — like Liszt, Heinrich Heine, and Mickiewicz — are merely mentioned in passing.

From the convent to which she had so implausibly retired, Solange had meanwhile begun corresponding with her mother. Perhaps God, in whom she had never had much faith till now, would in his infinite misericord be willing to listen to her prayers and give her back her daughter. George Sand, though doubting the depth of this sudden "conversion," adroitly suggested that God might be more inclined to grant her request if she agreed to exchange a "kiss of peace" with Augustine — a condition to which Solange submitted with unprecedented meekness.

In December of 1854 Nini's mother was overjoyed at the thought that her convent prayers had been heeded by the Almighty. The legal injunction establishing her separation from her husband decreed that the five-year-old Jeanne-Gabrielle be entrusted once again to the custody of her grandmother at Nohant. Clésinger's lawyer, however, contested the immediate enforcement of this injunction, declaring that it was going to be appealed to a higher jurisdiction. The unhappy Nini was thus forcibly retained at the boarding school, from which her careless father would occasionally take her out for midwinter carriage drives in a light summer frock. Not allowed to bring her home, Solange had to content herself with bringing her daughter toys to play with. In early January the poor child came down with scarlet fever, but it was several days before the headmistress would entrust her to Solange's care. By then it was too late: during the night of January 13, 1855, the feverish Nini died in her mother's arms.

Three days later Solange, accompanied by Emile Aucante and Eugène Lambert, came down to Nohant to be consoled by her mother.

"I slept after having wept away everything I had kept bottled up within me," George Sand noted in her agenda book on January 17. "I thought of her, and it seemed to me she answered. Sol is crushed and consequently calmer."

She herself was heartbroken. She could not take two steps in the garden without being haunted by the vision of her little Nini sprinkling the flowers with her watering can, filling her little wheelbarrow with leaves, or setting light to the faggots in the fireplace of the Trianon chalet. "I am the same as ever," she wrote to Solange, after her daughter had returned to Paris. "Every day I go and cry by myself in the chalet. I cannot master myself, I'm too old to be consoled." She did, however, find partial solace in a book entitled *Terre et Ciel,* written by Jean Reynaud, Pierre Leroux's former coeditor of the *Encyclopédie nouvelle*. Her faith in the reincarnation of the immortal human soul thus reconfirmed, George Sand started work on a piece of dream-sequence fantasy in which she imagined herself in Heaven meeting a slightly older, taller, slimmer, but still recognizable Nini.

To Alexandre Manceau it was soon clear that a change of scene was necessary. Maurice, who was back again in Paris fitfully trying to talk publishers into letting him illustrate their books, needed little persuading. Ever since 1838 he and his mother had talked and dreamed of making a winter trip to Italy. The moment had come to realize this project.

Finding the necessary money was once again a problem. As George Sand wrote to Victor Borie in mid-February: "I am preparing for our departure for Paris and Italy. Without Manceau, who is lending me his poor purse, it would be impossible for me to move, what with everything I have to pay before leaving. What frightens me is not being penniless — I'm used to it — it's feeling incapable of working since the death of this child."

In early March she and Manceau left Nohant for Paris to pick up Maurice. On the eleventh they took the train to Lyon, from where they traveled down the Rhone by river steamer, as she had done with Musset and Stendhal in 1833. At Marseille they called on the hospitable Dr. François Cauvière, who sixteen years earlier had rescued George Sand from her financial plight and helped nurse a cough-racked Chopin back to health. The septuagenarian surgeon had since given up his practice, but his experienced eye, if not his ear, may have warned him that George's new companion was also inclined to consumption.

Continuing on by sea, they reached Genoa on March 16 and spent a sunny morning visiting the Ducal Palace and lunching under the orange trees of an outdoor café with Etienne Arago, now living as an exile in the Kingdom of Piedmont. Later that same day they called on Bianchina Rebizzo, the Milanese wife of Pietro Pagello's friend Lazzaro Rebizzo, the dilettantish poet-plotter whose hopes of seeing Italy freed from the Habsburg yoke had been dashed by the collapse of the revolutionary uprisings of 1848. She was now running a young ladies' boarding school, to which George Sand's old friend Luigi Calamatta had sent his attractive dark-haired daughter Marcelina. What Maurice thought of the latter, we do not know, but he could not have realized that he was looking at his future wife.

The next stop was at Leghorn where, as she had done in 1834, George had herself driven inland in a hired carriage to Pisa — this time for a cold, mid-March glimpse of the deserted Campo Santo, the Orcagna frescoes ("too romantic for me," she later noted), and the tipsily inclined tower. Some twenty years earlier, Alfred de Musset's whim and a casual toss of a coin had sent her eastward toward Venice. This time, however, she was not going to be diverted from what she imagined would be the sunny south. With Manceau and Maurice, she reboarded the paddle-wheel steamer for the final lap to Civita Vecchia, which they reached on March 18. Climbing into a small stagecoach pulled by three black horses, they were driven over the coast-hugging Via Aurelia into Rome. Here they were welcomed by none other than the prefect of police, who had been warned that a highly suspect lady of letters was about to descend on the Eternal City.

Like Stendhal before them, they put up at the Albergo della Minerva, a hostelry which an enterprising Frenchman had opened in an old Roman *palazzo*. Frequented by itinerant prelates as well as gentlemen of letters, it featured a vast dining hall where the latest arrivals took their places at the long rectangular table d'hôte next to the other "boarders." This communal atmosphere was much to George Sand's liking and good-humoredly accepted by those compatriots who chose to call — like the fair-haired and pale-skinned Ida Ferrier, the estranged actress, mistress, and wife of Alexandre Dumas, who was now living in princely sin with a Sicilian grandee.

The several weeks George Sand spent in Rome proved singularly disenchanting. Republican Venice, though a ghost of its former self, had delighted her; pontifical Rome appalled her. She was unable to share the enthusiasm of her cicerones and to sink into "abysses" of Chateaubriandesque rapture before the "sublime" ruins of Imperial Rome. At fifty, she was no longer the naive Aurore Dupin whose romantic reveries had been kindled by Piranesi's idyllic engravings, nor could she forget that the city of the Caesars had long run red with the blood of early Christian martyrs. The reality she saw and smelled bore little relation to the grandoise myth. There were too many sheep and goats grazing in the meadows and vegetable gardens surrounding the "huge carcass" of the Colosseum for her to enjoy a spectacle which struck her as worthy of a "country fair." She was put off by the sight of oxen sinking their squat snouts into the rippling waters of the Fontana del Tritone, upset by the omnipresent stench of frying fish, rotting trash, and excrement, irritated by the dust stirred up on unpaved streets by carriage wheels and horses' hoofs. Most of all she was annoyed by the flocks of beggars and *facchini* waiting at every street corner with outstretched palms and eager offers to guide her and her companions to some as yet unexplored basilica or venerable relic.

Such was papal Rome, the Rome to which Prince Louis Napoleon had six years earlier dispatched General Oudinot — to reimpose a Pope whom a popular insurrection, backed by her friend Mazzini, had sent packing off to Naples. A city without a soul, a dead city, a city of abject slaves! A theocratic tyranny which was even more smug and crippling than the imperial tyranny that had been imposed on France.

The elements did nothing to temper her hostility. During much of their stay it rained, and Maurice even had to keep to his bed for a few days with a nasty sore throat. Refusing the overtures made to her by aristocratic hostesses who were dying to have a close look at the monster, George Sand finally withdrew with her two male companions to the tranquil heights of Frascati, with its sweeping view of Rome on one side and on the other the even more spectacular view of the Tiber threading its silvery way through the misty hills toward the slate gray expanse of the Mediterranean. "For a modest price," as she wrote to Solange, they had been able to rent the ground floor of the Villa Piccolomini. "The trees are in full bloom, it's already very hot out of doors, though very cold in our great vaulted chambers, designed for the summer and ill garnished with fireplaces (aside from the difficulty of obtaining wood) . . . Everywhere there is a dancing and babbling of waters which can truly be called crystalline without resort to metaphor. In a word, this is paradise on earth."

From this paradise she reluctantly consented to be dragged back into Rome for Easter Sunday, to see the Pope officiate at High Mass. But her egalitarian sentiments were more scandalized than ever by the sight of Vatican guards, "in their opera costumes," using their halberds to shield the luxuriously robed Princes of the Church from the sea of hideously scarred, diseased, and half-naked beggars which had flooded into the vast nave of Saint Peter's.

On April 23 a carriage and coachman were hired to drive George Sand, Manceau, and Maurice northward to Spoleto and Perugia. Their artistic sensibilities were deeply stirred by the soft skies and vistas of Umbria, and the sight of the western sun disappearing behind Lake Trasimemo with its rear guard of fiery lances moved George to describe it as "sublime" in her agenda book. The rains which had bothered them in Rome and Frascati were now replaced by radiant skies and starry nights which accompanied them as far as Florence. "The absence of civilization is frightful, and one is torn at each step between a desire to linger in these lovely spots and a haste to leave them," she wrote to Madame Dumas from the *pensione* where the three of them were at last able to wash away the accumulated dust and dirt. "The flea in particular is the deadly foe of gentle reveries. It follows you everywhere and assassinates your pure rejoicings. To become a poet at one's ease one should grow a bit *unclean* when traveling . . . Yet every time I see or feel something beautiful," she added, "I tell myself that if my poor little one had not died, I would not have had this pleasure, and then the pleasure turns bitter; for I had arranged my life for *her,* and it pains me to resume it for my own sake."

Florence, where they spent four busy days visiting picture galleries and chapels, had two surprises in store for her. The first was Elizabeth Barrett Browning, who honored her with a visit, much as she had done three years before in Paris. The second was the Cocomero theater, where a company of French actors were performing in one of her plays, *Le Mariage de Victorine.*

They reached Lucca, the next stop, in time to celebrate Manceau's thirty-eighth birthday. George even composed a few doggerel verses for the occasion, describing herself as *"l'aurore aux doigts de roses"* — rosy-fingered Aurore (a pun on "dawn") — weeping such bucketfuls of tears that the dry-riverbeds were flooded.

At Genoa, where she caught a fleeting glimpse of Lazzaro Rebizzo — enough to conclude that he was "madder than ever" — George Sand said goodbye to Maurice, who wanted to continue north to Turin to do a bit of Alpine sightseeing before proceeding to his father's country house at Guillery. With Manceau, she reboarded the paddle-wheel steamer for the final lap to Marseille. The passage was even rougher than the one she had experienced with Musset. As she later wrote to Maurice, "there was no way of sleeping, we were tossed around on our beds like omelets. Chinaware was flying all over the place, glasses were landing on people's heads and plates skidding under one's feet. The slumberers stretched out on the floor kept looking for their caps on the ceiling. The women wept, the children shrieked, the sailors swore. Manceau maintained a sickly smile, having no appetite and feeling his insides beginning to heave. We finally entered Marseille harbor after having eaten . . . in a scandalous manner. The vessel was magnificent and the fare excellent. Poor Manceau! Such good wine! . . ."

Back in Paris, after a twenty-hour train ride which seemed wondrously rapid to someone who had once spent three days covering the same distance by stagecoach and paddle steamer, George Sand found more proofs of *The Story of My Life* waiting to be corrected. This and a multitude of theatrical distractions — like the staging of *Maître Favilla* — kept her from writing up her Roman trip for another twelvemonth. The delay did nothing to temper the ferocity of the eventual product — a vehemently antipapist novel entitled *La Daniella,* which she began writing in the summer of 1856. Ostensibly it was a tale woven around a French painter's love for a lowly Frascati laundress. But the complexity of the novel's tragicomic intrigues could not mute the stridently anticlerical note, which kept recurring. In describing the Pope's appearance among the tattered paupers of Saint Peter's, the author abandoned all semblance of impartiality, roundly declaring that the "dreadful beggars" of Jacques Callot's engravings were like "dandies in comparison to these . . . It's something horrible to see! The morality of these wretches is as repugnant as their sores. Nowhere have I seen the human being so degraded" — by pontiffs whose love of pomp and circumstance was closer to the gory circuses of the Caesars than to the charity of Christ. Rome, she pointed out, was still ruled by pagan augury and superstition. Pope Pius IX, who had started out a liberal, had been held in such aversion in "high places" that there were cardinals who "to this day never approach him without keeping two fingers of the closed hand extended, an Italian custom designed to repel the evil eye."

To suggest that the Pope was in league with the devil was, of course, to provoke the imperial censors, as George Sand knew well. She was not prepared to forgive the military support Louis Napoleon had provided to the banished Pope for the cynical purpose of ingratiating himself with France's Catholic aristocracy and bourgeoisie. And she wanted the world to know it. Had she been willing to leave it at that, *La Daniella* would have been read and soon forgotten as just one more of George Sand's incorrigibly didactic novels. But in the course of her highly personal denunciations, she described Italy as "a virgin prostituted to all the bandits of the universe and whom nothing could purify," later pouring more fuel on the flames by quoting Joseph de Maistre's celebrated adage: "A people always gets the government it deserves." While the government took umbrage over the term "bandits" — which obviously included General Oudinot — the Italian nationalists and their French supporters were outraged to see the Italian people likened to a harlot. The result was a furious polemic which raged for weeks in the columns of *La Presse,* the newspaper which was serializing *La Daniella,* and in those of its rival, *Le Siècle.*

This time George Sand was assailed not only by conservatives for whom she had long been a prominent bête noire but also by liberals like the historian Henri Martin, the Dutch painter Ary Scheffer, and Daniele Manin, who had led the Venetian uprising against the Austrians in 1948. From Brussels her old friend Luigi Calamatta wrote to express his dismay, while Louis Blanc in London was equally disturbed by this intemperance of language. Though she was courageously upheld throughout this literary fray by the editor of *La Presse,* George Sand was finally forced to trim her sail after Napoleon III's censors had issued several warnings and finally had the paper suspended. Certain of the more incendiary passages were consequently omitted from the novel when it appeared in book form.

The year 1856, during which *La Daniella* was written, was not a particularly happy one for its author. Three new plays — *Lucie, Françoise,* and *Comme il vous plaira* (this last put on by the Comédie Française) — which she had dashed off with her usual facility, were poorly received, and this at a time when she was more than ever in need of funds to help the families of men who had been imprisoned or exiled for their continuing hostility to Napoleon III and his Empire.

George Sand's growing fame, not simply as an authoress but even more as a benefactress ever ready to put in a good word for the oppressed with the Emperor's influential cousin, Prince Jérôme Bonaparte, whom she now numbered among her friends, had become a permament embarrassment, attracting an almost daily stream of visitors to Nohant. To escape these harassing solicitations, she decided in late June of 1857 to make an excursion into the hill country of the Creuse — the "little Switzerland" of the Berry province, as she called it. She had always been fond of this picturesque river valley, with its cliffs and gorges, its foaming rapids and intermittent pools of tranquil water, its sudden patches of greenery and its scattered mills, each with its small wharf-hitched boat ready to be rowed by its owner across the bridgeless waters.

This time she was accompanied by Manceau and a noted Paris entomologist named Depuiset. Their first stop was Châteaubrun, where they picnicked on the grass next to the monumental ruins of the medieval fortress, whose roof- and floorless keep now played host to elusive swifts and lizard-eating kestrels. From these imposing heights they bumped their way down into the valley over a rough road which finally petered out near the confluence of the boulder-strewn Creuse and its torrential tributary, the Gargilesse. Here they ran into a trout fisherman and hunter named Moreau whose swarthy face — that of a "Spanish smuggler," as she later described it — broke into a sun-bronzed grin when he saw George Sand, whom he had guided about these rocky parts on donkeyback some eleven years before. With Moreau again acting as a guide, they followed a dusty and uneven footpath up the narrow side valley, between dark gorse- and heather-covered cliffs, as far as the little village of Gargilesse.

In the slanting rays of the setting sun the brown-tiled roofs and Gothic gables glowed, as in a colored illustration of *Grimm's Fairy Tales*. Dominated by a Romanesque church and a battlemented castle whose fortress walls dropped sheer into the waterbed of the ravine, the little village was quaintly sprawled over a rocky eminence in a sheltered valley full of gushing waterfalls. Everything about it — from the twisted weathercocks crowning the medieval turrets to the solitary tree shading the napkin-sized square — was a source of wonder and enchantment — and not least of all the thin sliver of a crescent moon, floating serenely in the warm evening sky, as though to welcome their arrival.

No less enthralling for George Sand was the friendly and open spirit with which this village seemed imbued. For when she asked the guide if there was any place where they might spend the night, he answered simply: "Here!" Leading them up a flight of seven large-stone steps, he pushed open a door whose lock was useless. Inside were two small whitewashed rooms, with plain wooden ceilings, cherry-wood beds, and rush chairs. The house and everything in it, the guide explained, belonged to a Madame Rosalie, who would gladly let them spend the night here provided they dined at her inn farther up the hill. The idea of spending the night in a place where no one needed to lock and bolt his front door, because theft was unknown, was as intriguing to George Sand as the unexpected stillness next to which the nocturnal quiet of Nohant seemed like an infernal "din" (as she later wrote, with pardonable exaggeration).

Another night and day spent in this secluded valley turned Manceau too into a Gargilesse enthusiast. He caught a most unusual black butterfly with pearl gray markings which was triumphantly identified as an *algira,* a species common enough in North Africa, occasionally found in certain regions of Italy and Provence, but totally unknown in central France. This was followed by the netting of another rare flutterer, identified by the Paris entomologist as a *gordius.* The explanation for these astonishing "finds" was simple: shielded from the sharp winds which raced across the flatlands and shook the elms, evergreens, and poplars of Nohant, the sunken valley of the Gargilesse was a kind of nature-made hothouse harboring an almost tropical exuberance of mosses, plants, and butterflies.

"I don't think I've ever been so hot, I'm as baked as a brick," George Sand wrote to Maurice, who was still in Paris at the time. This discovery was all she needed to make Gargilesse "her" village. "It's a bit as though one were to meet gazelles or antelopes in the forest of the Ardennes" was the way she later described this botanical wonderland. Why journey all the way to La Spezia in search of Mediterranean warmth when one could find it here, curiously preserved in a sheltered fold of earth, a bare twenty-five miles to the east and south of La Châtre?

This was, of course, a spur-of-the-moment fancy. Later, when she came to know Gargilesse better, George Sand discovered that it could be as cold as Nohant. The gushing waterfalls could freeze into cascades of brittle ice and the Gothic houses disappear in soft blankets of wintry fog which were wondrously described in *L'Homme de Neige* (*The Snowman*), a novel supposedly set in eighteenth-century Sweden, which she wrote in 1858. But during the summer of 1857 the picture she painted of this sun-blessed haven was positively rhapsodic. Maurice was so infected by his mother's contagious enthusiasm that on his return to Nohant in early July, he insisted on accompanying her and Manceau on a second exploration. The unlocked house they slept in being the only one available, Manceau dug into his hard-won savings and paid out 800 francs to Madame Rosalie, the owner. He spent another 300 francs on the installation of toilets and wardrobes to make it a suitable "present" to his benefactress. "There's no way of keeping him from arranging his shack much more to our liking than to his," George wrote to Maurice in late July, after her son had left for his annual visit to his father at Guillery. "He's turning it into a ship's cabin, measuring the centimeters so that each person can have his complete gear, his nail, his chamber pot, a place for each boot, etc., etc. He doesn't want you to have to go sleep in the castle; we've learned enough things about the filth it's in to make a dog vomit."

Thus fitted out by its self-appointed "skipper," the little house at Gargilesse became for George Sand a kind of literary ark in whose "cabins" she could seek refuge from the diluvial flood of visitors she had to face at Nohant. So precious to her did this rustic retreat eventually become that here, as her biographer Vladimir Karénine pointed out long ago, no less than thirteen novels were either begun, continued, or concluded. One of the first was the most controversial and ill-inspired of them all, *Elle et Lui,* which was finished at Gargilesse in May of 1858.

As an experiment in literary vivisection, *Lucrezia Floriani* had made painful reading for those who, like Delacroix, were close friends of both Chopin's and George Sand's. Given the nagging jealousy which had inspired it, it had some psychological justification. But even George Sand's most ardent admirers were hard put to justify this new experiment in literary exhumation. For the corpse George Sand now dug up and presented to a startled public in *Elle et Lui* was nothing less than her ill-starred romance with Alfred de Musset.

Alfred de Musset, the *him* in *Elle et Lui,* had died in March of 1857, the forty-six-year-old victim of desperate drunkenness and dissipation. But this was not a valid reason for writing a "novel" which struck many as being little better than an act of posthumous literary vengeance, as well as an excruciating exercise in self-vindication. *La Confession d'un enfant du siècle,* which Musset had written in 1835, at a time when his poetic powers were still at their height and the memory of his dark-eyed mistress fresh and searing, was a minor masterpiece of literary transformation in which his own backslidings and psycopathic weaknesses as a confused and crestfallen "child of the century" were contrasted to the maternal solicitude of the heroine, Brigitte. George Sand had been so moved by the novel that in May of 1836 she had written to Marie d'Agoult: "The tiniest details of an unhappy intimacy are so faithfully, so minutely recorded from the first hour to the last . . . that I wept like a dumb animal on closing the book. Then I wrote the author a few lines to say I know not what: that I had loved him greatly, that I had forgiven him everything, and that I never wished to see him again." To which she had added, less charitably: "With me forgiveness goes as far as never conceiving a bitter thought against the murderer of my love, but it will never go as far as to regret the torture suffered."

The wound which smarted in 1836 was still not healed twenty years later. Each new meeting with Musset — of which there were five or six over a period of a dozen years — seems to have left George more upset by the idea that she could ever have been so smitten by such a shameless debauchee, and on the occasion of their last encounter, in 1848, Musset had been hopelessly drunk. In *Elle et Lui* the hero, Laurent, is not exactly shameless and the reader is made to feel a certain sympathy for his periodic "aberrations." But the portrait which ultimately emerges is that of a carefree gigolo, sharply contrasted to his industrious mistress Thérèse, who works dutifully at her canvasses to keep the wolf from the door, while her irresponsible companion wastes his time in idleness and dubious frequentations.

François Buloz, with whom George Sand was now reconciled after a breach of fifteen years, was so embarrassed by the manuscript that he hesitated for some months before finally serializing *Elle et Lui* in the *Revue des Deux Mondes.* His apprehensions were fully justified, for this fragment of autobiography was draped in such flimsy fiction as to be utterly transparent. It provoked an immediate uproar in the salons of the capital. Paul de Musset, who had once been a welcome guest at the Quai Malaquais apartment, felt himself personally insulted by this unflattering portrait of his brother Alfred, whom George Sand had shorn of his genius but not of his pathetic vices. He retaliated by writing a counternovel, entitled *Lui et Elle,* in which the roles were neatly reversed: here a proud but untalented songstress named Olympe was unfavorably contrasted to a composer of genius named Edouard de Falconey. As a piece of "fiction," this roman à clef was certainly inferior to the "novel" which had inspired it, having little of the latter's psychological insights. But for the biographer or historian *Lui et Elle* remains a fascinating, if biased document, based on a good deal more than hearsay. Quite aside from what his brother Alfred was willing to confide to him over the years, Paul de Musset had actually witnessed one or two of the dramatic moments which George Sand had experienced in the town house of the Rue de Grenelle during those tense winter months of 1834–1835.

This literary duel hardly embellished the escutcheon of either party. But the totally unwarranted intervention of a third person turned the whole sorry business into a dismal farce. This person was Louise Colet, a pushy *femme de lettres* who had managed to seduce and then harried an increasingly reluctant Gustave Flaubert before concentrating her amorous attention on Alfred de Musset. At one point she had sought to ingratiate herself with France's most illustrious woman author, but George Sand had quickly sensed the shallowness of Louise Colet's intellectual snobbery and refused to have anything more to do with her. "There are some who seek to be talked about in a certain way, there are others who seek to be talked about no matter how. The first like celebrity, the second like noise.

Louise Colet was of this second category," Flaubert's friend Maxime du Camp was later to write. "The world absolutely had to know that Alfred de Musset had had a passing fancy for a talentless woman writer; Louise Colet undertook to enlighten it. After *Elle et Lui,* after *Lui et Elle,* Louise Colet published *Lui.* The *Him* is Alfred de Musset, whom one resists because one wishes to remain faithful to one's adored Léonce. Léonce is Gustave Flaubert. Ah! I know the story, for I was saturated *ad nauseam* with it. I have more than three hundred letters which Louise Colet wrote to me because she thought I was the confidant of the tender advances with which she persecuted Flaubert, who had had all he could take."

The controversial *Elle et Lui* was followed, a year and a half later, by one of George Sand's most popular and successful novels, *Le Marquis de Villemer* — an elaborate fresco of aristocratic salon and country chateau life which was obviously inspired by recollections of her grandmother's "old countesses" and the titled gentry she had met at Guillery and Chenonceaux.

Her next important novel, *Valvèdre,* was written while she was recovering from a severe attack of typhoid fever which came close to killing her in the autumn of 1860. Though this was not the first time she had struck an anti-Romantic note, never had she done so more strongly — which probably explains why Matthew Arnold, who was a moralist and critic as well as a poet, later singled it out for special commendation. Dedicated to Maurice, whose new passion for mineralogy had partly inspired it, the novel contrasted the meritorious labors of an aging scientist named Valvèdre with the devious and dishonest amours which his young wife Alida was carrying on with a dilettantish poet named Valigny. Didactic, like so many of George Sand's novels, it forthrightly criticized the Romantic cult of morbid introspection, extolling the study of nature and man's environmental world as an excellent therapeutic for lovesick souls. Reality once again was a major source of inspiration: though the author may not consciously have realized it, there was a good bit of Solange's talent for self-deception in the "heroine," as well as something of Maurice's dilettantish flightiness and tendency to self-indulgence in the poet Valigny, while her own and Manceau's taste for self-sacrifice and concentration were triumphantly epitomized in the person of Valvèdre.

To regain her health, George Sand undertook a long trip to the Riviera in the spring of 1861. Maurice, who was with her for the first weeks, finally left her to the care of Manceau, unable to resist Prince Jérôme Bonaparte's invitation to accompany him on a steamship cruise to Algeria, Spain, and ultimately America. Not until June did George finally return to Nohant, where she was at last able to consolidate a ten-year-old friendship by playing hostess to Alexandre Dumas *fils*.

Everything about this friendship was extraordinary, and not least of all the odd circumstances surrounding its inception. In 1851 George Sand had decided to end the row which a mischievous bon mot about Mérimée had touched off in 1833 by dedicating her play *Molière* to the author of *The Three Musketeers*. The elder Dumas, a spontaneous and exuberant human being who traded gossip as he traded mistresses, with a nonchalance totally devoid of malice, had immediately reciprocated by inviting George to dinner during one of her brief stays in Paris. At the time his son Alexandre was in Germany, where he was desperately pursuing a young Russian beauty, Lydia Nesselrode, who had been unhappily married to the son of Emperor Nicholas I's Foreign Minister. To put an end to what in Petersburg was regarded as a "scandalous" liaison — between the lovely Lydia and the captivating Alexandre *fils* — Dmitri Nesselrode had suddenly turned up in Paris and "carried off" his reluctant wife, to the despair of her twenty-seven-year-old lover, who, unwilling to give up, had set off in hot pursuit. The resultant chase, as heroically romantic as anything to be found in the older Dumas' novels, had taken the young Aramis from Brussels to Dresden and from Dresden to Breslau. But he had come a cropper at the frontier town of Mystowitz, where the tsarist police officials guarding the Russian-occupied area of Poland had received stringent orders to halt his further progress.

While vainly waiting for a visa which was never to be delivered, the frustrated Alexandre had befriended a Polish gentleman who had volunteered to show him a packet of letters that Chopin had received from some feminine admirer. The feminine admirer was none other than George Sand, and the letters in question were those, written between 1838 and 1847, which Chopin's sister Ludwika had acquired after her brother's death and decided to take back with her to Warsaw. On reaching the border, however, she had taken fright at the idea that this precious correspondence might be confiscated by the tsarist police, ever suspicious of things French, and had left the letters with a Polish friend.

Dumas *fils* had lost no time writing to his father to tell him that he had been allowed to read this correspondence, which struck him as "far more charming than the proverbial letters of Madame de Sévigné!" So charming indeed that he had decided to make copies. "I'm bringing back a full notebook for you, for unfortunately these letters were only lent to me . . . Nothing is sadder and more touching, I can assure you, than all these letters whose ink has yellowed and which were touched and joyfully received by a person who is dead . . . For a moment I hoped that the depositary, who is my friend, might suddenly die, that I might inherit his deposit and offer it in homage to Madame Sand, who might perhaps be happy to relive this past death a bit. The wretch, my friend, is in splendid health, and in the belief that I was leaving on the 15th [of May], I handed back all the papers which he did not even have the curiosity to peruse."

The older Dumas dutifully transmitted this news to Nohant. George Sand immediately replied, asking to get her letters back. From Mystowitz the young Alexandre wrote to her in early June of 1851 to say that he would undertake to bring the letters back, with or without the authorization of Chopin's sister. "The copy of this correspondence will also naturally be given to you at the same time . . . But believe me, Madame, no profanation was involved. The heart which so distantly and discreetly became the confidant of yours was long since attached to you, and its admiration has the stature and age of the greatest and oldest devotions."

Alexandre Dumas *fils* was as good as his word. In July he returned to Paris with this priceless trophy which — one can only say, Alas! — was finally dispatched to Nohant by post, when it became clear that neither of the two Dumas could bring it down in person. At Nohant the letters were destroyed by George Sand — to protect not Chopin's, but her daughter's reputation. As she wrote to Alexandre Dumas *fils,* in a long letter of explanation: "One tells one's children everything when they reach the age of manhood. I then used to tell my poor friend" — Chopin — "what I now tell my son . . . But these family revelations can take on great importance to malicious eyes, and it would greatly have pained me had I opened for all to see this mysterious book of my intimate life, wherein my daughter's name was so often written, amid smiles mingled with tears."

Not until the following February did George Sand and Alexandre Dumas *fils* finally meet — at the Théâtre du Vaudeville in Paris — during an entr'acte of his *La Dame aux camélias,* which had enjoyed a successful première (after being held up for months by obtuse censors) only a dozen nights before. George, who had spent years watching over the precarious health of a sick genius, could not but be profoundly moved by the younger Dumas' dramatic portrayal of his own amorous tribulations as the lover of the beautiful Marie Duplessis ("the most absolute incarnation of a woman that has ever existed," Liszt had once remarked of her), who had died of consumption two years before Chopin, in 1847.

This, however, was only one of several sentimental bonds which made for a special affinity between the twenty-seven-year-old dramatist and the forty-seven-year-old *femme de lettres.* The young Alexandre's mother, Catherine Labay, had been a humble seamstress, like Aurore Dupin's; and like her own half brother, Hippolyte, he had been born out of wedlock. Like Hippolyte, too, he had later acquired a half sister (Marie-Alexandrine), another product of the elder Dumas' promiscuous amours (which the father treated so casually that not until 1831 did he bother to recognize his six-year-old son). One year later the young Alexandre had been forcibly wrenched from his mother — much as Casimir Dudevant had sought to wrest Maurice from his wife's control — and placed in a boarding school where his classmates, having discovered the secret of his parentage, had made cruel sport of his bastard origin. These experiences had marked him for life, making of him a pessimistic idealist, a disabused romantic. He always felt that his humble, hardworking, and fundamentally virtuous mother had been wronged by his other parent, and though he later succumbed to the temptations of the flesh which his father so openhandedly tossed his way (more or less discarded mistresses from his ceaselessly replenished harem), he disapproved of Dumas *père*'s magnificently profligate existence.

Less exuberant than his overpowering father — that "instrument of permanent sonority" (in Maxime du Camp's words) who could talk for twelve hours at a stretch without the slightest trace of fatigue — Alexandre Dumas *fils* could be entertaining company, for he had a mordant wit and was an excellent mimic. His Herculean build and bright blue eyes, both inherited from his illustrious parent, enabled him to be a lady-killer when he chose, which was relatively seldom. For unlike his "prodigal father" (the title he gave to one of his plays), he preferred to play the role of "unprodigal son" — a bon mot apparently coined by George Sand.

Victor Hugo once remarked that the father was all genius and no talent (meaning that he was incapable of literary discipline), while the son was all talent and no genius. What the latter lacked in abundance of imagination, he made up for in control. He was also less of a literary opportunist. Though anything but allergic to success, he was opposed to the aristocratic doctrine of *l'art pour l'art* (art for art's sake) — "three words totally devoid of meaning," he once remarked — and was an advocate of "reformist" literature. This made him naturally sympathetic to George Sand, who was soon treating him — he was after all twenty years her junior — as another of her adopted "sons." In return, he gaily addressed her as "Very dear Mama" and generously offered to help her write her plays, going as far as to rewrite entire scenes, the final authorship of which he invariably ascribed to her.

The question of who most influenced the other is too complex to be unraveled here. But George Sand seems to have contributed at least as much as she received. She directly inspired two of Dumas *fils*'s plays — *Les Idées de Madame Aubray* and *L'Ami des Femmes,* the latter of which was considered so "disgusting" by a public of outraged hypocrites (it included an unhappy wife's description of the torments suffered on her bridal night) that it was closed after a brief run.

At the time of his first visit to Nohant, in July of 1861, the younger Dumas was depressed by a sense of uncertainty and failure, in his private life as much as in his writing. After his rebuff at Mystowitz, he had later transferred his affections to another Slavic siren, Princess Nadyezhda Naryshkin, who had journeyed all the way from Petersburg to tell him that her friend Lydia Nesselrode no longer wished to see him, succeeding so well that she had soon effaced the memory of her fickle friend. As the smitten Dumas wrote to his "dear Mama" George: "What I like in her is that she's absolutely a woman from the tips of her toes to the depths of her soul." He was bewitched by the slinking finesse of her physique, adding: "With her amber skin, her tigress claws, her long fox-colored hair and her sea-green eyes, *she suits me!*"

The siege, this time, proved to be a long one. Unhappily married though she was to a man far older than herself, Nadine Naryshkin was not one to give in to the first impetuous assault. To begin with, she had a daughter (Olga) whom she did not care to shock at too tender an age. Nor did she have much taste for casual affairs. This one had to be a genuine passion — everything or nothing. Dumas *fils* rose heroically to the occasion but had to admit at times that it was hard, uphill work: "The battle began seven or eight years ago, and it was only two years ago that I managed to *tumble* her at last . . . I rolled in the dust with her a bit, but I'm on my feet again, and I think she's definitely on her back," he added with characteristic Dumas bravado. "Her last journey did the trick."

These annual returns to her native land, where she picked up more funds, had her visa renewed, and obtained a bogus medical certificate prescribing prolonged "convalescence" in some distant French spa, were less troubling to the young Dumas than the realization that he could not marry his green-eyed siren because the Tsar was implacably hostile to all forms of divorce. The resultant dilemma was particularly painful for a moralist who had used the stage to condemn the illegitimate consequences of male promiscuity. It was doubly galling for a lover who had to live in semiclandestine sin with a mistress who, a few months before he visited Nohant, had brought another daughter into the world — one hypocritically christened Nathalie Lefébure and merely "adopted" by the parents.

In George Sand the troubled playwright found a sympathetic confidant, who did her best to cheer him up during his brief stay at Nohant. After he had left, she wrote him a long letter to say that she felt not the least inclined to be a "personality"; she only wished to be his mother: "So let us remain altogether young and trembling right into old age, and let us try to fancy that we are merely starting out in life right up to the very eve of death . . . I am an optimist in spite of everything that has torn me to shreds; it's perhaps my only quality."

In his reply, written in mid-September, Dumas *fils* informed his "dear Mama" that he had finally overcome the hesitations of "Great Russia" (as he called his Nadine), who was apparently awed by the prospect of meeting the notoriously anthropophagic Madame Sand face to face. She would also like to bring along "Little Russia," her daughter Olga, rather than leave her all alone in the "forty-four-room shack" — the Château de Villeroy, east of Paris — which the princess was then renting. "Little Russia" would be no problem: "as a young, much-traveled Moscovite" she would be glad to sleep on a couch in her mother's room. "But there's a hitch. I have a friend, a fat friend who somewhat resembles your Newfoundland dogs, who's named Marchal, weighs 182 pounds, and has wit enough for four. He'll sleep anywhere, in the chicken coop, under a tree, under the fountain. May we bring him along?"

The answer of course was Yes. At Nohant both "Great" and "Little Russia" were hospitably received and duly entertained by Maurice's sprightly puppet shows. Dumas *fils* startled everyone at the dinner table by greeting the dessert with some verses of Alfred de Musset. But the surprise of surprises was *Marchal le Gigantesque,* also known as *le Mastodonte,* a huge hunk of jolly manhood who ate like a horse and kept the company in stitches with lively accounts of his many feminine conquests. An artist, like Clésinger, he had a taste for models and made few bones about it. He even seems to have thought, in a moment of brash euphoria, that he could give his hostess a quick "tumble," for the entry in her agenda book for October 10, 1861, includes this curious sentence: "Long visit from Marchal. Evening spent reasoning with him, while downstairs they were rehearsing."

Nine days later another entry noted that the jolly "Mastodon" was now become "my fat baby," but exactly how much petting and caressing this promotion involved is anybody's guess. This was not the kind of information George was going to confide to a diary jointly kept by Manceau and herself. But after Dumas and his two Slavic beauties had departed, Marchal, who had added his boisterous wit and voice most effectively to Maurice's puppet dialogues, was persuaded to stay on for another month and put to work making sketches of the household.

"We are expecting the gay Lambert," George Sand reported in another letter to Dumas on November 20. "Right now we have Borie and his young wife, a fat turtledove and his slim, solemn pigeoness. We'll only keep them for eight days. Others you don't know keep coming and going. But my greatest regret has been to let your fat friend Marchal go. I don't know how this mastodon managed it, but he has made himself adored by everybody, beginning with myself. It is true he spoiled us greatly. He did portraits of all of us, wonderful and charming as drawings and of a likeness such as portraits have never had. He had no idea he could do them, and is amazed to have succeeded. My portrait is a masterpiece; like those of Maurice and Manceau" and several other houseguests "which he tried, just to amuse himself . . . He's going to photograph the portrait he did of me, and you will at last have something that is me and not another . . . I don't know if you were here when he did his two sketches of Alsatian paintings. They are most remarkable. He doesn't know how to paint; but he draws wonderfully well. It's a contrast to be studied, this fat nature so delicately doing such elegant things."

It was indeed a contrast to be studied, and this particular study was to be carried rather far — much farther than Dumas *fils* can have anticipated when he brought his rollicking friend down to Nohant. So far as we know, Charles Marchal was George Sand's last lover. He was also destined to be one of the most inconstant. Which is hardly surprising. He was, after all, one year younger than Maurice.

36. New Joys and Sorrows

In the early spring of 1862 George Sand made another trip to Paris where, as was their wont, she and Manceau dined almost daily at Magny's, a Left Bank restaurant also frequented by Sainte-Beuve and the two Goncourt brothers, Jules and Edmond. The latter, encouraged by a letter she had written two years before congratulating them on a book of literary portraits, now came to call on her at Manceau's fourth-floor studio-flat on the Rue Racine, which she had long since made her Paris home. Silhouetted against the fading light of a late March afternoon, she looked to them at first like a motionless gray shadow which neither spoke nor moved. Accustomed as they were to the oral pyrotechnics of the literary salons they frequented, they were struck by the tranquil monotony of her voice, the gravity of her bearing, which seemed to them almost that of a ruminant, and the methodical, semisomnambulistic slowness of her gestures — as when she leaned forward and struck a small wax match to light another cigarette.

Manceau, who knew how solemn and tongue-tied his mistress could be when in the presence of strangers, did his best to enliven the flagging talk, which only warmed up a bit when the conversation turned to the theater of Nohant — where, as Jules and Edmond Goncourt later noted in their journal, "they play for her and for her maid until four o'clock in the morning" — a good example of how fanciful were the notions entertained by many Parisians about the doings at Nohant. One of the Goncourt brothers mentioned her prodigious faculty for work, whereupon she answered that this was in no wise *meritorious,* work having always been easy for her. Manceau — "who does the explaining rather as though he were showing off a circus wonder" — undertook to explain to the two visitors that Madame Sand worked every night from one till four in the morning, then worked for another couple of hours during the day. "She doesn't mind being disturbed," he added, almost boastfully. "Suppose you have a tap running and somebody comes in, you turn it off. It's like that with Madame Sand." Well, she corrected him, she didn't mind being disturbed by "sympathetic people" — by which were meant the "peasants who come to speak to me."

"When the time comes to take our leave," the Goncourt journal continues, "she stands up, gives us her hand and accompanies us to the door. Now at last we see something of her good, soft, calm face, the colors faded but the features still delicately drawn in a dull, pale shade, the color of amber. There is a finely chiseled lightness in her features which has not come through in her portraits, which have thickened and fattened her face."

Maxime du Camp, who also paid a call on her at this same studio-flat, was equally surprised at first — but as much by the presence of Manceau as by the appearance of George Sand. As a former editor of the *Revue de Paris,* he had often been exposed to bohemian authors — such as Gérard de Nerval, Charles Baudelaire, and the irrepressible Théophile Gautier. Even so, he seems to have been taken aback by the "shifty gaze" and "doubtful hands" of the gaunt and ill-kempt engraver "whom she dragged around with her and who seemed to maintain a kind of anxious watch over her," as he later described it in his *Souvenirs littéraires.* "She rolled a cigarette which she offered to me, spoke little, and seeing that I was surprised by her silence, she said: 'I don't say anything because I'm stupid.' This was excessive; she was only shy, and like people who write a great deal, she found a certain charm in keeping quiet. In her grayish brown silk dress and her stout walking shoes, she looked like a good middle-class housewife skilled in housekeeping, and did not in any way suggest the picture one could conjure up of Lélia. Dolled up in a neatly placed black wig, she would have looked ugly, with her dull complexion, flat cheeks and overly long teeth, if the gaze of her deep eyes had not recalled her pristine beauty. I sought to detect . . . the delicacy in the sketch Delacroix did of her, in man's clothes and with a tortured face . . . There was not a trace left; all had vanished with the whiff of age . . . There was something immobile about her, as though she were steeped in a penetrating placidity which no longer let emotions touch her."

Alfred de Musset's former love had now become a matron and was soon to be a mother-in-law for a second time. In 1850 the irresolute bachelor Maurice, who had so lightheartedly missed the bus with Augustine, had one day surprised his mother by declaring that the kind of wife he needed was a *jeune première* — a young actress gifted enough to play leading roles in the Nohant theater. This irresponsible suggestion had moved George to pen a long epistle of maternal reprimand, in which she told her son to put away "this fancy without determined object" and to wait "till a definite object stirs deeper fibers than those of theater comedy."

Now, at the relatively late age of thirty-eight, a less irresolute and frivolous Maurice was ready to make the fateful plunge. The long-awaited miracle was incarnated by the nineteen-year-old Marcelina Calamatta, the pretty dark-haired daughter of George Sand's old friend Luigi Calamatta. Maurice had known her since she was a child, for though her father was Italian, little "Lina" — as she was known — had been brought up in Paris. The painter Ingres had agreed to be her godfather, while her mother, born Anne-Joséphine Rochette, was the granddaughter of the no less celebrated sculptor Houdon. She was also something of a Catholic fanatic, a disposition which made for almost permanent tension in the Calamatta household, since the engraver was a freethinking republican who harbored little sympathy for Pio Nono, the once liberal Pope who had grown so frightened of revolutions that he now preferred the Austrians to a "red" like Garibaldi. When, in 1854, he sent his daughter south to Bianchina Rebizzo's boarding school in Genoa, it was probably as much to free her from her mother's bigoted influence as to perfect her knowledge of Italian. The cure at any rate worked wonders, and Lina returned from her three years in the south as ardently patriotic and antipapal as her father. This, allied to her lively intelligence and charm, made her particularly sympathetic to both George Sand and Maurice when she visited Nohant in 1860. For Maurice at this point in his life was becoming even more anti-

Catholic than his mother. So anti-Catholic, indeed, that when he and Lina were finally joined in wedlock, on the seventeenth of May 1862, it was a good deal less than holy, sanctioned but not sanctified in a purely civil ceremony.

The young bride's twentieth birthday was celebrated one month later in a blaze of Nohant fireworks. Her father, who had journeyed up from Milan for the occasion, was welcomed with a puff of powder and a loud report, as Maurice set off the miniature cannon he had installed near the Trianon chalets. The delicate Manceau recited a few verses he had improvised for the occasion, there were presents after dinner, and never had George Sand felt happier to be called a "Little Mother" . . . by a daughter-in-law whom she could cherish, as she had never been able to cherish Clésinger.

At Nohant Lina soon filled the void left by Augustine's departure. While Solange pursued her adventurous career, moving from one European city to the next on the arm of some wealthy patron or aristocratic lover, George Sand once again had a daughter on whom she could lavish her formidable reserves of maternal affection. Lina's soft Italian features made her ideally suited for certain theater parts, and her full-throated Italian voice was even more valued by the musically inclined mistress of Nohant, who liked to enliven plays and marionette shows with rustic bourrées and comic adaptations of old Berrichon chants. Not one to turn up her nose at culinary chores as being beneath her "status," Maurice's wife kept surprising the household with succulent dishes prepared according to Genoese and Florentine recipes; and like her mother-in-law, Lina proved an adept seamstress, diligently sewing and hem-stitching the little clothes for the child which, in the early autumn of 1862, she knew herself to be carrying.

In early September George Sand learned that her old friend and one-time lover, Pierre Bocage, had died at the age of sixty-two. As ardently republican as she, he had suffered far more from Louis Napoleon's meteoric rise to power, first losing his position as director of the state-subsidized Odéon theater and later finding it increasingly difficult to get dramatic roles commensurate with his talents. The gifted actor whom Alexandre Dumas had prized above all others for his plays had thus fallen on hard times. His name in

1862, for much of the theater-going public, was little more than a memory, much as Marie Dorval's had been in 1848. But having heard that the playwright Paul Meurice was preparing a stage version of George Sand's novel *Les Beaux Messieurs de Bois-Doré,* he had come to call on her at the Rue Racine apartment during her February visit to Paris, and had talked both her and Meurice into letting him play the role of the aged marquis Sylvain. To see this tall, faintly stoop-shouldered, and now white-haired actor thus return to the stage was, for a nostalgic Romantic like Théophile Gautier, almost like seeing a Phoenix rise from its ashes. But this belated triumph was also Bocage's swan song. Only by locking himself into his room during the day and seeing no one had he managed to spare his failing voice sufficiently to see the play through a hundred successful evenings. In doing so he used up his last reserves of strength, and shortly after the last performance he died.

By the end of this same summer George Sand had completed two more plays — *Le Pied sanglant* (later renamed *Cadio*) and *Jean le Rebâteux* (later reentitled *Les Don Juan de village*) — which kept the amateur actors of Nohant busier than ever. She also completed a forthrightly anticlerical novel, *Mademoiselle La Quintinie,* which was to make its author the idol of Parisian youth. Like Lamennais, George Sand had always felt that Christ's Gospel preached pity for the poor rather than satisfaction for the rich, and she was no readier to accept the Second Empire's bogus religiosity than she had been prepared to condone the get-rich-quick ethos of the Louis-Philippe regime. "They are, I think, going to close the taverns on Sundays, and at the same time forbid work, because on Sunday the workingman should neither work nor amuse himself," she had written to Maurice in December of 1850, even before the Empire was formally established. "He must spend the day at church. It is amazing how religious this will make the workingman, who is all too little so, as it is." To which she had added, prophetically: "He is indifferent to all religion; they will make of him an atheist."

Nothing Louis Napoleon had since done, not even the eleventh-hour "liberalism" he had displayed in sending a French expeditionary force into Lombardy in 1859 to free northern Italy from the Habsburg yoke, had reconciled her to the Second Empire's sanctimonious smugness. While she had hailed her country's military intervention with two belligerent pamphlets (one of them devoted to Garibaldi — "the elect of God, the miracle man," she had termed him), she could not forgive Napoleon III for having hastened to make peace after the French victories of Magenta and Solferino, leaving the Italian peninsula disunited and Venice still in Austrian hands.

George Sand no more believed in the divine right of emperors to enforce religion than she did in the divine right of kings to rule. The same went for editors. When François Buloz, whom she had long regarded as a political opportunist, undertook to serialize a devoutly sentimental novel entitled *Sibylle,* the work of a forty-one-year-old author named Octave Feuillet, she retaliated by pointedly making Buloz's native province — he was, after all, a Savoyard — the setting of her next novel.

In *Sibylle* a devout young girl who had begun to suffer from religious doubts after her first communion was eventually reconverted to the Catholic faith after seeing a priest row out alone into a stormy sea to save some sailors in distress. George Sand's answer to this piece of pious sentimentalism was first to have been called *The Novel of a Priest,* but in the course of composition the spotlight shifted to the heroine, who, like Lina Calamatta, was of mixed French and Italian parentage. The religious conflict which had finally torn the Calamatta household apart (with the father and mother living separate lives) was now reenacted in the struggle of conscience between the devout young daughter of a strait-laced general, Lucie La Quintinie, and her persuasive wooer, a freethinking young scientist named Emile Le Montier. The freethinker was in essence a younger version of Maurice, sharing both his and the author's pet phobias: the Catholic Church's belief in hellfire and damnation, its insistence on confession, its fear and condemnation of the "flesh," and its rejection of the idea of Progress. The novel thus became the story of a freethinker's unremitting efforts to liberate his beloved from these "heresies" and to convert her to "true Christianity" — one singularly reminiscent of Pierre Leroux's. First serialized in Buloz's *Revue des Deux Mondes* in the late spring of 1863, *Mademoiselle La Quintinie* was gobbled up by Paris' university youth, already trained by the "positivistic science" of Auguste Comte to regard traditional Christianity as a form of superannuated myth.

Never one to rest on her laurels, George Sand was soon hard at work on another play (*Le Château de Pictordu*). When Lina's devout mother turned up at Nohant in early July of 1863, she was astounded to find her pregnant daughter still going down to the nearby Indre with George Sand and the consumptive Manceau for cool dips in the river, while the evenings were devoted to the staging of Madame Sand's latest play. So all-consuming was the hostess' passion for the theater that on the eve of Lina's delivery the midwife as well as the two Calamatta parents were dragged in to La Châtre to watch a performance put on by a troupe of itinerant players. The suffering Lina had to wait for their return before being delivered of a boy. Thanks in part to this enthusiasm for the stage, the young Marc-Antoine came into the world — most auspiciously for George Sand and her republican friends — on July 14, the anniversary of the sack of the Bastille.

The heroic Roman name of Mark Antony failed to stick. For when Dumas *fils* turned up in early September, he found that the tireless word jugglers of Nohant had nicknamed the tiny infant Cocoton — as they had once done with the pint-sized Eugène Lambert, who having now made a name for himself as a painter of bright-eyed cats (instead of still-life fowls), no longer merited this appellation.

Now happily married in his turn, Eugène Lambert was more than ever persona grata with George Sand. So too was Victor Borie's father-in-law, Charles de La Rounat, who had succeeded Bocage as the manager of the Odéon theater. Like Alexandre Dumas *fils,* with whom George had extensively discussed the project, La Rounat seemed interested in seeing her novel of aristocratic country life, *Le Marquis de Villemer,* turned into a play and performed on the Odéon's broad stage. The younger Dumas had accordingly undertaken to rewrite the first two acts.

The evening after his arrival at Nohant, his "dear Mama" insisted that he read both out loud in the blue-wallpapered drawing room. While the dashing Maréchal de Saxe, in his gleaming breastplate and powdered wig, looked approvingly down from the glowing portrait

Maurice Quentin de la Tour had painted of him, Dumas' gifted son kept the assembled company enthralled with his histrionic performance. "Ah, spellbinding! What work!" was Manceau's enthusiastic comment when the time came to record the day's events in his mistress' agenda book.

Two days later a cousin of Manceau's named Louis Maillard arrived, closely followed by that huge teddy bear Marchal. With Madame Calamatta occupying one bedroom, Eugène Lambert and his wife, Esther, occupying a second, it was an uncommonly full house which had to receive the ebullient Théophile Gautier when he turned up the following evening. Dumas *fils,* being younger, was sent off to join Marchal in the pavilion, which had now become a kind of guesthouse, while the famous Romantic chronicler and poet was lodged upstairs.

Gautier's account of his first visit to Nohant, given a few days later to the Goncourt brothers at the end of another Restaurant Magny dinner, is worth quoting, full of postprandial exaggeration though it is. Asked if he had found the atmosphere at Nohant amusing, Gautier replied: "Like a convent of the Moravian Brothers. I arrived in the evening. It's a long way from the railroad. They pushed my trunk through a bush. I entered by way of the farm, in the middle of dogs that frightened the life out of me . . . I was given dinner. The food is good, but there's too much game and chicken — which doesn't suit me . . ."

"And what is life like at Nohant?"

"Breakfast is at ten o'clock. At the last chime, when the minute hand is exactly on the hour, everybody sits down to table. Madame Sand arrives with the air of a somnambulist and stays asleep throughout breakfast . . . After breakfast everyone goes out into the garden. There are games of bowls, and that revives her. She sits down and starts talking. At this hour the conversation is usually about questions of pronunciation . . . But not the slightest word on the relations between the sexes. I think you would be flung out on your ear if you made the slightest allusion to it.

"At three o'clock Madame Sand goes back upstairs and turns out more copy until six. Then one dines, only one dines rather hurriedly, to give Marie Caillot [sic] the time to have dinner. She's the household maid, a *Petite Fadette* whom Madame Sand found in the country to act in her theater plays and who comes to the drawing room in the evening.

"After dinner Madame Sand plays patience without uttering a word, until midnight . . . For example, the second day I began by saying that if we weren't going to talk literature, I was leaving . . . Ah, literature! They looked at me aghast! I must tell you that at present there is only one thing with which everybody there is occupied: mineralogy. Each person carries a hammer, one doesn't sally forth without one. So I said that Rousseau was the worst writer in the French language, and that way we had a discussion with Madame Sand until one o'clock in the morning.

"Even so, Manceau has really rigged up this Nohant place for turning out copy. She can't sit down in a room without the quills, blue ink, cigarette paper, Turkish tobacco, and lined writing paper appearing from nowhere. And how she uses them up! For as you are doubtless aware, she starts working again from midnight till four in the morning. Do you know what once happened to her? Something monstrous. She finished a novel at one o'clock in the morning . . . and started another that same night. Providing copy is a natural function with Madame Sand.

"For the rest, one is very comfortable at her place. The service, for example, is silent. There's a box with two compartments in a corridor: one of them is destined for letters to be posted, the other for letters for the house. For the latter you write down whatever you need, indicating your name and room. I needed a comb. I wrote: 'M. Gautier, such and such a room' and my request. The next day at six o'clock I had thirty combs to choose from."

But for Dumas *fils,* the uncomprehending Théophile Gautier might well have left Nohant the morning after his arrival. When the playwright brought the poet into George Sand's study, to prove that their hostess' chain-smoking silence in the drawing room was anything but hostile, she exclaimed: "What! Didn't you tell him I was as stupid as they make them and that I don't know how to converse with witty people? Tell this dear Théo he's mistaken." Dumas countered with a pun (based on the French words *trompe* and *éléphant*), which she promptly trumped with another, and dear Théo was persuaded to stay on.* The "copy" he later joked about, while dining with the Goncourt brothers, was of course the drama version of *Le Marquis de Villemer,* on which she worked with Dumas privately, even going as far as to feign a blinding headache so as to be able to retire upstairs, while Maurice, Manceau, Marchal, and Lambert were instructed to keep Gautier entertained with games of bowls and conversations on the terrace. The restless Théo finally left after a four-day sojourn, taking Dumas with him; whereupon the Nohant household went back to rehearsing a new Sand play, aromatically entitled *Datura Fastuosa—The Gaudy Trumpet-Lily.*

Manceau, whose frequent fevers and consumptive coughing were a source of growing concern to George, had meanwhile been encouraged to write a verse play, *Une Journée à Dresde.* There is little doubt that this was a grave psychological faux pas on the part of Maurice's mother. But Nohant at this point had succumbed to a literary as well as dramatic fever fierce enough to turn the soberest heads. A few years earlier Manceau had helped Maurice illustrate a two-volume history of the Italian commedia dell'arte which he had been asked to write for George Sand's publisher Michel Lévy. She herself had contributed an introductory preface and had copies of *Masques et Bouffons,* as it was called, delivered by her friend Prince Jérôme Bonaparte to his father-in-law, Vittorio Emmanuele II. The man who was destined to become a united Italy's first king had been so pleased with the present that he had decorated Maurice with the Order of Sardinia. Emboldened by the success of this first literary effort, Maurice had later struck out on his own; he had written up his transatlantic steamship voyage with Prince Jérôme in a travel book entitled *Six mille lieues à toute vapeur* (*Six Thousand Leagues at Full Steam*) and followed this up in the spring of 1863 with an Etruscan novel, *Callirhoé,* inspired by memories of the trip he, his mother, and Manceau had made through Umbria and Tuscany in 1855. Buloz, to his and George's delighted surprise, had found the novel good enough to be serialized in the midsummer numbers of the *Revue des Deux Mondes.*

This was all Maurice needed to persuade himself that he had a

* For an explanation of these double meanings, see the notes to this chapter at the end of the book.

genuine literary vocation. As a would-be illustrator of books, he had failed to make his mark. He had never been blessed with the patience and control which had made Manceau a much-esteemed engraver, nor did he have the penetrating eye which had turned the elephantine Marchal into a first-class portraitist. It was galling to his manly pride, doubly sensitive now that he was a husband, to be overshadowed by his illustrious mother and to be thought of merely as an eccentric country gentleman with a gift for taming foxes and animating puppets. (There was a cage full of small foxes, as well as an aquarium with sticklebacks and tenches in the Nohant dining room.)

Maurice now decided to write a second novel called *The Deluge* — the inspiration for which was only forthcoming in driblets. Manceau, working with his usual tenacity, had already finished his verse play, while Maurice had yet to compose his first chapter. At this point George should have quietly locked Manceau's effort in a drawer, as a treasured memento. But compassion once again got the better of wisdom. "Superb weather but too hot — walks, etc.," she noted in her agenda book on September 19. "Lina sings divinely . . . We rehearse *Datura,* after which Manceau reads us his play . . . It's charming to hear once again."

For her no doubt it was. But it was less charming for Maurice — and the increasingly impertinent Marie Caillaud, the humble serving girl whom George Sand had democratically decided to make a part-time actress, for the greater glory of the theater of Nohant — and, one suspects, the deliberate stupefaction of the snobbish burghers of La Châtre. Her growing success as a feminine "star" had made this home-grown Fadette as headstrong and capricious as a diva who was not going to be told how to act by that parvenu Manceau. As George Sand noted all too laconically in her agenda book on September 25: "Lovely *clair de lune* . . . I spend the day restoring peace . . . and arranging Marie Caillaud's costumes . . . Dress rehearsal tonight. I make cigarettes." Two days later she noted: "*Datura Fastuosa* . . . The play a great success. *Manceau surpasses himself*" — the three words underlined in her usual blue ink. "Lambert excellent, Marie Lambert charming and Marie Caillaud very good and sympathetic."

This Marie Lambert, as it happened, was not Eugène's wife but a well-known actress. The next day she returned to Paris with a message for the Odéon's manager, Charles de La Rounat, who was invited to come down to Nohant for a reading of *Le Marquis de Villemer*. George Sand spent the next three weeks putting the final touches to her and Dumas' dramatic adaptation, trying out different scenes on old friends who came to call, like Charles Duvernet and Alexis Duteil. On October 22 the work was sufficiently advanced for "the invincible Manceau" (as George termed him in her agenda book) to be able to read the play from beginning to end — a vocal feat which consumed all of four hours. His chronic cough notwithstanding, the devoted engraver repeated the exploit six days later — for the benefit not only of Charles de La Rounat, but also of Jules Boucoiran and Luigi Calamatta, who had arrived the day before. The entire household was once again gathered in the blue drawing room for the occasion — with the significant exception of Maurice, who preferred to withdraw to his bedroom with a "headache." The real reason, one suspects, is explained by this agenda-book entry: "Manceau reads like an angel." So angelically, indeed, that La Rounat assured her on the spot that he would have *Le Marquis de Villemer* staged at his Odéon theater early in 1864.

Thirteen years earlier Pierre Bocage and his nephew Paul (a close friend of Maurice's) had vainly sought to persuade George Sand to break with Manceau, apparently feeling that this liaison was unworthy of her. Maurice had then backed his mother, probably not realizing just how long this new love affair would last. Alexandre Manceau was, after all, his friend. But of friendly feelings there was no longer a trace.

The next agenda-book entries (in Manceau's hand) betray little of the mounting tension. October 29: "Departure of Calamatta . . ." October 31: "Boucoiran does some botany . . ." November 1: "Madame Sand has an attack of bilious colic . . ." November 4: "Farewell to this poor Boucoiran" — the faithful factotum who, unlike Manceau, had never enjoyed the favor of George Sand's bed. Not until the fourteenth do we catch a hint of the trouble brewing, this time in George Sand's hand: "Manceau reads Villemer for the last trial run here . . . Manceau reads like a jewel . . . Maurice is unwell, headaches and sciatica."

More than headaches and sciatica were involved, however, when the storm finally broke nine days later. Manceau took Marie Caillaud to task; Maurice defended her. The argument grew heated, as all of Maurice's pent-up jealousies and resentments now came bursting forth. Who, after all, was master in this house, Maurice angrily demanded, he or Alexandre Manceau? George, who had sensed but been unable to avert the mounting crisis, sought to calm her son: obviously it was Maurice and no one else who was the master of Nohant. Very well, declared Maurice, then Manceau must go!

Shaken by this unexpected vehemence, for which she was not prepared, his mother meekly gave in. Sadly wiping the tears from her eyes, she told Manceau that he was now "free" to leave Nohant. She begged Maurice to give him a little time — a favor which was readily granted. Having triumphed, her son could afford to be magnanimous.

That night (November 23) Manceau noted bitterly in the agenda book: "I was informed that I am free to leave on the next feast day of Saint John. Tears were shed for me! Not for long! This is all I have amassed in the way of regrets after fifteen years of devotion. I wish to note it here, so as never to have to cry about it and in the hope of later being able to smile again. No matter, mankind for the most part is a sorry thing . . . So I am going to regain my freedom, and if I wish to love somebody and devote myself once again, since that is my whole joy, I shall be quite free to do so . . . Freedom! How lovely. . ."

George Sand, on reading these reproachful lines, must have been touched to the quick. Here was her devoted Manceau standing in judgment over her — a liberty he had never previously taken. But how could she blame him? Sixteen years earlier she had been faced with the same kind of cruel choice — between Chopin and her son. She had sided with her son, because Chopin, through his nagging jealousy, had poisoned her existence. Lucrezia Floriani, her heroine, had died of it, but though desperately unhappy, George Sand had been in no mood to die. Manceau in any case was different. What was there to hold against him? His fidelity had been exemplary, his care and patience inexhaustible, his devotion boundless. To abandon him now would be monstrous, inhuman. It would prove to those who were only too ready to believe it that her heart was made of stone. As for Maurice, he was happily married and forty years old; he could fend for himself. Let him keep Nohant. She would stick with Manceau.

A week later Manceau left for Paris to look after his mistress' affairs, and in early January of 1864 George Sand journeyed up to the capital in her turn. She found the studio-flat on the Rue Racine well heated and the atmosphere at Magny's as cordial as ever. On January 13 she and Manceau went to the Odéon theater, where his verse play, *Une Journée à Dresde,* was given its première as a curtain raiser. Salvos of applause greeted the most stirring lines, and to judge by a rhapsodic letter George wrote the next day to her daughter-in-law, Lina, there was not a dry eye in the house. Marchal, Dumas and his two "Russias," Théophile Gautier, and the usual pack of critical bloodhounds were all present for the occasion, but the most enthusiastic in his acclaim was Prince Jérôme Bonaparte, who shouted over the heads of the frowning spectators to Manceau, insisting that the bashful author come into his box to receive the congratulations of his young wife.

The prospect of living cooped up in Manceau's little studio-flat was a good bit less exhilarating than this auspicious opening. George felt the need for fresh air and greenery such as she had known at Nohant. Manceau's cousin Louis Maillard generously volunteered to scout the Paris suburbs for an inexpensive cottage and finally found what they were looking for in the little village of Palaiseau, south of Paris and not far from the Chevreuse valley. "Very cold, snow flurries but no more," George Sand noted in her agenda book on February 7. "We leave for Palaiseau at noon, are at the cottage at 1:30. Everything seen and considered, we decided on the spot. Maillard and Jacques study the ground plan. Manceau makes projects for our installation."

To finance the purchase of this ideally located cottage, George Sand decided to sell most of the pen and pencil sketches, pastels, and canvases which she had received from Delacroix, who had died a few months earlier. She kept only *The Confession of the Dying Giaour,* this being the first of the painter's gifts to her, and a strange picture of a cave. A pastel entitled *The Education of Achilles,* a canvas showing Cleopatra receiving the lethal asp in a basketful of gleaming fruit, another of an Arab shown climbing up a rocky slope to surprise a somnolent lion were among the treasures auctioned off, while the little painting of Saint Anne giving a lesson to the Virgin Child, which Delacroix had executed at Nohant, was given to Edouard Rodrigues, the philanthropic banker who had agreed to underwrite the purchase of the Palaiseau cottage.

Had George Sand realized what a triumph her new play was to be, she would probably have hung on to most of these pictures and relied on a loan to tide her over. But the last few years, marked by a severe crackdown on the press which had made it difficult for her to get her novels serialized, had been particularly hard financially. It had taken Bocage's unexpected success in *Les Beaux Messieurs de Bois-Doré* to restore her self-confidence as a dramatist, severely shaken after the failure of three successive plays (*Lucie, Françoise,* and *Comme il vous plaira*) in 1856. During these January and February weeks she was full of trepidation. The rehearsals were slipshod, the players slow to learn their parts. On February 25, just three days before the dress rehearsal, Ribes, the lead actor, "had a fight with his female" (i.e., the lead actress), as George noted in her agenda book. "Manceau is livid and it's I who have to cheer him up." But the next day she had to admit that "Ribes plays remarkably well."

Though she found the stage sets "rich and ugly," the dress rehearsal, on February 28, went off far better than she had dared hope. It was so unusually warm that the windows of the foyer could be opened and the first scents of spring waft in from the Luxembourg Gardens. In the finest Romantic tradition everybody at the Odéon theater — from musicians and stagehands to on-duty firemen and gas-lamp lighters — wept at the sadder scenes.

The news that Napoleon III and Empress Eugénie would be attending the première, along with a flock of cabinet ministers and other dignitaries, left the author characteristically cold. As George wrote to her "dear children" (Lina and Maurice), "the emperor's police take up too much room . . . We'd rather have artists in the forward boxes than diplomats and functionaries. These people don't ruin their white gloves to thwart a cabal" — for to the very last she seems to have feared that her many enemies would again try to hoot the actors off the stage, as they had once done with *Cosima.* "The orchestra will be full of police informers, nothing will be missing from the fete."

Eighteen hundred and sixty-four being, as luck would have it, a leap year, the opening performance of *Le Marquis de Villemer* had been scheduled for February 29. The date proved to be auspicious and the author's fears unfounded. The nearby Latin Quarter had been suddenly electrified by the realization that a new Sand play was in the offing, and throughout the day the four flights of stairs leading up to Manceau's studio-flat were black with top-hatted students tramping up to ask for seats.

"I've just come back escorted by students to cries of 'Long live George Sand! Long live *Mademoiselle La Quintinie!* Down with the clericals!' It's a wild manifestation and at the same time a success, they say, such as the theater has never seen," she was at last able to report to Maurice and Lina in the early hours of March 1. "From ten o'clock in the morning onward the students were gathered in the square of the Odéon, and throughout the performance a compact mass of people who had been unable to get in filled all the neighboring streets and the Rue Racine right up to my door . . . Inside there were shouts and stampings through every scene, despite the presence of the entire imperial family. Besides, everyone applauded, the emperor like the rest, and he even wept quite openly. Princess Mathilde" — the Emperor's first cousin and the sister of Prince Jérôme Bonaparte — "came to the foyer to shake my hand. I was in the manager's box with the Prince and Princess" — Jérôme and his young, recently married wife, born Clothilde of Savoia. "The prince clapped hard enough for thirty claqueurs, leaning out from his box and shouting his head off. Flaubert was with us and crying like a woman. The actors played very well and there were repeated curtain calls after each act.

"In the foyer more than two hundred people I both know and don't know came up to kiss me, until I could take it no longer. There wasn't a trace of a cabal, though many of those present were unfriendly. But even those who innocently blew their noses were hushed up.

"I don't know if it will be as warm tonight," she concluded. "It's thought so, and inasmuch as three to four thousand people were turned back for lack of room, the public is likely to be numerous and ardent . . ."

Only later did George Sand discover exactly how triumphal this première had been. There was such a mob outside that the imperial carriage could not approach the Odéon's pillared steps. Refusing to have the police clear the square, Napoleon III walked sedately to the waiting carriage, spontaneously cheered on by students overjoyed by this startling democratic spectacle. A few of them made fun of the devout Empress Eugénie by singing the irreverent "Sire de Framboisy." Others had to be restrained by constables from unhitching the horses from George Sand's hackney cab and pulling it all the way to the Rue Racine. The rest led a noisy procession of five to six thousand demonstrators down to the premises of the Catholic Club and the house of the Jesuits next door, before which they stood chanting, "Oh, Holy Ghost, descend upon us!" in mocking falsetto voices which were finally stilled by the arrival of the mounted police.

The second night, if anything, was even more delirious than the first. The pious Catholics who had come to boo the play were overwhelmed by the shouting and cheering that greeted almost every line. The uproar was maintained through the intermissions, with hundreds of students in the galleries, corridors, and lobby chanting in unison: "Black men, where are you? Long live *La Quintinie!* Long live George Sand! Long live *Villemer!*"

"*Villemer* is still going marvelously," she wrote again to Maurice one week later. "The big press is even more laudatory than the small, and this without restriction. These gentlemen who had declared me incapable of writing for the theater now claim that I'm *very good.* The Odéon has been making four thousand francs an evening in seat bookings, with another six hundred at the box office. The carriages are lined up all day long to book seats, they're lined up again in the evening, with a long queue to the box office . . . Travelers reaching Paris who drive by the Odéon in the evening stop their cabs in alarm and ask if there's a revolution on, if the Republic has been proclaimed." To which she added the next day, in another dithyrambic missive to her son: "The success of *Villemer* has brought the crowds back to me. Manceau is going off his head. The doorbell doesn't stop ringing. I am in good health, nonetheless."

Six days later, on the eve of their departure for Nohant, they dined once again with Dumas *fils* at Magny's. Later, at ten o'clock in the evening, when he came up to say goodbye to them with the massive Charles Marchal, Dumas reported that the queue of waiting carriages stretched from the Odéon theater all the way to the new Boulevard Saint-Germain, which Baron Haussmann had recently pierced through the labyrinth of narrow Left Bank streets.

Nohant, to which they returned on the evening of March 16, was already aglow with hyacinths and daffodils. "Everything is bursting into leaf, but I shall never see the spring flowering here again," Manceau noted sadly in his mistress' agenda book. But George was overjoyed at being able to hug and fondle the little Cocoton again. In mid-February Maurice had written to say that, all things considered, he and Lina had decided to become Protestants, and would she be willing to become the godmother of their child? George Sand may well have wondered for a moment if Nature, once again, were not imitating Art. Her Albert de Rudolstadt had been a Protestant, and here was her own son, who had also loved a kind of real-life Consuelo (Pauline Viardot), now deciding to become a Protestant in his turn. Her written response in any case was favorable: "If it was to become a Catholic, I would say: 'No. It brings bad luck.' But the free Church is different, and you should not doubt my adherence for a moment."

Shortly after their arrival Luigi Calamatta turned up to do a portrait of his and George Sand's grandson, the nine-month-old Cocoton. Ten days later it was finished. The grandmother found it "very pretty" and had Manceau frame it. Already she could feel a new novel stirring within her — a novel about a lost child. Manceau, to whom she read the first pages, found it "very interesting." But the atmosphere of Nohant was such that she found it hard to concentrate on her writing. Nor did it much improve after Manceau had left in April with Luigi Calamatta. To humor Maurice she listened dutifully to the chapters of a new novel (*Raoul de la Chastre*) he had begun to write. "Always original" was her indulgent comment. Beyond that, the entries in her agenda book tell us little — save that on April 15 she helped her son concoct "a nice climax" for his novel.

Five days later, feeling the sudden urge to be on her own, she left for a brief stay at Gargilesse, arriving in the evening with a kind of provision hamper. Though it was only the twentieth of April, it was warm June weather, with a brilliant moon. She was fifty-nine years old and the most famous woman author in France; she had recently seen the Emperor and Empress applaud her latest play, but she was not above making her bed, sweeping the floor, and clearing up.

Three days later she was back at Nohant, having used the lamplit solitude of her sleepless nights to make headway on her new novel. Never had the lawns seemed greener, the new leaves more tender, the lilacs more delicately hued. The pink peonies were out and the Judas tree was beginning to blossom. But the air was heavy with reproach and she was depressed by Manceau's absence.

To finance the furnishing of the new Palaiseau cottage, George Sand and her consort had decided to relinquish the studio-flat on the Rue Racine in favor of a smaller pied-a-terre on the Rue des Feuillantines. Maurice, who seems belatedly to have realized that Nohant without his mother was going to lose half of its former animation, resolved to do his bit of economizing by accepting his father's invitation to visit him at Guillery with Lina and their child.

On June 7 Manceau returned unexpectedly to Nohant, weathering a drenching thunderstorm which almost washed away his carriage on the road from Châteauroux. "Madame," as he invariably called her, was delighted to have him back to help her with the packing — a more than usually onerous undertaking, since she had decided to clear out her study and to take many of her manuscripts to Palaiseau.

"Last evening at Nohant," Manceau noted four days later in her agenda book. "I think we shall all remember it. There is thus nothing to be written about this last evening. But I can't help thinking that during the 14 years I have spent here, I have laughed and cried and lived more than in the thirty-three years that preceded them. Henceforth I shall be alone with Her. What a responsibility! But also, what an honor and what joy!" To which an impenitent Maurice later added his two-pence worth of spite: "What a fathead! What a fool!"

Accompanied by Manceau, George Sand left Nohant the next morning at 7:00, reaching Paris at 4:30 in the afternoon, after a six-hour train ride from Châteauroux. Louis Maillard was waiting for them at the station platform and drove with them to the Rue des Feuillantines flat, which George found "delightful, clean . . . charming . . . Departure for Palaiseau at 7, arrival at the house at 8," she noted that same night in her agenda book. "I am thrilled with everything — the countryside, the little garden, the view from the house, the furniture, the dinner, the maid, the silence. This good Manceau has thought of everything, and it's perfection."

Though the cottage was decidedly small, here she had something she had always lacked at Nohant: a view over a varied landscape of flat, carpetlike wheat fields and pastures, lush vegetable gardens and orchards full of spreading fruit trees which seemed to her "enormous" after the dwarfs she had become accustomed to at home. In places the vegetation disappeared, revealing chalky escarpments and shallow patches of fine sand, but everywhere else the earth was dark, fine grained, and rich. "The meals here are delicious and never have I eaten so well," she wrote in a letter to Maurice. "The fruits and vegetables, which is mostly what I live off, are from a Land of Plenty. If we had such a soil at Nohant, we would be rich."

On June 22 Alexandre Dumas *fils* came out to spend the day and must have found the little cottage somewhat subdued compared to the animation of Nohant. No plays, no marionettes, no evening word games in the drawing room. "We play cards, we dine, we play again, we do what we can to keep Dumas from being bored," Manceau noted that night in his mistress' agenda book. "Do we succeed? Manceau accompanies him back" — to the little suburban train — "at 7 h 18."

The next day George Sand had to finish the entry her consumptive lover had begun. "Manceau coughed up a bit of blood, but it's nothing surely." Did she really believe it, or did she add that hopeful ending to cheer up her unfortunate companion? The ordeal she had known with Chopin was beginning once again.

It took them ten days to get everything unpacked and rearranged. With living space now at a premium, George Sand decided to get rid of excess paper. The first to be sacrificed was the manuscript of *Engelwald,* the novel inspired by an Austrian's attempt to assassinate Napoleon at Schönbrunn in 1809, on which she had toiled through many a night during her tempestuous romance with Michel de Bourges. In 1858 an Italian fanatic named Orsini had similarly tried to assassinate Napoleon III. Though this act of folly and even more the moving letter of explanation Orsini had addressed to the Emperor had later prodded Louis Napoleon into helping the Italian patriots against the Austrians, the immediate result had been the tightening of press censorship and the closing down of "dissident" or "suspect" publications, like Maxime du Camp's *Revue de Paris.* This was not the moment to heave a new firebrand onto the embers of imperial discontent. Besides, George Sand was now as opposed to political murder as she was to revolutionary violence. On June 28 she accordingly noted: "We proceed today to a well-*deserved* execution. *We burn Engelwald.* The terrace fireplace scatters its ashes to the winds during a good quarter of an hour . . ."

The next day the holocaust continued — with unpublished fragments of *Mauprat, Cosima, Maître Albertus* (presumably an early draft of *Les Sept cordes de la lyre*), and *Paul de Villemer* being committed to the flames. Probably none of them were worth saving, but one can only regret the burning of a fragment entitled *Les Petits Piffoël* — presumably a description of Maurice and Solange, written at the time of the Chamonix excursion with Marie d'Agoult and Liszt.

In early July they made two brief trips to Paris to see Buloz, who had already informed George Sand that he could not publish Maurice's new novel in the *Revue des Deux Mondes* without making extensive cuts — essential to avoid the kind of scandal and lawsuit that had been caused by the publication of Flaubert's *Madame Bovary.* It was a polite way of saying that the literary products of the son were not up to the mother's level, as George immediately understood.

"60 years old today," she noted in her agenda book on July 5, "with magnificent weather, sun, air, a pure sky, a countryside as fresh as in the month of May. I receive letters from my children. The Lamberts come to see me at 2 o'clock . . ."

But the calm was not to last. Just five days later George received word from Guillery that Cocoton — her grandson — had come down with dysentery. Immediately fearing the worst, she asked her son to keep her daily informed through semaphoric telegraph. "No news of the little one," she reported in her agenda book on July 13. "I'm desperate, deep down within me" — though she did her best to hide her anxiety from Eugène Lambert and his wife, who came out again for a visit. July 14: "Sad birthday for my poor little one. But this evening the telegram is better. There is hope, provided it keeps up!" July 17: "The telegram is good. The *improvement continues.* At last!" But on the eighteenth there was no telegram, only a letter from Maurice explaining that the child's fever had not abated.

On the nineteenth, just as she and Manceau were about to sit down to dinner with two friends, the telegraph messenger turned up with a laconic message: *"Much worse, little hope."* The two guests were hastily dispatched to Paris to alert Maillard, while Manceau and George Sand hastily packed their bags. But the little suburban train was late, and they reached the Gare d'Orléans in Paris five minutes after the departure of the train for Bordeaux. The next one did not leave until the following evening, so that they had to spend the night in the Rue des Feuillantines flat. "We did well to bring along Lucie" — the maid — as Manceau noted that night in the agenda book.

Another telegram from Guillery, which they received the next morning, was even more alarming. "If you want to see him, come." Leaving nothing to chance, George Sand talked her doctor friend Camille Leclerc into accompanying her and Manceau. At midnight they were at Orléans, reaching Périgueux early the next morning. Here they dismounted from the train and took the stagecoach to Agen, which they reached at 10:30. Climbing into a chaise, they posted on to Guillery. At two o'clock they were there, but it was already too late. A postman they had met on the road had told them that the child had died at one o'clock that morning.

As the carriage rolled up the driveway, between two impressive rows of plane trees, a haggard Maurice came out on the steps to greet his mother. He was followed by his father, a decidedly embarrassed Casimir who (as George described it later in a letter) "was as affected as he can be and showed me a lot of friendship." The chief cause of his embarrassment was his servant-concubine, Jeanny Dalias, who had joined him on the threshold. Casimir instructed her to accompany *"Madame la baronne"* to her room, taking care to add: "It has not been occupied since your departure."

"We let Madame console the children," Manceau later reported in George Sand's agenda book, "and we take our dispositions — dinner — the little dead child is placed in the bier. This poor little body is very painful to see. Camille [Leclerc] and I go to Nérac for the night."

The little Marc-Antoine was buried the next day in the Dudevant family vault at Lanmaignan. The arrival of a Protestant clergyman, specially summoned by Maurice, must have surprised his father, who was not inclined to any faith, save perhaps that of Rabelais. Maurice cried his way through lunch, while his mother later shocked the servants by smoking cigarettes — which may well have been her way of trying to hide her own grief. They were also amazed (according to one "witness") by the red petticoat Madame la Baronne was wearing beneath the long, daintily caught up dress.

The evening of the twenty-third George left for Agen, where she, Manceau, and Dr. Camille Leclerc spent the night. The next evening they were back in the little flat on the Rue des Feuillantines in Paris, and the following day they returned to the cottage at Palaiseau. "Camille examined Manceau," George Sand noted on July 28, "found him well and put him on arsenic" — apparently in the belief that this would alleviate his consumptive coughing.

With the coming of autumn Manceau's poor health took a marked turn for the worse. They could no longer spend the evenings on the sun-warmed terrace as they had done during the hot summer days. "Auguste the mason works on the fireplace in the living room," George noted on September 4. "Poor Manceau grows impatient and coughs horribly . . ." September 6 (again in Geoge Sand's handwriting): "Manceau still coughs and chokes." Six days later it was Manceau's turn to note: "Madame slept badly. She is tired and unwell. One is also ill at Palaiseau" — a reference to the frequent stomach pains and headaches that had plagued her at Nohant.

It is difficult from these laconic agenda notations to reconstruct exactly what was going on in George Sand's mind. But the cumulative effect of so much unhappiness — occasioned by her little grandson's death, Manceau's consumptive coughing, and the news that her half sister Caroline's husband had just died — was such that it precipitated a new crisis. On September 12 she told Manceau that she was going to Gargilesse for a few days with Charles Marchal. The latter had come out to Palaiseau to thank her for having used her good offices with Prince Jérôme Bonaparte, who had persuaded his cousin the Emperor to award him the little red ribbon of the Légion d'honneur. Though there had been an extraordinarily playful intimacy in the letters he had long exchanged with his "little ivory beetle" and his "little darling treasure," the "good mastodon" Marchal must have been startled as well as flattered by this sudden invitation.

Manceau, curiously enough, does not seem to have taken umbrage at this sudden "flight." He may have thought the possibility of an affair between the massive Marchal and his "little darling treasure" too outlandish to warrant jealousy; or he may have reached a state of such apathetic resignation as no longer to care. It seems more than likely, as Casimir Carrère has suggested, that George Sand had by now ceased all sexual relations with Manceau, as she had done earlier to "save" Jules Sandeau, Alfred de Musset, and Chopin from a premature demise through erotic overindulgence. Manceau's consumptive coughing was by now so persistent that she must have feared the worst; only this time she knew that she would have to nurse her sick one to the end. She needed a change of air to restore her shattered morale and to give her the strength to carry on. Compared to the frail, cough-ridden Manceau, the huge Marchal was strength incarnate, exuding the same kind of fresh, robust health that had once drawn her to Pietro Pagello, as she sat, desperate and despondent, by the bedside of the feverish Musset. Her "big baby," her "fat darling," her *gros monstre,* as she teasingly called him, was possessed of that unfailing good humor and hearty joviality which portly men often exhibit.

On September 14 the two of them left for Gargilesse, apparently accompanied by a maid, while Manceau was left to the care of a new cook. Just what happened at Gargilesse there is no way of knowing, for George Sand left her agenda book at Palaiseau, and Manceau scrupulously refrained from making any entries during her weeklong absence. On September 22 he went in to Paris and waited for her at the Rue des Feuillantines flat. That evening's entry noted: "She returned at five o'clock with Marchal and Lucie" — the maid. "We were waiting for her with Maillard. Dinner at Magny's with Maurice and Lina . . . We go to Maurice's apartment, then to Mr. Rodrigues'. Rehearsal at the Odéon — of a new Sand play, *Le Drac*.

The next week was spent in Paris, with daily visits to the Odéon and the usual dinner at Magny's. September 26 (Manceau's entry): "Another dinner at Magny's. Maurice talks of returning to Nohant." September 29 (Manceau again): "Odéon. Dinner at Magny's with Maurice and his wife. Première of *Drac*. It is going fairly well. I am convinced it won't make a penny, but one's honor is saved. Maurice is as insolent as the hangman's valet. We say good-bye to the children and return home with Maillard."

Thus the autumn gradually settled into winter, a winter which was to prove even bleaker than the summer. In late January Manceau, who was coughing worse than ever, was immensely upset by the sudden death of his cousin Louis Maillard, stricken by an attack of peritonitis. Unwell though he was, he insisted on traveling into Paris with George Sand and on accompanying his cousin's coffin all the way to the Père-Lachaise cemetery, a walk of some six miles.

But soon the time came when Manceau could no longer travel into Paris at all, being wracked by convulsive coughing fits whenever he tried to do too much. In a despairing effort to cheer him up, George began writing a novel with him — *our* novel, as he called it. But the pleasure it gave him could no longer halt the steady deterioration of his condition. On June 6, 1865, Manceau made his last entry in George Sand's agenda book: "In the evening I cough a lot. Madame advises me to eliminate the gas" — that is, the oxygen he had been given to inhale. "In the evening lotion . . . compresses . . ."

From then on she made all the entries, Manceau being too weak and dispirited to try to write. "He is the same as ever," she noted on the eleventh, "weak and calm in the morning, coughing more and more as the day advances . . . The fever is hard to combat . . ." She tried giving him quinine, then came back to sulfates — all to no avail. "Sad day, rather cold, for us sunless and joyless . . . Manceau is stunned. He spends the whole day on the divan, listlessly, and says he doesn't suffer." June 27: "Morère, the doctor, comes to talk of the weather and one thing and another . . . everything he has proposed has failed to work. I suffer as much as ever and cannot regain my courage."

By July 5 she was no longer trying to conceal the note of mounting anguish. "How painful it is to see him so ill and desperate! What courage can I give him to overcome such crises! I haven't got it in me to see him suffer so. The Lamberts come this evening at 4 o'clock . . ."

Seeing that neither Dr. Morère nor her friend Dr. Camille Leclerc could do anything to improve Manceau's condition, she wrote to Montpellier and persuaded Dr. Fuster, a well-known "specialist" in the treatment of tuberculosis, to journey all the way up to Paris for an expert look at Manceau. His examination proved as fruitless as the others'. Among other things *cold water* frictions were prescribed which she did not have the heart to apply, though the shivering Manceau insisted that they be carried out to the letter.

By early August he was so weak that he could no longer rise from his bed. George now had to watch him by night as well as day. The following entries give some idea of the ordeal it must have been. August 9: "He eats in bed and then dozes off for the rest of the day. He speaks to me between 10:15 and 10:30. He is more lively, more irritable, more affectionate. He still thinks of everything." August 17: "One more sad day . . . . The diarrhea returns, his weakness is not diminished. His choking is perhaps less violent." August 18: "He coughs uninterruptedly all night and all day. 48 hours! It's heartbreaking, yet he's infinitely calmer than on the preceding days." August 19: "Same state, only worse . . ." August 20: "Alas! He's been reading everything I've written here, and here I was afraid of irritating him . . . . It's been several months now that I've known" — that Manceau was dying and could not be saved. "What a fight I've had to hide it from him!"

On August 21 the long ordeal was ended, just as she had sensed and feared for weeks. "*Dead* this morning at six o'clock, after a night that was seemingly completely calm. On waking up he spoke a bit in an already dead voice, and then came vague words, as in a dream, and then a few efforts to breathe, then a pallor, and then *nothing*. He was not conscious, I hope. At midnight he had spoken to me with willpower and lucidity. He talked of going to Nohant! . . . I changed his nightgown and arranged his bed. I closed his eyes. I put flowers round him. He is handsome and seems quite young. Oh, my God! I shall never watch over him again . . ."

Charles Marchal, who had said that she must let him know if and when she needed his help, came out immediately to see her, as did Victor Borie and Alexandre Dumas *fils.* Manceau's sister Laure, who also came out to Palaiseau, refused to go upstairs for a last look at her brother, saying that the sight of his dead face would be too much for her. She had written to George Sand, urging her to summon a priest to administer the extreme unction before Manceau died, but the request, typically enough, had been ignored. "So he's damned and one's not going to give him a last kiss," George wrote in disgust to her son, Maurice. "The mother didn't appear, it was she above all who wanted him to confess, without a fear for the mortal blow this would have dealt him: a mother! Such are the devout. We're not carrying him to the church, needless to say; so the beadle has refused us the bier and winding sheet. But the village workers, who adored him, want to carry him with a white sheet and flowers."

Maurice arrived in time to accompany his mother and the other mourners to the village graveyard. "What good he did me! What a day of emotion and tears!" George noted in her agenda book. But about her son's real feelings she had no illusions. "I'm so utterly worn out and dazed that I can't leave tomorrow," she wrote to her daughter-in-law, Lina, who had remained at Nohant. "I'll hurry down, rest assured. You were the first to say to him: 'Go fetch your mother.' I know it, I thank you and I bless you."

On August 27 Maurice and his mother set out for Nohant. Now that her lover was dead, George Sand could at last be reconciled with her son.

37. The Good Lady of Nohant

AFTER SEVERAL WEEKS spent at Nohant, where she found her daughter-in-law, Lina, already four months pregnant, George Sand returned to the little house at Palaiseau. Though she had a cook to prepare her meals and wait on her, as well as a gardener who lodged with his family in a pavilion beyond the shrubs and flowers, she was lonely and felt the need for human company. The friends who came out to see her, or who called on her during her frequent trips into Paris, were, however, amazed by her resilience and energy. It was almost as though, with Manceau dead, she had turned over a new leaf. Though haunted by his memory, she refused to yield to gloom and apathetic self-pity. After all, she was only sixty-one! There was still so much to learn and do, even at her age. There were new plays to be seen, new books to be read, new novels to be conceived. "Life for me is always the present instant," she had written three years earlier to Marie d'Agoult, with whom she still occasionally corresponded; and as she was soon to admit with equal frankness to Gustave Flaubert: "I forget so well."

The most adept, if not the most assiduous, in helping her to forget her loss was the rollicking Charles Marchal. With his pointed mustachios and Vandyke goatee, he looked more than ever like a nineteenth-century Porthos. But he was a Porthos with the temperament of an Aramis. By late October of 1865 George was beginning to use the familiar second-person *tu* in her letters to him, and in early November she playfully dubbed him *mon gros printemps* (my plump spring) — which would seem to indicate that by this time their friendship had ripened into a full-bodied liaison. She was obviously troubled by the marked disparity in their ages (twenty-one years) as much as by the marked disparity in their respective sizes, and she was not a little embarrassed by the pathetic pleas she had to make to be able to see this distinctly offhand cavalier. "Any way, take me as I am," she wrote to him in late November. To which she added, in the two-fisted style she often affected with her male friends: "I give you a formidable punch, to cheer myself up, for when I'm alone with myself I'm as sad as a donkey."

From Nohant, where she spent Christmas and New Year's, George wrote to complain in early January because her "dear fat child" had written her but once. She would soon be back in Paris, ready to lead her casual lover down the primrose path once more if he had time— or, she added with a sigh of resignation, "to applaud you in your work if you are working." The very next day — the tenth of January 1866 — another of her worries was happily resolved when Lina gave birth to a dark-eyed daughter, named Aurore in the good Koenigsmark tradition.

Three weeks later the contented grandmother returned to Paris and to Palaiseau from where she was soon bombarding Marchal with suggestive, not to say suppliant letters. She seems to have sensed, reluctantly, that this was to be her final "fling." For the title she gave to the new novel she was working on — a novel about an elderly husband's patience with his young wife's infidelity (the approximate reverse of George Sand's real-life situation) — was, significantly enough, *Le Dernier Amour — The Last Love.*

In Paris, whenever she had a free evening, she continued to dine at Magny's. Thanks in large part to Flaubert's insistence, the two Goncourt brothers and Sainte-Beuve, who had previously thrown cold water on Princess Mathilde Bonaparte's wish to be invited to their fortnightly dinners, had agreed to make an exception for George Sand. "They could not have welcomed me more warmly," she noted in her agenda book on February 12, 1866. "They were brilliantly witty, save for the great scientist Berthelot . . . Gautier as dazzling and paradoxical as ever; Saint-Victor" — a well-known literary critic — "charming and distinguished; Flaubert, an impassioned debater, is more sympathetic to me than the others. Why? I don't yet know."

George Sand's slight deafness made it difficult for her to keep up with the rapid-fire dialogue of several conversationalists — but, as was her custom, she preferred to listen rather than to "shine." Edmond de Goncourt noted in his journal: "She is there beside me, with her lovely and charming head and a mulatto complexion which has grown more pronounced with age. She looks at everyone with an intimidated air, whispering in Flaubert's ear: 'You are the only one here who doesn't put me off!' She listens, doesn't speak, sheds a tear for a verse play of Hugo's at the point where its false sentimentality shows through. What I find striking in this woman-writer is the marvelous delicacy of the little hands, lost and almost hidden in her lace sleeves."

This initial timidity, habitual with strangers, was soon overcome, however, and three months later she startled the Goncourt brothers by appearing for the fortnightly dinner in a bold peach-flower dress, "worn, I suspect, with the intention of raping Flaubert" — as one of them commented in the journal.

George Sand's growing friendship with Gustave Flaubert was one that honored both of them. For in literary tastes and conceptions they were poles apart. A firm believer in the aristocratic doctrine of "Art for Art's sake," Flaubert cared little for the kind of didactic fiction in which George Sand specialized. None of her early novels had found favor with him, with the curious exception of *Jacques* — a novel which today is virtually unreadable but which had shocked many middle-class readers at the time for its ostensible advocacy of "free love." In 1844 he had even boldly proclaimed, in his preliminary draft, that he was not writing *L'Education sentimentale* for fourth-form schoolgirls or seamstresses who enjoyed reading George Sand. He had not been impressed by the extracts of *The Story of My Life* which he had read in *La Presse,* and as late as 1859 he was still writing to friends, like Ernest Feydeau, the novelist, to warn them against the doctrines of "*la mère* Sand."

Doctrines, however, were one thing; personal feelings another. Four years later, in January of 1863, Flaubert, whose gory Carthaginian novel *Salammbô* had been rather poorly received by most Paris critics, was agreeably surprised by the flattering article George Sand devoted to it. The novel probably reminded her of Delacroix's fiery canvases of stormed cities and Sardanapalian orgies, while the author's historical research was reminiscent of the pains she herself had taken with the Bohemian background of *La Comtesse de Rudolstadt.* "His imagination is as fecund, his power of description as terrible as Dante's," she did not hesitate to write. "What a sober and powerful style to contain such an exuberance of invention!"

Flaubert had written to thank her, and she had courteously replied, in a letter addressed to "my dear brother," inviting him to visit her at Nohant. Though they do not seem to have exchanged many letters over the next eighteen months, George Sand was already sufficiently familiar with his powerful build, balding head, round chin, and swooping, thatchwork mustache to be able to invite Flaubert to her box and to see him weeping his sea green eyes out during the première of *Le Marquis de Villemer* in February of 1864. They probably met at Magny's Restaurant more than once over the next few months, and they had in Princess Mathilde Bonaparte (the sister of Jérôme and the first cousin of Napoleon III) a common friend, whose salon they occasionally frequented. By the summer of 1866 they had established a solid friendship, and when, in the late autumn of that same year, *Le Dernier Amour* appeared in volume form, it was not dedicated to Charles Marchal, who had partly inspired it, but to Gustave Flaubert.

Just how much she knew about the "old troubadour" (as she was soon to call him) when she accepted his invitation to visit him at his widowed mother's country house near Rouen, there is no way of saying. But a man capable of writing a novel like *Madame Bovary* was obviously no cold-hearted creator. George Sand must have sensed very quickly that "with his policeman's air" (as another of his feminine admirers, Madame Roger des Genettes, was to put it) "he had a delicacy that was quite feminine." To be sure, he was a cynic, capable of writing on the flyleaf of a gift copy of *Madame Bovary: "L'Amour est comme l'opéra. On s'y ennuie, mais on y retourne."* (Love is like the opera. One is bored, but one keeps going back.) He was also, unlike George Sand, a pessimist who mocked the cult of Progress. His own despair was born of a feeling of frustration at having been born too late — like Alfred de Musset. But if Musset had suffered from the realization that he had missed the heroic tumult of the Napoleonic age, he had at least been able to throw himself heart, soul and bearded body into the Romantic Revolution of the late 1820s and early 1830s. Flaubert, born ten years after Musset, in 1821, had been too young to take part in this literary and artistic orgy, and it had left him with a sense of frustration which he had brilliantly transcribed in the pathetic person of Emma Bovary, dying to join the "lyrical legion" of those adulterous heroines she had read about in novels (like George Sand's).

Instead of proceeding directly to Rouen to meet Flaubert, George Sand, in mid-August of 1866, took the train to Dieppe for a brief visit with Alexandre Dumas *fils*. Now married at last to his green-eyed goddess Nadyezhda (following on the death of old Prince Naryshkin), the younger Dumas had bought a seaside villa for himself and his family at the Norman fishing village of Puys. Enchanted though she was by the villa's setting — with the wooded hills sloping down to the chalky cliffs and flint-strewn beaches beyond which the pearl gray sea rolled its crested breakers in through the restless foam — George Sand could not have arrived at a worse moment. Her Russian hostess was ill, and Dumas, to keep his sick wife company, insisted on retiring immediately after dinner, at eight o'clock in the evening. For a night owl like George this was punishment indeed. In her upstairs bedroom she found there was only one candle to read by; for her ablutions there was "a vase and a salad bowl" (as she noted caustically in her agenda book); and the maid service was so poor that she had to go out to fetch her own water! The windows, warped by the sea air, would not properly close, and in the unheated bedroom she froze.

After two nights of this spartan regime she was happy to move on to Flaubert's home at Croisset, where the service was of a less casual order. The self-styled "recluse" was waiting for her at the Rouen station with a carriage in which he took her on a brief tour of the old town's medieval center, with its quaint, narrow streets, its flamboyant Gothic cathedral, and the fifteenth-century town hall in which Joan of Arc had been tried by a panel of British bishops. The pleasant eighteenth-century mansion in which Flaubert lived with his mother was situated several miles downstream in what was then a suburban village. Flanked by Lombardy poplars on one side, by a graceful avenue of linden trees on the other, with a garden rising gently toward the rolling hills behind, the house looked out over a terrace walk toward the tidal waters of the Seine. In his upstairs study Flaubert had even installed a telescope through which he could view the "thousand spires" of Rouen to the left and to the right the steamships plying up the estuary from the ocean.

George Sand found Flaubert's septuagenarian mother charming, and she was most agreeably impressed by the cleanliness of the house, the promptness with which the servants brought her water to wash with, and the quiet efficiency with which her every wish seemed to have been foreseen. She was also pleased to discover that her host was a night owl like herself and quite capable of working into the small hours of the morning. Normally so wary of inviting female guests to his home, he insisted after dinner on taking her upstairs to his book-lined study, where he read her fragments of the as yet unpublished *Tentation de Saint Antoine* — that strangely lush prose epic on which he had been working fitfully for over fifteen years. George Sand found what she heard "superb," but whether it was the lavishness of Flaubert's descriptions of the Nile or the vividness of the anchorite's tempting hallucinations, her agenda book unfortunately does not specify. All it records is that the two writers talked till two o'clock in the morning.

The next day Flaubert took his houseguest, with his mother and two friends, on a steamboat trip down the Seine. They were buffeted by pelting rain, but while the others huddled inside, George Sand, as resolute and sturdy at sixty-two as she had been at thirty with Musset, preferred to remain on deck, watching the windswept water. Still, it was a wonderful feeling to be back three hours later, able to dry out one's soaked clothes in front of a crackling fire while gulping down cups of hot tea. Later Flaubert led her round the property, showing her the garden, orchard, vegetable patch, farm, and finally what he termed the "citadel," an old wooden house which had been turned into a granary. He took her up the stairs to a little outdoor balcony from where there was a fine view over the Seine valley. This was followed by an excellent dinner, some card games with Madame Flaubert and a friend, and another long conversation with Flaubert which lasted until two in the morning.

This first visit left her more than ever intrigued by this curious bachelor whose earthy wit, she sensed, was essentially a mask. "You are a being quite apart, most mysterious, and withal as gentle as a lamb," she wrote to him from Nohant on September 21. "I much wanted to question you, but I was kept from doing so by too great a respect for you . . . Sainte-Beuve, who likes you nonetheless, claims that you are frightfully vicious."

"What! Me a mysterious being? Come, come, *chère Maître!*" Flaubert immediately replied. "I find myself abominably platitudinous, and I'm sometimes bothered by the bourgeois that lies concealed within me. Sainte-Beuve, *entre nous,* doesn't know me at all, no matter what he says. I even swear to you (by your granddaughter's smile) that I know of few men less 'vicious' than myself. I have dreamed a great deal but done but little . . . If you want my frank confession, I shall give it to you unstintingly. A sense of the grotesque has held me back on the downward slope of depravity. I maintain that cynicism borders on chastity. We shall have much to say to each other on the subject (if you are in the mood) the first time we see each other."

George Sand's reply to this was, if anything, even more cryptic: "Now that I am no longer a woman, I would become a man, if the good Lord were but just. I would be full of physical strength and I would say to you: 'Let's take a trip to Carthage or elsewhere.' But there it is, one advances toward infancy, which has neither sex nor energy."

Literally interpreted, this would seem to indicate that she and Charles Marchal were now no longer intimate but simply friends—on those rare occasions when she managed to see him. Which may well have been the case. But it is equally possible that this was a white lie, inspired by her own "sense of the grotesque."

In early November, at any rate, she accepted her unvicious tempter's invitation and made a second and longer visit to Croisset. Flaubert himself took the train with her to Rouen, where they were met by his mother and his brother Achille, a doctor. In her agenda book Flaubert was now called Gustave, a sure sign of the growing sympathy she felt for this deceptively gruff bachelor who had prudently shied away from marriage, which had so complicated her own existence. Even more than George Sand, Flaubert had been marked for life by his first great love — Elisa Schlesinger, by whom he had been smitten when he was barely fourteen years old. Unhappily married to Maurice Schlesinger, the same penny-pinching "Shylock" who had paid Chopin so shabbily for his priceless Mazurkas, Elisa Schlesinger had been for the young Flaubert what Aurélien de Sèze had been for Aurore Dudevant — a kind of unattainable ideal, a great and almost certainly platonic love. It seems inconceivable that at some point in their growing fondness for each other George Sand and Flaubert should not have talked about Elisa Schlesinger, the real-life model for Madame Arnoux in *L'Education sentimentale,* the novel on which an older and wiser Gustave was now working.

"I'm quite *unhinged* since your departure, I have the feeling it's been ten years since I've seen you," Flaubert wrote to her a few days later. "My one subject of conversation with my mother is yourself, everyone here is fond of you . . . I feel a *particular* tenderness for you which I haven't felt for anyone up till now. We got on well together, don't you think, it was charming . . . We parted just when we were about to let our lips say certain things. All the doors between us are not yet open."

George Sand, in her reply, was more guarded. "I was very happy during those eight days with you. Not a care, a comfortable nest, a lovely countryside, affectionate hearts, and your handsome and frank face which has something paternal about it. Age does not affect it; one senses in you an infinitely kind protection, and one evening, when you called your mother *my girl,* I had tears in my eyes. I was reluctant to leave, but I was keeping you from working, and then — a malady of my old age is to be restless. I am afraid of becoming too attached and of wearying others. The elderly should be of an extreme discretion. From afar I can tell you how much I love you without fear of harping on the same string. You are one of the *rare* beings who have remained impressionable, sincere, in love with art, uncorrupted by ambition, unintoxicated by success."

From Palaiseau she wrote again a few days later to describe the "utter loneliness" she now felt in the cottage which was still haunted by a dead man who had ended his days "like a lamp which has gone out but is still there . . . And what are you doing at this hour? . . . The night there must be lovely. Do you occasionally think of the old troubadour on the country inn's grandfather clock, forever coming out to sing of a perfect love?" To which Flaubert replied that, of course, he thought of the old troubadour — which was to become George Sand's nickname for him thereafter — and indeed regretted him. "How nice they were, those nocturnal talks of ours (there were times when I had to restrain myself from kissing you like a big child)."

This was as close as Flaubert ever came to admitting that he had been sorely tempted. Though they continued to discuss the temptations of the flesh and personal experience, it was for the most part within a literary context. "One must be neither spiritualist nor materialist, you say, one must be a naturalist," she replied to a later Flaubert letter. "This is a major question . . . No, I have no theories. I spend my life raising questions and seeing them resolved one way or another, without a victorious and unanswerable conclusion ever being given." Nor was she able to accept his single-minded devotion to his craft, which he put above all else. "*Sacrosanct literature,* as you call it, is merely secondary in my life. I have always loved somebody more, and my family more than that somebody."

Though their ideas and working methods differed, as writers they shared a common and recurring predicament. "So you are having money troubles once again?" she wrote in answer to a plaintive letter from Croisset. "That's all I've known ever since I was born. I live off my day's wages like a proletarian; when I'll no longer be able to do my day's fill, I'll be bundled off to the next world and I'll need nothing more." How could Flaubert not marvel at this dogged determination, particularly when he compared it to his own fitful inspiration? "You do not know, you, what it is to remain a whole day with your head in your two hands trying to press this unhappy brain into finding a word. The idea flows from you broadly, incessantly, like a flood. With me it's a thin trickle. I need great works of engineering to obtain a waterfall. Ah yes, I can say I've really known them, the *pangs of style!*" To which his *chère Maître* replied, with touching humility: "When I see the trouble my old one takes to write a novel, I'm discouraged by my own facility and I tell myself I'm turning out slipshod prose."

Much as she admired his painstaking efforts to produce a smooth, unruffled, absolutely limpid style, she could not share Flaubert's aversion to didactic novels or agree when he confessed to feeling "an invincible repulsion to set down on paper something of my heart. I even feel that a novelist doesn't have the *right to express his opinion* on anything whatsoever. Did God ever state His opinion?" This cold-hearted "neutrality" instinctively chilled her ardent, combative nature. "To put nothing of one's heart into what one writes? I don't understand at all, oh, but not at all! It seems to me one can't put anything else into it. Can one separate one's mind from one's heart?" she asked, adding, some eight or nine years later: "Perfect impartiality is antihuman, and a novel must be human above all."

In December of 1866 George Sand left Palaiseau for Paris, intending to continue on to Nohant for Christmas. But at the Rue des Feuillantines apartment she came down with a violent gastric attack that almost killed her. She was confined to her bed for more than two weeks, and not until January 10, 1867, could she finally make it to Nohant, in time to celebrate her granddaughter Aurore's first birthday. Maurice, who had feared the worst, now pleaded with his mother to give up the little Palaiseau house, where there was no one to look after her but the cook and gardener and such doctors as could be lured out from Paris. George Sand needed little persuading: the cottage, with Manceau's death, had lost most of its raison d'être, while at Nohant she had, in her daughter-in-law, a "treasure of a woman" to take care of her, as well as a velvet-eyed granddaughter — now nicknamed "Lolo" — to spoil.

"I am thinking of going to the Riviera when I have seen my children," she had written to Flaubert on the eve of her departure from Paris. But it was not until the following year — 1868 — that this longing was to be fulfilled, thanks to a new and fervent friendship with a writer of her own sex.

Almost forty years younger than George Sand, Juliette Lamber had been brought up in the increasingly scientific climate of the mid-nineteenth century by an extreme left-wing socialist and had been married off to a lawyer, La Messine, who was an Auguste Comte "positivist." In her daily battle against the masculine agnosticism of her father and husband she had found two heroines to sustain her faith and idealism. The first was George Sand, a fervent if somewhat heretical believer in a kind of pantheistic God; the second was Marie d'Agoult, who under the pen name of Daniel Stern had written a novel called *Nélida* about her love affair with Liszt before producing a masterly three-volume history of the 1848 revolution. In the late 1850s these two eminent ladies had aroused the withering scorn of Proudhon (the same iconoclast who had once proclaimed that "Property is Theft!"), and in a three-volume opus entitled *La Justice dans la Révolution,* the old communist curmudgeon had heaped ridicule on George Sand and Daniel Stern. Outraged by this misogynistic assault on her two idols, the twenty-year-old Juliette had locked herself into her bedroom with her young daughter, and while her lecherous husband was fornicating with a maid in another part of the house, she had burned the midnight oil forging a counterblast to which, when it was ready, she gave the ringing title of *Idées anti-Proudhoniennes.* The book had finally been published by a humble bookseller after being rejected by a score of publishers who had mocked her desire to become a "bluestocking" like George Sand. It had made her a celebrity and one of the attractions of Marie d'Agoult's fashionable Paris salon.

George Sand's response to the paeans of praise heaped upon her by the young Juliette La Messine was at first distinctly wary. She had never felt much sympathy for women authors. It had taken her years to overcome her initial distaste for Hortense Allart's gushing admiration, while she could not stand the literary wiles of adventuresses like Caroline Marbouty and Louise Colet, who seemed to think that the easiest way of acquiring something of the genius of men like Balzac, Flaubert, and Alfred de Musset was to have it rub off on their quivering bodies while making love to them. But after receiving favorable reports from several Paris friends, George sent her young admirer a copy of *Monsieur Sylvestre,* a novel she had written in 1865 around the theme: is happiness in this world possible? In this novel the idealism of her own generation was personified by Monsieur Sylvestre, a disillusioned 1848 revolutionary who has withdrawn from the world in disgust, persuaded as he is that all forms of society are inevitably bad, while the skepticism of the younger generation was epitomized by Pierre Sorrède, who is convinced that the dream of universal fraternity cannot be realized from "without" through the mere establishment and imposition of "perfect" laws.

"Virtue and faith, when decreed, are no longer faith and virtue; they become detestable," the latter was made to say, obviously expressing the author's maturer wisdom. In short, revolutions are nefarious and tyrannical to the extent that they have to be rammed down the throats of unwilling subjects.

Without realizing it, George Sand had ceased to be an ardent revolutionary and become a cautious "reformer." Juliette La Messine was frankly shocked by her heroine's abandonment of the political idealism that had marked her youth and middle age — a shift she attributed to Flaubert's sardonic turn of mind and to the social skepticism of the Goncourt brothers. She wrote as much to George Sand, who was much amused by the criticism of this young admirer, now more trenchantly Sandist than Sand herself.

Thus began a correspondence which slowly blossomed into a deep friendship. It was retarded, on Madame Sand's part, by the realization that Juliette La Messine was a good friend of Marie d'Agoult's, who rarely lost an opportunity for denigrating George. But this stumbling block was removed by the providential death of Juliette's husband. Free at last, she made no secret of her wish to marry the man she loved — Edmond Adam, a political journalist. Marie d'Agoult, who had borne three children to Franz Liszt without trying to marry him, felt that this was a deplorable concession to bourgeois respectability. "The trouble with being a widow," she declared with characteristic hauteur, "is that one has the stupid longing to remarry. A woman who thinks must remain free and the absolute mistress of her thought, do you hear, Juliette?" Refusing to hear, Juliette replied: "I need happiness more than I need freedom." This retort unleashed an incredible fit of rage on the part of Marie d'Agoult, who accused her young protégée of wanting to develop a rival politico-literary salon aimed at "killing" her own.

Unburdened at last of this crippling love-hate friendship, Juliette La Messine asked George Sand to receive her the next time she came to Paris. It was as curious a first meeting as we know of in the life of George Sand. For it was even more wordless than usual. When the intimidated young authoress was ushered into the Rue des Feuillantines apartment, she was frankly taken aback by the short, matronly woman who pointed to the armchair next to hers while her fingers continued to roll a cigarette. The cigarette lit, she lapsed into a pensive frown, apparently not quite knowing how to break the ice. Overcome with emotion, Juliette La Messine burst into tears. George Sand then opened her arms and the two embraced. Without exactly willing it, she had acquired one more "daughter."

In Paris the two soon became inseparable companions. "He has a loyal hand, you should be proud to give him yours," George declared in the familiar Sand style after meeting Juliette's "fiancé." No less firmly she insisted on bringing her young protégée to the fortnightly Magny dinner — no matter how the Goncourt brothers might feel about this feminine "invasion." Charles Baudelaire had just died, and this gave rise to a discussion of his erotic inclinations. Jules de Goncourt contributed a salacious story, and George Sand, as usual, declared herself shocked. "Then we'll repeat it all over again!" declared Flaubert with a challenging laugh. Juliette La Messine was struck by his beady blue green eyes, long lashes, flushed face, and Vercingetorix moustache, but even more by the covert friendliness she sensed behind the bristling physique. Merciless in puncturing pompous expressions or sloppy phraseology, the author of *Madame Bovary* could not forgo the pleasure of poking fun at the young authoress for having written a short story in which a farm laborer who had lost an arm in a threshing machine was later described as taking a money box into his "two hands."

Visibly impressed by her good looks, Alexandre Dumas *fils* felt that the young Juliette's literary lapses were a good sign, indicating a salutary lack of talent. For what was a young lady with such a charming face and figure doing in wanting to become a "bluestocking"? The disrespectful playwright was promptly put in his place by his "dear Mama." "Young Alexandre, I beg you to restrain your scorn for bluestockings . . ." And so the banter went, with one repartee following the next, while the pitiless Flaubert made fun of everything and everyone — from George Sand's "detestable memoirs" to the celebrated journal of the Goncourt brothers, put together, he claimed, from shorthand notes furtively scribbled on Edmond's shirt-cuff underneath the table.

When the time came for George Sand to return to Nohant, in October of 1867, her new friend Juliette made her promise that she would come and spend the winter in her Riviera villa, near the Golfe-Juan. George agreed, provided that she would not have to meet Prosper Mérimée or her daughter, Solange. A discreet neighbor, Mérimée posed no problem, but Solange was another matter. In 1862 George Sand had let her snobbish daughter team up with her brother, Maurice, in a joint lawsuit against their father, who was planning — or so it was thought at Nohant — to disinherit his legitimate children in favor of the illegitimate daughter he had had by his housekeeper and bedmate, Jeanny Dalias. This unsavory episode did little credit to any of the persons involved, but it was revealing of the lengths to which Madame Sand was prepared to go to defend her "little ones" against what, rightly or wrongly, she thought to be an injustice. Nor did this legal venture do much to improve the strained relations between mother and daughter, who had since removed herself to Cannes with a new aristocratic lover. George had pointedly refrained from inviting Solange to Nohant lest she be tempted to vent her own frustrations, as a disappointed wife and mother, on her happily married sister-in-law, Lina. Solange, to avenge herself, had let it be known that she was not going to "permit" her mother to spend the winter with Juliette La Messine at her Golfe-Juan villa.

Lina being pregnant once again, it was finally decided that she would remain at Nohant with "Lolo." George Sand would be accompanied to the Riviera by Maurice, who could shield her, if necessary, from Solange's "persecutions." At the last moment a second bodyguard was added in the person of Maxime Planet. The twenty-five-year-old son of Gabriel Planet had, since his father's death in 1853, been adopted into the Nohant "family," and, charitable as ever, George felt that his poor health would profit from a visit to the Mediterranean.

The weather lived up to their expectations. After leaving a foggy Paris the three of them stepped off the train onto the sunny, mimosa-scented platform of Cannes, where Juliette, parasol in hand, was waiting in an open carriage to take them to her villa. Maurice, who had never met her before, immediately hit it off with his hostess. He presented Juliette with a gift copy of a novel he had recently completed, *Le Coq aux cheveux d'or — The Golden-Haired Cock*) and addressed her facetiously as *mon cher confrère* (dear fellow-writer). He also hit it off with Edmond Adam, an armchair strategist who was impressed by Maurice's military knowledge. Indeed, such was the enthusiasm he displayed for Napoleonic battles and the First Empire's panache that he was soon dubbed *le sargent* (a deliberately English mispronunciation of the French word *sergent*). Eventually all the members of the household acquired military ranks. Edmond Adam was the general; George Sand was promoted to the rank of colonel; Juliette became a lieutenant colonel, and the young Maxime Planet a simple "rifleman" — along with another "recruit" who was lured over from Nice: the forty-four-year-old Edmond Plauchut, who had by now replaced Marchal as George Sand's most assiduous *cavalier servant*.

Plauchut's story was by all accounts an odd one. An ardent republican who was almost exactly Maurice's age, he had first attracted George Sand's attention by writing to her, in the aftermath of the 1848 revolution, to take issue with certain of the arguments Victor Borie had propounded in his pamphlet *Travailleurs et Prolétaires*. She had been sufficiently impressed by this criticism to write two long letters which the young journalist from Angoulême had preserved as hallowed treasures. Preferring exile to life under the Second Empire, Plauchut had later embarked at Antwerp for distant Singapore, only to be shipwrecked on the Cape Verde islands. He had lost all his baggage, saving only a small iron box which contained, among other things, George Sand's two letters. These had proved an extraordinary talisman, gaining him the hospitality and succor of a wealthy Portuguese settler, who had clothed and housed him and sent him on his way. This extraordinary adventure had sufficed to endear him to his unintentional "benefactress," to whom he was finally introduced in 1861. Since then he had become a frequent houseguest at Nohant. At Les Bruyères — as Juliette's villa was called — the ship-wrecked voyager was made to repeat the tale of his misfortune and salvation, not once but a dozen times, by a stony-faced Edmond Adam, who seemed maliciously determined to prove to everyone that Plauchut was a bogus Sindbad and no more than a "drawing-room castaway."

Altogether, it was a merry household, in which any pretext served for joyous pranks and laughter. Here, as at Nohant, the evenings were enlivened by ingenious word games in which farcical questions, jotted down on scraps of paper, were passed around to elicit the absurdest answers. "Madame Sand, who claimed to have no wit, would write out the drollest thoughts, which became minor masterpieces," Juliette Adam was later to recall. Masterpieces matched by the pompous phrases which *le sargent* Maurice, in the finest trooper style, would bestow on the prizewinners at the conclusion of the evening's entertainment.

Here too, as at Nohant, Madame Sand was permitted to keep late hours. In the morning, after having spent part of the night correcting the heavily annotated proofs of her latest novel, *Mademoiselle Merquem,* which Buloz kept sending her from Paris, she would wake to the soft scent of blossoming mimosa and spring roses and to the oaths and exclamations of the menfolk playing bowls on the fragrant terrace. News of George Sand's presence on the Riviera was not long in spreading, and her hostess was amazed by the flood of letters which began pouring in from Toulon, Grasse, Nice, and even Marseille, from needy strangers asking for financial help or her indulgent intercession (with Prince Jérôme Bonaparte) on behalf of some unfortunate victim of administrative injustice. "The Good Lady of Nohant," as Juliette observed, had now become "the Good Lady of Bruyères." Most of the requests for personal visits had to be refused, though exception was made for certain letter-writers whom Maurice wanted to "pillory" with a mocking caricature. One of the victims of his sketches was a viscount, promptly dubbed *"de Vilain XIV"* (Ugly the Fourteenth). Another was an eccentric Englishwoman who wanted to find out which of her novels George Sand personally preferred. "I don't remember what I've done and I never reread myself" was the imperturbable answer.

Before returning to the cooler north, hosts and guests undertook a short trip to Nice, Monte Carlo, and Menton. At Monte Carlo they strolled through the palm-shaded casino grounds, where Maurice began accosting passers-by, asking them, in the assumed accent of a Berrichon country bumpkin, if they could give him a few tips about gambling. Inside the gambling halls he continued to play the fool — so successfully that he was finally ejected by the outraged croupiers and ushers. His mother followed him out with the rest of the party, declaring, typically enough, that the "smell of the passion for gambling" had made her feel sick.

A letter from Lina, asking them to return in time for the childbirth, due in about a month, put an end to the merriment. Regretfully George Sand, Maurice, and the young Planet took leave of their hosts and boarded the train to Paris. Here, on March 13, 1868, they were startled by the news that Lina had already given birth — to a second daughter. She had somehow miscalculated the expectancy period. Weary though she was, George immediately left with Maurice for Nohant, where they were greeted by a fat, happily gurgling baby — "lovely, dark, with big black eyes . . . in a word, a Lolo Number Two" — as she wrote to Juliette. This second granddaughter was christened Gabrielle.

Four months later Juliette and her husband were invited to Nohant on the occasion of George Sand's sixty-fourth birthday. They journeyed down on the train with Edmond Plauchut and Henry Harrisse, an American writer and self-appointed "authority" on George Sand's writings whose pedantry quickly exasperated his companions. The welcome at Nohant was gay and the banter at the dinner table as uninhibited as at Les Bruyères. The windows had been left open in the salon next door, and the warm summer evening with its heady scents and twinkling stars seemed to have taken possession of the room. George Sand entertained her guests by sitting down at the newer Pleyel piano (the other, on which Chopin had given lessons to Solange, was still in the drawing room but never used) and by playing some Mozart and Gluck pieces she had learned by heart. Juliette was deeply moved by the delicate artistry of the performance, which struck her as that of an "incomparable musician."

The next morning, when Juliette and her husband came downstairs, they found the house festooned with flowers and garlands which had been secretly tressed by villagers and local peasants. While the rest of the household slept, Maurice had spent the night decorating the ground-floor corridor and rooms as a surprise for his mother's birthday. The midday meal was solemnly announced by the traditional firing of the miniature cannon, and when George Sand finally appeared at the top of the stairwell, the servants gathered in the vestibule cried: *"Vive la bonne dame!"* (Long live the Good Lady!)

The first to offer his congratulations on her three score years and four was Maurice, who unfolded a parchmentlike scroll and proceeded, in mock military language, to read a flattering Order of the Day which he had illustrated with pen-and-ink flourishes. Her eyes a trifle moist, the Good Lady of Nohant laughingly embraced her son, saying: "How adorably stupid you are!" Dolled up and beribboned in a flouncy dress, the two-year-old Lolo was laboriously heaved up by Juliette's daughter to kiss and be kissed by her grandmother, into whose smiling face she babbled her childish felicitations. Edmond Adam, whom George Sand had nicknamed her "Wa-Wa" (because his spade beard and walrus mustachios reminded her of his Newfoundland dog), came forward to assure her that "the *Wa-Wa* will love you more and better this year than last." His wife chimed in with a presurrealistic compliment inspired by the cobalt skies of the Côte d'Azur which George had so enjoyed: "Happiness at Nohant is as blue as at Bruyères." There were other gay greetings from the "salon castaway" and "rifleman" Planet; after which Henry Harrisse launched into a ponderous encomium of George Sand's literary achievements, while the irreverent Juliette Adam and others made mocking faces behind his coattails.

The evening was marked by a gala marionette performance — the première of a new Maurice Sand production: *Alonzi Alonso the Bastard, or The Brigand of the Sierras.* Almost a month of work had gone into the preparation of this latest birthday surprise, which included a dazzling new curtain screen, painted by Maurice. The puppet show was the occasion for the usual heckling from the audience. When Balandard, the puppet troupe's "stage manager," appeared in the riding coat, impeccable white waistcoat, and sweeping musketeer's hat which George Sand had personally tailored for him — as he kept proudly pointing out — Plauchut made fun of his introductory speech. "Silence in the ranks!" was Balandard's immediate retort.

The action which followed was declared incomprehensible, the plot preposterous. There were cries of protest from the spectators against the turpitude of the villains, pleas of mercy for the threatened victim — to all of which Maurice replied, from behind the miniature stage, with perfectly in-character repartees. When the misogynistic Coq-en-Bois appeared, he who had always disdained the fair sex, Juliette Adam decided to put his antifeminine prejudices to the test by making a public declaration. The flattered misogynist cooed unexpectedly in response.

"What!" cried Lina. "You, Coq-en-Bois, who till now have been faithful to your name, you too have been hooked, you wretch!"

"How can I help it?" Coq-en-Bois replied. "Juillette has spoken to me." With that the unhardened bachelor launched into an impassioned avowal, which ended with the suggestion that he and his "love" dine, *en tête-à-tête,* in the private chambers of a famous Paris restaurant.

"Well I'll be damned!" Juliette's husband couldn't help exclaiming, amid a roar of laughter.

The days that followed were full of pranks, and any guest who was sent out on a flower-plucking expedition in the fields — for as George Sand explained, she *never* cut her garden flowers — was likely to discover that his absence had been used to prepare some practical joke. During one such absence Maurice emptied the wood chest in Edmond Adam's room and installed a cock. At two o'clock in the morning the imprisoned fowl began to crow. While Juliette and her daughter, Alice, hid under the blankets, trying not to laugh, a disgruntled "general" lit the candle on his night table and made a vain inspection of the chimney flue. The cock renewed its crowing, while behind the bedroom door George Sand, Maurice, Lina, Plauchut, and Planet were gathered, like giggling children. Uttering a terrible oath, Edmond Adam finally yanked open the wood chest and cried: "There he is! I bet Maurice put him there!" The irate fowl was finally caught and flung out of the window, but only after a wild chase in the course of which the candle was extinguished. Then the crowing was unexpectedly renewed, with a mocking *Cocorico!* which came this time from behind the tittering door.

That there was something childish about these practical jokes there can be no doubt. But like the evening word games, Maurice's puppet shows, and the dips she continued to take in the shallow waters of the Indre on hot summer days, they were part of the rejuvenating stimulus George Sand needed to sustain her vitality. If human beings, as the sardonic Flaubert was convinced, are a sorry lot and life a vale of tears, then the world of make-believe and the luxury of laughter were more than ever necessary for one's spiritual well-being. To prove it, she devoted the spring of 1869 to the composition of a "comic modern novel"—*Pierre qui roule* (a typical George Sand pun on the proverbial "rolling stone" and which might best be translated by "Peter grows no moss")—in which Maurice's commedia dell'arte figures became the protagonists of a nineteenth-century plot. The novel, significantly enough, was dedicated to Gustave Flaubert.

This is not to say that George Sand was blind to the literary merits of Flaubert's "naturalism" or totally unaffected by his pessimism. Eighteen sixty-nine was not a particularly happy year for either of them. In March she was much affected, as was Lina, by the death of Luigi Calamatta, who had finally settled down in Milan. In July Flaubert lost his closest friend, the poet Louis Bouilhet, who had acted as a kind of literary "midwife" for the birth of *Madame Bovary*. In October Sainte-Beuve died, a loss which made George Sand feel her full age, since her old literary mentor was of the same vintage year—1804—as herself, having been born a couple of weeks after Napoleon's imperial coronation.

The 1860s, after almost twenty years of coolness, due in large part to her infatuation with Pierre Leroux's ideas, had brought them together once again, and it was to "Sainte-Beuve, the soft and precious light of my life," that she had dedicated *Monsieur Sylvestre*. She traveled up to Paris for the funeral, which was attended by Flaubert and Ernest Renan, the learned author of *The Life of Christ*, who never lost a chance, at the fortnightly Goncourt dinners, of praising George Sand as the greatest of contemporary French novelists. Also present was the aging Alexandre Dumas, who hobbled along painfully on his son's arm, and another ghost from the romantic past: the white-haired Albert Grzymala. The spontaneous doffing of top hats which greeted George Sand, as Edmond Adam and Edmond Plauchut escorted her out of the Montparnasse cemetery through the waiting crowd to her carriage, could not make her forget that this funeral marked the end of an age. She had the feeling that the onlookers were cheering a national monument, a relic of the past, for it was now the fashion to mock the idealism of her own exalted generation.

A few weeks later Flaubert published *L'Education sentimentale*, one of the great novels of the century and indeed of all time. Its painstaking composition had taken almost five years and frequently led the author to interrogate George Sand, who unlike himself had been an active participant in the heady turmoil of the 1848 revolution. Though she could never endorse the aristocratic scorn he felt for the "masses," urging him more than once to show pity for the "vanquished," she shared Flaubert's abhorrence of France's smug bourgeoisie and could not but approve of the irony with which he had depicted the vapid, moneygrubbing middle-class milieu in which the novel's "hero," Frédéric Moreau, moved. The author of *Horace* was also honest enough to realize that Flaubert had succeeded far more brilliantly than she in evoking the confused, turbulent, and scatterbrained student world of Paris' Latin Quarter.

Yet hers was a minority opinion. The Paris press was largely hostile and the public on the whole indifferent, apparently unable to accept a novel whose "hero" was so unsparingly portrayed as an indecisive, frivolous, alternately self-indulgent and self-despising Romantic. Saint-Victor, one of the privileged participants of the Goncourt dinners, refused to defend the novel. Another critic undertook to demolish it in Buloz's *Revue des Deux Mondes,* while Barbey d'Aurevilly tore it to pieces in the *Constitutionnel.* But nothing so outraged George Sand as Emile de Girardin's reluctance to publish the article of praise she wrote for his newspaper, *La Liberté*.

Two days before Christmas Flaubert finally let himself be talked into coming down to Nohant with Edmond Plauchut. He proved a most exacting guest and was particularly "insupportable" during the puppet shows, criticizing everything. *La Tentation de Saint Antoine,* parts of which he read out loud to the company assembled in the drawing room, was declared "superb," but he seems to have been too upset by the dismal response to *L'Education sentimentale* to be much comforted by his hosts' enthusiasm for this new work. George Sand even had to write to Juliette Adam, begging her to read Flaubert's novel and to convey her own enthusiasm to the "big, fat, half-understood" recluse of Croisset, who was in need of more tenderness than he had been able to find in his art and in his life. "He is brusque, violent, but infinitely good."

Much to Juliette's chagrin, George Sand did not come down to the

Riviera during the early months of 1870. She decided to stay at Nohant "for a change," to finish a new novel, *Malgrétout.* "Come what may, we shall see each other in the summer, but alas, what may not happen in the interim! They are again beginning what was stupid and bad in 1848; the reds who are in too much of a rush, the whites who are too stupid . . ." The "reds," of course, were the left-wing proletarians and republican extremists; the "whites" were the Legitimists and other monarchists, who had never really accepted the second Bonapartist "usurper."

George Sand's hostility toward the Second Empire had gradually mellowed with the years. In 1859 her republican friend Alphonse Fleury had been able to return to La Châtre thanks to an amnesty Napoleon III had introduced in the immediate wake of his North Italian war with Austria. This had been followed in 1860 by a more liberal policy, slightly enlarging the powers of the two legislative chambers. More, of course, was needed to disarm George Sand's deep-rooted antipathy for a "fraudulent" and opportunistic regime which had cynically exploited universal suffrage and imperial plebiscites to sway the uneducated and gullible masses. As much as personal pride, this explains her refusal of the 20,000 franc award which Napoleon III had generously offered to her as a kind of consolation prize for the French Academy's refusal to bestow its annual Literary Prize upon her in 1861.

Napoleon III's later concessions to an ever stronger opposition finally convinced her, however, that she could live with a liberal Empire, which would have been a constitutional monarchy in all but name. In 1864 strikes were legalized, and four years later another law permitted the creation of trade unions. The press was simultaneously freed from the crippling control of the Ministry of the Interior, while public meetings were authorized for the open discussion of current problems. The result was a dramatic upsurge of movements and feelings that had long been suppressed. France was swept by a wave of strikes as left-wing extremists flocked to join the Marxist First International. In the parliamentary elections of 1869 the opposition parties managed to pile up more than three million votes, compared to 4.4 million for the government. Two months later what had come to be known as the "Third Party," led by Emile Ollivier (who had married Marie d'Agoult's daughter, Blandine Liszt), forced Napoleon III to agree to a drastic extension of parliamentary power.

In February of 1870, at a moment when the Second Empire was in a state of unprecedented ferment, the *Revue des Deux Mondes* began the serialization of *Malgrétout.* The recent shooting, in a duel, of a prominent Paris journalist by a member of the Bonaparte family had already provoked an uproar, and the appearance of this new Sand novel did nothing to still the tumult. For it contained a scathing portrait of a beautiful and madly ambitious *parvenue* which was widely thought, and nowhere more insistently than at the Tuileries palace, to have been inspired by the Empress Eugénie.

What George Sand could not forgive in the Empress Eugénie — other than the coquettishness which she had always regarded as a weak point in the *sexe faible* — was the blighting effect her intransigent Catholicism had had upon Napoleon III's liberal inclinations. In March of 1856, when she had borne him a son and heir, she had insisted that the reactionary Pope Pius IX be invited to become his godfather. Eight years later there had been a momentary falling-out with the Pope when the Emperor, yielding to the entreaties of his liberal cousin Jérôme, had agreed to withdraw his French troops from Rome, where they were the mainstays of papal power, and had subsequently refused to allow the publication in France of Pio Nono's *Syllabus of Errors,* in which national patriotism and universal suffrage were specifically condemned. In Mexico, however, Napoleon III was simultaneously pursuing a hairbrained scheme for establishing a new Catholic empire under the aegis of the Austrian Emperor's brother Maximilian, and in November 1867 he alienated the liberals and republicans in France by sending another French expeditionary force into Italy to defeat Garibaldi at Mentana.

The only conclusion one could draw from these extraordinary zigzags was that Napoleon III was a confused and indecisive personality, an opportunist who was at one moment a bogus liberal and at the next a bogus Catholic, torn as he was between his desire to further the unity of Italy and his desire to curry favor with his Catholic subjects. It is only fair to add that his freedom of maneuver on the diplomatic chessboard of Europe was limited. He could not promote the cause of Italian independence too vigorously without antagonizing the Austrians, whom he needed as a counterweight to the growing power of Prussia. His cousin Jérôme Bonaparte, not being seated on the throne, was less inhibited. A genuine liberal who was all for unifying Italy regardless of the Pope, he was so open-minded about religious questions that he readily agreed to be the godfather of Maurice Sand's daughter Aurore and to attend the *Protestant* baptism which was celebrated at Nohant for George Sand's two granddaughters in 1868. Having married the King of Piedmont's daughter, it was only natural that the prince should have made the Italian cause his own. This made him, like George Sand, a hater of the "reactionary" Habsburgs, one who, like many liberal Frenchmen, cheered when Bismarck's Prussians defeated the Austrians at Sadowa.

It seems incredible, in view of what was shortly to follow, that so many "enlightened" Frenchmen could have been so obtuse, yet such was the case. These "freethinkers" insisted on judging the problems of European diplomacy in essentially religious terms. Thus, under the editorship of Adolphe Guéroult (the one-time Saint-Simonian who had often visited George Sand at the Quai Malaquais apartment), Prince Jérôme Bonaparte's liberal paper *L'Opinion Nationale* could confidently proclaim: "We are for the diminishment of Austria because Austria is a Catholic power which should be supplanted by Prussia, the boulevard of Protestantism in the center of Europe. Now Prussia's mission is to Protestantize Europe, just as Italy's mission is to destroy the Roman pontificate. These are the two reasons why we are at one and the same time for the aggrandizement of Prussia and the aggrandizement of Italy."

George Sand's rabid Italianophilia (so marked that a good third of her novels, plays, and short stories were given Italian settings or character names) made her ill prepared for the catastrophe that finally overtook France in 1870. Only a couple of years before she had been quite ready to applaud Flaubert in his tirades against Adolphe Thiers: "Nothing can give you an idea of the nausea inspired in me by that old diplomatic simpleton, fattening his foolishness off the dung heap of the bourgeoisie." Yet it was this "diplomatic simpleton" who, more than any other parliamentary orator, had been warning his compatriots against the growing might of Prussia.

Now, belatedly, on the very eve of the Franco-Prussian War, George Sand began to realize that the man she had so long detested as the main architect of the July Monarchy of 1830 and the prototype of the self-satisfied bourgeois was the most lucid and levelheaded of French politicians. At a time when Paris was being worked up to a feverish pitch of anti-Prussian bellicosity, Thiers — the Cassandra who had predicted that Napoleon III's Mexican venture would culminate in disaster — was once again counseling caution, at the risk of being called a "cowardly" pacifist.

The person most responsible for reversing George Sand's negative opinion of Thiers was Edmond Adam, a professional observer of parliamentary debates. In late June of 1870 he and his wife, Juliette, made another visit to Nohant. George Sand seemed at first more concerned by the recent deaths of Jules de Goncourt and Armand Barbès than by the gathering crisis in Europe, remarking to Juliette that the two Goncourts were antifeminist haters of "the nineteenth-century woman," whereas her old friend Barbès, who had preferred to die in exile in Holland rather than return to imperial France, was, with Lamennais, the "noblest and purest soul" she had ever known. Maurice, on the other hand, seemed to have succumbed to the general war fever, for he entertained his guests with a military puppet show, introduced by the stage manager Balandard with these words: "Lieutenant Colonel Juliette, riflemen Plauchut and Planet, Colonel George, General Adam, you must get used to the smell of powder; there's no telling what may happen."

Several days later, when George Sand and "General" Adam read the bellicose report that the French Foreign Minister, the Duc de Gramont, had just made to the two legislative chambers, they both had the same reaction: "What imprudence!" For some months past Bismarck, to provoke the French into a war for which they were not prepared and which he needed to press the South German states into joining his North German Confederation, had been astutely promoting the candidacy of a Hohenzollern-Sigmaringen prince to the vacant throne of Spain. The proposal had aroused French fears of a new diplomatic "encirclement," reminiscent of the "vice" in which France had once been caught, in the sixteenth and early seventeenth centuries, between a Habsburg Spain, a Habsburg Lowlands, and a Habsburg Austria which dominated southern Germany and northern Italy. At the last moment the head of the Hohenzollern-Sigmaringen family agreed to withdraw the controversial candidacy. But instead of seizing this olive branch, Napoleon III's Foreign Minister publicly instructed the French ambassador in Berlin to "show more firmness." George Sand could not conceal her consternation: "Does God want to do in the imperial government by striking it blind?" she exclaimed.

Going upstairs, she dashed off an urgent letter to Prince Jérôme Bonaparte, imploring him to reason with the Duc de Gramont, who seemed to have lost his head. But it was already too late. The foolhardy duke had compounded his initial blunder with an even more provocative note instructing his ambassador to obtain a written apology from the Prussian King, who was then "taking the waters" at Ems. This amounted to an ultimatum, which the King of Prussia was honor-bound to reject. Bismarck now had the casus belli he needed. The Duc de Gramont's rash note — the famous Ems telegram — was made public in Berlin after being doctored by Bismarck, negotiations over the Hohenzollern candidacy were peremptorily broken off, and on July 15 Marie d'Agoult's hotheaded son-in-law Emile Ollivier told a wildly cheering French Assembly: "War is necessary, and my colleagues and I accept the responsibility for it *with a light heart!*"

The French parliament's declaration of war against Prussia put a brusque end to the usual Nohant festivities. There was no further mention of military marionette shows, as Juliette Adam, her "general" husband, and "rifleman" Plauchut packed their bags. Their last lunch at Nohant was a somber one, enlivened only by a letter Lina had received from an Italian deputy: in it he told how Prince Jérôme Bonaparte, on a hurried diplomatic mission to Turin, had obtained Victor Emmanuel's promise to send an army of 60,000 Italians to "invade" southern Germany through the Austrian Tyrol. Even Napoleon III had never thought up a more scatterbrained scheme than this, but it was greeted at Nohant with something close to cheers.

But there was no jubiliation later that afternoon when an ashen-faced Maurice appeared on the terrace steps, rhythmically beating an old wooden drum which was still decorated with the tricolor sash and rosette of the First French Republic. Everyone stood up. *"Vive la France!"* cried Maurice in a broken voice. *"Vive la France!"* the others repeated. George Sand and Juliette Adam burst into tears.

The month of August was a nightmare. While the Prussians overran Alsace, a Saharan heatwave ravaged the province of Berry. The forty-seven-year-old Maurice proclaimed his intention of signing up for military duty but could find no properly equipped unit to join. Put to the cruel test, the Second Empire of "Napoleon the Little" (as Victor Hugo had dubbed him) proved itself a poor copy of the First. Instead of an Austerlitz, all it could produce was a succession of Waterloos. The chaos and confusion, at La Châtre as elsewhere, were boundless. There were not enough rifles to arm the young, let alone the middle-aged, while food was scarce. The peasants, interrupted in their harvest labors, were incensed by the outbreak of a war provoked by some incomprehensible dynastic squabble. The draft dodgers were legion. As Lina wrote to Juliette Adam in Paris: "I'm sickened by the sight of all these mothers trying to prove that their sons are good for nothing, that they have neither legs, nor eyes, nor health, and then truly I weep for France."

"We must sweep away the Prussians and the empires at the same time," George Sand wrote to Juliette in her turn. But if the Second Empire proved an easy thing to sweep away, the invading Prussians were another matter. In early September the news reached Nohant that Napoleon III had capitulated with an entire French army at Sedan. On the fifth Maurice woke his mother with the news that the Republic had been proclaimed in Paris without a shot being fired — "an immense feat, unique in the history of the peoples of mankind," George noted lyrically in her agenda book. "May God protect France! She is once again worthy of being looked upon." She penned a message of enthusiastic support which was dispatched to Paris and duly published in *Le Siècle.* Its resonance was considerable. From central Italy, where he was preparing to march on Rome, Ludovico Frapolli, a fervent Garibaldian and Masonic anti-Catholic, wrote to congratulate her: "You have undone the Empire, we are undoing the Papacy."

In the circumstances, however, undoing the Second Empire was also France's undoing. By mid-September the Prussians were laying siege to Paris, while a second French army was hopelessly bottled up in Metz. In the midst of these disheartening setbacks La Châtre was plagued by the outbreak of a smallpox epidemic. George Sand and Maurice hastily packed their bags, and to keep Lina and her two children from being infected, they all drove off to the hill country of the Creuse, where they spent several weeks with friends. Arming themselves with bamboo stalks and reeds, the four-year-old Lolo and the two-year-old Titite (as her younger sister was now called) sought to imitate the distant Prussians and the youths they saw, drilling in the village squares with sticks. Their grandmother fretted, racked by a feeling of frustration.

The inhabitants of Paris were now cut off from the rest of the country by an iron ring of German troops, and there was no way of getting news from friends like the Lamberts, Edmond Plauchut, Juliette and "General" Adam. In early October two balloons, one named the *Armand Barbès,* the other the *George Sand,* rose from a piece of empty ground behind Montmartre carrying several beleaguered Americans as well as the minister of the interior, Léon Gambetta, to "safety." The besieged Parisians were doing what the besieged inhabitants of Richmond had done eight years before. Landing at Amiens, Gambetta proceeded southward to Tours, avoiding the German lines, and sought to organize a makeshift Army of the Loire. For George Sand it was all painfully reminiscent of what she had witnessed in 1815. Flattering though it was to have her name thus publicly associated with the patriotic cause, she was frankly skeptical and pessimistic.

It was soon obvious that Gambetta's Army of the Loire was too weak and ill equipped to break the iron ring which the Prussians had forged around Paris. A stirring orator he might be, but Gambetta was clearly no Bonaparte. What France needed was not a Cicero but a Caesar. And a Caesar who did more than talk and purge the provincial administration of all who seemed war-weary or faint-hearted. "It's a great misfortune to believe oneself apt for a task beyond one's powers," George Sand commented acidly. Like Flaubert, she was irritated by the plethora of ready-made phrases which kept pouring out of the resistance centers of Tours and Bordeaux: heroic injunctions like — "France will rise again! One must not despair! Patience! Courage! Discipline!" etc. Enough to make her write: "When Monsieur Gambetta adds a few exclamation marks to the bottom of his dispatches, he thinks he has saved the country."

In mid-November George returned with her family to Nohant, after spending a few days in Charles Duvernet's nearby country house. The war by now was entering its fourth month, and the plight of the Parisians was grimmer than ever. From his seaside villa near Dieppe Alexandre Dumas *fils* wrote to inform her of his father's death. The old literary warrior who had fought on the 1830 barricades, rushed to Naples to join Garibaldi, and whose last novel, prophetically entitled *La Terreur prussienne,* had been laughed off as one more piece of Dumas "fantasy," had dragged himself back from Marseille with exactly two golden louis in his pocket. This was all the prodigal and repeatedly bankrupt father had been able to salvage from close to forty years of prodigious literary effort. "Even if you weren't for me what you are," his son wrote to George Sand, "you would be the first to whom I would announce this death. He loved and admired you more than any other woman."

Christmas came and went with no trace of a let-up or sign of success. From Cannes, where he had been momentarily reconciled with his wife Solange after raising a volunteer force to defend Besançon, the former cuirassier Clésinger dispatched a lieutenant to Nohant, beseeching his mother-in-law to take refuge in the south. George Sand, however, refused to panic, rightly judging that Paris, not La Châtre, was the Prussians' primary objective. The continuing resistance of the Parisians, now reduced to eating cats, dogs, rats, and zoo animals, struck her as dismally quixotic. Unlike Flaubert, who had written to her in September to say that he would rather see Paris burned to the ground, like Moscow, than yielded to the Prussians, she felt that surrender was the only sensible course for the starving population. The war had been lost, whether one liked it or not, and the best thing to do was be honest and admit it rather than prolong the needless bloodshed and suffering. Why should the French people have to suffer for the giddy follies of an emperor who had now been deposed?

The momentary success of Garibaldi, who had rushed northward with a few thousand Italian volunteers and helped to stem a Prussian assault on Dijon, left her unimpressed, and when, on January 29, 1871, she learned that Paris had finally surrendered, she heaved an immense sigh of relief: "My children and I embrace each other, weeping," she noted in her agenda book. "For three months now I have been up in arms against this awful theory that France must be martyrized to be woken up . . . The sous-préfet who brings us the dispatch at two o'clock thinks that Gambetta will resist. So there will be a civil war? He's capable of wanting one, rather than agree to relinquish his authority." Had George Sand lived seventy years later, it seems likely she would have been a Pétainist in 1940. And an equally acid critic of De Gaulle's trans-Channel heroism.

The national elections of early February showed that she was closer to the national mood than the radical diehards who wanted to fight on to the bitter end. Two thirds of the delegates elected to the provisional parliament of Bordeaux were conservatives, prepared to follow Thiers's lead in negotiating with the conqueror. But the terms imposed — a forced levy of five million francs, the cession of Strasbourg, Metz, all of Alsace and a good chunk of Lorraine — were unexpectedly harsh. Nor was Thiers's thankless task facilitated by the strutting arrogance of the victors. Already humiliated by the elaborate ceremonial which Bismarck had staged on January 18 in the Hall of Mirrors of Versailles, where King Wilhelm I of Prussia was crowned Kaiser of the Second German Reich, the Parisians had to stand by in sullen silence as columns of spike-helmeted Prussians tramped and trotted up the Champs-Elysées in early March. Cafés and shops were closed, the polluted pavements were scrubbed clean with soap and disinfectants, and the republican goddesses of Strasbourg and Metz, solemnly seated on their stony posteriors on the Place de la Concorde, were veiled in black crepe. But there was no calming the mounting indignation.

On March 8 George Sand received a letter from her American admirer Henry Harrisse in which he wrote that Paris was gradually coming back to life: the gas lamps were being lit at night, the provocative cocottes were once again twirling their parasols and promenading their bunny-tail bottoms up and down the boulevards. But the atmosphere was tense and popular feeling running high against a "reactionary" parliament which, under Thiers's cautious guidance, had now established itself at Versailles. Harrisse's forebodings were well founded. Refusing to accept the reality of defeat, the radical extremists of the Paris National Guard seized the cannon on the heights of Montmartre and nominated a Central Committee to rule the city in defiance of the edicts issued by the parliamentary government at Versailles. The troops of the line which Thiers sent in to Paris to recapture the seized guns of Montmartre were surrounded by proletarian militiamen from the neighboring suburb of Belleville, and refused to fire on the opposing crowds. The two generals leading the detachments were seized by the fraternizing mutineers and shot. The Hôtel de Ville was invested, and a "commune" — which is to say, a revolutionary government — was established by radical republicans, Proudhon anarchists, Blanqui egalitarians, and followers of Karl Marx's First International.

At Nohant George Sand watched this new turn of events with anguished consternation. She had always dreamed of a *fraternal* republic in which the middle-class bourgeoisie and the working-class proletariat would at last be reconciled, but here was an insurrectionary movement which seemed determined to reopen all the old wounds. "They are ransoming, threatening, arresting, and judging," she noted in her agenda book on March 23. "They are keeping the law courts from functioning. They have squeezed a million from the bank, five hundred thousand francs from Rotchild [sic]. People are scared, have been giving in. They have started to fight in the streets; on the Place Vendôme they opened fire on an unfriendly manifestation" — unfriendly because it was opposed to the pulling down of the Napoleonic victory column, as though Bonaparte the Great were responsible for the imperial foolishness of Bonaparte the Small — "and killed several people. They have occupied all the town halls, all public establishments. They are pillaging stocks of food and ammunition . . . They are loutish and ridiculous, and the impression one gets is that they don't know what to do with their *coup* . . ."

Though she felt little sympathy for the "stupidly reactionary" assembly of Versailles, she felt even less for the band of diehard fanatics who had chosen this desperate moment to launch a communist utopia. In their furious desire to take it out on their bourgeois "oppressors," they seemed to have forgotten that the Germans were still occupying most of northern France. George Sand blamed her republican friends, and none more severely than the ultrapatriotic "rifleman" Plauchut, for succumbing to this myopic euphoria. "He is one of those I compare to the tenant who lets his house burn, to spite the landlord," she commented in her agenda book.

The senseless war against Prussia was now replaced by an even more senseless civil war. No mercy was shown by either side, as the fanatic Communards shot their hostages (including the Archbishop of Paris and other priests) and the Versailles regulars summarily executed many of those who surrendered. By the time the carnage was over and order finally restored in late May, twenty thousand French men, women, and children had been killed — almost three times as many as during the Robespierre Terror of 1793. The revolutionary knitters who had gleefully watched the tumbrels carrying their aristocratic victims toward the guillotining knife had this time been succeeded by an equally ugly breed of female fanatics — the *pétroleuses,* who worked off their social frustrations by setting fire to bourgeois houses with bottles of flaming petroleum (nineteenth-century precursors of our Molotov cocktails). Flaubert, who visited Paris in early June, was appalled by the orgy of destruction to which the frenzied mobs had yielded in the final throes of the struggle. The Tuileries, the Palais-Royal, and the Hôtel de Ville had been gutted, the Place Vendôme victory column pulled down, the lampposts on the Place de la Concorde uprooted and its graceful fountains disfigured. "The stench of corpses sickens me less than the stink of selfishness which emanates from all mouths," he wrote sadly to George Sand. "The sight of ruins is nothing compared to the absolute imbecility of the Parisians. With few exceptions everyone seemed to me to be raving mad. Half of the population wants to strangle the other half, which shares the same craving."

To her friends, George Sand made no attempt to conceal her condemnation of this fratricidal folly. "Don't justify me when I'm accused of not being *republican enough,*" she wrote to Edmond Plauchut. "On the contrary! Tell them I'm not a republican after their fashion. They have ruined and will always ruin the Republic, exactly like the priests who ruined Christianity. They are proud, narrow-minded pedants, and never have a doubt as to what they can or can't do."

The recent disasters notwithstanding, George Sand remained a communist — a spiritual believer, however, not a militant activist. As she wrote in late July to Prince Jérôme Bonaparte, who had asked if she felt he should return to France: "If we are persuaded to adopt some kind of royalty as a panacea, we are lost, we shall take a backward step and more surely leap into the void. Then the *International* will resume its work and plunge us into anarchy. I believe in the future of the *International* if, renouncing the crimes and mistakes its stupid adherents have just committed, it transforms itself and pursues its principle without wishing to apply it violently. All it has brought forth has been a pack of madmen and scoundrels, but it can purify itself and become the law of the future. For this time is needed. If it is brought back through *coups d'état,* it will likewise be dead and unworkable. Its formula is basically good, but its program is detestable, impossible . . ."

Yes, by all means, she concluded, the prince should return to France, ignoring the inevitable charges that would be leveled against his Bonapartist "plotting." As for herself, she had no desire to go to Paris, where "gold and muck" were now indiscriminately mixed. "I have not left Nohant, and I won't leave it this year. I prefer the shade of my linden trees and the possession of myself, my judgment, my freedom and my dignity."

The return of peace and the gradual consolidation of a new republic, though warmly welcomed, did not make George Sand feel any younger. Alfred de Vigny had died in 1863, the same year as her old friend Delacroix; Berlioz had followed them in 1869, and 1870 had claimed Mérimée as well as Dumas *père.* Of the great Romantic generation which had so exuberantly burst upon the stage in and around 1830, she and the white-bearded Victor Hugo were now the solitary survivors. Twice a grandmother, she could consider herself doubly widowed as well. For her spiritual mentor, Pierre Leroux, who (like Hugo) had lived in exile in the Channel islands throughout the 1860s, had returned to Paris after Napoleon the Small's collapse only to die in April of 1871. He had already been preceded to the grave by Casimir Dudevant, one of whose last fatuous acts had been to write to the Emperor in the Tuileries Palace, suggesting that the hardships he had suffered as the husband of Lucile Dupin, better known to the world as George Sand, merited his being awarded the Cross of the Legion of Honor.

Her old friend François Rollinat, whom she had loved like a brother, had died in 1867, but Gustave Papet and Charles Duvernet were still around to enliven the long autumn and winter evenings at Nohant with their wives, sons, and daughters. So too was the tall, if now less robust "Gaul" — Alphonse Fleury — whose stoutly republican opinions had caused him to be named prefect for the department of the Loire-Inférieure from September of 1870 to March of 1871. Unwilling to die a bachelor, Jules Boucoiran had finally chosen to get "hitched" in his turn. In early September of 1872 he journeyed up from Nîmes with his wife and a young son. What George Sand thought of the first we do not know, but the son was described as "lovely as an angel" in her agenda book.

They were followed, a few days later, by Pauline Viardot, who came with two of her three daughters, the twenty-year-old Claudie and the eighteen-year-old Marianne. Maurice's youthful "flame" had trouble recognizing "her" Nohant, which she had not visited in more than twenty years, having been forced to live a life of exile in England and Germany because of her husband's outspoken hostility to Napoleon III's Second Empire. Her voice, though it had suddenly cracked in 1859, provoking a precipitate retirement from the opera stage, was still as rich and crystalline as ever for the singing of drawing room lieder. George was no less astounded by the prodigious memory Pauline displayed in entertaining the six-year-old Lolo by singing a number of Berrichon songs she had picked up a quarter of a century before, when Chopin was at Nohant.

"What a day, what emotion, what musical penetration!" George Sand noted in her agenda book at the conclusion of the second day. "Pauline sings in the afternoon and evening. *Panchito la cagna, Verdi prate, Las muchachas* and ten other things of the first order. She is even more sublime, more incomparable than ever. I cry like a calf . . . Lolo *drank up* the music with her big eyes. The Viardot girls sang delightfully, they are charming, with voices of crystal, but Pauline, Pauline, what a genius!"

The next day Pauline treated her "Ninoune" to five hours of Schubert, Saint-Saëns ("too complicated" for her hostess' taste), and a number of other songs which were once again termed "sublime." What the once bewitched Maurice must have felt, George Sand's agenda book unfortunately does not tell us. Now happily married to a sprightly wife and the father of two dark-eyed daughters, he had no reason to regret the hopeless infatuation he had once felt for the most gifted female singer of the nineteenth century. But that same evening he outdid himself in a marionette performance of *Alonzi Alonzo* (the Brigand), which kept Pauline and everyone else in stitches.

The week of entertainment that followed left George Sand "drunk" with happiness. There were musical afternoons, dancing and the usual word games in the evenings. On October 3 the Russian writer Ivan Turgenev made a last-minute appearance, having been delayed in Paris by a painful attack of gout. Like Maurice, but to an even more compelling degree, he had been fatally smitten by Pauline Viardot almost from the moment he had first heard her sing in Berlin in 1845. For a full quarter of a century already she had been his great platonic love — one is even tempted to say, his "sacred" love, as opposed to the profane love (with one of his mother's house servants) which had produced an illegitimate daughter, whom he had asked Pauline to bring up for him — first at Courtavenel, and then, after its sale in 1861, at the Viardots' villa in Baden-Baden. During her triumphal seasons at Petersburg and Moscow, Turgenev had been Pauline's leading champion. He had even helped Pauline to write several operettas — one of which, *The Last Sorcerer,* Liszt had partly orchestrated and Brahms had undertaken to conduct at a musical festival given at Baden-Baden in 1869.

George Sand found her eminent Russian guest "gay, amiable and charming," but she was particularly impressed by his talents as a raconteur. "Last day of musical bliss," she noted in her agenda book on October 4. "Pauline and her daughters sing bits of her operettas, as explained by Turgeniev. It's charming. Turgeniev told Lolo and all of us a story, seated on the garden bench." In a variation on the usual marionette performance, Maurice had each of his puppets appear and greet Turgenev with a witty phrase, and the evening ended with charades and the usual word games in the drawing room. After which, as George noted in her agenda book, hosts and guests embraced each other in a fond farewell, already regretting "these happy days which have passed so quickly."

Flaubert, now more than ever a lonely bachelor since his mother's death in the spring of 1872, finally accepted George Sand's repeated invitations and made a second visit to Nohant for Easter of 1873. She found him somewhat thinner and much affected by another recent death — that of his friend Théophile Gautier, who had died the previous October. Once again Flaubert proved himself an exacting as well as exhilarating houseguest, preferring to engage the radical Edmond Plauchut in heated arguments over the vices of democracy to a forced participation in "boring" games of dominoes. After being taken to admire Gustave Papet's nearby stables, he subjected the Nohant library to meticulous scrutiny, finally declaring to his hostess that there wasn't a book on its shelves he hadn't read! Caustic as ever, he made witty fun of everything, sparing only Maurice's impressive butterfly collection. He did not even spare himself during the after-dinner dancing, when the members of the household appeared in fancy dress; hastily taking possession of a woman's skirt, the mustachioed Gustave threw himself into as strange a fandango as had ever been seen at Nohant.

Much of Easter Monday was spent listening to Flaubert's histrionic reading of *La Tentation de Saint Antoine,* which he had at last completed. George Sand found it "splendid," Lina was enthusiastic, Plauchut was bowled over, and Maurice was so overwhelmed by this six-hour tour de force that he retired to bed with a headache. Turgenev's arrival, two days later, brought the festivities to a new crescendo — with evening dances and noisy games in the drawing room which Flaubert vainly sought to interrupt in order to talk literature with his friend Ivan. But the bearded Russian seemed to revel in this atmosphere of noisy mirth and merriment. "He is as much a child as we are," George noted approvingly in her agenda book. "He dances, he waltzes. What a good and stalwart man of genius!" she concluded, slightly altering the phrase Pauline Viardot had once coined about herself, calling George Sand "a good woman of genius."

Flaubert avenged himself the following day with such a torrential display of vivacity and wit that he completely dominated the conversation. Virtually reduced to silence, the more diffident Turgenev had trouble slipping in a word every now and then — to George Sand's personal regret, for she was less familiar with his ways of thinking and fund of knowledge and experience, far broader and more European than Flaubert's.

In September of 1873 Pauline Viardot made another visit to Nohant, accompanied this time by her sixteen-year-old son, Paul, as well as by her two daughters, Claudie and Marianne. The "two nightingales," as George Sand now called the latter, sang divinely. Their mother, as usual, was "sublime" in singing a number of new Schubert songs George had never before heard. But the sensation of this new musical season was Paul Viardot, a skilled violinist who had clearly inherited the musical gift of the Garcías. Turgenev, who arrived on the twenty-third, stayed for almost one week. In the absence of the overpowering Flaubert, he could now at last unfold his talents as a raconteur without fear of verbal sabotage. George was particularly impressed by a story of shipwreck which he related with such mastery that it left even Plauchut ("the drawing-room castaway") enviously open-mouthed.

Industrious as ever, the "Good Lady of Nohant" still devoted a few hours of each day to "blackening the paper," though her literary powers were now clearly waning. In addition to the voluminous correspondence she still maintained she derived a rare pleasure from entertaining Lolo and Titite with what she called "Grandmother's Tales" — tales she later had published under the title *Contes d'une grand-mère*.

Her feelings toward Solange, on the other hand, were strangely mixed. For years she had hoped that her daughter would finally rescue herself from her shiftless and haphazard existence by following her own example — that is, by concentrating on some form of serious literary work. Alternately encouraged and criticized by her mother, Solange had tried her hand at poetry, then announced that she was going to write a "major work" on their illustrious ancestor, Maurice de Saxe. The projected magnum opus never got beyond the outline stage, interrupted as it repeatedly was by Solange's flighty need to rush off to Turin, Aix-les-Bains, or Baden-Baden in search of "diversion" — presumably with some new lover. For a while she toyed with the idea of going her mother one better by writing a series of *Lettres d'un voyageur amoureux* — a project which hardly enchanted George Sand — and at one point she even persuaded the powerful newspaper magnate, Emile de Girardin, to send her to Florence to write some articles for *La Presse.* (Three of them were actually published.) This is not to say that Solange was lacking in literary talent. She had enough wit and verve to be able to preside over a modest literary salon in Paris during the 1860s, and in 1869 she even managed to complete a novelette entitled *Jacques Bruneau,* which was first serialized and then published in volume form on the eve of the Franco-Prussian War.

What Solange lacked, of course, was what her mother had in such incredible abundance: tenacity and perseverance. Nor did her mother much help her to develop these two virtues through her financial generosity. She may even be said to have pushed Solange in the opposite direction by making life too easy for her. Had George Sand foreseen all the consequences it would entail, she would probably have been less zealous in persuading Maurice and Solange to take legal action against their father, simply to keep him from leaving the Dudevant country house at Guillery to the illegitimate daughter he had had with Jeanny Dalias. Having lost the lawsuit, the aging baron was obliged to sell the country house for some 280,000 francs. Of this he was allowed to keep 150,000, while the remaining 130,000 francs were divided between his two legitimate heirs.

Solange used her share to buy a plot of land near Cannes, on which she began building a villa. She named it "Malgrétout" — supposedly in filial homage to the novel her mother had thus entitled — but there may well have been a note of challenging irony in so asserting that "in spite of everything" (*malgré tout,* in French) she was at last accomplishing something constructive. Solange was too intelligent not to realize that her failings were now grist for her mother's literary mill and that it was she above all who had inspired the haughty, capricious, and contradictory character of Erneste de Blossay in *Mademoiselle Merquem,* a novel George Sand had written in the autumn and winter of 1867. She may likewise have suspected that she had also provided the real-life model for the headstrong and unscrupulous heroine of *Césarine Dietrich,* which her mother had written during the early summer of 1870.

Being the daughter of George Sand was not easy for a former "lioness" whose one persistent craving in life had been to shine and dazzle. "Solange is destined for the absolute in both good and bad," Marie d'Agoult had forecast more than thirty years before. "Her life will be full of struggles and combats." The prophecy had been fulfilled with a vengeance. Now, at the age of forty-three, Solange was ruefully forced to admit that she had not really succeeded in anything she had tried; her marriage had been a disaster and she had lost her two daughters. In a pathetic letter to her mother, written in October 1871, Solange wrote that her childless state was for her a source of radical despair — "a despair which lodges like solitude in the heart, and which burrows and spreads like a cancer as one grows older. To grow old alone is awful for a woman."

She had hardly finished building and furnishing her Riviera villa when, in the summer of 1873, a wealthy gentleman offered her twice the sum all this work had cost her. Solange finally agreed to sell, using the proceeds to buy the Château de Montgivray, near Nohant, from Hippolyte Chatiron's debt-ridden daughter, Léontine Simonnet. The last thing George Sand wanted was to have her headstrong daughter for a neighbor. But the deal, shrewdly engineered through the connivance of another woman who acted as Solange's stalking horse and representative, left her with no choice in the matter. Confronted with this disagreeable fait accompli, George Sand made her displeasure felt by terminating the allowance she had up till then paid to her daughter. She did not, however, have the heart to close her door to Solange, who took advantage of Montgivray's proximity to pay frequent visits to Nohant. These, as often as not, were unannounced. Sometimes, to save appearances, Solange was invited to stay to dinner and even to partake of the evening's entertainment. But at other times it fell to Maurice's little daughters, Lolo and Titite, to mount guard outside their grandmother's study and to inform their imperious aunt that she could not enter the sanctum.

And so the years passed, each bringing its new and surprising crop of novels and articles of reminiscence (most of the latter published in *Le Temps,* to which George Sand was a regular contributor). Nobody, least of all herself, would have dared to claim that *Nanon, Ma soeur Jeanne, Flamarande, Les Deux Frères, Marianne Chevreuse,* or *La Tour de Percemont* were works of genius, but they did bear witness to her extraordinary vitality. As Henry James, who spent most of 1875 in Paris, was to write with such sympathetic insight: " 'Realism' had been invented, or rather propagated; and in the light of *Madame Bovary* her own facile fictions began to be regarded as the work of a sort of superior Mrs. Radcliffe. She was antiquated; she belonged to the infancy of art. She accepted this destiny with a cheerfulness which it would have savored of vanity even to make explicit. The Realists were her personal friends; she knew that they did not, and could not, read her books; for what could Gustave Flaubert make of *Monsieur Sylvestre,* what could Ivan Turgenieff make of *Césarine Dietrich?* It made no difference; she contented herself with reading their productions, never mentioned her own, and continued to write charming improbable romances for initiated persons of the optimistic class."

Flaubert, whatever his personal sentiments may have been, was kind enough to write her a few lines of praise after having read *Flamarande* and *Les Deux Frères* "at one sitting," as he put it. He wrote again a few months later, in the hope that she would come up to Paris to see the new staging of *Le Mariage de Victorine,* which, he claimed, had caused him to weep his eyes out when he had seen it with Turgenev and Pauline Viardot. But George Sand, who had spent the summer of 1875 going from one gastric crisis to the next, was in no mood to leave Nohant in midwinter, now that it was blanketed in snow — "a weather I adore: this whiteness which is like a general purification, and when indoor amusements are sweeter and more intimate," as she wrote to her dear "troubadour."

For some years past George Sand had suffered from periodic bouts of colic which, though often extremely painful, she had done her best to ignore, following a "remedial" regime prescribed to her by a Paris doctor, Henri Favre. In mid-May of 1876 she was once again afflicted by prolonged constipation, with a serious swelling of the stomach. A local doctor who visited Nohant on the twentieth, to treat Maurice for neuralgia, gave her some mildly laxative pills, which seem to have brought her momentary relief. But not for long. When he returned on the 29, the same doctor (Chabenat, a newcomer to the Nohant household) was asked to go upstairs for another look at Madame Sand. He found her writing in her study with her customary concentration, but he was disturbed by the enormous volume of her abdomen. She had had no movements since the twenty-third and had great difficulty in eating. Afraid that she might be affected by an ulcerated intestine, the doctor prescribed another mild laxative of castor oil mixed with barley water, which she took on May 30, but with no remedial effect.

By three o'clock that afternoon it was clear that she was seriously ill. Summoned to her study, Maurice found his mother stretched out on the couch, suffering dreadful gastric pains. That evening she began vomiting. Gustave Papet was hastily called over from the nearby Château d'Ars. He was appalled by his old friend's condition. After examining her, he took Maurice aside and said: "Your mother is done for." She was suffering, Papet realized, from an intestinal occlusion, which could only be cured by an immediate operation. (With the surgical methods then used, this was likely to be fatal.)

Papet prescribed a treatment of baths and stomach massages which had little effect. The vomitings ceased, but the gastric pains were so intense that George Sand's cries of suffering could be heard far out into the garden for a good part of the night.

The following morning two more doctors were called in. They noted that her pulse beat — eighty-eight per minute — was abnormally high, her usual beat varying from a remarkably low fifty to fifty-five a minute (comparable to that of many long-distance runners). Her condition being obviously extremely serious, they asked Maurice to telegraph to Paris for a specialist. Maurice told them that he was going to telegraph to Dr. Favre, in whom his mother had unlimited confidence. The two doctors frowned and insisted that

Dr. Favre be accompanied by a man of "uncontested practical science" — the intimation being that this Favre was something of a charlatan.

The next day Favre turned up alone, claiming that he had been unable to persuade any of his medical colleagues to accompany him. He examined George Sand and then declared with fatuous complacency that so far as he could tell, she was suffering from dysentery or perhaps hernia and that he was going to give her a friction bath: an incredible diagnosis which caused the other doctors to grind their teeth in silent rage.

On June 2 two more physicians were summoned to the scene. One of them, a surgeon, undertook a minor operation, which momentarily reduced the intestinal pressure. But the abdomen remained dreadfully swollen. By June 4 the pulse beat had risen to 100 per minute. George Sand now had trouble breathing, so intense was the pressure on her lungs of the blocked intestinal gases. A new operation was tried, again without success.

A messenger was sent over to Montgivray to inform Solange, who was found to be away in Paris. Alerted by telegraph, she arrived the next morning. Maurice took her into his arms and kissed her on both cheeks, but his wife, Lina, would only accord her a cold nod. Suddenly abashed, Solange addressed her as "Madame." Maurice then took his wife by one hand and his sister by the other and had them embrace. The ice was broken, superficially at any rate.

On seeing her daughter appear by her bedside, George Sand showed no trace of emotion. Her attention was clearly absorbed by her terrible discomfort and a feeling of dryness inside her swollen mouth which made it difficult for her to speak. She was also wracked by a hideous thirst, which grew progressively more pronounced.

From then on Lina and Solange, usually accompanied by the children's nurse, seldom left her bedside. It was clear to all that the end was near. George Sand understood it too. At nine o'clock on the evening of June 7 she made a special effort to speak, but all she could manage to say was: *"Adieu, adieu, je vais mourir . . . ,"* followed by two mysterious words — *"Laissez verdure."*

At one o'clock on the morning of the eighth she asked to be washed, and at two o'clock she groaned: *"La mort, mon Dieu, la mort!"*

At six o'clock Solange moved the iron bed on which she was resting so that her mother could see the trees of her beloved Nohant garden through the window. At nine George Sand asked for her grandchildren. "Farewell, farewell, I'm going to die . . . *Adieu Lina, adieu Maurice, adieu Lolo, ad —*" She wanted to say "Farewell, Titi," but had not the strength to finish the sentence. Shortly thereafter she lost consciousness and died.

A long and many-sided discussion followed as to just how George Sand was to be buried. Solange, who took her mother's place at table for the noonday meal, insisted that it had to be a religious and not simply a civil burial, like Sainte-Beuve's in 1869. She even claimed to have found a blue satin satchel belonging to her mother inside of which was a slip of paper indicating her last wishes: "Death not being a misfortune, I want no emblem of mourning on my tomb, I wish on the contrary that there be flowers, trees and greenery." Though this slip of paper later disappeared in the most mysterious fashion, the message sounded sufficiently authentic to carry conviction. There is little doubt that the two words she had uttered on the eve of her death — "*Laissez verdure*" (Leave the greenery) — meant that she wished to be buried beneath a simple mound of grass, like her father and grandmother, and that she did not want her final resting place to be marked by white slabs and crosses.

If her mother had wanted a civil burial, so Solange argued, already gesticulating and laying down the law, she would have said so in her will. But her will was silent on the matter. Her daughter-in-law, Lina, who had been as close to her as anybody in the last years of her life, had to admit that they had never discussed the subject, though she was convinced that Madame Sand wanted a civil burial. Maurice, with whom the final decision lay, was undecided. He was privately convinced, like Lina, that his mother would have wished a civil burial, but he was afraid that a purely civil ceremony would be misinterpreted in the Nohant countryside as proof that George Sand had become an atheist and that her sympathies had really been with the godless "reds" and Communards. He himself had chosen to become a Protestant, a step his mother had refused to take — enough to suggest that she had remained deep down within her a Catholic.

Little persuasion was needed to get Maurice to consent to a religious burial — particularly since Solange had the support of George Sand's nephew Oscar Cazamajou, of Hippolyte Chatiron's grandson, René Simonnet, and even that of Gustave Papet, who (according to one witness) let it be known that neither he nor any member of his family would attend a purely civil ceremony. Solange accordingly telegraphed to the Archbishop of Bourges, who gave his official consent to a regular church burial. Telegrams were sent off to all George Sand's closest friends in Paris. Emile Aucante and Edmond Plauchut were already at Nohant. Gustave Flaubert, Ernest Renan, Alexandre Dumas *fils,* and Prince Jérôme Bonaparte were among those who traveled down to Nohant on a gray rainy day. Henry Harrisse, her American admirer, Calmann Lévy, her publisher, Edouard Cadol and Paul Meurice, who had acted in George Sand's plays, also made the trip, as did Victor Borie, the only one of her ex-lovers who was present. Dumas' portly friend Marchal was conspicuously absent.

The illustrious mourners, like the less well known, were led upstairs for a final glimpse of George Sand in her bedroom. Her face had been covered with flowers, and all that was visible, as Dumas noticed, was her small right hand, which looked like a piece of polished ivory. There was a last-minute crisis when it was discovered that the lead coffin sent down from Paris was too small to contain her vastly swollen stomach. While correspondents from the *Figaro* and other Paris papers wandered up and down the lanes of the Nohant garden, wondering how it was that the author of *Mademoiselle La Quintinie* could have arranged for a religious burial, a new coffin was hastily ordered. It arrived in the nick of time, a bare hour before the service was to begin.

It was still raining when the coffin, draped in black velvet, was borne out of the house on sturdy peasant shoulders. Prince Jérôme Bonaparte walked immediately behind, holding a tasseled cordon in one hand and a laurel sprig in the other. The little Nohant chapel was already filled with peasant women, and not all of those in the procession could squeeze their way in. Some of them had to stand outside in the rain, with the throng of uninvited onlookers who had tramped and ridden over from near and far away.

After a brief service, the little chapel's bells took over from the singers. The priest, dressed in a worn purple chasuble, emerged with a choir boy, who carried the cross. All made their way into the graveyard separating the little chapel from the manor house's garden wall. After several prayers, priest, choir boy, and chief singer withdrew. Jules Néraud's son-in-law Ernest Périgois (who like Alphonse Fleury and many another of George Sand's friends had been forced into exile under Napoleon III) read a speech he had prepared for the occasion. He was followed by the playwright Paul Meurice, who read a typically high-flown message from Victor Hugo. ("The human form is an occultation. It hides the true divine countenance, which is the idea. George Sand was an idea; she is now beyond the flesh and free. Dead, she now lives . . ." etc.) While Renan thought it full of "amphigoric" commonplaces, the normally sardonic Flaubert found it sublime. Prince Jérôme Bonaparte, who was of Renan's opinion, had also prepared a funeral oration, like Dumas. But they finally decided that between the Church and Victor Hugo there was no room left for their eloquence. They remained mercifully silent.

"This ill-tended graveyard, this throng of peasant women wrapped in their dark cloth mantles and kneeling on the wet grass, the gray sky, the cold drizzle which kept pelting our faces, the wind whining through the cypresses and mingling with the aged sexton's litanies, touched me far more than this conventional eloquence," Henry Harrisse later recalled. "Still, I couldn't help thinking that nature, in this solemn moment, owed a last ray of sunshine to George Sand."

"Poor, dear Madame Sand," Turgenev wrote to his friend Flaubert when the news was brought to him in distant Russia. "She loved both of us, but you above all, which was natural. What a heart of gold she had! What absence of every petty, mean, or false feeling! What a brave man she was, and what a good woman!"

Replying from his home in Normandy, Flaubert admitted that during the burial ceremony he had "wept like a calf, and twice: the first time when kissing her granddaughter Aurore (whose eyes that day so resembled hers that it was like a resurrection), and the second time on seeing the coffin pass by . . . You are right to regret our friend, for she loved you dearly and always spoke of you as 'the good Turgeneff.' . . . The good country folk wept a great deal around the open grave. There was mud up to the ankles in that small country graveyard. The rain was falling softly. Her burial was like a chapter from one of her books."

To another friend, Mademoiselle Leroyer de Chantepie, Flaubert had already written to say that he and George Sand had often talked about her. "One had to know her as I knew her," he added, "to realize how much of the feminine there was in that great man, the immensity of tenderness there was in that genius. She will remain one of the splendors of France and unmatched in her glory."

A Word about Nohant and Gargilesse

After Maurice Sand's death in 1889 the Nohant estate was administered by his widow, Lina Calamatta Sand, until her death in 1901. (Solange had died two years earlier, in 1899.) In the subsequent division of property Aurore Sand acquired her grandmother's manuscripts and certain lands, while her younger sister, Gabrielle (the former "Titite"), was granted the usufruct of the country house and garden. The latter were subsequently donated to the Institut de France by Gabrielle, who had married and then divorced a M. Romeo Palazzi without having any children.

The elder granddaughter, who assumed the name of Aurore Lauth-Sand after her marriage, was also without heirs. Shortly before her death in 1961 she repurchased the Gargilesse cottage, which had previously been sold, and bequeathed it to her godson, M. Georges Smeets, who died in his turn in 1970.

A large part of George Sand's library had been sold off in the early 1890s. Some of the letters, including those to and from Alfred de Musset, were later sold to the Bibliothèque Nationale, while a far greater number were sold or donated to the Bibliothèque Historique de la Ville de Paris. Many others had been painstakingly gathered or copied by the Belgian collector and connoisseur Vicomte Charles Spoelberch de Lovenjoul. Today both the country house at Nohant and the cottage at Gargilesse are museums and open to the public.

Acknowledgments

Notes

Bibliography

Chronological List

Index

Acknowledgments

For graciously authorizing my publishers to reproduce Auguste Charpentier's portrait of George Sand on the jacket cover of this book I owe special thanks to Señora Bartomeu Ferra, proprietor of the Chopin-Sand cell at the Charterhouse of Valldemosa. I am likewise indebted to M. Marquet-Lempert, curator of the Carnavelet Museum in Paris, and to M. Gourvest, curator of the George Sand Museum at La Châtre, for kindly letting me reproduce certain of the drawings and portraits in their collections.

I would also like to thank M. Jean Garnier for permission to quote from the ten-volume edition of George Sand's letters that he has published with the aid of Georges Lubin; M. Marcel Thomas, of the Bibliothèque Nationale, and M. Henry de Surirey de Saint-Rémy, of the Bibliothèque Historique de la Ville de Paris, for being allowed to consult the precious letters, diaries, and other manuscripts now placed in their safekeeping; and M. Jacques Suffel for making me feel so much at home in that little treasure-trove of French nineteenth-century source material — the Spoelberch de Lovenjoul library at Chantilly.

To M. Georges Lubin, as perfect a gentleman as he is a scholar, I owe more than I can say; as I do to my dear friend Robert Cowley, whose manly struggle with the "longest article" he ever had to edit was clearly above and beyond the call of duty.

C.C.

Notes

The following abbreviations have been used:

GS	George Sand.
HV	*Histoire de ma vie,* George Sand's autobiography, as published in
OA	*Oeuvres autobiographiques,* 2 vols., edited with notes by Georges Lubin (Gallimard, Pléiade, 1970–1971).
Corr.	*Correspondance.*
GS, *Corr.*	George Sand's *Correspondance,* as published by Maurice Sand in 6 vols., from 1882–1884.
Cor	George Sand's *Correspondance,* as published in a more complete and accurate 10-volume edition by Georges Lubin (Garnier, 1964–1973).
CSM	*Correspondance Sand-Musset,* ed. by Louis Evrard (Monaco, 1956).
GS-GF	*Correspondance entre George Sand et Gustave Flaubert,* ed. by Henri Amic (Paris, 1904).
GS-PV	*Lettres inédites de George Sand et de Pauline Viardot, 1839–1849,* ed. by Thérèse Marix-Spire (Paris, 1959).
LV	*Lettre* or *Lettres d'un voyageur.*
JI	Journal intime.
CGS	*Le cas George Sand,* subtitle for Thérèse Marix-Spire's *Les Romantiques et la musique* (Paris, 1954).
GSB	*George Sand et le Berry,* vol. I (subtitled "Nohant"), by Louise Vincent.
IVGS	*L'Italie dans la vie et dans l'oeuvre de George Sand,* by Annarosa Poli.
RDM	*Revue des Deux Mondes.*
RGM	*Revue et Gazette musicale de Paris.*
RHLF	*Revue d'Histoire littéraire de la France.*
RSH	*Revue des sciences humaines.*
Lov. fol.	Ms. and folio number at Spoelberch de Lovenjoul library at Chantilly.
BHVP	Fonds Sand at the Bibliothèque Historique de la Ville de Paris.
BN, n.a.f.	Bibliothèque Nationale, ms. department, nouvelles acquisitions françaises.

Page *lines*

1. MAJOR DUPIN'S DAUGHTER (*Pages 3–12*)

3 GS's first reminiscences are described in *HV*, Part II, Ch. 11. (*OA* vol. I, pp. 530 f. Lubin's notes, pp. 1375–6.) The house in which Aurore

Page *lines*

Dupin was born — 15 (now 46) Rue Meslay — still exists near the Place de la République. It was then the home of her aunt, Lucie Maréchal (GS, *Album,* p. 11, and *OA* I, pp. 477, 1362). The date of her birth — 12 Messidor An XII — corresponded to July 1, 1804, though for much of her life GS was persuaded that she had been born on July 5, which was accordingly celebrated as her birthday (*OA* I, pp. 13, 464–6, 1236–7).

Maurice Dupin, who had inherited his parents' musical talents, also composed music and even tried to write an opera (*OA* I, p. 490). At the time of his daugher's birth he was a lieutenant and twenty-six years old. His wife, baptized Antoinette Sophie Victoire on July 26, 1773, was thirty at the time of their marriage, celebrated in Paris on June 5, 1804 (*OA* I, pp. 461, 467–71, 1359–60). As a child she was called by her first name in honor of Queen Marie Antoinette. Later she was known as Victoire, in keeping with the militant spirit of the Republic and Napoleon's first campaigns. Maurice Dupin preferred Sophie, the Christian name thereafter used (*OA* I, p. 341).

Maurice Dupin's descent from Maurice of Saxony, after whom he was named, is explained by the genealogical chart accompanying the notes to Ch. 3. Antoine-Claude Delaborde, the bird seller and tavern keeper, died in December 1781, when his daugher, Antoinette Sophie Victoire, was only seven (*OA* I, pp. 1238, 1363). His wife, born Marie-Anne Cloquard, was an ironmonger's daughter. She died in 1790, when her elder daughter, Sophie Victoire, was seventeen and her younger daughter (the future GS's aunt), Lucie, fourteen years old (*OA* I, pp. 71–5). Both of her maternal grandparents were dead long before Aurore Dupin came into the world, and as GS candidly admitted in her autobiography, her mother could tell her absolutely nothing about Antoine Delaborde's parents (*OA* I, p. 71).

4 *2–3* The house, then numbered 22 (today 13), still exists on the Rue de la Grange-Batelière, which runs parallel to the Boulevard Montmartre (*OA* I, p. 1376). Caroline Delaborde, Aurore Dupin's half sister, was born out of wedlock in 1799. She was thus five years older than the future George Sand. It is not known who her father was. Georges Lubin's diligent research has uncovered the fact that Aurore's mother had had another child in 1790, as the result of a liaison — it was probably not a marriage — with a certain Claude-Denis Vantin Saint-Charles, who was arrested as a Royalist suspect during the Robespierre Terror of 1793. The child disappeared during these revolutionary upheavals, while Saint-Charles later married another woman (*OA* I, pp. 1255–6).

4 *20 ff.* For GS's elaborate description of the Rue de la Grange-Batelière apartment, see *HV* I, Ch. 11 (*OA* I, pp. 529–47). Aurore's aunt, Lucie Delaborde, was married to Amand Maréchal on July 25, 1804 (*OA* I, p. 1358). A former noncommissioned officer, Amand Maréchal had found a job with the army's quartermaster department. Their daughter Clothilde was born in August 1805 and was thus a

Page *lines*

year younger than her first cousin, Aurore Dupin (*OA* I, pp. 1369, 1452). The Maréchals later moved to a house in Chaillot, then a suburb of Paris (*OA* I, Chs. 11, 12).

5 *31 ff.* Maurice Dupin's military peregrinations are described at length in the first two parts of GS's autobiography. At the time of Aurore's birth he was attached to the staff of General Dupont and officially stationed near Boulogne, where Napoleon had assembled a large army for the projected invasion of England. In September 1805 Dupont's division, which was part of Ney's army corps, proceeded by forced marches to Ulm, where it helped encircle Mack's Austrian army. Severely mauled in subsequent battles with the Russians, the Dupont division, which had lost half its men, was later sent to Vienna to recuperate. Maurice Dupin thus missed the battle of Austerlitz in early December of 1805. He was promoted to Captain of Hussars two weeks later, took part in the Jena campaign of 1806, and spent the following winter in Poland. In March 1807 he was promoted to Chef d'Escadron, the equivalent of Major, in the Hussars. Two weeks later Murat made him one of his aides-de-camp. From Tilsit, after the signing of peace treaties between France, Prussia, and Russia in July 1807, Maurice Dupin returned briefly to Paris before accompanying Murat and Napoleon to Venice and Milan.

6–12 The trip to Madrid and back is described in vivid detail in Ch. 13 of GS's autobiography (*OA* I, pp. 564–76). The Infanta was María
7 *10–19* Luísa, daughter of Carlos IV, who had married the Duke of Parma's son. Napoleon, deciding to annex the duchy, had given them Tuscany, elevated to the status of a kingdom, whence the title of *reina* — queen.

9 *24–29* Maurice Dupin's mother had bought the Nohant property in August 1793 from Pierre-Philippe Péarron de Serennes, formerly royal governor of Vierzon. The price paid was 230,000 pounds (*livres* in French) (*OA* I, p. 1252).

2. NOHANT (*Pages 13–24*)

13 GS's first impressions of her grandmother and Nohant are described
14 *3 ff.* in *HV* II, Ch. 15 (*OA* I, pp. 585–8). Aurore's half brother, Hippolyte Chatiron, had been brought into the world in 1799 by Catherine Chatiron, the twenty-year-old daughter of a La Châtre carpenter. The illegitimate child was officially baptized Pierre Laverdure (*OA* I, p. 1304) but indulgently adopted by his grandmother, Madame Dupin de Francueil, who had him brought up by a peasant woman inhabiting a house next to the Nohant stables. The importunate Catherine Chatiron was sent back to La Châtre, but according to GS (*OA* I, p. 249), Madame Dupin de Francueil helped her out financially.

Page	lines	
14	*10 ff.*	Born in 1761, Deschartres was forty-seven years old in this autumn of 1808.
19	*18–24*	Maurice Dupin met his future wife, Sophie Victoire Delaborde, in Milan in December 1800 (*OA* I, pp. 338–41, 1323–4). The "hussy" was then the mistress of a forty-nine-year-old quartermaster general named Claude-Antoine Collin, who was attached to General Dupont's headquarters (see Georges Lubin's revealing note, *OA* I, p. 1326). Her pursuit of Maurice Dupin occupies most of Chs. 2, 3, and 6 of the second part of GS's autobiography (*OA* I, pp. 334–76, 422–64).
19	*34–37*	An anonymous portrait of Aurora of Koenigsmark (1670–1728) is to be found at the Carnavalet Museum in Paris. There is a copy at Nohant.
20	*20–25*	Friedrich Augustus of Saxony (1670–1733) had himself elected King of Poland in 1697, was deposed in 1706, but managed to regain the throne in 1709 and to keep it until his death. His heart, cut out and preserved in Dresden, was found to be twice the normal size. Maurice de Saxe's affair with Marie-Geneviève Rainteau (1730–75) took place when she was seventeen and the victor of Fontenoy a ripe fifty years. After bearing him a daughter (Aurore de Saxe) she started an affair with the writer Marmontel and then moved on to the Duc de Bouillon, to whom she bore a son (the Abbé de Beaumont). She and her sister, Geneviève-Claude Rainteau (1734–91), were the daughters of an enterprising lemonade merchant who helped to launch both of them on their careers as gallantly kept ladies (*OA* I, pp. 31–2, 1241–2).
21	*4 ff.*	GS in her old age wrote a charming portrait of the Abbé de Beaumont entitled *Mon Grand-Oncle* (*OA* II, pp. 475–96, usefully annotated by Georges Lubin, pp. 1410–16). His visit to Nohant is described in GS's autobiography (*OA* I, pp. 621–6).
22	*28–33*	Shortly after signing the treaties of Tilsit, Napoleon, in August of 1807, had established the Kingdom of Westphalia, half of whose domains he annexed for his own purposes. The income from one of these domains provided Sophie Dupin with a kind of widow's pension (*OA* I, p. 1388).

3. BETWEEN TWO WORLDS (*Pages 25–55*)

The material in this chapter is drawn from the first ten chapters of Part III of GS's autobiography (*OA* I, pp. 643–861).

Page	lines	
28	*13 ff.*	On Aurore's first music lessons and her grandmother's extraordinary knowledge of eighteenth-century music, see *OA* I, pp. 625–6, 803–5, and Marix-Spire, *CGS*, pp. 47–134.
37	*18–20*	The pastel portrait of Louis-Claude Dupin de Francueil is now part of the Carnavalet Museum's collection in Paris. There is a copy at Nohant (*OA* I, pp. 760, 1403).

Page *lines*

51 *14–18* Contrary to what GS asserts in her autobiography (*OA* I, p. 33), Antoine de Horn, who was born in 1722, could hardly have been a bastard son of Louis XV. The latter was born in 1710 and would have had to father the Count at the precocious age of eleven. See Georges Lubin's pertinent comment, *OA* I, p. 1243.

52 *4–8* The father of Louis-Claude Dupin de Francueil (1715–1786) was the opulent Claude Dupin (1686–1769), who was twice married. His first wife, born Marie-Jeanne Bouilhat de Laleuf, was the great-grandmother of Aurore Dupin and her first cousin, René de Villeneuve. Claude Dupin's second wife was Louise de Fontaine (1707–1799), whose mother, married to a French naval commissioner, had been the mistress of the wealthy banker Samuel Bernard. GS, quoting Jean-Jacques Rousseau (*OA* I, p. 42), claims that Samuel Bernard was Louise de Fontaine's real father. She brought Claude Dupin a handsome dowry when they married in 1724, thus enabling him to buy the Hôtel de Lambert, on Paris' Ile St. Louis, in 1729, and the Château de Chenonceaux in 1733.

Rousseau served for a while as private secretary to Claude Dupin and was so smitten by the charms of his beautiful wife (Louise de Fontaine) that he made an abortive attempt to seduce her (*OA* I, pp. 42–4). The young Louis-Claude Dupin (GS's grandfather) was thus brought up in the same chateau with Rousseau. The chateau having been jointly purchased by Claude Dupin and his second wife, it was inherited by their son, Louis-Armand Dupin, a terrible spendthrift with a passion for gambling who finally died of yellow fever at the early age of thirty-seven. It was in part to pay his son's debts that Claude Dupin was forced to sell the Hôtel de Lambert in 1751 to Voltaire's friend, Madame du Châtelet. The Château de Chenonceaux was inherited, after Claude Dupin's death in 1769, by his grandson, Claude Dupin de Rochefort (1752–1788), who died childless at the age of thirty-six. Ownership then passed to a nephew of Louise de Fontaine's named Pierre-Armand de Villeneuve, who had ingratiated himself with the octogenarian Claude Dupin by marrying his granddaughter by his first marriage, Madeleine Dupin, in 1768. See the genealogical chart and *OA* I, pp. 51, 1247–51.

4. FROM DEVILTRY TO "SACRED SICKNESS" (*Pages 56–68*)

The material in this chapter is drawn from GS's lengthy description of her three convent years in Chs. 10–14 of Part III and the first two chapters of Part IV of her autobiography (*OA* I, pp. 861–1010, and Lubin's notes, pp. 1414–33). The Couvent des Anglaises no longer exists, part of its grounds now being occupied by the Ecole Polytechnique.

64 *29–32* William James, *Varieties of Religious Experience,* London, 1912, p. 381.

Genealogical Table showing Aurore de Saxe's kinship to the Kings of France

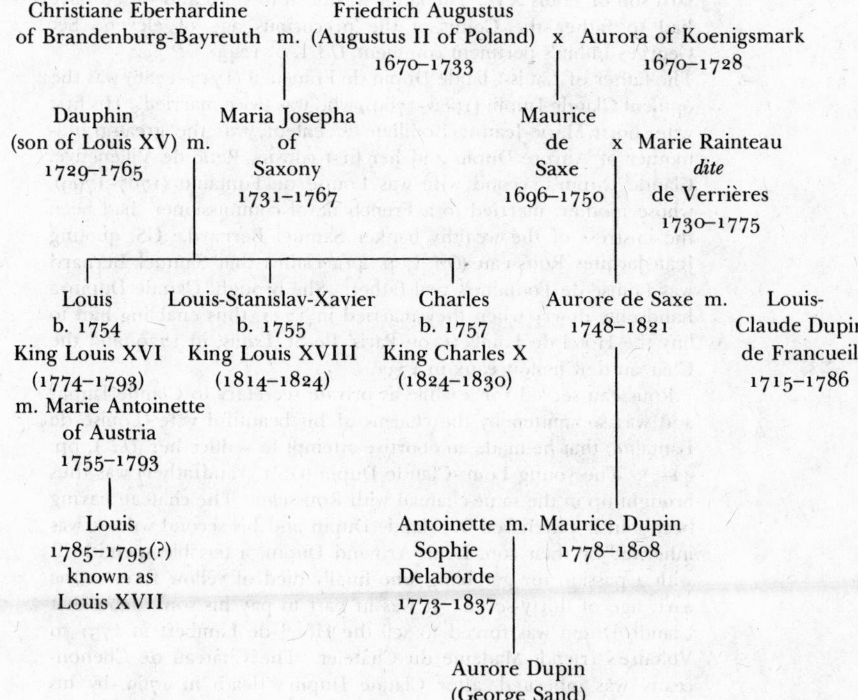

Genealogical Table showing Aurore Dupin's kinship to René de Villeneuve and his family

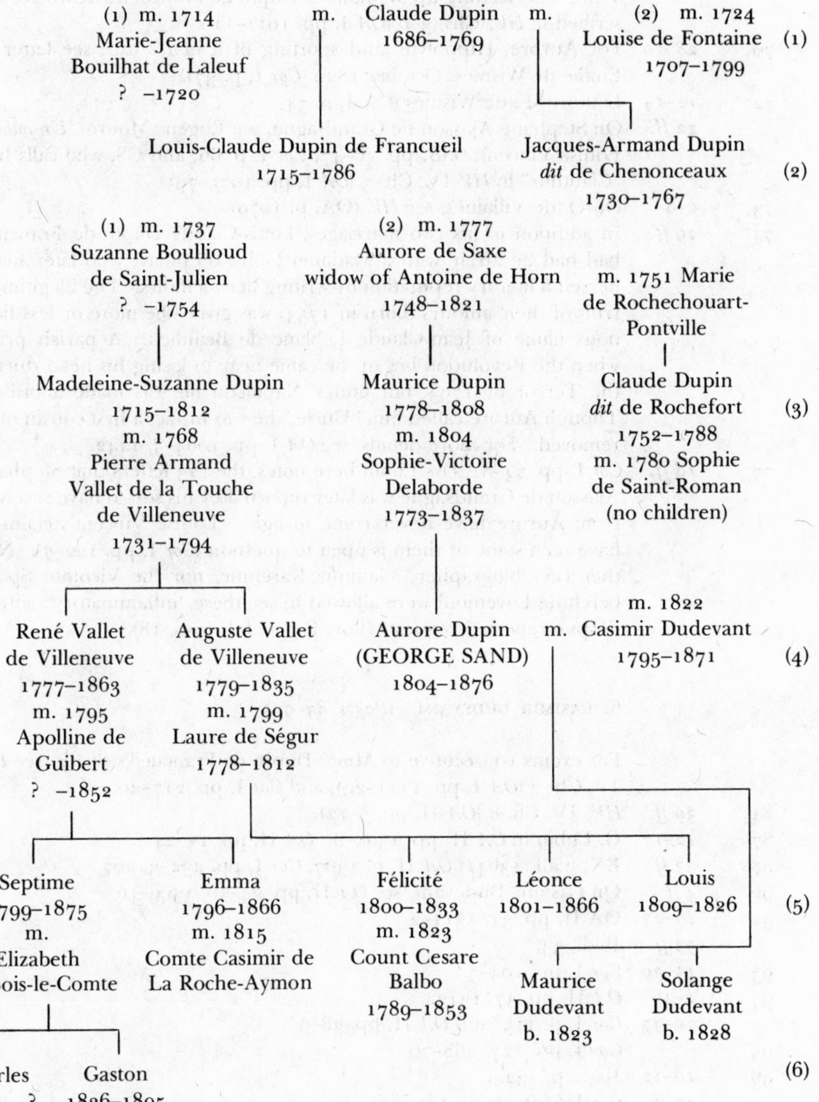

Figures on the far right indicate the generations.

Page lines

5. HELLION ON HORSEBACK (*Pages 69–79*)

The events leading up to Madame Dupin de Francueil's death are described in *HV*, Chs. 3–6 (*OA* I, pp. 1011–110.

70 *28–30* For Aurore, Hippolyte, and sporting of a man's cap, see letter to Emilie de Wismes, October 1820 (*Cor* I, p. 37).

72 *11–14* Letter to E. de Wismes (*Cor* I, p. 54).

22 ff. On Stéphane Ajasson de Grandsagne, see Eugène Mourot, *Un oublié;* Louise Vincent, *GSB,* pp. 46–47; *Cor* I, p. 66; and GS, who calls him "Claudius" in *HV* IV, Ch. 5 (*OA* I, pp. 1075–79).

73 *2–8* On O. de Villaines, see *HV* (OA, p. 1079).

74 *29 ff.* In addition to his two marriages, Louis-Claude Dupin de Francueil had had an affair with a Madame Lalive d'Epinay, who later made herself a literary reputation by writing her memoirs. The illegitimate fruit of their amours (born in 1753) was given the more or less fictitious name of Jean-Claude Leblanc de Beaulieu. A parish priest when the Revolution began, he came near to losing his head during the Terror of 1793, but under Napoleon he was made a bishop. Though Aurore called him "Uncle," he was in fact a first cousin once removed. For more details, see *OA* I, pp. 1064–5, 1442.

77 *18 ff.* *Cor* I, pp. 74–81. As Lubin here notes, the 123 letters that Stéphane Ajasson de Grandsagne was later reported by his son to have received from Aurore have never come to light. Louise Vincent's claim to have seen some of them is open to question (*Cor* I, pp. 122–7). Neither GS's biographer, Vladimir Karénine, nor the Vicomte Spoelberch de Lovenjoul were allowed to see these "inflammatory" letters, despite repeated requests (Lov, E 954, fols. 3–8, 18).

6. CASIMIR DUDEVANT (*Pages 83–99*)

For events consecutive to Mme. Dupin de Francueil's death, see *HV* IV, Ch. 7 (*OA* I, pp. 1111–29), and *Cor* I, pp. 217–20.

84 *30 ff.* *HV*, IV, Ch. 8 (*OA* II, pp. 5–12).

87 *12–17* G. Lubin in *OA* II, pp. 1305–6. *OA* II, pp. 13–24.

88 *33 ff.* BN, n.a.f. 13641; *OA* II, p. 1307; *Cor* I, pp. 232–3, 267.

90 *4 ff.* On Casimir Dudevant, see *OA* II, pp. 24–30, 1309–10.

92 *17–23* OA II, pp. 31, 1311–2.

33 ff. Ibid., 33.

93 *13–30* *Cor* I, pp. 103–5.

94 *1–20* *OA* II, pp. 37, 1313.

30–37 *Cor* I, p. 115, and *OA* II, pp. 38–9.

95 *Cor* I, pp. 127, 268–70.

96 *10–12* Ibid., p. 132.

27 ff. *Cor* III, pp. 75–6, 135.

97 *6–12* *Cor* I, p. 137.

28–34 Ibid., pp. 270, 139.

Page	lines	
	35 ff.	On Ormesson, *OA* II, pp. 43–7, and *Cor* I, p. 142.
98	*20–22*	Ibid., p. 269.
98–99		*OA* II, pp. 48–51.

7. ROMANCE IN THE PYRENEES (*Pages 100–111*)

Page	lines	
100	*1–14*	BHVP, G 3474, 3480; *Cor* I, p. 159; *OA* II, pp. 53–4, 1317.
	15 ff.	On Cauterets, see J. Fourcassié, *Le Romantisme et les Pyrénées,* pp. 5–59, and José Ortega y Gasset, *Obras Completas* II, pp. 601–5.
101	*8–19*	*OA* II, p. 58, and *Cor* I, pp. 160–1.
	20 ff.	*OA* II, pp. 58–63, 1319, and *Cor* I, pp. 271 ff.
103	*24 ff.*	On Zoé Leroy, see *OA* II, pp. 62–9, 1319. On Basque guides, *Cor* I, pp. 163–6.
104	*12 ff.*	On Aurélien de Sèze, see *Cor* I, pp. 244, 258, 272–3, and Auguste Nicolas, *Notice Biographique.*
104–111		*OA* II, pp. 64–72, and *Cor* I, pp. 239–40, 244–5, 251–3, 272–9.
111	*33–37*	Ibid., p. 169.

8. A CURIOUSLY PLATONIC TRIANGLE (*Pages 112–126*)

A brief but interesting account of the months spent at Guillery is given in Part IV, Ch. 9, of GS's autobiography (*OA* II, pp. 73–84). For the rest I have relied on letters written at the time.

Page	lines	
112	*8–13*	*Cor* I, pp. 170–1.
113	*1–19*	Ibid., pp. 239, 280–1.
	20 ff.	Ibid., pp. 192–5, 240, 281–2.
117	*1–9*	Ibid., pp. 225–6.
	10–14	Ibid., p. 180.
	10 ff.	Ibid., pp. 180–5, 226.
118	*15–35*	Ibid., pp. 175–7.
	36 ff.	Lov. E 902, fols. 4–21, and *Cor* I, pp. 177–261.
119	*15–23*	Lov. E 902, fols. 15–6, and *Cor* I, pp. 231–6.
	24–32	Lov. E 868, fols. 25–6, and *Cor* I, pp. 235–8.
	33–37	Lov. E 902, fol. 21. *Cor* I, p. 260.
120	*3–28*	Ibid., pp. 271, 287–8, 305. Lov. E 868, fol. 209.
	29 ff.	*Cor* I, pp. 288–9. Lov. E 902, fols. 22–4.
121	*12–34*	Lov. E 868, fols. 211–22.
	34 ff.	Lov. E 868, fols. 229–31, and *Cor* I, 293–8.
122	*9–18*	Lov. E 902, fols. 15–21, and *Cor* I, pp. 231–4, 239–261.
	19 ff.	Lov. E 868, fols. 30–40, and *Cor* I, pp. 262–292.
124	*9–21*	Lov. E 902, fols. 78, 43–5, and *Cor* I, pp. 308–9.
	22–27	Lov. E 868, fol. 227, and *Cor* I, p. 314.
125	*7–19*	Lov. E 869, fols. 34–5, and *Cor* I, pp. 321, 347.
	29–36	BHVP, G 106–7, and *OA* II, p. 1324.
126	*5–11*	Lov. E 902, fol. 68, and *Cor* III, p. 406.

Page	*lines*	
		9. A DISTINCTLY MACULATE CONCEPTION (*Pages 126–141*)
127	*3–15*	*Cor* I, p. 326, 329.
	16 ff.	Letter of A. de Sèze, BHVP G 5332, fols. 152–3. *Cor* I, pp. 357.
128	*9–21*	Lov. E 902, fol. 51, and *Cor* I, pp. 337, 340, 344–9.
	22–27	Lov. E 902, fols. 91–4. *Cor* I, pp. 341, 347, 343, and L. Vincent, *GSB,* p. 102.
	28–37	*Cor* I, pp. 333, 348. See *OA* II, pp. 543–51, for GS's description of a similar mad outing during the 1829 carnival season.
129	*5–15*	Lov. E 902, fols. 58–9, and *Cor* I, pp. 362–3.
	16–24	Lov. E 902, fol. 97, and *OA* II, p. 94.
	24 ff.	*Cor* I, pp. 361, 367, 371, 376–80.
131	*1–22*	BHVP, G 447, and *Cor* I, pp. 383–5. In March 1823 Hippolyte Chatiron had married Emilie Devilleneuve, who was already pregnant with the child (the future Léontine) she was to bear him the following August. Her dowry included a house on the Rue de Seine, in Paris, which was bequeathed to her by her father, a well-to-do Berrichon landowner. BHVP, D 218, 220, 221; *Cor* I, p. 107; and *OA* II, p. 1318.
	23–36	*Cor* I, pp. 388, 391, and BHVP, G 3494.
132–5		The journal Aurore kept of this trip to Mont-Dore is preserved at the Spoelberch de Lovenjoul library in Chantilly (E 850) and has been published in toto in *OA* II, pp. 503–27.
134	*17–20*	On Blavoyer, see *OA* II, pp. 212, 1419, and *Cor* I, pp. 472–3.
135	*20 ff.*	*Cor* I, p. 396. On Jules Néraud, *"le Malgache,"* see *OA* II, pp. 107–8; GS's sixth *Lettre d'un voyageur, OA* II, pp. 796–9, 1328; L. Vincent, *GSB*, pp. 109–12; and *Cor* I, pp. 416–9.
136	*5–19*	For GS's account of the Châteaubrun incident, see *Cor* III, pp. 77–8, and the testimony of Fleury and Duvernet, Lov. E 948, fols. 85, 91.
	25 ff.	*Cor* III, pp. 78–9.
137	*1–24*	*Cor* I, pp. 401, 403–9.
	25 ff.	Ibid., pp. 410–28.
138	*35 ff.*	BHVP, G 5348–9, and *Cor* I, pp. 443–40.
139	*9–13*	Lov. E 902, fols. 62–3, 105.
	30 ff.	Lov. E 902, fols. 107–8, and *Cor* I, pp. 441–4, 451.
140	*15 ff.*	Lov. E 902, fol. 101; *Cor* I, pp. 454, 481–2; and *OA* II, pp. 90–1, 1326.
141	*8–15*	Lov. E 888, fols. 5–6, and *Cor* I, p. 457. Louise Vincent's claim (*GSB,* p. 122) that Aurélien de Sèze returned to Bordeaux in a state of heartbroken "consternation" is contradicted by the letter from Bordeaux, dated October 21, 1828, in which Zoé Leroy speaks of Aurélien's elaborate descriptions of Nohant. His subsequent "madness" and "imbecility" were in no wise caused by chagrined "surprise" over Solange's birth; they were Zoé's ironic way of poking fun at Aurélien's "superhuman intelligence" and at his (for her) incomprehensible predilection for philosophical meditation and "learned discourse" with the man she loved — R. de Vignemale — but could not marry (Lov. E 902, fols. 113–5, corroborated by Aurore's reply, fols. 39–40, this last published *Cor* I, pp. 492–5).

Page	*lines*	
		10. THE END OF AN IDYLL (*Pages 142–152*)
142	*1–7*	L. Vincent, *GSB,* p. 122.
	8–12	Boucoiran's later testimony, as recorded in Lov. E 948, fol. 101.
	17 ff.	Lov. E 948, fols. 19, 99; *Cor* I, p. 483; and *Cor* III, p. 77.
143	*17 ff.*	Lov. E 902, fol. 113. *Cor* I, pp. 491, 501–8, and *OA* II, pp. 88–9.
144	*6–18*	*Cor* I, pp. 510–2, and GS *Dernières Pages,* pp. 27–33.
	19–29	Lov. E 948, fol. 40, and *Cor* III, p. 848.
	30 ff.	*Cor* I, pp. 511, 524–34.
145	*9 ff.*	Lov. E 902, fols. 122–3, and *Cor* I, pp. 544–7, 551–5.
146	*3 ff.*	*OA* II, pp. 104, 100, *Cor* I, pp. 560–2.
147	*9–29*	On Boucoiran, see *Cor* I, pp. 540–2, 548–50, 1000.
	30 ff.	On Desgranges, the Bordeaux "shipping merchant," see *Cor* I, pp. 530, 560, 570. Aurore was long persuaded that Félicie Molliet's real father was Maurice Dupin and that they were thus half sisters, but Georges Lubin has shown that this could not have been the case (*OA* II, pp. 1326, and *Cor* IV, pp. 424–5). On this Périgueux trip, see *Cor* I, pp. 564–71, 574–5, 601–2.
148	*13–23*	*OA* II, pp. 91, 1326–7, and Lov. E 948, fol. 40.
	24 ff.	*Cor* I, pp. 572–3, 577. Lov. E 948, fol. 99.
149	*12–33*	*Cor* I, pp. 577–9, 582–6.
	34 ff.	Ibid., pp. 595, 598, and *OA* II, pp. 105.
150	*15 ff.*	*Cor* I, pp. 629, 642–7, 666.
152	*5–33*	Ibid., pp. 546–7, and *OA* II, p. 99.
		11. JULES SANDEAU (*Pages 115–167*)
155		*Cor* I, pp. 638–41, 656, and *OA* II, pp. 106–7.
156	*21–38*	Quotation from a long entry entitled "Fragments de souvenirs personnels" which GS probably wrote in 1833 and then pasted into an album labeled in English "Sketches and Hints" (BN, n.a.f. 13506, fols. 134–48). Reproduced in *OA* II, pp. 601–9.
157	*14–17*	*Cor* I, p. 667.
	20–26	*Cor* III, p. 78, and Lov. E 948, fol. 100.
	27–34	*Cor* I, pp. 670–3.
158	*6 ff.*	Ibid., pp. 682–5, 688, 692, 708.
159	*7 ff.*	Aurore's first meeting with Sandeau was later written up by Ch. Duvernet in his unpublished "Memoirs" (see Mabel Silver, *Jules Sandeau,* pp. 11–20 and pp. 21–2, for details about his youth and upbringing). Though called a chateau, Le Coudray was a country house, like Nohant. The Château d'Ars, belonging to Gustave Papet's family, was on the other hand a turreted edifice more in keeping with our notion of "chateau." See Plates 52–4 in Lubin's *George Sand en Berry* and Plates 47 and 52 in his Pléiade *Album.*
160	*16 ff.*	*Cor* I, pp. 877–8. On the Couperies, see *OA* II, pp. 573–81; *Cor* I, p. 743; GS's ninth *Lettre d'un voyageur* (*OA* II, pp. 874–9).

Page *lines*

161 *12–30* *Cor* I, pp. 690–1.

31 ff. Ibid., pp. 704–7.

162 *14–25* Ibid., pp. 710–13; *Cor* III, p. 78; Boucoiran's later testimony in Lov. E 948, fol. 99.

26–37 *Cor* I, pp. 716–8.

163 *5–18* *Marianna,* pp. 241–2.

19–32 *Cor* I, p. 963.

33 ff. Ibid., pp. 715, 719–22.

164 *7–16* Ibid., p. 720.

18–21 *Cor* I, p. 735.

22–33 *OA* II, pp. 102–5.

164–5 *Cor* I, pp. 736–9.

166 *13–35* *OA* II, p. 108, and *Cor* I, pp. 751–5, 760–1.

167 *4–14* On Félix Pyat, see Ségu, *Le Premier Figaro,* p. 44; GS's letter, *Cor* I, pp. 761–3; Lubin's biographical note, ibid., p. 1015.

15–23 OA *II,* p. 109.

12. "VIVE LA VIE D'ARTISTE! (*Pages 168–191*)

Many details in this chapter are drawn from GS's autiobiographical reminiscences, written more than twenty years later (*HV* IV, Chs. 13, 14).

168 *1–14* *Cor* I, pp. 771–5.

15–24 Ibid., pp. 853–5, 862, 884.

169 *1–3* On Gustave Papet, the future friend of Alfred de Musset, as well as Chopin's doctor, see Lubin's biographical note, *Cor* I, pp. 1012–3.

4–18 *Cor* I, pp. 781–2, 855, 858–9, 867, 875, 881–2, 891. For a novelistic portrayal of Aurore and Sandeau eating off a narrow table and drinking from the same glass, see *Marianna,* p. 270.

19 ff. *Cor* I, p. 777. On Duris-Dufresne and Kératry, see *OA* II, pp. 148–150, 1338, and *Cor* I, pp. 792–7, 806–7, 812–3.

170 *1–13* Ibid., pp. 801, 819, and satirically reported in *Figaro,* March 1, 1831.

14 ff. See H. Monnier, *Mémoires de M. Joseph Prudhomme* II, pp. 85–112, and F. Ségu, *Un journaliste dilettante.*

171 *30 ff.* On "l'affaire Fualdès" and the subsequent *Mémoires de Mme Manson,* see F. Ségu, *Un Romantique républicain,* pp. 64–73; on *Les Dernières Lettres des deux amants de Barcelone,* ibid., pp. 71–6; on *Correspondance inédite de Clément XIV et Carlo Bertinazzi,* ibid., pp. 306–9.

172 *7–12* On Maurice Dupin's musical association with the Duvernets and Latouche's father, see Marix-Spire, *CGS,* pp. 94–5, 121.

15–25 *Cor* I, pp. 779–80. GS's letters to Latouche, along with others written by Stendhal, Balzac, and Condorcet, were carelessly destroyed in 1871 when the Prussians occupied his "hermitage" at Aulnay. Many, if not all, of his letters to her were preserved and are now part of the Lovenjoul and BHVP collections.

26–32 Ségu, *Un Romantique républicain,* p. 34, and *Cor* I, pp. 783–4, 790.

33 ff. *Cor* I, p. 801.

Page	*lines*	
173	*3–13*	Ibid., p. 783.
	14–36	Ibid., pp. 783–4, 790.
174	*1–9*	Ibid., p. 796.
	10–14	Ibid., pp. 818–9.
	15–22	On Paris in 1831, see Chopin, *Correspondance* II, pp. 56–7; Théophile Gautier, *Histoire du romantisme,* pp. 1–6. Robert Burnand, *La Vie quotidienne en 1830* (Paris, 1957); Bernard Gavoty, *Chopin,* pp. 141–72.
	23–32	*Marianna,* pp. 68–72.
	33 ff.	*Cor* I, pp. 808–10.
175	*14–24*	Ibid., pp. 810–15. and *Figaro,* March 5, 1831, article entitled "Vision."
	25 ff.	Ségu, *Le Premier Figaro,* pp. 2–51; *Cor* I, pp. 818–9; *OA* II, pp. 151–3.
176	*16–30*	*Figaro,* March 3,1831, article entitled "La Molinara"; March 5, bogus decree; March 10, article on Paganini.
	31 ff.	*Cor* I, pp. 822–5.
177	*17–22*	Ibid., pp. 818–9.
	23 ff.	*OA* II, pp. 116–8.
178	*7–15*	*Cor* I, pp. 789–90.
	16–30	On Paris as a music center, see Marix-Spire's fascinating introduction to *CGS,* pp. 11–45, and Gavoty, *Chopin,* pp. 176–8. On María Malibran, see *CGS,* pp. 207–28, and Chopin, *Correspondance* II, pp. 44–6.
	31 ff.	On *La Prima Donna,* see *CGS,* pp. 232–4.
179	*13–21*	On Charles Lassailly and the *paroxystes,* as they were called, see *OA* II, pp. 117, 1341, and Emilien Carassus, *Le Mythe du Dandy* (Paris 1971). Lassailly's novel, *Les Roueries de Trialph,* had been published in 1828.
	21–28	*Cor* I, pp. 825–6. Balzac's two tales, recently serialized in the *Revue de Paris,* were *Sarrasine* (the story of a Roman castrato) and *Une passion dans le désert.*
	29 ff.	On Latouche's literary judgment, see *OA* II, pp. 159–160; on his dislike of Hugo and his coterie, Ségu, *Un Romantique républicain,* pp. 345–55; on his musical taste, Marix-Spire, *CGS,* pp. 229–30. On Habenek, the Conservatoire, and Malibran, see *CGS,* pp. 207, 212–3, 224.
180	*18–35*	*CGS,* pp. 215–20. *Cor* I, pp. 821, 830, and *Figaro,* March 23, 1831.
181	*1–12*	On *La Fille d'Albano,* see *Cor* I, pp. 670, 790, 818, 871, and *CGS,* pp. 234–5.
	19–29	*Cor* I, pp. 840, 855, 871, 897.
	30 ff.	Ibid., pp. 854, 861. None of the letters Aurore wrote to Sandeau at this time have come down to us. To keep his jealous wife from getting her hands on them — Marie-Louise Pailleron claimed to have actually seen her burning one of them (*GS* II, p. 59) — Sandeau, some time before his death in 1883, entrusted them to a bookseller named Sapin. The latter unfortunately died before the Vicomte Spoelberch de Lovenjoul could discover their whereabouts and offer a good price for them. Sapin's widow presumably disposed of them as "trash."
182	*8–12*	Balzac, *Correspondance* I, pp. 522–3, and *Cor* I, p. 858.

Page	*lines*	
	13–24	*Cor* I, pp. 875, 881–3. A major source of information about her love affair with Jules Sandeau, these and other letters written to Emile Regnault are now part of the BN's manuscript collection (n.a.f. 13507, with copy at Chantilly, Lov. E 898).
	25 ff.	*Cor* I, pp. 909–10.
183	*8–15*	Ibid., pp. 915–6.
	16–29	Ibid., pp. 918–23, 929, 936–8. See also Pierre Reboul, *RSH,* October–December 1959, pp. 379–84.
	30 ff.	*Cor* I, pp. 919–20.
	11–22	Ibid., pp. 922–3.
184	*23 ff.*	Lov. E 868, fols. 238–9. *Cor* I, pp. 930–1.
185	*9–33*	Ibid., pp. 936–8.
186	*1–21*	*Cor* I, pp. 936–43.
	22 ff.	Ibid., pp. 958, 944–6, 953, 962, and M. Silver, *Jules Sandeau,* p. 43.
188	*6–20*	*Cor* I, p. 955.
	21 ff.	Ibid., pp. 961–3.
189	*16–25*	*Cor* I, pp. 969–71, 897, and *OA* II, pp. 133–4, 160.
	26–34	*Cor* I, pp. 972–3.
190	*1–17*	On Giuditta Pasta, see Marix-Spire, *CGS,* pp. 210–2, 225–8, and Chopin, *Correspondance* II, pp. 44–5.
	18–37	*Cor* I, pp. 984, 988–9, and *OA* II, pp. 138, 1335–6.
191	*1–17*	*Cor* II, pp. 16, 41–2, and *Figaro,* December 17, 1831. Ségu, *Un Romantique républicain,* p. 95, quotes Latouche as later remarking: "If I have cause for literary pride, it is for two recollections: that of having published André Chénier and of having kept George Sand from busying herself with watercolor portraits."

13. INDIANA *(Pages 192–206)*

Page	*lines*	
192	*1 ff.*	*Cor* I, pp. 979–80, 991–3, and *Cor* II, pp. 9–13.
193	*12–30*	*Cor* II, pp. 22–30.
	31 ff.	On *Indiana,* see Pierre Salomon's introduction to the Garnier (1962) edition; Marix-Spire, *CGS,* pp. 280–1; *OA* II, pp. 164–70; *Cor* II, pp. 42–53.
195	*35 ff.*	On A. de Sèze's wild oats, see A. Nicolas, *Notice Biographique,* pp. 15–6. On Claire's pregnancy, *Cor* I, p. 980.
196	*24 ff.*	*Indiana,* pp. 168–9, 225–6, 242.
199	*2–8*	*Cor* II, p. 48.
	9 ff.	Ibid., pp. 62–77, and *OA* II, pp. 141–2.
200	*10–19*	*Cor* II, p. 78.
	20–34	Ibid., pp. 87–8.
	32	I have translated here by "francs," though the word used by Aurore in her letter to Duvernet was *livres,* meaning "pounds." The French *livre* was originally a gold coin having the same value as the later franc. Though the currency had been streamlined at the time of the

Page	*lines*	
		Revolution, many French men and women continued to use the old pre-Revolutionary terms.
201	*1–20*	Ségu, *Le Premier Figaro,* pp. 63–80; *Un Romantique républicain,* pp. 442–4, 666; *Cor* II, pp. 88–9.
	21 ff.	*OA* II, pp. 173–4, 1342–3.
202	*3–37*	On Balzac, see *OA* II, pp. 154–8, and *Cor* II, pp. 86–7.
203	*1–19*	*Cor* II, pp. 89–90, and *OA* II, pp. 138–9, 1336.
	20–32	*Cor* II, pp. 115–6.
	33 ff.	*OA* II, pp. 142–6, and *Cor* II, pp. 97–8, 102–5, 112–3.
205	*14 ff.*	Ibid., pp. 118–20.
206	*16–26*	Marix-Spire, *CGS,* p. 253.

14. DISENCHANTMENT AND DESPAIR (*Pages 207–216*)

Page	*lines*	
207	*1–19*	*Cor* II, pp. 110–1, 123–4, 152, and Lov. E 864, fols. 216–7.
	20 ff.	*Cor* II, pp. 129–39.
208	*17–30*	Lov. F 1031, fol. 177, and M. Silver, *Jules Sandeau,* pp. 38–43.
	10–35	On François Rollinat, a young Châteauroux lawyer, see *OA* II, pp. 122–5, and Lubin's biographical note, *Cor* II, p. 934.
209	*1–7*	On *La Marquise,* see *Cor* II, pp. 159–69.
	8–33	On *Valentine,* see V. Karénine, *GS* I, and Marix-Spire, *CGS,* pp. 254–60.
210	*17 ff.*	BHVP, G 4410, and *Cor* II, pp. 160–1.
211	*16–21*	All told, some 34 letters, written by A. de Sèze between November 1825 and 1829, are now preserved at the BHVP (Fonds Sand, G 5339). For the fate of Aurore's letters to him, see foreword, note to page 398.
212	*1–15*	*Cor* I, pp. 692–3, 708–9, and *Le Roman d'Amour d'Aurore Dudevant et d'Aurélien de Sèze,* Paris 1928, pp. 210–11.
	16–38	BN, n.a.f. 13507, fols. 26–8, and *Cor* I, pp. 894–8.
213	*1 ff.*	*Cor* II, pp. 155–8, 162–6, 168.
214	*9–17*	*Cor* II, pp. 114, 150.
	18–38	Ibid., pp. 170–2.
215	*1–38*	*Marianna,* pp. 271–2, 277, 293.
216	*1–19*	*Cor* II, pp. 178–80.

15. LÉLIA (*Pages 217–240*)

Page	*lines*	
217	*1–20*	On the success of *Valentine* and *La Marquise,* see *Cor* II, p. 193, and on the Quai Malaquais apartment, ibid., pp. 185–94, 204.
	21 ff.	See Maurice Regard, *L'adversaire des romantiques. Gustave Planche* I; *OA* II, pp. 280–8, and Lubin's pertinent *mise au point* in *Cor* II, pp. 195–8.
218	*16 ff.*	On Buloz and the *RDM,* see the book of reminiscences written by his granddaughter, Marie-Louise Pailleron, *François Buloz et ses amis.*
219	*1–7*	Lov. E 861, and *Cor* I, pp. 188–9.

Page	lines	
	7–15	Ibid., pp. 234–6.
	16–25	On *Trenmor* and its subsequent development, see Pierre Reboul's introduction to *Lélia* in the Garnier edition (1960).
	26 ff.	*Cor* II, pp. 195–8. Planche's diatribe against Latouche, entitled "De la haine littéraire," had appeared in the December 1, 1831, issue of the *RDM*.
220	*1–5*	Regard, *Gustave Planche* II, pp. 62–3, and *Cor* II, pp. 205–6.
	6–34	Ernest Renduel, Charles Gosselin, Mame-Delaunay, and of course Dupuy, with whom she signed the contract for *Lélia*. See *Cor* II, pp. 199, 217–21.
	35 ff.	Lov. E 899, fols. 6–6; *Cor* II, pp. 260–1; Jean Bonnerot, *Correspondance générale de Sainte-Beuve* I, p. 368. See also Bonnerot, *Une grande amitié littéraire: Sainte-Beuve et George Sand*.
221	*2–12*	On *Joseph Delorme*, see *Cor* II, pp. 289–90; Maurice Allem, *Portrait de Sainte-Beuve*, pp. 50–3; Harold Nicolson, *Sainte-Beuve*, pp. 17–9; Ségu, *Un Romantique républicain*, pp. 349–60.
	23 ff.	These and other biographical details are drawn from Françoise Moser's *Marie Dorval* and GS's elaborate portrait, Part V, Ch. 4, of *HV*. On the start of this friendship, see Lubin, *RHL*, April–June 1958, pp. 205–9; *Cor* II, pp. 241–2; *OA* II, p. 228.
222	*28 ff.*	Vigny, *Journal d'un poète*, p. 173, and *Cor* II, p. 369.
223	*11–18*	M. Regard, *Planche* I, pp. 103–4, and *Planche* II, p. 69.
	19 ff.	*OA* II, pp. 223–4.
225	*32 ff.*	*Cor* II, p. 242.
226	*7–15*	Ibid., p. 251.
	16–26	"Mlle Mars et Mme Dorval" in February 17, 1831. issue of *L'Artiste*, later republished in GS, *Questions d'art et de littérature*, pp. 13–23. Charles-Maurice's furious rebuttal in February 19 issue of the *Courrier des spectacles*, quoted by Lubin, *Cor* II, pp.254–5.
	27 ff.	*Cor* II, pp. 257–60.
227	*11 ff.*	Houssaye, *Confessions* II, pp. 13–4. See *Cor* II, p. 290, regarding infrequency of GS's visits to Marie Dorval.
228	*6–16*	*Lélia*, pp. 153–8.
	17–36	*Marianna*, pp. 296–313.
229	*1–8*	H. Amic, in the *Figaro*, November 2, 1896; repeated by V. Karénine, *GS* I, p. 388, and M-L. Pailleron, *F. Buloz et ses amis* I, p. 342, but contested by M. Silver, *Jules Sandeau*, p. 45, and Lubin, *Cor* II, pp. 178–9.
	9–32	*Cor* II, pp. 268–9, 272–5.
	33–7	M. Silver, *Sandeau*, pp. 69–70.
230	*1–9*	Ibid., pp. 50–5. March 28, 1833, entry in Ch. Didier's diary, Lov. E 940, fol. 25; also published by M. Regard, *Charles Didier et GS*, in *RSH*, October–December 1959, pp. 459–66. First cousin of the poetess Delphine Gay, Hortense Allart had been Chateaubriand's mistress before becoming Henry Bulwer's. Barbey d'Aurevilly, an ultraconservative royalist who detested "bluestockings," i.e., women authors, called her a "female Rousseau." See André Billy, *Hortense et ses amants*, and Léon Séché, *Muses romantiques*.

Page	lines	
	10–19	Ch. Didier diary entry, July 13, 1832. Lov. E 940, fol. 19.
	19–21	Lov. D 583, and *Cor* II, p. 261.
	21 ff.	Didier entries — February 4, March 21 and 30, 1833. Lov. E 940, fols. 24–6.
231	*7 ff.*	Planche's influence on GS and the composition of *Lélia* is well discussed by Pierre Reboul in his introduction to the 1960 Garnier edition, pp. xxv–xxxvii. On Balzac and *La Peau de chagrin,* ibid., pp. lvi–lviii; on Nodier, pp. lix–lxiii.
	18–22	*Cor* II, p. 183.
233	*21 ff.*	*OA* II, pp. 280–9.
236–8	*5 ff.*	*Lélia,* pp. 172–6.
239	*5–9*	The fate of these 123 letters remains a mystery. Louise Vincent, *GSB,* p. 124, was told by friends of Paul de Grandsagne (Stéphane's son) that he had entrusted them to a Mademoiselle Naud, who died in 1906, or thereabouts, after marrying a M. Chauvet. Louise Vincent managed to track down one of Chauvet's two daughters, who said that she had never heard of any such letters having been in her stepmother's possession. About Stéphane de Grandsagne's letters to Aurore we know even less. Presumably she burned them as too compromising.

16. FROM CELEBRITY TO SCANDAL (*Pages 241–251*)

Page	lines	
241	*6 ff.*	*Cor* II, pp. 290–2.
243	*1–11*	Ibid., pp. 270–2.
	12 ff.	Ibid., p. 293, and *OA* II, pp. 177–9. See also Marix-Spire, *CGS,* pp. 274–5.
244	*10–13*	*Jacques,* eighty-ninth letter.
	14 ff.	See Albert de Luppé, *Prosper Mérimée,* and A. Billy, *Mérimée.*
245	*3–5*	*Cor* II, p. 155 — reference to Mérimée's "Les Voleurs en Espagne" in the August 26, 1832, issue of the *Revue de Paris.*
	5–9	Regard, *Planche* II, pp. 69, 72, and *Cor* II, pp. 237, 239–40, 244, 246, 262.
	13–18	On Mérimée, GS, and Spain, see Marix-Spire, *CGS,* pp. 295–302.
	22–7	A. de Pontmartin, *Mémoires* II, p. 66. Also, pp. 127–8 for Marie Dorval on the subject of GS.
	35 ff.	*Cor* II, pp. 374–5.
246	*6 ff.*	I have followed Maurice Parturier's account of what followed in *Une Expérience de Lélia.* In a biographical essay devoted to Mérimée and published in 1885, Paul d'Haussonville gave a far tamer account of what took place, doubtless feeling that it ill behooved a former minister of justice to descend to the level of bedroom farce.
247	*9–16*	*Cor* II, pp. 295–6.
	17–33	Vigny, *Journal d'un poète,* pp. 239–40, and *Cor* II, pp. 369–70.
	34 ff.	Ibid., p. 375.
248	*22–9*	Ibid., pp. 322–3, 329–30.
	34 ff.	Charge later leveled by Casimir against GS, *Cor* III, p. 849.

Page	*lines*	
249	*3 ff.*	See Didier's diary entry, June 9 (or possibly 29), 1833, Lov. E 940, fol. 27; also *Cor* II, p. 309; Lubin's fns. to pp. 321, 336–8; Regard, *Planche* II, pp. 74–8; Sainte-Beuve, *Correspondance* I, p. 370.
250	*1–16*	*Cor* II, pp. 351–2. On Alessandro Poerio, see Poli, *IVGS,* p. 44.
251	*6–9*	*Lélia,* p. 244.
	10–25	*Cor* II, pp. 369–71.
	26–30	Ibid., pp. 372–9.

17. A YOUNG DANDY OF GENIUS (*Pages 255–274*)

Page	*lines*	
255	*1–6*	*Cor* II, p. 326.
	8–10	*Lélia,* pp. 283–4.
	18–22	On the Paris cafés and gambling clubs frequented by Musset, see Léon Séché, *La Jeunesse dorée sous Louis-Philippe,* and Musset's own description, "Le boulevard de Gand," published by Maurice Allem in *Oeuvres Complètes en Prose,* pp. 1104–8.
256	*1–5*	*Cor* II, pp. 277.
	6–10	Lubin's detailed footnote to *Cor* II, pp. 331–2, explains why GS's first meeting with Musset did not take place, as previously thought, in a restaurant. The date was probably June 19, 1833 (see J. Pommier, *Variétés sur A. de Musset et son théâtre,* pp. 36–39).
	11–19	For descriptions of Musset, see L. Séché, *Musset* I, p. 72; Maurice Toesca, *Vie d'Alfred de Musset,* pp. 59, 65, 69–70; M. Allem, *Oeuvres en Prose,* p. 1105; GS's barely fictionalized description of his arrogant gaze and the lids that had lost their lashes, in *Lélia,* p. 250.
	20 ff.	Paul de Musset, *Lui et Elle,* p. 32.
257	*11–15*	BN, n.a.f. 10369, fol. 78; L. Evrard, *CSM,* p. 22; *Cor* II, pp. 332–3; Toesca, *Musset,* p. 100.
	16–34	Musset, *Poésies,* pp. 273–92, and Allem's commentary, pp. 707–24.
258	*1–31*	Toesca, *Musset,* pp. 101–2; "Après la lecture d'*Indiana,*" in Musset, *Poésies,* pp. 512–3, 871–2.
	32 ff.	*Cor* II, pp. 339–41; Allem, *Musset,* pp. 84–5; Pommier, *Variétés,* pp. 197–9.
259	*8–15*	Second Chant, twenty-fourth stanza of *Namouna.* On Hoffmann and *Don Juan,* see Marix-Spire, *CGS,* pp. 196, 273, 308, 325–7.
	16–21	*Cor* II, p. 343, letter to Papet, thought to be the handsome young man with the swagger stick.
	22 ff.	Paul de Musset, *Lui et Elle,* pp. 41–3. In this semifactual novel Gustave Planche became the slovenly Diogène, Papet and Boucoiran were merged into the country bumpkin figure of Caliban, and Alphonse Fleury became Hercule, also known as Don Stentor.
260	*8–14*	Paul de Musset, *Biographie d'Alfred de Musset,* pp. 88–9, and Regard, Planche I, pp. 48–9.
	20–28	As related by Musset's friend, Mme Martellet, to Dr. Cabanès in his article, "Un Roman Vécu a trois personnages," *Revue hebdomadaire,* August 1, 1896, p. 134.
	29 ff.	Evrard, *CSM,* pp. 23–4, and *Cor* II, pp. 353–4.

Page	*lines*	
261	*22–26*	"Les Secrètes pensées de Rafael," in Musset, *Poésies,* p. 121.
	27–31	"A la Pologne," ibid., p. 491, and *Cor* I, p. 949.
	31–34	Paul de Musset, *Biographie,* p. 100; Marix-Spire, *CGS,* pp. 303–30; "Les Marrons du feu," Scene V, Musset, *Poésies,* pp. 37–8.
262	*2–10*	Evrard, *CSM,* p. 25, and *Cor* II, pp. 366–7.
	11–15	Mme Martellet, *Alfred de Musset, intime,* pp. 295–6.
	16–20	Evrard, *CSM,* pp. 26–7, and *Cor* II, p. 368.
	23–28	Paul de Musset, *Lui et Elle,* pp. 45–6.
	33 ff.	The incident with Mme Beaulieu was described by Musset himself in Ch. 3 of his *Confession (d'un enfant du siècle)*. See also Paul de Musset, *Biographie,* p. 80, and Allem note in *Poésies,* pp. 625–6.
263	*15–23*	Evrard, *CSM,* p. 24, and *Cor* II, pp. 380–1.
	24–34	Evrard, *CSM,* pp. 27–8.
	35 ff.	See Musset, *Confession,* Part IV, Ch. 1., and Lubin's note on these pages torn from GS's "Sketches and Hints" album, *Cor* II, p. 382.
264	*2–33*	Evrard, *CSM,* pp. 29–31, and *Cor* II, pp. 382–5.
	34 ff.	On the start of the Sand-Musset liaison, see L. Séché, *A. de Musset* II, p. 8; J. Pommier, *Variétés,* pp. 36–51; and *Autour du drame de Venise,* pp. 11–19; *Cor* II, pp. 385, 395, 563; GS, *Elle et Lui,* pp. 100–102; Musset, *Confession,* Part III, Ch.11; Musset's poem celebrating his conquest, "Te voilà revenu, dans mes nuits étoilées . . ." in *Poésies,* pp. 513–4, 873.
265	*21 ff.*	*Cor* II, pp. 394–6.
266	*20–26*	"Sketches and Hints" album, BN, n.a.f. 13506. *OA* II, p. 589.
	24 ff.	On Musset's need to torture GS by mocking allusions to his dissolute past, see *Confession,* Part IV, Ch. 2; on his morbid jealousy and suspicions regarding Planche and others, J. Pommier, *Variétés,* pp. 59–65; on previous hysterical fits, Toesca, *Musset,* pp. 39, 51.
266–7		GS, *Elle et Lui,* pp. 103–14.
267	*22–30*	*Elle et Lui,* pp. 115–6, and *Confession,* Part IV, Ch. 3.
	31 ff.	Paul de Musset, *Biographie,* pp. 117–8.
268	*12–29*	*Cor* II, pp. 397–401.
	30 ff.	Didier diary entries, August 9, 10, 12, 14, 19, 20. Lov. E 940, fols. 28–9.
269	*13–27*	*Cor* II, pp. 406–10.
	28 ff.	For Capo de Feuillide article, "Les Bas Bleus," see Sp. de Lovenjoul, *La Véritable histoire de "Elle et Lui,"* pp. 258–74.
270	*5–20*	M. Regard, *Planche* I, pp. 118–21, and Vol. II, pp. 79–81; *Cor* II, pp. 410–1; Musset, *Poésies,* pp. 514–9.
	21–33	*Cor* II, pp. 418–9; Musset, *Poésies,* pp. 520, 522–3.
271	*1–11*	In French: "Je soussigné, Mussaillon ler, déclare que mon album n'est pas si cochoné que ça." His drawings of himself and GS — Plates 21 and 22 — come from this album (Lov. E 956).
	12–13	Musset, in *Confession,* Part IV, Ch. 1, even describes Brigitte (i.e., GS) composing an air he took for one of Stradella's.
	14–37	Paul de Musset, *Biographie,* pp. 119–20. On Deburau, the mime, see *OA* II, pp. 135–6, 1334.
272	*1–6*	*Cor* II, pp. 421–2.

Page *lines*

7–31 Ibid., pp. 419–20, 435, and Toesca, *Musset,* pp. 121–2. On "The Conspiracy of 1537" and *Lorenzaccio,* see *Cor* I, pp. 893, 900; Paul Dimoff, *La Genèse de Lorenzaccio;* A. Poli, *IVGS,* p. 28; J. Pommier, *Variétés,* pp. 117–41; M. Allem, Musset, *Théâtre,* pp. 1240–9.

32 ff. *Cor* II, p. 427.

273 *3–6* See ibid., pp. 432–3, Lubin's reasons for suggesting that two excursions were made to the forest of Fontainebleau.

6–12 *L'Artiste,* November 3, 1833, and *Cor* II, p. 432.

18–23 *Cor* II, p. 405, and *OA* II, pp. 176–7.

24 ff. *Cor* II, pp. 434–5, and Napoléon Peyrat, *Béranger et Lamennais,* p. 81.

18. WINTER IN ITALY (*Pages 275–306*)

In attempting to unravel the tangled skein of events related in this chapter, I have relied on the following sources: (1) GS's letters, *HV,* and her later novel, *Elle et Lui,* (2) Musset's *Confession* (*d'un enfant du siècle*) and a later "testament" dictated to his bother, Paul, (3) Pietro Pagello's diary and later reminiscences (as quoted by A. Poli in *IVGS*); (4) Paul de Musset's semifactual novel, *Lui et Elle;* (5) Louise Colet's novel, *Lui,* an elaborate embellishment of Alfred's indiscretions.

275 *1–3* *Cor* II, p. 367.

5–7 *Childe Harold,* Canto IV, stanza 26.

7 ff. On Italian influences, see A. Poli, *IVGS,* Ch. 1; Pommier, *Autour du drame de Venise* (henceforth *Venise*), pp. 114–5; Marix-Spire, *CGS,* pp. 329–30.

13–16 "Mémoires de Casanova" in *Le Temps,* March 20, 1831 (Musset, *Prose,* pp. 871–5).

276 *1–6* On Hoffmann's influence, see Pommier, *Variétés,* pp. 67–73, and Marix-Spire, *CGS,* pp. 325–7.

17–23 *Cor* II, pp. 434, 444–5. On *Le Secrétaire intime,* see Regard, *Planche* I, pp. 103–4, 118–21; Pommier, *Variétés,* pp. 60–73.

277 *1–5* 60 centimes a line, according to Stendhal's calculations (see Paul de Musset, *Biographie,* p. 367).

6–17 *Cor.* II, pp. 442–4. The "Italian" novel was named *Jacques* in honor of GS's "foster-father," James Roëttiers du Plessis (*OA* II, p. 21).

17–21 *Cor* II, pp. 446–7.

22 ff. Ibid., pp. 448–57. The contract for *Le Secrétaire intime* gave Buloz the right to print 1300 two-volume copies. The December 9 contract for *Jacques* called for a first edition printing of 1500 two-volume copies; a second printing would require a new payment, to be fixed by mutual agreement. This followed the practice established with Dupuy, who had agreed to a first edition printing of 1200 copies for *Valentine* and of 1300 for *Lélia* (*Cor* II, pp. 123–4, 219–21).

278 *19–24* *Cor* II, pp. 458–60. Boucoiran, who would have liked so much to be in Musset's shoes, contributed as much as Pagello to the later portrait of Smith in *Confession,* Part V, Ch. 3.

Page	*lines*	
	25–35	L. Séché, *Musset* I, p. 99.
279	*1–24*	Paul de Musset, *Biographie,* pp. 125–6. Sp. de Lovenjoul, *La Véritable histoire de "Elle et Lui"* (henceforth *VHEL*), p. 17.
	25 ff.	As described in *Lui et Elle,* p. 63. On Alfred's superstitiousness and his sister's, see Séché, *Musset* II, pp. 8–9.
280	*7 ff.*	*OA* II, pp. 204–6. Copy of the album, Lov. F. 976.
280–1		*Cor* II, pp. 460–5, and Marix-Spire, *CGS,* p. 349.
281	*9–17*	Pommier, *Venise,* pp. 127–32.
281–2	*18–31*	*Lui,* pp. 71–2. *OA* II, p. 206; Lov. E 948, fol. 12; *Cor* II, pp. 465–6.
282	*26 ff.*	GS's own description of their arrival in Venice (Sp. de Lovenjoul, *VHEL,* pp. 140–3), and P. Mariéton, *Une Histoire d'amour,* pp. 74–7.
283	*15–34*	Poli, *IVGS,* pp. 60–1.
283–4		See Musset's later description of the beauties of Venice in *Le Fils du Titien* (*Prose,* pp. 429–30).
284	*9 ff.*	GS, *OA* II, p. 207, and *Cor* II, p. 730.
	17–31	For Byron's influence on Musset, see Pommier, *Venise,* pp. 102–15; Poli, *IVGS,* pp. 62–4; Musset, *Histoire d'un merle blanc* (*Prose,* p. 705), and his comic drawing of the Mocenigo Palace footman in album (Lov. F 976).
285	*6–13*	*Elle et Lui,* p. 133, and *Lui,* pp. 163–4.
	15–19	Raffaello Barbiera, *Nella citta dell'amore,* p. 107.
	20–27	*Cor* II, p. 730. Henri Guillemin's attempt to dismiss this letter because it was later written by GS and was thus a "fake" is as arbitrary as the rest of his diatribe, *La Liaison Musset Sand.* See Lubin's rebuttal in *RHLF* I, 1973.
285–6		Pommier, *Venise,* p. 21; *Lui et Elle,* pp. 92–3, and Musset's satiric drawing of this clumsy doctor, with caption "non ve arteria" (Lov. F 976).
286	*1–20*	A. Cabanès, April 1, 1896, issue of the *Revue indépendante,* pp. 143–5; Poli, *IVGS,* pp. 65–6, quoting from Pagello's unpublished memoirs, fol. 8.
	21 ff.	*Cor* II, pp. 483–4; *Lui,* pp. 164–7; Séché, *Musset* II, p. 25; and *OA* II, p. 170, on GS's only needing milk or lemonade for inspiration.
287	*3–12*	Poli, "Les Amants de Venise et Casanova" in *RHLF,* January–March 1959.
	13 ff.	*Elle et Lui,* pp. 132–6, 128, 142–4; *Cor* II, pp. 730–1, 492; *Lui,* pp. 161–248; Poli, *IVGS,* p. 64; R. Barbiera, *Nella citta dell'amore,* p. 105.
287–8		BN, n.a.f. 10369, fols. 121–2. In French: ". . . je ne sais ce que tu devenais le soir et un jour tu me dis que tu craignais avoir une mau-
288	*1–4*	vaise maladie." As Lubin points out (*Cor* II, p. 730), the damning words "d'avoir une mauvaise maladie" were so carelessly crossed out by GS as to seem underlined. This carelessness was almost certainly deliberate. Gustave Papet, who was both a doctor and a friend, never revealed what GS must have told him about Musset's sexual idiosyncracies, but there are two revealing clues at the Lovenjoul library in Chantilly. The first is a letter from Maxime Du Camp (G 1169, No. 11) written to Sp. de Lovenjoul in October 1882, in which

Page *lines*

he wrote that GS had retained her letters to Musset as "terrible" weapons to be used, if needed, against his brother, Paul: "The true story of Sand and Musset will never be more than suspected; it would be necessary to unveil its secret, the shameful part of it, and require a courage which I, for my part, will never have, although I know many things about all this." The second is a letter written to the Vicomte in September 1890 in which Maurice Clouard expressed his conviction that most of what had been written about this Venetian drama was nonsense, Paul de Musset and even more his wife (the former Aimée d'Alton) having "played a very ugly role in this matter. You should, furthermore, be apprised of a *physical* detail concerning *Him* which will give you the explanation for certain reproaches made to him by the partisans of the *other,* but not by Her, who knew more than enough on this score" (G 1163, No. 166).

These insinuations, as Lubin pertinently points out (*Cor* III, pp. 812–3), are regrettably discreet. The conclusion I have drawn from the available evidence is that Musset told GS he feared he might have contracted a case of the "clap" — or whatever he chose to call it. This is not to say that he actually had. But the mere fear would have been enough to chill GS's amorous ardor for the next few weeks, helping to explain (though not necessarily to condone) her subsequent behavior with that embodiment of healthy manhood, Pietro Pagello.

16–21 *Cor* II, pp. 730–1, and Musset, *Le Fils du Titien* (*Prose,* pp. 435–6), where making love by moonlight in a gondola "between sky and sea" is specifically referred to. In *Elle et Lui* (pp. 140–1) these nocturnal escapades are referred to more cryptically as "lessons" in baiting and casting supposedly administered to the hero by a local fisherman.

22–32 *Cor* II, pp. 478–81.

288–9 Ibid., pp. 486–92, and Evrard, *CSM,* pp. 46–8.

290 *22–33* *Cor* II, pp. 493–7, and Poli, *IVGS,* pp. 68–9.

290–1 Leslie Marchand, *Byron* II, pp. 686–7; *Cor* II, pp. 563–4; *Elle et Lui,* pp. 134–5; and GS's later reminiscence of these nightmarish days in J. Adam, *Mes Sentiments et nos idées avant 1970,* p. 218. Musset, in *Confession,* Part V, Ch. 4, made a pathetic avowal of the debauchee's need to use foul language, in defiance of the "hypocritical" parlance of "genteel" society.

291 *15–35* *Cor* II, pp. 496–8, and Poli, "La Véritable histoire de la correspondance Sand-Pagello" in *RHLF,* July–September 1957.

292 *1–8* *Cor* II, pp. 499–500, and Lubin's biographical note on S. de La Rochefoucauld, ibid., pp. 926–7.

8–13 This explains GS's furious outburst against Sandeau in her letter to Emile Regnault in June 1833 (*Cor* II, pp. 325–6). Cf. *Marianna,* p. 328.

18–36 *Cor* II, pp. 504–7. Cabanès, *Revue indépendante,* August 1, 1896, p. 149.

293 *1–17* On Pagello, see Poli, *IVGS,* pp. 73–5; Pommier, *Venise,* pp. 45–50; *Lui et Elle,* p. 93.

Page *lines*

18 ff. Musset's account, as dictated to his brother, Paul, in Mariéton, *Une Histoire d'amour,* pp. 104–6, and *Lui et Elle,* pp. 96–100. The tea cup scene also figures in *Confession,* Part V, Ch. 4.

294 *13 ff.* *Cor* II, p. 527. On the extraordinary effect of spring on her, see Aurore's revealing letter to Zoé Leroy in June 1826, in which she spoke of becoming positively "foolish at a certain period each year" (*Cor* I, pp. 340–1).

18–27 Pages later pasted into notebook entitled "Sketches and Hints" which GS had left behind in Paris (BN, n.a.f. 13506, fols. 73–4, quoted by Marix-Spire, *CGS,* pp. 353–5, and published by Lubin in *OA* II, pp. 620–2).

295 *1–18* As described by Pagello in preface to unpublished memoirs (quoted in original Italian by Poli, *IVGS,* p. 70) and as related to Professor Vittorio Fontana and repeated to Dr. Cabanès, op. cit., pp. 144–5.

19 ff. Mariéton, *Histoire d'amour,* pp. 94–7; *Cor* II, pp. 501–3; Poli, *IGVS,* pp. 70–3.

297 *4 ff.* *Cor* II, pp. 507–11.

298 *31 ff.* *Confession,* Part V, Ch. 4 (*Prose,* p. 248).

299 *5–20* As noted by Buloz, after conversation with Musset (M-L. Pailleron, *François Buloz et ses amis,* pp. 415–6). Confirmed by *JI* (Journal intime) entry of November 1834 (*OA* II, p. 957).

21–26 *Confession,* Part IV, Ch. 2 (*Prose,* p. 201).

27–35 *Cor* II, pp. 511–4.

36 ff. Ibid., pp. 526–7.

300 *9 ff.* Poli, *IGVS,* pp. 82–8; *Cor* II, pp. 517–8, 544–8; *Cor* IV, pp. 476–7; Marix-Spire, *CGS,* pp. 354–8. On Tattet, see Séché, *Jeunesse dorée,* pp. 6–12, and his *Musset* I, pp. 95–113.

301 *31 ff.* *Cor* II, pp. 526–30.

302 *6–34* On Leone Leoni, see Poli, *IVGS,* pp. 154–6; Marix-Spire, *CGS,* pp. 379–80; *Cor* II, pp. 520–2, 530–8.

303 *1–8* *Confession,* Part V, Ch. 5; *Cor* II, p. 548; and *Cor* IV, p. 477.

9–14 The Danieli hotel register, which R. Barbiera was able to consult, showed GS and Musset leaving on March 13. See A. Poli, *IVGS,* p. 78, and "Il romanzo Sand, Musset, Pagello" in *L'Illustrazione italiana,* November 15, 1896, p. 347.

14–33 *Cor* II, pp. 541–4.

33 ff. *Cor* II, p. 546. The idea of dying of erotic excess in the arms of a beloved mistress, as had happened to the painter Raphael, had already helped inspire Balzac's *La Peau de chagrin,* a novel which had made an extraordinary impression on Aurore at the time of her liaison with Sandeau. To judge by *Le Fils du Titien* (see *Prose,* pp. 447–8), which dates from 1838, Musset was also much intrigued by this "glorious" demise. In *Confession,* Part IV, Ch. 6, there is a pointed reference to "nights of terrible voluptuousness," charged with enough emotional electricity to kill both heroine and hero. In real life, however, GS was not prepared to contribute to such an amorous apotheosis. On her fear of killing Musset through frenzied fornication, see her early April letter to Boucoiran and the later letter

Page lines

to Papet, in which the case of Alfred Périgois is specifically mentioned (*Cor* II, pp. 554, 580); also her June 25 letter to Emile Paultre in which she declared that she had "no taste for the role of the *Fornarina,*" i.e., Raphael's mistress (*Cor* II, p. 638). Later, GS was similarly convinced that excessive lovemaking, as much as consumption, had hastened the early end of Marie Dorval's daughter Gabrielle, who died in April 1837, two months before her lover, Antoine Fontaney (*OA* II, pp. 232–3, 1358).

304 *4 ff.* As dictated by Musset to his brother and later published by Mariéton, *Histoire d'amour,* pp. 115–9.

305 *3–15* The wild trip across the lagoon to the Lido does not figure in Alfred's dictated account, but was added by Paul de Musset in *Lui et Elle,* pp. 106–8. The "night of the letter" was later referred to by Musset in writing to GS from Paris on April 30 (Evrard, *CSM,* p. 92): here Alfred gave her the benefit of the doubt and concluded that she had not lied to him about herself and Pagello. Much later, after Musset's death and the publication of *Lui et Elle* and *Lui,* GS felt the need to throttle the idea that she had threatened to have Musset locked up in a lunatic asylum. She then forged a brief, anxious note to Pagello, asking him to hurry over since Musset was seeing ghosts around his bed and hysterically shouting: "Je deviens fou!" To suggest haste in composition, she used a pencil on the back of a printed score entitled *Canzonetta nuova sopra l'Elisire d'amore.* The first to suggest that this penciled message might be a fake, concocted long after the event, was Antoine Adam in *Le Secret de l'aventure vénitienne,* pp. 281–2. But it took Georges Lubin to point out the essential flaw: that this penciled message was written in the round handwriting of the later GS, not in the tenser and more cramped hand that was hers in the early 1830s. See *Cor* II, pp. 538–40.

16–34 Ibid., pp. 542–4; Evrard, *CSM,* pp. 70, 93; Adam, *Secret,* pp. 144–5, 278–9.

306 *1–14* Evrard, *CSM,* pp. 67, 63; *Cor* II, p. 550; Poli, *IVGS,* pp. 88–90.

15–22 First *LV* (in *OA* II, p. 663); *Cor* II, pp. 554, 645–6, 695.

23–30 Pommier, *Venise,* pp. 133–4; 155–75; Second *LV* (in *OA* II, p. 683); Evrard, *CSM,* p. 154.

30–37 *Cor* II, p. 569, and first *LV* (in *OA* II, p. 670).

19. PIETRO PAGELLO'S VENICE (*Pages 307–317*)

307 *1–11* *OA* II, p. 208, and *Cor* II, pp. 550–2.

12 ff. This hiking tour into the Dolomites is described in GS's first *LV* (*OA* II, pp. 651–78). See also *Cor* II, pp. 557, 559–60, and Poli, *IVGS,* pp. 90–7.

308 *18–24* *Cor* II, pp. 546, 557, 564, 574, 651.

25 ff. On GS's life with the Pagello brothers, see Poli, *IVGS,* pp. 98–110, and Cabanès, op. cit., pp. 610–4.

Page	lines	
309	*25 ff.*	*Cor* II, pp. 565–7, 570–4.
310	*24 ff.*	The blue-eyed Giulia Puppati is described under the name of Beppa in GS's second *LV*, and Roberto Pagello as Giulio. See also *Cor* II, pp. 591–3, 692, and *OA* II, pp. 1441–2.
312	*19–25*	*Cor* II, pp. 603, 626.
	26–32	Ibid., pp. 564, 569–70; Evrard, *CSM*, pp. 97–102.
	32–38	Pailleron, *Vie litt.*, pp. 419–21.
313	*1–3*	*Cor* II, p. 601, fn. 2.
	3–8	On *André*, see L. Vincent, *GSB*, p. 115, and Poli, *IVGS*, pp. 152–4.
	10–21	*Cor* II, pp. 584–6, 594, 600–20.
	22–30	On Blavoyer, see *OA* II, pp. 211–2, 1351; *Cor* I, pp. 472–3, 512; *Cor* II, 632, 643, 911–2; Marix-Spire, *CGS*, p. 569.
	31–37	*Cor* II, pp. 629–31.
314–7		GS's second *LV*, in *OA* II, pp. 679–713. See also Ch. 3 in Poli, *IVGS*, and chapter entitled "Venise, ville chantante," in Marix-Spire's *CGS*, pp. 349–90.

20. A TENSE HOMECOMING (*Pages 318–332*)

Page	lines	
318–9		GS's third *LV*, written in July 1834, published in *RDM*, September 15, 1834 (*OA*, II, pp. 713–35).
319	*10–20*	*OA* II, p. 217.
	21–29	Poli, *IVGS*, pp. 149–60.
	30 ff.	Evrard, *CSM*, pp. 69–71.
320	*4–17*	*Cor* II, pp. 561–4.
	18 ff.	Evrard, *CSM*, pp. 80–4.
321	*12 ff.*	*Cor* II, pp. 569–70, 587–90, 597.
322	*12–23*	*Cor* II, pp. 617–20, 623, 645–9, 655, 666–7. BN, n.a.f. 10369, fols. 48–9; Evrard, *CSM*, p. 147.
	24 ff.	Poli, *IVGS*, pp. 131–8; *OA* II, pp. 212–4, 1352; *Cor* II, pp. 668–72.
324	*10 ff.*	From Pagello's unpublished ms. in Poli, *IVGS*, pp. 131, 138–40, and *Cor* II, pp. 672–9, 686.
325	*12 ff.*	Evrard, *CSM*, pp. 153–4; *Cor* II, pp. 676–7.
326	*9–13*	For "crown of thorns" see GS's June 15 letter to Musset (*Cor* II, p. 624).
	14–21	Ibid., pp. 678–9.
	22 ff.	Adam, *Secret*, pp. 172–7; Evrard, *CSM*, pp. 157–60.
327	*27–38*	*Cor* II, pp. 680–1, 682–3; Adam, *Secret*, pp. 178–81; Evrard, *CSM*, pp. 161–2, 170–1.
328	*1–24*	Poli, *IVGS*, p. 141; *Cor* II, pp. 684–8, 696–8; *OA* II, pp. 217–9; *Cor* III, p. 83.
	25 ff.	*Cor* II, pp. 694–7.
329–30		Evrard, *CSM*, pp. 161–5; *Cor* II, pp. 691–5.
330	*10–17*	Ibid., pp. 708, 714; Adam, *Secret*, pp. 183–4.
	18–37	Duchesse de Dino, *Chronique* I, pp. 246–8. "Le Prince" in *RDM*, October 15, 1834, later republished as GS's eighth *LV* (*OA* II, pp. 851–69).

Page	lines	
	21–29	*Cor* III, p. 83.
	30–35	*Cor* II, pp. 718, 744.
331–2		Poli, *IVGS,* pp. 140–8. *Lui et Elle,* p. 186.
332	*3–8*	*Lui,* pp. 287–9; Adam, *Secret,* pp. 182–3. There is no mention in Pagello's journal of this *RDM* dinner, which may well be literary legend.

21. TWO WOUNDED EAGLES (*Pages 333–351*)

The title for this chapter is taken from Musset's August 18 letter to GS (quoted on page 326): "Let ours . . . be the farewell of . . . . two suffering minds, two wounded eagles who meet in the sky and exchange a cry of pain before parting forever." Evrard, *CSM,* pp. 169–72.

333	*1 ff.*	Ibid., pp. 172–3. A mutilated copy of the letter GS had written to Musset from Nohant around September 7, asking him to return the fateful August letter, still exists (BN, n.a.f. 10369, fols. 119–20), but as Lubin points out (*Cor* II, pp. 691–5), it was later recopied and censored by GS. The August letter has disappeared, like all of Pagello's to GS, which she probably burned as too compromising for her later reputation. She may also have burned them to please the jealous Alfred, who in *Confession,* Part V, Ch. 5, depicts Brigitte as burning a former lover's letters after declaring that she had to be his (*OA* II, pp. 257–9). Musset had GS's letters before him when he wrote his *Confession.*
334	*6–21*	Adam, *Secret,* pp. 187–94.
	22 ff.	*Cor* II, pp. 722–3.
335	*12 ff.*	Adam, *Secret,* pp. 195–7; *Cor* II, pp. 724–5; Poli, *IVGS,* p. 146.
336	*12–35*	*Cor* II, pp. 729–32; Evrard, *CSM,* pp. 177–9.
337	*1–15*	Adam, *Secret,* pp. 198–201; *Cor* II, pp. 733–6. On Liszt, see Marix-Spire, *CGS,* pp. 392–9, 419–448, and J. Vier, *La Comtesse d'Agoult et son temps,* vol. I.
	16–21	Though written in Venice, almost half of GS's third *LV* was devoted to Lamennais.
	21–30	*Correspondance de Liszt et de Madame d'Agoult,* vol. I, pp. 118–20, and J. Vier, op. cit., p. 375.
	31 ff.	On Planche's anti-Musset rumor-spreading, see M. Regard, *Planche* I, pp. 133–5, and vol. II, pp. 93–4, 98–100.
338	*1–26*	Adam, *Secret,* pp. 202–4; Evrard, *CSM,* p. 184; *JI* ("Journal intime") in *OA* II, p. 954, and Lubin's comments, p. 1499.
	27–35	*Indiana* (Garnier ed., 1962), p. 298.
339	*6–30*	*Lui et Elle,* pp. 132–5; *Lui,* pp. 312–4. The Mary Magdalene comparison was GS's — see *JI* entry, November 19 (*OA* II, pp. 959–60).
	31–37	Lov. E 861 bis, fol. 70, quoted by Lubin in *OA* II, p. 1498.
340–1		*JI,* in *OA* II, pp. 953–4, 963; *Cor* II, pp. 745–7.
341	*19 ff.*	*Lui et Elle,* pp. 144–53.
342	*28–30*	See end of Part IV, *Confession,* for mention of GS's "Journal intime"

Page *lines*

(presented as a testament) and the poison-powder the heroine kept to put an end to her days.

30–36 *JI,* in *OA* II, p. 966; *Cor* II, pp. 747–9.

343 *1–14* Marie d'Agoult, *Mémoires,* p. 45, and J. Vier, op. cit., p. 389.

15 ff. *JI,* in *OA* II, pp. 958–60. In P. de Musset's *Lui et Elle,* Liszt is called Hans Flocken (pp. 130, 154–6).

344 *3 ff.* *JI,* in *OA* II, pp. 966–8, 971, 1503–4; *Cor* II, pp. 750–762. Antoine Adam's contention that at this point a hopelessly frustrated GS went and flung herself into the "perverse" arms of Marie Dorval in an effort to "extinguish the blaze that was consuming her" is an unfortunate lapse in an otherwise excellent book (*Secret,* pp. 219–24).

345 *9 ff.* *Cor* II, pp. 757–9, 765–7.

346 *2–13* *Cor* III, pp. 83–4; corroborated by Fleury, Rozanne and Jean-Joseph Bourgoing, Ch. Duvernet, and G. Planet (Lov. E 948, fols. 85–9, 91, 98).

14–24 Dedicated to François Rollinat and published under the title "Lettres d'un oncle" (*OA* II, pp. 735–57).

25 ff. *Cor* II, pp. 785, 781–2; Evrard, *CSM,* p. 221.

347 *6–36* *OA* II, p. 312; *Cor* II, pp. 780–7; *Lui et Elle,* p. 150; Part IV, Ch. 6, of *Confession,* one of several passages where Musset makes a frank avowal of his sado-masochistic inclinations. GS, in *Elle et Lui* (pp. 274–5), described Musset's outbursts as a form of "intellectual epilepsy."

347–8 *Cor* II, pp. 791–7.

348 *2–6* Ibid., pp. 798–9.

13–20 Toesca, *Musset,* p. 177; *Cor* II, pp. 800–1.

21–33 Evrard, *CSM,* pp. 227–8; *Cor* II, pp. 811–2.

348–9 Similar scenes are described in *Elle et Lui,* pp. 279–84, *Lui et Elle,* p. 155. In Part V, Ch. 6, of *Confession,* Octave (i.e., Musset) comes near to stabbing Brigitte (GS) with a knife while she is sleeping, and the same incident is more briefly described in *Elle et Lui,* p. 285.

349 *5–10* Evrard, *CSM,* p. 231.

11 ff. *Elle et Lui,* pp. 294–300, and Musset, *Correspondance,* p. 119.

350 *10 ff.* *Cor* II, pp. 814–7, 819, 830.

351 7 The phrase "enfant du siècle" had already been applied by GS to Sténio in *Lélia* (1960, Garnier ed., p. 277).

19–21 Musset, *Corr.,* p. 120. In French: ". . . c'est encore la femme la plus femme que j'aie jamais connue." On Musset's capacity for mnemonic self-torture and his pathetic ability to relive the past in all its emotional and voluptuous intensity, see the scene described by Liszt in Janka Wohl's *Souvenirs d'une compatriote,* pp. 162–7 (pp. 122–6 of original German edition).

22. THE FIREBRAND OF BOURGES (*Pages 355–369*)

355 *1–21* *Cor* II, pp. 837, 859.

21–25 Ibid., p. 711.

Page	*lines*	
356	*1–13*	*OA* II, p. 301; *Cor* II, pp. 736–7, 834.
	14–21	Lov. E 948, fols. 14–17; *Cor* II, pp. 798–9, 820, 841–2; *Cor* III, p. 85.
	22 ff.	*OA* II, pp. 293–5, 345–6; *Cor* II, pp. 849–50, 876–7, 887–9.
357	*3 ff.*	*OA* II, pp. 310–22. On Michel de Bourges, see Magon-Barbaroux's
357–9		*Etude biographique,* and Part V, Ch. 8, of *HV,* where he is called Everard, as in GS's sixth *LV*.
359–60		*Cor* II, pp. 870–2, 813–4, and Marix-Spire, *CGS,* pp. 608–9.
361	*1–29*	Sixth *LV,* in *OA* II, pp. 779–817.
	30–37	Ibid., pp. 800–1.
362	*7–9*	On Michel's wife, see *OA* II, p. 362, and Lubin's note, p. 1375.
	19 ff.	On the "procès monstre," see *HV,* Chs. 8, 9 of Part V, and Louis Blanc, *Histoire de dix ans,* vol. IV, pp. 225–427.
363	*10 ff.*	On Lamennais, see *OA* II, pp. 347–54; A. Molien and F. Duine, *Lamennais* (Paris, 1899); J-R. Derré, *Lamennais, ses amis à l'époque romantique* (Paris, 1962); Heine's negative opinion in *Lutèce,* pp. 230–1.
364	*33*	Laski, *Authority in the Modern State* (Oxford, 1919), p. 255, quoted by D. O. Evans, *Social Romanticism in France,* p. 39.
365	*1–3*	Marix-Spire, *CGS,* p. 435.
	13–28	As reported by Edmond Leclerc, *Mercure de France,* June 15, 1835 (*CGS,* p. 449; *Cor* II, p. 888).
	28	Johannes Kreisler, composer-hero of E. T. A. Hoffmann's unfinished novel, *Kater Murr* (Tom-cat Murr).
	29–36	*OA* II, p. 329.
366	*1–20*	*Cor* II, pp. 884–5; Marix-Spire, *CGS,* pp. 448–51; *OA* II, pp. 349–50, 846.
	21 ff.	*OA* II, pp. 325–7; *Cor* II, pp. 904–5.
367	*26 ff.*	*HV,* Part V, Ch. 9, and Louis Martin, *Michel de Bourges, Plaidoyers et discours* (Paris, 1909).
368	*8–19*	*Cor* II, pp. 889–90; *OA* II, p. 846.
	20 ff.	*OA* II, pp. 344–5; *Cor* II, pp. 896–7, 903–5; *Cor* III, pp. 7–9.
369	*1 ff.*	BN, n.a.f. 13646, fol. 53; *Cor* II, p. 903; *Cor* III, p. 850.
	10–18	*Cor* III, pp. 9–21; *OA* II, pp. 347–8, 846–7, 1381, 1470–1.
	19–31	Lov. E 948, fol. 42; *Cor* III, pp. 782, 850.

23. BARON DUDEVANT'S BLIND RAGE (*Pages 370–386*)

370	*1–11*	*Cor* III, pp. 24–6, 32–4.
	12 ff.	Ibid., pp. 34–5.
	22–26	On *Engelwald,* see P. Reboul, *RHLF,* January–March 1955.
371	*3–17*	On *Simon,* see Marix-Spire, *CGS,* pp. 468–9, and Poli, *IVGS,* pp. 168–70.
	18–25	*Cor* III, pp. 64–5.
	26 ff.	On Duteil, see Vincent Moreau's testimony, Lov. E 948, fol. 95.
372–4		GS's detailed account of the October 19 explosion and the events leading up to it is to be found in her memo to M. de Bourges (*Cor* III, pp. 74–90). I have added a few details from the accounts later

Page lines

given by Fleury, Papet, Rozanne and Jean-Joseph Bourgoing (Lov. E 948, fols. 86, 88–90, 96–7).

374 *19 ff.* *OA* II, pp. 367–76; *Cor* III, pp. 68–9.

376 *15–37* Lov. E 948, fol. 84, and *Cor* III, pp. 101–2, 132, 138–9.

377 *1 ff.* Ibid., pp. 122–4, 145–7, 165–70, 232, 261, 308, 176–7, 193, 251–2.

378 *1–18* Ibid., pp. 275, 219, 235–7. Boucoiran's testimony is included in Lov. E 948, fols. 99–101. Félicie Molliet and Ch. Duvernet also declared having heard Casimir call Solange an "enfant de grue" (a harlot's child) and a future whore (". . . elle ne sera qu'une putain" — by implication, like her mother).

19–27 Lov. E 948, fols. 101–3; *Cor* III, pp. 240–2, 249–50, 254.

378–9 *OA* II, pp. 376–7; *Cor* III, pp. 278–9, 282–3, 301–2, 312–3; BHVP, G 3181.

379 *15–17* On Emmanuel Arago, see Lubin's biog. note, *Cor* III, p. 860.

19 ff. See J. Sellards, *Dans le Sillage du Romantisme: Charles Didier*. André Maurois' description of Didier as a "sensual" man is as arbitrary and misleading as his claim that Didier had been Hortense Allart's lover in Italy (*Lélia,* English ed., pp. 147, 219). At the time Hortense Allart was giving birth to a child. Her passing mention of him in *Les Enchantements de Prudence,* written in 1872 — "Un homme m'a ravi (Libri), un homme m'a plu (Antonio Bargagli), un homme a touché mon âme (Charles Didier); aucun ne l'a su" — flatly disproves it. Armand de Pontmartin was closer to the truth in considering Didier to be "un fruit sec, mélange d'orgueil et d'impuissance" (A. Billy, *Hortense et ses amants,* p. 63).

33 ff. *OA* II, pp. 289–91.

380 *7–15* On D'Aragon, see *Cor* III, p. 383, and Lubin's biog. note, ibid., p. 861.

17 ff. These and other quotations are taken from M. Regard's careful transcription of Didier's diary in *RSH,* October–December 1959.

382 *29 ff.* *Cor* III, pp. 332–9, 390, 362, 374, 447–8, 844.

383 *3–18* Lov. E 948, fols. 40–2, published by Lubin in *Cor* III, pp. 847–51.

19–31 *Cor* III, pp. 343–4, 348–9; Lov. E 948, fols. 55–8.

383–4 BN, Mss. fr. 7633, fols. 7–8; Lov. 948, fols. 107–8; *Cor* III, pp. 425–7.

384 *12–20* *Cor* III, pp. 353–7.

34–35 Neither the diatribe against Talleyrand nor the January 1835 essay on boredom and suicide had been called an *LV*. The essay inspired by Michel de Bourges, though really the seventh in order of composition, was published in the June 15, 1835, issue of the *RDM* as *LV* IV. The next essay, dedicated to Liszt, appeared as *LV* V in the *RDM* of Sept. 1, 1835. The new "Letter" on which GS was now working, though comprising elements written as far back as September 1834, became the sixth *LV* when published in the June 1, 1836, issue of the *RDM*. It was listed more accurately as the ninth *LV* when these and later essays were published in volume form in 1837. See *OA* II, pp. 869–81, and Lubin's comments, pp. 635–44, 1447–80.

385 *1–20* *Cor* III, pp. 320, 365–7, and *OA* II, p. 378. One of Maurice's school-

Page *lines*

mates was already spreading the word that D'Arago (did he mean Emmanuel Arago or Charles D'Aragon?) was his father and GS's husband, simply because he often came to take the boy out of boarding school on Sundays when his mother was at Nohant. *Cor* III, pp. 358–61.

386 *1 ff.* *Cor* III, pp. 389–90, 367–9, 845–6, 394, 435–6; *OA* II, pp. 378–9; Lov. E 948, fols. 104–6.

24. THE MISCONDUCT OF WOMAN OR THE INFAMY OF MAN? (*Pages 387–399*)

387–9 *1 ff.* On the Saint-Simonians, see *Doctrine de Saint-Simon,* ed. by C. Bouglé and E. Halévy (Paris, 1924); Sébastien Charléty, *Histoire du Saint-Simonisme;* M. Allem, *Portrait de Sainte-Beuve,* Ch. 3.

389 *13–19* See Didier's diary entry for August 29, 1832, describing Enfantin's attempt to "magnetize" his followers, including H. Allart (Lov. E 940, fol. 21), and A. Billy, *Hortense et ses amants,* pp. 115–27. For GS's first critical reactions, see *Cor* I, p. 796; *Cor* II, pp. 854–6, 862.

21–26 The quotation from *Jacques* in the Preface comes from p. 38 of the 1834 edition. On its extraordinary impact in places as distant as Russia, see J. Adam, *Mes Sentiments,* pp. 221–5, and Karénine, *GS* II, pp. 81–2.

390 *1–18* *Cor* II, pp. 739–42.

19 ff. BHVP, G 3158, and *Cor* III, pp. 57–62.

391 *12–20* Karénine, *GS* II, pp. 281–3.

21 ff. *Cor* III, pp. 325–9.

392 *11–37* "A.M. Nisard" published in the *Revue de Paris,* April 29, 1836, later became GS's twelfth *LV* (*OA* II, pp. 936–43).

393 *1–20* *OA* II, pp. 383–4, and *Cor* III, pp. 402–3, 460.

21–32 Karénine, *GS* II, pp. 254–6, and *Cor* III, pp. 373–4.

393–4 *Cor* III, pp. 442, 428–36; Didier diary entries, May 19–20, 1836, as published by M. Regard in *RSH,* October–December 1959.

395 *11–20* *Cor* III, pp. 441–3.

396 *30 ff.* For GS's attempt to persuade S. de La Rochefoucauld that she wasn't M. de Bourges' mistress, see *Cor* III, pp. 419–20, and for embarrassment caused by Didier's visit to La Châtre, pp. 453–4.

397 *6–20* *Cor* III, pp. 473–80.

21–34 *OA* II, pp. 385–8, 1386–7; *Cor* III, pp. 482–508.

398 *1 ff.* This account of the trial is based on the July 30–31 issue of *Le Droit,* with a detail or two added from GS's letters (pp. 482–508). In the autumn of 1833 GS had written to Aurélien de Sèze to congratulate him on his recent marriage to a Mlle de Villeminot (who was to bear him nine children) and to ask if she might have back the letters she had written to him. Already embarrassed by the number of family references in *Indiana,* Aurélien preferred to burn most of Aurore's letters, lest she be tempted to use them for some future "composition." He fortunately kept the notebook into which she had poured

Page lines

out her heart at Guillery. When GS wrote to him again in May 1836, suggesting that this candid avowal of her platonic love might help her to combat her husband's base accusations, Aurélien sent it to her with a letter asking if he might have it back once the trial was over. GS finally decided to keep it after toying with the idea of turning it into a novel. See GS, *Roman d'amour,* pp. 212–20, and *Cor* III, pp. 776–7.

25. DR. PIFFOËL AND THE HUMANITARIANS (*Pages 400–414*)

400 *1–16* *Cor* III, pp. 507, 510–1, 525, and Didier's diary, August 4, 1836.

17 ff. On Switzerland, see *Cor* II, pp. 897–8, 903–5. Also J. Vier, *Comtesse d'Agoult,* vol. I, Part II, Ch. 1. This first daughter was Blandine Liszt.

401 *3 ff.* *Cor* III, pp. 521, 525, 531–8, 540–5. GS gave her own account of this trip to Autun, Lyon, and Geneva in another *LV,* dedicated to "Herbert" (Ch. Didier) and published in *RDM,* November 15, 1836 (*OA* II, pp. 881–95).

402 *1 ff.* *Cor* III, pp. 545–7. On Pictet, see J. Vier, *Comtesse d'Agoult* I, pp. 200–6, 397, and Robert Bory, *Une Retraite romantique en Suisse.* My description of this Alpine excursion is partly based on GS's tenth *LV* and partly on Pictet's equally ebullient *Une Course à Chamounix.* T. Marix-Spire devotes a well-documented chapter to this "equipée suisse" in *CGS*.

11–15 These "poetic cigars" may well have contained a touch of opium. The leaf was that of the *datura fastuosa,* later made the title of one of GS's plays.

21–23 In GS's tenth *LV* Gévaudan is referred to simply as the "légitimiste" — the term then used, like "carliste," to designate the ultra-Royalists who had remained faithful to Charles X and hostile to the Orléanist "usurper," Louis-Philippe.

404 *24–30* Marie d'Agoult later described herself to Henry Bulwer as being "a funny fellow" — which may well have been the words this red-faced Briton had first applied to Liszt. See J. Vier, *Comtesse d'Agoult* II, p. 46.

405 *25–27* *Cor* III, pp. 565–6. On GS's stay in Geneva, see Vier, op. cit. I, pp. 393–7; *Cor* III, pp. 551–2; *CGS*, pp. 502–21.

406 *22 ff.* *Cor* III, pp. 549–50, 553–69.

408 *12–15* Copies of ten GS letters to Michel de Bourges are to be found at the Sp. de Lovenjoul library. Forty-one others were published in five issues of the *Revue illustrée* from November 1, 1890 to January 15, 1891. V. Karénine was allowed to copy a number of others written in the spring and summer of 1837, but Michel's heirs were less generous with Georges Lubin (see his comments, *Cor* IV, pp. 112–3). In November or December 1836 M. de B. wrote GS an angry letter demanding that she return the letters he had written to her. Though at first outraged by this request, she later complied (*Cor* III, pp. 627–8, 644). He probably destroyed his letters to her, and she

Page	*lines*	
		may have done the same with the few she received from January 1837 on.
	19 ff.	*Cor* III, pp. 569–71.
	35 ff.	Didier's diary, October 25, 1836, entry, and ff. for rest of this chapter in *RSH,* October–December 1959.
409	*3 ff.*	*OA* II, pp. 390–2, 1389; *Cor* III, pp. 574–84, 597–8; *Cor* IV, pp. 200–9. J. Vier, *C. d'Agoult* I, p. 233. On the Hôtel de France, ibid., Part II, Ch. 2; Marix-Spire, *CGS,* pp. 552–34, and earlier ch., "Musique et Philosophie."
411	*13–18*	Emile Barrault had just returned from the Near East, where he had gone to find a Woman Messiah, a nineteenth-century Queen of Sheba worthy of sharing the power and glory of Enfantin's Solomonian throne. Lady Hester Stanhope had for a while fancied herself for the role, particularly after Lamartine had written her up in *Voyages d'Orient.* See Chaléty, *Les Saint-Simoniens,* Bk. II, Ch. 3, and Bk III, Chs. 1–2.
	27–30	On Adolphe Nourrit, see Marix-Spire, CGS, pp. 449–56; on Musset's mockery, the second of his "Lettres de Dupuis et Cotonet" (*Prose,* pp. 837–49).
412	*1 ff.*	As reported in *Vert-Vert* (*CGS,* pp. 530–1).
412–3		Heine, *Lutèce,* p. 187.
413	*3 ff.*	On his first impressions of GS, see Friedrich Niecks' *Chopin,* Vol. II, Ch. 20; on their first two encounters, Marix-Spire, *CGS,* pp. 526–8; Casimir Wierzynski, *Chopin,* pp. 232–5; *Cor* III, p. 596.
414	*33–37*	On GS's spiritual distress, see *Cor* III, pp. 594–5, 597–600, 627–8, 641–4; on invitations to Chopin and Grzymala, ibid., pp. 664–5, 699, 765.

26. TWELVE MONTHS OF DRAMA (*Pages 415–441*)

Page	*lines*	
415	*1 ff.*	*Cor* III, pp. 607–22.
416	*1–31*	*Cor* III, pp. 637–47, 654, 664, 696–7, 738, 568–9; *OA* II, pp. 986, 1507.
	32 ff.	See first six chapters of J. Vier, *C. d'Agoult* I.
417	*15–21*	Ibid., pp. 241–54; *Cor* III, pp. 680–1, 684; Marix-Spire, *CGS,* pp. 535–42; S. Rocheblave, "Une Amitié romanesque, GS et Mme d'Agoult," *Revue de Paris,* December 15, 1894.
	22 ff.	"Lettres à Marcie" in *Le Monde,* February 12, 19, 25, March 14, 23, 27.
420	*1–17*	*Cor* III, pp. 711–4; *Cor* VI, p. 486.
	18–26	On GS's relations with Lamennais, rumored to be her lover, see *Cor* III, p. 623; on her annoyance with Sainte-Beuve for mocking him, ibid., pp. 160–4.
421		*Mauprat,* finished May 13, 1837 (*Cor* IV, p. 48).
422	*4 ff.*	Lov. E 881, fols. 12–13, and *Cor* III, pp. 730–8.
423	*16 ff.*	*Cor* III, pp. 740–53, 781–2, 785–8, 777–9, 788–828.

Page	*lines*	
424	*21 ff.*	Ibid., pp. 768, 775–6, 803–8, 816, 838.
425	*7–22*	*Cor* IV, pp. 23–37, 49–51, 71–2, 112–3.
	22–29	Marix-Spire, *CGS,* pp. 543 ff.; Cor *III,* pp. 769, 779.
	30 ff.	*Cor* IV, pp. 38–42.
426	*12–32*	Ibid., pp. 48–9, 69–88; *Cor* III, pp. 826–7.
426–7		From journal entitled "Entretiens journaliers avec le très docte et très habile docteur PIFFOËL professeur de botanique et de psychologie," June 3 entry (*OA* II, pp. 980–2).
427	*20 ff.*	On Liszt and Marie d'Agoult, see diary entries for April 1837 in J. Sellards, *Ch. Didier,* p. 69; J. Vier, *C. d'Agoult* I, Ch. 7; Marie d'Agoult's Nohant diary, in *Mémoires,* pp. 73–95.
428	*5–16*	*OA* II, pp. 981–2.
	17 ff.	*Cor* IV, pp. 83–8, 100–2, 112–3.
429	*25 ff.*	Ibid., pp. 114–7, 163–4; Piffoël journal (*OA* II, pp. 987–90).
430	*9 ff.*	Marie d'Agoult, *Mémoires,* pp. 87–8.
431	*7–9*	Marix-Spire, *CGS,* p. 624.
	27 ff.	*OA,* II, pp. 991–1000, and diary entries in Sellards' *Didier,* pp. 70–2.
432	*16 ff.*	On Pierre Touzé, alias Bocage, see Paul Ginisty's biography; also C. Carrère, *GS amoureuse,* pp. 284–92; Lubin's biog. note, *Cor* IV, pp. 891–2.
432–3		Marie d'Agoult, *Mémoires,* pp. 79–80, 95–7.
433	*12–21*	*Cor* IV, pp. 153–5.
434	*4 ff.*	*OA* II, pp. 393–401; *Cor* IV, pp. 159–79.
435	*8 ff.*	On GS's new row with Casimir, see *Cor* III, pp. 691–2, 719–20, 726, 739–40, 756–7, 782–4; *Cor* IV, pp. 56–60.
436	*16–21*	On Mallefille, see C. Carrère, *GS amoureuse,* pp. 296–301, and Lubin's biog. note, *Cor* IV, p. 913.
437	*11–30*	On *Les Maîtres Mozaïstes,* see Poli, *IVGS,* pp. 175–81, and Marix-Spire, *CGS,* pp. 557–61.
	31–37	*Cor* IV, pp. 178, 187, 290–1.
438–9		*OA* II, pp. 402–5; *Cor* IV, pp. 189–223.
439	*33 ff.*	*Cor* IV, p. 226, and Lubin's fn., p. 222.
440	*7 ff.*	Ibid., pp. 221–3, 226–30, 233–8, 271–2, 260.
441	*13–15*	Abbé Georges Rochet. See *Cor* IV, pp. 105–7, 280–2, 295–6.
	19–36	Marie d'Agoult, *Mémoires,* p. 97; Fleuriot de Langle, "F. Liszt et Daniel Stern," in *Mercure de France,* February 1, 1929; Lov. E 861, fols. 304–5; *Cor* IV, pp. 278, 290–3, 334–6.

27. LESS MALLEABLE THAN WAX (*Pages 445–458*)

445	*1 ff.*	*Cor* IV, pp. 317–9, 324–9, 337, 341–3, 351, 286, 291–2, 369. On *Spiridion,* see J. Pommier, *GS et le rêve monastique.*
446	*5 ff.*	*Cor* IV, pp. 364–72; Balzac, *Corr.* III, pp. 374–80, 390–1. Balzac, *Lettres à Madame Hanska* I, pp. 584–8. Balzac had already turned GS's love affair with Sandeau into a novel, *Less Illusions perdues,* causing Didier to remark that it was an act of "perfidy and base impropri-

Page	*lines*	
		ety; but there are character traits which are unfortunately too well captured" (Sellards, *Didier,* pp. 68–9).
447	*32 ff.*	Lubin, *GS en Berry,* p. 27, and *Cor* IV, pp. 403–5.
448	*20–32*	This Charpentier portrait, reproduced on the dust jacket, hangs today in the Sand-Chopin cell at the Charterhouse of Valldemosa. There is another Charpentier portrait in the Carnavalet Museum in Paris.
	33 ff.	*Cor* IV, pp. 384–413.
449	*4 ff.*	Ibid., pp. 476–8
	12–26	Ibid., pp. 394–5; Chopin, *Corr.* II, pp. 234–5. This Chopin album was destroyed, along with the National Library in Warsaw, during the Second World War.
	27 ff.	*Paris Elégant,* May 16, 1838, and *Cor* IV, p. 449. For Custine's influence on Proust, see Jacques de Lacretelle's preface to Custine's *Souvenirs et Portraits* (Monaco, 1956) and Rebecca West's review of George Kennan's appraisal of "Russia in 1839" (*Sunday Telegraph,* March 26, 1972).
450	*1–10*	*Cor* IV, pp. 403, 407–8.
	24–30	On GS's bashfulness in public, see her letter to Heine (January 1843): "I am very much afraid of strangers and I feel myself dying of embarrassment and coldness with people who examine me curiously" (*Cor* VI, p. 12).
451	*14–17*	On Chopin's and GS's admiration for Mozart, see Marix-Spire, *CGS,* pp. 272–3; *GS-PV,* p. 283; Delacroix, *Journal* I, pp. 283–4; *OA* II, pp. 421–2.
452–3		*Cor* IV, pp. 409, 412–3, 428–39.
454	*21 ff.*	Ibid., pp. 441–7, and Chopin, *Corr.* II, p. 265.
455	*9–17*	Now 21, Rue Visconti. Delacroix, *Corr.* II, p. 19.
	18 ff.	*Cor* IV, pp. 468, 473, 479, 481, 485, 498–9; on Switzerland, pp. 453, 457, 467, 472; on Casimir, pp. 446–7; on Buloz, pp. 457–9.
456	*9–16*	*Cor* IV, pp. 480–4.
	26–29	Maurois, *Lélia* (Eng. ed.), p. 274. See also René Bourgeois' introduction to *Les Sept Cordes de la Lyre* (Flammarion, 1973); D. O. Evans, *Le Socialisme romantique,* pp. 111–5; Marix-Spire, *CGS,* pp. 470, 583.
457	*12–19*	*Cor* IV, p. 473.
	20 ff.	*RGM,* September 9, 1838; Chopin, *Corr.* II, pp. 255–7; *Cor* IV, pp. 486–90.

28. THE SOLITUDE OF VALLDEMOSA (*Pages 459–476*)

Page	*lines*	
459	*1 ff.*	For this chapter I have relied essentially on GS's own account of this ill-starred journey, "Un Hiver à Majorque" (*OA* II, pp. 1029–177, with notes by G. Lubin, pp. 1515–50). I have added a few details from her autobiography (*OA* II, pp. 417–23), letters, and other sources.
	1–6	*Cor* IV, p. 505.

Page	*lines*	
	21 ff.	Chopin, *Corr.* II, pp. 271, 287–92.
460	*1–10*	*Cor* IV, pp. 492–6.
	11 ff.	Ibid., pp. 503–14.
461	*13 ff.*	*Ibid.*, pp. 514–27.
463	*12–20*	Chopin, *Corr.* II, pp. 265–6.
	21 ff.	*Cor* IV, pp. 528–34.
464	*32–37*	Chopin, *Corr.* II, p. 274.
466–7		On the charterhouse of Valldemosa as it was in 1838, see Bartomeu Ferra, *Chopin et GS à Majorque,* pp. 23–6.
468	*4–16*	*Cor* IV, pp. 538–40, and Chopin, *Corr.* II, pp. 282–3.
	28–29	The decree had been issued by the Spanish liberal Prime Minister, Juan Albarez y Mendizabal, whom GS and Chopin had befriended in the Marlianis' salon in Paris. He had traveled down to Perpignan in the same stagecoach with Chopin.
472	*1–4*	See Marix-Spire, *CGS,* pp. 499–502, 549–50, on "picturesque" or descriptive music — a problem GS had discussed in her eleventh *LV*, begun while in Geneva in September 1836. To this *LV,* dedicated to Meyerbeer, Liszt had replied with a *Lettre d'un bachelier ès-musique à un poète voyageur,* published February 1837 in Maurice Schlesinger's *RGM.* In her autobiography (*OA* II, pp. 420–2) GS claimed that Chopin was quite satisfied with the distinction she later established in her novel *Consuelo* between a slavishly "imitative" and a sublimely suggestive music. See also GS, *Impressions et Souvenirs,* pp. 87–8.
	5–8	*OA* II, pp. 422–3. Ten years later Chopin had to interrupt a piano recital in London when the "damned spirits" of Valldemosa suddenly rose before his haunted eyes (letter to Solange, September 1848, in Gavoty, *Chopin,* p. 299).
473	*3–31*	*Cor* IV, pp. 551–63, 569, 710; B. Ferra, *Chopin et GS,* pp. 53–62.
475	*7–9*	Chopin, *Corr.* II, pp. 323–4, 350. On Gaspar Remisa, the Spanish banker who lived in the same Paris house as the Marlianis, and his Mallorcan correspondent, Ernest Choussat de Canut, see *Cor* IV, pp. 563–7, 571–2, and M. Godeau, *Le Voyage à Majorque.*
476	*9–25*	*Cor* IV, pp. 576–80. As Lubin notes, a royal edict promulgated by Fernando VII in October 1751 made it mandatory to burn all clothes, bed linen, and furniture used by persons suffering from consumption or other contagious diseases in Spain.

29. THE TIGRESS OF ARMENIA AND HER LITTLE ONE
(*Pages 477–487*)

Page	*lines*	
477	*1–19*	*Cor* IV, pp. 568–81.
	20 ff.	Ibid., pp. 492–3, 575, 595–7, 606–8, 612–8; Chopin, *Corr.* II, pp. 303–7, 316–8.
478	*17–30*	*Cor* IV, p. 624, and Balzac, *Corr.* IV, p. 476.
	31 ff.	*Cor* IV, p. 623, and Chopin, *Corr.* II, p. 305.
479	*7 ff.*	*Cor* IV, pp. 589–90, 626, 608, 619, 635, 646.
480	*8–17*	Chopin, *Corr.* II, pp. 322–5, and *Cor* IV, p. 633.

Page *lines*

18–26 *Cor* IV, pp. 616, 634–5.

27–38 Ibid., pp. 600, 645–6, and Marix-Spire, *CGS*, pp. 338–9.

481 *1–8* *Cor* IV, pp. 651–8, 711; *OA* II, p. 425; Poli, *IVGS*, pp. 195–7.

9–20 *Cor* IV, pp. 647, 654–660. The carriage that GS had left behind at Chalons-sur-Saône had been brought to Marseille by riverboat.

21–27 Chopin, *Corr.* II, pp. 339–40, and *Cor* IV, pp. 663–5.

482 *1 ff.* *Cor* IV, pp. 504–5, 601–5, 614, 619, 628–32, 665–71, 740–4.

483 *5 ff.* Ibid., pp. 689–94, 698–708, 713–5, 731–2, 750–4.

484 *9–20* Ibid., pp. 735–8, 684, and G. Lubin, *GS en Berry*, p. 28.

21 ff. *Cor* IV, p. 627; *OA* II, p. 432.

485 *7–21* *Cor* IV, pp. 715–6.

486 *1–4* See GS's May 1847 letter to Grzymala, *Cor* VII, pp. 699–702.

5–15 *OA* II, p. 433.

27–28 In a letter written to GS in August 1840 Solange claimed to have been weighed at 84 lbs. and Chopin at 97. (BN, n.a.f. 14279, fols. 33–4, and *Cor* V, p. 100.

28 ff. *Cor* IV, pp. 588, 685, 730–1; Chopin, *Corr.* II, pp. 345–6, 348, 371, 374–6.

30. THE CAPUCIN PHILOSOPHER'S DISCIPLE (*Pages 488–498*)

488 *1 ff.* Chopin, *Corr.* II, pp. 351–72; *Cor* IV, pp. 749, 752, 755, 764, 780–3, 790–1, 928–9; *Cor* V, p. 456, 850–1, Balzac, *Lettres à Madame Hanska* II, pp. 7–8.

489 *1–12* *Cor* IV, pp. 806, 819, 829.

12–19 *Gazette musicale,* October 31, 1839; Wierzynski, *Chopin,* p. 292; Gavoty, *Chopin,* p. 308.

20–31 *Cor* IV, pp. 812–27; *RDM,* December 15, 1839, and January 1, 1840.

32 ff. *Cor* IV, pp. 770–97, 805, 848–9, 862–7, 883–5.

490 *28–35* Ibid., pp. 872–4; *Cor* V, pp. 48–50, and Sainte-Beuve, *Corr. gen.* III, p. 259. GS had taken Sainte-Beuve to task for criticizing Lamennais, and he had retaliated by ridiculing her, Liszt's and Lamennais' clownish *pas de trois* in launching *Le Monde* (early 1837). See *Cor* III, pp. 160–4, and Sainte-Beuve, *Nouveaux Lundis* XI, p. 364. Sainte-Beuve celebrated their reconciliation by terming GS "the most manifest, original, and glorious apparition to have emerged during the past ten years," in French literature (*RDM,* March 1, 1840).

35 ff. Balzac, *Corr.* IV, pp. 95–6; *Cor* V, pp. 21–3, 26, 34–45.

491 *6 ff.* *Cor* V, pp. 19–21, 44–7, 55. Heine's interesting review of *Cosima,* dated April 30, 1840, was written for the *Augsburger Allgemeine Zeitung* and later republished in his *Sämmtliche Werke* (*Collected Works*), vol. XI, pp. 282–94 (see also *Lutèce,* pp. 35–45).

29–36 Regard, *RSH,* October–December 1959, pp. 486–7; *Cor* V, pp. 51–3.

492 *1–11* *Cor* V, pp. 37, 87.

12–21 Chopin's teaching fee was twenty francs an hour. GS later persuaded him to raise it to thirty francs for lessons given outside his apartment (*Cor* V, pp. 160, 522–3).

Page	*lines*	
	25–32	*Cor* V, pp. 67–8, 86–7, 221–2, 250–1. None of GS's novels had yet been translated into English. After Hortense Allart's departure for Italy in 1839 Henry Bulwer (brother of the famous novelist Edward) had started flirting with Marie d'Agoult, who had thus vainly hoped to arouse Liszt's jealousy. Rebuffed in his advances, Bulwer may well have turned his attention to GS — enough to stimulate Marie d'Agoult's acid wit. Balzac's *Béatrix* (mentioned in the next chapter) had already been published and there was now little love lost between Dr. Piffoël and Princess Arabella (J. Vier, *Comtesse d'Agoult* II, pp. 44–8, 262).
	33 ff.	On Perdiguier, see *Cor* V, pp. 61–4, 103–5, 887; GS on *Compagnon*, *Cor* VII, pp. 186–7; Buloz's reaction, *Cor* V, pp. 112–3, 137–8.
493	*31 ff.*	D. O. Evans, *Le Socialisme romantique*, p. 115.
494	*5–15*	Heine, *S.W.* XI, pp. 300–1, and *Lutèce*, pp. 51, 367–76.
	22 ff.	*Cor* V, pp. 576–7. On Leroux, see D. O. Evans, op. cit., and GS, *OA* II, pp. 354–6.
495	*16–25*	M-L. Pailleron, *Les Années glorieuses de GS,* pp. 45–6.
	26 ff.	*Cor* V, pp. 187–90.
496	*16–23*	*RDM*, January 15, February 15, March 15, 1841.
	24 ff.	*Cor* V, pp. 133–6.
497	*10–12*	Ibid., p. 590.
	19–28	*Cor* V, pp. 316–7, 415, 418–25, 437–9, 453–7.
	29–32	Ibid., p. 390.
498	*1–9*	Ibid., p. 301–4.
	21–33	See Dostoevski, *Dnevnik Pisatelya,* June 1876 (*Journal d'un écrivain,* pp. 227–36), and D. O. Evans, *Le Socialisme romantique,* p. 129.

31 PAULINE GARCÍA AND *CONSUELO* (*Pages 499–531*)

Page	*lines*	
499	*1 ff.*	*RGM,* May 2, 1841, pp. 245–8.
500	*1–18*	*Cor* V, pp. 282–3, and Marix-Spire, *GS-PV,* pp. 104–7.
	30–38	*Cor* V, pp. 290–1.
501	*14–29*	J. Vier, *Comtesse d'Agoult* I, pp. 252–3; Liszt-d'Agoult, *Corr. romantique,* pp. 140–2, 165–8.
	30 ff.	Marix-Spire, *CGS,* pp. 620–1, and *Cor* V, pp. 254–5.
502	*1–14*	Vier, *Comtesse d'Agoult* II, Ch. 3, and Janka Wohl, *Liszt* (Fr. ed.), pp. 73–6. Marie d'Agoult's malevolence toward Chopin deepened the chill that had descended over his once warm friendship with Liszt, who had cavalierly used his Chaussée d'Antin apartment for an amorous assignation with Camille Pleyel's wife (*Corr. Liszt-Mme d'Agoult, 1833–1840,* p. 360).
	15–28	Lov. E 872, fols. 4–6, and Maurois, *Lélia* (Fr. ed.) pp. 311–2.
	30–37	*Cor* IV, pp. 720–1, 727–9; Lov. E 885, fol. 448.
503	*1–27*	See M. Regard's introduction to the Garnier 1962 ed. of *Béatrix;* Balzac, *Corr.* IV, pp. 18–20; J. Vier, *Comtesse d'Agoult* II, pp. 71–83.
	27 ff.	*Corr. Liszt-d'Agoult, 1833–1840,* p. 361. GS's long letter of explanation to Marie d'Agoult, quoted at length by Maurois, *Lélia* (Eng. ed.),

Page	*lines*	
		pp. 287–9, was no more than a rough draft, and G. Lubin (*Cor* IV, pp. 798–803) thinks that a polished version was never sent.
504	*1–6*	Didier diary entry, January 13, 1840 (Regard, *RSH,* October–December 1959, p. 485).
	7–23	*Corr. romantique,* p. 141, and J. Vier, *Comtesse d'Agoult* II, pp. 96–101, 275.
	24 ff.	On Marie d'Agoult and the Vicomtesse de Chailly, see Karénine, *GS* II, pp. 278–85, and January 7, 1841, entry in GS's Piffoëlesque journal (*OA* II, pp. 1010–3).
505–6		On Pauline García, see introduction to Marix-Spire's *GS-PV* and April Fitzlyon's biography, *The Price of Genius.*
506	*13–21*	*GS-PV,* pp. 27–8; *RDM,* January 1, and November 1, 1839 (Musset, *Prose,* pp. 986–1000).
	21–31	*GS-PV,* p. 22; Karénine, *GS* II, pp. 17–18.
	32 ff.	*Cor* IV, pp. 829–31.
507	*9–16*	This comic strip has been published in A. Fitzlyon's *Price of Genius.* For a verbal description, see Musset, *Prose,* pp. 1290–3.
	23–36	*OA* II, pp. 1014–5, and *Cor* V, p. 337.
508	*1–17*	*Cor* V, pp. 138–42, 316–7, 446, 344, 348, 353–4, 364–7, 372–5, 404, 391; Chopin, *Corr.* III, pp. 57–65.
	18–25	*Cor* V, pp. 401, 412–4. Marix-Spire, *CGS,* p. 184.
	26 ff.	*Cor* V, pp. 178–80, 350, 391–2.
509	*15–25*	Balzac, *Corr.* III, p. 668.
	26–37	*Cor* V, pp. 441–50, 461–6, 535.
510	*1–22*	*Cor* V, pp. 422, 454–6, 474, 485–6, 497–8, 522–3, 530; Chopin, *Corr.* III, pp. 74–8, 83–90.
	23–30	*Cor* V, pp. 449–50, 475–98.
	30 ff.	Ibid., pp. 482, 521–2, 531–47.
511	*12–19*	Sainte-Beuve, *Corr.* IV, p. 180.
	26–36	*Cor* V, pp. 522, 516, 544, 550–3.
512	*1–15*	Marix-Spire, *GS-PV,* pp. 32–43; Fitzlyon, *Genius,* pp. 90–1, 98–9.
	16 ff.	*Cor* V, pp. 558, 605–8; *GS-VP,* p. 154.
513	*10–20*	*Consuelo* (Garnier, 1959 ed.), p. 82.
	21–25	On Baillot, see Marix-Spire, *CGS,* pp. 212–20, and *OA* II, p. 813.
	25–31	"Le Théâtre italien et Mlle Pauline García," in *RDM,* February 15, 1840 (p. 589), later republished in *Questions d'art et de littérature.*
	34–38	Marix-Spire, *CGS,* pp. 555–6.
514	*1–20*	*RGM,* February 27, 1842; Chopin, *Corr.* III, p. 103; Marix-Spire, *GS-PV,* pp. 134–6; *Cor* V, pp. 534, 598–600, 607.
	21–30	Marix-Spire, *GS-PV,* pp. 44–5; *Cor* V, pp. 625, 632–6, 646–7.
	31 ff.	Ibid., pp. 616, 619–20, 672–3; Delacroix, *Corr.* II, p. 105.
515	*21–27*	*Cor* V, pp. 647–8; *OA* II, pp. 445–6; Wierzynski, *Chopin,* pp. 314–5.
516	*1–10*	*Cor* V, pp. 657–75, 682–3.
	11 ff.	Delacroix, *Corr.* II, pp. 89, 105–12, 128–9; *Cor* V, 634–6, 659–60, 702–3, 705, 709, 714–5; GS, *Impressions et Souvenirs,* pp. 84–6.
517	*12–26*	*Cor* V, pp. 692–5, 701, 708, 731, 740–2, 750–2, 759.
518	*1–9*	The idea of religious purity had already been expressed in an un-

Page	*lines*	
		published story, *Jehan Cauvin,* started by Aurore in 1831 (*Cor* I, p. 837).
	14–34	*Cor* V, pp. 617–9.
519	*1–8*	Ibid., pp. 775–7, 788, 506–7.
	9–25	*Cor* VI, pp. 52–3, 63. For Leroux's influence on the composition of *Consuelo,* see introduction by Cellier and Guichard to 1959 Garnier edition.
	26 ff.	Chopin, *Corr.* III, p. 126; *Cor* V, pp. 767–74; *GS-PV,* pp. 154–68.
520	*4–35*	*Cor* V, pp. 778–9, 635, 733–7, 743, 781–4, 788, 799; *Cor* VI, pp. 917–9; *OA* II, pp. 435–6; Niecks, *Chopin* II, pp. 133–5, 145; A. Houssaye, *Confessions* II, p. 19.
521	*1–21*	*Cor* VI, pp. 102, 171; Chopin, *Corr.* III, p. 127; Niecks, *Chopin* II, pp. 148–9.
	21–26	For references to GS's "undemonstrative" timidity and dislike of social functions, see *Cor* II, pp. 37–8, 261, 277, 292, 322, 329, 334, 376; *Cor* VI, pp. 12, 15–6; on her growing deafness, *Cor* IV, p. 855, and *Cor* V, pp. 809–10. Princess Anna Czartoryska bought the Hôtel de Lambert, which had once belonged to GS's great-grandfather, Claude Dupin, in 1843 (*Cor* V, pp. 79–80; *Cor* VI, pp. 204, 286).
	27–35	Karénine, *GS* III, pp. 423–30.
522	*1–10*	*Cor* V, p. 800.
	11–19	Ibid., pp. 717–9, 793–5, 608, 804–5, 842–3.
	20 ff.	Marix-Spire, *GS-PV,* pp. 48–61, 170–80; *Cor* V, pp. 783–4, 798–9.
523	*25 ff.*	*Cor* VI, pp. 133–4, 148–71; Chopin, *Corr.* III, p. 110 (misdated 1842).
524	*17–32*	*Cor* VI, pp. 117–8, 124–6, 173–80, 208–9.
	33 ff.	Ibid., pp. 191–2, 197–202.
525	*29 ff.*	Ibid., pp. 223–5, 230–1; Marix-Spire, *GS-PV,* pp. 61–2, 180–7.
526	*3–13*	*Cor* VI, pp. 250–5, 257–67; Chopin, *Corr.* III, pp. 136–42.
	14–16	On the petite Fanchette scandal, see *Cor* VI, pp. 248, 260, 264, 290–1, and Karénine, *GS* III, pp. 374–81.
	16–29	On *L'Eclaireur de l'Indre,* see *Cor* VI, pp. 283, 290, 296, 302–322, 333–7, 367–71, 380–99, 486–7.
527	*3–9*	Ibid., p. 431.
	10 ff.	Ibid., pp. 469, 495–7, 532–3.
528	*4–7*	Balzac, *Corr.* IV, p. 747, and *Lettres à Madame Hanska* II, p. 456. Also Dostoevski, *Dnevnik Pisatelya,* June 1876 (*Journal d'un écrivain,* p. 233).
	8–12	Letters to Hetzel, Charles Poncy, and François Barrillot (*Cor* VI, pp. 405–17).
	13–17	On Chopin's coughing, ibid., pp. 455, 460, 464.
	18–30	Ibid., pp. 520, 528–9, 538, 552, 557–8.
	31–33	On Latouche, see ibid., pp. 365–6, 370–1, 381, 392, 399; *OA* II, pp. 176–7.
	34 ff.	*Cor* VI, pp. 610, 589; Chopin, *Corr.* III, pp. 160–1; Marix-Spire, *GS-PV,* pp. 196–210, and *CGS,* pp. 568–9.
529	*5–15*	*Cor* VI, pp. 555–65; Chopin, *Corr.* III, pp. 150–9; *OA* II, p. 446.
	16 ff.	*Cor* VI, pp. 574–5, 579, 586–9, 596; Chopin, *Corr.* III, p. 206.
530	*6–25*	*Cor* VI, pp. 572–3, 584–5, 594–5, 600, 608.

Page	*lines*	
	26 ff.	Ibid., pp. 597–606, 622, 628; Chopin, *Corr.* III, pp. 201, 207–8, 210–1, 213.
531	*1–30*	Ibid., pp. 606–7, 617–9, 632.

32. THE DEATH THROES OF A ROMANCE (*Pages 532–570*)

Page	*lines*	
532	*1–19*	Marix-Spire, *GS-VP*, pp. 214–5; *Cor* VI, p. 693; Chopin, *Corr.* III, p. 170.
	24–26	*Cor* VI, p. 626.
533	*1–21*	Ibid., pp. 616–21, 625–6, 638–42, 645–6, 656–65, 671–4, 679–82, 701–5.
	22–37	Ibid., pp. 67–8, 278, 401, 620–1, 629–30.
534	*1–18*	Ibid., pp. 695, 707, 882–6, 461–2, 903, 907, 911–2; Chopin, *Corr.* III, p. 211.
	19–26	*Cor* VI, pp. 718–9, 726–7, 736–7; Karénine, *GS* III, pp. 392–3.
	27 ff.	*Cor* VI, pp. 754–5, 785–8, 800, 834; *Cor* VII, p. 27.
535	*16–22*	*Cor* VI, pp. 844, 850, 862, 880–1; *Cor* VII, pp. 24–7, 65, 70–1.
	23 ff.	*Cor* VI, pp. 895–907; Chopin, *Corr.* III, pp. 198–202; *Cor* VII, pp. 8–10.
536	*3–25*	*Cor* VII, pp. 43, 47–74, 77, 83, 94–6; Winwar, *Life of the Heart,* pp. 246–7; Karénine, *GS* III, pp. 659–60.
	26 ff.	Chopin, *Corr.* III, pp. 200, 213; *OA* II, pp. 446–7; *Cor* VII, pp. 159, 133–4.
537	*15–26*	Chopin, *Corr.* III, pp. 206–7, 223; *Cor* VII, pp. 69, 83–90, 45–50.
	27 ff.	On Augustine Brault and her family, see *Cor* IV, pp. 270–1, 893–4; *Cor* VI, pp. 890–1, 895, 902, 911; *Cor* VII, pp. 63, 103, 149–51; *Cor* VIII, pp. 552–7.
538	*15–27*	*Cor* VII, pp. 48, 87–9, 126, 159, 182–3, 196; Chopin, *Corr.* III, p. 211.
	28 ff.	*Cor* VII, pp. 151–2. See P. Salomon's and J. Mallion's introductory preface to *La Mare au diable* (Garnier, 1962).
539	*3–31*	Chopin, *Corr.* III, pp. 221–5; *Cor* VII, pp. 20–3, 155–6, 171–6, 181, 197–8, 208–13.
	32 ff.	*Cor* VII, pp. 261–3. See Marie d'Agoult's April 1837 warning that it would be GS's fault if Solange turned into a devil for having been spoiled "to death" (J. Vier, *Comtesse d'Agoult* I, p. 407) and H. de Latouche's June 1844 remonstrance (*Cor* VII, p. 569). In a July 1837 letter GS called Solange and Maurice *"il lione e il colombo"* — the lion and the dove. In another, dating from February 1840, GS wrote: "Solange is well, eats like a horse, swears like a teamster, and lies like a dentist" (*Cor* IV, p. 622). On the idea of marrying her to Louis Blanc, see Karénine, *GS* III, pp. 537–8; *Cor* VII, p. 749. For other references to Solange's impertinence, vanity, coquettish jealousy, domineering and indocile temperament, see *Cor* IV, pp. 622, 867; *Cor* V, pp. 120, 125, 180–1, 190, 274, 305–6, 398, 435, 479, 568, 662; *Cor* VI, pp. 56–7, 94, 158–60, 214.

Page	*lines*	
540	*11–23*	*Cor* VII, pp. 264, 287–8.
	24–34	Ibid., pp. 328–30, 341–2, 351, 366, 314–6, 348–9, 365–6.
541	*1–16*	Ibid., pp. 391–2, 370–1, 379–81, 395–6.
	17–19	On Duvernet, Liszt, and Chopin, see Marix-Spire, *CGS*, pp. 544, 184.
	20 ff.	G. Lubin, *GS en Berry*, pp. 28–9.
542	*13–38*	Matthew Arnold, *Mixed Essays* IV, pp. 236–9.
543	*1–20*	*Cor* VII, pp. 367–9, 424–6, 430. On Chopin's jealousy, see *Cor* VI, pp. 400–1, 915; *Cor* VII, pp. 93–4, 561.
	21 ff.	Chopin, *Corr.* III, pp. 245–6; *Cor* VII, pp. 381, 463–4, 495.
544–5		Ibid., pp. 368–70, 376, 389; Karénine *GS* III, pp. 514–37; Poli, *IVGS*, pp. 135, 220–2.
545	*31 ff.*	As recorded in Caroline Jaubert's *Souvenirs*, pp. 43–4.
546	*6–21*	*Cor* VII, pp. 348, 435, 453, 460, 464, 476–7.
	22 ff.	Ibid., pp. 382–92, 491, and *Cor* VIII, p. 19.
547	*4–25*	*Cor* VII, pp. 436–8, 478–82, 491, 488; Chopin, *Corr.* III, p. 245.
	26–34	*Cor* VII, pp. 511, 489, 498, 491, 559.
548	*1 ff.*	Ibid., pp. 538–41, 608–9, 546, 551, 559–60, 571–5, 590.
549	*23 ff.*	Ibid., pp. 613–5, 517, 571–3, 620–1, 638–41; *Cor* VIII, pp. 19–23.
550	*22–28*	*Cor* VII, pp. 507–9, 544, 672–5; Chopin, *Corr.* III, p. 265.
551	*1 ff.*	Chopin, *Corr.* III, pp. 282–9; *Cor* VII, pp. 615–6, 623–7, 677–9, 683.
552	*12–19*	On D'Arpentigny, see Lubin's biog. note, *Cor* VII, pp. 790–1, and Mme Martellet, *Dix ans chez Alfred de Musset,* pp. 56–7.
	19–30	*Cor* VII, pp. 668, 679–80, 696–7.
553	*1–28*	Ibid., pp. 648–61; *Cor* VIII, pp. 23–4.
	29 ff.	*Cor* VII, pp. 663–4, 668, 684; *Cor* VIII, pp. 25–7, 555–6.
554	*26–30*	*Celio Floriani* was published four years later under the title *Le Château des désertes.* See *Cor* VII, pp. 667, 677, 681; Chopin, *Corr.* III, pp. 274, 287.
	31 ff.	*Cor* VII, pp. 677, 668; Delacroix, *Journal* I, p. 223.
555	*5–18*	Chopin, *Corr.* III, p. 282; *Cor* VII, pp. 685–92, 698; "Sketches and Hints," May 1847 (*OA* II, pp. 625–7); Delacroix, *Journal* I, pp. 224–5.
	19 ff.	BHVP, G 5921, and *Cor* VII, pp. 699–703.
556	*18 ff.*	*Cor* VII, pp. 708–27, 737; *Cor* VIII, pp. 27–8.
557	*17–27*	*Cor* VII, pp. 706–8, 720, 730, and (on Rousseau) Lubin's biog. note, *Cor* V, p. 893.
558–9		*Cor* VII, pp. 752, 771–9, 727–9; *Cor* VIII, pp. 24–30.
560	*10 ff.*	*Cor* VII, pp. 745–53, 762–70; *Cor* VIII, pp. 30–2, 561.
561	*18–26*	*Cor* VII, pp. 741–2, 753, 759; Chopin, *Corr.* III, p. 284.
562–7		*Cor* VII, pp. 771–80; *Cor* VIII, pp. 32–44.
563	*36 ff.*	*Cor* VII, pp. 753, 772; *Cor* VIII, p. 55.
568	*3–13*	Chopin, *Corr.* III, pp. 294–5.
	14–29	*Cor* VIII, pp. 7–18, 42–8.
	30 ff.	Letters to Arago, *Cor* VIII, pp. 18–49, 68–9; to Chopin, pp. 10, 50–1.
569	*1–3*	Delacroix, *Journal* I, pp. 235–6.
	4–20	Chopin, *Corr.* III, pp. 295–7.
	25 ff.	BN, n.a.f. 24811, fols. 218–9, and *Cor* VIII, pp. 54–5.

Page	lines	
		33. 1848 (*Pages 573–603*)
573	*1 ff.*	*Cor* VIII, pp. 44–50.
574	*5–22*	Ibid., pp. 71–3, 85–7, 152–7, 173–4, 183.
	23 ff.	Delacroix, *Journal* I, p. 236; *Cor* VIII, pp. 52–4, 91–2, 104–7, 110–3, 149–50; Marix-Spire, *GS-PV*, pp. 235–8.
575	*7–10*	See *Cor* VI, pp. 886–90, for GS's unforgiven critique of M. de Rozières.
	11–25	*Cor* IX, p. 219. See also Léon Séché, *Sainte-Beuve* II, p. 109, where Mickiewicz is quoted as fearing that Chopin had become GS's "evil genius, her moral vampire, her cross . . ." On Victor Borie, see C. Carrère, *GS amoureuse*, pp. 377–83; *Cor* VII, pp. 780–1; *Cor* VIII, pp. 67, 169, 186–8, 775; P. Salomon's and J. Mallion's introduction to *François le Champi*, pp. 185–6.
	26 ff.	*Cor* VIII, pp. 73, 99–103, 114–6, 138–41, 159–61, 166–72, 179–89, 195–203, 207, 238–40.
576	*19 ff.*	Ibid., pp. 119–20, 136–7, 160–1, 181–2, 213.
577–8		Ibid., pp. 82–4, 113, 128–39, 155–8, 204–6, 216; Chopin, *Corr.* III, pp. 299–309.
579	*1–27*	*Cor* VIII, pp. 125–7, 164, 174–5, 241–8, 263.
	28 ff.	Ibid., pp. 262–3, 292, 296–301.
580	*9 ff.*	See Arnold Whitridge, *Men in Crisis*, pp. 22–30, and A. de Tocqueville, *Souvenirs*, pp. 3–61.
582	*9–11*	Figures given in *Bulletin de la République* No. 14, dated April 11, 1848.
	12–15	*Cor* VIII, p. 470.
	16–28	Lord Normanby, *A Year of Revolution* I (London, 1857), pp. 205–7.
	29–37	*Cor* VIII, pp. 304–6; Delacroix, *Corr.* II, p. 343.
583	*3–7*	Normanby, op. cit., pp. 122–5. Also Tocqueville, *Souvenirs*, pp. 62–82.
	16 ff.	*Cor* VIII, pp. 315, 320, 308, 447.
584	*4–15*	For GS's opinion on Lamartine, see *Cor* VIII, pp. 240–1.
585	*10–13*	Maxime Du Camp, *Souvenirs littéraires* I, pp. 413–5.
	26 ff.	*Cor* VIII, pp. 308–326.
586	*19 ff.*	Ibid., pp. 318–9; *Cor* IX, pp. 220–1; Chopin, *Corr.* III, pp. 331–2.
587	*20–24*	*OA* II, p. 448.
	27–37	*Cor* VIII, pp. 330–1.
588	*5–11*	"Lettre au peuple," partly reprinted in third *Bulletin de la République*, dated March 17, 1848.
	12–23	"Aux Riches," reprinted in fourth *Bulletin de la République* (March 19, 1848) and later in *Questions politiques et sociales*, pp. 225–30.
	24 ff.	*Cor* VIII, pp. 351, 327–346; "Souvenirs de mars-avril 1848" (*OA* II, pp. 1185–6).
590	*11–28*	*Cor* VIII, pp. 355–8; Normanby, *Year of Revolution* I, p. 246.
	32 ff.	Whitridge, *Men in Crisis*, pp. 67–75; *Cor* VIII, pp. 431–5, 450–3.
591	*32–36*	*Cor* VIII, p. 371.
592	*1–17*	Ibid., pp. 359–90, 434, 440, 447.
	18 ff.	Lockroy, who had bowed out of *Cosima*. See *Cor* VIII, pp. 365, 382–3, and T. Gautier, *Histoire de l'art dramatique en France*, vol. V, pp. 242–55.

Page	*lines*	
593	*1–12*	*La Cause du Peuple,* April 9, 1848, p. 16.
594	*13 ff.*	*La Réforme,* April 9; *La Vraie République,* April 10, 1848; *Cor* VIII, 391–2, 400–8.
595	*15–25*	*Cor* VIII, pp. 345, 351, 466; Chopin, *Corr.* III, pp. 333–4.
	26 ff.	"Plan de gouvernement pour la seconde République," commented by P. Salomon, *RSH,* October–December 1959, pp. 391–7.
596	*29 ff.*	*Cor* VIII, pp. 390, 424, 434–5, 371, 411–424; *OA* II, pp. 1187–8.
599	*1–16*	Whitridge, *Men in Crisis,* pp. 67–75; *Cor* VIII, pp. 431–5, 450–3.
	24 ff.	Tocqueville, *Souvenirs,* pp. 204–6.
600	*29 ff.*	Ibid., pp. 173–192; *Cor* VIII, pp. 458–62, 467–9, 477–82, 522–3.
602	*3 ff.*	*Cor* VIII, pp. 456–7, 463–7, 469–474, 477–8.

34. FAREWELL TO POLITICS (*Pages 604–629*)

Page	*lines*	
604	*1 ff.*	*Cor* VIII, pp. 473, 503, 536, 481–6, 493–5, 524, 530; *GS-PV,* pp. 251–5.
605	*4–17*	*Cor* VIII, pp. 511–7.
	18–32	Brault, *Une Contemporaine — Biographie et Intrigues de George Sand, avec une lettre d'elle et une de M. Dudevant;* also *Cor* VIII, pp. 509–10, 521–2, 528, 565–6.
	33 ff.	Whitridge, *Men in Crisis,* pp. 56–60, 96–103.
606	*4–15*	On GS and Godefroid Cavaignac, see *Cor* VI, pp. 117–8, 140, 311, 319, 726, 737, 742, 931; on General Eugène Cavaignac, *Cor* VII, pp. 44–5, 90–1, 671, 737–8, 793, and *Cor* VIII, pp. 323–4, 569; on Hetzel, ibid., p. 532.
	16–33	*Cor* VIII, pp. 527–8, 540–1, 528, 544–5.
	34 ff.	Ibid., pp. 537–41, 546–50.
607	*4–24*	Ibid., pp. 584–91, 619–20, 623–5.
	25–37	Ibid., pp. 666–7.
608	*1–11*	Ibid., pp. 573–4, 599–604; Karénine, *GS* III, p. 676.
	12–32	*Cor* VIII, pp. 618–9, 602, 667–73, 677, 686, 568–9, 625–6.
609	*1–33*	On sale of the Hôtel de Narbonne, see *Cor* VIII, pp. 613, 605–6, 611–2, 615–6, 622, 648, 683, 687–90, 694–5, 699–700, 704–5, 719–20, 724–5, 730, 738–9, and Marix-Spire, *GS-PV,* pp. 259–65.
610	*1–15*	*Cor* VIII, pp. 710–1; Whitridge, *Men in Crisis,* pp. 104–10.
	16–21	*Cor* VIII, pp. 633, 647, 655–7, 671–2, 708.
	22–31	Karénine, *GS* IV, pp. 156–65; *Cor* VI, pp. 708–11, 720, 779–80, 833–4, 901; *Cor* VII, pp. 40–1, 364.
	31–38	*Cor* VIII, pp. 710, 696, 715.
611	*1 ff.*	*La Réforme* (December 5), *La Démocratie pacifique* (December 5), *Le Peuple* (December 6, 1848); *Cor* VIII, pp. 717–9. Also, ibid., pp. 725–7, 735, 732.
612	*9–18*	Ibid., pp. 744, and *OA* II, pp. 449–50.
	19–23	*Cor* IX, pp. 117–21, 366–85.
	23 ff.	Ibid., pp. 170–1, 185–8; *OA* II, pp. 235–49.
613	*17 ff.*	Chopin, *Corr.* III, pp. 354–5, 366, and Fitzlyon, *Genius,* pp. 229–30. On Chopin's earlier detestation of that "unbearable pig" (M. de Ro-

Page	*lines*	
		zières), see *Corr.* III, pp. 68, 73; on her present wiles, pp. 353, 376–7, and Marix-Spire, *GS-PV*, pp. 241–2.
614	*13–32*	*Cor* VIII, pp. 727, 738–9; Marix-Spire, *GS-PV*, pp. 262–6.
615	*1–25*	BHVP, G 5925, and *Cor* IX, pp. 218–221, 255–7.
	26 ff.	BHVP, K 217; *Cor* IX, pp. 297–8; letter to Hetzel, ibid., pp. 320–1.
616	*22 ff.*	BHVP, K 218; *Cor* IX, pp. 303–5.
617	*12–28*	On Bocage and *François le Champi,* see *Cor* IX, pp. 216–7, 251–3, 261–3, 277, 281, 300–3, 313–5, 337–8; Arago's reaction, pp. 343–4.
618	*1–21*	On Borie, ibid., pp. 294, 327, 341, 386–8, 408, 414, 448, 727.
	22 ff.	On Müller-Strübing, see Karénine, *GS* III, pp. 138–9; A. Fitzlyon, *Genius,* pp. 256–7; *GS-PV,* pp. 267–70; *Cor* IX, pp. 61, 126–7, 196, 388–91.
619	*24 ff.*	Ibid., pp. 420–1, 449–51, 500, 510, 516, 608, 614, 678, 450.
620	*6–11*	Ibid., pp. 785, 805–6, 828–30, 833.
	12–35	On Alexandre Manceau, see C. Carrère, *GS amoureuse,* pp. 389–400, and *Cor* IX, pp. 419–21, 427–8, 456.
621	*1–10*	Ibid., p. 484. The play GS wanted to redo was *Claudie.*
	11–18	For Maurice's drawing, now at the GS museum at La Châtre, see Pl. 13 of *Cor* IX.
	19 ff.	*Cor* IX, pp. 516, 542–5, 726.
622	*32 ff.*	On Charlotte Marliani, ibid., pp. 633, 640, 647–53.
623	*1–3*	Letter to David Richard, ibid., pp. 662–3.
	4–12	Ibid., pp. 62, 178, 197; Marix-Spire, *GS-PV*, pp. 281–2.
	13–14	*Cor* IX, pp. 820, 832, 845, 851; *Cor* X, pp. 45–6.
	16–22	*Cor* IX, pp. 815–8, 837–43, 889–95; *Cor* X, pp. 37–50, 546–68.
	23 ff.	See "Journal de novembre–decembre 1851" (*OA* II, pp. 1195–222).
624	*26 ff.*	Karénine, *GS* IV, pp. 173–239.
625	*12–24*	For GS's letters to Louis Napoleon, see *Cor* X, pp. 659–64, 693–5, 712–3.
	29 ff.	Ibid., pp. 681–2.
626	*7–10*	Ibid., pp. 683–738, 741–50, 758–60, 778–80, 786–9, 794–803, 807–12, 818–25, 829–35.
626–7		Elizabeth B. Browning, *Letters* II, pp. 39–40, 49–50, 55–64; *Cor* X, p. 711. For EBB's admiration for GS, see *Letters* I, pp. 233, 357, 363, and vol. II, pp. 26, 66, 70, 222, 230. See also *The Letters of Robert Browning and Elizabeth Barrett Browning,* 1845–1846, vol. I, pp. 100–3, 117, 161, 349.
628	*10–21*	*Sonnets,* pp. 346–7, and GS's reaction, *Cor* VI, pp. 745–6.
	22–28	*Cor* X, pp. 708–9, 825–6, 829–33.
629	*6–14*	E. Quinet, *Lettres d'exil* I, p. 27, quoted by Karénine, *GS* IV, p. 237.

35. INDIAN SUMMER (*Pages 633–659*)

633–4		See "Le Théâtre des marionnettes de Nohant" (*OA* II, pp. 1247–76).
634	*32 ff.*	On Maurice's bedroom, see *Cor* IX, pp. 796, 802–3. On Emile Aucante, see Lubin's biog. note, *Cor* VIII, pp. 769–70.

Page	*lines*	
635	*6–12*	On Eugène Lambert, see C. Carrère, *GS amoureuse,* pp. 732–6, and *Cor* X, p. 866; on his penchant for still lifes, *Cor* VIII, pp. 371, 379, 434; on talents as a portraitist, *Cor* IX, p. 851, and as stage designer, *Cor* VIII, pp. 753–4.
	17 ff.	*Cor* X, pp. 63–4, 66, 72, 97.
636	*4–26*	Rocheblave, *GS et sa fille,* pp. 148–85, and *Cor* X, pp. 189, 207–8, 234–5, 269, 282–4, 288–90, 331–2, 367–73, 376–9, 383–4, 403–4, 409, 414, 429–36, 480–2, 498–500, 520–2, 535–7, 546–8, 569–71, 633, 667–8, 670–1, 674, 680, 721, 743, 764, 768, 781–4, 790.
	26–29	Rocheblave, *GS et sa fille,* pp. 173–4. The twenty-five agenda books, covering the years 1852 to 1876, are now part of the BN's ms. department (n.a.f. 24813–24838). The 1853 agenda book is n.a.f. 24814.
637	*5–9*	February 9, 1854, entry (n.a.f. 24815).
638	*4–12*	On *Maître Favilla,* see Poli, *IVGS,* p. 301; Marix-Spire, *CGS,* pp. 219, 584; Karénine, *GS* IV, pp. 186–7.
	15–16	April 26, 1854 entry.
	17–31	G. d'Heylli, *La Fille de GS,* pp. 77–8, who was however in error as to the identity of Solange's lover. According to G. Lubin, her affair with Count Carlo Alfieri started later. (Error repeated by Maurois in *Lélia,* Eng. ed., p. 384.)
	30–31	May 8, 1854, entry.
639	*1–15*	*HV,* serialized in Emile de Girardin's *La Presse,* from October 5, 1854 on.
	15–18	H. Taine, *Derniers Essais de critique et d'histoire,* p. 128.
	23 ff.	Rocheblave, *GS et sa fille,* pp. 188–92.
640	*19–31*	*OA* II, pp. 1225–33: "Après la mort de Jeanne Clésinger."
641–4		My brief account of this trip to Italy is based on Ch. 10 of Poli, *IVGS.*
641	*21–30*	Pietro Pagello had left Venice years before, settling down in Belluno with a stupid, ugly wife, as Marie d'Agoult described her in a letter to GS written in July 1838 (J. Vier, *Comtesse d'Agoult* I, pp. 300, 305–6, and Lubin, *Cor* IV, p. 450). On Pagello's painstaking efforts to safeguard GS's more compromising letters, see Poli, *IVGS,* pp. 387–402.
643	*18–26*	Rocheblave, *GS et sa fille,* pp. 208–11, and Poli, *IVGS,* p. 278.
644	*1–2*	April 16, 1855, entry (BN, n.a.f. 24816), and Poli, *IVGS,* pp. 288–90.
	23–27	BN, n.a.f. 13648, fols. 2–3, and Poli, *IVGS,* p. 292.
	35 ff.	BHVP, G 1620, and Poli, *IVGS,* p. 297.
645	*8 ff.*	Poli, *IVGS,* pp. 299–301. On *La Daniella* and ensuing controversy, pp. 309–16.
647–9		On the discovery of Gargilesse, see Karénine, *GS* IV, pp. 372–82; L. Vincent, GSB, pp. 451–5; GS, *Promenades autour de mon village* (Paris, 1869).
649	*3–9*	On *L'Homme de neige,* see Karénine, *GS* IV, pp. 301–10.
	26–32	Ibid., p. 384.
650	*17–26*	*Cor* III, pp. 398–9.
	27–32	For GS's discussions with Musset on the subject of their letters, see *Cor* III, pp. 239, 586–8, 602–3, 811–2; *Cor* V, pp. 116, 127–8; also a

Page	lines	
		long letter to Sainte-Beuve, dated January 20, 1861 (Lov. F 976, fols. 225–231).
651	*3–6*	Maxime Du Camp, *Souvenirs littéraires* II, p. 357.
	26 ff.	On Louise Colet, see Ch. 16, "The End of the Affair," in Enid Starkie's *Flaubert: The Making of the Master.* For GS's letters to her, see *Cor* V, pp. 73–4, 506–7; *Cor* VI, pp. 48–53, 61–3, 70–2, 753, 804–6.
652	*1–11*	Maxime Du Camp, *Souvenirs littéraires* II, pp. 359–67.
	12 ff.	On *Le Marquis de Villemer,* see Karénine, *GS* IV, pp. 392–4; on *Valvèdre,* ibid., pp. 390–2, and Matthew Arnold, *Mixed Essays* IV, p. 241.
653	*3–8*	Karénine, *GS* IV, pp. 397–8.
	11–19	For letters exchanged between GS and Dumas, see *Cor* III, pp. 355–6; *Cor* V, pp. 34–5; and later (after *Molière*) *Cor* X, pp. 272–3.
	19 ff.	On Alexandre Dumas *fils* and his adventures, see A. Maurois, *Les Trois Dumas,* particularly pp. 327–34.
654	*8–22*	On the discovery of GS's letters to Chopin, etc., see Karénine, *GS* IV, pp. 627–32.
	23 ff.	*Cor* X, pp. 272–4, 384, 393, 405–6, 442–3, 446–7, 454–6.
655	*10–20*	Ibid., p. 805, and Janka Wohl, *Franz Liszt* (Fr. ed.), pp. 170–3.
	21 ff.	On Dumas *fils'* youth, see Maurois, *Les Trois Dumas,* pp. 91–3, 117, 155–221.
656	*5–9*	M. Du Camp, *Souvenirs litt.* II, pp. 246–7. On his talents as a mimic, see J. Adam, *Mes Sentiments,* p. 168.
	12	In French, "le fils peu prodigue" (Maurois, *Trois Dumas,* p. 549.).
	15–17	Ibid., pp. 399–401.
	29–36	Ibid., pp. 431–5, 446–9.
657	*1 ff.*	Ibid., pp. 383–5, 421–3.
658	*1–22*	Karénine, *GS* IV, pp. 405–9; GS, *Corr.* IV, pp. 295–6; *Trois Dumas,* pp. 423–8.
	23–36	On Marchal, see C. Carrère, *GS amoureuse,* pp. 415–7.
	35–37	Agenda book entries, October 10 and 19, 1861 (BN, n.a.f. 24822).
659	*9–27*	*GS, Corr.* IV, p. 298; Karénine, *GS* IV, pp. 409–10; BN, Don Balachovsky, nos. 20–22.

36. NEW JOYS AND SORROWS (*Pages 660–686*)

660	*4 ff.*	Goncourt, *Journal* I, p. 316; vol. II, pp. 24–6.
661	*17 ff.*	Maxime Du Camp, *Souvenirs litt.* II, pp. 351–3.
662	*6 ff.*	*Cor* IX, pp. 851–6. On Lina Calamatta, see Poli, *IVGS,* pp. 346–9, and GS, *Corr.* V, pp. 324–5.
663	*5–13*	June 26, 1862, agenda entry (BN, n.a.f. 24824).
	30 ff.	On Bocage's last years, see P. Ginisty, *Bocage,* pp. 124–66; A. de Pontmartin, *Mes Mémoires* (Paris, 1882), pp. 180–3. He died on August 31, 1862.
664	*26–33*	*Cor* IX, p. 844. On GS's admiration for Garibaldi, see Poli, *IVGS,* Ch. 12 (pp. 331–345); on Napoleon III's "clerical autocracy," see her letter to Prince Jérôme, February 1862 (GS, *Corr.* IV, pp. 314–6).

Page	*lines*	
665	*8 ff.*	On *Mademoiselle La Quintinie,* see Karénine, *GS* IV, pp. 429–432; Poli, *IVGS,* pp. 352–3; Sainte-Beuve, *Nouveaux Lundis* V, pp. 40–1.
666	*3–17*	Agenda entries for June–July 1863 (BN, n.a.f. 24825); GS, *Corr.* V, p. 353.
	18 ff.	September 3–7 agenda entries.
667	*15 ff.*	Goncourt, *Journal* II, pp. 144–6.
668	*29 ff.*	Edmond Plauchut, *Autour de Nohant,* pp. 71–3. The dialogue, as recorded by Plauchut, went as follows: GS: ". . . Dis à ce cher Théo qu'il se trompe . . ." Dumas *fils* (in a low base voice): "-d'éléphant . . ." GS (covering her "copy" with a blotter): "Alors, défense d'y voir." *Se tromper* in French means "to be mistaken," while *trompe* is an elephant's trunk. Gautier, in the first exchange, had supposedly got the wrong elephant. GS's rejoinder — "défense d'y voir" — meant literally "You're forbidden to see it", but it was also an elephantine pun on the French word for "tusk" (*défense*). There was a lot of calembouric fencing at Nohant.
669	*8–10*	In a July 1842 letter to Delacroix (*Cor* V, p. 722) GS had written: "I am back with my carnations and the Datura fastuosa has blossomed." Jules Néraud had probably brought back the seed or bulb of this trumpet-lily tree from a trip made to Algeria in 1836.
	17–25	On *Masques et Bouffons,* see Poli, *IVGS,* pp. 325–6, 338–41.
	26–28	On *Six mille lieues à toute vapeur,* see Karénine, *GS* IV, p. 398.
	29–34	On *Callirhoé,* see Poli, *IVGS,* pp. 353–4.
670	*11–12*	GS, *Corr.* V, p. 63.
	35–37	On Marie Lambert, see Karénine, *GS* IV, pp. 221, 269, 405; *Cor* VIII, p. 789.
671	*21–25*	*Cor* IX, pp. 725–8.
673	*4–10*	Agenda book entries for 1864 (BN, n.a.f. 24826).
	10–18	Karénine, *GS,* IV, pp. 454–5.
	31 ff.	On Delacroix's death, see GS, *Corr.* IV, pp. 359–60; on sale of his paintings, L. Vincent, *GSB,* pp. 551–2, and GS, *Corr.* V, p. 14, where sale is described as having brought in 200,000 francs.
674	*10–12*	On Napoleon III's crackdown on the press, see *Cor* IX, p. 647.
675–6		GS, *Corr.* V, pp. 15–24.
676	*36–38*	Karénine, *GS* IV, p. 470.
677	*1–7*	March 16, 1864, agenda entry.
	8–11	March 21 agenda entry.
	13–23	GS, *Corr* V, p. 13.
	32–36	On *Raoul de La Chastre,* see GS, *Corr.* V, p. 63; agenda entries, April 5–6, May 19–21.
678	*7–12*	Agenda entry, April 24, 1864.
	13–19	GS, *Corr.* V, pp. 24, 30–1. In a later letter to Maurice GS noted that the Palaiseau cottage had cost half of what *Le Marquis de Villemer* had brought her in box-office royalties (Karénine, *GS* IV, pp. 496–7).
	27–35	Agenda entries, June 11, 12, 1864.
679	*9–19*	GS, *Corr.* V, pp. 36–40.

Page	*lines*	
680	*2–8*	On Orsini, see Poli, *IVGS,* p. 318; M. Du Camp, *Souvenirs litt.* II, pp. 214–8.
	22–29	Agenda entries for July 1, 4, and GS, *Corr.* V, pp. 40–1.
681	*29–37*	GS, *Corr.* V, pp. 46–7; L. Vincent, *GSB,* pp. 622–3; agenda entries, July 21, 22.
682	*32–37*	Pierre Cazamajou, father of Oscar; agenda entry of September 6, 1864.
683	*1–9*	BN, n.a.f. 24812, fol. 152; Carrère, *GS amoureuse,* pp. 419–20.
684	*7–8*	Maurice and Lina had gone to Savoie after their son's death (GS, *Corr.* V, pp. 60–2.
	11	In French: "Maurice est insolent comme le valet du bourreau." Misquoted by Maurois, *Lélia* (Fr. ed., p. 470, Eng. ed., p. 413) to read Marchal.
	12–18	Agenda entries, January 23–5, 1865 (BN, n.a.f. 24827); Karénine, *GS* IV, pp. 485–6.
685	*9–16*	Agenda entries, July 7–9.
686	*5–7*	BHVP, E 53702, n.a. 9, 10; Carrère, *GS amoureuse,* pp. 420–1; agenda entries, Aug. 22–3; Karénine, *GS* IV, pp. 491–2.

37. THE GOOD LADY OF NOHANT (*Pages 687–732*)

Page	*lines*	
687	*14–17*	GS, *Corr.* IV, p. 330, and GS, *Corr.* VI, p. 258.
	19 ff.	Carrère, *GS amoureuse,* pp. 421–4; BHVP, E 53702, n.a. 15, 17.
688	*14–17*	Agenda entry, January 10, 1866 (BN, n.a.f. 24828).
	28–30	J. Richardson, *Princesse Mathilde* (London, 1969), p. 107.
689	*1–12*	Goncourt, *Journal* III, p. 21.
	13–17	May 21, 1866, entry, ibid., p. 51.
	18–32	On Flaubert and GS, see Carrère, *GS amoureuse,* pp. 433 ff.
	33 ff.	"Lettre sur Salammbô," later reprinted in GS, *Questions d'art et de littérature,* pp. 305–12.
690	*7–10*	*GS-GF,* pp. 3–5; Carrère, *GS amoureuse,* p. 435.
	11–15	GS, *Corr.* V, pp. 17, 23–4.
	29–31	Mme R. des Genettes, quoted by E. Starkie, *Flaubert the Master,* p. 43.
	32–33	Starkie, *Flaubert: The Making of the Master,* p. 353.
691	*3–8*	Ibid., pp. 297–8.
	9–27	Maurois, *Trois Dumas,* pp. 435–44; GS agenda entries, August 26–7, 1866.
	28 ff.	GS agenda entries, August 28–30, quoted by Maurois, *Lélia* (Eng. ed.), p. 425.
692		On Croisset, see Starkie, *Flaubert: The Making of the Master,* Ch. 15, and GS, *Corr.* V (wrongly dated), pp. 126–30.
693	*1–25*	*GS-GF,* pp. 13–7.
	31 ff.	GS agenda entries, November 3–10, 1866.
694	*2–8*	On Elisa Schlesinger, see Starkie, *Flaubert: The Making of the Master,* pp. 25–6, 110, 178, and *Flaubert the Master,* pp. 115–20, 159–60; on Maurice (Moritz) Schlesinger, editor of the *RGM,* of which GS was a

Page	*lines*	
		sponsor, see Marix-Spire, *CGS,* pp. 36–7, 231, 535–7, 623; *Cor* VI, pp. 10–1; Chopin, *Corr.* II, pp. 255, 284, 307–9, 315–7, 374–5.
	13 ff.	*GS-GF,* pp. 25–39.
695		Ibid., pp. 39–40. GS, *Corr.* V, p. 371.
		GS-GF, pp. 49–50, 435.
696	*10–26*	Karénine, *GS* IV, pp. 515–6, and GS, *Corr.* V, pp. 159–60.
	27 ff.	Juliette Adam, *Mes Premières Armes litt. et pol.,* pp. 4–96, and *Mes Sentiments et nos idées avant 1870,* pp. 20–55.
697	*25 ff.*	On *Monsieur Sylvestre,* see Karénine, *GS* IV, pp. 481–4.
698	*5–11*	J. Adam, *Mes Sentiments,* pp. 106–7.
	13–28	J. Adam, *Mes Premières Armes,* pp. 201–3; *Mes Sentiments,* pp. 136–7.
	29 ff.	Ibid., pp. 143–6, 161–8.
700	*3–11*	L. Vincent, *GSB,* pp. 623–5.
	11–28	*Karénine,* GS IV, p. 540; J. Adam, *Mes Sentiments,* pp. 193–200.
700–2		Ibid., pp. 202–47.
701	*12–28*	See GS's letters to Plauchut in *Cor* VIII, pp. 634–7, 654–6; Lubin's biog. note, p. 795; Plauchut's *Tour du monde en cent vingt jours* (Paris, 1872).
703	*4–11*	GS agenda entries, March 13–20, 1868 (BN, n.a.f. 24830).
	12 ff.	J. Adam, *Mes Sentiments,* pp. 265–90.
705	*5*	Juillette, a deliberate deformation of Juliette inspired by Mme Adam's sunny, July-like (in French, *juillet*) disposition.
706	*1–12*	On *Pierre qui roule* and Luigi Calamatta's death, see Poli, *IVGS,* pp. 362–4.
	15–36	On Sainte-Beuve's funeral, see GS agenda entry, October 16, 1869 (BN, n.a.f. 24831); Karénine, *GS* IV, pp. 618–9.
707	*1–23*	Starkie, *Flaubert the Master,* pp. 135–7; Flaubert, *Oeuvres* XII, pp. 473–9; *GS-GF,* pp. 182–93. GS's article was published in the December 22 number of *La Liberté,* and later included in *Questions d'art et de littérature,* p. 415.
	24–36	GS agenda entries, December 22–27, 1869; J. Adam, *Mes Sentiments,* pp. 414–6.
708	*3–9*	Ibid., p. 415.
709	*1–4*	Blandine Liszt, whom Emile Ollivier had married in September 1857, had died in October 1862. See Vier, *Comtesse d'Agoult* III, pp. 134–7, 275–9.
	7–10	Victor Noir, killed by Prince Pierre Bonaparte. On *Malgrétout* and Flaubert's intercession on behalf of GS, see Karénine, *GS* IV, pp. 240–9.
	18–20	J. Adam, *Mes Premières Armes,* pp. 20–2.
	21 ff.	On French liberal sentiment and Italy, see Vier, *Ctsse d'Agoult* V, pp. 135–78.
710	*4–29*	Karénine, *GS* IV, pp. 255–8; J. Adam, *Mes Sentiments,* pp. 332–3, 85–8.
	35–37	Flaubert, *Corr.* V (Conard ed.), pp. 346–7.
711	*3 ff.*	J. Vier, *Ctesse d'Agoult* VI, pp. 9–10; J. Adam, *Mes Sentiments,* pp. 449–64.

Page	lines	
713	*5 ff.*	GS agenda, August 1870 (BN, n.a.f. 24832); J. Adam, *Mes Sentiments,* pp. 464–79.
	30–36	*Le Siècle,* September 8, 1870; Poli, *IVGS,* pp. 366–8. On these balloons, see *Icare,* No. 56 (Spring 1971).
714	*28 ff.*	"Journal d'un voyageur pendant la guerre," in *RDM,* April 1, 1871, pp. 422–32.
715	*1–4*	Flaubert, *Oeuvres* XII, p. 577.
	8–19	Maurois, *Trois Dumas,* pp. 455–72. Lov. E 882, fol. 527.
	20–25	Rocheblave, *GS et sa fille,* pp. 282–3; agenda entries, December.
	25–31	Flaubert, *Corr.* VI (Conard ed.), p. 151; GS, *Journal d'un voyageur pendant la guerre,* p. 259.
		GS agenda entry, January 29, 1871 (BN, n.a.f. 24833).
716	*20–23*	The First German Reich (the Holy Roman Empire) had been dissolved by Napoleon in 1806, after the battle of Austerlitz.
	32–36	Agenda entry, March 8, 1871.
718	*21–32*	Flaubert, *Oeuvres* XIV, p. 89.
	33 ff.	GS, *Corr.* VI. pp. 135–6.
719	*6–25*	Ibid., pp. 152–6.
720	*1–6*	Karénine, *GS* IV, pp. 259–60; Maurois, *Lélia* (Eng. ed.), pp. 442–3.
	14–18	GS agenda entry, September 7, 1872 (BN, n.a.f. 24834).
	19 ff.	GS agenda entries, September 25–October 4. On Pauline Viardot's children and her life abroad, see A. Fitzlyon, *The Price of Genius.*
721	*9–10*	"la plus grande cantatrice du XIX siècle" — Marix-Spire, *GS-PV,* p. 13.
	16–31	On Turgenev and Pauline Viardot, see *Ivan Tourgenev, Nouvelle correspondance inédite* (ed. by A. Zviguilsky), 2 vols.
722	*7 ff.*	GS agenda entries, April 12–19, 1873 (BN, n.a.f. 24835).
	20–24	April 13 entry and Plauchut, *Autour de Nohant,* pp. 68–9.
723	*10–23*	GS agenda entries, September 16–29, 1873.
	24–26	See GS agenda entries for December 19, 21, 22, 1873, in which she writes, "je vis de mes rentes," to indicate she has done no writing that day.
	31 ff.	Rocheblave, *GS et sa fille,* pp. 230–80; *Cor* X, pp. 414, 429–32.
724	*21–30*	L. Vincent, *GSB,* pp. 623–4.
	31 ff.	Rocheblave, *GS et sa fille,* pp. 266, 282–9; Maurois, *Lélia* (Eng. ed.), p. 441; Karénine, *GS* IV, pp. 581–2.
725	*8–12*	Marie d'Agoult, *Mémoires,* p. 82.
	16 ff.	Rocheblave, *GS et sa fille,* pp. 289–92; Karénine, *GS* IV, pp. 540–2, 614.
726	*10–23*	Henry James, *French Poets and Novelists,* p. 168.
	24–30	*GS-GF,* pp. 445–6.
	30–35	GS, *Corr.* VI, p. 373.
727–31		*Corr* IX, pp. 876–7; Karénine, *GS* IV, pp. 597–630.
731	*27 ff.*	Flaubert, *Lettres à Tourgueneff,* pp. 104–6; *Oeuvres* XVI, pp. 174–82.

Bibliography

Adam, Antoine, *Le Secret de l'aventure vénitienne* (Paris, 1938).

Adam, Juliette (Lamber, Mme Edmond), *Mes Premières Armes littéraires et politiques* (Paris, 1904).

———, *Mes Sentiments et nos idées avant 1870* (Paris, 1905).

Agoult, Marie (de Flavigny), comtesse d', *Nélida* (published under name of Daniel Stern), (Paris, 1845).

———, *Histoire de la révolution de 1848,* 3 volumes (Daniel Stern), (Paris, 1868).

———, *Mes souvenirs, 1806–1833,* (Paris, 1877).

———, *Mémoires, 1833–1854* (Paris, 1927).

———, *Correspondance de Liszt et de la comtesse d'Agoult,* 2 volumes (Paris, 1933–1934).

———, *Une Correspondance romantique. Mme d'Agoult, Liszt, Henri Lehmann* (Paris, 1947).

Allart de Méritens, Hortense, *Les Enchantements de Prudence* (published under pseudonym of Mme de Saman, with preface by GS, Paris, 1873).

Allem, Maurice, *Musset* (Paris, 1940).

———, *Portrait de Sainte-Beuve* (Paris, 1954).

Amic, Henri, *Mes Souvenirs* (Paris, 1893).

Arnold, Matthew, *Mixed Essays,* vol. IV (London, 1880).

Balzac, Honoré de, *Correspondance,* 5 volumes, edited by Roger Pierrot (Paris, Garnier, 1960–1970).

———, *Béatrix,* with preface by M. Regard (Paris, Garnier, 1962).

———, *Lettres à Madame Hanska,* 4 volumes, edited by Roger Pierrot (Paris, Delta, 1967–1970).

Barbiera, Raffaello, *Nella citta dell'amore* (Milan, 1923).

Barine, Arvède (Cécile Vincens), *Alfred de Musset* (Paris, 1893).

Billy, André, *Sainte-Beuve, sa vie et son temps. Le Romantique (1804–1848)* (Paris, 1952).

———, *Hortense et ses amants* (Paris, 1961).

Blanc, Louis, *Histoire de dix ans, 1830–1840* (Paris, 1841–1845).

Bonnerot, Jean, *Une grande amitié littéraire — Sainte-Beuve et George Sand* (Paris, 1933).

Bory, Robert, *Une retraite romantique en Suisse* (Geneva, 1923).

Brault, Joseph, *Une Contemporaine: Biographie et Intrigues de George Sand* (Paris, 1848).

Browning, Elizabeth Barrett, *Letters,* 2 volumes (London, 1897).

———, *Letters of Robert Browning and Elizabeth Barrett Browning, 1845–1846,* 2 volumes (London, 1899).

Cabanès, Dr. A, "Un Roman vécu à trois personnages: Alfred de Musset — George Sand — et le Docteur Pagello," *Revue hebdomadaire,* Aug. 1, 1896.
———, "Une Visite au Docteur Pagello," *Revue hebdomadaire,* Oct. 24, 1896.
Carassus, Emilien, *Le Mythe du Dandy* (Paris, 1971).
Carrère, Casimir, *George Sand amoureuse* (Paris, 1967).
Charléty, Sébastien, *Histoire du Saint-Simonisme* (Paris, Gonthier, 1964).
Chopin, Frédéric, *Correspondance,* 3 volumes (Paris, Richard-Masse, 1953–1960).
Clouard, Maurice, *Documents inédits sur Alfred de Musset* (Paris, 1900).
Colet, Louise, *Lui* (Paris, 1860).
Delacroix, Eugène, *Correspondance générale,* 5 volumes (Paris, 1937–1953).
———, *Journal,* 3 volumes (Paris, 1950).
Denis, Ferdinand, *Journal, 1829–1848* (Paris, 1932).
Derré, Jean-René, *Lamennais, ses amis et le mouvement des idées à l'époque romantique* (Paris, 1962).
Didier, Charles, *Journal* (fragments relating to George Sand transcribed by Maurice Regard in the *Revue des Sciences Humaines,* Oct.–Dec., 1959).
Dostoevski, Fyodor, *Dnevnik Pisatelya,* June 1876 (Fr. translation, *Journal d'un écrivain,* Paris, 1904, pp. 225–236).
Du Camp, Maxime, *Souvenirs littéraires,* 2 volumes (Paris, 1882–1883).
Evans, David Owen, *Le Socialisme romantique: Pierre Leroux et ses contemporains* (Paris, 1948).
———, *Social Romanticism in France* (Oxford, 1951).
Evrard, Louis, *Correspondance Sand-Musset* (Monaco, 1956).
Ferra, Bartomeu, *Chopin et George Sand à Majorque* (Palma de Mallorca, 1960).
Fitzlyon, April, *The Price of Genius. A Life of Pauline Viardot* (London, 1964).
Flaubert, Gustave, *Correspondance entre George Sand et Gustave Flaubert,* with preface by Henri Amic (Paris, 1904).
———, *Lettres inédites à Tourgueneff* (Monaco, 1946).
———, *Correspondance inédite,* 4 volumes, edited by L. Conard (Paris, 1953).
———, *Oeuvres,* 16 volumes, Rencontre edition, by M. Nadeau (Paris, 1960 –1965).
Fourcassié, Jean, *Le Romantisme et les Pyrénées* (Paris, 1940).
Gautier, Théophile, *Histoire de l'art dramatique en France depuis vingt-cinq ans* (Paris, 1858–1859).
———, *Histoire du romantisme,* new ed. (Paris, 1882).
Gavoty, Bernard, *Chopin* (Paris, 1974).
Ginisty, Paul, *Bocage* (Paris, 1926).
Godeau, Marcel, *Le Voyage à Majorque* (Paris, 1959).
Goncourt, Edmond et Jules de, *Journal,* 3 volumes (Paris, 1888).
Guillemin, Henri, *La Liaison Musset-Sand* (Paris, 1972).
Gutzkow, Karl, *Briefe aus Paris* (Leipzig, 1842).
Haussonville, Comte Paul Othenin d', *George Sand, Prescott, Michelet, Lord Brougham* (Paris, 1879).
———, *Etudes biographiques et littéraires, Mérimée, Hugh Elliot* (Paris, 1885).
Heine, Heinrich, *Lutèce* (Paris, 1855).
———, *Sämmtliche Werke,* vol. XI ("Französische Zustände") (Hamburg, 1862).
Heylli, Georges d' (Edmond Poinsot), *La Fille de George Sand* (Paris, 1900).
Houssaye, Arsène, *Les Confessions — Souvenirs d'un demi-siècle,* 6 volumes (Paris, 1885–1891).

James Henry. *French Poets and Novelists* (London, 1884).
Jaubert, Caroline, *Souvenirs, Lettres, et Correspondance* (Paris, 1881).
Karénine, Vladimir (Varvara Komarova), *George Sand,* 4 volumes, (Paris, 1899 –1926).
Karlowicz, Mieczyslav, *Souvenirs inédits de Frédéric Chopin* (Paris & Leipzig, 1907).
La Rochefoucauld, Sosthènes de, *Esquisses et Portraits,* 3 volumes (Paris, 1844).
Liszt, Franz, *Lettres à la Princesse Caroline Sayn-Wittgenstein,* 4 volumes (Leipzig, 1900).
———, *Correspondance de Liszt et de Madame d'Agoult,* 2 volumes, (Paris, 1933–1934).
———, *F. Chopin* (Paris, 1852; new ed., 1949).
Lubin, Georges, *George Sand — Correspondance,* 10 volumes (Garnier, 1964–1973).
———, *George Sand en Berry* (Paris, Hachette, 1967).
———, *George Sand — Album* (Paris, Pléiade, 1973).
Luppé, Marquis Albert de, *Prosper Mérimée* (Paris, 1945).
———, *Astolphe de Custine* (Monaco, 1957).
Magon-Barbaroux, A., *Michel de Bourges* (Marseille, Flammarion, 1897).
Mariéton, Paul, *Une Histoire d'amour* (Paris, 1903).
Marix-Spire, Thérèse, *Les Romantiques et la Musique — le cas George Sand, 1804–1838* (Paris, 1954).
———, *Lettres inédites de George Sand et de Pauline Viardot,* 1839–1849 (Paris, 1959).
Martellet, Madame (Adèle Colin), *Dix ans chez Alfred de Musset* (Paris, 1899).
———, *Alfred de Musset, intime — Souvenirs de sa gouvernante* (Paris, 1906).
Maurois, André, *Lélia, ou la vie de George Sand* (Paris, 1952).
———, *Olympio, ou la vie de Victor Hugo* (Paris, 1954).
———, *Les Trois Dumas* (Paris, 1957).
———, *Prométhée, ou la vie de Balzac* (Paris, 1965).
Monnier, Henri, *Mémoires de Joseph Prudhomme,* 2 volumes (Paris, 1857).
Moser, Françoise, *Marie Dorval* (Paris, 1947).
Mourot, Eugène, *Un Oublié — Stéphane Ajasson de Grandsagne* (Paris, 1900).
Musset, Alfred de, *Correspondance, 1827–1857,* ed. by Léon Séché (Paris, 1907).
———, *Poésies complètes,* edited by Maurice Allem (Paris, Pléiade, 1957).
———, *Théâtre complet,* edited by Maurice Allem (Paris, Pléiade, 1958).
———, *Oeuvres complètes en prose,* edited by Maurice Allem (Paris, Pléiade, 1960).
Musset, Paul de, *Lui et Elle* (Paris, 1859).
———, *Biographie d'Alfred de Musset* (Paris, 1877).
Nicolas, Auguste, *Aurélien de Sèze* (Paris, 1870).
Niecks, Friedrich, *Frederick Chopin,* 2 volumes (London, 1888).
Pailleron, Marie-Louise, *François Buloz et ses amis, vol. I: La Vie littéraire sous Louis-Philippe* (Paris, 1919).
———, *François Buloz et ses amis, vol. II: la Revue des Deux Mondes et la Comédie Francaise* (Paris, 1920).
———, *George Sand, Histoire de sà vie* (Paris, 1938).
———, *Les Années glorieuses de George Sand* (Paris, 1942).
———, *George Sand et les hommes de 48* (Paris, 1953).
Parturier, Maurice, *Une Expérience de Lélia, ou le Fiasco du comte Gazul* (Paris, 1934).
Peyrat, Napoléon, *Béranger et Lamennais* (Paris, 1861).
Pictet, Adolphe, *Une Course à Chamounix* (Paris, 1838).
Plauchut, Edmond, *Autour de Nohant* (Paris, 1897).
Poli, Annarosa, *L'Italie dans la vie et dans l'oeuvre de George Sand* (Paris, 1960).

Pommier, Jean, *Autour du drame de Venise* (Paris, 1958).

———, *George Sand et le rêve monastique: Spiridion* (Paris, 1966).

———, *Variétés sur Alfred de Musset et son théâtre* (Paris, 1966).

Pontmartin, Armand de, *Mes Mémoires* (Paris, 1882; 2 volumes, 1886).

Regard, Maurice, *L'Adversaire des Romantiques: Gustave Planche, 1808–1857* (Paris, 1955).

Rocheblave, Samuel, *George Sand et sa fille* (Paris, 1905).

Roz, Firmin, et Hugues Lapaire, *La Bonne Dame de Nohant* (Paris, 1898).

Sainte-Beuve, Charles-Augustin, *Correspondance générale,* 16 volumes, edited by Jean Bonnerot (Paris, 1935–1970).

Sand, George, *Souvenirs et impressions littéraires* (Paris, 1862).

———, *Autour de la table* (Paris, 1862).

———, *Promenades autour d'un village* (Paris, 1866).

———, *Journal d'un voyageur pendant la guerre* (Paris, 1871).

———, *Impressions et Souvenirs* (Paris, 1873).

———, *Dernières Pages* (Paris, 1877).

———, *Questions d'art et de littérature* (Paris, 1878).

———, *Questions politiques et sociales* (Paris, 1879).

———, *Souvenirs de 1848* (Paris, 1880).

(For other GS works, see Chronological List.)

Sand, Maurice, *Masques et Bouffons,* 2 volumes, illustrated by A. Manceau, Preface by George Sand (Paris, 1860).

———, *Six mille lieues à toute vapeur* (Paris, 1862).

———, *Callirhoé* (Paris, 1863).

———, *Raoul de La Chastre* (Paris, 1865).

———, *Le Coq aux cheveux d'or* (Paris, 1867).

———, *Miss Mary* (Paris, 1868).

Sandeau, Jules, *Marianna* (Paris, 1865).

Séché, Léon, *Sainte-Beuve,* 2 volumes (Paris, 1904).

———, *Etudes d'histoire romantique: Alfred de Musset,* 2 volumes (Paris, 1907).

———, *Muses romantiques: Hortense Allart de Méritens* (Paris, 1908).

———, *La Jeunesse dorée sous Louis-Philippe* (Paris, 1910).

Ségu, Frédéric, *Un Maître de Balzac inconnu: H. de Latouche* (Paris, 1928).

———, *Le Premier Figaro* (Paris, 1932).

———, *Un Romantique républicain: H. de Latouche* (Paris, 1931).

———, *H. de Latouche et son intervention dans les arts* (Paris, 1931).

Sellards, John, *Dans le sillage du Romantisme: Charles Didier* (Paris, 1933).

Silver, Mabel, *Jules Sandeau* (Paris, 1936).

Spoelberch de Lovenjoul, Charles, vicomte de, *La Véritable Histoire de "Elle et Lui"* (Paris, 1897).

Starkie, Enid, *Flaubert — The Making of the Master* (London, 1967).

———, *Flaubert the Master* (London, 1971).

Stern, Daniel, see Agoult, Marie.

Taine, Hippolyte, *Derniers Essais de critique et d'histoire* (Paris, 1894).

Tocqueville, Alexis de, *Souvenirs* (Paris, 1893).

Toesca, Maurice, *Alfred de Musset ou l'amour de la mort* (Paris, 1970).

Véron, Louis, *Souvenirs d'un bourgeois de Paris,* 6 volumes (Paris, 1853–1855).

Vier, Jacques, *La Comtesse d'Agoult et son temps,* 6 volumes (Paris, 1955–1963).

Vigny, Alfred de, *Journal d'un poète,* Conard ed. (Paris, 1935).

Vincent, Louise, *George Sand et le Berry: vol. I, Nohant; vol. II, Le Berry dans l'oeuvre de George Sand* (Paris, 1919).

West, Anthony, *Mortal Wounds,* (New York, 1973).

Whitridge, Arnold, *Men in Crisis* (New York, 1949).

Wierzynski, Casimir, *Chopin* (London, 1957).

Winwar, Frances, *The Life of the Heart* (New York, 1945).

Wohl, Janka, *Franz Liszt — Erinnerungen einer Landsmännnin* (Jena, 1887).

———, *François Liszt — Souvenirs d'une compatriote* (Paris, 1887).

Zviguilsky, Alexandre, *Ivan Tourguenev — Nouvelle Correspondance inédite,* 2 volumes (Paris, 1971–1972).

Chronological List of George Sand's More Important Works

(The page numbers following the book titles refer to the pages in this book on which each of GS's works is discussed.)

1832	*Indiana* 193–206
	La Marquise 208–9
	Valentine 207–9
1833	*Lélia* 231–40
	Métella 269, 272
	Le Secrétaire intime 276–7
1834	*Leone Leoni* 301–2
	André 301–2
	Lettres d'un voyageur (1–4) 312–9
	Mattea 355
	Jacques 289, 302, 323–4
1835–1836	*Lettres d'un voyageur* (5–8)
1836	*Simon* 371, 377
1837	*Mauprat* 420–2
	Les Maîtres Mosaïstes 437
	La Dernière Aldini 437
	L'Uscoque 445
1838	*Les Sept cordes de la lyre* 477–8
	Spiridion 445
1839	*Gabriel* (play) 478, 480, 483
	Cosima 489–492
1840	*Le Compagnon du tour de France* 492–3
1841	*Horace* 496–8
1842–1843	*Consuelo* 512–24
1843–1844	*La Ccmtesse de Rudolstadt* 524–7
1844	*Jeanne* 527
1844	*Le Meunier d'Angibault* 531–3
1845	*Tévérino* 535
1845	*Le Péché de Monsieur Antoine* 536
1845	*La Mare du diable* 538–9
1846	*Lucrézia Floriani* 544–6
1847	*François le Champi* 575
1848	*La Petite Fadette* 608
1848–1854	*Histoire de ma vie* 639
1851	*Claudie* (play) 623
1851	*Le Mariage de Victorine* (play)
1853	*Les Maîtres sonneurs*
1854	*Maître Favilla* 638
1856	*La Daniella* 645–6
1857	*Les Beaux-Messieurs de Bois-Doré* 664
1858	*L'Homme de neige* 649
1858	*Elle et Lui* 649–52
1860	*Le Marquis de Villemer* 652
1860–1861	*Valvèdre* 652

Index